A HISTORY OF
WESTERN
MORALS

BOOKS BY CRANE BRINTON

THE POLITICAL IDEAS OF THE ENGLISH ROMANTICISTS
THE JACOBINS: AN ESSAY IN THE NEW HISTORY
DECADE OF REVOLUTION: 1789-1799
THE LIVES OF TALLEYRAND
FRENCH REVOLUTIONARY LEGISLATION ON ILLEGITIMACY, 1789-1804
ANATOMY OF REVOLUTION
NIETZSCHE
THE UNITED STATES AND BRITAIN
FROM MANY ONE: THE PROGRESS OF POLITICAL INTEGRATION
AND THE PROBLEM OF WORLD GOVERNMENT
ENGLISH POLITICAL THOUGHT IN THE NINETEENTH CENTURY
IDEAS AND MEN: THE STORY OF WESTERN THOUGHT
THE TEMPER OF WESTERN EUROPE

Editor
THE PORTABLE AGE OF REASON READER

with others
WHAT DO WE EXPECT OF OUR TEACHERS TODAY?
THE WORLD OF HISTORY
THE HISTORY OF CIVILIZATION
MODERN CIVILIZATION: A HISTORY OF THE LAST FIVE CENTURIES

CRANE BRINTON

A HISTORY OF WESTERN MORALS

PARAGON HOUSE
NEW YORK

First Paperback edition, 1990

Published in the United States by

Paragon House
90 Fifth Avenue
New York, NY 10011

10 9 8 7 6 5 4 3 2 1

Library of Congress Cataloging-in-Publication Data

Brinton, Crane, 1898–1968.
A history of Western morals / Crane Brinton. —
1st pbk. ed.
p.   cm.
Reprint. Originally published: New York : Harcourt
Brace, 1959.
ISBN 1-55778-370-5 : $14.95
1. Ethics—History. I. Title
BJ71.B69 1990
170'.9—dc20 89-71057
CIP

This book is printed on acid-free paper.
Manufactured in the United States of America

TO THE CENTER AND THE FARM

Acknowledgments

I AM MOST GRATEFUL for the opportunity of spending a year as Fellow of the Center for Advanced Study in the Behavioral Sciences at Stanford, California, a most remarkable institution, already legendary in spite of its youth. The legends describe it variously, as the "rest cure," the "country club," the "think-shop," the "bee-hive"; for me, it has been the Abbaye de Thélème and its motto truly "Do what thou wilt." Without this year of complete freedom, I could not have completed the book at this time, nor, indeed, have written *this* book at all. In fairness I should list as those to whom I owe a debt for help in this book all of my colleagues at the Center. There is nothing vague about this debt, though it was incurred in the apparently fugitive course of informal discussion, often mere conversation. I am sure that many of these colleagues could hear the echo of their voices almost anywhere in the course of this book. I am grateful to them, and to Ralph Tyler and the rest of the most permissive "administration"—the irony always implied in such quotation marks here carries no trace of malice—who made life so easy for us all. I wish also to express my gratitude to the many in the Stanford community with whom the Center lives in a fruitful symbiosis.

More specifically, I thank David Landes, who has read large parts of the original manuscript and made discerning criticisms, which I have tried hard to take into account; Roy Willis, my assistant, who did much, much more than mere leg work for me—though he did a great deal of that, and most uncomplainingly; Mrs. Jeanne Gentry and Mrs. Mary Hurt of the secretarial staff at the Center, who struggled successfully with my untidy manuscript;

J. Elliott Janney, who, along with Lecky, showed me the value of the concept of the moral type or ideal; William Pullin, who set me at this difficult task; my secretary in Cambridge, Miss Elizabeth F. Hoxie, whose help as usual has been invaluable.

CRANE BRINTON

Cambridge, Mass.
27 October 1958

CONTENTS

Contents

I

Introduction

IN SEPTEMBER 1957 there appeared in most American newspapers a news photograph that showed a Negro girl in Little Rock, Arkansas, after a vain attempt to enter a white high school, leaving the premises with a group of whites trailing and abusing her. The face of one white girl was contorted in a shocking way; the Negro girl looked dignified and self-controlled. Commentators in the North were unanimous that the expression of the Negro girl symbolized the good and the expression of the white girl the bad; and commentators in the South were at least much disturbed by the picture, for they could not help making the same specific classifications of good and bad that their Northern colleagues did. My point here, however, is not so much the fact that in a certain sense moral goodness and moral badness were in this striking photograph made real, concrete, even "objective" or "universal." My point is, rather, that, dismissing for the moment the great philosophical problems lurking here, it is clear that no one could look at that photograph in quite the way he could look at a diagram of the occultation of Saturn by the moon that might well have appeared in the same issue of his newspaper or news weekly as did the photograph from Little Rock. Even the diagram of the occultation of Saturn might conceivably have stirred the emotions of an occasional reader, for it might have acted as a trigger to release a chain of thought-feeling about the vastness and impersonality of the astronomer's universe and the smallness and helplessness of man, a chain for which much in popular contemporary culture supplies the materials. But the picture of the good Negro girl and the bad white girl (some editorial writers preferred

1

to call the white girl "evidently neurotic," a fact again good grist for the historian of morals) roused very strong emotions indeed, emotions best described as those of moral indignation.

One very obvious difference in the two cases cited above throws light on the special conditions under which moral emotions are commonly felt. The newspaper reader knew and felt at once when he saw the faces of the two girls that "something should be done about it," that he himself might do something about it, write a letter to the editor, to his congressman, join something, pay dues, demonstrate, at the very least express an opinion. To no sane reader did the thought occur that he could do anything at all about the occultation of Saturn; in that form, the thought probably did not even occur to the reader who happened to be a devotee of the newspaper's daily column on astrology.

Not very long ago, as historical time goes, almost everybody would have felt that he could, by himself or with the help of priest or magician, *do something* about matters we now dismiss from our minds—and our adrenals—as concerns of the astronomer, the meteorologist, or some other expert who himself can do no more than follow Bacon's aphorism "Nature is not to be conquered save by obeying her." Call it growth of natural science, or of rationalism, or of common sense: something has pushed whole areas of our experience quite out of what we take to be our power, our will, even out of the customary field of action of any god or cosmic "force" capable of concern for humanity.

A great deal, however, is left for us to do something about as moral beings inspired by moral emotions. Any newspaper, any newscast, will supply all that the most hopeful or the most indignant need for moral exercise. A group of determined pacifists set out in true Western style as witnesses to the eternal verities to sail from Honolulu to the banned area in the Pacific where American authorities are testing atomic weapons; their little ketch is duly stopped only a mile or so from port by court injunction. A teen-aged girl stabs to death her divorced mother's lover and is gently handed over by the court to the custody of her maternal grandmother. Peruvian university students greet a good-willing Vice-President of the United States with a shower of vegetables, mixed with a few stones. The French government and people behave toward the Algerians as the British government and people forty years ago behaved toward the Irish. A Russian representative at the United Nations once more asserts that the United States is striving to subject the whole world to its capitalist tyranny; an American representative once more replies that it is the

Russians who seek to subject us all to Communist tyranny. An Italian bishop is sued in a secular court for libeling a freethinking couple married in a secular ceremony by declaring from his pulpit that the couple is living in sin. American automotive engineers add ten more pounds of chromium and twenty more unneeded horsepower to their next year's models, and the company business executives, who, as a liberal weekly points out, are the masters of the engineers and the real villains in the case, add another two or three hundred dollars to the price of their cars. A newspaper editorial points out that Americans spend more money on cosmetics than they do on books. A sociologist in an interview gives our society twenty years at most before its final destruction.

I have in the above paragraph, which could be indefinitely expanded, mixed the high and the low, the dignified and the undignified, quite without ironic intent. It is surely a good rigged random sample. I should be astonished if anyone could read it in this mid-twentieth century without experiencing at least a trace of what I have called moral indignation. The reading, and the train of associations set off by the reading, would surely also bring to many at least a trace of moral satisfaction. The historian of morals in the West, however, is pretty well forced to conclude from the record that there is in this human world of ours more moral indignation than moral satisfaction, that man as moralist is essentially a complainer. It is always easy to recognize man the moralist: the sequence is clear to an observer, and can be clear to the willing self-analyst. First the experience—another French cabinet falls; then the emotion, which may run from tired annoyance to refreshed anger; then the blaming, the censuring—these damn fool French, why can't they . . . ; then the doing something about it—we ought to. . . . Note carefully that in this sequence there is little room for any attempt to "understand" why that cabinet fell in the first place.

Yet this analysis of the moral process may well be itself—in fact, it is—stained with our inescapable human nature, or at least with the nature of an "intellectual." For the historical record is for the most part made by the kind of people we must call intellectuals; and intellectuals live, succeed, shine, by making us all aware of how much is wrong with the world. This statement would appear to be particularly true of intellectuals in the twentieth-century Western world.

Yet it will not do to exaggerate the gap between the intellectual and his fellow men. There are many definitions of man, from the "forked radish" and the "animal with opposable thumbs," to the "image of his Maker" and the "animal that knows it is going to die." Not the least far-reaching would be simply: the moral animal. For though we may grant to the physiologist that the emotions of man are bodily functions of a kind that go on also in other animal bodies, it seems unlikely that any other animal is stirred to fear, or anger, or contentment by any awareness of a difference between right and wrong, justice and injustice. We may fashionably amend the old philosophic tag to read, "Nothing in the intellect unless previously in the endocrines," but there in the intellect stands, nevertheless, the moral inheritance of our species, the bewildering, fascinating, unavoidable rights and wrongs of our past—and present.

II

It should be clear indeed that our subject is full of difficulties that have to be called philosophic. The semantic grace that begins so many books in these days seems especially needed in a history of morals. I shall try throughout this study to make consistent use of three closely related words which I shall now define, not as all readers would define or understand them—such unanimity about the full meaning of words of this sort is wholly impossible in the modern Western world—but not, I trust, in any erratic and private way. At least they are all exceedingly common words, so common that not even the pure in taste can object to them.

First, I shall use the word "conduct" to refer to the reported actions of human beings, alone or in groups. The historian, of course, must almost always deal with reports, usually written reports, of the actions or events with which he is concerned; such reports vary in accuracy, but the historian has at his command ways of testing their accuracy, ways not identical with those of the laboratory experimenter but good enough so that he is justified in using to describe these actions the blessed word "facts."[1] The actions that make up what I shall call "conduct" cover the whole range of human capabilities, from words to blows—and detonations of bombs. Perhaps the word "conduct" has some overtones of formality, even artificiality: "conduct in the bed" is a phrase that hardly comes naturally. "Behavior" is certainly a very close synonym, and may seem preferable to some. But in the form "behaviorism" the word refers to a specific set of doctrines—or dogmas—in the history of

---

[1] I forbear further discourse on the nature of "facts," which we all know nowadays is less obvious than our grandfathers thought it. To the interested reader I recommend a meaty little essay of L. J. Henderson's, "An Approximate Definition of Fact," University of California, *Publications in Philosophy*, XIV, 1932, p. 179.

formal psychology, to the work of a whole school which goes far beyond reporting or describing human conduct, which does, indeed, try to explain and control human conduct. I wish to use the word "conduct" as far as possible in a descriptive, not an explanatory, sense. But the distinction between these two words, which both denote human *doing,* is perhaps near to hairsplitting; both "conduct" and "behavior" quite readily take those indispensable adjectives "good" and "bad."

Second, I shall use the terms "ethics" or "ethical principles" to refer to the statements men make about what their conduct, or the conduct of others, or of both, *ought to be.* Only the very self-conscious semanticist will try to pursue that word "ought" further; it is surely one of the clearest of words, usually, one hopes, clearer to the individual using it than "is." Much of the time I shall use the words "ethics" and "ethical" to designate some specific part of the great and varied body of formal philosophical writing that commonly goes under that name and that is well-enough known in the United States as the subject matter of college courses in ethics. Here a caution is necessary. Philosophers have built up a tradition that, especially in the field of ethics, commonly does not list as philosophers many writers who seem to a layman to have philosophized. Nietzsche, for example, usually makes the grade as a philosopher, perhaps because he was a German and left behind him fragments of a book, *The Will to Power,* which he may have meant to be what the philosophers call a systematic treatise; but Pascal does not often make the grade, nor does Rousseau; and La Rochefoucauld almost never makes it. These, it seems, are "men of letters," and members of a nation known for its lack of philosophic depth. La Rochefoucauld, in particular, is usually labeled a "moralist." I shall here pay little attention to such distinctions, and shall treat as "ethics" all expressions of opinion as to how men ought to behave, from the Mosaic code through folk proverbs and newspaper columns of "Advice to the lovelorn" to the *Ethics Mathematically Demonstrated* of Spinoza, which last is a singularly lofty flight of pure philosophy.

Third, I shall use "morals" and "morality" in a somewhat less obvious sense, but one that seems to me to underlie the original Latin *mos, moris* and its descendants in our modern Western languages. If "conduct" is used consistently to indicate what men do, and "ethics" to indicate their appraisal of the *value* of their actions, then "moral" may be used to sum up the whole human situation involved in the existence of both conduct and evaluation of conduct, of both the "is" and the "ought" in human awareness of past, present, and future. Our moral awareness is a state of tension familiar to us all, no matter what our religion or our philosophy, a state of tension summoned up in us all by the common-sense word "conscience." I realize that there are all sorts of difficulties about this use of "morals." For one thing, such a use implies that what I call "ethics" has some effect on what I call "conduct," and even that what I call "conduct" has some relation to what I call "ethics"; both these conclusions have been rejected by some thinkers, simplifiers, it is true, and, like the solipsist, at the extreme or lunatic fringe of philosophic thought. Most of us would agree that there *is* a relation between human thinking, even about ethics, and human doing. About the nature of that relation there has always in the West been great dispute.

Conduct, ethics, morals are not here used to stand for "real" entities, but as instruments of analysis, that is, of convenience. To fall back as one must in such matters on a figure of speech: conduct, ethics, morals are not like so many separate islands in the sea; they are *more nearly like,* but not *just like* chemical elements which combine in various proportions to make compounds, elements moreover never or rarely found in a pure state in nature. In particular I wish to be firmly understood as *not* here maintaining that writers I have classed as primarily concerned with ethics are therefore concerned with "mere" words, with something therefore not quite real; nor do I maintain that such writers are wholly concerned with the "ought," with standards of value, and pay no attention to the "is," to the ways in which men establish and employ standards of value. The great systematic philosophers, an Aristotle, an Aquinas, a Locke, have much to say about conduct as well as about ethics, and about the resolution of these two in morals. Even in the sermon, where the preacher is making a special use of human awareness of the "ought," there is often a great deal of information for the historian interested in the "is." There are, of course, degrees of possible concern with "pure" ethics and with "pure" conduct. If you want to feel the difference between the two extremes, read Kant's *Metaphysics of Ethics,* or his *What Is Enlightenment?,* and then turn to any clinical case history, from one by Hippocrates to one by Freud or to the work of any good naturalist.[2]

We may indeed go further into metaphor. Morality is at once a part of man's being and the whole of it. The easy metaphor is the familiar one of a strand, a thread, interwoven with others in a fabric that would not be the fabric it is without *all* the threads. But the part of morals in the human whole

[2] Emphatically *not* to naturalists who figure in most histories of literature, and especially not to Thoreau, who could never look at a bird without seeing the universe—and Henry Thoreau.

is not neatly separable by the mind's eye as a thread. In a less dignified figure of speech, the moral is simply an ingredient in a mixture, a dish, in which the ingredients as we experience them are inextricably melted or mingled, not to be separated in this real world, but only in the unreal world of analysis—at most, to be subtly distinguished one from another by our moral taste buds.

Thus the moral in our human situation is not to be separated from the rest of our universe; yet the *good* we seek as moral beings is not, under analysis, the *true* we seek as thinking beings, nor is it the *beautiful* we seek as emotional beings. Our conventional vocabulary separates these as well as they can be separated. Our universe of moral discourse does not—I nearly wrote the revealing "should not"—deal with terms like "truth," "common sense," "reason," nor with terms like "beauty," "taste," "manners," "civility," but with terms like "good" and "evil," "justice" and "injustice," "struggle," "victory," "defeat," "conscience," "guilt." As moral beings, we all bear an uneasy burden from which most of us can hardly escape with serenity by making truth, beauty, and justice quite synonymous—or by separating them out in closed compartments of meaning. In particular, we cannot avoid thinking about morals, yet we cannot, peace to Spinoza, think about them, demonstrate them, after the manner of mathematics.

I shall try to adhere to the common use in matters of morals; "good" evaluates conduct or ethical standards as morally desirable, "bad" evaluates conduct or ethical standards as morally undesirable. Both words have also a common descriptive use, nicely brought out in a casual remark about a young professor who could never be relied on to keep appointments or serve on committees or in general do the little drudgeries expected of him: "Is Blank *really* good enough to be that bad?" Modern ethical philosophers have been very conscious—justifiably so—of the semantic difficulties of these and other words the moralist has to use: "right," "wrong," "just," "unjust," "duty," "conscience," and a great many more.[3]

The historian of Western morals must record a very wide range, a whole spectrum of specific contents of recorded conduct and recorded ethics. He must also note that there is a persistent belief in the West that in spite of this range—in conduct, for example, from that of St. Anthony to that of the

[3] The reader will find helpful here C. L. Stevenson, *Ethics and Language*, New Haven, Yale University Press, 1945; Richard M. Hare, *The Language of Morals*, Oxford, Oxford University Press, 1952; C. D. Broad, *Five Types of Ethical Theory*, New York, Harcourt, Brace, 1930.

Marquis de Sade; in ethics, from the belief that war is always bad to the belief that it is always good—there is really both in conduct and in ethics a kind of center, norm, or average which does not vary much with place or time. Here again, however, there is no full agreement as to just where the center lies, as to just what ordinary human nature and ordinary human capacities really are. All this will be clearer as our story progresses.

But first I must, speaking as historian, as recorder, note that from the very beginning of Western history in Greece and in the Ancient Near East there have been constantly recurring problems in ethics that have not in three thousand years been solved to the common satisfaction of all men. Can the individual really choose between doing what he thinks good and what he thinks evil? Is it right for the individual who happens to be born a Moslem to have several wives, but wrong for the individual who happens to be born a Christian? Does the kind of thinking you who are struggling with these lines are now doing really affect your conduct? These are the old problems, indeed, one may say the old chestnuts, of freedom of the will, ethical relativity, and the place of reason in human conduct. Socrates and his friends threshed them all out long ago; one may say that in the first book of Plato's *Republic* the principal ethical positions Western men have taken are already clearly stated. The voice of Thrasymachus, who said that justice is what you can get away with, but said so rather more elegantly than this, has echoed down the ages; but so, too, has the voice of Socrates, who said much nicer things much more nicely about justice.[4]

Now there is a sense in which to say that these and similar problems have not been solved, that men still give the sorts of attempted solution to them given millennia ago, is to take a definite philosophical position toward them. I have above tried to take refuge in my role as a mere historian, a mere recorder, but something in me—perhaps, appropriately enough in a history of morals, my conscience—compels me to admit that no refuge will do in the end. The historian, like the scientist, can keep awareness of these and similar problems out of his daily work; but both historian and scientist are human beings, and ethical, indeed metaphysical, concern is part of the human condition.

Some of the popularizers of a current of contemporary philosophy for

---

[4] Polemarchus, Thrasymachus, Glaucon, Adeimantus, and Socrates himself do not, of course, exhaust the range of ideas on ethics, but they do sketch the outlines of what would be the range of such ideas in the West, from conformism and traditionalism to pragmatism, opportunism, and idealism; they set up the spectrum in its broad lines.

which there is no good name, for "logical positivism" will not quite do, have come close to a kind of skepticism, even nihilism, about ethical propositions. Mr. Stuart Chase, who in his successful *Tyranny of Words* (1938) would have us say "blah-blah" instead of, for example, "natural rights," comes close to the proposition often attributed to the logical positivists: that if any kind of statement cannot be tested by an "operation," essentially like that done by a natural scientist seeking to verify a theory, it is "nonsense," and had better never have been entertained in the mind. We cannot here attempt to disentangle the many complexities of this semantic problem as it appears to our age. Suffice it to note that there *is,* if only among popularizers, not among true philosophers, a current tendency to put all statements not basically like those the scientist makes ("empirically verifiable," if you wish, although these, too, are weasel words) in one class of "nonsense," "drivel," somehow, unfortunately, communicable almost as if it were rational sense.[5]

The "blah-blah" or "no-nonsense" school of popularizers are, no doubt, extremists; and they do not, of course, by any means dismiss from their concern—and that of their readers—the age-old, insoluble, unavoidable, essential problems of philosophy they claim they are trying to get rid of entirely. But they make us all a little more self-conscious about our attitudes toward these problems. I feel that I owe the reader some account of my own attitudes toward—most emphatically not my solution of—some of these recurring problems of ethics, and, therefore, of morals. These attitudes are so affected by my training as a historian that I shall hardly seem to the philosopher to do more than beg the question, for I start with the assertion that on these great problems many, perhaps most, thoughtful men in the West hospitably accept and cherish simultaneously in their conscious, not just in their unconscious, minds, logically quite incompatible conclusions. For the modern Westerner exposed to any natural science, from popular to pure, it is impossible not to believe in some sort of determinism; but it is also impossible for him not to believe in some sort of freedom of the will. He therefore

5 One example among many. The discoverer of "Parkinson's Law" comments on the famous passage in the *Social Contract* in which Rousseau states his problem as finding "a form of association . . . by means of which each, coalescing with all, may nevertheless obey only himself and remain as free as before" as follows: "There might be no great harm in reading *this* piece of eighteenth-century rhetoric provided that the antidote were to follow. The student who is advised to read drivel should at least be warned that it is drivel he is being asked to read." C. Northcote Parkinson, *The Evolution of Political Thought,* London, University of London Press, 1958, p. 10. Professor Parkinson's antidote to drivel turns out to be a mixture of prehistory, social anthropology, and comparative history, taken in a fine mood of faith in a real world of no-nonsense.

believes in both, believes that he has a will, indeed *is* a will, not to be further defined in physiological terms, which makes "free" choices, and also that there is an unbroken and unbreakable chain of cause and effect in the universe, of which he is part.[6]

It is true that there are various systematic ways of thinking by which a Westerner can soften, disguise, or, if you prefer, reconcile, these logical opposites. He may, for instance, believe in "determinism" but reject "fatalism." Theology, metaphysics, ethics, common sense, all contribute to this process of reconciling logical opposites, a process indispensable for almost all of us. The *Vulgärpositivismus* which declares that such activity of the mind is quite unprofitable, *mere* nonsense, cuts itself off further from humanity than does the most otherworldly of idealisms. Indeed, a system like the famous Hegelian dialectic of thesis-antithesis-synthesis, though no "operation" approaching that of the natural scientist can be performed on it, is a kind of recognition that human beings in this real world *must* eat their cake and have it; all of us are common-sense Hegelians and common-sense Benthamites when we need to be.

So, too, with the old problem of ethical relativity. It was impossible even for the Greeks, sure as they were that their own ways of living were the only right ones, to deny that their barbarian neighbors had different ways. The first few generations of anthropologists, not unmoved by the pioneering scientist's desire to expose the errors of accepted belief, were perhaps too insistent on the respectability in Africa or New Guinea of conduct shocking to nineteenth-century Western man: "The Wadigo regard it as disgraceful, or at least as ridiculous for a girl to enter into marriage as a virgin."[7] Indeed, it has never been possible for a sane Westerner to deny that human conduct showed unmistakable variations in different times, places, and even individuals, and, furthermore, that the justification or evaluation of such conduct, that is, ethics in our sense, also varied widely and unmistakably. Yet again it has been difficult for most Westerners to accept full radical ethical rela-

[6] Denis de Rougemont has put with epigrammatic neatness what I have been trying to say: in these "necessary tensions" (he cites "transcendence" and "immanence," "freedom" and "authority," and others, much like those I here bring up) "the two terms are *true, contradictory,* and *essential.*" *Man's Western Quest,* New York, Harper, 1957, p. 116. Italics mine. Also Arthur Koestler, "for we are moving here through strata that are held together by the cement of contradiction." *The Invisible Writing,* Boston, Beacon Press, 1954, p. 349.

[7] E. Westermarck, *Origin and Development of the Moral Ideas,* 2nd ed., London, Macmillan, 1917, Vol. II, p. 422, quoting from O. Baumann, *Usambara* (1891).

tivism, that is, the doctrine that right and wrong are for each individual what at a given moment he thinks or feels they are. The polar-opposite doctrine, that right and wrong are absolute, universals unaffected by what we call time and place, the same always and everywhere, has surely been at least as far from ordinary Western acceptance. Nevertheless, some residual belief that the distinction between good and evil is not one rooted solely in human convenience and human history, but has something to do with the structure of the universe, has in our world survived even among those who have given up the Judaeo-Christian belief in a God who made both good and evil. Most Westerners today would surely be reluctant to accept the concept of "evil" as on a level with the concept of "weed," neither more nor less absolute, neither more nor less built into the structure of the universe, neither more nor less a matter of our convenience.[8]

Our third old chestnut of a problem, though it, too, is as ancient as the Greeks, looks today a bit fresher, which is to say that the debate about it is livelier than that about free will or ethical relativism. The unpalatable extremes are there: the intellectualist doctrine that at least potentially men can reason logically, even, as Spinoza held, mathematically, about the distinctions between right and wrong, arrive at demonstrably correct and perfectly communicable conclusions about them, and, finally, make their conduct conform to the results of their reasoning; and the anti-intellectualist doctrine that reason is in these matters of conduct either quite helpless, or at most the "slave of the passions," that all reasoning is rationalizing, that even if philosophers could agree—and they cannot agree—as to standards of right and wrong, even the philosophers, let alone the rest of us, would still follow drives, urges, impulses, instincts, sentiments, species-specific acts, conscious and unconscious. Though perhaps, in terms of metaphysical concern, this question of the role of reason in morals is as insoluble as our others, the inevitable compromises men make about it in their own minds are in these days at least fairly obvious. Few of us can dismiss the work of two generations of psychologists and go back to what really was the common belief of the eighteenth-century Enlightenment, that is, that only bad environment, especially faulty

---

[8] I make the above statement in full awareness that it is infinitely debatable, and can be misleading. But I do think it is a statement that can help *focus* the problem of ethical relativity. Thistles and roses *sub specie aeternitatis*—perhaps even *sub specie Linnaei*—are not what they are to gardeners. But liars and honest men? Or even Hitler and Lincoln? Surely in ethical matters are we not reluctant to think of ourselves as *mere* cultivators of our gardens?

education, mistaken religious training, and bad political and economic institutions, prevents all men from thinking alike on ethical matters, and from adapting their conduct to the results of their thinking. We agree, if not with the Freudians, at least with much of Freud, that the obstacles to clear thinking and to acting in accord with such thinking are much more complex and persistent than our predecessors thought they were. We are alerted to the presence everywhere of rationalizing, wishful thinking, propaganda, prejudice, brainwashing, motivational research, and other evidences that the world is not yet the world Condorcet foresaw, nor even the world young H. G. Wells foresaw.

Yet a chastened belief in the uses of the instrument of thought has survived modern anti-intellectualism. Indeed, in precisely the field of ethics we are here concerned with, our century has seen the rise not, perhaps, of a "school" in the old sense, but of a number of writers on ethics who—though they might not like it put this way—seem to have as a common aim the salvaging of a place for reason in the establishment of ethical standards for the effective guiding of human conduct.[9] It is no longer fashionable, and probably was never quite possible, to "think with the blood." We shall, in short, here concern ourselves with ethics, with "ideas" about good and bad, right and wrong, with "values," with no worries lest we are dealing with "mere froth on the surface of the waves," nor even with "mere superstructure." Morality is a *relation* between ethics and conduct in human societies, a relation that always includes what we may here unworriedly call "thinking," or, more self-consciously, some sort of activity in the frontal lobe of the brain.

Whether this is a causal relation and if so what kind of causal relation are most certainly questions of the kind we have above called "old chestnuts." In its simplest form, one much influenced by popular, or, rather, pseudo-, Marxism in our day, the question can be put: Do ethics—that is, ideas about what a person's conduct should be—cause, or initiate, or at least affect that person's conduct? I have elsewhere suggested that such questions, if not, perhaps, to be dismissed as "meaningless," as the purveyors of popular semantics like to do, can at least be bypassed with profit by the historian, much as the engineer and, one suspects, a good many physicists bypass

[9] C. L. Stevenson, *Ethics and Language,* is a good sampling, and through its notes and references a good guide to recent work in the field. See also the list of "pertinent literature" in Arthur Pap, *Elements of Analytic Philosophies,* New York, Macmillan, 1949, pp. 64-65.

certain questions of an "ultimate" kind as to the nature of matter, energy, and the like.[10]

A concrete case should be useful here to dismiss this problem, and prepare the way for a somewhat different problem, our *sources* of information about the conduct of men in the past, which will concern us in the next section of this chapter. In the troubles over desegregation in the South of the United States, troubles touched off by the Supreme Court decision of 1954 that segregation in public schools is unconstitutional, it is quite clear, is, indeed, a "fact," that a number of Negroes in many Southern towns and cities want desegregation and are actively organized to try to get it. They are refusing to accept a specific kind of social and political inequality. But that kind of inequality is condemned as *wrong* in almost all the sources of ideas about the nature of our society available to the educated or partly educated Negro. Certainly there are other reasons for the *conduct* of these Negroes than their training in American *ethics* (I am here deliberately using these terms as I have earlier defined them). But surely is it not absurd to expect that they can be so trained, exposed in a society like ours to creeds and codes like the preamble to the Declaration of Independence, the Bill of Rights and the like, and to the constant examples of the American drive toward many specific kinds of social equality with which all our cultural life is filled, and then calmly accept the status of an Uncle Tom?[11] Surely can we not now reject

10 In my *The Shaping of the Modern Mind* (New York, New American Library, 1953, p. 9), I suggest that the automotive engineer does not ask whether the spark or the gasoline "causes" the motor to run, or whether spark or gasoline is more "important," or "fundamental." Applied to the present problem of the relation between "ideas" and "interests," "drives," "*material* conditions," "sentiments," this analogy no doubt presents all the shocking weaknesses of such imprecise uses of the human mind. But I do not mean to suggest that the "ideal" is the spark and the "material" the gasoline, nor vice versa. All I mean to suggest is that as for the engineer no internal combustion engine without both gasoline and spark, or their equivalents, as in diesel engines, so for the historian: he can fearlessly assert that nothing happens in history without the presence of both ideas and material conditions. In concrete instances of human conduct, it is no doubt useful to try to estimate the part played in such conduct by intellectual elements and the part played by emotional elements; but no formula will work for an average or generalized case. Compare Stevenson, "To ask whether beliefs in general direct attitudes in general, or whether the causal connection goes rather in the opposite direction, is simply a misleading question." (Stevenson, *Ethics and Language*, p. 5.)

11 I had just come to review and possibly revise the above sentences when I found the following: A Negro businessman in Montgomery, Alabama, comments: "We've got the fatherhood of God, the brotherhood of man, the Bill of Rights, the United States Supreme Court, American democracy and democratic principles and sentiment, Republican and Democratic sympathy, national politics and world history all on our side." New York *Times*, December 29, 1957, Section VI, p. 38.

the despairing innocence of an Orwell? Even with constant repetition from above, the Orwellian slogan "All men are created equal, only some are more equal than others" will not always work on the underdog. Motivational research has not yet quite eliminated, or explained, moral man.

It is tempting to go on to a much broader generalization that ideas about human equality, the "dignity of man," and the like have played a part in other risings of underdog groups, at least since with the Stoics and the Christians such ideas clearly enter the record. But the record of what the underdog thought and felt is so incomplete! We know that most members of the National Association for the Advancement of Colored People are aware of the ideas of Thomas Jefferson on human equality, that they *feel* the kind of pressures toward egalitarianism our culture exerts. But we have no information as to what went on in the mind even of a leader like Spartacus in the so-called slave revolt of the first century B.C. We know that he was a Thracian, perhaps enslaved by force, and that he was clearly a leader, a "superior." But had he ever heard of Stoic ideas on human equality, which, though stated somewhat coldly and abstractly, are clear and far-reaching? Had his followers any glimmering of such ideas? We just do not know. It is, however, most unlikely that thousands of Spartacists could have held together as a fighting group unless some of them had "ideas" about what they were doing there in their fortified camp in the crater of Vesuvius.

Even for the Middle Ages we do not have by any means the kind of information needed to be certain that Christian ideas on equality played a part in risings of the underdogs. But there are intriguing straws of evidence, on which the not-too-cautious mind can build. The well-known slogan of the English Peasant War of the fourteenth century

> When Adam delved and Eve span
> Who was then the gentleman?

would seem to be evidence that the Christian holy writings were playing then the revolutionary role they have so often played—and which is so obviously there, built into them. With the sixteenth century we do, however, begin to get a great deal of the necessary information about what the active participants in social and political movements wanted.

I have dwelt perhaps too long on this problem of the part "ideas" play in human conduct; but I confess to harboring the hope that some of my readers may at least worry it over a bit in their minds. For it seems to me that most educated and interested Americans, or, at any rate, many such, do accept uncritically certain attitudes toward this problem, attitudes I find unrealistic and perhaps unprofitable. Put negatively, there is the common American attitude that "abstract" ideas in particular are mere disguises for real, hard motives; put positively, there is the attitude that these real, hard motives are limited to the kind of rational self-interest the economist takes as his starting point—and ending point—that the great clue to all human conduct is in the old tag *cui bono,* with the *bonum* very clear, very material, preferably hard cash. Now I am willing for the moment to assume the correctness of the view of human nature that lies behind these attitudes—a view rather oddly close to some aspects of Christian pessimism and remote from the attitude of the Enlightened—but I insist that in real life these basic drives or urges or what you will emerge into actual human conduct only through a long process which involves sentiments, emotions, symbols, "ideas," some of them very "abstract," like the idea that abstract ideas have no activating part in human conduct. I dare not here attempt any refutation of these great national beliefs of ours. For one thing, I have been much snubbed by my countrymen for displaying my ignorance of the realities of life. Only a few months ago a ranger in the Craters of the Moon National Monument crushed my suggestion that perhaps the Indians pitched their tepees in a particularly Dantesque spot in the monument— pure devilish black lava—because men have always been fascinated by any hell that moves them religiously; on the contrary, he insisted, they came there because, in spite of the apparent desolation of the spot, it really was full of game that came there to drink from pools accumulated in the contorted lava. He may well have been right; but there are not always pools in the lava flow.

I submit, as a mere parting shot or so, that though the phrase "abstract ideas" has in our centemporary culture a pejorative sense, we usually mean by abstract ideas those we dislike, or do not share, or are somewhat ashamed of confessing we entertain. I am not even wholly persuaded that American G.I.'s in our last two wars were quite as contemptuous of the noble, the good, and the true in our war aims as the investigators insist they were. There is a long and dignified Western masculine tradition of concealing the nobler sentiments except in epic or dramatic moments. And as for the common American belief in the economic interpretation of everything, this, too, is partly a pose, and even more a habit of thought which has hopelessly ennobled economic activity into a form of the agon, and thus quite removed from it the nice rationalism of self-interest with which economic theorists still tend to endow it.

There remain a few more introductory explanations about which I shall try to be specific. I have already said that morals are not, under analysis, identical with manners, nor even in quite simple discourse "related to," or "a variety of," manners. The student of human conduct cannot, however, hope to work effectively with the kind of precise systematic terms the taxonomic biologist, for instance, must insist upon. Human thought and feeling about manners and morals clearly do not separate them rigorously; "good" and "bad" do the needed work in both realms of discourse. There is, indeed, commonly among Westerners a feeling that morals are concerned with loftier matters; that taste, at least in the fine arts, is concerned with less lofty but still serious and important matters; and that taste in cookery and other not-fine arts is a rather low thing, and manners in the sense of civility somehow basically an artificial, ideally unnecessary, though actually important, thing. Yet there is nothing like agreement in the West on such usage, and the above sentence could hardly have been written save by an American. An Englishman or a Frenchman, though he might well agree that morals are at the top of this particular order of rank, would surely rewrite the rest of the sentence —and not in the same way. Everywhere there are individuals who, by the test of what symbols arouse their indignation—we are here well beyond simple animal rage—find matters of taste at least as important as matters of morals. Even in the United States, where the finest of arts is not quite as dignified a matter as morals, there are those who find crooners more evil than gangsters.

Indeed, the kind of mind that likes to stretch words into great blankets could claim that a history of morals is necessarily a complete history of all human activity. In the sense I am here giving to "morals"—the relation between ethics and conduct—it seems clear that man is inevitably a moral creature, and the only one. For man alone is capable of the kind of thinking —"symbolic thinking," a now generally accepted phrase, will do well enough here—which can produce an ethics. I certainly do not propose in this book to consider, as so many treatises on ethics do, the moral sense in the higher animals. I grant that a scolded dog can look guilty, but in my use of the term the dog cannot have ethics and therefore cannot be moral or immoral, simply because he is incapable of symbolic thinking. You can say "naughty dog," and your dog will "understand" you: but no two dogs ever discussed together whether "naughty" is a relative or an absolute, or even whether in a given instance the use of "naughty" was just or unjust.

I shall not here attempt to study in detail the morals of our prehistoric Western ancestors directly or by analogy with the primitive peoples the anthropologist studies; nor shall I, save incidentally, study the morals of children. These studies are of great importance. In the long reaction (which may have passed its peak) against the late eighteenth-century belief in the power of right thinking to change rapidly and completely the conduct of large numbers of men, it has come to seem probable that human conduct is influenced by our biological as well as our cultural inheritance from the millennia before Plato and Isaiah, and by our immediate interpersonal relations with our parents, siblings, and child companions, much, much more than by our cultural inheritance from the last twenty-five centuries of Western history. Moreover, all that anthropologists, prehistorians, and psychologists have begun to find out begins to look rather fundamental, rather hard to change. But such studies have really only just begun, and can hardly yet be incorporated into a history of this kind. I am, furthermore, quite incompetent through lack of training to appreciate critically the literature in these fields. I shall therefore begin in the old-fashioned way, after a hopeful nod to the anthropologists, with the peoples of the Ancient Near East and the Greeks.

I shall not attempt to write about the moral history of peoples other than those generally understood nowadays as Western. Here, again, this limiting choice is by no means a sign that I think the story of the ethics and the conduct of the Chinese, the Japanese, the Hindus, the Aztecs, and all the rest unimportant. It is a sign partly of my own ignorance and partly of my deliberate intention to keep this book within manageable limits of length, for the reader's sake as well as my own. Furthermore, it seems to me clear that a history of Western morals need not be greatly concerned with what, in Toynbee's words, we know as "contacts between civilizations." The fact is that in the time and places covered by the old classic school sequence of Ancient, Medieval, and Modern, the "cultural narcissism" clear in the Greek distinction between "Hellenes" and "Barbarians" has been the pattern for the West. No doubt *within the West itself* the narrow limits of the national or racial in-group have never in historic times kept out for long "foreign" influences. Juvenal was, for a Roman satirist, reasonably accurate: the Syrian river Orontes did flow into the Tiber, though in the long run it turned out to be even more important that the Jordan, too, flowed into the Tiber. But though there were faint contacts between Rome and China, though with the Polos and da Gama and Columbus the West began its expansion, Europe and the Near East did not really "learn"—and in particular did not learn morality —from the peoples they subdued, traded with, and taught so much. Even today, the Yangtze and the Ganges by no means empty into the Hudson—nor does the Volga.

III

The historian of morals must try to find out what the actual conduct of all sorts and conditions of men has been. He encounters—or so it seems to one engaged in the effort—even more difficulties than does the historian of politics, war, economic activity, and other human pursuits. Some of these difficulties, both in getting source material and in organizing what he does get, are worth brief attention here.

Especially for the conduct, but also for the ethics, of the ordinary man, reliable information is hard to come by, and sometimes, as in the early medieval centuries, almost wholly lacking. The problem is real enough for the sociologist or the psychologist studying contemporary and recent societies. It is perhaps sufficient to ask the question: How near the *real* truth of the actual sexual conduct of representative or typical mid-twentieth-century American men and women—let alone of the universal "male" and "female" of his titles—did the late Dr. Kinsey get? But we do have such studies, and since about 1750 increasingly elaborate and, to be fair, increasingly accurate statistics about a great deal of human conduct, good and bad, of great value to the historian of morals. We have no such wealth of evidence for earlier periods. It would be rash indeed to entitle a book "The Sexual Behavior of the Human Male in the Roman Empire." We know reliably enough that the Greeks did expose newborn children, especially females, but we can hardly pretend to give statistics as to what proportions were so exposed, or what, if any, were the variations by class, city-state, or period of time.[12]

Nevertheless, there are sources from which with caution it is possible to get rough notions of the actual conduct not only of the upper or ruling classes, but also of ordinary men and women. The conclusions based on such sources cannot, it must be insisted, satisfy anything like the going standards of the social scientist concerned with the conduct of human beings in contemporary society; and if the precedents of the last few centuries of historical investigation hold for the future, our successor will do better than we can hope to do. Dire predictions that we shall not get any more facts about, say, well-worked periods like the English Middle Ages have so far not come true.

The most important body of information for us surely lies in the great body of Western literature. For the purposes of the historian of morals, almost

[12] But for an interesting attempt to reconstitute something like statistics, using the comparatively objective and nonliterary source afforded by inscriptions, see W. W. Tarn, *Hellenistic Civilisation*, London, Arnold, 1927, p. 87. The inscriptions are those of the third and second centuries B.C.

none of it is without value. Some of it, however, presents very great dangers for the interpreter. These dangers are greatest in the writings commonly catalogued as dealing with morals. An extreme case often proves most illuminating. The Roman satirists, Horace, Martial, Juvenal, and the rest, were gifted writers indeed. To judge from their writings, Romans, and, in particular, upper-class Romans, spent most of their time in fornication, gluttonous eating, drunkenness, langorous hot baths, backbiting, informing, betraying their friends, imitating and exceeding the example set by the corrupt Greeks and Syrians—in short, setting something like a record in iniquity. Here is a good sample:

> Who now is loved, but he who loves the Times,
> Conscious of close Intrigues, and dipt in Crimes;
> Lab'ring with Secrets which his bosom burn,
> Yet never must to publick light return?
> They get reward alone who can Betray:
> For keeping honest Counsel none will pay. . . .
> The Barbarous Harlots crowd the publick Place:
> Go, Fools, and purchase an unclean embrace;
> The painted Mitre court, and the more painted Face.[13]

The pattern thus set has had many imitators in the West ever since. Yet it is as certain as anything of the sort can be that Juvenal and his fellows cannot be taken as reliable authorities for the actual conduct even of the Roman upper classes who read their work. The sensitive, the indignant, especially when they have literary gifts—the Orwells, the Koestlers—are untrustworthy reporters.

The difficulty here is central and familiar to readers of newspapers—and one hopes to their writers. The really wicked deed is much more interesting than ordinary conventional behavior; it is news. In my brief service with the federal government I had occasion to make an "evaluation" of the horrendous reports of what French Resistance groups were doing to the occupying Germans in 1943. I began my report with the suggestion that it was dangerous to generalize for all of France from the fact—if it was a fact—that a truckload of German soldiers on the way to a movie in Orléans had been bombed. I suggested that even what the army called "intelligence" was subject to the ways of journalism; the headline is "Banker found in love-nest," never "Ten thousand bankers spend night at home." My analogy was found unsuited

---

[13] The reader will find the whole gamut run in this Third Satire of Juvenal's. I have quoted from Dryden's good liberal translation.

to the dignity that should mark government reports, but I assume that my point was made.

To this basic fact, that the exceptional is more interesting than the usual, and the exceptionally wicked especially interesting, there must be added other facts about the literary that make some of the greatest monuments of literature quite untrustworthy for our purposes. It is again an observed and continually observable fact that the writer, as perhaps the most characteristic intellectual, shows to the full a characteristic of the Western intellectual tradition, the tendency to use the mind to exhort, to correct, to complain, to do with the written word a great deal that has indeed to be done, that is surely worth doing, but that is not reporting the results of accurate observing so organized as to distinguish clearly between the exceptional and the usual, and degrees in between. This last sentence was written heavily and cautiously. I may risk more brevity: just man watching, a task much harder than bird watching, is rare among moralists. Moreover, the writer in recent times, and to a degree throughout Western cultural history, has felt himself shut out from ordinary men by his superior sensitiveness, or superior brightness, or some other superiority. Where he is not tempted to exhort or complain, he is then often tempted to shine. The aphorist, La Rochefoucauld, for example, or Nietzsche at his best, however admirably they say certain things —"true" things, even—are particularly unreliable as reporters of what ordinary people are like, and of what such people believe to be right and proper. Or, to underscore the obvious, the introductory paragraphs of the *New Yorker* do not do the job of man watching for our contemporary United States. Even the *Reader's Digest* is probably a better man watcher.

Yet it must be repeated that the whole body of Western literature is a priceless store of source material for the historian of morals. He cannot begin to know this whole body, not even indirectly through literary histories. He can but sample. On the whole, the most useful genre from our present point of view is the novel and its analogues—Chaucer's *Canterbury Tales,* for example, and even some of the epics—where the writer sets himself up as observer and narrator rather than as moralist. The great histories, of course, are useful, more so when they are the work of a restrained and conscientious moral philosopher like Thucydides or a bright but not too Voltairian a storyteller like Herodotus than when they are the work of a deeply injured moralist like Tacitus, or a soured one like Henry Adams. There is a residue of observation of actual human conduct even in the work of writers whom the French, who used to be masters of the genre, call *moralistes*. La Rochefoucauld's

"There are those who would never have loved had they not heard love talked about" is penetrating though clever; note that La Rochefoucauld wrote "loved," not "made love."

With the beginning of printing in the fifteenth century and of journalism in the seventeenth, the record of human activity of all sorts in the West begins to be very complete; with the beginnings of statistics and of the behavioral or social sciences in the eighteenth, it begins to be better organized. There are still gaps and difficulties, but what the historian calls source material is for these centuries almost too abundant. Moreover, the technological revolutions of the modern West have also been revolutions in scholarship. The labors of generations of scholars have unearthed a great deal of information about the Western past, so that even though the past—especially the Greco-Roman past—may be gradually pushed out of higher education, there is already on our great library shelves an accumulation of "facts" about this culture that would have amazed, delighted, and perhaps disillusioned a humanist of the Renaissance.

The historian of morals will find in the work of social historians one of his most valuable sources of material on what ordinary men and women have done. Social history is often an amorphous mass of details, but it is a splendid mine—or, rather, heap of tailings—in which the historian of morals will find much good ore. It is not an altogether new kind of history; Herodotus was a fine social historian. But it offered the nineteenth century a convenient repository for much information about the past the scholars were digging up, and which couldn't be fitted anywhere else. A work like Ludwig Friedländer's *Roman Life and Manners under the Early Empire,* though it seems to have hardly any structure and barely even a point of view, brings together in one place an immense amount of fragmentary information about what the Romans were doing. There are many others of the sort.

The great problem remains: How can these odds and ends of facts be put together? Is there a describable *normal* human conduct in a given time and place? Certainly in the sense of a statistical mean or average, let alone a distribution curve, there is not much use in the historian's attempting to achieve anything of the sort. I have already noted as a warning the work of the late Dr. Kinsey. We do, however, constantly try to form notions of the typical, the normal, the "ideal," if you do not object to the word, where we lack not so much facts for the mind to work on as a good, reliable guide or tool for the mind to work with. The scientist has in mathematics such a tool. The humanist will maintain that he has tradition-developed methods which, aided by intuitive familiarity with the human activities he is studying, and supported by scholarly conscientiousness and, if possible, by a little common sense, will enable him to draw not wholly invalid generalization out of even imperfect or incomplete data. The humanist may well be right. I shall do my best in this book to live up to his standards.

Our supply of material information in the field of *ethics* is abundant, even for the earlier periods of written Western history. The historian of formal philosophy must regret lacunae, such as the lack of works of the pre-Socratics, or of whole texts of the two great founders of the rival schools of ethics, Epicurus and Zeno the Stoic. It would be a great addition to our heritage to have more, for instance, from the Heraclitus who could leave the brilliant fragment "character as fate." Still, the historian of ideas can hardly complain that he does not know what Greek and Roman formal philosophers thought about the good life. Man is an incurably moral animal, and almost every written record, and much of his other records, such as the fine arts, give some hint as to what he thought good and what he thought evil. Formal philosophical ethics are probably a much less unreliable guide to what ordinary men thought right and proper than it is fashionable in certain intellectual circles even now to admit. But we can supplement the work of ethical philosophers by much that unquestionably does touch the lives of ordinary men—codes of conduct for religious groups, law codes, folk wisdom and its reflection in such works as Franklin's *Poor Richard,* folk art of various kinds, and a great deal of the literature I have mentioned above as a source of information about the conduct of ordinary men. Special care, of course, needs to be taken in special cases; the harsh criminal law codes of most Western European countries in the eighteenth century, for instance, are by no means a reliable indication of what anybody thought was right and proper at the time. Nor from the fact that in popular literature at most times and places in the West the cuckolded husband is a lamentable figure, the wife and the lover quite admirable ones, would it be safe to conclude that ordinary men and women *really* felt adultery to be an ethical good.

But abundant though our information about what Westerners have considered to be ethically good and ethically bad may be, the problem of organizing this information is at least as difficult as for actual human conduct. The problem of the typical or normal, and of the nature and extent of variations, remains a serious one for the study of the ideal as for the study of the actual, as difficult for the study of attitudes as for the study of performance. Here there can hardly be mention of statistical treatment. It would be wonderful to have the results of a properly conducted public-opinion poll of attitudes in times past. What did the English think about "corruption" under Walpole in 1734? What did Parisians think about the St. Bartholomew's massacre in 1572 (strongly approve, mildly approve, mildly disapprove, strongly disapprove, don't know)? What did they think about the same event a hundred years later? Two hundred years later? Three hundred years later? Of course, one cannot give even retrospective guesses in terms of figures. Londoners may have disapproved more strongly of Walpole's regime of graft in 1834 than in 1734; there should have been more "don't knows" in 1834 than in Walpole's own lifetime, for the British have the gift of forgetting the less noble parts of their past. Parisians would probably have shifted from approval to disapproval of St. Bartholomew's Eve by 1772. In spite of the humane aspects of nineteenth-century culture, it is possible that the poll in 1872 would show some rise in approvals over the one in 1772, for the great French Revolution had reawakened religious fears and hatreds. I feel pretty sure that even after four centuries the "don't knows" of indifference or ignorance would not have increased greatly in Paris, for the French feel fully the weight of their history.

But these guesses little befit so serious a matter as history, which can hardly afford to indulge in the relaxation of putting itself in the conditional mood. I shall try in this book to achieve by the methods of the humanist reasonably good generalizations—not mere guesses—about the moral preferences of men in past times. In particular, I shall try to rescue this study from the rag-bag incoherence of much social history by trying to describe as concretely as possible the varieties of what men have held up as the *admirable human being*—the *moral ideal,* to use a good, simple, concrete term.[14]

Word trouble looms here, of course. "Hero" is an obvious possibility; but that word is stained by Carlyle's private misuse of it, and has, moreover, much too specific associations with simple early societies and noble cultures to do what is necessary here. Words like "type," "pattern," or some compound of "figure," as in "father-figure," seem to me either too flat or too closely associated with the vocabulary of formal psychology. As for the "admirable," I shall not mind if you prefer the "enviable" human figure, though I should think it better to *add* enviable to admirable, for admiration and envy often go together, though one or the other may be a mere trace, in the human soul. The word "ideal" has also the advantage that it at least

[14] W. E. H. Lecky in his introductory chapter to the *History of European Morals from Augustus to Charlemagne* (New York, Braziller, 1955, Vol. I, pp. 153 ff.) has some interesting remarks on what he calls "moral types" and "rudimentary virtues." (Two volumes are in this edition printed as one, paged as two.)

suggests that the admired figure is not any single human being. Of course, the ideal can sometimes be "embodied" in a real living person, or in a fictitious character who is quite as much a living person. Achilles embodies or personifies much of the old Greek ideal. Abraham Lincoln does so for Americans. But there remains a residue no one real figure can quite encompass. If it is at all possible to make sensible generalizations about the American ideal—and the old problem of accurate generalization is most acute in problems of national character in our modern world—the final form or picture must be a composite to which, in addition to Lincoln, Henry Ford, Jefferson, Washington, and even Emerson make their contributions. It is tempting to add to this list Paul Bunyan, Babe Ruth, and Gary Cooper, with Marilyn Monroe thrown in for good measure.

This last remark suggests a further difficulty. Even if you grant that with due caution and by adding all sorts of variations for nationality, class, religion, even personality, one can arrive at a most complicated picture, there will still remain the question: Is this what people *really* admired, or did they merely *say* they admired it, thought it proper to admire it, but actually admired something else, something very different? Or in terms I have been using in this book, is this a purely *ethical* ideal, wholly an "ought" without any influence over the "is," and therefore not really a moral ideal in which the "ought" and the "is" are organically related? There is a point of view from which such a question is wholly unanswerable, and, indeed, presumptuous. No one can get inside another person, *be* another person.

But all science is presumptuous, as the Greek Prometheus and the Hebrew Job learned long ago, with very different results, at the beginnings of our story; the social sciences are even more presumptuous than the natural. We shall have to go ahead with as little as possible of the pride that makes presumption. In daily life we all encounter in others the contrast between what is said and what is done, a contrast that in particularly glaring and unpleasant circumstances we call "hypocrisy." Now the hypocrite, who by definition knows he does one thing and says another and contrary thing, is much rarer than is commonly supposed. For the most part, by a system the psychologist calls our "defenses" we actually manage to keep the inconvenient reality which contrasts with the pleasant ideal altogether out of our minds, or, at any rate, out of our consciousness. *Not by any means always.* The naïve notion occasionally professed in the West that all ethics is hypocrisy is nonsense. Significantly enough, the complementary notions that all actual human conduct is of a piece, not to be judged as good or bad, but just taken as "material," or that actual human conduct really is as ethics states it should be, and evil an illusion, have hardly ever been held here in the West. We do not in daily awareness usually divorce what I call "ethics" and what I call "conduct."[15]

Once again, a concrete example should help. The Christian saint was one of the ideals of the Middle Ages, an ideal that spilled over in part on just ordinary churchmen. But in the contemporary French popular tales known as the *fabliaux,* in the amusing wood carvings on the choir stalls which often make fun of the monks who propped themselves up on them during the long services, in the works of a Chaucer or a Boccaccio, in page after page of the interesting miscellany of medieval documents assembled by the late G. G. Coulton, there is unmistakable evidence of popular irreverence toward the clergy.[16] Priests and, more especially, monks, appear as fornicators, liars, gluttons, drunkards, idlers, hypocrites. Did the medieval peasant and townsman then at heart reject the Christian ethical ideal? Was their true moral preference for something a good deal more worldly, not to say fleshly, than the saint? Did they perhaps most admire the outlaw, the rebel against conventional standards, the Robin Hood? These questions I hope to struggle with in their proper place in our story; here I pose them as examples of difficulties that face us.

The difficulty here may be partly overcome by trying to distinguish between admiration and envy in particular instances, for admiration is, in common usage, considered good, and envy bad. Neither good nor bad—this is a cliché I have not yet permitted myself, but it is a sound and unavoidable cliché—is often found in human conduct in the simple and mutually exclusive state they are often found in ethics; they are mixed, though, again, almost always in varying proportions, which can be, not mathematically weighed or measured, but humanly weighed and measured. For the human ideal type of a given culture, men almost always feel a kind of admiration not necessarily unmixed with envy, but an admiration that makes them even in their secret conscience unaware or at least unashamed of the tincture of envy present. Thus the Greeks admired Achilles; thus we admire Lincoln. In our American

[15] I realize that there are in our Western tradition pantheistic and universalist philosophies and theologies which get rid of evil completely—and sometimes of good also: and I know that the followers of Mrs. Eddy find illusory much that the rest of us find only too real. But I think that those who deny the reality of *evil* are much more nagged by something inside themselves that rejects this world view than are those who deny the reality, or, at any rate, the prevailing, of *good.* The pure pessimists seem perversely to *enjoy* their metaphysics more than do the pure optimists.
[16] *Life in the Middle Ages,* four volumes in one, New York, Macmillan, 1931.

culture the gangster hero is envied for his success, his wealth, his fame, but he is not admired as a moral ideal. One good test is that failure ruins a gangster with all but the most fanatically devoted of his "admirers"; there are no martyrs save among the good.

The problem of the winning scoundrel is certainly a real one. I should not question for a moment the common verdict that Satan comes out for many readers as the hero of Milton's *Paradise Lost*. But Satan in this poem is by no means what I mean by a "moral ideal" in the West. The old Latin tag puts the matter more clearly: *Video meliora proboque; deteriora sequor.*[17] Poor Ovid has had a bad press. I think he really meant this, as I think another rather spotted moral being, La Rochefoucauld, meant his basically identical statement: Hypocrisy is the tribute vice pays to virtue.[18] Our morals are as real as our digestion; the good and bad no more and no less mysterious in one than in the other.

There will be a long line of these ideal figures or patterns, none of them to be treated without qualifications, without some question as to how universal their appeal, how real the esteem in which they were held by various groups in the community. These figures will inevitably be varied and in one sense disparate, since the degree of moral dignity, the extent to which they seem to reflect conduct as well as ethics, and much else about them will not be the same. We shall encounter the Homeric hero, the beautiful-and-good of the Golden Age of Greece.[19] We shall have to measure the Roman citizen–soldier–country gentleman of the great days of the Republic, the Christian saint, the Renaissance man of *virtù,* the French aristocrat of the best days of Louis XIV, the English gentleman, the French *philosophe* of the eighteenth century, the Prussian *Junker,* the Byronic artist, the pure scientist, the American frontiersman or "pioneer," and many others. They will not be as real as the flesh-and-blood individuals who figure in narrative history, nor as varied and as complex. But we can hope they will prove quite as interesting. And they are even more important, for they are a distillation of men's hopes and fears. They are the guides, the myths, the symbols, of which our hope-ridden,

---

[17] Ovid, *Metamorphoses*, VII, 20. (I see the better course and approve it; I follow the worse.)

[18] *Maximes*, No. 218.

[19] *kalokagathia*. This deceptively ordinary phrase has been the despair of generations of translators; it is, of course, untranslatable. So, too, are *virtù* and *philosophe*, which also appear on this list. I shall try, as such terms arise, to make their meaning clear in a translation which will be necessarily a periphrasis; but I shall often use the original terms in the text, preferring exactness to good taste, these two being, unfortunately, not always identical.

fear-ridden age—or at least the prophets, publicists, and analysts of our age —are so conscious.

This concept of a moral ideal will, I hope, help tie together in some kind of unity the diverse materials of this book. I shall also make frequent use of a unifying concept worth brief semantic notice here, for I do not find quite the right word or phrase in common American usage: I am going to make much use of the word "agon." Western men have always striven among themselves, as individuals and as groups. Our own society likes to use the term "competition," and, especially, the misleading term "free competition," which have for our purposes here much too narrow connotations from economics. "Conflict" is a good and necessary word—and thing—but its use might to some readers carry the suggestion that men commonly fight for the sake of fighting, that they are "naturally" bellicose, competitive, instinctively and masculinely inclined to mauling. So, no doubt, are many men. But I prefer to emphasize by my choice of words what they fight, or compete, for; this I hope to achieve in part by borrowing from the Greek the word "agon" (ἀγών), which I shall translate, with an ironic glance at the social Darwinists, as the "struggle for prize."

The agon was originally the formal religiously ritualized assembly of the Greeks to witness their games, and only later came to mean any struggle, trial, or danger, which, given overtones of harshness and pain, made the word *agonia* (ἀγωνία) and our own "agony." But simply as agon, the word can carry a great and complex weight of meaning—the desire of men to gain honor and esteem by winning out in competition with their fellows, the need for ritual recognition of such achievement, the need for rules of the game, for a code, in short, for morality—since a genuine free-for-all, "nature red in tooth and claw," is simply not humanly enjoyable, not even bearable, for long— the reality of conflict, of bitter, heart-rending struggle even when it is so regulated and moralized, the pain, the tragedy (*agonia*) of success as well as of failure, the driving animal force of living that makes even "blessed are the meek" a kind of battle cry, man's need of much, so unreasonably much. No single word or phrase can carry all the weight of human nature; that is why the struggle for life, the class struggle, competition, co-operation, the lust for wealth, the will to power, the will to shine, the desire of the moth for the star, cannot sum up what makes us what we are. I do not claim for "agon" a magic I deny these other terms. I use it in this book largely because I think that, especially for American readers, who are likely to have inclinations toward a misleadingly innocent economic interpretation of human conduct, toward the often naïve *cui bono,* it may help redress the balance toward recognition of the great part ritual combat or competition, fully integrated with religious and moral sentiments, has played in our Western past, and still plays in our Western present. The agon, originally knightly and heroic, has spread to the full range of human interests, from head-hunting to the acquisition of honorary degrees. It seems, indeed, to have played a part in that extraordinary phenomenon of our contemporary Western society the rise in the birth rate among the comfortably off. To have many children is to give proof of being fully adjusted; and adjustment, oddly enough, perhaps, after all, democratically enough, has become a prize in the agon.

IV

This introduction must not swallow the book. We are all, in contrast to most of our Victorian predecessors, so aware of the gaps between ethics and conduct, or, more fundamentally and specifically, so aware of the inadequacy of the explanations of human nature and human conduct—and the consequent anticipations of future human conduct—which the Victorians took over from the eighteenth-century Enlightenment, that I am tempted to call here at least part of the whole roll of questions at issue: What, if anything, does the term "moral progress" mean? What is there in the old debate on "heredity versus environment" for the historian of morals? Is there, perhaps, some foundation for the vulgar modern notion that problems of morals are essentially problems of sex, and is that notion exclusively modern or exclusively vulgar? How important is the structure of classes in a given society and its distribution of incomes for the historian of morals? Was Weber right about Calvinist ethical justification for worldly wealth?

Many of these problems will come up in their due place in this study. Here we must as a last introductory word note that for the historian of morals and of ethics on the one hand and of religion and of theology on the other, there arises another one of these intricate problems of breaking down in analysis a relation so close as to be, in real life for real people, a felt unity. The old debate as to whether religion and morals *can* be divorced ought at least to be somewhat affected by what seems to me to be the fact that in Western experience they *never have been* divorced. Such a statement does, indeed, imply a definition of religion that by no means all Westerners will accept. I consider that in addition to the classic revealed monotheisms of the West, Jewish, Christian, and Moslem, and the classic polytheisms of Greece and Rome and the much less classic ones of Germans, Celts, and Slavs, there has been a whole series of what the eighteenth century liked to call "natural" religions for which it is difficult to find a good common term. I am being quite fashionable today when I note modern Marxism as one of these religions without a supernatural godhead. What the Marxist believes about the nature of the universe—his religion—seems to me to have some relation to what he believes about the nature of man and his place in that universe—his morals. The same is true of the positivist, the rationalist, the member of an ethical-culture society, and all the other varieties of what M. Raymond Aron calls a "secular religion." Here again a final warning: I shall not assume either that a man's religion "determines" his moral beliefs and practices or that a man's moral beliefs and practices "determine" his religion. Once more, they are mutually dependent.

But difficulties—difficulties of securing from all my readers that suspension of moral indignation I wish as a historian of morals to obtain as often as possible—force me to use another pretentious term, one most offensive to the purist in language. Since words like "religion" and "theology" applied, say, to modern Western nationalism, or to Marxism, or to any form of Enlightenment clearly do offend many Christians, I shall reluctantly fall back at times on that horrid Germanism "world view" (*Weltanschauung*). No theist, I think, will deny that the Marxist, or even the Enlightened democrat, has at least a world view; and we need not pay much attention to the Marxist or other Enlightened when they say they have no such thing, but merely a way of finding the truth—scientific truth. Everyone who tries to read this book has a world view, or a set of world views; indeed, I suspect that world views are held by those well down in that already old-fashioned order of rank we call the I.Q.

We are ready, then, to embark on a brief survey of a phase of Western history that with the imperialistic drive so natural to man I am here tempted to call the most important, the most essential, phase of that history. But I will settle for less: the history of morals is simply an important, difficult, and relatively neglected part of that history.

Origins: The Ancient Near East

THE DISTINGUISHED AMERICAN EGYPTOLOGIST J. H. Breasted once wrote a book about a phase of ancient Egyptian culture which he entitled *The Dawn of Conscience*.[1] Breasted's love for his subject led him to claim for the Egyptians a priority that is hardly theirs. It is indeed quite possible that the Jews found in earlier Egyptian writings the basis for much of the "wisdom literature" of the Old Testament. It may even be possible to claim for the Egyptians the first recorded examples of men thinking about ethical problems, though the specialist in Mesopotamian studies might maintain that the creation myths of that area, which may well be at least as old as anything of the sort we have from Egypt, show men definitely aware of moral good and moral evil, and their implications for conduct.

We need not here take sides on this issue, for the actual dawn of conscience—it must have been a very gradual one—is hopelessly lost in prehistory. At a minimal definition, the notion of conscience demands an awareness of a future. *Homo sapiens* must have had that awareness very early in his evolution, if not from the very beginning. With that awareness there must have come long, long ago the symbolic expression of a mood Robert Frost put into our words just yesterday in his familiar poem "The Road Not Taken" from *Mountain Interval*. The man of the Stone Ages must have regretted that he took one road, not the other: this is surely the dawn of conscience. These men were moral beings, and had a moral history, but that history will never be written. The skeletal remains and the tools and other artifacts which give

[1] New York, Scribner, 1933.

30

us all the information we are likely to get about these men and women simply do not answer the kind of question the historian of morals must ask. It is quite clear, for instance, that axes and arrows were used to kill human beings as well as game, but we do not know how the killers felt about the killing. It seems likely that some primitive ancestors of Western men did *not* fight much; but were they *moral pacifists?* Anthropological studies of modern "primitives" permit a very safe inference that at least within a specific in-group the ethical concept enshrined in our word "murder" existed among these men of the Stone Ages. We can on the same basis make a good many inferences, such, for instance, as that they did not take sex in their stride; they must have worried about it, talked about it, and would, if they could, have written about it.

All our sound knowledge of recent and existing primitive societies does remain inference when it is applied to Western prehistoric societies. It has been of very great use in eliminating, or at least cutting down the general acceptance of, certain misleading simplifications about human nature, and hence, of course, about morals, that we have inherited, above all, from eighteenth-century notions about an original "state of nature" in which men were, to put it mildly, believed to have been very different from Westerners in 1780. Indeed, what can be, not immodestly, called the cumulative knowledge about human beings that the social scientists have gradually built up does enable the historian of Western morals to start off with some broad generalizations about the possible ways in which what went on during the hundreds of centuries of prehistory help explain what went on in our brief Western history—or, at the very least, to sketch out some limits of Western conduct not always recognized as limits by those who set up Western ethical standards.

We are, of course, on the unsettled ground of analogy. There are, for example, good grounds, the biologists believe, for the statement that when we fall we "instinctively" put up our arms because the "instinct" to do this was part of the physiological equipment of our tree-borne ancestors. But this action, which helped these very distant ancestors to grab the nearest branch when they fell by accident, is of no help to us, and is likely to give us a broken arm we should not have had were we able to fall with the instincts of the cat, or like the *trained* actor in a death scene, loosening up generally.[2]

Now a parallel case might be found in an activity more obviously involved

[2] The instance is from Fred Hoyle, *Man and Materialism*, New York, Harper, 1956, pp. 25-26.

in a history of morals than a physical fall. We are all subject to the kind of emotion I have in my introductory chapter called moral indignation; indeed, the news photograph of the good Negro girl and the bad white girl there cited will do as our concrete example. A large number of Americans were certainly made angry by the sight of that photograph. In the process that makes us "feel" this anger, the body produces a flow from the adrenal glands, a flow that in the primitive past of *Homo sapiens* moved him to anger or fear, and hence to fighting or running away, either action in its proper place a response useful to his survival. But the action of the adrenal glands we get from reading the daily newspaper can hardly end in any such direct action; the letter to the editor is no substitute for hitting someone hard—and quickly. It is possible that this misdirected adrenal flow may have something to do with all sorts of human ills now fashionably called psychosomatic.[3]

At the very least, it does seem likely that in civilization men face in the relation between their thought-sentiment and their "rational" or "scientific" thought a kind of problem that did not disturb prehistoric men. I should guess that all the very real troubles of conscience—yes, conscience—suggested to so many of us by terms like "prejudice," "wishful thinking," "a priori," "unscientific" are recent indeed in the long evolution of mankind. We cannot often make so simple a confession of the strength of our made-up minds as the following, from an Englishman concerned with the horrid dangers of Americanization:

I have long viewed with alarm the influx of American television programmes. It is one of our biggest social problems. *I have never seen the American programmes* but I am convinced, after considerable study, that they are a bad influence.[4]

Another broad generalization is even more hazardous than these last, since it involves that dangerous and attractive intellectual device, the concept of a social or cultural "organism." But it is worth our brief attention. From the admirable studies of children made by Jean Piaget and his assistants, it is clear that very young children go through a stage, roughly from four years or so to nine, but varying with individuals, in which they regard the rules of their games—the moral code of an important part of their lives—as absolutes, as part of a reality wholly external to them. Moreover, since they are unable

[3] For an interesting sketch of this problem in nontechnical but scientifically respectable language, see Joseph Pick, "The Evolution of Homeostases," *Proceedings* of the American Philosophical Society, XCVIII, 1954, p. 298.
[4] Quoted in Terrence O'Flaherty's column in the San Francisco *Chronicle*, September 27, 1957. Italics mine. The man who made this statement would probably explain that his "study," though not direct observation, still gave him the "facts" that made up his mind. We lack the courage of our prejudices.

to distinguish among rules, laws, and "natural" events, their concepts of agency, responsibility, and guilt are quite different from those of adults.[5] Now it is risky to appeal to the familiar biological notion of recapitulation—the human fetus, for instance, briefly has something like gills, retracing, so to speak, almost instantaneously the stage of our evolution when we were fishes. The morals of Piaget's child subjects do bear striking similarity to the morals of Western societies we think of as "young," say, the Greeks of the Homeric epics or the Jews of the Pentateuch, not so much in their actual content, of course, as in the moral attitude toward rules as absolutes. It is less risky to say simply that, quite apart from any parallelism between biological and cultural development, it may well be that our Western culture has preserved over the last few dozen centuries strong traces of an ethical absolutism characteristic of earlier Western societies.

Even more apposite, perhaps, is the recent work of the biologists and naturalists who call their field "ethology." The work of Konrad Lorenz, N. Tinbergen, and many others suggests that the higher animals develop certain elaborate forms of behavior they are *not* born with, in the old sense we used to think of as "instinct," but which they do not have to "learn" either. We moralists are perhaps too much influenced by the assumption that since human morals can be and are so thoroughly verbalized, they must be wholly learned, wholly the product of much symbolic thinking embodied and even codified in "culture." It goes against the grain to think of "releasers" and "imprinters" that bring the human conscience into play—or work; but this is a line of investigation that many believe will prove fruitful for the social sciences. In the balance, surely, the Western turn in the Age of Reason *was* a turn to excessive intellectualism and to even more excessive meliorism.[6]

Finally, there remain the much-disputed efforts to find leads—indeed, whole theories—for sociology and anthropology from modern depth psychology. Freud's own attempts in *Totem and Taboo* and in *Moses and Monotheism*, the application of Jung's concept of a "collective unconscious" to actual social problems, the recent tendency within psychoanalysis itself to study the social and cultural environment of the patient—all this work has so far failed to attain general acceptance among students of human relations. It is fashionable now to make fun of Freud's efforts, as a good Jewish nonreligious Jew, to find the origins of old Jehovah, not in a volcano, but in the

[5] J. Piaget, *The Moral Judgment of the Child*, trans. by M. Gabain, New York, Harcourt, Brace, 1932.
[6] The reader will find an interesting—and not at all ponderous—introduction to this field in Konrad Lorenz, *King Solomon's Ring*, New York, Crowell, 1952.

patriarch, the old bull of the herd. But the hope lingers on that we shall find in the continued study of human behavior, and with the full collaboration of the students of anthropology and prehistory, some clues to the reasons why men so obstinately and firmly continue to behave like human beings, and not like the happy, rational, natural MAN of the eighteenth-century Enlightenment.

At the very least, we can conclude that the work of biologist, anthropologist, and sociologist—though not all of them would be willing to admit this —does suggest that a great deal of our conduct is "determined" by what happened to our ancestors, more particularly to our human and anthropoid ancestors in the million or so years before written history began a mere five thousand years or so ago. The biological aspect is clear indeed: no significant change in historic times. Even for the subgroups the ethnologist studies, the degree of mixture of different "races" within the West has probably not changed significantly in historic times. The last few decades in particular have certainly submitted some specimens of Homo sapiens to material environments wholly unprecedented. It is sufficient here to mention the airplane and the possibilities of space flight.

But such matters must be left to the final chapter, when we face such difficult questions as whether our total human equipment is good enough to stand up against what science and technology have done for us and to us. Here we need no more than suggest that, in many ways which we cannot fully understand, our distant past may well be the most important thing in our lives. We were all nomads ten thousand years or so ago, and our Celtic and Germanic ancestors were nomads or seminomads much more recently than that. Clearly men *did* make the transition from the life of hunting and food gathering to the grinding toil of farming, the disciplined sociopolitical life of village and city, the simple *staying put* made necessary for the masses by the so-called "neolithic revolution." Perhaps survivals of old nomad days have had a part in the recurrent phases of cultural "primitivism" in the West, the last of which, the eighteenth-century cult of Nature and the Noble Savage, is not yet quite dead. Perhaps the nomad of 20,000 B.C. had some part in that very modern miracle, the settlement of the American West.

One more very large topic will suggest the range and difficulty of these problems. The human family is an old and universal institution. We find it at the beginnings of history in all societies, and though the prehistorian can tell us little about the family in our Western Stone Ages, it is inconceivable that the family did not exist. A great deal of human conduct is tied up with the family—sex, child rearing, economic activity, law, and much else. The anthropologists, who have taught us so much, have told us that the Christian monogamous family in its nineteenth-century Victorian form is not the only successful form of the family, and they have, perhaps without always intending to do so, shaken the belief that this nineteenth-century Western family is the best form of the family, the apex of moral evolution. Now, in the mid-twentieth century, the prophets of doom find the family disintegrating—in the United States, already disintegrated.[7] The historian of morals, indeed the historian *tout court,* can suggest that hundreds of centuries of the family—granted, not quite in the Victorian tradition—make it extremely unlikely that the family will disappear in our day, or even change its ways greatly. But he cannot go much further than that. He can note that over the ages, biology and important phases of culture have combined to put women in a position "inferior" in some sense to that of men in the West; he can even go further, and suggest that some of the resistance men still make to complete equality between the sexes is probably a survival from the distant past. And so for many of our attitudes in matters of sex, incest, for example, or less shocking forms of sexual abnormality; they go back to the beginnings of our record, and presumably further, though by no means as constants in form and intensity.

To take another and less serious instance, many of us feel special pleasure in a fireplace or a campfire. It has been, indeed, a favorite literary device to take this pleasure back through the ages to our distant ancestors basking in the warmth and security of the safe, controlled little fire in the cave. Certainly simple utilitarian explanations seem here inadequate. Modern American houses are overheated successfully enough without a fireplace. Nor does the motive of snobbery, a perfectly good "rational" motive, seem quite enough by itself, for the usual development of snobbery in these matters in the United States is in the direction of pride in the very latest thing possible. The chimneyless house, however, has not taken hold.

The difficulty in this and our other instances is to set up a satisfactory explanation of just how these attitudes were transmitted over thousands of years. Our high-school course in general science set our minds straight about the genetics of peas, and even of blue eyes in human beings. But it is hard to believe that there is a gene which bears a love of fireplace fires, or even a horror of incest. Certainly those particular genes have not been found. Yet

---

[7] I am exaggerating, but not much. For an example of such a prophet, see P. A. Sorokin, *The American Sex Revolution,* Boston, Porter Sargent, 1956.

the concept of *cultural* inheritance remains vague, a vagueness well brought out if you try to use realistically a term like "cultural genetics." Clues there are, such as Walter Bagehot's happy phrase "unconscious imitation." In the broadest sense, it is quite certain that the adult generation does "transmit" attitudes to the younger generation, that the young reach adulthood "conditioned" to these attitudes, which they then find difficult to change. But some of them do get changed—or, obviously, there would be no history.

As always, there is a nagging metaphysical problem at the bottom here: permanence versus change. As usual, the twentieth-century Westerner has to settle as comfortably as he can on both sides. "Something" changes, but "something" is *relatively* permanent.[8] We must note the particular form the problem takes here, since one of the great and unsolved questions of morals in our own mid-twentieth century is how great and how rapid *changes* in men's *conduct*—for example, in their conduct as members of existing "sovereign" in-groups known as nation-states—are possible. The problem has many sides, but one important side involves the degree to which we are all imprisoned in our past. If the disposition to do certain things has, so to speak, been built into us by thousands of years of human social life, the normal assumption would be that we shall continue to do, or try to do, those things. In mid-eighteenth century, as we shall see, the enlightened Westerner believed substantially that no such historically determined disposition, *at least no such disposition toward what he regarded as evil,* existed in human beings as individuals or in groups. In mid-twentieth century, such a belief is barely possible anywhere in the West.

If the last two centuries of work in the social sciences by no means tell us what part—if any—of our morals we owe to our prehistoric ancestors, it has on the whole made it quite clear that those who make plans to reform men and their institutions ought not to neglect human history and prehistory, since only through such history and prehistory can they learn what kind of materials—to use a deliberately provocative word—they are working with. They may well have to learn that those materials are really limited, let us say, like "natural" fibers; there are no possible human equivalents of the synthetic "miracle" fibers. Moreover, these last two centuries of work in the social sciences—in the wider sense, also the work of scholars, novelists, philosophers, of all concerned with human conduct—have made it clear that

[8] I owe to my friend Albert Léon Guérard the very apposite tale of a doctor's oral in which the badgered candidate was pushed into a more and more intransigent position. One of his tormentors commented, "Well, Mr. So-and-So, you *are* an absolutist, aren't you!" This time the candidate scored: "I suppose I am, sir, relatively."

36

such conduct has long been exceedingly varied. Primitive men and primitive societies studied in modern times have turned out not to be simple, not to conform to any one pattern, and its seems hardly likely that our own Western prehistoric ancestors were simple either. More particularly, the search for some original forms of human personality and human society which we could use in good practical propaganda and planning in our own society has proved pretty fruitless. Over thousands of years and over the whole planet, there have been communist societies and societies based on private property, there have been really bewilderingly complex variations in kinship and marriage systems, there have been variously defined in-groups and out-groups, there have been peaceful societies and bellicose societies, and there have even been societies other than our own postmedieval Western society in which individual economic success was esteemed. Herbert Spencer's famous summing up of the evolution of human society, from "homogeneity to heterogeneity," from the simple to the complex, has to be amended into that formula so inevitable in the sciences, so repugnant to us all as human beings, heirs of that confused and confusing cultural evolution: with respect to A, yes; with respect to B, no. The motorcar is more complex than the horse-drawn wagon. The division of labor in modern Western society is more complex than it was in the Stone Age. But grammatically, at least, our modern Western languages are far simpler than earlier ones and our kinship system is simplicity itself compared with those of many "primitives." In respect to the still-little-understood working of what we call memory, it is likely that the central nervous system of our primitive ancestors was more complex than ours; it had to be, for a man's mind was then his whole reference library.[9]

In sum, the thing we human beings are and have been, the "human nature" we shall shortly see was first systematized as a master concept by the later Greeks, is not universally and rapidly malleable; but it is extraordinarily

[9] I do not wish to be understood as suggesting in the above passage either that our own contemporaries have abandoned all concepts of a "cultural evolution" of humanity, or of Western humanity, or even that among such concepts of evolution they have wholly given up the basic notion of some savage, earlier, and "lower" stages and later civilized "higher" stages of the process; nor do I wish to imply on the other side of the contrast that Herbert Spencer's contemporaries were all in agreement with him in these matters. Nevertheless, the range of our contemporary theories about such cultural evolution is great indeed, from the Marxist to the Toynbean and the Sorokinian; and the more moderate ones, such as those of the anthropologist A. L. Kroeber and the historian and sociologist of religion Christopher Dawson, are far from Victorian unilinear evolutionary concepts. And as for the Victorians themselves, though some of them did reject all notions of evolution, biological as well as cultural, those who accepted such notions were not very far apart—no further, let us say, than were Comte, Buckle, and Spencer in their belief in unilinear "scientific" evolution.

varied and complex. We must reject the kind of metaphor that suggests that planners or "cultural engineers" can do with this human stuff anything like what the plant breeder does with his plants or the organic chemist with his.[10] But we must also reject the kind of metaphor that suggests that this human stuff is really just *one thing,* unchangeable—yet somehow corruptible. So much, it seems to me, the historian of Western morals can risk concluding even before he begins his story.

II

The story can appropriately begin with the ancient Egyptians, even though we cannot accept Breasted's claim that they first knew what we call "conscience." In particular, thanks to the remarkable achievements of several generations of Egyptologists, we can for these people know a great deal about a part of human life of the utmost importance for the historian of morals— their religious beliefs and practices. For earlier peoples, such as the Magdalenians who made the famous cave paintings some ten thousand years ago, we can only guess at their religion. The paintings of bison, the deer, the outlined human hands, often with a finger missing, found on the walls of caves can hardly have been merely the equivalents of our own contemporary decorative or representational arts. The pictured animals were probably put there so that the hunters could thereby somehow kill real animals in the hunt; they probably were not god animals or totem animals, though it is not inconceivable that they may have been. Archaeologists have also found in these earlier times sculptured female figurines with buttocks and breasts greatly exaggerated; the inference is obvious—they have some relation to a cult of fertility. As for the mutilated hands, they suggest a possible form of ritual sacrifice, perhaps even a substitution of a finger for an earlier total sacrifice. But even with the aid of comparisons with known primitive peoples, interpretation of these archaeological materials falls well short of a theology or a sociology of religion, and tells us little about ethics.

For the Egyptians, however, we have a substantial part of all these latter. We must therefore pause for a moment and examine the very thorny problem of what we mean by religion and what religion has to do with morals. The problem is thorny for us largely because a great number of educated Westerners today consider that they have no religion but do have morals, and that the separation of religion and morals is a natural, normal part of Western

[10] We must reject it even when the metaphor is expanded into a book, as in B. F. Skinner's *Walden Two,* New York, Macmillan, 1948.

life. Historically speaking, this is simply not so; religion and morals have been intimately related, though it makes little sense to say that either is the "cause" of the other. It is thorny also because for the faithful Jew, Christian, or Moslem, what he believes about God and God's ways to man can never be wholly explained by a historical-naturalistic approach; even a term like "sociology of religion" must, in view of the secularist origins of the study of sociology, have for the faithful of a revealed religion some unpleasant overtones. The Western monotheisms make a place for history, and therefore for uncertainty and doubt; but they are obliged to put God and God's work *ultimately* outside history and beyond doubt. Finally, any sort of religious belief, including most emphatically our own secular religions like nationalism, Marxism, the various positivist or rationalist beliefs stemming mostly from the eighteenth-century Enlightenment, gives our judgments on all forms of religion an inescapable emotional bias.

Two closely related distinctions commonly made by students of comparative religion here make good guides in an attempt to sort out the complexities of primitive religion and morals. First, the distinction between a *contractual* view held by the believer as to his relation with his god or gods, and a *dependent worshiper*'s view of these relations. The former is nicely summed up in a Latin phrase, *do ut des*—I give that thou mayest give. In this view, the believer complied with certain ritual requirements his faith told him the god insisted on, and in return the god did what the believer wanted him to do; the relation was not unlike that of buyer and seller, with an implied contract. The latter is summed up in such a phrase as "prayer of contrition." The believer loves, fears, is in awe of a Being whom he would never dream of approaching in the mood of a man seeking to make a contract. Second, there is the related distinction between magic and religion, or "true" religion. In magic the magician claims to have a special knowledge of the ways of the gods, or of nature, by which he can produce results; he is a *manipulator*. In religion the priest is the creature of the gods, at most a specially placed intermediary between the believer and the gods, but wholly dependent on the gods; he is, like the laymen from whom in many religions he is hardly distinguishable, a *worshiper*.

Now these distinctions are indeed useful; even one who believes himself free of Western religious influences should be willing to grant that the attitude of the prayerful worshiper is morally superior to that of the self-seeking practitioner of contract or magic. But in applying these distinctions to the stuff of history the gap between the real and the ideal opens clearly. On this earth, Christian life itself has shown varying admixtures of all these attitudes. The familiar Christian opposition of faith and works is at bottom a form of the first opposition noted above. Pure faith is pure worship; pure works are certainly close to pure contract. Again, historical Christianity has never, for the mass of believers, meant the practice of either pure faith or pure works. But then, neither has the practice of the earlier polytheisms, one may hazard, been purely *do ut des*. Above all, the historian is confronted with the difficulty of finding out the attitudes in matters of this sort of the man in the street, the average, the ordinary man. The saint, the noble soul stands out in history at least as firmly as the wicked, the villainous. The good, which in the abstract or even in the average flesh is perhaps less interesting than the bad, is in its exceptional and heroic forms conspicuous indeed. Ikhnaton, the pharaoh who tried, apparently, to purge Egyptian polytheism of its grosser elements, stands out as a lofty idealist. But for the ordinary Egyptian believer, we tend to assume that the formal structure of his religion, the named gods, the sacrifices, the whole ritual is an index of his actual state of mind. All these factors tend overwhelmingly on the side of polytheistic and magical beliefs.

Here, for instance, is an Egyptian mother protecting her child from the powers of darkness.

> Run out, thou who comest in darkness, who enterest by stealth. . . .
> Comest thou to kiss this child? I will not let thee kiss him.
> Comest thou to soothe him? I will not let thee soothe him.
> Comest thou to harm him? I will not let thee harm him.
> Comest thou to take him away? I will not let thee take him away from me.
> I have made his protection against thee out of *Efet*-herb, it makes pain; out of onions, which harm thee; out of honey which is sweet to (living) men and bitter to those who are yonder (the dead); out of the evil (parts) of the *Ebdu*-fish; out of the jaw of the *meret;* out of the backbone of the perch.[11]

The latter part of this invocation is obviously magic, and not at all lofty. Let us put it beside another survival from the long centuries of Egypt.

CREATION OF MAN

> Creator of the germ in woman,
> Who makest seed into men,
> Making alive the son in the body of his mother,
> Soothing him that he may not weep,
> Nurse even in the womb,
> Giver of breath to sustain alive every one that he maketh!

[11] Quoted in Breasted, *Dawn of Conscience,* p. 248. Chapters 13 and 14 of this book give many more examples of magical formulas.

When he descendeth from the body (of his mother) on the
   day of his birth,
Thou openest his mouth altogether,
Thou suppliest his necessities.[12]

This passage from a hymn to the sun-god Aton, whom the pharaoh Ikhnaton in the fourteenth century B.C. tried to establish as center of a universalist monotheistic religion, is quite as clearly high-minded worship. Indeed, Breasted quotes this and other passages from the hymn in the midst of parallel passages from Psalm 104 of the Old Testament, a device perhaps a bit unfairly helped by the lofty mood which anything approaching the style of the King James version automatically produces in the reader of English, but still a fair parallel, no mere trick. Magic and religion here stand confronted; they are not the same thing.

And yet something more needs to be said. In morals as in taste the drastic separation of higher and lower must seem to the observer trying to divest himself of either morals or taste to hide sometimes a certain underlying set of emotions felt both by the experiencer of the high and the experiencer of the low. The Egyptian mother was not just muttering a spell; she was singing a lullaby. All the first part of her song might well have been sung by a mother any time since in the West. There is in her song maternal love, maternal concern over the helplessness of the infant, maternal fear of the unknown. These are all emotions that in more dignified expressions we should accept as humanly desirable; only yesterday, at least, the child psychologist would have said that the existence and strength of such emotions in the mother, even though they were accompanied by the use of magic, was much better for the child than their absence or weakness in the mother, even though accompanied in the latter instance by the best external help our modern medical technology can provide and by good intentions on the part of the mother.

Moreover, we must note here what seems to be a fact of human conduct, however objectionable the mere recognition of this fact may be to many very admirable partisans of the best in human life. Words, gestures, rites of all sorts once firmly become custom lose the referential immediacy which the mind freshly focused on them finds in them. The simple example is afforded by the blasphemies of everyday Christian life, which are not blasphemies at all, but merely emphatic grunts or groans where there is any real emotion, and often no more than obsessively repeated sounds. The Egyptian mother conceivably did not even bother to make the witches' brew to which her song refers; and almost certainly her state of mind was one that the modern intel-

12 Breasted, *Dawn of Conscience*, p. 283.

lectual apparently has difficulty in recognizing, a mood of serene and unthinking acceptance of routine, of custom, of conditioning in almost the Pavlovian sense.

Finally, to draw what we can from these two contrasting passages, it must be noted that there is in the hymn to Aton a touch of what has to be called rhetoric. It is a noble rhetoric, but it wipes no infant's nose. Whether you will go on and infer that Ikhnaton and the courtiers and priests who helped him in his attempt to purify Egyptian religion were perhaps not as good parents as our mother with the spell depends a bit on how much of Rousseau there is in you. The whole Aton movement, of which we know nothing like the details we know for most Christian reform movements, may really have been basically political in intent, an effort to centralize and unify a state and society that often tended to break apart. It is also possible to see in Ikhnaton himself an early example of a moral type we shall not infrequently meet in these pages, the idealist of highest ethical standards, the intellectual too pure for this harsh world of affairs, the martyr, for his reforms failed miserably; and yet also a man by no means without the will to power and the will to be admired, and capable, to gain his ends, of actions that look to outsiders immoral. Again, we don't really know enough to judge him. I suspect that he was an "unprincipled idealist."[13]

The firmest mark the ancient Egyptians have left in the history of culture is their extraordinary awareness of—I am tempted to jargon, obsession with—life after death. Some sort of belief in the survival of something of the individual after the obvious death of the body known to common sense is very common in all sorts of cultures; and the least patronizing of anthropologists has to link this belief with some relatively primitive notions about ghosts and the like, and with simple human desires not to die. But the linkage of all this with the conduct of the deceased in life on earth is far from universal. With the Egyptians the concept of a divine judgment weighing the good and evil of a man's career and assigning reward or punishment after death is clear as early as the third millennium B.C. For the upper classes, at least, there were elaborate ritual forms involving this principle of moral judgment, as well as the well-known efforts to insure at entombment for the dead a physical existence as much like the earthly one as possible. The suppliant to the god Osiris, the judge of the dead, is made to put the best possible case for his innocence. The following passage from the Book of the Dead has a touch of the earthly law court which is certainly not in the purest Christian tradition

[13] This useful and penetrating phrase I owe to the late A. Lawrence Lowell.

in these matters, and has a touch of pride offensive to both Jewish and Christian developed tradition. Indeed, it must be noted that the Jew at Yom Kippur does the exact opposite—he recites his sins. So, too, does the Christian under confession. Yet the moral code has surely more of the Western, if not of the universally human, than the specifically religious psychology of the sacrament itself would show.

Hail to thee, great god, lord of Truth. I have come to thee, my lord, and I am led (hither) in order to see thy beauty. I know thy name, I know the names of the forty-two gods who are with thee in the Hall of Truth, who live on evil-doers and devour their blood, on that day of reckoning character before Wennofer (Osiris). Behold, I came to thee, I bring to thee righteousness and I expel for thee sin. I have committed no sin against people. . . . I have not done evil in the place of truth. I knew no wrong. I did no evil thing. . . . I did not do that which the god abominates. I did not report evil of a servant to his master. I allowed no one to hunger. I caused no one to weep. I did not murder. I did not command to murder. I caused no man misery. I did not diminish food in the temples. I did not decrease the offerings of the gods. I did not take away the food-offerings of the dead. I did not commit adultery. I did not commit self-pollution in the pure precinct of my city-god. I did not diminish the grain measure. I did not diminish the span. I did not diminish the land measure. I did not load the weight of the balances. I did not deflect the index of the scales. I did not take milk from the mouth of the child. I did not drive away the cattle from their pasturage. I did not snare the fowl of the gods. I did not catch the fish in their pools. I did not hold back the water in its time. I did not dam the running water.[14]

For the rest, it is possible to find in the surviving fragments of Egyptian writings a surprisingly representative range of moral attitudes, at least as they are reflected in the writings of the moralists. *The Maxims of Ptahhotep* are believed to be the work of a high official of the twenty-seventh century B.C. It takes no historical imagination at all to confuse Ptahhotep with Polonius, especially as the maxims are his advice to his son. Here is a sample, I trust a fair one:

If thou hast become great after thou wert little, and has gained possessions after thou wert formerly in want, . . . be not unmindful of how it was with thee before. Be not boastful of thy wealth, which has come to thee as a gift of the god. Thou art not greater than another like thee to whom the same has happened.

Be not avaricious in a division, nor greedy (even) for thy (own) goods. Be not

---

14 Breasted, *Dawn of Conscience,* pp. 255-256. The last sentences refer to tampering with rules for the use of irrigation water, as wrong today in Arizona as it was thousands of years ago in Egypt.

43

avaricious towards thy own kin. Greater is the appeal of the gentle than that of the strong.

Follow thy desire (literally "thy heart") as long as thou livest. Do not more than is told thee. Shorten not the time of following desire. It is an abomination to encroach upon the time thereof. Take no care daily beyond the maintenance of thy house. When possessions come, follow desire, for possessions are not complete when he (the owner) is harassed.

If thou hearkenest to this which I have said to thee, all the fashion of thee will be according to the ancestors. As for the righteousness thereof, it is their worth; the memory thereof shall not vanish from the mouths of men, because their maxims are worthy.[15]

Nor is there lacking in Egypt another moral attitude, one in much greater credit among the Western literary, at least, than the admirable commonplaces of Polonius. To some ancient Egyptians, as to James Russell Lowell, right was ever on the scaffold, wrong forever on the throne. Here again one need but sample:

THE CORRUPTION OF MEN

To whom do I speak today?
Brothers are evil,
Friends of today are not of love.

To whom do I speak today?
Hearts are thievish,
Every man seizes his neighbour's goods.

To whom do I speak today?
The gentle man perishes,
The bold-faced goes everywhere.

. . . .

To whom do I speak today?
Robbery is practised,
Every man seizes his neighbour's goods.

. . . .

To whom do I speak today?
There are no righteous,
The land is left to those who do iniquity.

Calamities come to pass today, tomorrow afflictions are not past. All men are silent concerning it, (although) the whole land is in great disturbance. Nobody is

[15] Breasted, *Dawn of Conscience*, pp. 132-137.

free from evil; all men alike do it. Hearts are sorrowful. He who gives commands is as he to whom commands are given; the heart of both of them is content. Men awake to it in the morning daily, (but) hearts thrust it not away. The fashion of yesterday therein is like today. . . . There is none so wise that he perceives, and none so angry that he speaks. Men awake in the morning to suffer every day. Long and heavy is my malady. *The poor man has no strength to save himself from him that is stronger than he.* It is painful to keep silent concerning the things heard, (but) it is suffering to reply to the ignorant man. . . .[16]

The very last passage, attributed to a priest of Heliopolis during the difficulties of a period of crisis often called a "feudal age" (second millennium B.C.) has clearly the marks of a moralist in the midst of a "time of troubles." The priest of Heliopolis is indeed worrying, complaining, but his complaints are somehow more dignified than those of the author of "The Corruption of Men." The priest, for one thing, appears to be puzzled, indeed to be thinking; the author of "The Corruption of Men" is merely relieving himself.

It is hardly possible to conclude much about the moral ideal of the Egyptians. Theirs is a long history, which research has shown to be by no means one of frozen uniformity. It is true that there is an early period of growth and consolidation, a comparatively long period, broken into peaks and valleys of high artistic and literary creativity, and then some dozen final centuries of marking time. In terms basically of ethical theory, there is a definite development from earlier contractual relations with nature gods who get blind obedience from men, to moral relations with gods who approve virtue in their worshipers and condemn vice in them, and thence to the monotheistic worship of Aton and the self-conscious wisdom literature from which we have just quoted. But there is also in the last millennium or so a clear lapse into magic and conformity, a loss of freshness and originality. Even at the height of the culture, however, we cannot from present available sources outline an Egyptian equivalent of the Hebrew prophet, the Greek beautiful-and-good, the European knight of chivalry.

It is, however, possible to discern some phases of what might be called the national character, phases not unimportant for the historian of morals. For all their reaching and overreaching toward another world—their monumental art, their preoccupation with the mysteries of death, the touches of not accepting the things we Westerners feel we know and accept so well from our senses and our science—for all this, there is in the Egyptian record a strong element of what has to be called "realism," the realism that believes itself to be holding a mirror to nature. In sculpture, figures like that of the

16 Breasted, *Dawn of Conscience,* pp. 172-179.

scribe are familiar; he looks busy, capable, and unworried.[17] And in ethics we can always summon up the figure of Ptahhotep of the maxims, maxims much more like those of Franklin than like those of Vauvenargues or La Rochefoucauld. Moreover, though they had a few brief moments of imperialist expansion, though they were a "great power" in the earliest of Western balance-of-power systems, the Egyptians were not very good at war, not by any means a military people. Of course, a great hot fertile valley does not breed warriors—this much we must concede to the "materialistic" interpretation of history. It took invaders from harsher lands, settled in Egypt but still remembering their past, to stir her to expansion. But again the material on this earth always translates itself into the spiritual, or at least into the habitual. The successful long-term militarist is no realist, no accepter of this world and these human beings, but a heaven stormer who would shake us all out of our senses. A military caste is so unnatural, even in the West, that it needs, as we shall see, special educating and conditioning, special moral ideals, to keep going. These apparently the Egyptians did not, over long periods, develop.

They were also gifted inventors, skilled in the practical arts, characteristics the American will list at once as signs of a realistic people. The Greeks, as we know from Herodotus and others, though they were puzzled by the mysterious sides of what they thought was a priest-ridden society, were greatly impressed with the practical side of Egyptian life, with what we should call Egyptian know-how. Moreover, these skills were, in the balance, rather based on the empirical tradition of the craftsman than on anything close to scientific speculation. Astronomy and mathematics owe more to the Babylonians than to the Egyptians; the latter were good at medicine, an art that goes naturally enough with an acceptance of this world and an unwillingness to leave it long for any other. All in all then, it looks as though we can find in ancient Egypt a moral attitude, a moral type, very characteristic of the West, though it has never perhaps quite set the moral tone anywhere. This is the firmly unheroic, indeed not even athletic, unimaginative, undespairing, practical man of common sense. He is not quite Sancho Panza (though Cervantes has come close to him), not quite Poor Richard (though Franklin himself has touches of him); Molière's M. Jourdain misses him as badly as does Sinclair Lewis's Babbitt. In fact, the men of letters are not very good at getting at and reporting a creature so different from themselves; the artist sometimes does better. Take another look at that four-thousand-year-old Egyptian scribe.

[17] See for example Plate 66 in *The Art of Ancient Egypt,* Vienna, Phaidon Press, 1936, or Elie Faure, *Ancient Art,* New York, Garden City Publishing Co., 1937, p. 33.

III

It is hardly necessary here to pay great attention to ancient Mesopotamia. To the general historian, to the historian of culture, there is much in the record of great importance. The historian of Western morals can content himself with noting that the creation myths of the Chaldeans got incorporated into the Hebrew cosmogony—though he will, if he is, above all, concerned with his own modern world, be even more interested to note the glee with which nineteenth-century rationalist opponents of Christianity lighted on evidence that God had not begun his work of creation with the Jews. He will note that in the Code of Hammurabi (about 1800 B.C.) we have a very early and very complete code of laws which, for the moralist, shows the violence and cruelty of punishments one would expect, but which also shows clearly the legislator's attempt to recognize degrees of guilt, a distinction that implies practical recognition of men as independent moral beings, responsible for their acts— just the kind of recognition Piaget's young children were unable to make.

Two peoples do stand out in the long and complex history of the Mesopotamian state system in the kind of relief that interests the historian of morals.

The Assyrians, who from the margin of the great Mesopotamian Valley came to dominate it in a sudden rise in the eighth century B.C., are known as militarists. They seem to have deserved their historical reputation. Their art is highly masculine, bullish and lionish. Their surviving literature is mostly imitative of the Babylonian, for, though successful soldiers sometimes come to admire literature, they do not often create it. There are surviving inscriptions left by conquering heroes in which one of the abiding traits of the military caste stands out in almost caricatural sharpness—their love of boasting by hyperbole, so different from the intellectual's boast by litotes.

But we do not know about these warriors what the historian of morals most needs to know: how they were keyed by education to the hard job of professional heroism. It would be nice to know what the Assyrian equivalent of the Prussian *Junkers'* cadet school was like—there must have been an equivalent—but we do not have for them even the kind of information we have on the education of the Greek warriors who took Troy. Perhaps the Assyrians did not do a good job of military education; at any rate, they held their empire briefly, going down to a revival among the Babylonians they had conquered—perhaps evidence that the Babylonians were not quite as corrupt as the Jewish prophets made them out to be. Here are two specimens from Assyrian remains:

At that time I received the tribute of the land of Isala—cattle, flocks and wine. To the mountain of Kashiari I crossed, to Kinabu, the fortified city of Hulai I drew near. With the masses of my troops and by my furious battle onset I stormed, I captured the city; 600 of their warriors I put to the sword; 3,000 captives I burned with fire; I did not leave a single one among them alive to serve as a hostage. Hulai, their governor, I captured alive. Their corpses I formed into pillars; their young men and maidens I burned in the fire. Hulai, their governor, I flayed, his skin I spread upon the wall of the city of Damdamusa; the city I destroyed, I devastated, I wasted with fire. . . .[18]

And now at the command of the great gods my sovereignty, my dominion, and my power, are manifesting themselves; I am regal, I am lordly, I am exalted, I am mighty, I am honored, I am glorified, I am pre-eminent, I am powerful, I am valiant, I am lion-brave, and I am heroic! (I), Assur-Nasir-Pal, the mighty king, the king of Assyria, chosen of Sin, favorite of Anu, beloved of Adad, mighty one among the gods, I am the merciless weapon that strikes down the land of his enemies. . . .[19]

The Babylonians, especially after their final conquest of the Jews in the sixth century B.C., do appear as the first example of the sensual, corrupt, materialistic big-city men. Clearly, the Jewish priestly men of letters to whom we owe our impressions of the Whore of Babylon were not engaged in an effort at objective analysis of a culture. But we do know that the religion of the Babylonians was a polytheism that goes with settled agriculturalists of such early areas of civilization, with a fertility cult, ritual magic, and a general lack of high-mindedness. The Babylonians seem to have been devoted to business. We simply do not have the evidence in the scattered sources to hazard a guess as to whether the merchant was in any sense considered an admirable person, a moral ideal; probably not. But it is clear that the Babylonians led the kind of life that stank in the nostrils of the puritanical Jews of the Captivity, that the Jews felt toward them the righteous horror of the monotheist for the polytheist, the kind of horror felt today by the Moslem in India for Hindu beliefs and practices, mixed with the kind of indignation Martin Luther felt in the streets of Renaissance Rome. The Babylonians, alas, have left no good record of their own feelings about the Jews. One may guess that they were not greatly afflicted with feelings of guilt.

[18] D. D. Luckenbill, *Ancient Records of Assyria and Babylonia,* Chicago, University of Chicago Press, p. 146. Assur-Nasir-Pal—from the pavement slabs of the entrance to the temple of Urta at Calah (Nimrud).
[19] *Ibid.* Pavement slabs as above, following the invocation to Urta.

III

Origins: The Jews and the Greeks

THE JEWS must bulk very large in any history of Western morals. The very familiar notion that modern Western culture has two roots, one in Judaea and one in Greece—its most representative statement is perhaps in the works of Matthew Arnold—is one that must annoy the revisionist historian, and any inquirer distrustful of formulas, anxious to qualify, to note variants, to avoid nice big ideas that simplify what he knows to be reality. Nevertheless, the formula keeps cropping up even in the mind that tries to reject it. We shall have to return to it. Here we shall be concerned with the very difficult problem of what the morals of the Jews really were in the centuries before the prophets, before the defeats which marked so deeply the minds of the intellectual leaders of the nation. But the problem can be put more sharply: other peoples in that cockpit of early international conflict, the great valleys of Mesopotamia and Egypt and the connecting fertile crescent, were beaten, lost their independence, were absorbed by their conquerors, died and were forgotten, producing no Isaiah, no Jesus, no Maimonides, and, very definitely, nothing like a Theodor Herzl or a Chaim Weizmann.

For the early Jews, our surviving record is, in a sense, no longer fragmentary. Yet for the historian the Old Testament is about as full of pitfalls as a source can be. In the form we have, it was clearly edited by various priestly hands and at various times, most notably after the great disasters of the Jewish "national state" in the seventh and sixth centuries B.C., but continuing on down to the second century B.C., commonly given as the date of the Book of Esther, the latest of the Old Testament. It can be analyzed into

49

constituent elements; indeed, scholars are nowadays in substantial agreement as to its composition, subject to the usual scholarly debate over detail, an agreement that should do much to refute the notion that there is nothing cumulative in humanistic scholarly studies. There are elements of a cosmogony which looks to be substantially a development of old Babylonian cosmological myths, including that much worked-over topic the Flood. There are elements of what it is not unfair to call an epic of the heroic ages, the "Jewish Iliad," with its echoes of the wandering days of the Hebrews before they settled in Canaan, and with a fine central theme, the story of Moses and the deliverance from Egypt. There are elements of a running historical account (the Books of Joshua, Judges, Samuel, and Kings) clearly not the work of any "lay" historian like Herodotus, indeed, in a sense even more obviously "clerical" and anonymous, than the work of medieval monkish chroniclers, which is perhaps the best Western parallel familiar to most of us. There are elements of what we are accustomed to call, simply, "literature"—the poetry of the Psalms, the aphoristic wisdom of the Book of Proverbs, stories like those of Ruth and Job, didactic, philosophical, poetic, patriotic, but, still, stories. There are the books rather tamely called the "prophetic books," which—if you can forgive the kind of generalization that laughs at distribution curves—are the heart, the essence, of what the Jew has meant to Western history. And, most important for us in this chapter, there are, especially in the first five books, known as the Pentateuch (Genesis, Exodus, Leviticus, Numbers, Deuteronomy), a record of theological growth toward monotheism, an elaborate set of liturgical and other priestly rules, which make up the Law, and important ethical writings of which the heart is the Ten Commandments.

The major difficulty for us is to discern the earlier Hebrews through the later editing. No one seriously maintains that the editors faked, doctored, or invented; bad as was the world for these Jews of the centuries of disaster, it was not quite an Orwellian world. But there were no complicated techniques of historical criticism known to them; these editors could not be what we hopefully call "historically minded." They wrote with a present much in mind. That present they reflected back as, for example, high ethical monotheism into an age when the recently nomadic Jews could hardly have conceived of a single God, not even their jealous tribal god Jehovah.[1]

---

[1] The Hebrew form is, of course, Yahweh, or, more pedantically transliterated, YHWH. But I cannot quite give up a form sacred not only to Christians, but, as Ethan Allen's famous use of it at Ticonderoga shows, to anti-Christians.

Yet it is quite possible that the general impression left by the last two or three centuries of Western scholarly work on the early Jews exaggerates the gap between the Jews of Moses' day and those of the last few centuries B.C. In the English-speaking world in particular, anti-Christian debunkers, who have been numerous and vocal, have enjoyed showing just how different the religion of the Old Testament really was from what it appeared to be as seen from the Baptist Sunday schools of Birmingham, England, and Birmingham, Alabama. Jehovah appeared in the pages of these debunkers as a horrid tribal tyrant-god, the Jews as primitives somehow nonetheless already endowed with many of the traits modern anti-Semitism finds in them. They were already unnaturally clannish, unable to get on with their neighbors, addicted at once to a particularly libidinous sex life in polygamy and to a kill-joy puritanism, cruel and treacherous in war (the story of Judith, for instance), double-crossers (Moses in Egypt, the tale of Joseph and his brothers), perversely ingenious, as witness the complexity of their Law; in sum, rather worse than most early peoples in their conduct, whited sepulchers, in fact, to quote a much later Jewish writer.[2]

Even when the animus of such accounts is allowed for, even when one says simply that the historical evidence makes it seem that the Hebrews were one of the nomadic tribes of Semitic origin in the arid or semiarid regions around the Nile-Mesopotamian "cradle of civilization," who like so many over so many centuries penetrated these areas and *were absorbed by the peoples and cultures they found there,* the basic question still remains: Why are the Jews and their history part of our lives today, while the many known and the many more unknown tribes that came out of the desert or the mountains to the valleys and the fertile crescent are at best part of specialized historical scholarship?

A good answer, that God chose the Jews, is one impossible for me, and surely for many of my readers, not all by any means necessarily in these days

2 The above is, I admit, synthetic, but I hope not a caricature. Almost all writers hostile to orthodox Christianity since the Enlightenment have seemed to enjoy insisting on the phases of early Jewish life most inconsistent with the spirit of the Beatitudes. The Nietzschean H. L. Mencken will do as a sample. See his lively but too damned sensible *Treatise on the Gods,* New York, Knopf, 1930, and *Treatise on Right and Wrong,* New York, Knopf, 1934, both *passim* or as the indexes under "Jews" and "Yahweh" indicate. The following passage is typical: "The Old Testament, as everyone who has looked into it is aware, drips with blood; there is indeed no more bloody chronicle in all the literature of the world. Half of the hemorrhage is supplied by the *goyim* who angered Yahweh by flouting His Chosen People, and the other half issues from living creatures who went down to death that He might be suitably nourished and kept in good humour." *Treatise on the Gods,* p. 158.

bad religious Christians or bad religious Jews. A sort of background for an answer can be found in a familiar, if dangerously broad, generalization well known to the contemporary sociologist of religion. The early settled agricultural societies tended toward lush polytheisms based on a tamed "nature," reflecting the preoccupation of such societies with the comforts of the flesh, with the need for vegetable and animal fertility, with trade, property, and the like; the early nomads, closer to an untamed "nature" and to the ways of preagricultural hunters and food gatherers, tended toward a more austere polytheism of sky-gods and mountain-gods (among the latter, old Jehovah, not just a mountain, but a volcano!). As the chief or father god of these pastoral peoples grew in importance, he tended to become the sole god of monotheism, though originally the sole god of the tribe or people only, not by any means a universal God.[3]

There is something in this distinction between the religions and morals of agricultural peoples on one hand and those of pastoral peoples on the other, especially if it is not held as a simple dualism. It becomes especially misleading, however, if it is developed into a Spenglerian metaphor of Western religion emerging from the shadowy desert "cave" of a Semitic Near East. Perhaps Jehovah, the Father of Jesus, and Allah did start their careers in the desert or semiarid country, but so, too, did many Semitic Baals who never got beyond their own little shrines. The Phoenicians and their Carthaginian heirs, also Semitic, continued, into their greatness, devotion to their Moloch, their graven images, their by no means higher religion. Nor did the Aryan and other invaders from the north, who, if they did not emerge from deserts, were surely pastoral nomads originally, attain to high ethical monotheism. Their sky-gods and other thunder wielders never became more than firsts among equals. The most famous of them, Zeus-Jupiter, became, as befits the king amongst his nobles after the nobles have acquired arts and letters, rather less than that, to judge from recorded squabbles on Olympus.

There is no single broad explanation either of Jewish survival as a people or of the Jewish achievement of a religion that is a base of Christianity—the two achievements being, indeed, related. The foundations were surely laid before the Babylonian Captivity began in 586 B.C., and some of them go back to the desert, back to Abraham and the other patriarchs. What was built up in the earlier centuries and in the successful establishment of Israel was a

---

[3] On this contrast of the gods of settled agricultural and wandering pastoral peoples, see a good résumé in Christopher Dawson, *The Age of the Gods*, Boston, Houghton Mifflin, 1920, Chap. XI.

society extraordinarily knit together in self-consciousness. The phrase the bluff Menckens have had such an ironic time with—the Chosen People—deserves to be taken in full sociological seriousness. Here it is in all its clarity from the Pentateuch:

> . . . the Lord thy God hath chosen thee to be a special people unto himself, above all people that are upon the face of the earth. The Lord did not set his love upon you, nor choose you, because ye were more in number than any people; for ye were the fewest of all people: but because the Lord loved you, and because he would keep the oath which he had sworn unto your fathers, hath the Lord brought you out with a mighty hand, and redeemed you out of the house of bondmen, from the hand of Pharaoh king of Egypt.[4]

It will not do to assume that the feelings behind this passage were limited to the priestly intellectuals who wrote it. The Hebrew religion as it developed spread these feelings to the common people. Moreover, the Jews were, in spite of their quarrels among themselves, their frequent backslidings into idolatry—the "familiar spirits, and the wizards, and the teraphim, and the idols and all the abominations"—one of the great *religiously and morally disciplined* peoples of history. Most of the well-known analysis that Polybius and, after him, Machiavelli give of the role religion played in the disciplining of the early Romans applies to the Jews. In addition, the Jews had, in the Biblical account of creation, in the great epic of the exile and the exodus, in all their early national literature, an emotionally and intellectually satisfying justification for the discipline to which they submitted—no, "submitted" is here the natural and wrong word of a culture-bound twentieth-century American; let us say "which they embraced." Finally, there is the possibility that Moses was a great man, not just a myth, and that in the very critical years when the Hebrews were becoming the Jews of Israel they were well served by a series of good leaders.

Above all, however, it will not do to assume, as we of this day of nationalism and racism are inclined to, that the Chosen People felt themselves chosen unconditionally, by themselves and for themselves, to satisfy individual pride in the pooled pride of the in-group. The conscientious Jew from the time of the exile on, at least, and, we may assume, from much earlier, felt that the Jews were chosen *for* something, chosen as witnesses for God's will toward men, chosen to set the example of a moral life. The Jew—and, here, the pagan-loving, Greek-loving critic who dislikes the Jewish element in our tradition as "repressive" or "puritanical" is not without some justification in fact

---

[4] Deuteronomy 7:6-8.

for his attitude, though he usually neglects this same side of his beloved Greeks—this Jew did go through life worrying about his righteousness, did submit himself to extraordinary ritual tasks which carried specific moral implications, did, in the matter particularly of sex relations, spell out for himself a code that fully took account of the grave complexities and difficulties men and women have with that obstinately "unnatural," that is, moral, phase of human conduct. The Jew, clearly, did not grow up in the South Seas, nor in the pages of an Enlightened eighteenth-century devotee of nature's simple plan. Our real feelings and our customary behavior in matters of sex continue to bear firmly the mark of Jewish experience.[5]

Thus endowed in the course of the centuries, of which the Pentateuch and the early historical books are a record with an unusually closely meshed cosmogony, theology, liturgy, priesthood, and received historical epic culminating in the concept of the Chosen People, with a moral code and moral habits in turn closely meshed with the above and culminating in a tight national discipline, with a national culture hero like Moses, the Jews became the people of Israel. But—and this is most important—they never became, like the Romans, a successful expansionist people. Even at its height, the kingdom of Solomon was, beside such great powers as Egypt, Assyria, or Babylonia, a minor state. The Jews could keep the kind of discipline that is always lost in a successful imperialist expansion. Their history had prepared them for their extraordinary feat of survival.[6]

In the face of this survival, the harshness of early Jewish culture is not of

[5] On Jewish moral puritanism, I suggest the reader not directly familiar with the sources go to them, if only briefly for such a good sample as Deuteronomy, chapters 21-28. If in this reading he finds only absurdities, irrationality, superstition, unnatural restraints, if he thinks himself superior to all this, then I suggest he had better not bother to go on with this book. He has shown himself too enlightened in the narrow rationalist sense to profit from the record of the long centuries of the unenlightened.

[6] An American can perhaps best get some feeling for how the Jews, molded by a consciousness of being chosen, by a firm belief in theologically explained history, by a discipline strengthened by the resistance of neighboring peoples, by a moral code that set them off from their neighbors, and by gifted leadership, survived as a people if he will reflect on the achievement of the Latter-day Saints. In the midst of an American democratic society that presses and persuades to conformity, that "assimilates" at least as rapidly and completely as any early civilized society could, the Mormons have for a century maintained themselves as a peculiar people. I am not suggesting that the Mormons are not at all like other Americans, but merely that they preserved a corporate identity of their own. Nor do I suggest that they will preserve even that as long as the Jews have theirs. But, for the present, I submit that not even the firmest devotee of the explanation of history by geographical environment or by any other simple "materialistic" factor can get at the *moral* difference between those two geographical twins Utah and Nevada or those older ones Israel and Phoenicia.

great importance. A cultivated, artistic, peaceful people, a people smilingly accepting a world in the balance to be enjoyed—such, for instance, as from their artifacts alone we perhaps mistakenly picture those delightful Minoans —could not have done what the Jews did in Israel. You need at least an island for such a delightful culture, a Crete if not a Bali. There is a streak of austerity in these early Jews, not an ascetic turning away from the delights of the flesh (the Song of Solomon is surely concerned with sex in a way well short of sublimation) but, rather, a certain heaviness of spirit. The laughter of the gods is not there, nor even the smiles of men.

The great moral code of the Jews is still taught most Westerners in their childhood. Here are the Ten Commandments:

1. Thou shalt have no other gods before me.
2. Thou shalt not make unto thee any graven image, or any likeness of any thing that is in heaven above, or that is in the earth beneath, or that is in the water under the earth: thou shalt not bow down thyself unto them, nor serve them: for I the Lord thy God am a jealous God, visiting the iniquity of the fathers upon the children unto the third and fourth generation of them that hate me; and shewing mercy unto thousands of them that love me, and keep my commandments.
3. Thou shalt not take the name of the Lord thy God in vain; for the Lord will not hold him guiltless that taketh his name in vain.
4. Remember the sabbath day, to keep it holy. Six days shalt thou labour, and do all thy work: but the seventh day is the sabbath of the Lord thy God: in it thou shalt not do any work, thou, nor thy son, nor thy daughter, thy manservant, nor thy maidservant, nor thy cattle, nor thy stranger that is within thy gates: for in six days the Lord made heaven and earth, the sea, and all that in them is, and rested the seventh day: wherefore the Lord blessed the sabbath day, and hallowed it.
5. Honour thy father and thy mother: that thy days may be long upon the land which the Lord thy God giveth thee.
6. Thou shalt not kill.
7. Thou shalt not commit adultery.
8. Thou shalt not steal.
9. Thou shalt not bear false witness against thy neighbour.
10. Thou shalt not covet thy neighbour's house, thou shalt not covet thy neighbour's wife, nor his manservant, nor his maidservant, nor his ox, nor his ass, nor any thing that is thy neighbour's.[7]

This is not the code of pastoral nomads, and it could not have been de-

[7] Exodus 20:3-17. I number in the common Protestant tradition. Roman Catholics and Lutherans combine 1 and 2, and separate 10 into two by distinguishing between wife and goods as objects of covetousness. Thus, allusion to, say, the "sixth commandment" is in itself misleading; it may refer to adultery or murder.

livered to a historical Moses at the time and place described in Exodus. Its feeling for private property—such as "thy neighbor's house"—even the Sabbatarian provisions of the fourth commandment and its firm monotheistic theology, are the work of a people already settled, and could hardly have come directly out of the desert. In spite of the harshness of the second commandment—that phrase "visiting the iniquity of the fathers upon the children unto the third and fourth generation of them that hate me" has long been particularly offensive to modern Western liberals of all sorts—the code as a whole is not a cruel, harsh, or "primitive" one. Granted that it is in form an imposed and absolutist code, it has nonetheless been able to survive with honor among modern peoples who do not really feel it as either, but as something springing from the experience of the race.[8] The code has quite simply been part of our lives, not something outside us, nor outside nature. It seems likely that over the long centuries some men and women have halted on the brink of theft, or perjury, or even adultery, have "resisted temptation," because they had been "brought up on" the Ten Commandments—or so it must seem to all but disastrously naïve deniers of the power of the Word.

The Ten Commandments of course by no means exhaust the ethical teachings of the Old Testament. The books of the Pentateuch, variously edited as they were, contain a really extraordinary variety of ethical precepts and commands. Leviticus itself, the most priestly of the books, has not only ritual precept after ritual precept, on diet, cleanliness, sacrifices, and the like, the Law as duly spelled out under the authority of Moses; it has also a great many ferocious laws on matters sexual, prescribing death penalties for a great and specific range of spelled-out misconduct from adultery to sodomy and incest. It has much on keeping the Sabbath, and on preserving the in-groupness of Israel. But it also has, among many prescriptions that are essentially concerned with social and political relations—part of the fields and the gleanings shall be left "for the poor and the stranger," for instance—a sentence that the evangelists were to echo word for word: "Love thy neighbor as thyself."[9]

---

[8] W. T. Stace makes a common, but also misleading, distinction, to which I shall return, between the two sources of European [Western] ethical thinking which he calls the Palestinian "impositionist"—that morality is imposed on man from *outside* humanness—and the Greek "immanentist"—that morality grows *out of* humanness. *The Destiny of Western Man*, New York, Reynal and Hitchcock, 1942, Chap. I.

[9] Leviticus 19:18. See also Matthew 19:19; Luke 10:27. Chapters 19 and 20 of Leviticus are a good cross section of these priestly ethics. There are also some fine "primitive" prescriptions in Exodus 21 following immediately after the Ten Commandments.

Origins: The Jews and the Greeks

Not even from the body of the Old Testament we are in this section concerned with (the books from Genesis to Isaiah) is it quite possible to draw an embodied Jewish ideal person. Moses was, as we have noted, a culture hero, but it does not seem as though the Jew of those years would quite dare to think of himself as being "like" Moses in the way an American might want to be like Lincoln. It is not that early peoples were incapable of conceiving what I have called the moral human ideal; as we shall see in the very next section of this chapter, such an ideal emerges very clearly from the pages of Homer. Nor are the elements lacking from which some generalizations can be made; they just do not fit neatly together. Job's final surrender to a God beyond any possible formal and logical theodicy is surely too complete to be Western, or, even in the ordinary sense, Jewish. The wisdom of Proverbs and, still more, that of the Protestant-rejected Ecclesiasticus seem to err too far on the other side from that of the Book of Job, that of irony, worldly wisdom, intellectual disgust with the ways of man (and, perhaps, of God?). The Book of Psalms is probably the best source for the moral "tone," and the moral "style," of conventional Jewry before the downfall of the two kingdoms. It is grave, pious, conventional, not heaven-storming, but fully aware that the Way and the Law are not easy to keep. The figure of *walking* —"uprightly," "in the way of the Lord," "righteously," and the like—is common in both the Old and the New Testaments. It is a good figure, suggesting effort but not strain; above all, carrying with it no menaces, no commands from above. Here is the beginning of the Fifteenth Psalm:

> Lord, who shall abide in thy tabernacle?
> Who shall dwell in thy holy hill?
> He that walketh uprightly, and worketh righteousness,
> And speaketh the truth in his heart.[10]

Yet, to point up our difficulties in generalizing about the moral tone of early Jewish life, this very same psalm turns at once to the *negatives,* to the denials—unaccompanied, it is true, by any threats beyond the very common Old Testament coupling of "Lord" and "fear," but still negatives, still threats:

> He that backbiteth not with his tongue,
> Nor doeth evil to his neighbour,
> Nor taketh up a reproach against his neighbour.
> In whose eyes a vile person is contemned;
> But he honoureth them that fear the Lord.

[10] Psalm 15:1, 2. And see C. S. Lewis, *Reflections on the Psalms*, New York, Harcourt Brace, 1958.

He that sweareth to his own hurt, and changeth not.
He that putteth not out his money to usury,
Nor taketh reward against the innocent.
He that doeth these things shall never be moved.[11]

There is an easy test of the tone of the Old Testament. Take any concordance to the Bible, and glance at the entries under the neighboring words "laugh" and "law" and their various grammatical forms. "Laugh" is snowed under by "law"; if you subtract from the instances under "laugh" those in which the authors of the King James version translated by "laugh to scorn" a single Hebrew word perhaps better translated "mock," and if you also subtract the ironic use of "laugh" in the wisdom literature, you have very little real and joyful laughter left.[12] Such a test must not be taken to mean that the Jews spent their time in lofty misery, that they never enjoyed themselves simply and thoughtlessly. The Old Testament is, after all, a product of the literary, the priestly literary, and not a piece of social-psychological research into attitudes and mental health. Moreover, it is all we have. It is arresting to reflect that if all we had for the early Greeks was the *Works and Days* of Hesiod, we should have to conclude that their hearts, too, were overwhelmed with the harshness of this world.

Yet even a fragment of the accepted great literature of a people is not altogether misleading as to their moral ideals and even as to their conduct. A later age that found of all American writings only, let us say, a copy of *Walden* would by no means understand what we had been like, not even what the old Yankees had been like; but if the age were still Western, still interested in history, it would not be wholly without understanding of us. It would in Thoreau's work have a good clue to the exaggerated, almost, but not quite, unlivable form the eternal coexistence of Don Quixote and Sancho Panza takes with us Americans. The first twenty books of the Old Testament, as we have noted, are a great deal more than a fragment; edited and composed as they were, they are less and more than an anthology, a "course" in Jewish cultural history.

From them there stands out clearly a feeling of need for discipline, for the Law, an acceptance of the need to struggle against men and nature, an attitude the New Testament often reflects: "Because strait is the gate, and

[11] Psalm 15:3-5.
[12] Examples: "The virgin the daughter of Zion hath despised thee, and laughed thee to scorn" (II Kings 19:21); "Even in laughter the heart is sorrowful; And the end of that mirth is heaviness" (Proverbs 14:13).

narrow is the way. . . ."[13] Some of these feelings are those of any early people struggling for a living in a harsh environment. Canaan flowed with milk and honey only in comparison with the desert. The Jews did not have it easy. But however you care to explain them, those feelings are there, so put, so preserved, that they have guided—some of the time, and for some of the people—lives in lands that flowed with richer stuff than milk or honey.

To conclude, there is need to make briefly a few cautionary remarks. The early Jews had the concept of an afterlife, and of a heaven and a hell; but it was not a firm concept, let alone a preoccupation, like that of the Egyptians—and that of the early Christians. The Jewish *sheol,* or hell, often seems no more than that of their Babylonian neighbors, a colorless limbo, a threat, but not a vigorous one. They had a firm notion of sin, a word that bulks large in these early books of the Old Testament. But even a hasty reading confirms the commonplace; sin is, before the prophetic writings, no Calvinistic or Freudian horror within a man, but a simple transgression of a clear law, a crime against the ordinances of the City of God, disarmingly illustrated in the words attributed to Moses: "And I took your sin, the calf which ye had made, and burnt it with fire, and stamped it, and ground it very small, even until it was small as dust."[14] Again, there is not much use trying to revise the commonplace: up to the time of the prophets, Jehovah (the Lord, God) is indeed the sole god of *Israel.* There is no solid evidence that the Jews believed the gods of their neighbors to be nonexistent, or in any way fakes. These gods quite literally did not compete with Jehovah, had nothing to do with him, except indirectly as their adherents tried to tempt the Jews to go whoring after other gods. It seems to me probable that these early Jews did not even think of Jehovah as "superior" to other peoples' gods, for they could hardly have yet had the modern national habit—at its extreme, apparently, today with us and with the Russians—of thinking always in terms of a kind of big-league international competition in everything. Finally, it need hardly be said that these Jews differ in many important ways from their modern heirs. They were still farmers and herdsmen, the merchants among them much less important than those of the Babylonians, for instance. The history of their kingdoms is the history of political rivalries and political crimes; these Jews were no lotus-eaters. But they do not seem, to use a current word of social psychology, a very competitive society; or their society is by no means the ritually combative society we find among

13 Matthew 7:14.
14 Deuteronomy 9:21.

the Greeks. Nor are these Jews notably hard workers, that is, they work no harder than their rough land and primitive technology make necessary; there is no Calvinistic cult of work, and the famous text "Go to the ant, thou sluggard; consider her ways, and be wise" is rather out of line.[15] Finally, not even in the wisdom literature is there much trace of two attitudes, two personalities, we know in modern Jewry: the witty, cynical, sentimental Heine and the rationalist, optimistic, enlightened, reforming Eduard Bernstein. True, these types belong to a much later and in some ways more advanced and more complicated society. But is it not also possible that the two are European, indeed German, types, not Jews at all?

II

The Greeks, too, were a people of the Book. Their Bible was Homer. We need not here concern ourselves with the problems, interesting though they are, which have long occupied scholars: Was there an individual Homer who composed these epics, or are they the work of, to us, forever anonymous professional bards over many generations? If there was a Homer, did he compose *both* the *Iliad* and the *Odyssey?* Have the two poems perhaps quite different sources? There are many more questions. Scholars are agreed that both poems were handed down in oral form by professional bards for several centuries; they are reasonably well agreed that the written version of the *Iliad* the Athenians used and which has come down to us was brought to Athens in the sixth century B.C. and may even have been given something like its final shape in Ionia by a "Homer" of the ninth century. There is great debate as to how much interpolation, how much editing the texts of both poems underwent before they were reasonably fixed by writing, as to how good "history" (in contrast to "poetry") they are, and as to just what society and what culture they came out of. It would seem pretty clear that the poems were not nearly as much altered by later and interested emendations as were the books of the Old Testament which record the Jewish epic; and it is not very risky to use them, with due caution, as documents "reflecting" the moral life of the Greek aristocracy of the Mycenaean Age just before the last or Dorian wave of Greek invasions or no later than just after those invasions, that is, of the thirteenth to the eleventh centuries B.C. Achilles was, roughly, a contemporary of Moses.

[15] Proverbs 6:6.

We may find it difficult to realize that the poems of Homer, and, more especially, the *Iliad,* which to us are "literature," certainly better, greater, than *Hiawatha,* but, like that poem, "literature," were as much "religion" to the Greeks as was the Bible to the Jews. But the educated Greek of the great ages, and right on to the triumph of Christianity in the West, was brought up on Homer. Plato himself, not, for reasons of principle, an admirer of poets, though he was, of course, one himself, called Homer the "educator of Greece."[16] It is true that the poems were composed to amuse and elevate, and certainly to hold the attention of, audiences of nobles, squires, and retainers who were presumably in no mood to be preached at, let alone indoctrinated with a theology. The priestly touch unmistakable even in the most straightforwardly historical books of the Old Testament, bloody and warlike though they are, is not in these poems. Indeed, Oswald Spengler insists that Homer was what we should call an antisacerdotalist, a fine, free, noble warrior-spirit contemptuous of the weak, womanish, priestly intellectual, in fact, an anticipation of Schopenhauer-Nietzsche-Spengler, as masculine as a Mediterranean man could be.[17]

One may suspect that even the bards of the Greek heroic age, however, were modern enough, intellectuals enough, even human enough, to wish to improve the morals of their audience. There is, incongruous though the notion may seem, a good deal of the didactic in Homer; Homer knew well how a gentleman ought to behave, and he keeps reminding his audience of what they, too, well knew. Of course, he was not directly concerned with problems of cosmogony, theology, or even of that most universal element of all religions—including the Marxist, which passionately justifies the ways of the god Dialectical Materialism to man—that is, a theodicy. Yet it is equally clear that Homer was no more making a purely literary use of the

---

[16] On this see H. I. Marrou, *A History of Education in Antiquity,* trans. by G. Lamb, New York, Sheed and Ward, 1956, Chap. I. This work is a great deal more than a narrow and conventional interpretation of its title would indicate. It is, in fact, an excellent history of morals in antiquity—as a history of education should be. Herbert J. Muller, *The Loom of History,* New York, Harper, 1958, Chap. III, is very good on Homer.

[17] O. Spengler, *The Decline of the West,* New York, Knopf, 1950, Vol. II, p. 281. Alas, "Homer," like these Germans, probably never cracked an enemy's skull. Still, the purely literary fighter, his mind berserk, his bottom quietly chaired, is, I think, in the West a product of the post-Christian and, in our modern world, increasingly sharp conflict between the two aristocracies of the sword and the pen. I do not think Homer felt any contrast between the world of the gods and the world of Achilles and his peers; in fact, I do not think he was much like Spengler.

Olympian gods than were the authors and amenders of the Pentateuch so using Jehovah. Perhaps that last is not put sharply enough. Homer *believed in* Zeus and Athena and the rest.

Of these Greek gods of Olympus, it is often said that, especially in Homeric times, but to a degree right down through to the end of Greco-Roman paganism, they were just like human beings, only more powerful, that the world of Olympus was simply a mirror image of this world, even a kind of huge realistic folk novel, in which the gods conducted themselves as human beings do in our realistic fiction—that is to say, rather worse than in real life. This is largely true, but it must not be interpreted as meaning that the Greek Olympian religion "taught" its believers that men could and should imitate the ways of the gods. The early Christian apologists were very fond of using the argument that the pagans could hardly help lying, cheating, whoring, and the like, because the gods did so.

Nor is it difficult to show why the worshippers of the gods cannot be good and just. For how shall they abstain from shedding blood who worship bloodthirsty deities, Mars and Bellona? Or how shall they spare their parents who worship Jupiter, who drove out his father? . . . how shall they uphold chastity who worship a goddess who is naked, an adulteress, and who prostitutes herself as it were among the gods. . . . Among these things is it possible for men to be just, who, although they are naturally good, would be trained to injustice by the very gods themselves?[18]

It was no doubt a good argument, and like most such arguments more consoling to the already converted than actually useful as a means of converting unbelievers. But it was poor history, poor social psychology. The devotees of these early Western polytheistic faiths were by no means as inclined to try to make their own conduct godlike as are the believers of our modern higher religions. The central Greek concept of *hubris,* to which we shall return, warned men firmly that the gods punished such presumption as prideful indeed. The magic world of charms, incantations, and the like existed in Greece as the world of astrology, fortunetelling, and similar charlatanries exist with us, definitely below the accepted religion of dignified worship.

[18] Lactantius, *Divine Institutes,* in *Works,* trans. by W. Fletcher, Edinburgh, 1871, Vol. I, p. 316. I admit that our Western training makes us feel that Lactantius must be substantially right. I would not wish to overdo anti-intellectualism by denying that there is *any* connection between what men believe about the supernatural and their actual conduct. But I feel sure that Lactantius is wrong about those who are "naturally good"; the quiet, faithful Roman wife even in the Late Empire was *not* driven by her ideas about the gods to an *imitatio Veneris.*

True, lovers might appeal to Aphrodite—but not quite at the purely magic level of the philter. Lovers later were to appeal to the Virgin Mary.[19]

In this whole problem, the intellectualist error—that the Greek thought cheating a moral good because his god Hermes was a slippery customer (or, as we shall note shortly, because his hero Odysseus was one also)—is indeed an error. But so, too, is the anti-intellectualist error that the kinds of gods, the kinds of heroes, a man believes in has *no* effect on his morals or his conduct, no relation with them. Unfortunately, there is no neat mathematical formula for striking a mean between the intellectualist and anti-intellectualist position, which mean is an accurate account of reality. There is a relation between what men think the gods are like and what they think good and evil, but it is a relation that varies with time, place, and persons. It is no doubt a variation within limits; the *ideals* of both good and evil tend clearly to exceed the limits of all but the most newsworthy *real*. And always there is that pressure—rather, that suasion—of ritual, habit, custom, institutions whereby the ideal gets short-circuited out of the human conscious, where it is a stimulant, and into less noble parts of the mind, where it is a sedative.

There is, indeed, in the relations between mortals and gods the element of contract: *do ut des*. But there is more. Odysseus is a favorite, a protégé, of Athena, who intrigues for him at court, struggles with Poseidon, whom Odysseus has offended, exults in his successes, mourns his misfortunes. Athena is the patron saint of Odysseus; but Odysseus has to deserve her support, not just by ritual acts, but by being the kind of man Athena approves, wise, resourceful, by Christian ethical standards often unscrupulous, but never stupidly unscrupulous, persistent in the face of setbacks, courageous in combat. The reciprocal relation of contract is a *moral* one; men must merit the support of the gods, and the gods must merit the support of men.

They are both aristocracies. Homer is not really concerned with the common people, the *demos*. Eumaeus, the faithful swineherd in the *Odyssey*, is the only conspicuous commoner in the epics; and he is there to point up, it is true in almost heroic degree, the standard virtues of the commoner in a noble household. The warriors who fought the Trojan War were officers and gentlemen, among themselves, as such, equals, and meeting in council to make important decisions. Their leaders are the characters we know by name, Agamemnon, Menelaus, Odysseus, and the rest, older, wiser chieftains, but

---

[19] I do not write the last sentence with intent to shock. I do not equate Aphrodite and the Virgin—they are very different. But part of their provinces in human terms do overlap.

hardly, even in the later medieval European sense, monarchs. And, above all, there is the young Achilles, the hero, in no mere literary sense, of the *Iliad*.

Achilles is the man all of Homer's listeners would like to be, the man of *aretē*. The untranslatable word comes out in the dictionaries as, among other things, "virtue," but "honor," even "proper pride," come closer. Achilles is young, handsome, the conspicuous and admirable person, the athlete of grace. Agamemnon, leader of the expedition against Troy, in order to appease an offended Apollo, is forced to take a series of steps culminating in a mortal offense to the honor of Achilles. Military ethics forbids Achilles to challenge the old leader to a duel, so Achilles simply withdraws. In his absence his dearest friend, Patroclus, is persuaded to impersonate him in a ritual combat with the Trojan champion Hector, and is killed. Achilles—though he knows from a prophecy that he will die—now follows what *aretē* in such a case demands of the hero. He fights Hector, kills him, drags his body in triumph from his chariot—but dies from a wound in the heel by which his mother had held him when she dipped him as an infant in the waters of the Styx, an immersion she had intended to make him proof against wounds.

Now the *aretē* here brought to a tragic peak is very far from Christian virtue, and almost as far from modern secular, utilitarian morality. It is no trouble at all to outline the story of Achilles in terms, for most of us at least, of strong moral condemnation. The initial offense that outraged the hero was Agamemnon's taking away a concubine from Achilles in a kind of politico-religious deal with Apollo. The hero withdraws, thus endangering the cause of his fellows, his country, the whole expedition, out of jealous pique. He is roused to' fight again by a purely personal matter, the death in fair combat of his friend Patroclus, with whom he may have had pederastic relations. He takes a vainglorious revenge on the vanquished Hector. He is moved throughout by vanity; he is about as moral—and as human—as a fighting cock.

The above is, of course, unfair. Homer is setting forth in the framework of the customs of his time a heroic agon, a struggle in which a man who has become what his fellows most admired goes deliberately to what he knows must be his death—to keep that admiration. More nobly put, Achilles sacrifices his life for an ideal, an ideal that has never ceased to be part of Western moral life, though fortunately not often at the frenetic intensity of the Homeric hero's life. We are back again at *aretē*.

It is the virtue of the man, always measuring himself against others, who is determined to do better than they the things they all want to do. In Homer's day those things were the things young, athletic fighting men of a landed aristocracy wanted to do and be. But the element of agon, the ritual struggle, could and would be later in Western history transferred to many other kinds of human activity, a fact that Americans hardly need to be reminded of. The ideal of the Homeric hero can be put pejoratively. He is the obsessively competitive man, always aware of his place in an elaborate order of rank—indeed a human peck order—always trying to move himself up and push someone down, the jealous egalitarian who somehow manages to treat with appropriate differences those above and those below him, the man who must be a success. Perhaps only the archaic dignity of Homer's poetry and the excellence our educational tradition has always found in the Greeks really make the difference between these Homeric competitors and the vulgar big shots of our vulgar business world today. The ultimate prize in the Homeric agon, however, is not mere success, not mere leading the league, any more than it is in business with us. Honor, in a curious way, is its own reward. Achilles followed his father's most Homeric advice, αἰὲν ἀριστεύειν καὶ ὑπείροχον ἔμμεναι ἄλλον, to a martyr's death.[20]

Homer is an admirable source for the ways of the Greek fighting aristocracy of the first few centuries after these northern wanderers settled down in the Aegean world and appropriated for themselves, after the fashion of such conquerors, the benefits of the civilization they found there. It is already an established aristocracy, in many ways reminiscent of the early feudal aristocracy of Europe, whose bards have also left us a great epic, the *Chanson de Roland*. The *aretē* of the Homeric hero will reappear, altered indeed, in the perfect gentle knight of chivalry. But Homer tells us very little about the rest of the Greeks, who clearly were not even in this stage, before the city-state, or polis, quite simply divided into warriors and serfs. For a period of a few centuries later, however, still well before the great age of Athens in the fifth century, we do have in the works of Hesiod, and in those attributed to him, information about aspects of Greek life not developed at length in the Homeric poems, the more practical, day-to-day wisdom of the didactic poet, and some reflection of the ways of the Greek farmer. Hesiod himself was no nobleman, but also no serf or slave. He came of what we might call yeoman farming stock in Boeotia, a region that later Greek literary tradition was to label slow-witted, boorish. He probably wrote the *Works and Days,* a series of didactic poems dealing with the life of the small farmer, though most

[20] "To be always among the bravest, and hold my head above others." *Iliad,* VI, 208, trans. by R. Lattimore, Chicago, University of Chicago Press, 1951; I should like to translate unpoetically: "Always to be best in masculine excellences and come out on top of the others."

critics now think he did not write the *Theogony* the later Greeks attributed to him. "Hesiod," at any rate, formed with "Homer" the staple of Greek education right down to the end of pagan days. Hesiod clearly supplied the common touch lacking in Homer.

The *Theogony* is the first surviving attempt to systematize what the Greeks had come to believe about their gods; it is a kind of canon of their Olympian religion. There is in this straightforward account none of the prettiness, the literary savoring, the playing with a mythology which is found in so much later Greek and Roman writing, and which is at its worst perhaps in the *Metamorphoses* of Ovid. Hesiod surely *believed in* the Olympian gods, and not self-consciously. The line between the life of the gods and that of men was clear, but it was not for Hesiod and surely not for most Greeks of his time a line between what we should call the supernatural and the natural. Within a century or so in Ionia we may believe that the first "philosophers" on our record were to begin to make this distinction, and to push the boundaries of the natural toward the point where the existence of any supernatural is denied; Thales, the earliest name in the long history of Western philosophy, is said to have predicted an eclipse in 585 B.C. This, it may be noted, is one year after the fall of Jerusalem and the beginning of the Babylonian captivity of the Jewish elite.

These early Greeks certainly did not expect a *dramatic* supernatural interference by an Olympian in the routine of their daily lives; but it seems unlikely that they commonly felt the distinction between the everyday prevailing of the kind of regularities the scientist discovers and the rare, direct, miraculous intervention of the deity in the affairs of men. Whatever else it was, the Olympian faith was an immanent one. Perhaps an ordinary Westerner today can best understand the distinction as the Greek felt it if he will try to think of the distinction between the rulers and the ruled in the old monarchic sense, where the ruled have no direct voice in choosing their rulers, but do know the difference between good times and bad, good rulers and bad, and feel, however obscurely, that some actions of theirs may somehow get home to their rulers and influence them. The Greek was even capable of cursing a god who failed to respond satisfactorily to what the petitioner felt was a ritually correct demand; and this must not be thought of as blasphemy.

Yet one must not assume that these Greeks were unduly familiar with their gods. They would not at this early date—and, save for a minority of rationalist intellectuals, would not at any time—have understood the common phrase in our history textbooks that the ancient Greek gods were like men except that they were immortal and much more powerful. Both immortality and power, for one thing, would have had more absolute reality for them than for us. The Greek did have the feelings we still can associate with the word "blasphemy," if we take the trouble. More particularly, if he did not get what he wanted from his petition—let us say frankly, prayer, for there are many kinds of prayer—he could feel that either he had failed to carry out the prescribed ritual forms as they should be carried out, or that he had made not so much an unreasonable demand of the god as a presumptuous one, one that would, after all, offend the god's immortal majesty. The former was perhaps no more than an error, but the kind of error in carrying out a rational process that can still upset the scientist when he makes a similar one; the latter was a sin, which we shall again meet in the great days of Greece, the sin of *hubris.*

For the rest, the works collected under the name of Hesiod, together with a few fragments of gnomic wisdom from various sources, do give us some notion of what Homer had to omit, the daily moral life of ordinary Greeks. They expect to work, indeed to toil. They know they should honor the gods, take care of their families, tell the truth, and keep their word. They do not look forward with anything like Egyptian awareness to reward or punishment in a future life; they would appear to have some sense of individual immortality of the soul, but not an *operational* one. They do not have any concept of "moral progress," or of historical progress. Indeed, in this cosmogony we get the first clear notion of human collective life as a decline from a Golden Age to an Iron Age, with no relief in sight. In short, the tone of these works and fragments is pessimistic, a pessimism not really far from the classic phrase of the Book of Job: "But man is born to trouble, as the sparks fly upward."[21] Again it must be insisted that from writings like these one must not conclude that Greek lives were spent in unrelieved unhappiness; but it must also be insisted that these Greeks were not the happy, smiling children of the Mediterranean sun, their lives clouded only by a few interesting passions, that they seemed to some Victorians to have been. The Greek common people could never be sure enough of tomorrow—let us be clear and colorless and say, could not have anything like enough economic security—to be optimists. There is this much truth in the doctrine of dialectical materialism; it took the steam engine to produce Pollyanna.

21 I incline to believe that not until the eighteenth century in the West did large numbers of human beings come to feel the antithesis of this, that "man is born to happiness, as the sparks fly upward."

III

There is not much point in dwelling in a history of this sort on the West European equivalents of the archaic or heroic early periods we have been dealing with in this chapter; or, rather, consideration of the Germanic and Celtic, perhaps also the Slavonic, myths and heroes should come only under the nineteenth-century heading. Though Moses and David, Achilles and Odysseus have never ceased to play an important part in the moral history of the West, Wotan, Siegfried, and the druids of eld went underground several thousand years ago, with the advent of Christianity, and stayed underground until quite recently; and it is very hard to trace them underground. In the sense that I discussed in the very first section of this chapter, your *conduct* and mine may well be in part "determined" by what went on among our Celtic, Germanic, or Slavic ancestors long, long ago, but I do not see any way in which the historian can establish the nature and importance of such an effect, if it exists. Historians, men of letters, and at least one very distinguished composer of operas did in the nineteenth century combine to inform the Germans, for instance, that they were braver and more profound than ordinary people because Siegfried had gone even Achilles several better in heroics. Some, indeed, went so far as to prove that Achilles himself had in fact been a German. We cannot leave Siegfried, nor even the druids, out of a history of Western morals, because they, through their legends, figure in some of the great modern religions of nationalism. But they do not belong here, at this moment.

As a matter of fact, and in spite of the often successful efforts of scholars to reconstitute objectively as much as possible of these cultures, we know the moral and religious elements of the culture of the ancient German and the Celtic peoples through a double refraction, that of medieval redactions like the Arthurian cycle and the song of the Nibelungs and that of the modern romantic nationalists which begins with eighteenth-century figures like James McPherson and Justus Möser. Each of these groups reflects more clearly the concerns of its own age than the nature of the past ages it was trying to bring back to mind. The peoples of Northern and Western Europe simply did not record in writing what they thought and felt until after they had come into contact with the Roman Empire or Christianity. The Greek and Roman writers of later times do give us valuable bits of information about the barbarian tribes who were breaking into the empire, but the most skeptical toward what our modern social sciences have achieved will have to admit that our standards for such information are vastly higher than those even of an Ammianus Marcellinus, who had no ax to grind. The best known, and in many ways the best, of Roman accounts of the Germans is the *Germania* of Tacitus, a man with a very sharp ax indeed against his fellows of the Roman ruling classes of the late first century A.D. Tacitus was certainly a stern moralist, and in this little tract he is using the "primitive" and unspoiled Germans as a foil to the civilized and very spoiled upper-class Romans of the Flavian Age. But he does bring out the fact that the Germans were addicted to drunkenness, brawling, outbursts of temper, and knightly honor, as well as to preserving the chastity of their women and to maintaining the simplicity of honest rural life.

It would be useful if we could be sure that certain tendencies toward conduct of a specific sort in peoples of Northern and Western Europe today could be traced back to the ways of their ancestors of the first millennium B.C. Take the German tendency toward disciplined obedience to orders from their rulers, their feeling for what they call *Obrigkeit* (not quite our "authority"). This tendency, which cannot be described with perfect exactness, would probably be accepted as "real" by all save the hopeless nominalists who refuse to admit that there is anything at all that can be described as a national trait, a national character. Does this feeling for *Obrigkeit* go back to Arminius and beyond, or is it, rather, the product of the last few centuries of Prussian and Hohenzollern success? Even the assumption that the older such a tendency is the more firmly embedded in a people's habits it is, and, therefore, the less likely to change or be changed, may not be correct; but if it is, we must regret that we know so little about just such aspects of the early history of these peoples. Perhaps the problem of the source of a trait almost the opposite of this Germanic sense of *Obrigkeit,* the fiery unruliness and irresponsibility attributed to the Celts, is no longer important, since even in Ireland the fire seems almost extinct. Yet for the sake of Franco-American relations it would be good to know whether the reluctance of the French to obey our behests is the fault of Vercingetorix, or merely of Louis XIV and Napoleon. And of course it would be good to know whether the "Slavic soul" really was formed in the Pripet Marshes, or was invented by nineteenth-century Slavophile intellectuals. But unfortunately we cannot know this, and much else of the sort we should like to know. We shall have to get back to those remarkable Greeks of the fifth century B.C., about whom we do know a great deal.

Greece: The Great Age

MODERN HISTORIANS are very aware of the problem of what, in space and time, constitutes a valid "unit" of history. Mr. Arnold Toynbee keeps telling us that it is impossible, or at least immoral, to try to write the history of so parochial a group as the modern nation-state. Others have so far pushed back in time what as schoolboys we knew as the "Renaissance," and dated even in Italy as beginning with the mid-fifteenth century, that Renaissance and Middle Ages seem to melt together. In all this critical revision, however, the old-fashioned concept of a Great Age of Greece, beginning in the eighth century B.C., culminating in the fifth, and ending neatly with the fourth and Alexander the Great, has stood up pretty well. The Greeks were no longer in this age recent invaders under tribal chieftains and a warrior aristocracy of landholders, as they had been in the Homeric Age. They had already formed the characteristic Greek society, the polis, or city-state. These small states were established through the Aegean, in Asia Minor, the Greek mainland and islands, and in the colonies scattered on coasts of the Mediterranean and Black seas not held by those other colonists the Phoenicians. Note that this city-state was not confined to what Americans know as their "city limits," nor even to their city and suburbs, but, territorially considered, was nearer to an average American county with county seat and surrounding small towns and farms. The Greek city-state, even Athens, which was a manufacturing and trading city, had its farming population. There is no great distortion involved if you will think of it as a small-scale equivalent—especially as to the emotional allegiances of its members—of the modern Western nation-state.[1]

These city-states, big (*relatively* big, of course), middle-sized, and small, formed a kind of system, an "international society" within which there were wars, sports (the original Olympic games and the like), diplomatic relations, trading, travel, immigration in varying degrees of freedom, and, again in varying degrees of freedom, interchange of ideas. Their wars among themselves culminated in the supremacy of a marginally Greek tribal state on the north, Macedonia, and the spread of Greek armies and culture eastward under Alexander. After about 300 B.C., though Athens, Sparta, and the other major city-states took a while to realize it, the classic city-state gave way to a differently organized Mediterranean world, the world of "Greco-Roman" culture we shall study in the next chapter. That world owed a great deal—did a great deal as it did, thought and felt as it did—because of the world of the Greek city-state we are about to study. So in their turn did the Greeks of the Great Age owe much to their ancestors of the Homeric Age. But as periods, ages, cultures, and suchlike devices that the historian must use to cut his cloth go, these are all three—Homeric, Greek, Greco-Roman—justifiable, perhaps even "real," and genetically related.

If historians are fairly well agreed that there was a Great Age of Greece, they are, as might be expected in mid-twentieth century, by no means agreed on what the age was really like. Indeed, the history of the reputation of the Greeks is itself a fascinating one. Over the last 2,500 years it is safe to say that, to those in charge of Western formal education and to almost all members of the Western intellectual classes, these Greeks seemed to have set the highest standards men have ever set in manners, taste, and morals, in art, letters, and philosophy. There has been over the centuries a remarkably stable set of evaluative notions—let us carefully *not* say "myth," "legend," or even "pattern"—about the Greeks of the Great Age, which, since I cannot here dwell on it at book length, I shall rashly try to summarize in a sentence. The Greeks, more especially the Athenians of the Age of Pericles, who represent in the tradition the topmost peak, enjoyed and admired physical health and "classic" beauty, as embodied in their statues; were temperate and sensible individuals for whom these enjoyments never became obsessions; had a highly

---

[1] The pattern is not, of course, perfect. Some parts of Greece itself, notably the northwestern sections north of the Gulf of Corinth, were even in the fifth century organized tribally on an earlier pattern. Where Greek colonies were planted in lands inhabited by alien peoples, there were always special problems of relations between the urban Greeks and the surrounding "natives," who probably were mostly farmers.

developed sense of duty to the state but also a determined sense of individual rights and freedom; admired and practiced the use of what men still call "reason," but were not narrow rationalists, since they had a lofty, even tragic, awareness of man's middle state between beast and god; had a firm sense of right and wrong, but no nagging, puritanical worries about sin; had, in fact, the best of this world and the next, with no hell, no torments of the damned; had psyches singularly unlike the psyches charted by Sigmund Freud, good Greek psyches in which the unconscious, if it were there at all, was as serenely temperate as the conscious. The Pericles of the famous funeral oration was in this tradition a realist:

Our form of government does not enter into rivalry with the institutions of others. We do not copy our neighbours, but are an example to them. It is true that we are called a democracy, for the administration is in the hands of the many and not of the few. But while the law secures equal justice to all alike in their private disputes, the claim of excellence is also recognised; and when a citizen is in any way distinguished, he is preferred to the public service, not as a matter of privilege, but as the reward of merit. . . . For we are lovers of the beautiful, yet simple in our tastes, and we cultivate the mind without loss of manliness. Wealth we employ, not for talk and ostentation, but when there is a real use for it. To avow poverty with us is no disgrace; the true disgrace is in doing nothing to avoid it.[2]

Perhaps Walter Savage Landor was a realist, too:

> Tell me not what too well I know
> About the bard of Sirmio . . .
>   Yes, in Thalia's son
> Such stains there are . . . as when a Grace
> Sprinkles another's laughing face
>   With nectar, and runs on.[3]

This view of the happy Greeks of the Great Age and their cultivated Roman imitators has twice been severely attacked. First, to the Fathers of the Christian church the Greeks were pagan idolaters, and what the world most admired in them was to the Christian simply sinful. We shall see in a later chapter how far early Christianity did in fact set up ideals the polar opposite of the beautiful-and-good. At any rate, with the reception of Aristotle in the medieval West through the Arabs, some part, at least, of the culture of the Greeks returned to high honor. With the Renaissance in Italy

[2] Thucydides, *The Peloponnesian War*, trans. by B. Jowett, Oxford, Clarendon Press, 1881, Book II, §§37-40, Vol. I, pp. 117-119.
[3] "On Catullus," in *Poetical Works*, ed. by Stephen Wheeler, Oxford, Clarendon Press, 1937, Vol. II, p. 413.

the whole Greek model was raised to the highest point it has ever attained as a model. Only with the French "Quarrel of the Ancients and the Moderns" and the British "Battle of the Books" in Western Europe at the end of the seventeenth century did a group of intellectuals, in spirit on the whole on the defensive, dare suggest that "classic" cultural achievements might be equaled or even in some fields surpassed by contemporaries. The modernists did not really turn to the attack until the nineteenth century, when the more ardent devotees of science and technology, the more confident heirs of the Enlightenment, began to suggest that things Greek had been rather petty—the Englishman Richard Cobden said they were "Lilliputian"—and that it was really shocking that young men all over the West should spend the best years of their lives in formal education, learning the dead languages and the dead cultures of the Greeks and Romans. Herbert Spencer put it neatly:

Men who would blush if caught saying Iphigénia instead of Iphigenía, or would resent as an insult any imputation of ignorance respecting the fabled labours of a fabled demi-god, show not the slightest shame in confessing that they do not know where the Eustachian tubes are, what are the actions of the spinal cord, what is the normal rate of pulsation, or how the lungs are inflated.[4]

What we may call the utilitarian attack has not yet been as successful as was the first wave of Christian attack; but then, Western higher education has not, in spite of the gloomy predictions of the humanists, broken down as did Greco-Roman pagan education after the fourth century A.D. The Greeks, even if only in translation, are still in high honor among us. They are—and this is surely characteristic of our multanimous age, as yet very far from mass uniformity—very variously interpreted. There are the individual crotchety interpretations. Samuel Butler, the Victorian rebel against a Victorian father, wrote a book to prove that the *Odyssey* was written by a woman. To Nietzsche, Socrates was almost as guilty as St. Paul in bringing about the perversion of the Greek warrior ideal. More seriously, modern anthropological studies have focused interest on sides of Greek life in the Great Age, such as the cults of Demeter and of Dionysus, in which the initiates behaved more like Holy Rollers than like sober devotees of sweetness and light. Social and economic historians have called attention to the always precarious material basis of Greek culture, political historians to the disastrous struggles among the city-states by which they destroyed the very independence each

4 Herbert Spencer, *Education: Intellectual, Moral, and Physical*, New York, Appleton, 1890, p. 43.

one cherished so greatly.[5] The late Gilbert Murray, one of the most distinguished of classical scholars, even suggested a major heresy in interpretation: the Greeks of the Great Age were perhaps not even classicists in the sense of being poised, gentlemanly, reasonable followers of the Golden Mean, but were at bottom romanticists, rebels, undisciplined yearners and mystics who very much needed to praise, and even to set up ethical and artistic standards of self-restraint, just because they were such wild men at heart. Traces of these romanticists still remain, as in much of the work of Euripides, but, Murray suggested, generations of schoolteachers and conventional moralists have probably worked to mold the heritage of the Great Age in accordance with their schoolmasterish "classic" tastes, a task made possible by the scarcity of manuscripts in days before printing.

The classical view of the classic Greeks, however, still persists. One of the most esteemed of American commentators on the Greeks, Miss Edith Hamilton, whose *The Greek Way* has had wide distribution in paperback form, still sees them as the Renaissance saw them, as quite simply the best yet, as Apollos incarnate—and in something like the Christian sense of an incarnation. So strong still is the acceptance of the Athenians of the fifth century and of all Greeks of the time as incarnations of the humanist's virtues, that the historian is strongly tempted into revision, if not into actual debunking. It is certainly a temptation I shall rather note here than wholly resist.[6]

II

The ideal of the beautiful-and-good, the καλοκἀγαθία, as it stands out from the very considerable body of art, literature, and philosophy that has survived is attractive, one must say, to most Westerners not predisposed by other devotions—or perhaps by some inner resistance to the human lot—to find it repelling. The Athenian gentleman who strove to attain this ideal was a member of an aristocracy new in the West. With undue but useful simplification, we may say that throughout Western history—and, one suspects, Western prehistory, at least from the Neolithic times—two groups of gifted, specially trained, and privileged human beings have stood out from the masses. We

[5] On this whole topic, nothing more is necessary for the general reader than the admirable *The Greeks and the Irrational* by E. R. Dodds, Berkeley, University of California Press, 1951, now available in a paperback edition, Boston, Beacon, 1957.

[6] In strictness, I suppose one should be careful not to use "Athenian" and "Greek" interchangeably; but it is difficult to avoid some such usage. At any rate, the great tradition *does* take Athens as typical, Sparta as atypical. This usage is not without justification.

may call these, with Spengler, the warriors and the priests, and symbolize them by heart and head, or sword and pen. The neat dualism of course breaks down in concrete application: individuals display various admixtures of both, and additions of something that is neither, and this is true whether we classify them in terms of the roles they play or of their temperaments, their personalities. Above all, for our present purpose, ruling or upper classes themselves are often mixed, a class of warrior-priests, a monarchy headed by a priest-king. Yet often, if only roughly, the division holds, and the relation between the warrior class and the priestly class and the prestige of each in the eyes of the other and of the common people are extremely useful facts for the historian of ideas and of morals.

Now the point about the Athenian aristocratic ideal is this: the beautiful-and-good man is both a warrior and a priest—or, if the last word throws you off a bit, let me use a current, shop-worn, but not, I hope, too misleading word, an "intellectual." It is, however, in many ways a most unsatisfactory word, for it can start a powerful flow from the adrenal glands. Americans often think of "intellectual" as meaning "intelligent," and not "one who preaches, teaches, writes, acts on the stage, paints, designs, or who is chiefly concerned with appreciating the results of such activities." Physicians, who are in our United States rarely *intellectuals* in this sense (though they may have an intellectual's hobbies), are usually very *intelligent,* very well-educated, and aware of so being. When they read about intellectuals in my sense of the word, they know they are not intellectuals, and they think they are being excluded from the class of the intelligent. This makes them angry.[7]

At first sight it may well seem that these two, warrior and intellectual, are in happy and useful balance in Athens, each respecting and influencing the other, the warrior refined but not softened in the intellectual, the intellectual toughened but not stultified in the warrior. So, at least, the ideal has appeared in the great tradition. And the record of the lives of these gentlemen is there to show the ideal was not wholly unrealized. The warrior is no vain, boastful

[7] See S. M. Lipset's "The Egghead Looks at Himself," New York *Times,* October 17, 1957, Section VI, and especially a "letter to the editor" signed "Robert Zufall, M.D." a fortnight later, December 1, Section VI, p. 31. The letter is worth quoting as a documentary: "I am moved to comment on Professor Lipset's article. It upsets me greatly to see any group of people call themselves 'The Intellectuals,' as if they had some sort of monopoly on brains. Webster defines 'intellectual' as 'much above the average in intelligence.' The Professor defines it as anyone who depends for his livelihood on 'culture,' including, obviously, a lot of people who aren't even intelligent at all. It strikes me that this assorted group of singers, dancers and ivory-tower types would get a bit more respect from the rest of us if they stopped calling themselves, so ridiculously, 'the smart ones.' "

Homeric fighting chieftain; he is Xenophon, recording not only the successful fight against great odds of the *Anabasis,* but the conversations of Socrates and the admirably balanced education, or *paideia,* of young Cyrus. Or if, as it must be admitted the Achilles of Homer seems to have, the hero must have his interesting complexities, these complexities are now, as in the charming Alcibiades, ambivalences worthy of the modern novel. So, too, starting from the side tradition lists as primarily that of the intellectual, we know that Socrates himself was an Athenian soldier, that Aeschylus was proud of his part in the Persian Wars.

Was he prouder of this, perhaps, than of his work as dramatist? Commentators have often noted that in the famous epitaph in the Palantine Anthology there is no mention of the plays:

Aeschylus son of Euphorion the Athenian this monument hides, who died in wheat-bearing Gela; but of his approved valour the Marathonian grove may tell, and the deep-haired Mede who knew it.[8]

It will not do, however, to question the genuineness of the admiration which the Athenian gentleman of the Great Age felt for the work of the mind. If, in a culture that so prized bodily strength and beauty, a culture still held so much in thrall by the spell of Homer, one feels that the warrior primes the priest-intellectual, it is still true that the balance between the two was remarkably even. What a closer examination does reveal is not so much a failure of balance—Athenians could in the Great Age hardly have understood the situation aptly put by Bernard Shaw for his England as the contrast between Horseback Hall and Heartbreak Hall or have sympathized with Kipling's very mixed feelings toward his "flanneled oafs and muddied fools"—but, rather, that the agonistic warrior ideal we saw as one of the keys to the moral ideal of the Homeric Age took almost complete possession of the intellectuals of the Age of Pericles.

We confront another useful but dangerous dualism, that between competitiveness and co-operativeness in human nature and human society.[9] Certainly a complete opposition, the warrior and the warrior class always for competition, the priest and the priestly class always for co-operation, warriors always

---

[8] *Select Epigrams from the Greek Anthology,* trans. by J. W. Mackail, London, Longmans, 1938, p. 48.
[9] The subject is of major importance for the historian of Western morals, and I shall return to it. The reader who wants a clear, forceful—and exaggerated—statement of the contrast should read P. A. Kropotkin, *Mutual Aid, a Factor of Evolution,* New York, McClure, Phillips, 1902.

pouring oil, priests always pouring water, on the fires of human aggressive-ness—such an opposition is very misleading indeed. Even for Christianity, the observation dear to hostile rationalist critics is true enough: no rivalries more bitter than those inspired by hatred theological. Yet it is certainly true that the Christian ideal, as we shall see in Chapter VI, if not by any means pacifist (it *does* have pacifist elements), nonetheless exalts brotherly love, self-abne-gation—co-operation, in short—and severely condemns just those physically agonistic elements of human life the Greeks of the Great Age so admired.

Their admiration was no merely theoretical one, but was translated into almost every sphere of the good, the dignified, the aristocratic life. The Greeks not only competed in the Olympic and other athletic contests, but they com-peted in all the arts and letters, and not merely in the possibly ambiguous competition of the market place and the coteries, from which the wounded author of our day can always—well, almost always—salvage some kind of *succès d'estime.* The Greek creative artist engaged in a firmly ranked compe-tition from which he emerged as clearly placed—and as widely known—as a major-league batter in the United States. The dramatists of Athens entered their plays, which, if accepted, were staged and performed at public expense, in a competition and came out ranked first, second, third, and also-ran. Sculptors, painters, architects all submitted to this sort of athlete's competi-tion. Politicians, it need hardly be said, had to win votes, though the complex machinery of Athenian political institutions did not make for such clear numerical ranking as we Americans are used to in our elections. Pericles him-self was a boss rather than a direct people's choice. But the agonistic element in Greek politics and war hardly needs emphasis.

This everlasting competition, as yet not softened by humanitarian and egalitarian sentiments, was far more ferocious than it appears to most modern lovers of ancient Greece to have been. It was at its most intense in the con-stant wars that culminated in the great Peloponnesian War at the end of the fifth century. Actual fighting among human beings is clearly never a gentle pursuit, but there is, nevertheless, a remarkable range between the extremes of stylized and not very murderous fighting, as in the knightly combats of the later Middle Ages, and all-out fighting like that of our own wars and those of the Greeks of the Great Age. It does not become us, whose culture has pro-duced Auschwitz, Katyn, and Hiroshima, to reproach the Greeks of the Great Age with Melos and Corcyra. But read—and no one concerned at all with public affairs today should fail to read—the pages of Thucydides in which he describes what went on at Melos and Corcyra. Here, certainly, that ambiguous and perhaps meaningless commonplace that a sufficiently great difference in degree can be a difference in kind does not hold. In numbers of victims, our outrages exceed those of the Greeks a thousand to one; morally they are identical.

Quite outside war and politics, one gets the impression that competition in Greek life, save perhaps in "business," was at least as extensive as in ours, and somewhat more extreme. The old Homeric theme, which can be translated into good American as "winner take all," still prevailed. One aimed always for the very top; only the championship counted. There were no seconds or thirds in the Olympic games and no team scores. It is, incidentally, enlightening to note that when the games were revived in a very different world in 1896, the planners, quite aware of Greek history, refused to admit team scores by points; the press, and especially the American press, proceeded to work out "unofficial" team scores which counted placing down through fifth.

Moreover, though there were certainly rules for all these competitions, intellectual and athletic, in ancient Greece, though as in all aristocracies the concept of honor was a very real one, there are indications in the literature that the kind of unscrupulousness certainly not condemned by Homer in his wily Odysseus persisted into the Great Age. We are dealing with intangibles; but it looks as if the standards of "fair play" both in ethics and in conduct of these Greek aristocrats fell rather below that of later aristocracies at their best. Aristophanes, Thucydides, and Plato together cover a lot of ground. They share little, perhaps, but a common feeling that their Athens is going wrong—morally wrong. The first two in particular are good observers as well as good moralists. From them all there emerges the sense of a society in which the desire to win, to excel, to shine, to rise, is breaking down the conventional restraints of morality, the rules of the game.[10]

The Greeks of the Great Age were then engaged in an agon that often looks like a mad scramble. But their ideal of the beautiful-and-good was by no means without influence on the goals, at least, of the competitors. The Greek aristocrat of the Age of Pericles would not have cared to succeed as Rockefeller succeeded, nor as St. Francis succeeded, nor as St. Simeon Stylites

---

[10] These are war and postwar writers, and I should grant that they and their society reflect the deep wounds such wars make, especially on intellectuals. But I do not think one can find a more golden and moral age in the years immediately preceding 431, not even among the men who fought at Marathon. Themistocles turned traitor; Demaratus, king of Sparta, took refuge with the Persian enemy. Alcibiades was not the first.

succeeded. All three of these men would have seemed to the Greek to have pursued unworthy ends—money, mystic poverty, self-castigating austerity; indeed, the latter two would have been, probably, quite incomprehensible pursuits to a Xenophon. But here Rockefeller gives us a better start. The Greek of the Great Age did not disdain wealth; it was for him an indispensable moral good. The poor man could not, in this ethics, be a good man. The *pursuit* of wealth, though, was beneath this aristocrat, as we shall soon see. He would have counted Rockefeller out of the moral community of the beautiful-and-good merely because he was a businessman. But he would *also* have thought that Rockefeller—like the Croesus of his own legends—had simply too much money, indecently too much, even had it been inherited.

We are at perhaps the most familiar part of Greek ethics, the concept of the Golden Mean, of nothing in excess. Aristotle has in the *Nicomachean Ethics* given it classic expression. Courage is a virtue, for the beautiful-and-good one of the very highest virtues. Cowardice, which is insufficiency of courage, is a vice; but so, too, is foolhardiness, rashness, the caricatural "courage" of the show-off, which is the excess of courage. This kind of analysis can be applied to a great range of human conduct. Prudent care of one's money, good stewardship, is a virtue; the spendthrift is a bad man, but so, too, is the miser.

We may here note that there has been a good deal of hostile criticism of this ideal of the Golden Mean, criticism no doubt basically directed at the implications for conduct of the ideal, but framed as criticism of the logical implications of its wording in specific cases. Does a term like "excess" of courage make sense? Has foolhardiness *any relation* to courage? Or, to take a modern instance, the rationalist J. M. Robertson writes that a pickpocket could "claim to observe the mean between robbery with violence and the spiritless honesty which never steals at all, and to be thus, on Aristotelian principles, a virtuous man in that respect."[11] The phrase "in that respect," which the reader does not notice and is not supposed to notice, no doubt saves Robertson's logic in this particular piece of casuistry, a somewhat suspect but often useful way of thinking about moral problems. To Aristotle, of course, the instance would have been pointless; pickpockets are just not allowed to compete for the prize of the beautiful-and-good.

The real objections to the ideal of the Golden Mean are more deeply rooted in human attitudes toward this world and the next than casuistry, at

11 John Mackinnon Robertson, *A Short History of Morals,* London, Watts, 1920, p. 120.

least on the surface, usually reveals. The ideal of these Greek gentlemen seems to most of those who dislike it to be commonplace, pedestrian, dull, unheroic. It seems to seek compromise where the truly good man ought to fight to the death. It is earth-bound, wingless. We are here at our first clear confrontation with another of the inevitable dualisms we shall have to deal with throughout this history, one we know best as the contrast of the *romantic* with the *classical,* a contrast that has as much meaning for the historian of morals as for the historian of art and letters, a contrast we can by no means summarize here. An old pair of symbols will have to do: the romantic is the soaring Gothic cathedral; the classical, the confined Greek temple, clinging to the ground.[12]

Now it is the romantic to whom the ideal of the Golden Mean is unacceptable. To the classicist, it has been, ever since it was first so clearly stated by the Greeks, one of the foundations of his view of life. And the views are certainly different. Where the romanticist sees in the Golden Mean an ignoble contentedness with the easy, the ordinary, the average, the classicist sees in it a difficult striving, quite as heroic as any ascent to heaven or descent to hell, to attain on earth something by no means there for all to snatch; above all, no average, no compromise, such as mere common sense takes those terms to mean, but a standard, an ideal; no product of statistics, but, rather, of the very human drive to transcendence the romanticist likes to claim as his sole property. There is nothing ordinary or average, the classicist will insist, about the Venus de Milo, nor Pericles, nor the Parthenon. He is likely to go further, and maintain that basically the ideal of the beautiful-and-good is for the moralist not unlike what the ideal of health is for the physician, only more difficult to attain, and rarer. We must return to this theme when we come to Christianity.

Still another set of attributes needs to be added to this Greek ideal of the Golden Mean, attributes that have a moral as well as a more obvious aesthetic character. The Greek admired restraint, spareness, simplicity. Here, too, the "classical" canon, as it has developed, no doubt distorts and exaggerates. Those calm, now weathered Greek statues were once gilded, painted in bright colors. Greek joy was often unrestrained. Greeks of the Great Age employed

---

[12] Spengler's antithesis of Faustian (romantic) and Apollonian (classical) remains one of the fullest and most interesting developments of this theme. See the *Decline of the West,* Vol. I, pp. 183 ff. I suppose to the old-fashioned nominalist, who often disguises himself today as a scientist—especially a social or behavioral scientist—all this, and the very concepts "romantic" and "classical," is nonsense. But it is singularly useful nonsense, indeed indispensable nonsense, for the student of human affairs.

hyperbole—witness Aristophanes—as well as litotes; *both* words and things are Greek. Yet surely no one would use the word "lush" of fifth-century Greece; indeed, the connotations of "lush" are overwhelmingly romantic, Faustian. Morally, there is more than a trace of the Stoic in Greece even before Zeno taught on the Stoa.

The ideals of the agon and the Golden Mean are very specifically ideals meant in their Athenian fifth-century origin to be valid only for an aristocratic minority. Work, undignified, necessary work, as the world knows it, makes the good life impossible.[13] The smith has to develop his muscles to a point well beyond Apollonian symmetry; the bookkeeper bending over his accounts starves both his body and his soul. Workers of any sort are bound to be specialized professionals; and the beautiful-and-good was as firmly an ideal of the amateur, the all-around man, as was the ideal of the modern British upper classes, who used to be, of course, brought up on a nice version of Greek culture. For the activities that disqualify for the attainment of true virtue, the Greeks had a word which sometimes attains unabridged English dictionaries in the form "banausic," though we do not have much use for it. Banausic are most of the activities which engage us all today, for few of us can even try to live up to the letter of the Greek ideal of the beautiful-and-good.[14] Many modern commentators on the ancient Greeks have seemed to feel a need to apologize for the very concept "banausic." Yet the ideal lives on, as it did in Athens itself, in a society committed to democratic egalitarianism.

The ideal of the beautiful-and-good man is not as selfish as it must seem from the foregoing, not as individualistic as we today usually take the term to imply—that is, in something like the frame of reference of Spencer's *The Man versus the State.* There is no need here to take back the remarks I have made above concerning the extreme competitiveness of Greek life among these gentlemen. But, to qualify a bit, it was a competitiveness that had as a balancing force, even in Athens, the soldier's acceptance of discipline, the citizen's acceptance of law and custom, the believer's acceptance of the pieties of religion, even a touch of the old patriarch's sense of responsibility for the

---

13 The familiar brief statement is: "No man can practice virtue who is living the life of a mechanic or laborer." Aristotle, *Politics,* Book III, Chap. 5. The word translated "virtue" is, of course, the untranslatable *aretè.* It is sometimes translated as "excellence."

14 It is interesting to consider how many of our stereotypes would have made no sense to the Greeks of the Great Age. What would Socrates have thought of Edison's "Genius is one per-cent inspiration and ninety-nine per-cent perspiration"?

family. Another commonplace of the manuals is here essential: the Greeks, even again the Athenian, were, in the oft-cited phrase of Aristotle, *political animals,* men made to live in a polis; and the man who showed some signs of setting himself up as a rugged individualist to the neglect of the conventional duties of the citizen was known by a word which has become our word "idiot." Again, a needed complementary consideration, the strong element of the Homeric hero and his drive to compete, and win, which survives in the fifth century, a really frenetic competitiveness, was limited to activities, shall we say, not banausic—to art, letters, sports, to the life of the country gentleman. Unbridled competitiveness in matters of business was never what it was to be in the nineteenth-century West—a truly important matter. It is perhaps unfortunate that war and politics were not also thought banausic in Athens; here the spirit of the agon quite gainsaid, with disastrous results, the ideal of the Golden Mean.

Though much of the ideal of the Great Age was real, and realized, the gaps between real and ideal began opening widely with the Peloponnesian War. The shades again are subtle. But what with Pericles sounds as lofty as the Gettysburg Address begins with the later Isocrates to sound faintly like George Babbitt, to have a touch of that vulgar "pooled self-esteem" that the sensitive detect in modern patriotic loyalties. Pericles, as reported by Thucydides, is certainly proud of Athens, "an education to Greece"; but his tone is not that of Isocrates, who boasts, "Our city was not only so beloved of the Gods but so devoted to mankind . . . that she shared with all men what she had received." There follows the Rotarian touch, "service of mankind."[15] Pericles at least spoke before Mytilene, before Melos, before Syracuse; Isocrates spoke *after* Athenians had given in these places somewhat paradoxical evidence of their devotion to the "service of mankind."

Perhaps the gap between ideal and real in Athens had never been a small one, even in the best days of Pericles. Yet it was certainly smaller than it became in the days of Cleon, or the Thirty Tyrants, or the restored democracy of the fourth century. There is the possibility, hopeful or discouraging as you may feel it, that the failure of Athens was at bottom the failure of a democracy to live up to an aristocratic set of goals, choosing a Cleon rather than a Pericles or an Aristides, perhaps even choosing a Cleon in the belief that it was choosing a man like these. This is an oversimplification, no doubt,

[15] Isocrates, *Panegyricus,* 28, trans. by George Norlin, London, Heinemann, Loeb Classical Library, 1928, Vol. I, p. 135.

like the parallel notion that Christianity, which also sets most aristocratic standards, has kept alive only by *not* trying to apply those standards to the conduct of the many.

Yet we need not add to the long list of those who, from Plato on, have blamed the ills of Athens on the spread of egalitarian and democratic ways; Sparta, where these ways never were followed, failed as miserably and as quickly as did Athens in the dog-eat-dog military competition among the Greek city-states. Sparta, too, has left her mark on the moral history of the West. Among the ancients, the Spartan tone and the Spartan achievement were admired perhaps more than were the Athenian. It was the Italian Renaissance that set Athens up so firmly as the symbol for the Greek achievement; Florence, even the Florence of Savonarola's brief triumph, could never have felt an affinity for Sparta.

We know about Sparta chiefly through the writings of Athenian contemporaries of the Great Age, men like Plato, Thucydides, and Xenophon, who were shocked by what seemed to them the democratic indiscipline of Athens and sought in Spartan virtues a cure for Athenian laxity, and through later writers like Plutarch, whose sources were hardly better than ours. Yet the main facts about Sparta are clear enough. The inland plain of Lacedaemonia was settled by one of the last bands of Dorian invaders, who subjected earlier inhabitants to an inferior but not fully servile status. Sparta seems at first to have gone the normal way of Greek city-states, fighting with her neighbors, but also nourishing a vigorous artistic and intellectual life. Then there came, within a generation or so, what looks in the Spartan society like a kind of transformation we know well enough in the personality of the rare individual—the sudden turn that made Francesco Bernardone into St. Francis of Assisi, for instance—but that we do not expect in a whole society even from what we call a "revolution." Sometime in the seventh century B.C., Sparta—all Spartans—gave up poetry and music, save as aids to military ardor, gave up talking—always a Greek delight—gave up even the private and normal forms of family life to become an aristocratic communist city-state and society.

The Greek ideal of the beautiful-and-good gets twisted almost, but not quite, out of recognition in the great barracks that Sparta became. The ideal of bodily health and strength is focused on the toughness of the soldier, on a superhuman endurance of hardship and pain. The agon is there, but among the Spartiates it is narrowed to a competition in military prowess, and, even more than in the rest of Greece, channeled, controlled, into a collective effort to keep Sparta first among the Greek city-states. The old Odyssean note of admiration for *successful* cunning and deceit is there, it, too, oddly contorted in this barracks air. Perhaps the best-known tale from Sparta is the one made familiar by Plutarch of the Spartan lad, trained to thieve but with the proviso he must never get caught in theft, who stoically, Spartanly, endured a stolen fox gnawing at his vitals under the folds of his cloak rather than admit his guilt. The restraint is there, now made austerity, if not insanity; the Spartan would not even permit himself the luxury of speech. He spoke laconically.

The Golden Mean has quite vanished. The Spartan had no use for the middle of the road, for compromise; for him the Greek folk wisdom of "nothing in excess" did not hold. He could not have too much discipline, could not be too literal-minded in obeying commands, could not remain too much aloof from the undignified business of managing his estate, could not banish art and letters too completely from his life. No major society in the West, perhaps, ever tried so thoroughly to transcend the limitations of Homo sapiens as did the Spartan. It was an extraordinary attempt, and it succeeded for a few generations. We cannot here attempt to trace the decline of Sparta and the failure of the attempt to perpetuate so inhuman a way of life. But a few of the contributing factors must especially interest us. For one thing, it is clear that Spartan contempt for the intellectual life coupled with their devotion to tradition, to doing what always had been done, made it difficult for them to solve problems involving new factors. Even in their specialty, war, they could not change fast enough to cope with the Theban innovation of the phalanx, and went down in defeat. The Spartan Thermopylae surely deserves its place in a noble tradition that has helped men to find a courage they never cease to need. And yet, was it that much better than the charge of the Light Brigade, on which we now surely accept French Marshal Bosquet's verdict: *C'est magnifique, mais ce n'est pas la guerre?* True, Tennyson now sounds empty, silly.

> Theirs not to make reply,
> Theirs not to reason why,
> Theirs but to do and die,
> Into the valley of Death
> Rode the six hundred.

And Simonides has still the perfect word:

O passer-by, tell the Lacedaemonians that we lie here obeying their orders.[16]

The Greek spell is hard to break, hard, above all, for the chaste realist to break, who has no trouble with the Loreleis and the *belles dames sans merci* of mere romance.

Again, the fine Spartan soldierly contempt for economic matters, and the curious communistic life the adult males spent in barracks and on campaigns, meant that their wives and stewards got control of property, with results disastrous to the necessary economic basis of equality among the Spartiates. Finally, the Spartiates in the fourth century simply began to die out, to fail to propagate, a result probably linked with their long absences from home on campaigns, and the exaggerated military communism which actually made it hard for them to sleep at all with their wives. But most narrow aristocracies tend not to perpetuate themselves by natural births, and have to recruit new members one way or another. Spartan excessive exclusiveness made this way impossible; one had to be born a Spartiate, and fewer and fewer were born such.

The historian of morals must ask the obvious question: How did Sparta happen to develop so unusual, so "unnatural," a society? The occasion is clear enough. In a first war at the end of the eighth century, Sparta conquered neighboring Messenia, but instead of merely exacting a tribute and a few border settlements—in the Greek, as in the later Western world, there *were* international decencies—she proceeded to outrage these decencies and annex Messenia and make Helots, or serfs, of the Messenians. Almost a century later, a ferocious revolt of the Messenians, crushed with difficulty, seems to have alarmed the rulers of Sparta, who then put through an extraordinary set of reforms which made the Spartiates the military communists we meet at Thermopylae and many another field. But surely Messenia was but the pull on the trigger. The gun was loaded. The real problem is why the Spartans responded as they did to a problem other peoples had solved quite differently, by assimilating the conquered, by compromises of all sorts, even by retreat from a difficult position, the favored solution among the wicked imperialist powers of today. The answer can never be certain, but it looks as if there were perhaps a certain analogy with the experience of the Jews. The Dorian band or bands that settled in Laconia may well have been especially hardened

[16] Tennyson, "The Charge of the Light Brigade," in *Works,* Boston, Houghton Mifflin, 1898, p. 226; Simonides, "On the Spartans at Thermopylae," in *Select Epigrams from the Greek Anthology,* trans. by J. W. Mackail, 3d ed. rev., New York, Longmans, 1911, Section III, No. 4.

by their wanderings. In their early years in Laconia even their art bore a stamp of warlike energy of stubborn weight. Tyrtaeus, while Spartans were still poets, could write so symbolically Spartan a line as

So let each man bite his lip with his teeth and abide firm-set astride the ground.[17]

In the critical years of decision, a man or group of close-knit leaders almost certainly swung the balance. Lycurgus, to whom legend attributed the great reform, may be in strict historical rigor as shadowy, if not as mythical, a figure as Moses. But some one or some few surely did—and in a crisis—what Lycurgus is supposed to have done.

III

The beautiful-and-good, then, even in its Spartan caricature or perversion, is the moral ideal, the concept of the admirable and enviable person the Greeks of the Great Age of the polis cherished. Presented and preserved in an art and literature that has survived the praise of its many admirers, it is still a living ideal in the West. We must, however, try further to probe what kind of moral lives these ancient Greek admirers of the Golden Mean really led. As almost always until very recent times, we can tell very little of how the masses lived. Certainly for Athens of the fifth century it seems pretty clear that this culture, moral as well as intellectual, spread downward to most of the actual urbanized population. Sources like the pamphleteer known as the Old Oligarch, who complains that the very slaves in Athens do not respect their superiors, Aristophanes, above all, give us a glimpse—the first in Western history—of a lively, slick, "sophisticated" city people, quick to imitate and, if you like, vulgarize the tastes and ways of their betters. We get again a glimpse of the fact that the sober country folk, only a few miles away in Attica, thought the city dwellers morally loose and untrustworthy. This remains a pattern even in contemporary America, where technological advances have almost eliminated material differences between city and country. Like most such patterns, it has elements of truth; the Athenian, like the later Parisian and the Cockney, was no slow, steady, wordless follower of established routine. But one element in the pattern, the belief that these bright talkative city people lacked stamina, endurance, manliness, was probably as untrue then as aerial bombardment proved it to be of great Western metropolitan centers in our day. The Athenians did not lose their great war through any failure of nerve among

[17] *Elegy and Iambus,* trans. by J. M. Edmonds, London, Heinemann, 1931, Loeb Classical Library, p. 71.

the common people, nor through a lack of public spirit among them. Here Arnold Toynbee seems to be right: their betters led them into a series of only outwardly successful conquests which did violence to the habits and ideals of the polis.

Two things need to be kept in mind in any attempt to judge the moral level of Greek life in the Great Age. First, the Greeks were very few generations removed from a relatively primitive tribal society. The notion embodied in what used to be called the "miracle of Greece" has been abandoned. Study of the Aegean civilization centering on Crete, which had been highly developed before the Greek bands came down on it, has made it clear that the Greeks did not create their mature civilization out of nothing, and in a few hundred years. Still, however much they may have taken over from their predecessors, the fact remains that their poleis were new institutions. If old tribal habits do survive, if there is such a thing as cultural lag, we should expect the Greeks to show signs of them. Second, the Greeks were always poor. Their land was mountainous and rocky, their soil thin. The wealthiest of the poleis—Athens, Corinth, the cities of Ionia—depended on commerce and production of pottery and similar work of craftsmanship. The rich by no means attained the kind of luxury that was to be made possible later in the Greco-Roman world; the poor were poor indeed, and numerous.

With this background, it is not surprising that this Greek world should be a world of violence, a world in which death, disease, human suffering of all kinds were accepted in something like the way we accept the weather. Care is necessary here: I do not mean that the Greeks took suffering callously; nor do I mean to imply that our own is a culture that is without violence. Our recent wars have killed on a hitherto unequaled scale; our technological progress, and especially the internal-combustion engine, has meant that what we call accidents are relatively far more frequent than they were in the ancient world. But we rebel against such suffering, and try, however unsuccessfully, to do something about it; the Greeks of the Great Age, though they felt deeply the extent of human misery, seem not to have believed that the group, society, "reforms," could do much to lessen it. Plato, who was in almost all the modern connotations of the word an idealist, accepted in his Utopia, the *Republic,* war as a normal function of the perfect state. In all the literature that has come down to us from the Great Age, you will find it hard to note anything you could classify as an expression of what we should call desire for humanitarian reform. There is, indeed, pity, compassion, eloquently expressed, though mostly in the tragedies, which do not deal with the lives of ordinary people.

In Euripides, this pity seems at times to direct itself to the oppressed, the underdog, but even in Euripides there is really no trace of what we might call a "social gospel." We shall return to this theme with the Middle Ages.

Acceptance of violence and insecurity in ordinary daily life is the normal human lot until almost our own day. But later Greek ethical systems, and the Christian ethic, did at least introduce a concern for victims of violence, injustice, and misfortune, which really is hard to find in the Great Age. Spartan exposure of infants who did not measure up to the high physical standards set for males—and females, too, for the Spartans were among the earliest eugenicists—is hardly surprising in that abnormal society. But infants in the rest of Greece, exposed to poverty and overpopulation, were very commonly exposed. As a good British reformer of our own day puts it, "Socrates (son of a mid-wife) is made in Plato's *Theaetetus* to speak of putting away the new born infants as he might of the drowning of kittens."[18]

Slavery was an accepted part of the society of Greece. The slaves were for the most part prisoners of war, or victims of some other misfortune. They were not in these early days of a very different racial background from that of their masters. Their condition varied greatly from city-state to city-state, and within a given one, in accordance with what work they did. The Helots of Sparta, serfs in formal status rather than chattel slaves, were nonetheless very badly treated and were greatly feared by their masters. The familiar tales from Plutarch are revealing. The Spartan leaders would at intervals get a Helot drunk and exhibit him to the young Spartiates as an object lesson; a special secret police was organized to spy on the Helots and scent out plans for revolt. The state slaves who worked the silver mines at Laurium in Attica had a hard life indeed; on the other hand, the police at Athens were commonly Thracian slaves, and a policeman's lot is not usually an unhappy one. It is perhaps true that an Oxford philhellene like the late Sir Alfred Zimmern makes the position of the slave in Athens a bit too good; "fellow-worker"— a term that sounds like an American corporate personnel manager a few decades ago—is no translation for δοῦλος. "Slave" is the word. Yet, with the exception of Sparta, the Greek world of the free polis was not one in which slavery appears at anything like its worst. Emancipation was easy, and not uncommon; the slave could actually earn money and buy his freedom. But there is almost no protest against the institution itself; and Aristotle's opinion that a slave is likely to be by nature a slave is no doubt representative enough

[18] Robertson, *Short History of Morals,* p. 91. The reference is to the *Theaetetus,* §§149, 151.

to deserve its position in the history manuals. The slave is simply not a free moral agent. Plato, in the *Laws,* has the physician to slaves dictate without explanation, the physician to freemen make the patient understand the disease and treatment.[19]

The state of the family is no doubt correlated with the moral state of a given society. Yet the correlation is nothing as simple as our contemporary American worriers about the divorce rate like to make out. In earlier Western societies one expects to find the family ties strong, and the father of the family powerful. The family in the Greek polis was such a family. It should be noted at the start in a society entirely without any provision for "social security," either through state laws or through private insurance, the family was the one possible form of old-age insurance. The Greek expected his children to take care of him in his old age; the children expected to take care of their parents. In Athens, before a man could become a magistrate, evidence had to be produced that he had treated his parents properly. A man who refused his parents food and dwelling lost his right of speaking in the assembly. It must be noted that ordinarily laws of this sort are meant to take care of the exceptional case, the case that makes the news. We need not conclude that Athenians commonly let their parents starve.[20] These were firm sentiments, the kind Pareto called "persistent aggregates," and they were strong even in Athens, the least traditionalist of the poleis. Greek literature from the earliest days is full of evidence of the strength of these family ties. Again, only in Sparta in its final decline is there evidence of the kind of dissolution of the family, including loose behavior of upper-class wives, that is found at certain later stages of Roman history.

This was no society for the feminist. The "subjection" of Athenian women in particular was one of the phases of life in that much-to-be-admired society that called for most regrets from Victorian liberal philhellenes. The Athenian wife in the upper classes, and, indeed, rather far down the social scale, was held firmly to her domestic duties of supervising the household and educating her daughters and young sons; she did not go abroad unattended, nor take any part in public life, nor in the social life of her menfolk, the dinners, symposia, chattings in the market place. Yet the gynaeceum was not quite a harem, and even the Athenian wife was hardly in an Oriental seclusion. There is in the

---

[19] Plato, *Laws,* §720, in *Works,* trans. by B. Jowett, Oxford, Oxford University Press, 1892, Vol. V, pp. 103-104.
[20] E. Westermarck, *Origin and Development of the Moral Ideas,* Vol. I, p. 536, quoting L. Schmidt, *Die Ethik der alten Griechen* (1882).

surviving literature little sign that she was discontented with her lot, which, after all, was for those days a secure one. The remarkable Euripides, who can usually be trusted to anticipate the nineteenth century, does show traces, notably in the *Medea,* of what, if you do not mind anachronisms, you can call feminism. But there is little else. Masculine supremacy was taken for granted in the Greek, and in the Greco-Roman, world, a fact amusingly reflected in the universal assumption that the queen bee was a *king.*[21] Demosthenes could say almost incidentally of the Greek male—always, of course, of the upper classes, for poverty makes monogamy quite bearable—"Mistresses we keep for the sake of pleasure, concubines for the daily care of our persons, but wives to bear us legitimate children and to be faithful guardians of our households."[22]

We come at last to sex relations, a topic which, to the pain of sensitive moralists, does seem to be in contemporary vulgar English and American the first, if not the only, thing suggested by the word "morals." It is a topic of major concern to the historian of Western morals, and one to which we must recur. Here a few generalizations may help to guide us through the thickets that lie ahead—and they are thickets, of clinical reports, of pornography, sermons, theological writings, poems, novels, *faits divers,* in all of which the clinical and the pornographic are almost always inextricably mixed—for no one can take sex in stride, not even the historian, who, according to Lytton Strachey (who should have known), tends to be not very strongly sexed.[23]

First, human sexual activities would seem to be an especially clear and often extreme example of the fact that the word and the deed are not necessarily very closely united in human life. It may even be true that Homo sapiens spends more time and energy fantasying, thinking, talking, and writing about sex than in doing anything about it. In the frank language of our era— or, at any rate, of our novels—there is a great deal of paper tail in the world. One doubts whether Don Juan actually enjoyed—no, not enjoyed, for we all know now that the Don was a neurotic incapable of genital satisfaction, but one doubts that he had at all—those famous 1,003 Spanish ladies. In the West generally, and especially after the introduction of Christian prohibitions added

[21] See Vergil, *Georgics,* IV, 67. Of course, Vergil's use of "kings" in this passage may be no more than metaphor. But the ancients could not have understood the sex life of the bees.

[22] Demosthenes, *Private Orations,* trans. by A. T. Murray, London, Heinemann 1939, Loeb Classical Library, Vol. II, *Neaera,* pp. 445-447.

[23] L. Strachey, *Portraits in Miniature,* London, Chatto and Windus, 1933, "Essay on Macaulay," p. 177.

zest to fornication, men and women have found in sexual conquests a great reinforcement of their egos, a real sense of achievement. Moreover, from the very fact that love-making is almost always conducted in privacy, it is easy indeed to claim a conquest never in fact achieved. Again, in a great many periods of Western history, not just in our own, verbal frankness about sex has been fashionable. There are no doubt many other, and deeper, roots for this conduct. The upshot of it all for the historian of morals should be clear: Do not conclude, and especially not for brief periods, such as, say, from 1880 to 1920 in our day, that because there is a change in the way men talk and write about sexual matters there is a corresponding change in their conduct.

Second, it may be possible to go even further and entertain at least the possibility that in routine matters of private morality—sex relations, personal honesty, family loyalties, in short, much of the moral realm of the Ten Commandments—there is for the inarticulate many something like a rough constant of *conduct* over long periods, that in the whole of our short Western history there has been relatively little change in this respect. I suggest this very tentatively. I do not mean to deny that there are times and places, and especially social classes or other groups, of great moral looseness, and others of great moral strictness, in terms of the great Western moral codes. But I think it possible, for instance, that if we could construct a kind of Kinsey report on the sexual behavior of the Western male since 600 B.C., we should find variations much less striking than those we find in our literary sources. I feel very sure that we should find nothing remotely like the simple development Mr. Sorokin traces from an "ideational" period in which men are wholly innocent and continent in matters of sex relations to a "sensate" period (we are right in it now) in which men are wholly guilty and heroically incontinent in such matters. We must recur to this problem of "cyclical" changes in conduct and morals, and in the end to the wider one of moral dynamics or evolution. It is a very difficult one, hardly to be solved with our present analytical means. But it can only be further befuddled if we assume that changes in taste, manners, and in what the imperfect historical record tells us about what men have said about their conduct are in themselves proof that ordinary men and women have in fact changed their conduct. The upper classes, for one thing because they can afford change, may be expected to change more rapidly than the lower classes. The degree to which the lower classes trust and admire and imitate the upper classes—if you dislike this way of putting it, say "ruling classes," or "elites" and "ruled" or "followers"—is certainly subject to great variations. *Morale*—not in English identical in meaning with *morals*—is also subject to change. To all this we must return in a final chapter, but it will be well to keep these problems in mind throughout.

The Greek in the street of the Great Age seems to have been sexually normal enough, if that word has any meaning in relation to sex. His religion held up to him no warnings that the gods objected to love-making—quite the reverse, for Zeus outdid Don Juan, and seems, on the whole, unlike the Don, to have enjoyed himself in the process. On the other hand, there is no evidence that the Greek in the street was notably promiscuous; he had trouble enough providing for his family. He seems not to have been greatly addicted to romantic, or obsessive, or any other vicarious sexual satisfaction of the kind we symbolize by the word "Hollywood." It is true that we do not have the sources we need to have to be sure of this. But we do have the Old Comedy of Aristophanes, much of which is clearly directed to the tastes of the many, of the "pit," who must, the suspicion lingers in the mind of all but the blindest lover of old Athens, have often found Sophocles and Euripides hard going. Now Aristophanes is often obscene, but there is in him no trace of boudoir or Palais Royal sex, let alone of Hollywood sex. When he actually brought the bed onto the stage in *Lysistrata,* the audience must have been so interested in the high comedy—and high politics—involved in the situation as to have suffered no sexual stimulation at all. Aristophanes seems to find sex amusing, an attitude often by no means unfavorable to comparative continence in actual conduct.

There is, however, evidence in the Greek literature of high seriousness, of an attitude toward sex very different from ours. In a familiar passage at the very beginning of the *Republic,* Plato has the aged Cephalus, who appears as a thoroughly conventional old gentleman, remark:

How well I remember the aged poet Sophocles, when in answer to the question, How does love suit with age, Sophocles—are you still the man you were? Peace, he replied; most gladly have I escaped the thing of which you speak; I feel as if I had escaped from a mad and furious master.[24]

Hesiod, too, thought of love in terms not of modern romance:

[24] *The Republic of Plato,* § 329, trans. by B. Jowett, Oxford, Oxford University Press, 1921. Jowett made this translation in High Victorian times. I cannot, as a historian of morals, resist the temptation to cite the version of this passage that the late A. D. Lindsay made in Georgian times: "Take the poet Sophocles, for example. I was with him once, when someone asked him: 'How do you stand, Sophocles, in respect to the pleasures of sex? Are you still capable of intercourse?' 'Hush, sir,' he said. 'It gives me great joy to have escaped the clutches of that savage and fierce master.'" *The Republic of Plato,* trans. by A. D. Lindsay, London, J. M. Dent, 1923, p. 3.

. . . and Eros (Love), fairest among the deathless gods, who unnerves the limbs and overcomes the mind and wise counsels of all gods and all men with them . . .[25]

Sex, in short, is a nuisance, or at best an appetite likely to interfere with the conduct of life according to the Golden Mean. This, be it noted, is very different from the attitude that sex is a form, if not *the* form, of original sin. We cannot know whether most Greek gentlemen agreed with the aged Sophocles; the guess is that they did not. This view of love as a misfortune is almost certainly an upper-class intellectual's view, a part of that complex, and by no means wholly sunny, ideal of the beautiful-and-good.

Sex figures in that ideal in a form even stranger to us, a form that has greatly disturbed modern lovers of Greece. In Voltaire's *Dictionnaire philosophique* the topic is treated under the heading "Amour Socratique," a phrase that at least avoids the misunderstandings of one like "Greek homosexuality." The Greek warrior-gentleman and his young man were indeed lovers in the physical sense; of that we should not be led into doubt even by the reluctance of ancient authors to approach clinical details, nor by the idealization with which Socrates, as reported by Xenophon as well as by Plato, surrounds the relation. But it was not the furtive homosexuality of an unfortunate few born into abnormality, and, above all, it was not usually a homosexual relation in which one of the partners assumed a female or passive role. Both the younger man and the older were assumed to play psychologically a masculine, and, therefore, noble, role, the older man essentially teaching the younger, preparing him for his future part in this world of heroes, fighters, competitors, *men,* still in so many ways of the spirit of the world of Homer.[26]

The sociologist can hardly avoid seeing in Greek pederasty a by no means unprecedented form of a relation common among warriors. At the simplest level, sexual relations among males are supposedly common where there are no females available, notably among sailors in the days of long voyages. No such complete isolation existed among the early Greeks, but with them warfare was endemic and seasonal, and it did involve long periods in camp and in sieges and expeditions where women were not accessible. Some have maintained that the Greek relegation of women to housekeeping and childbearing,

---

25 Hesiod, *The Creation,* quoted in W. H. Auden, *The Portable Greek Reader,* New York, Viking, 1948, p. 52.
26 The whole subject is treated with masterly compression and full command of the sources—and with a quite mid-twentieth-century attitude—in Marrou, *A History of Education in Antiquity,* Chap. III, entitled "Pederasty in Classical Education." M. Marrou even permits himself the statement that *"paideia* found its realization in *paiderasteia,"* a statement a bit too sweeping and a bit too clever, but basically accurate.

the semi-Oriental exclusion they suffered, was itself the "cause" both of pederasty and of the growth of that very Athenian form of professional female prostitution to which Demosthenes refers, the *hetairai* ("mistresses") who bring pleasure because they are bright and attractive. The Greek gentleman, in this notion, turned to boys and *hetairai* since his *wife*, because of her faulty upbringing, could not keep up with him in conversation. This seems a somewhat overintellectualized reason. In fact, the actual situation among the Greek gentlemen of the Great Age seems to be an admirable example of the interaction of mutually dependent variables. The warrior-established relation worked to increase the undesirability of the wife; the wife's relegation and, presumably, resignation worked to increase the desirability of the young male beloved, the *eromenos*.

Greek pederasty, however, got well beyond the sociology of the family and into the sociology of knowledge, if not rather into the sociology of religion, for in the Great Age *l'amour socratique* became a means of symbolizing, turning into a faith, an ideal, the act and fact of love. The pederast became the seeker, the transcendentalist, the mystic, soaring far above the gentlemanly limits of the beautiful-and-good. No doubt with most of these pairs of lovers the relation was one in which this earth was no more than decently, moderately, briefly, left for a better one, as when we are moved to hope for better things. The older man and the younger were partners in an effort to rise above, but not too far above, the common-sense acceptance of an untranscended world that does play an essential part in the beautiful-and-good. Certainly, generations of commentators have tried to show that Socrates himself, and even his *rapporteur* Plato, meant by "Eros" in those famous dialogues that deal with love nothing really Faustian, northern, and indecently, wildly mystical, but no more than "the joint attainment by lover and beloved of self-mastery."[27] It remains true that for the small group of aristocrats who practiced it, this love became what conventional love between men and women did not become in the Great Age, a subject for poet and philosopher, an inspiration for the artist—many of the Athenian vases are dedicated to a male lover —no mere habit, however pleasant, but a goal. Whether that goal was, in fact,

[27] The phrase is from Denis de Rougemont, *Love in the Western World*, trans. by Montgomery Belgion, New York, Pantheon, 1956, p. 61, note. M. de Rougemont compresses in a brief note this contention that in the *Phaedrus* and in the *Symposium* Socrates is putting a bridle on Eros, not applying the spur. He adds, what most commentators would accept, I suppose, that whatever Socrates-Plato may have meant originally, subsequent interpreters have made the Eros of the dialogues into "boundless desire," that is, something transcendental, romantic, "Faustian."

a "romantic" one—that is, an *unattainable* goal—is a question that cannot be firmly answered. Even here, however, one must doubt that the Greek of the Great Age could ever quite sympathize with Shelley's

> . . . . where we taste
> The pleasures of believing what we see
> Is boundless, as we wish our souls to be.[28]

IV

With Socrates we have come to that body of writings that for so many generations has stood for the greatness of the Greeks. There is no need, perhaps, to repeat here warnings against assuming that even so varied and wide-ranging a body of writing as what we may call the Greek canon tells the historian of morals all he wants to know about the Greeks of the Great Age. But it does tell us a great deal, and especially for Athens, where we know the many were at least attracted by the standards of the few, it does not leave us wholly in the dark even about the moral attitudes of the average man.

The canon is varied and inclusive. There is, first of all, the not very formal theogony of the Olympians, the gods themselves, not yet as much embroidered as it was to be in the Greco-Roman world. Then there are the tales of the mortals of old, who had commerce with the gods, and who sometimes from heroes became gods; these are the tales, the "myths," of which the tragedies of the Great Age are made. Then, woven of the same stuff, but a very different thing in the end, there are the "mystery cults" of Dionysus and of Demeter, religious beliefs in which a modern Westerner can recognize a communion, an emotional experience he has difficulty recognizing in the formal Olympian faith. Finally, there is already by 300 B.C. a very substantial body of what might be called "lay" literature, philosophy, lyric and gnomic poetry, history, even the Old Comedy, in some of which the gods and heroes are treated in a skeptical and realistic temper that can hardly be classified as in any sense one of the varieties of religious experience.

As to the formal Olympian faith, I need add little to what I have said above (p. 62ff.). The gods are indeed in a sense and in part like mortals, save for their power and their immortality. The believer does negotiate with them, make a contract with them, he does not seem to pray, to worship, as we understand those words. Yet it must be said emphatically that there is no good evidence that the Greek in the street, as long as he believed in them at all, ever felt that what the gods are permitted to do he was permitted to do. The Greek

[28] Shelley, "Julian and Maddalo," line 15.

moral code—the usual code that condemns dishonesty, greed, adultery, that backs up law codes—does not come directly from Olympus as the Hebrew code comes from God on Sinai; but there *is* such a code, a part of the *nature of things,* in a sense antedating the Olympians, even superior to them. The Olympians themselves may often violate it with impunity, especially in such matters as adultery, much, perhaps, as the conspicuous people on earth, the people whose doings history records, seem to violate it. But for the ordinary man, the gods themselves act as moral agents, their authority reinforcing custom and law. Even for Alcibiades, imitation of the doings of the Olympians is a risky piece of *hubris;* for the plain man, it is unthinkable. This attitude is a difficult one for contemporary American intellectuals in particular to understand; it is probably much easier for John Doe, reading in his tabloid about the goings on of "café society," to understand.

It must be noted that the *leaders* of Greek thought had long anticipated the Christian complaint to come; a Zeus who conducts himself as immorally as does the Zeus of the Olympian faith cannot be a good god, and, therefore, cannot be a god at all. Either Zeus lives up to the best that has been thought and said here on earth or he does not exist. Plato has Socrates say something like this often, and had clearly arrived himself at an idealistic monotheism that really dismisses the whole Olympian theogony and most of Greek "mythology" as unprofitable and often downright wicked storytelling. Euripides, too, often criticizes the view of the Olympians we have attributed to the man in the street.[29] Here, in fact, would seem to be the beginnings of an important and never really greatly narrowed gap between what the educated, the ruling classes as well as the pure intellectuals, of the Greco-Roman world made of the formal, organized religion of their society and what the masses made of it. This was the gap through which Christianity and its great rivals, Mithraism, the cult of Isis, and the like, were to enter Western society.

The gap was in the Great Age only partially filled by the mystery cults. Our sources for understanding the nature of these cults, and in particular for understanding their effect on the morals of the masses, are, of course, defective. For one thing, they were cults about which their initiates were sworn to secrecy; for another, the intellectuals who made and transmitted the great tradition of the beautiful-and-good were apparently rather ashamed of the emotional abandon of these rites. Even Euripides, whose *Bacchae* is the

[29] For Socrates-Plato, the last few pages of Book II of the *Republic* will do as an example. Note that Jowett regularly translated θεός as God with a capital letter. For Euripides, see the *Iphigenia in Tauris,* line 391.

fullest great literary source for the worship of Dionysus, can hardly be said to approach the subject in the frame of mind of the calm observer. Nevertheless, thanks to the labors of generations of scholars, we can be quite sure of the most important facts about the mystery cults. The worshiper took part in a *sacrament* by means of which he communed directly with a god, indeed became through theophagy a part of a god, and hence immortal. In both Demeter and Dionysus there lives the old Western belief in an earth-god or -goddess who dies and is born again. At the height of the ritual the worshipers underwent an experience that exalted them into the kind of mystic transport which, whether it be violent frenzy or quiet rapture, is quite unintelligible, if not indecent, to the rationalist temperament.[30]

As to the moral consequences of participation in these mysteries, we have no substantial evidence. The rationalist is likely to feel about them, as about their modern equivalents, that they are at best comparatively harmless psychological outlets for needs the *really* mature person ought not to have, at worst debauches that may lead to immoral conduct. The Christian mystic must feel that these Greek cults were too much manifestations of mass feelings, too public. The American observer can hardly help comparing them to revivalist camp meetings, Holy Rollerism, and suchlike manifestations of communicable excitement. At any rate, the cults in their original form did not survive the rival excitements of all sorts of other Eastern cults in the later centuries. Their very existence is, however, an important and necessary modification of the oversimple view of the Greeks of the Great Age as universally calm and dignified embodiments of the ideal of the Golden Mean. The Greek in the throes of communion with Dionysus could not have looked much like those serene statues of the Parthenon.

There are still more exceptions to this textbook pattern of the Olympians and their human followers. If the mystery cults suggest an emotional incontinence unworthy of the "classical" ideal, the Sophists, as reported to us, it is true chiefly by their enemy Socrates-Plato, are quite as clearly extremists in another direction. Their famous "man is the measure of all things" has been variously interpreted, but it does seem inconsistent with deep religious feeling.

[30] As an example of the difficulties of interpretation that face the historian interested in human conduct and motivation, the dispute over the *Bacchae* will do very well. Interpretations range from the view that in this play Euripides is the rationalist showing by example the horrors of religious intoxication to the view that he is here the wise humanist showing by example the dangerous narrowness of the matter-of-fact rationalist. The play itself, duly and romantically translated by Gilbert Murray, is of major importance in any scheme of "general education." See the well-known A. W. Verrall, *Euripides the Rationalist*, Cambridge, Cambridge University Press, 1913.

It must be repeated that Socrates and his pupils may have completely mis-represented Protagoras and his. I should guess it much more likely that these Sophists were in fact the first large and well-developed group of the kind most familiar to us in the *philosophes* of the eighteenth century, no-nonsense rationalists who held that properly directed thinking could answer all questions worth asking and guide men's conduct alike for the individual and the general good. No doubt the individualism they taught could act as a dissolvent of old traditional morality, as Aristophanes shows wittily in the *Clouds,* but they probably sincerely believed, as the *philosophes* did, that the new rational morality would lead to a better commonwealth, not to unprincipled struggle among "anarchistic" and selfish individuals.

On the other hand, Plato himself clearly goes beyond the limits set by the ideals of the beautiful-and-good, the Golden Mean, the human super-humanity of the sculptured Apollos and Aphrodites; or perhaps it would be safe to say merely that the accumulated weight of centuries of interpretation of Plato's writings pushes him over to the side of the mystics, the other-worldly, the seekers, or, mildest of words here, the idealists. Plotinus and the other neoplatonists in a later age most certainly heightened Plato's transcendental flights—or, if you see things this way, made his nonsense even more nonsensical. But surely the Plato who in the familiar parable of the cave decides that the world of human sense experience as interpreted by common sense is somehow not the "real" world belongs among William James's "tender-minded," not among his "tough-minded." More riskily, perhaps, one may list him as a Faustian, not as an Apollonian.[31]

Plato's metaphysics, however, need interest us here only as they add to the complexities of the "classic" view of life, as they cast doubt on the view that the Greeks of the Great Age were too gentlemanly to display their metaphysics. As a moralist he almost always speaks as Socrates, and here, too, he presents us with a problem: Does he deepen and widen the ideal of the beautiful-and-good, but still within the tradition of his countrymen, or does he twist it into an unearthly, and un-Greek, striving for the annihilation of the flesh? His Socrates does arrive at the formula "Knowledge is virtue"; and this formula was Greek enough so that many of his critics at the time seem to have

[31] Aristotle, who is usually classified as more worldly, nearer the conventional Greek tough-mindedness than Plato, nonetheless arrives at an ethical ideal, *theoria,* which has firm overtones of some kind of transcendence of this practical and inconvenient world, a sort of quiet, soulful, thoroughly decent ecstasy, far removed from Bacchic intoxication, but still an ecstasy, no mere detached philosophic calm. The more you look at these Greeks, the less they look like the Elgin marbles.

confused him with his opponents the Sophists. But for the Sophists knowledge was apparently instrumental, utilitarian, "practical" almost in our modern sense; and for the Socrates of Plato knowledge was the intuitive appreciation of God's ordering of the universe, the things his daimon told him were true, the things the poor captives in the cave could not really see in their half-light. We are almost at the German distinction between *Verstand* and *Vernunft*— the Sophists with their prudent, indeed banausic, bookkeeper's reason (*Verstand*), Socrates with his profound insights (*Vernunft*) into a world where there are no bookkeepers, and no books.

Plato does, especially in the *Republic* and in the *Laws,* come down to concrete cases. Yet it is precisely in these details of what he regards as the good life, and in the spirit behind them, that he seems most clearly to deviate from the Greek, or at least the Athenian, way, the way of Pericles's funeral speech. Plato's Utopia is, in fact, an aristocratic communist society, divided on lines of caste, though not without possible careers open to *approved* talent, ruled firmly by a chosen few, and pervaded by an austere discipline under which the ruling classes, at least, would appear to have to give up the very Greek delights of poetry, music, the arts of living, even family, and to have to embrace poverty, virtue, the higher life. There are echoes of Sparta and a foresight of Christian monasticism, the monasticism of the Teutonic knights, perhaps, rather than that of the Benedictines.[32]

The Athenian tragedies of the Great Age are no doubt a fairer reflection of what the Athenian gentleman thought about the good life than are the works of the great philosophers. Yet here, too, there must be a warning. Tragedy— Greek tragedy, at any rate—is loftily, serious, dignified. A great deal of living, even for the best of us, must be a matter of routine, of trivial matters, relieved by absence of high thinking, if not actually by lightheartedness. Still, the work of Aeschylus, Sophocles, and Euripides, supplemented by that of Thucydides, and even of writers like Herodotus and Xenophon, can take us intimately into Greek concern with matters of high seriousness. The ideals we have sought to summarize under such words as the beautiful-and-good, the Golden Mean, the agon, are *conventional,* loftily so, aristocratic, but still a con-

---

[32] I am aware that the above is a one-sided interpretation of Plato. He is, in fact, a kind of litmus paper for separating the "realists" from the "idealists." (You may put this dualism, which is, I think, almost as clear-cut as that between sheep and goats, in your favorite terms.) Jefferson, for instance, a realist, reacted violently against Plato. See his letter to John Adams, July 5, 1814, and Adams's reply July 16, 1814. *Correspondence of John Adams and Thomas Jefferson,* selected by Paul Wistach, Indianapolis, Bobbs-Merrill, 1925, p. 107.

ventional moral idea; and the high philosophic mysticism of Plato, the madness of the mystery cults, are simply out of line. We get a more just sense of what the sensitive Greek of the Great Age felt about man's fate from Greek dramatic literature.

This Greek came nearer the view of the world as a vale of tears than many later Hellenists like to admit. He had as yet little of Job's final resignation—that will come later with the Stoics, though not by any means in identical form—but he was not very far from Job's feeling that man is born to trouble. Even granting that tragedy as a literary genre has to deal with somber matters, even granting that the Greeks held that tragedy, through what Aristotle called "catharsis," purged the soul through pity and terror to leave it filled with courage, perhaps even with hope, granting that Greek tragedy by no means leaves in the spirit the gnawing, rather nasty despair the modern "problem play" leaves, it is still true that, once more, this is not the sunny, lighthearted, untroubled Greece of the Apollonian smile. The world of the tragic poets is not a world designed for human happiness; or, if you prefer, man is, for the tragic poets, born with a flaw that prevents his attaining the happiness he wants, a flaw as real to the sensitive Greek as the flaw of original sin to the sensitive Christian. This flaw is *hubris* (ὔβρις), still best translated as pride, which is also the great Christian sin.

The parallel with the Judaeo-Christian moral tradition can be carried further. Greek *hubris* is the overweening individual's rebellion against the ordering of the universe; Adam's sin, which is ours, is also rebellion, disobedience. There are obvious and important differences, at bottom the differences between Prometheus and Adam as rebels. Prometheus is a hero, for the Greek could not quite believe his gods loved men; the Jew does really believe his God loves men. Not even in Aeschylus, the earliest and simplest of the three great Greek dramatists, is there rebellion against a personal god, but against an impersonal necessity, and therefore a rebellion clearly heroic, justified, perhaps; and only in Euripides is there a trace of the complaining against the rest of the world that is the mark of the romantic Ibsen. Adam is not in the canon a hero, and the tradition hardly motivates his disobedience in ordinary human ways; it is just stupid sinful disobedience. Again, both the Greek and the Hebrew traditions are rooted in early concepts of hereditary guilt. Of the Greek house of Atreus, the dark tale of which was a favorite topic of classic tragedy, the words of the fourth commandment can certainly apply: visiting the iniquity of the fathers upon the children, upon the third and upon the fourth generation.

On the moral base for Greek tragedy, on such problems as how far necessity (ἀνάγκη) is a blind force ruling the universe with no concern for man, how far *hubris* itself in a man is the product of his own free will, of his blindness to the warnings from the gods, to the "facts of life," how near to our own conceptions of guilt that of the tragic poets is, are questions on which generations of interpreters have not agreed. To us, at least at first glance, Oedipus, who killed his father and married his mother all unknowing, seems a victim of mere accident. He did kill a stranger in a crossroad row, which can seem to us as crudely motivated as a fight in a movie Western. But this scuffle itself is an example of the normal violence of Greek life, a violence I have already noted (see p. 87); it seems to me difficult to read into Sophocles's text any idea that this initial act of violence by Oedipus is, in fact, the act of *hubris,* the beginning of the stain. It is perhaps fairer to say that Oedipus's whole career, up to the point where fate overtakes him, seems to have been the career of a fortunate but insensitive man, a career open to talents not quite tuned to the subtleties of the beautiful-and-good, a tragic career at once guilty and innocent.

However you interpret these tragedies, and the complex of tales out of which they are built, you can hardly deny that they display men struggling against something not men, something hostile or indifferent to men, yet something that has to be reckoned with, adjusted to, in the kind of tension we call "morality." That morality is not an easy, "natural," "immanent" thing, the true human nature, to be contrasted with the harsh and unnatural dictated code of a Jehovah. Necessity seems often to be as harsh and distant a master of man as any ever have conceived. Only slowly, and surely only among an intellectual elite of a somewhat later age, does the full force of the Heraclitean fragment come home: character as fate. This was perhaps the final lesson of Greek tragedy. These Greeks by no means saw and felt the universe as did the optimistic enlightened of the eighteenth century, our own closest spiritual fathers.

One major element in the moral history of the Greeks remains to be noted: their civic morality, their feelings about the relation of the individual to the polis. Here there is no need to question the accepted verdict that the Greeks, who made the *word* "democracy," also made the thing. The spotted reality was, of course, quite different from the ideal as set in the funeral speech of Pericles or in the writings of modern romantic philhellenes. There is no need to bring up the slavery, the *coups d'état,* the horrible internecine wars among the poleis; nor is there need to insist that democracy was not invented by, say, a Solon or a Cleisthenes much as an Edison invented the phonograph. Spartan democracy—for among the Spartiates themselves there was a kind of democracy—still looks a good deal like the old tribal war council out of which it developed. But Athens about 400 B.C. looks modern indeed, in spite of slavery, a society of great freedom of discussion, of party rivalry, of decisions made by some kind of balancing, and a great deal of talking, among conflicting interest groups.

Of the individual—the free adult male individual—in such a society, we must note, first of all, that he was a "citizen," a word one would hardly use of a Jew, an Egyptian, an Assyrian. He felt, if he were a good citizen, strong obligations toward the society; he was a citizen-soldier, and a taxpayer, and a voter; he took full part in politics, not always a very "moral" part. Above all, he did feel that in his relations with the agents of his society—its "government"—he was no slave, no subject, not even an obedient product of social conditioning (these last terms would have been wholly incomprehensible to him). He felt that in obeying the laws he was obeying himself. I am aware that these are idealistic terms, and I by no means believe that the Athenian in the street went through a process of thinking out high philosophical problems like this in the manner of Rousseau's *Contrat social*. But he *felt* something of the sort, and we have ample evidence of it. Here is a small but significant fragment: Simonides's epitaph on the Spartan dead at Thermopylae is usually translated as "We lie here, having obeyed their [the Spartan lawful rulers] commands," but the word πειθόμενοι is the passive of the verb best translated "persuade," and the passage is literally close to "having been persuaded to comply with their commands." Again, there is a famous passage in Herodotus, often quoted by lovers of Greece. Demaratus, exiled Spartan king, is at the court of the invading Persian despot Xerxes; he is there, be it noted, as a result of one of those rough political adjustments, well short of the best political morality, that occur in the *practice* of Greek democracy, and is, in fact, a traitor. But when Xerxes doubts that the tiny Spartan group will fight his host, doubts that they will fight against such odds even if they were on his side, and threatened with the whip, Damaratus replies:

So likewise the Lacedaemonians, when they fight singly, are as good men as any in the world, and when they fight in a body, are the bravest of all. For though they be freemen, they are not in all respects free; law is the master whom they own; and this master they fear more than thy subjects fear thee. Whatever he commands they do; and his commandment is always the same: it forbids them to flee in battle, whatever the number of their foes, and requires them to stand firm, and either conquer or die. . . .[33]

The Greek would have fully understood Henry de Bracton's phrase *non sub homine, sed sub Deo et sub lege,* a government of laws, not of men. Once more, the tough-minded cynic can insist that law is simply what men have made, and are making, it, but he misses the point that is clear in the moral logic of the sentiments. The *Antigone* of Sophocles is here the *locus classicus.* Antigone resists Creon, himself as king a legitimate source of commands, because his command that her brother, for willful, and unsuccessful, rebellion, be buried without proper funeral rites is to her an *arbitrary* act, an act contrary to religion, an act he had no "right" to command. Here, surely, is the essence of the moral history of the West, perhaps of mankind: this is the Promethean gesture of human defiance of not-man in the guise of other-man, conscience asserting that higher and lower for the moralist are not what they are for the physicist; this is Luther's *ich kann nicht anders.* Is this perhaps *hubris,* a sin become a virtue, the final victory of Dionysus over Apollo?

Greek moral life, like all moral life, was not perpetually keyed to the intensity of tragic poetry. Indeed, through all Greek history to the present there runs a sly little thread of a most pedestrian, if not immoral, dye. From Odysseus on through the clever and handsome young men of Athens, the brilliant sophistic manipulators of the new logic, the exiled traitors, the *Graeculus esuriens of Juvenal,* on to the traditional Levantine—a word no one now dare use—of the nineteenth century, the Greeks have had a reputation for untrustworthy sharpness. No doubt the Roman and the British examples are "race prejudice," the lion's eternal contempt for the fox. But the tradition, the reputation, are there, in their way, facts also.

Yet the sum total of what the Homeric Greeks and their successors of the Great Age of the poleis have meant to us for two millenniums is overwhelmingly on the side of sweetness and light, on the side of the good, not the bad. The beautiful-and-good, the Golden Mean, the agon, *hubris,* Necessity, *aretē,* democracy, above all, perhaps, the effort to state clearly what these concepts mean in the daily round of life, the effort to set up communicable standards of *human nature,* the effort to think about man's fate, at bottom to *alter* man's fate, all this we owe the Greeks. To them, more surely than to that other source of our moral traditions, the Jews, for whom God was much

---

[33] *The History of Herodotus,* trans. by George Rawlinson, New York, Tudor Publishing Co., 1928, pp. 387-388.

too invested with earthly concreteness to arouse worry over transcendence or "idealism," we owe the characteristic Western tension between acceptance of the world of the senses and transcendence of such a world, between conformity and rebellion, between—but the polar dualisms could fill pages. The Greeks by no means established a fine, healthy, normal middle way in all these tensions. But they did experience them all, and have left us an extraordinary record of their experience. Above all, they sought at the height of their cultural blossoming to combine the two excellences—the two great prides, the two great snobberies, if you are Christian enough, or democrat enough, to want to put it thus—of the warrior and the priest, the athlete of the body and the athlete of the soul. They did not wholly succeed in combining these excellences; what success they had did not last long. But they have drawn from this attempt their haunting hold on the imagination of the West.

Yet perhaps we should be most grateful to these Greeks for the fascinating, complex, almost always clearly and beautifully expressed account of the varieties of human experience we have in their theogony, their mythology, their literature, art, and philosophy. Looked at as no more than a great clinical record of human conduct under the spur of human hopes and aspirations, this record of Greek achievement is invaluable. It is complete, finished, and yet never-ending. Even if it is no more than a clinical record, that record is ours, still.

The Greco-Roman World

IT WAS THE ROMANS who put an end to the wars among the Greek city-states and who finally united all the Mediterranean world. It is through the Roman Western world that the cultural inheritance of the Greeks came to our West European ancestors, at least until with the Renaissance men tried to get back directly to the work of the Greeks themselves. We cannot, in fact, get away from that awkward hyphen; what we have is Greco-Roman. The Roman component is a major one.

For several centuries after the legendary date of the founding of the city, 753 B.C., the little agrarian and trading city-state on the Tiber grew slowly in the obscurity of its remoteness from the then Greek center of the Western stage. The Roman ruling classes were later to become very conscious of their place in the now widened world, and of their need for a Homeric past. They had their own religion, their own "mythology," their own political, legal, and moral traditions, but they hardly had a true "heroic age," or, if they did, it is lost forever to men's memories. We can, with the help of archaeology, work our way through the prose lays of ancient Rome that Livy left us, the noble, moving, but very self-conscious, epic past that Vergil gave his countrymen, the Tocquevillean study that the Greek Polybius made of his strange captors, and a great deal of miscellaneous materials, laws, formal records, and the like, to some firm notions of the moral and psychological base from which the Romans started.

It was a solid base indeed. The old Romans were a people of steady habits, disciplined, good citizen-soldiers, distrustful of the arts of the intellect, hard-working, and—the cant term will not be kept down—"practical." They have something in common, in terms of social morality, with all peoples known for their cohesiveness, their devotion to routine and discipline, the piety of their religious practices—not, be it noted, for the intensity of their religious emotions—for their firm attitude of no damned nonsense—in short, for their apparently successful and unneurotic suppression of much we today think of as essential to the human lot. The Romans have something, at least, in common with the early Jews, with the Spartans, with those children of Calvin and a stony soil, the Scots and the early New Englanders.

Here at the very start we encounter in the concrete a factor of great importance in any account of what the Romans have meant to the world: their persistent, direct borrowings from the Greeks, who attained the prestige of cultural ripeness several centuries ahead of the Romans, and toward whom educated Romans even into the late Empire always had most mixed feelings of admiration, envy, distrust, and contempt.[1] The Romans had a polytheistic religion of their own, though no doubt built up from many sources in their distant Indo-European past and from borrowings from the Etruscans, with named gods and goddesses of specific attributes. The early Roman, however, seems to have had a fairly simple and even dull pantheon. When their intellectuals ran up against the dazzling Olympian pantheon of the Greeks, they did their best to fit the two together. Mercury and Hermes, Venus and Aphrodite, and the rest were paired, and gradually the whole body of Greek theogony, myth, and fable took over and swamped the Roman.

It is likely, however, that for the early Romans the major gods of their pantheon were less important than the host of intimate gods and goddesses of the hearth, the bed, the field, the market place. To the Roman, as Polybius pointed out, religion meant a sober, steadying, ritual approach to the tasks of living in a world in which a man always needed steadying, always needed to feel that the nonhuman could be brought to help him, or at least to be less hostile. This Roman faith is indeed—and the phrase is Latin—a religion of *do ut des.* But the warning we have made already in noting that many primitive polytheisms—and even monotheisms like the early Jewish worship of the tribal Jehovah—bring man and god together in a contractual relationship needs to be repeated here. The very word "contractual," the whole attempt to state the relation in our modern languages, especially since the eighteenth-century Enlightenment, distorts and falsifies the moral facts of the relation.

[1] Juvenal's Third Satire (see above, p. 19) is here the *locus classicus,* especially lines 58-125.

The early Roman who did his duties to the gods, who displayed *pietas,* was in a state of mind and heart equally far from a man making a business transaction and from a man "going through the motions." He was trying to do what he "ought" to do as a moral agent, trying to adjust, or, better, to mold his conduct to the scheme of things cosmic his faith outlined for him. Now "mold," unlike, say, the contractual term "adjust," does suggest the disciplined, moderate, obedient citizen-soldier the Roman was; it does not, of course, suggest the self-abnegation of the mystic, which the Roman was not.

"Contract" also connotes for us something like a relation between equals. But no pious Roman could ever feel himself an equal even in his relation with his household gods. The steady moral ways of the Romans of the Republic were sanctioned by commands from above. Again, though we can find in these early years little sign of the humble contrition of a believer overwhelmed by the feeling still conveyed to us in the Judaeo-Christian tradition by the word "sin," we can be sure that the Roman knew that if he did wrong he would be punished, punished in an afterlife. Polybius, who lived at just the time the educated Romans were cutting themselves free, very free, from the restraints of the old-time religion, remarked:

For this reason I think, not that the ancients acted rashly and at haphazard in introducing among the people notions concerning the gods and beliefs in the terrors of hell, but that the moderns are most rash and foolish in banishing such beliefs.[2]

Indeed, it should be noted at this point that the accepted notion that the formal religion of the Greeks and Romans had very little place for the doctrines of the immortality of the soul and of judgment after death needs some qualifying. Our tradition makes too much of the famous passage in the *Odyssey* in which Achilles complains of the dullness of the afterlife; Dante's hell and even his paradise are a good deal sharper. But the fact is that the immortality of the soul had a definite place in the Olympian faith, and one that should not be minimized. We may reasonably believe that for the ordinary man, even down into the end of the pagan culture, the kind of moral sanction such a belief carries with it does exist. Even for the literary, there is a kind of wistful reality in the other world. In a famous passage in the *Aeneid,* Vergil describes the crowd coming to Charon's ferry, perhaps not as if he really saw the shades, but at least in an elegiac, not in a rationalist and rejecting, mood:

2 Polybius, *The Histories,* trans. by W. R. Paton, London, Heinemann, 1923, Loeb Classical Library, Book VI, §56:12.

> To the bank come thronging
> Mothers and men, bodies of great-souled heroes,
> Their life-time over, boys, unwedded maidens,
> Young men whose fathers saw their pyres burning,
> Thick as the forest leaves that fall in autumn
> With early frost, thick as the birds to landfall
> From over the seas, when the chill of the year compels them
> To sunlight. There they stand, a host, imploring
> To be taken over first.[3]

We cannot make explicit and symbolic the ethical ideal of these Romans of the first centuries of the Republic; we cannot quite set up the equivalent of the Homeric hero, the Periclean beautiful-and-good. But we can get hints of what the Roman gentleman—the word is not perfect, but it will have to do, for it is better than "noble"—thought proper and admirable. Livy unquestionably was writing deliberately to encourage old-fashioned virtues that he thought, quite correctly, were dying out among the Roman ruling classes of the Augustan Age. Still, the tales he records, or perhaps even invents, are almost certainly "genuine" in the sense that tales like those of Alfred and the cakes, Bruce and the spider, even that of Washington and the cherry tree are genuine parts of a national tradition. These Roman tales emphasize courage against odds, soldierly obedience, individual heroism, simplicity of manners, *gravitas,* dignity, high seriousness, and *pietas,* loyal, respectful feelings toward the established moral order; here are Horatius at the bridge, Lucretia's chastity, the patriotism of her avengers, the Iroquoian fortitude of Mucius Scaevola, Cincinnatus at the plow; all the long list makes for a firm, even rigid, sense of moral obligation. Sparta, of course, comes to mind, but there is here a note by no means so clearly sounded in Sparta, a note of straightforward honesty, of piety in the old Roman sense. If you read together the early books of Livy and the *Lycurgus* of Plutarch and some Spartan speeches in Thucydides, you will feel at once a difference in the moral tones of early Rome and Sparta.

Moreover, the Romans had a very different attitude toward the uses of the human mind than had the Spartans. This fact, indeed, might be deduced —if the historian dare indulge in deduction—from the given fact of Roman success in creating the One World of their empire. The Spartans could not adapt themselves to any change, could not summon the minimum diplomatic and governmental skills necessary for successful expansion. The Romans, though it is not unfair to say that there runs through their whole history a

[3] Book VI, 305-314, *The Aeneid of Vergil,* trans. by Rolfe Humphries, New York, Scribner, 1951, p. 154.

108

certain distrust of the speculative intellect, and, at the very least, a certain excessive if not awkward seriousness among their intellectuals, nonetheless made excellent use of their minds to adapt their resources to the drive toward expansion. They were, as we all know, good lawyers, diplomatists, engineers, administrators. Their civic life was by no means an unprofitable adherence to custom; on the contrary, out of the struggle of patricians and plebeians, out of the wars with their neighbors, they acquired the skills with which, luck aiding, they were to conquer what was for them almost the known world.

Cicero, a conventional person on the defensive in a time when many of the old ways were vanishing, is throughout his numerous writings a good, platitudinous authority for the old Roman moral outlook. Here he is at his average pace:

But when with a rational spirit you have surveyed the whole field, there is no social relation among them all more close, none more dear than that which links each one of us with our country. Parents are dear; dear are children, relatives, friends; but one native land embraces all our loves. . . .[4]

Yet the ideal seems warmer and more sympathetic in the fragments we have of less deliberately improving literature, notably in the inscriptions, which are no doubt not without contrivance, but which often ring true. Here is an epitaph from one of the lower trades, that of butcher:

Lucius Aurelius Hermia, a freedman of Lucius, a butcher of the Viminal Hill. She who went before me in death, my one and only wife, chaste in body, a loving woman of my heart possessed, living faithful to her faithful man; in fondness equal to her other virtues, never during bitter times did she shrink from loving duties.[5]

But the Romans could not keep intact the morality of their earlier and simpler days. The old Roman qualities of *gravitas, pietas, virtus*—all subtly but very definitely different from what the English words derived from them suggest to us—never wholly disappear, if you look for them, in Roman history. But they do not, after the conquest of Carthage and the East, make the style, the tone, of the Greco-Roman culture. The loss of the close-knit discipline, the virtues of the simple life, and the cohesion of the patriarchal family can be noted in the very articulate effort of high-minded reformers to revive them. These moralists, from the elder Cato, who caricatures the early Roman type, to the Augustan generation, including emphatically that tardy strict

---

[4] Cicero, *De Officiis,* trans. by Walter Miller, Cambridge, Mass., Harvard University Press, 1951, Loeb Classical Library, 1.17(57).
[5] E. H. Warmington, *Remains of Old Latin,* London, Heinemann, 1940, Loeb Classical Library, Vol. IV, p. 23.

moralist Augustus himself, certainly exaggerate the completeness of the loss. The historian, however, if he must have a general rule in such matters, will find the folk wisdom of "where there's smoke there's fire" a bit safer than the folk wisdom of the tale of the boy who cried "Wolf, wolf!"

Livy's own diagnosis was oversimple. As he makes clear in his preface, he blames the loss of the old virtues chiefly on increasing wealth and luxury. He writes, for instance, of the first part of the second century B.C.:

At that time the cook, to the ancient Romans the most worthless of slaves, both in their judgment of values and in the use they made of him, began to have value, and what had been merely a necessary service came to be regarded as an art. Yet those things which were then looked upon as remarkable were hardly even the germs of the luxury to come.[6]

Cato, though he blanketed his whole age in blame, and thought the younger generation was going soft, was especially bitter against the rising intellectualism of education, and the admiration for those slippery creatures the Greeks. The censors in 92 B.C. issued an edict against the new schools of rhetoric which is typical enough:

Our fathers determined what they wished their children to learn and what schools they desired them to attend. These innovations in the customs and principle of our forefathers do not please us nor seem proper. Therefore it appears necessary to make our opinion known to those who have such [newfangled] schools and those who are in the habit of attending them, that they are displeasing to us.[7]

One may believe that earlier when the censors said "displeasing" the word was strong enough. In the later years of the Republic not even vigorous edicts of prohibition worked. The Roman housewife of the early days seems to have been in a position not unlike that of the Athenian housewife, or, at any rate, if not so secluded, held to rigorous standards of quiet obedience. Her emancipation is a clear index of the disintegration of the early Roman moral world. Yet already in the Republic one finds efforts to keep the ladies good by edict, as, for instance, by forbidding them to drink wine. In a similar frame of mind the Roman authorities early in the second century B.C. sought to suppress not only in Rome but throughout Italy the celebration of the newly imported Bacchic rites. This "persecution" was based on much the same arguments that were later to be used against the Christians: the rites

---

[6] *Livy*, trans. by Evan T. Sage, Cambridge, Mass., Harvard University Press, 1936, Loeb Classical Library, Book XXXIX, vi, 9.
[7] Quoted in N. Lewis and M. Reinhold, *Roman Civilization*, New York, Columbia University Press, 1955, Vol. I, p. 492.

were held to lead to all sorts of vile practices, and to make the worshipers untrustworthy citizens.[8]

We here encounter clearly for the first time another persistent theme in the moral history of the West, and one that confronts the sociological historian with some difficult problems: sumptuary, prohibitory, "blue law" legislation accompanied by official or semiofficial educational propaganda toward a return to "primitive" virtues. There is no simple formula available, certainly no extreme statement that such efforts are always in vain, always efforts to go against the tide, always an indication that a given society is in fact already completely corrupt, decadent, "loose," doomed. The historian must try to judge each case separately, in the hope that effective comparisons may eventually permit some generalizations. On the whole, what the old republican reformers sought to preserve was indeed lost in the later Rome, where, as we shall shortly see, the ruling classes and the urban masses in Rome itself and in the great metropolitan Eastern centers have left in history an indelible and surely not wholly undeserved reputation for conduct below not only the best Western standards of ethics, but below the actual standards of conduct in most Western societies.

Yet the Rome that seemed to be about to go to pieces in the second century B.C. did survive and even grow for many more centuries. The Roman Empire was by no means what we think of as the welfare state, but it was no Oriental despotism, and it could not have been held together by cowardly soldiers and corrupt administrators. Even at the top, the balance is not wholly on the side of Nero, and wholly against Marcus Aurelius; at the level of the now nameless men who did the work, the Empire was served by civil and military administrators with high, if not precisely Platonic or puritanical, standards of morality. And we can be pretty sure that all over the Empire, in the soft East as well as in the hard West, there were at all times thousands of country gentlemen as conscientious, as sober and hard-working, as civilized, in the best sense of the word, as was Plutarch, who lived in Boeotia at the turn of the first to the second centuries A.D. At the very end of the Empire we come across a work of the Gallic poet Ausonius, Roman consul in 379, the *Parentalia,* in which he describes several generations of his family in Auvergne and Aquitaine in a spirit of old Roman piety and realism. The men are not in the least like the vile plotters of Tacitus, nor the women like the scandalous ladies of Suetonius. In fact, we seem to be in nineteenth-century

8 *Livy,* Sage, trans., Book XXXIX, viii-xix; Lewis and Reinhold, *Roman Civilization,* Vol. II, pp. 600-601.

Lyons, or Edinburgh, or Boston, with one of those sober dynasties of pillars of society so characteristic of these centers of virtue.[9]

The competitive spirit survived to the last, certainly at the very top. The struggle for the imperial purple is among the most ruthless on record. Even in an age of violence, one would suppose that a rough statistical awareness that the odds were against an emperor's dying a natural death might deter candidates, which it clearly did not. Huizinga suggests that the baths, theaters, halls, and other public works given by wealthy donors all over the Greco-Roman world were not inspired by feelings of charity, nor even, as they really do seem to have been in Athens of the great days, by public spirit, but by the desire to show off, by what he calls the "potlatch spirit."[10] Certainly the Trimalchio of Petronius was moved by the potlatch spirit; he constantly boasts to his guests about the cost and rareness of their food, and has the wine brought in with the jars labeled conspicuously *Falernian Opimian one hundred years old.*[11] Vergil, as usual, puts it nobly in the old heroic way. The crews are waiting for the signal to start a boat race:

> They are at their places, straining,
> Arms stretched to the oars, waiting the word, and their chests
> Heave, and their hearts are pumping fast; ambition
> And nervousness take hold of them. The signal! . . .

> *Considunt transtris; intentaque brachia remis:*
> *Intenti expectant signum, exsultantiaque haurit*
> *Corda pavor pulsans, laudumque arrecta cupido.*[12]

The key phrase is *laudumque arrecta cupido,* which I have seen translated "and the wild thirst for praise." Humphries's "ambition and nervousness," whether you think it Vergilian or not, is a fine description of the eternal Western aristocratic agon.

II

Rome at almost any time after the end of the second century B.C. has long been a symbol for moral looseness, for evil, not only in public but in private

[9] I expect the convinced primitivist will argue that Ausonius's family came from an as yet uncorrupted provincial region, and cannot be taken as typical. This point cannot be decisively proved or disproved. But Ausonius did move in the highest circles at Rome itself. See Samuel Dill, *Roman Society in the Last Century of the Western Empire,* London, Macmillan, 1910, Book II, Chap. III, pp. 167-178. Also pp. 158-159 for Ausonius's advancement under Gratian, and pp. 402-403 for his influence in increasing the salaries of teachers.
[10] Johan Huizinga, *Homo Ludens,* Boston, Beacon, 1955, p. 178.
[11] Petronius, *Trimalchio's Dinner,* trans. by Harry Thurston Peck, New York, Dodd, Mead, 1908, p. 85.
[12] *The Aeneid of Vergil,* Rolfe Humphries trans., pp. 117-118, Book V, 136-138.

life. As usual, our sources deal almost wholly with the doings of the small group at the top of the social pyramid. We may then begin by fixing our attention on these people, fully aware that at the very least, since the masses could not afford the luxuries of the rich, they could not practice their vices, certainly not as extensively and as intensively. But we cannot assume that there is *no relation* between the conduct and ethical standards of the few and the conduct of the many. Like the related problem of how far sumptuary and other moral legislation to restore primitive virtues is really effective, a problem briefly noted just above, the historian has to do his best to judge each case as it presents itself. A corrupt aristocracy and a sober, steady, virtuous populace seem hardly to go contentedly and in equilibrium together, but the historian cannot close his mind to the possibility that they may, at least in the short term.

There must be made the caution once more that our sources for the horrid conduct of the ruling classes of the late Republic and, subject to some irregular cycles of good emperors and bad, of the Empire in the whole period of its nearly five hundred years of life certainly do not do much whitewashing. We have so far passed the days of complete reverence for whatever was written in classical Greek or Latin that it may be permissible to assert that Suetonius and some of the lesser historians of the Augusti had tabloid mentalities. And Tacitus, a great historian and no doubt a good man, displays that preoccupation with wickedness characteristic of the high-minded reformer as well as of the good newspaperman.

Yet the wickedness is certainly there. To begin with a simple and in a way constant or endemic form of misconduct, there is always sex. The exploits of Messalina, third wife of the Emperor Claudius, are still familiar in our best homes. Her lovers were legion, chosen from all sorts and conditions of men. Her sexual endurance—one lover after another all night—challenges belief even in such a record-conscious age as our own. The normal vocabulary of sexual abnormality—nymphomania, erotomania, and the like—pales before her achievements. Is she a legend? Perhaps to a degree she is, but there can be no doubt that the Empress was a very loose woman, and a palace plotter and unscrupulous participant in the murderous competition of high politics. There can be no doubt that Augustus's own womenfolk, his wife, Livia, and his daughter, Julia, let this restorer of virtuous living down rather worse than Napoleon's promiscuous sister, Pauline, let him down in a somewhat similar attempt to make a renewed aristocracy respectable in the eyes of the world. But there is no need to insist further on this point; all but the most bowdlerized of history books will give you the details.

The literary confirm the sexual looseness of the ruling classes. The corpus of Greek and Latin writings together, of course, form the first and still one of the major sources of pornographic pleasure available to the Western reader; for not until quite recently have men dared to read pornography into the Old Testament. We shall come again to the complexity, the range, the modernity of this society of the One World of the Roman Empire. In the field of actual physical exercise of the sex organs, after all, by no means the richest and most complicated field open to human activity, it may well be true that the Greco-Roman experience pretty well exhausted the possibilities, that we have since invented little really new. The clinical record, though it was hardly composed in a clinical spirit, is there, for the normal as well as for the abnormal. Indeed, most of the actual terms in sexual abnormality are of Latin, old Latin, or Greek, not new medical, coinage—*cunnilinguis, fellatrix, tribades,* and the like. Nor, at least among the literary, is there a lack of the stepped-up psychological tortures of the erotic competition, of what we might fashionably call the meta-erotic. Catullus and his Lesbia, Propertius and his Cynthia, are evidence that the Roman could build up as complicated a relation between the sexes as any modern French novelist. Catullus in particular can range from the frankly indecent through the pleasantly romantic and the gently cynical to the depths of self-analysis in love, as in the famous and exceedingly modern:

> *Odi et amo: quare id faciam, fortasse requiris*
> *Nescio, sed fieri sentio et excrucior.*[13]

The vices of less complicated self-indulgence are there as well. The Roman upper classes have left a reputation for luxury that still echoes—delicate foods imported from all over the world, warm baths, warm houses, a comfort not attained by European upper classes again until our own time, and not always then, hosts of slaves waiting on every movement, town house and country house, in short, all that very great wealth can bring. Already in the last years of the Republic, Lucullus, no mere idler, but a distinguished soldier and politician, was to establish such a reputation for what Veblen called "conspicuous consumption" that the Lucullan banquet has endured as a cliché right down to the present, when Latin clichés have almost vanished. Lucullus was a gentleman, and—though no Greek would admit it of a Roman, any more than a Frenchman today of an American—may be assumed to have some sense of security in good taste. Closer to what inspired Veblen

---

[13] *Carmina,* LXXXV. Literally, "I hate and I love; should you ask me why, I do not know, but I feel it, and I suffer exceedingly."

to his wrath, the Romans, too, had their newly rich. The tasteless excesses of conspicuous consumption in which these *arrivistes* indulged themselves and their retainers have been duly reported by the intellectuals who witnessed them, and doubtless, after their fashion, enjoyed them. Petronius, in his satirical novel, of which we have but fragments, tells in detail about a feast given by the fabulously wealthy freedman Trimalchio (he did not quite remember where all his estates were): toward the end, Trimalchio, in his cups, tells about a funeral inscription he has devised for himself.

HERE LIES
GAIUS POMPEIUS TRIMALCHIO
MAECENATIANUS

Elected to the Augustal College
in his absence. He might have
held every civil post in Rome;
but he refused. A worthy citizen,
brave and true. A self-made man,
he died worth 30,000,000 sterling.
Yet he had no college training.

Farewell to him—and thee.[14]

It should hardly be necessary to note that the Roman imperial upper classes pursued many of the conventional activities of an upper class, activities the censorious moralist lists among the vices. Gambling was high among these, and, as almost always, was by no means limited to the upper classes. Nor, of course, were the gladiatorial games and the chariot races so limited. Aristocrats, emperors themselves, "descended" into the arena, usually with a degree of safety not granted to the professional gladiators; that this was a moral descent was certainly the general opinion of the solid responsible people we shall shortly study as the Stoic gentlemen of the civil and military services. Actually, these Roman aristocrats did not have the outlet for personal athleticism the medieval knight and the nineteenth-century English gentleman—and the Americans, too—had in field sports, organized games, hunting with the horse, jousting, and the like. The horse is important in Rome, but in war and work and in the professional horse racing of the circus, not in the hunting field. We must come again to this sporting side of Roman life. Meanwhile, it is sufficient to note that some of the vices of the upper classes of the Empire were a reflection of their exclusion from many ordinary

14 *The Satyricon,* trans. as *Leader of Fashion* by J. M. Mitchell, London, Routledge, 1922, pp. 104-105.

aristocratic physical games of agonistic competition. They, like all aristocrats, wanted to make records; they made them in vice.

This was a society so firmly built on great social and economic inequalities that the good intentions of the virtuous moralists among the upper classes must seem ludicrous to us, who take our egalitarian faith with increasing seriousness and literalness. Seneca, a conscientious Stoic not untouched by a mild moral primitivism of the kind that attacked the French aristocracy just before 1789, begins one of his contrived "letters" on the virtues of the simple life:

My friend Maximus and I have been spending a most happy period of two days, taking with us very few slaves—one carriage load—and no paraphernalia except what we wore on our persons. The mattress lies on the ground, and I upon the mattress. There are two rugs—one to spread beneath us and one to cover us. Nothing could have been subtracted from our luncheon; it took not more than an hour to prepare. . . .[15]

Seneca, a philosopher whose part in high politics by no means confirms Plato's hopes for his philosopher-statesmen, reminds us that, in the actual business of ruling, these Roman privileged classes indulged in one of the most ferocious struggles for power on record, one in which plotting, spying, informing, bribery, treason usually work up to murder or suicide. With certain interludes of stability, the best known of which is the period of the "five good emperors" from 96 to 180, in which Gibbon thought any man would elect to have lived if he could, imperial Roman history at the top is a record of instability and violence. Perhaps we note it more conspicuously than as bad a record, say, among the Merovingians or among the Turks—or even Latin Americans and Soviet Russians—because in the back of our minds we expect better of the law-abiding Romans of old. But the reality of this shocking instability of the throne and of palace politics is unquestioned, and it sets for the historian of morals another of his many unsolved problems: murder, slander, lying, bad faith, all the role of evil so eloquently, and basically accurately, called by a Tacitus are morally far more wicked than the fleshly vices of gambling, eating, drinking, and promiscuous love-making we have noted above. (Do not let nineteenth-century anticlericals persuade you that in the Judaeo-Christian tradition the mere vices of the flesh are ranked as deadlier sins than the great evils of pride, bad faith, cruelty; as we shall shortly see, this is not so.)

[15] *Epistolae Morales*, trans. by Richard M. Gummere, London, Heinemann, 1920, Vol. II, lxxxvii, 2.

Is there, however, such a relation between the vices of the flesh and the sins of the spirit that, as with, for instance, the Roman ruling classes of the Empire, one can say that given their luxurious self-indulgence, their more serious vices follow in consequence? Almost certainly there is here no direct causal sequence. A murderous struggle for power went on among the Italian upper classes of the Renaissance, accompanied by great luxury and self-indulgence; such luxury and self-indulgence among the upper classes of Western Europe in the seventeenth and eighteenth centuries were *not* accompanied by unusual political violence and the immorality of power. Moreover, it must never be forgotten that almost always in Western history the ferocious competition that results in unrestrained abandonment of moral decencies and the self-indulgence of an exceedingly rich class go on among the very few, and that just beneath them there is a larger group of administrators, professional men, even intellectuals, whose conduct is usually vastly better. The Victorians and the Marxists have persuaded us that the middle class and middle-class morality are consequences of the industrial revolution, and did not exist in earlier societies; actually, something very like this solid group has long played a part in Western society. Finally, even in the Roman upper classes at their worst, there were always men and women who strove to lead the good life their cultural tradition made clear to them. We must not forget those five good emperors in a row, topped by Marcus Aurelius.

III

If the violence and corruption of the imperial aristocracy make one of the darker, and naturally more interesting, pages of Western history, the ideal of moral excellence that emerges from this very aristocracy and from the groups just beneath it in the social pyramid has ever since been one of great prestige in our tradition. The Greco-Roman Stoic ideal, embodied in many a soldier, scholar, and gentleman who did the work of the Empire and left no trace on history, is recognizably a successor to the old Greek ideal of the beautiful-and-good. It treasures the past that had produced that ideal. It retains a respect for the body, a moderation, a temperateness, reminiscent of the Aristotelian Golden Mean. In this real world, it still retains some flavor of the Greek sense of an order of rank in which the mechanic cannot be truly virtuous and the slave is marked by nature as an inferior. In ideal, of course, these Greco-Roman gentlemen were firm believers in the equality of all men.

The formal philosophical tag Stoic is not altogether fortunate here, but

I have sought in vain for a brief phrase to describe this moral ideal as effectively as does the beautiful-and-good for the old Greeks, and for an embodied hero who incorporates and makes tangible this ideal as does Achilles for the Homeric Age. The truth is that we have now arrived at a late age and a most complicated society for which it is difficult to find a neat symbol of the dominant tone or style. Yet there was such a style or ideal among the upper classes. And it was this tone or style that stood for centuries as the major cultural heritage left to later times by the Greco-Roman world. Only since the Renaissance has Periclean Athens seemed more typical of classical antiquity than the Rome of Augustus or of the Antonines.

Stoicism goes back in the genealogy of ideas to the successors of Plato and Aristotle in the formal schools of Athenian philosophy. Zeno, the founder of what one easily falls into calling a "sect," taught in the Stoa, or porch, in Athens at the beginning of the third century B.C. He was an almost exact contemporary of Epicurus, the founder of a rival sect, the Epicureans, which can easily be made to come out much like the Stoics. Both philosophies, though they of course have metaphysical and epistemological implications—often made explicit in the course of their long histories—are chiefly concerned with ethics. Indeed, it is not misleading to say that they arose in the world of the disintegrating city-state to give hope, faith, and guidance to men for whom the old Olympian faith had become impossibly naïve, and who could no longer simply find their moral place as citizens in a world of competing superpowers.

There is a sense in which the now often used term "secular religion" or "surrogate religion" as applied to communism, positivism, "humanism"— the kind that comes out of Yellow Springs, Ohio, not the kind that comes out of Florence—and other modern cults may be applied to Stoicism, Epicureanism, and their variants. The Painted Porch of Zeno and the Garden of Epicurus were both retreats, closets of the philosophers, from which, nonetheless, there emerged a form of faith, aristocratic, never widespread among the masses—Epictetus, the slave who was one of the masters of Roman Stoicism, is simply one more example of the eternal Western career open to talents— but a great deal more than an academic philosophical doctrine.

Stoicism finds its highest ideal in ataraxia (ἀταραξία), "impassiveness," clearly a derivation of the Aristotelian *theoria,* and equally clearly one of the many forms of a Western ideal of mystic serenity, of nonstruggle, which the West and these same Stoics rarely attain in practice. Ataraxia is a state of mind untroubled by the petty cares of this world, unaghast at its many horrors, above the melee, the Western sage's approach to the Buddhist nirvana. But the

Roman—and the Greek—Stoics by no means fled the world and its responsibilities, and they are not much like even the Buddhists of the Mahayana, who
nobly forsook their own nirvana to lift others nearer to it; and they are certainly not in monastic retreat from the world. One feels about the Roman
Stoics that their ataraxia was a singularly unreal abstraction, a gesture toward
the philosophic origin of their faith. There is even a Stoic contempt for this
world of the flesh; but contempt led the Stoic to no desert, to no monastery.
He would not bow to the world in so extravagant a gesture as that of the
monks. Ataraxia visibly meant no more than calm, dignity, self-control, the
traditional gentlemanly virtues, held a bit self-consciously.

The Stoic held firmly to his earthly station and its duties. There is even
a touch in someone like Marcus Aurelius of the pride of the martyr, the man
who deliberately does what is difficult and unpleasant because clearly he
wants to do it, gains stature with himself by doing it. For the most part, however, the Stoic seems as serene as he says he is, aware that his world is a
harsh one, that he cannot make it much better, but that he can hardly avoid
trying to make it such. His self-control curbs even his moral indignation.
Seneca even "declares his belief that the contemporaries of Nero were not
worse than the contemporaries of Clodius or Lucullus, that one age differs
from another rather in the greater prominence of different vices."[16] He is not,
in short, a moral innovator, a meliorist; but neither is he a despairing or
simply lazy and indifferent spectator of life. He does his duty. He keeps at
the job of cleaning the Augean stables, with no illusion that he is Hercules.
He is, in fact, quite incapable of the engineer-inventor's skill by which Hercules solved his problem. The Augean stables that faced the Greco-Roman
soldier and administrator were never really cleaned.

The Stoic held firmly a philosophical doctrine of necessity, which, as it
consistently has in our Western history, seems to have sharpened his sense of
the badness of much of the necessary, as well as his desire to change the
necessary. It is true he would not like the matter put this way, true that the
textbooks sometimes accuse him of fleeing the world. But his actions are
unambiguous; the Stoic was a fighter. Seneca's rhetoric is firm indeed:

All things move on in an appointed path, and our first day fixed our last. Those
things God may not change which speed on their way, close woven with their
causes. To each his established life goes on, unmovable by any prayer.[17]

16 Dill, *Roman Society from Nero to Marcus Aurelius,* New York, Macmillan, 1905,
p. 10, paraphrasing Seneca, *De Beneficiis,* 1.10.1.
17 *Seneca's Tragedies,* trans. by F. J. Miller, Cambridge, Mass., Harvard University
Press, 1953, Vol. I, *Oedipus,* 987-992.

But this is rhetoric, not analysis or description. Marcus Aurelius was the slave of Duty, not of Necessity.

The Christians were later shocked by the Stoic—in fact, generally, Roman —feeling that suicide is legitimate, even praiseworthy under certain conditions. One doubts very much whether at the moment of slashing his veins, the Stoic seriously went over the doctrine of necessity in his mind and decided that some will not his own was guiding the knife. Even the Stoic's approval of suicide (how approve the inevitable?) was not unconditional: the suicide must not involve any harm to others, directly or indirectly.[18]

The Stoic did not "believe in" the gods of the traditional Olympian pantheon, but neither did he reject the gods—at least, he did not reject them in the ferocious mood of the modern "materialist" and atheist rejecting Christianity. There is some trace of the attitude that a gentleman does not openly practice a disbelief that will be imitated with disastrous results to their morals by the masses, who do not have the gentleman's sense of *noblesse oblige*. But in fairness to what we may believe to be the ordinary, inarticulate Stoic gentleman, it may be said that he conformed religiously out of patriotism, out of respect for the past, perhaps out of a feeling that, though the gods were not what the vulgar thought them to be, still, there was in the Olympians what we should nowadays call a symbolic value. The Stoic was no skeptic, though he does have a touch of the modern Christian existentialist.

He was not wholly a rationalist either; that is, he did not suppose he had an answer to all problems of the universe. But what the Ionians had started had by Greco-Roman times so grown as to penetrate into ordinary lives. The Stoic's reason told him a great deal that common sense could hardly have told him. One of his central doctrines was that all men are created equal, that the differences of race, status, and conduct so conspicuous to the unreflective observer are superficial and artificial. Cicero put it baldly in absolute if also abstract terms: *Nihil est unum uni tam simile, tam par, quam omnes inter nosmet ipsos sumus* (Nothing is so like another thing, so equal to it, as we [human beings] all are amongst ourselves).[19] Slavery could not be reconciled with principles such as these, and the Stoic writers insist that the slave is a fellow human being, endowed by nature with basic human rights, and that fate and human injustice have made him what he is. The great law code which

[18] Westermarck, *Origin and Development of the Moral Ideas*, Vol. II, p. 248 ff., gives a good brief outline of classical opinion and practice of suicide, with many references to the sources.
[19] Cicero, *De Legibus*, I.29.

sums up so much of Roman ideals as well as Roman experience puts it quite clearly: slavery is "an institution of the Law of Nations, by which one man is made the property of another, in opposition to natural right."[20]

The same Seneca we have just now seen contenting himself with a single carriage load of slaves was one of the most articulate in his moral condemnation of slavery. I do not wish to give aid and comfort to the naïvely cynical anti-intellectual who maintains that men always keep their ideals and their conduct in separate compartments of their being, but it does seem as though some of these Greco-Roman gentlemen carry the thing too far. Their real world was, in fact, one of extreme inequalities of all sorts, one in which slavery formed the economic base of the labor force, one in which there was a true urban proletariat—the word itself is Latin—in the great cities, one in which there was surely no less than the usual suffering and deprivation that has gone with the human civilized lot. Yet they talk and write about the equality and dignity of man, about the law of nature so superior to our petty particular laws, about that state of self-mastery they call "ataraxia," so difficult for most of us to attain on an empty stomach. They are cosmopolitans, above the narrow patriotism of the city-state; yet do these Roman gentlemen really feel they are no better than the motley set of peoples they rule? Was not Pontius Pilate perhaps at heart an anti-Semite?

It is not easy to answer these questions from our very miscellaneous sources. There are signs that the attitude put neatly in Juvenal's *Graeculus esuriens* never wholly left the Roman gentleman; he must have felt himself superior to the painted Britons as well as to the already somewhat Levantine Syrians. Yet we, who are so used to great systems of moral values based on theories of race or other form of group superiority, Nordic, Latin, Anglo-Saxon, American, Slavic, must be struck by the absence of any such *systematic* concepts among the Greco-Romans of the Empire. The Stoicism we are dealing with here takes, as we have seen, just the opposite view, that racial differences among men are superficial and unimportant.

One part of the answer to our difficulty here must lie in the fact that the One World of the Empire was *one* only at the top, among the officers, civil servants, lawyers, financiers, landlords, and intellectuals (these categories are, of course, not mutually exclusive), Greek, Roman, or bilingual in language,

[20] *Institutes,* i.3.2. quoted in Westermarck, *Origin and Development of the Moral Ideas,* Vol. I, p. 693. Westermarck on pp. 689-694 of this work gives a good summary of Greek and Roman ideas and attitudes toward slavery, with many still-useful references.

Greco-Roman in education and culture, who ran the Empire. Even among the masses there was no doubt in that very modern world a great deal more actual moving about, physical as well as social mobility, than we culture-bound moderns, who feel that no one ever moved much or far before the steam engine, can readily admit. Christianity, which was *not,* as was Islam, at first spread by physical conquest, could hardly have spread as it did in a world of compartmentalized territorial units. Still, in the sense that we expect a nation-state today to have a certain homogeneity of culture, right down to the bottom of the social pyramid, it is clear that the Roman Empire had nothing of the sort, save at the top. The Stoic gentleman was by no means isolated from "reality," by no means living in an ivory castle, but he did not have the facts of life among the masses constantly nagging at him, could generalize, rationalize, in the company of his equals, in a long serene tradition that no vulgar concern for immediate practicality, and certainly little concern with what we know as science-*cum*-technology, could disturb.

Yet, you may observe, the Romans were a "practical" people, great engineers and builders, civilian as well as military. Surely they never talked about ideal sewers, or entrenchments that only *seemed* to be different, but were in accord with natural law identical, did they? The answer here, I should think, would be, first, that the Romans did succeed in keeping the practical and the ideal nicely separated, a separation made easier, perhaps, by the fact that the ideal was imported from the Greeks. The later Romans who wrote on practical matters, Pliny, Varro, and the rest, do not attempt to philosophize abstractly about farming, stock raising, estate management. Again, there lingered in their education much of the old Greek feeling about *banausia;* technical skills, even engineering skills, were certainly necessary to the gentleman-officer. But he learned them by apprenticeship and practice, not in formal schooling. Civilian engineering seems generally to have been the work of craftsmen of great skill, but not members of the ruling classes. This separation of the real and the ideal is no hypocrisy; it is merely a habit, a consolation. Here, as so often, Marcus Aurelius, fighting the Marcomanni on this earth, meditating eternal peace in the next, is typical enough.

Epicureanism may seem to the determinedly pragmatic mind to counsel in real life much that Stoicism counsels, indeed "to come out at" much the same thing. Epicurean apraxia ($\dot{\alpha}\pi\rho\alpha\xi\dot{\iota}\alpha$), "not acting," like Stoic ataraxia, was a withdrawal from the petty struggles of an active life, the attainment of a balanced serenity, but still no full retreat into seclusion. Epicurus and his followers did, however, insist on a "materialist" cosmology, and they did use that dangerous word "pleasure" (ἡδονή, *hēdonē,* whence hedonism) to describe the good life. In vain—and this is clear in the few fragments we have from Epicurus himself—did they protest that *true* pleasure is not swinish behavior, not the coarse indulgence of the senses, but quite the opposite, the difficult mastery of the low senses by the higher ones, and the cultivation of the higher arts—not so much self-indulgence as self-denial. At the very least, this is the Aristotelian ethics of the Golden Mean; but in keeping with the general high seriousness of Hellenistic and later Roman ethical thinking, and with the pessimism common among intellectuals of these centuries, Epicureanism developed into a most austere and existentialist ethics. Its best representative is the Roman Lucretius of the last years of the Republic, whose long philosophical poem *On the Nature of Things* must owe its preservation in part to the admiration even his religious and philosophical opponents have felt for it. Indeed, after two thousand years, no one has yet succeeded in investing the bleak world view of atomistic materialism and rationalist resignation in the face of necessity with the emotions appropriate to the religious spirit as does Lucretius. The poem has remained a consolation, a *sursum corda,* to many a rebel against conventional Christianity in the modern world.

Yet the old tag "a hog from Epicurus's sty" has stuck to Epicureanism and to hedonistic ethical systems of all kinds ever since—even, to the despair of the least sensual and sensuous of thinkers, John Stuart Mill, to the English Utilitarianism of the eighteenth and nineteenth centuries.[21] No doubt Lucretius is a most stoical Epicurean, far out toward the immaterial, the spiritual, on the spectrum of definitions of "pleasure"; there is no doubt in the balance that conventional Epicureanism did lean toward a softer life, toward abandonment of the struggle with himself that the Stoic so enjoyed. Still, the historian of morals must record that the bitterness of the attacks on the preachers of swinish self-indulgence who set up pleasure as an ethical standard seems, in view of the most unswinish nature of the pleasure most ethical hedonists preach, to be most unjust. It is, however, not unreasonable, for ethics even more than other branches of formal philosophy does seep down to the average educated person; and "pleasure" in all our Western tongues does to the unreflective mean . . . well, something closer to what "immoral" means to him than what "moral" does. We must return later to this obvious theme that our supposedly materialistic and practical West has never widely professed a purely hedonistic *ethics.*

---

21 Horace, "Epicuri de grege porcus," in *Epistolae,* Book I, No. 4, line 16. This light hearted piece of irony has been taken in earnest.

Still another current of Greco-Roman thought mingled with Stoicism and Epicureanism in various ways, and contributed to the world view of these centuries. For this current the best word is still "rationalism." It is a current clear in what we know of the earlier Sophists, but in the Greco-Roman world this current developed to a point as extreme as any it has yet reached. The rationalist must always admit that some men—indeed, he usually thinks that most men—sometimes behave irrationally, do things that reason can show will not in fact attain the end the doer aims at, give reasons for acts that are not *real* reasons, believe in the existence of supernatural beings reason shows cannot exist, and so on; but the rationalist also holds that there is always a rational explanation for the irrational, that he can correct and ultimately eliminate the irrational, at least among the enlightened few. These Greco-Roman times produced a characteristic figure of this sort, one whose name still sticks to the effort to root the unreasonable in reason, or, at least, given early ignorance, in a "reasonable" error. Euhemerus, a Greek who flourished at the beginning of the third century B.C., sought systematically to explain the gods and goddesses of the Olympic pantheon as heroes and heroines of olden times transmuted into supernatural beings by folk imagination. We have only the barest fragments of his work, but his reputation grew, and the term "euhemerism" is still used for the effort to explain mythologies by naturalistic-historical methods at their simplest. It is a method that tends to be revived in any rationalistic era; many *philosophes* in the eighteenth century simply could not believe that those admirable unprejudiced Greeks and Romans, happily free from the superstitions of Christianity, could have had their own superstitions and irrationalities, save as heirs of sensible but uninformed "primitive" ancestors.[22]

These rationalists occasionally express clearly another position that recurs in the eighteenth century, the view that for the unenlightened masses atheism is a dangerous thing, since they need the moral policing religion, in spite of its superstitions, gives them. Strabo observes that

It is impossible to lead the mass of women and the common people generally to piety, holiness and faith simply by philosophical teaching; the fear of God is also required, not omitting legends and miraculous stories.[23]

You will note here the implication that women even in the privileged classes

---

[22] On this see the forthcoming *The Eighteenth Century Confronts the Gods* by Frank E. Manuel, Cambridge, Mass., Harvard University Press, 1959.
[23] Strabo, quoted in L. Friedländer, *Roman Life and Manners under the Early Empire*, Vol. III, trans. by J. H. Freese, London, Routledge, 1909, p. 85.

are not to be trusted as rational creatures. This is one of the constants of Western culture, certainly not weakened by the advent of Christianity, and not unknown even in our own day.

Rationalism turned on the dissection of the classical pantheon becomes religious skepticism—not, be it noted, necessarily full philosophical skepticism. The controlled, or incomplete, rationalism of the Socratic tradition rejects the anthropomorphic gods of Olympus but insists on a spiritual reality superior to this world of the flesh and the senses, and not to be approached by mere prudential and instrumental thinking. There is a strong strain of this pagan monotheism—its god is a bit less remote than the god of eighteenth-century deism—in so representative a man as Plutarch.[24]

The Epicureans took another and more clearly deistic tack. This is the position, eloquently put by Lucretius, that the gods are indifferent to the fate of mankind. A fragment of an early Latin poet, Ennius, puts very clearly the basis of this distrust in a simple question of theodicy: the gods cannot care about men, for if they did the good man would be happy and prosper, the bad man unhappy and fail, which is not so.[25]

It is not far from this grave doubt to lighthearted doubt, or at least to whistling in the dark. We have from the second century A.D. abundant writings of a Greek rhetorician, satirist, and popular lecturer, Lucian of Samosata. It is certain from these writings that Lucian was very clever, very gifted verbally, and that he was fully aware, as most of his sort are, that the clever rarely are entrusted with the work of the world, even though they know so well how to do it. What is not at all clear, since we know little in detail of his life, is whether he accepted this badly run world or rejected it. He has been compared to Swift, a superficial comparison indeed, for there is little trace in Lucian of the moral horror Swift has for the world. He is at least as witty as Voltaire, and more fanciful, but it is hard to think of Lucian fighting for the rehabilitation of a Calas. You can argue that Lucian was just a good entertainer, that the spectacle of human folly amused rather than outraged or elevated him. He is certainly irreverent. One of his dialogues, "Zeus Cross-examined," is a fine sample of the lighthearted rationalist playing with some old metaphysical problems. The central issue is one familiar to Christians: how to reconcile determinism with any system of rewards and punishment for human exercise

---

[24] For example, Plutarch's *Moralia, De Iside et Osiride,* 78.
[25] *Nam si curent, bene bonis sit, male malis, quod non est.* Quoted in Albert Grenier, *The Roman Spirit in Religion, Thought, and Art,* London, Kegan Paul, Trench, Trubner, 1926, p. 125.

of free will. Zeus grants the difficulty at once, but he will by no means give up determinism. The dialogue is bright and charming, more like the work of a Diderot than a Voltaire, and most reminiscent of the French eighteenth century. Lucian was much surer that God and the gods were dead even for the mass of mankind than the *philosophes* could be. In "Timon the Misanthrope" he has Timon act, one guesses, as his own mouthpiece in addressing Zeus:

Mankind pays you the natural wages of your laziness; if anyone offers you a victim or a garland nowadays it is only at Olympia as a perfunctory accompaniment of the games; he does it not because he thinks it is any good, but because he may as well keep up an old custom.[26]

The most difficult problem Lucian presents to the historian of morals is this: How far does he represent a state of mind common to at least an important minority in his world? Lucian does not urge his listeners to go out and lead immoral lives—immoral by the relatively constant standards of Western ethics. But he does not preach, and he does report without censoring it directly an immense amount of trickery, backbiting, pretense, irresponsibility, downright vice and evil. There is a quality in Lucian that must seem to the very serious-minded moralist about as repugnant as any human attitude can be, actual amusement over the spectacle of human wickedness. And it would seem that a society wholly composed of Lucians would be at least as bad as a society wholly composed of Messalinas, and, fortunately perhaps, even more impossible. But the historian of morals, in contrast to the moralist, can hardly entertain such hypotheses. Lucians did not exist in large numbers. Lucian himself was certainly listened to, supported, but by a fashionable minority of intellectuals and would-be intellectuals. He is, granted, inconceivable in early republican Rome, in Judaea at any time; the Victorians had their doubts about him. There is a problem, to which we must return in a final chapter, of the relation between fashionable skepticism, devotion to the clever and the cutting, contempt for conventional morality as dull, and so on, and the *morale* of a whole society, its ability to keep on going. Here we may note that the popularity of Lucian and his like is an indication that some part of the literate classes of the Roman Empire at its height did admire fashionable cleverness and a degree of skepticism.[27]

[26] Lucian, *Works*, trans. by H. W. and F. G. Fowler, Oxford, Oxford University Press, 1905, Vol. I, p. 32.
[27] A minor problem from our point of view, but an interesting one, is set by the very survival of the manuscripts of Lucian's work. He should have been about as objectionable to the early Christians as any pagan author. One suspects that at crucial points

We have already noted, however, that probably even more of these literate classes of the Empire were high-minded Stoics, serious men who took their responsibilities seriously. There are even signs of a continuing pagan orthodoxy, no doubt on the defensive, but not despairingly so. The minor historian and moralist Aelian, who flourished in the early third century A.D., finds even the philosophers of virtue dangerous, and believes the old gods are still good gods. He tells the exemplary story of Euphronius, who did not believe in the gods, but who, having fallen seriously ill, dreamed that he must burn the writings of Epicurus, knead the ashes with wax, and apply the whole as a poultice to his belly in order to recover. He was so impressed with this dream that he became a pious believer and a good influence forevermore. In a passage in his *Various History,* Aelian "praises the barbarians, who have not become alienated from the faith by excessive education like the Greeks; amongst the Indians, Celts and Egyptians there are no atheists like Euhemerus, Epicurus, and Diagoras."[28]

Finally, there were in this One World of the Empire a very great many pagan cults and beliefs, surviving forms of the older pagan mysteries, importations of sacramental faiths from Egypt, Syria, Persia, and, of course, the rising Christian faith. Among the intellectuals for whom Stoicism was too austere, rationalism and skepticism quite unsuitable, there flourished an elaborate *amalgame* of philosophy and theology known as Neoplatonism, of which the chief exponent was the third-century Greek writer Plotinus. We cannot here possibly go into the twists and turnings of this very cerebral set of beliefs, which, as Gnosticism, once threatened to take over Christianity. It is otherworldly, mystic, eternity-seeking, but also very verbal, and, in the primary sense of an overworked word, sophisticated. Its adepts, whatever else they may have been, were certainly no skeptics, no materialists. We have no evidence that they led low lives of self-indulgence; but we have no evidence that they led simple lives of altruistic devotion. The odds are firmly against the latter. They seem to have been few in numbers, but most articulate. Some of them were certainly charlatans, exploiting the need of a privileged and edu-

---

in the lives of various manuscripts some of the good Christian fathers yielded to the temptation to play with the forbidden. Also, of course, Lucian made formal pagan religious beliefs ridiculous indeed. The historian will note that W. H. Auden in his *Portable Greek Reader* refuses to include any Lucian in his anthology, on the grounds that Lucian is not fit reading for us today, "haunted by devils" as we are. See his comment in his preface, p. 7.

[28] L. Friedländer, *Roman Life and Manners,* Vol. III, pp. 97-99. Aelian's own words are: He told all that he had heard to his nearest relatives, who were full of joy, because he had not been rejected with contempt by the god. Thus the atheist was converted and was ever afterwards a model of piety for others.

cated but often idle and irresponsible upper class for a faith, an interesting faith, a privileged faith, and one that does not demand much real or symbolic sweat or worry—a theosophy, in short. Lucian has fun with them, a fun that seems for him almost bitter. In his "Sale of Creeds," Hermes as auctioneer puts up for sale "Pythagoreanism"—Pythagoras was the pre-Socratic founder of the first of these sects of illuminati and long a good butt for common sense —and goes into his spiel:

Now here is a creed of the first water. Who bids for this handsome article? What gentleman says Superhumanity? Harmony of the Universe! Transmigration of souls! Who bids?[29]

Yet out of all this welter of beliefs—among which, as I have insisted, it seems fair to conclude that a kind of moderate Stoicism was in fact the accepted faith of the great majority of the working ruling classes of the Empire right down to the end—a history of Western morals must emphasize the ripening of a way of thinking about ethical problems that transcends the actual specific content of these many creeds. Here there comes out fully what had been begun far back in Ionia, the concepts of *nature,* of *natural law,* and of *human nature,* concepts in which the "is" and the "ought," the descriptive, the explanatory, and the evaluative are mingled—it is not unfair to say, often confused—in a characteristic Western manner. The "natural" is, in this classical tradition (definitely *not* in the romantic tradition), what the correctly thinking thinker discovers as the uniform element in the apparently diverse and changing phenomena which his sense experience, as organized by unthinking common sense and habit ("conditioning"), presents to him. The natural is thus the regular, the predictable, in contrast to the sporadic intervention of an unpredictable supernatural. Thunder is natural, the result of the working out of regular meteorological forces; Zeus hurling his thunderbolts when the mood strikes him is unnatural, and in fact nonexistent, a "myth." The specific prescriptions and penalties in actual law vary from people to people, in earlier days from town to town; but the student of jurisprudence who will examine with this tool of rational analysis which is his *mind* these diverse laws will be able to classify them in accordance with what they have in common. He will note that for a valid contract there will be certain minimal requirements everywhere; he will thus arrive at the concept of a universal law, the law of nature. Finally, the man who simply looks at his fellows in the street without thinking will see them as so many separate individual beings, tall and short, handsome and ugly, Roman and Syrian, slave and free, and so on

[29] Lucian, *Works,* Fowler trans. Vol. I, p. 190.

indefinitely; the thinker will see in these varied individuals *man,* the human being who is everywhere the same beneath these apparent differences.

This last statement may be misleading. The familiar statement that human nature is everywhere the same did not mean to the Stoics and the other thinkers of the Empire that differences in individuals—say, in bodily build or in disposition or temper—are nonexistent, but, rather, that they do not exhaust what can be said about human beings; from their point of view it was even more important to note that there are limits to the range of variation in individuals, that all have certain minimal bodily functions in common, that all have minimal spiritual characteristics in common. What is in common, the regularities and the uniformities that the discerning mind sees are not just what we should call statistical averages, any more than the Aristotelian Golden Mean is a statistical average or mean. The regularities are nature's plan, what men *ought to be.*

By an easy transition the man thinking along such lines slips from analysis, classification, the search for uniformities that will allow prediction, into moral purposiveness, into a search for uniformities that will provide goals toward which other men can be persuaded, or forced, to strive to mold their conduct. In the purest tradition of modern natural science this transition is a kind of betrayal, a piece of intellectual dishonesty. To the historian, it is one of the abiding ways Western men think and feel, which in practice has proved to be an effective means of changing, above all, of widening, the economic, social, and political organizations in which men live. This paradoxical use of the concept of Nature as *what ought to be* so as to bring about changes in the unnaturally natural of the given moment has really worked. Remote as some of the more extreme and abstract concepts of what this Nature, and human nature, were—those of the Stoics, for instance, or those of the eighteenth-century *philosophes*—from the "facts of life," there remained this curious intellectual and, therefore, moral link with these same facts, an inescapable link. The classical tradition of "reason" has never quite been able to deny, escape, transcend, suppress the vulgar here, now, and imperfect. Even Plato is not a very good mystic, not in the sense that St. Teresa or St. John of the Cross are good mystics; Plato cannot help arguing.

It is this never-quite-severed Greco-Roman link with the world of our sense experience—shall we say, the "minimally organized world"—that makes the real basis for the commonly exaggerated distinction between the Hebraic and the Hellenic in our Western moral and intellectual tradition. Mr. W. T. Stace, as I have noted above (Chapter III, p. 56) puts the distinction in morals as one between a Hebrew *imposed* code and a Greek *immanent* one, a Hebrew supernatural and authoritarian source and sanction for morals, a Greek source and sanction flowing from within human beings, inside human "nature." Now the Nature that advised Cicero or Seneca seems to me about as remote from this world as the God that commanded Moses and David, and actually rather more remote than the God that inspired Isaiah. No doubt Spengler is giving way to his anger against the classical tradition when he writes that "Nature [the concept of nature] is a function of the particular Culture."[30] Still, the curiously hypostatized concept of nature as moderation, regularity, order, decency—the list could be long, scandalously *not* composed of logical synonyms, but with a strongly consistent affective tone—the concept of nature which gets fully developed in the later Empire can hardly seem to most of us today to describe, let alone flow "immanently" from, nature as it appears in geophysics, meteorology, biology, or human nature as it appears in formal psychological studies.

Such a Nature as that of Cicero or Seneca must seem rather the ideal of a privileged class in a culture that no longer sought to apply its ideals to all of its members. It is an ideal that still attracts, perhaps because it is at least as unattainable and, therefore, attractive to Western man as any boundless desire. Martial, whose life, to judge from most of his poetry, did not much resemble the ideal, has left a fine statement of it.

> Martial, the things for to attain
> The happy life be these, I find:
> The riches left, not got with pain;
> The fruitful ground; the quiet mind;
> The equal friend; no grudge, nor strife;
> No charge of rule nor governance;
> Without disease, the healthful life;
> The household of continuance;
> The mean diet, no delicate fare;
> Wisdom joined with simplicity;
> The night discharged of all care,
> Where wine may bear no sovereignty;
> The chaste wife, wise, without debate;
> Such sleeps as may beguile the night;
> Contented with thine own estate,
> Neither wish death, nor fear his might.[31]

[30] Spengler, *Decline of the West,* Vol. I, p. 169.
[31] Martial, Book X, No. 47. This poem of Martial's has been often translated. I give in modern spelling that of the sixteenth-century Henry Howard, Earl of Surrey. The

IV

All told, we know quite a bit about the condition of the masses, the common people, of the One World of the Roman Empire. We do not by any means know enough to risk comments on the general level of sobriety, of steady ways, of chastity in contrast to the more lurid vices in all parts of this great territory. We may believe that the country folk were simpler, perhaps more honest, though probably not much more chaste, than the city folk. Such, at least, was the common belief of most intellectuals of the time, as it was to be at later periods of European cultural life when great cities give the moralist something to complain about. But at least for Rome we have evidence that here were some million human beings living, on the whole, in one of the moral troughs of Western history.

More particularly, we know a great deal about one of the pursuits of the urban masses that has almost always shocked later commentators—the gladiatorial games. It should be clear that we are here dealing with a special and peculiar phase of moral history, a *case*, like that of Greek pederasty in the Great Age, not a common phase of human moral development. There are recurring examples of crowds of men and women witnessing with interest and pleasure the physical suffering of their fellows. The histories all bring out the hangings at Tyburn in London right down almost to Victorian times; Huizinga devotes a whole chapter to the fascination people in the Middle Ages felt for the spectacle of human suffering.[32] But these are relatively sporadic and isolated instances, not organized and regular mass displays for public amuse-

---

reader may be amused to see what the twentieth century makes of it. Here is Mr. Gilbert Highet:

> To bring yourself to be happy
> Acquire the following blessings:
> A nice inherited income,
> A kindly farm with a kitchen,
> No business worries or lawsuits,
> Good health, a gentleman's muscles,
> A wise simplicity, friendships,
> A plain but generous table,
> Your evenings sober but jolly,
> Your bed amusing but modest,
> And nights that pass in a moment;
> To be yourself without envy,
> To fear not death, nor to wish it.

Latin Poetry in Verse Translation, ed. by L. R. Lind, Boston, Houghton Mifflin, 1957, pp. 272-273.

[32] J. Huizinga, *Waning of the Middle Ages*, London, Arnold, 1927, Chap. I.

ment, as at Rome. And such horrors as the French Reign of Terror, the mass murders by the Nazis, those of the Yezhov period in Russia, are obviously very different things indeed, in no sense part of the daily delights of their participants. The Spanish bullfight of our own day does have its analogies with the Roman games; automobile racing probably holds some of its fans by the attractive possibility of witnessing sudden death. Let us content ourselves with observing that in the West there seem always to be numbers of people who do not find it repugnant to witness the public display of cruelty to men and animals, or at least to await the dramatic possibility of violence. The fact remains that only in Rome has this been an organized and widely approved public pursuit. Undergraduate American editorials that equate our football with the gladiatorial games are wide of the mark.

The shows were many and varied. The bloodiest were the various forms of individual and group combats to the death, and the combats between beasts and men and among beasts. Mercy could be shown, as we all know, for a beaten fighter who put up a good show; but "thumbs up" could hardly apply to mass combats, and there is no evidence that the Roman crowd was a kindly one. Even where blood was not deliberately planned to flow, the circuses, the chariot races, the spectacles were expensive, full of accidental violence, and by no means demanding on intellect or taste. Rome with its great Colosseum and its Circus set the pace, but in the West of the Empire, at least, the provincial centers aped the metropolis, though they could not afford the lavishness of display and bloodshed the emperors and other donors felt obliged to give the Romans. Crowds were large even by our modern standards; the Colosseum held about 45,000 spectators.

The games are by no means without precedent in earlier Roman history. Though bigger and better after Augustus, they go back to republican days, before Rome was a world power. The first triple duel among gladiators on record was in 264 B.C.; there had been single fights earlier. The fights do seem to go with the Roman character or disposition. Another modern notion about the games is wrong: the crowds were by no means limited to the lower classes. Many of the emperors enjoyed the games; others came even if they did not enjoy them, because they were part of the ceremonial and ritual that symbolized the Empire. The people expected to see their rulers do their public duty by presiding at the arena. Many individuals among the upper classes clearly delighted in the games, followed the gladiators and the charioteers in public eye, mixed with them socially, kept their own "stables," human as well as animal, behaved, in short, about mass sports as the nonintellectuals of Western aristocracies generally do when civilization deprives them of the relaxation of serious fighting. The world of the arena and the race course was truly a world of consuming interest for all sorts of Romans. There are all the signs one would expect to find in mass spectator-sport—statistics of records, worship of the successful athletes, wide publicity. At Pompeii some of the informal transcriptions found scribbled in public places tell us the Thracian Celadus, probably a gladiator, was a "man the girls yearned for"; an inscription tells us that Crescens, a Moor, a Blue charioteer, drove a four-in-hand at the age of thirteen, and between A.D. 115 and 124 ran 686 races, getting first prize forty-seven times, second, 130 times, and third,111 times, winning, in all, 1,588,346 sesterces.[33] Martial wrote, perhaps not altogether without the intellectual's envy of the attention the athlete gets, an epitaph for Scorpus, dying young:

I am that Scorpus, glory of the shouting circus, thy applauded one, Rome, and brief delight; whom a jealous fate cut off at thrice nine years, believing, having counted my victories, that I was already an old man.[34]

Juvenal says in clear indignation that a successful jockey of the Red gets a hundred times what an advocate gets.[35]

The Roman stage furnishes another example of a decline in taste, a vulgarization as its audience gets increasingly unable to discriminate between the amusing and the titillating. Terence and Plautus wrote plays in imitation of Menander and other Greek playwrights of the New Comedy, plays in which the wit is partly, at least, a matter for the mind. By imperial times what takes place on the Roman stage is hardly more than stylized exhibition of mimes, often very obscene, and clearly far from subtle in content, though the art of the individual actor was very highly developed. The people of the stage, like those of the arena and the circus, were interesting and enviable persons in the eyes of the urban masses and of many of their patrician hangers-on, but they were definitely not respectable. Indeed, the moral disrepute of the actor, the professional athlete, the denizen of the underworld of amusement is first clear in the West in this Greco-Roman society. We Westerners admire, envy, and scorn those who amuse us, as we admire and scorn our best friend, the dog. This worldly underworld of the Romans is a vast Bohemia, as yet without romantic overtones.

33 L. Friedländer, *Roman Life and Manners,* Vol. II, pp. 51, 23.
34 Martial, Book X, no. 53.
35 Juvenal, Satire VII, lines 112-114.

Yet, save from the Christians, there is not much vigorous condemnation of the games. There is, though, not much defense of them either. Pliny the Younger has a famous passage in his panegyric of Trajan in praise of the contempt for death the spectacles teach; but the rhetoric of the piece makes it hard to guess whether Pliny really thought the games toughened the spectators up in good Hemingway style.[36] But for the most part what strikes one is the naturalness with which the games were taken. Symmachus, a late fourth-century pagan whose contrived letters seem by no means those of a harsh person, reports the suicide of some Saxons he was having groomed to fight in the arena; he clearly is very sorry for himself, but not at all for the Saxons.[37]

The Stoics included the mob in that world they sought to rise above. They were no crusaders; they were willing to leave the populace to its own bad ways. The rulers knew they had to provide bread and the circuses, and that the circuses were more necessary than bread. Trajan, writes the historian Fronto, knew that

the goodness of government is shown both in its earnest aspects and its amusements; and that while neglect of serious business was harmful, neglect of amusements caused discontent; even distributions of money were less desired than games; further, largesse of corn and money pacified only a few or even individuals only, but games the whole people.[38]

The world of the Roman Empire was a varied, lively, interesting world, not very sensitive, not at all simple, from which the anecdotist can draw on a vast range of human conduct. Aulus Gellius, the source for the well-known tale of Androcles and the lion, finishes his story with a touch usually omitted in the retelling: Androcles, manumitted after the touching episode in the arena, went the rounds of the taverns leading his lion by a leash; the customers threw money to Androcles, sprinkled the lion with flowers.[39] St.

[36] Pliny, *Panegyricus Trajano,* Chap. XXXIII. "You [Trajan] provided a spectacle, not of the sort that softens and weakens the spirit of men, but that serves to harden men to bear noble wounds and be contemptuous of death." That *pulchra vulnera* is quite untranslatable, but very much part of the agon of a noble warrior class. It just does not go with the Roman games of the Empire, where the wounds must have been most unlovely.

[37] *Epistolae,* Book II, 46, quoted in L. Friedländer, *Roman Life and Manners,* Vol. II, p. 55.

[38] Fronto, *Preamble to History,* quoted and translated in L. Friedländer, *Roman Life and Manners,* Vol. II, p. 3. See the Loeb Classical Library edition of the fragments of Fronto, trans. by C. R. Haines, Cambridge, Mass., Harvard University Press, 1955, Vol. II, p. 217.

[39] Aulus Gellius, *Attic Nights,* trans. by J. C. Rolfe, London, Heinemann, 1927, in Loeb Classical Library, Book V, 14, Vol. I, p. 427.

Augustine reports, on the authority of Seneca, that women used to sit on the Capitoline by the temple of Jupiter, believing, probably on the strength of dreams, that they were beloved of the god.[40] Suetonius notes that each spring, after the death of Nero, flowers were laid by an unknown hand on his grave. This is the charisma exercised by the captivatingly wicked; one supposes that it is an ever-present element in Western society, but clearly it is usually repressed in a society of simple ways—or at least, in such societies, the wicked are Robin Hoods, not Neros or Capones.[41]

In Rome a good many thousands of the urban proletariat did live off the state dole. They needed the circuses, if only to make their idleness bearable, and they seem to have got something like one day in three as public holidays. They certainly did not make a sober, steady, soldierly people; they were not virtuous; but they could hardly afford the expensive vices of their betters. Theirs was no doubt the short and simple fornication of the poor, the vicarious satisfactions of the arena, the stage, the spectacle of the wickedness of their rulers, the melodrama of high imperial politics. The masses of the great cities of the East, Antioch, Alexandria, and the rest, were probably less dependent on state handouts, but clearly were poor, crowded, restless, and aware of their plight. Theirs is the strange world of superstitition, vagabondage, big-city fashionable alertness, and moral laxness we begin to get glimpses of in Hellenistic times, and which is nicely reflected in one of the few almost-novels we have from antiquity, the *Golden Ass* of Apuleius, who flourished under the Antonines.

And always there was slavery, an institution to which even the triumphant Christianity of the fourth century was to adapt itself. Slavery in the Greco-Roman world was not by any means throughout a harsh and thorough subjection of the slave. One can even make a good case for the assertion that on the whole the Greco-Roman was one of the milder forms of slavery. Rank-and-file prisoners of war, often forced to fight against hopeless odds in the arena, were victims of the violence normal to the West throughout most of its history. Galley slaves had an especially grueling task. Apuleius has a grue-

---

[40] St. Augustine, *City of God*, Book VI, Chap. 10. "But some sit there that think Jove is in love with them: never respecting Juno's poetically supposed terrible aspect."
[41] Suetonius, *Nero*, 57, quoted in Dill, *Roman Society from Nero to Marcus Aurelius*, p. 16. Suetonius says, "Yet there were some who for a long time decorated his tomb with spring and summer flowers. . . ." Some gangsters do have their faithful after death. In fact, I think I perhaps have underestimated in the text the strength throughout Western moral history of a folk worship of the exciting, picturesque, romantically wicked. Not only in the United States of the 1950's have the Becks and the Hoffas been heroes to their followers.

some passage about some unfortunate slaves.[42] And W. E. H. Lecky writes that

numerous acts of the most odious barbarity were committed. The well-known anecdotes of Flaminius ordering a slave to be killed to gratify, by the spectacle, the curiosity of a guest; of Vedius Pollio feeding his fish on the flesh of slaves; and of Augustus sentencing a slave, who had killed and eaten a favorite quail, to crucifixion, are the extreme examples that are recorded. . . . Ovid and Juvenal describe the fierce Roman ladies tearing their servants' faces, and thrusting the long pins of their brooches into their flesh.[43]

Yet much can be set against this black picture. The inscriptions show many instances of manumitted slaves who did well in craft or small business, and left enough to get proper funeral inscriptions. Freedmen rose high in the service of the emperors—scandalously high in the opinion of the old Romans. The career open to talents was not shut to the capable slave, for whom his handicap could sometimes act as a stimulus in competition. No doubt the slaves who did the work of the great estates, which, especially in Italy, but to a degree elsewhere, took the place of the yeoman farms of the early Republic, had the lot usual with plantation slaves. The bright ones might manage to get into the household of the master, and eventually into the city and on the road to manumission. The masses of the slaves were at least spared the worst by increasingly great legal protection from bad masters, and by the economic good sense of the ordinary master. Varro, a contemporary of Cicero, who wrote on agriculture, has much to say on the treatment of slaves. He sounds very sensible, almost as if he had studied nineteenth-century economic writings. He counsels humane treatment on prudential grounds, and advises special concern to encourage efficient foremen, themselves slaves, by "incentive pay," possibility of eventual freedom, and so on.[44]

On slavery as an institution, as I have noted briefly above, the fashionable rationalist philosophy was driven to the conclusion that if the mind finds men equal, it can hardly find slavery natural. Cicero, Seneca, and many others register their disapproval; Epictetus, himself a slave, sounds more sincere:

What you avoid suffering yourself, seek not to impose on others. You avoid

[42] Apuleius, *The Golden Ass,* IX, 12.
[43] *History of European Morals from Augustus to Charlemagne,* Vol. I, pp. 302-303.
[44] Varro, *Rerum Rusticarum,* Vol. I, p. 17. Lewis and Reinhold, *Roman Civilisation,* Vol. I, pp. 446-448. On legal protection, Westermarck, *Origin and Development of the Moral Ideas,* Vol. I, pp. 691-692, gives many examples.

slavery, for instance; take care not to enslave. For if you can bear to exact slavery from others, you appear to have been first yourself a slave.[45]

But there is no record of a Roman Society for the Abolition of Slavery. Of course, in the bureaucratic Empire there was no place for what we call pressure groups. Still, the protests of the literary and the philosophic against slavery seem more than usually remote from the habits and conduct of ordinary men. We must conclude that slavery was an accepted part of this great society, exhibiting the widest range from cruelty to gentleness, from economic exploitation to legal moderation, and from melodramatic gestures of psychopathic origin to the daily routines of convenience. We may perhaps go a bit further, and conclude that the kind of anecdote Lecky has culled from the sources is no sounder social and moral history than any other case history of the monstrous, the psychopathic.

One final topic: it is possible for the later Empire to list for the first time some "intellectuals" among the many, if not quite among the masses. At least, we know from our sources that there was a relatively large public for whom, in the absence of a printing press and other marvels of modern mass communication, there existed professional lecturers, schools at which tuition was paid, and which indulged in a certain amount of what we call adult education —in short, a public with leisure enough to talk about "ideas." This public was served by a motley group of rhetoricians and "philosophers" who have had a thoroughly bad press. Some of them do smell of the ancient equivalent of Grub Street, if not of still lower reaches of ill-paid masters of the word. Lucian, who at one time in his life was perhaps one of these, has left some very stinging satire on them. They numbered charlatans, poseurs, hawkers of all sorts of salvation. They deliberately made themselves up as philosophers. Epictetus, a true blue himself, wrote indignantly of these pretenders:

> When people see a man with long hair and a coarse cloak behaving in an unseemingly manner, they shout, 'Look at the philosopher': whereas his behavior should rather convince them that he is no philosopher.[46]

Even when this intellectual life was not downright charlatanry, it was pitched at a somewhat low level of casuistry. Here is a topic on which the young rhetoricians exercised themselves:

[45] Epictetus, *Moral Discourses*, trans. by Elizabeth Carter, London, Dent, 1910, Fragment 38.
[46] IV, 8, 4, quoted in L. Friedländer, *Roman Life and Manners*, Vol. III, p. 237. Friedländer's Chapter III of this volume on "Philosophy as a Moral Education" gleans many interesting details from the sources.

In this case the law is that if a woman has been seduced she can choose either to have her seducer condemned to death or marry him without bringing him any dowry.

A man violates two women on the same night. One asks for him to be put to death, the other chooses to marry him.[47]

Something has certainly happened to "philosophy" since the pre-Socratics!

V

I have hitherto restrained myself from making the obvious comparisons. When the million and more sesterces of the charioteer Crescens's prize money came up, I said nothing of Eddie Arcaro; nor did I suggest that Celadus, the *suspirum et decus puellarum* of the Pompeian graffiti had anticipated Elvis Presley by two thousand years. But we cannot here sensibly dodge the much-discussed topic: Are we now somewhere in our own modern Western version of the Greco-Roman world? From Spengler through to Toynbee and the latest appeal to history as a clue to the future, our time has seen dozens of versions of the parallel between the Greco-Roman world and our own. A history of morals in the West can by no means be extended into an attempt to examine all sides of this problem; but neither can such a history wholly avoid considering this problem, if only because for the moral temper of our own age this appeal to history, or to historicism, is most important.

Toynbee and his fellows have made the cyclical form almost as much the accepted form of our thinking on these matters as unilinear evolution was for our grandfathers. It is difficult today to avoid thinking of all sorts of human group activities as subject to ups and downs, growth, decay, and death, spring, summer, fall, winter, and other such conceptual schemes or figures of speech. From business firms through sports clubs to nations and civilizations, we have before us what we must think of as the fact of cyclical processes. We understand thoroughly none of them, can control fully none of them, not even the business cycle. It is probably true that the wider the net of human activity we gather together to study as a cycle, the less accurately we can analyze it. The Spenglerian civilization, the Toynbean society, are so great, so complicated, so much a series of cycles within cycles within cycles, that we cannot possibly use them to place our own society in a single position analogous to these. We cannot say the West is now just where the Greco-Roman society was in such and such a year, or century.

Any attempt to analyze the varied human activities from which the master

[47] Seneca, *Controversiae*, I, 2, quoted in H. I. Marrou, *Education in Antiquity*, p. 287.

cycle of the whole society is usually constructed shows at once that we cannot really fit the parts together. If one takes the relations among the independent states making up a given society—international politics—one can see with Toynbee a certain parallel between our day and the Greco-Roman day of about 250 B.C. The superpowers Rome and Carthage become the superpowers U.S.A. and U.S.S.R.; one or the other will give the "knockout blow" and there will be a new universal state, American- or Russian-inspired. Indeed, Mr. Amaury de Riencourt has already decided that the Americans are the Romans of the modern world. If one takes morals in the vulgar modern sense, with emphasis on luxury, "sensate" self-indulgence, sophistication at the top, and some effort at the bottom to keep up with the top, in short, if one is Mr. Sorokin, then we now appear to be, not in 250 B.C., but three hundred years later, along with the contemporaries of Martial and Juvenal, along with all the shocking conduct we have just above briefly and decently reviewed. If one takes over-all economic productivity, the application of any cyclical theory is impossible, because so far there has been no *secular* trend in modern Western society, since the end of the Middle Ages at least, save upward. The horrors of twentieth-century destructiveness have not, statistically speaking, destroyed; two world wars and a great depression have left the West richer in things of this world than it has ever been.

If we cannot then *apply* cyclical theories to our own society with diagnostic success, can we, perhaps, consider the whole development of the Mediterranean world in "classical" antiquity as a kind of case history? If we take "case history" seriously, as at least an effective working tool of the sort the clinician in medicine uses, clearly the answer is no. The clinician who concluded anything at all from *one* case history would be thought ill of by his colleagues. Even if with Toynbee and others we judge that history gives us something to work with for maybe a dozen or so civilized societies, these are few indeed; and, more important, they are perhaps so different as to be useless for the diagnostician, for we may be comparing the incomparable, and our actual knowledge of their histories is often slight. We do know the "classical world" quite well, too well, if we are sensible, to suppose that what has happened there is going to happen here. All that we can do with the history of the Greco-Roman world is what we can always do with any history—treat it as a record of human experience which we can add with due caution to what we know of our own times. We can draw all sorts of generalizations from that sort of experience, but no master generalization about man's fate, human destiny, "whither mankind?"

There remains, however, the old chestnut about the causes of the fall of the Roman Empire. Surely the historian of morals cannot decently side-step that question, though he cannot pretend to answer it completely. He will not in mid-twentieth century go along with any variants of naïve materialistic determination which rule out morals from the variables to be considered. The fall of Rome was not *simply* a moral fall, but it was in part a moral fall. One cannot even say that, given the conduct our sources report for these centuries, a society in which men and women conducted themselves as did the Greco-Romans was corrupt, decadent, bound to collapse under attack from the outside if not under revolt from the inside. One can make the rough generalization that at least in the ruling classes and its hangers-on the kind of conduct that we most readily label "immoral"—the vices of self-indulgence and display—tend to diminish somewhat after what was perhaps their peak early in imperial times. This is by no means a sure generalization. It may be that our sources for later periods lack the moral intensity of a Tacitus. The later historian Ammianus Marcellinus has two good passages of moralistic attack on the weaknesses of the upper classes, but they are not very vehement or very extensive, and are perhaps no more than the conventional scornful feelings of the soldier toward the rulers back home. The society reflected in the *Saturnalia* of Macrobius is, as Samuel Dill points out, simpler than the luxurious one of old, with no fantastic foods, no dancing girls, no extravagant display.[48]

The tough-minded may infer that the comparative poverty of the last years of the Empire explains this comparative chastity and decency; the tender-minded will remind us that Christianity ought to have had some effect on the conduct of those who espoused it. Certainly the Christian writers found no improvement in the morals of the many. Salvianus of fifth-century Aquitaine found his fellows living in one vast whore house, found no one chaste—except, one hopes, himself.[49] Even after the gladiatorial games were finally suppressed early in the fifth century, the mimes continued to carry on with the usual indecencies, acting out Leda's loves, and the like. So reports Sidonius, a provincial of Gaul, and thus an early Frenchman, perhaps already saddled with the French national obligation to note these matters saltily.[50]

Still, it is difficult to escape the conclusion that the moral tone of life at Rome itself, and to a degree throughout the Empire, was not one in keeping

[48] Ammianus Marcellinus, XIV, 6 and XXVIII, 4; Dill, *Roman Society in the Last Century of the Western Empire*, p. 161.
[49] Dill, *op. cit.*, pp. 140-141, quoting Salvianus, *On God's Governance*, Book VII, 16.
[50] *Carmina*, Book XXIII, 286-288, quoted in Dill, *op. cit.*, p. 56.

with the maintenance of a state and a society able to stand off its enemies. This is surely true if one is concerned with the *civic virtues,* those of the citizen-soldier, the citizen participant in community political life. Even in the upper classes, there was a sharp division between the workers in war and administration, the admirable Stoic gentlemen who manned the Empire, and the corrupt aristocracy of Rome and high politics. There was the horde of Romans on the dole, a people no longer good for war or peace. There was the slave proletariat, and the many tribes and peoples of this huge political entity, none of them really *sharing* in the common thing of the Empire. The commonplace is unavoidable; even with the final spread of Roman citizenship in a legal sense throughout the Empire (slaves were never, of course, full citizens), even with the development of emperor worship as some kind of symbolism to remind ordinary people that there was an Empire, this huge state never really was more than a congeries held together by its armies and its bureaucrats, and by sheer habit.

I do not wish to be understood as maintaining that the civic virtues at their best in fact—let alone at their best in words, as in worship of Swiss cantons or New England town meetings—are an essential to a going state. I mean merely that with all the variables allowed for, including by all means the economic weaknesses of the later Empire, the "lack of Romans," the taxing away of the responsible middle class of curiales, even, perhaps, the malaria and the sunspots, all the long, long list of "causes" of the fall, a moral weakness, not so much a matter of the picturesque vices as one of softness, lack of civic responsibility, lack of drive toward a shared earthly betterment of material conditions, perhaps even, toward the end, a vague feeling of despair, must be on the list.

Softness? Despair? Is this the old tale of Gibbon once more? Am I about to list Christianity as at least partly responsible for the fall of the earthly Roman Empire? I am indeed, though not in a spirit of gloating irony. It may well be—I think it is—true that no men and no institutions we can realistically imagine in a restrained exercise of history-in-the-conditional could have held the congeries of the Roman Empire together. Let us grant Toynbee that the Empire was in a sense born dead. Still, it would also seem true that the kind of virtues that are indispensable to an imperial ruling elite were not those of early Christianity, and that for the many what early Christianity brought was by no means a set of civic virtues they had previously lacked. We must turn now to the moral implications of the Judaeo-Christian tradition as it grew in the Greco-Roman world and embodied itself in the Roman Catholic Church.

141

VI

The Beginnings of the Judaeo-Christian Tradition

THE TAXONOMY—to say nothing of the genetics—of morals is a difficult business. What I have in this chapter heading called the "Judaeo-Christian" tradition is perhaps better called, in spite of the unwieldiness of the phrase, the "Judaeo-Helleno-Romano-Christian" tradition. Certainly as to ethical concepts there can be no doubt that as early as St. Paul himself Greek ways of thinking and feeling, with difficulty, if at all, to be discerned in previous Jewish culture, come into Christian thought and feeling. Nothing is easier than to draw from the works of Greco-Roman writers from Plato on expressions of ideas that seem clearly Christian. I shall shortly give a brief sample of this familiar procedure of finding classic Greece in Christianity. But in the balance it still looks as if so much of what made Christianity different from Stoicism, or Neoplatonism, or any of the actual cults of the Empire, those of Mithra or of Isis, for example, does come from the Jews that the term "Judaeo-Christian" is justifiable. Job, Isaiah, Jeremiah, and Jesus must, even to the natural historian of morals—and most certainly to the Christian believer—mean more than Plato, Zeno, Marcus Aurelius, Plotinus, and all the rest of the pagans put together.

From the disasters that overcame the Jewish independent polity and culminated in the fall of Jerusalem and the Babylonian captivity at the beginning of the sixth century B.C., the intellectual leaders of the Jewish people were stirred to a heart searching out of which came the prophetic books of the Old Testament, and what looks like a revolutionary shift of Jewish theology into a universalistic monotheism, and into much else new. These results of loss of

142

political independence are in themselves remarkable. Carthage was destroyed —and rebuilt eventually—with no such results. The loss of independence by the Greek city-states, if more gradual and unaccompanied, as a rule, by razing of temples and deportations of intellectuals, was still a real loss, and one that produced no moral renewal. From the point of view of an engaged intellectual, the blows that have fallen on France in the twentieth century are certainly heavy, and they have in the existentialist movement produced something in high culture; but though some of our French existentialists sound at moments like Jeremiah at his worst, the comparison is for the natural historian of morals pretty silly. Not even a relatively intense modern nationalism of the sort prevalent in France seems to produce the reaction to defeat produced in Jewish nationalism by the downfall of the kingdoms of Judah and Israel.

The kind of secular "nationalism" we can understand is clearly not quite what filled Jewish heads and hearts. The Jews by the sixth century B.C. had been molded into a community of extraordinarily disciplined cohesion. They were already a, but not yet *the,* Chosen People. Jehovah had laid down the Law for them: the Jew who followed the Law could be certain, morally certain, that Jehovah would take care of him. We are here at a most delicate point. Christian terms like "salvation," "grace," and even "heaven" are not right here; and though there is something shocking in the suggestion that the Jew who followed the Law was "well-adjusted," free from anxiety, full of ego satisfaction, yet if these phrases of our time are taken freely and not too naïvely, they·may be useful in understanding why the fall of Jerusalem upset so much.

Disaster shook this certainty, but it did not shake the moral and intellectual habits on which the certainty was founded. Above all, it did not lead the Jews to doubt Jehovah, and certainly not, in the pagan Greek manner, to curse him for letting them down.

> Thou, O Lord, abidest for ever;
> Thy throne is from generation to generation.
> Wherefore dost thou forget us for ever,
> And forsake us so long time?
> Turn thou us unto thee, O Lord, and we shall be turned;
> Renew our days as of old.
> But thou has utterly rejected us,
> Thou art very wroth against us.[1]

The prophets were sure that it was the Jews who had let Jehovah down.

[1] Lamentations 5:19-22.

143

They were articulate, and managed to record a great number and variety of sins and backslidings. Some are the kind of sin we have noted before—whoring after strange gods, lapses in following the Law—but many are lapses in conduct of the sort Western tradition generally recognizes as immoral. The prophets do write in a figurative and lofty style of a kind likely to throw off the modern realist; but it seems possible that often when they talk of whoring they mean it unfiguratively. Here, at any rate, is a sampling from Jeremiah:

Why then is this people of Jerusalem slidden back by a perpetual backsliding? they hold fast deceit, they refuse to return. I hearkened and heard, but they spake not aright: no man repenteth him of his wickedness, saying, What have I done? every one turned to his course, as a horse that rusheth headlong in battle. Yea, the stork in the heaven knoweth her appointed times; and the turtle and the swallow and the crane observe the time of their coming; but my people know not the judgment of the Lord. How do ye say, We are wise, and the law of the Lord is with us? But, behold, the false pen of the scribes hath wrought falsely. The wise men are ashamed, they are dismayed and taken: lo, they have rejected the word of the Lord; and what manner of wisdom is in them? Therefore will I give their wives unto others, and their fields to them that shall inherit them: for every one from the least even unto the greatest is given to covetousness, from the prophet even unto the priest every one dealeth falsely. And they have healed the hurt of the daughter of my people lightly, saying, Peace, peace; when there is no peace. Were they ashamed when they had committed abomination? nay, they were not at all ashamed, neither could they blush: therefore shall they fall among them that fall: in the time of their visitation they shall be cast down.[2]

The·logic would be neat indeed: Jehovah is punishing the Jews, not because they transgressed the Law as of old understood, but because their very concept of Jehovah and the Law as theirs and theirs alone was a sin against the one true universal God of all men. I do not think that even Isaiah thought explicitly in this way—there are those who hold that he was mainly concerned with international politics, being pro-Assyrian and anti-Egyptian—and yet somehow he *did* make the leap from the tribal to the universal.

Ye are my witnesses, saith the Lord, and my servant whom I have chosen: that ye may know and believe me, and understand that I am he; before me there was no God formed, neither shall there be after me. I, even I, am the Lord; and beside me there is no saviour.[3]

[2] Jeremiah 8:5-12. The first few chapters of Jeremiah are a good specimen of prophetic moral writing, less lofty than Isaiah, but still hardly earth-bound. Eric Hoffer has dared suggest that the prophets were the first revolutionary intellectuals. The new labor-saving device of the alphabet, he argues, produced a new class of intellectuals who could not find employment, and who were thus "alienated" and turned to attack on, not support of, existing ways. *Pacific Spectator,* Vol. X (1956), p. 7.
[3] Isaiah 43:10-11.

Here, however, the next turn is clear. This one universal God has chosen the Jews in a different sense from the old way of Jehovah, chosen them to lead the other peoples to Him.

> For Zion's sake will I not hold my peace, and for Jerusalem's sake I will not rest, until her righteousness go forth as brightness, and her salvation as a lamp that burneth. And the nations shall see thy righteousness, and all kings thy glory: and thou shalt be called by a new name, which the mouth of the Lord shall name. Thou shalt also be a crown of beauty in the hand of the Lord, and a royal diadem in the hand of thy God. Thou shalt no more be termed Forsaken; neither shall thy land any more be termed Desolate:[4]

There is no use insisting on the obvious: we are not here in the midst of the eighteenth-century Enlightenment and its cosmopolitan rationalist theory. Isaiah's God was, at least during the process of adjustment after this victory, going to behave toward these now momentarily triumphant gentiles much the way jealous old Jehovah behaved toward backsliders.

> And kings shall be thy nursing fathers, and their queens thy nursing mothers: they shall bow down to thee with their faces to the earth, and lick the dust of thy feet; and thou shalt know that I am the Lord, and they that wait for me shall not be ashamed. Shall the prey be taken from the mighty, or the lawful captives be delivered? But thus saith the Lord, Even the captives of the mighty shall be taken away, and the prey of the terrible shall be delivered: for I will contend with him that contendeth with thee, and I will save thy children. And I will feed them that oppress thee with their own flesh; and they shall be drunken with their own blood, as with sweet wine: and all flesh shall know that I the Lord am thy saviour, and thy redeemer, the Mighty One of Jacob.[5]

Here, then, are already the broad foundation lines of the Christian interpretation of man's fate: one universal righteous God, sinful and disobedient men who transgress God's ways, God's plan to set up a minority as an example of men who do not so transgress, and who will be rewarded for setting this example, not only by winning the world, but by winning eternal salvation in the next world. I have deliberately and I dare say successfully put this last flatly and with no spark. It was, as we all know, put in splendid language that did justify God's ways to man. Cherished and developed in the Jewish communities within the world of Greco-Roman culture we have just studied, given added intensity by the concept of a single earthly leader, the Messiah, who should do what the prophets had said would be done, the Word seems already clear: it is a universalist high ethical monotheism.

4 Isaiah 62:1-4.
5 Isaiah 49:23-26.

The successors of the Babylonian exiles did come back to Jerusalem. David and Solomon had no heirs, but Jewry was not yet wholly dispersed. Babylonian gave way to Persian hegemony, Persian to Greek, Greek to Roman, but the Jews lived on in Palestine, a Palestine increasingly made part of this Levantine One World of trade, war, politics, increasingly subject to inflow and outflow of men and ideas. The Jews responded variously. A few of the ruling classes accepted assimilation to Greek and later Roman ways. The best known of these is the Herod who ruled at the time of the birth of Christ, a kinglet who formed part of the elaborate chain of Roman control of the East. Jews had already begun, not the forced later migration known as the Diaspora, but individual migration to the great cities of the Empire, still chiefly in the East. Of these, many learned, as did Saul of Tarsus, a great deal of Greece and Greek ways, without ceasing to think of themselves as Jews, and without ceasing to follow the Law. At the opposite extreme there were groups that lived apart in intensified and perhaps quite altered Jewishness. The recent discovery of the so-called Dead Sea scrolls—a discovery that by the wide interest it has aroused throughout the West at least casts some doubt as to the worrier's complaint that we have all quite forgotten the Bible—has focused attention on the Essenes. These seem to have been communists who lived together in brotherly sharing and simplicity in quiet places, rejecting the worldly ways of the Greco-Roman Levant, yet contemplating a better world that might yet be the world of the prophets. From these and other "advanced" groups, perhaps through Persian and Hindu influences that they would for the most part have denied indignantly, there came into Jewish religious life a much more strongly emphasized concept of an afterlife, of sin, repentance, and cleansing. There came, also, a heightening, or at least a broadening into wider circles of the Jewish people, of the prophets' conception of a Saviour, a Messiah (the anointed one, in Greek, *Christos*), a conception that still arouses scholarly debate over its origins, development, and degree of acceptance among the Jews before the birth of Christ.

There were also people whose place and reputation in Jewish history is very different from the place they occupy in our New Testament. The Pharisees carry through Western history a quite undeserved reputation for wickedness. They were old-fashioned religious conservatives, upholders of the decencies of the Law, distrustful of innovation and of what the eighteenth century called "enthusiasm" in religion, but surely not more wicked, not more insensitive, not even more self-satisfied than such folk (who come out badly in the history of ideas in the West) usually are. They were probably no more hypocrites than are any other high-minded routine conservatives. Jesus shocked their sense of decency, and, perhaps even more important, seemed to them by his conduct to be making for Roman armed intervention. Let us note that heroism in a satellite nation can have consequences most unpleasant for the many who are not heroes.

II

There were, then, Jewish beliefs, attitudes, and experiences which anticipate, make possible, prepare the way for, Christianity. The Greco-Roman world, too, found much of Christianity familiar. Something like monotheism was well established, at least, quite well known, among the educated classes, in both East and West. It was indeed a deistic or pantheistic, and not very fervent, belief in one God, and it was hardly worship—merely poetry and philosophy. Lucan has Cato the Stoic say:

All that we see is God; every motion we make is God also. Men who doubt and are ever uncertain of future events—let *them* cry out for prophets: I draw my assurance from no oracle but the sureness of death. The timid and the brave must fall alike; the god has said this, and it is enough.[6]

Still, such beliefs are a long way from pagan polytheism. Even closer parallels with Christian ethics can be found. The motto of Epictetus, "Suffer and renounce," is Stoic, but also Christian. Nietzsche, at least, might find what he thought the perverse Christian pride of the humble in Epictetus's "How do I treat those whom you admire and honor? Is it not like slaves? Do not all, when they see me, think they see their lord and king?"[7] Long ago Plato had Socrates say in the *Crito* that "we ought not to retaliate or render evil for evil to anyone, whatever evil we may have suffered from him." It is true that he went on to add, "this opinion has never been held, and never will be held, by any considerable number of persons." Is this last, too, perhaps not wholly incompatible with the facts of Christian life?[8]

Such parallels, it must be insisted, are abundant. Their study is often interesting and even useful, but a listing of them is no more an explanation of Christianity than a listing of Shakespeare's sources is an explanation of Shakespeare. We cannot here go into the many problems of early church his-

[6] Lucan, *The Civil War*, trans. by J. D. Duff, London, Heinemann, 1928, Loeb Classical Library, Vol. IX, p. 580.
[7] Epictetus, *Discourses*, iii. 22. Quoted in L. Friedländer, *Roman Life and Manners under the Early Empire*, Vol. III, pp. 272-273.
[8] *Crito*, 49, *The Dialogues of Plato*, trans. by B. Jowett, New York, Macmillan, 1892, Vol. II.

tory, the sources of Christian theology and ritual, and much else essential to the study of Christianity.[9] From the point of view of the outsider, Christianity is in all its aspects, from the purely theological through the ethical to the details of liturgy and church government, a syncretic faith; the elements are all there, ready to hand. But the putting together was a remarkable achievement in making something new.

On what the triumph of Christianity meant for the moral life of the West, there has, at least since with the Renaissance anti-Christian sentiments could come out in the open, been warm debate. We may simplify a bit, and distinguish two kinds of attack on Christian moral achievement. The first, typically that of modern high-minded rationalism of the Enlightenment, takes the position that, though most or even all of Christian ethics is good, Christianity has failed dismally to make them prevail in the real world, largely because of its wicked priesthood, who developed and spread its absurd theology. The second, that represented, but by no means exhausted, by Nietzsche, takes the position that Christian ethical principles are in themselves bad—low and ignoble—but seem, unfortunately, to have been sufficiently successful to prevent the prevailing of the true good. We shall have to return to both these positions in later chapters, for they form an important part of Western moral history. Here we need but note them briefly.

The late J. M. Robertson, a kindly and fervent freethinker, will do well to point up the first attitude.[10] Robertson works hard to show that established Christianity by no means made the morals of the Roman Empire any better than they had been under the pagans, indeed, made some human conduct worse. Slavery was not abolished; what there was of improvement in the workings of the institution was due to pagan philosophers and pagan lawyers. The Christians did not stop the gladiatorial games, in spite of the noise the Fathers made about them; the games withered on the vine as the economy of the Empire declined to the point where they could not be supported. In an

[9] I have dealt summarily with some of these matters in Chapter V of my *Ideas and Men* (New York, Prentice-Hall, 1950), and have made reading suggestions on p. 567 of that book. See also M. Hadas, "Plato in Hellenistic Fusion," *Journal of the History of Ideas,* Vol. XIX, January 1958, p. 3.

[10] "Freethinker" is not the perfect word, but apparently there is no single word to gather together the materialists, positivists, rationalists, deists, "humanists," ethical culturalists, Unitarians, agnostics, believers in natural science as a religion, anticlericals, Marxists, and the rest. You may say that these all stand for different beliefs; yet the variations among them are hardly greater than among Christians who have broken with Rome, and for these we have an accepted blanket word: "Protestant." I propose generally throughout this book to use for these groups from eighteenth-century deists to twentieth-century Marxist-Leninists the blanket word "Enlightened," duly capitalized.

analogous way, slavery itself declined in the Middle Ages—not because of Christian doctrine. Sex morals were not improved. The insanities of early monasticism actually meant worse, more perverse, sexual conduct. This all leads up to the familiar attack by Gibbon: Christian contempt for this world led to the disastrous failure of civic morality and of military capacity, and to the fall of the Empire.[11]

Those who claim to reject Christian ethics entirely are wilder men. Some, indeed, are no more than admirers of what they think those admirable Greeks of the fifth century B.C. were like; in the opinion of these classical humanists from the Renaissance on, Christianity destroyed the ideals and the practice of the beautiful-and-good. But more recent attackers go far beyond this, and find that Christian ethics is the prevailing of the weak over the strong, a flying in the face of Darwin, "slave morality," an exaltation of Mediterranean vices above Nordic virtues, and more, too much more, to the same effect.

It is hard for anyone in the West, Christian, anti-Christian, or, if such there be, skeptic, to write about Christian morals without being influenced at all by the long controversies that have been the life of Christianity. I shall do my best, with a few further words of warning. First, the inevitable problem of effective generalization from varied concrete instances comes up sharply in any use of the word "Christianity." Since for centuries all Westerners were in a formal sense Christian, the actual conduct of men called "Christians" has run the gamut of Western capacities, which are many and varied, and seems to have been fully exploited. It is at least clear that many different beliefs, many different human personalities, many different kinds of conduct—some of them in conventional logical use actually antithetical—have been given "Christian" as an attribute. There are those, some of whom would claim to be Christians, who find an antithesis between Jesus and Paul, at the very beginnings of Christian history. I shall rarely mean by Christian *all* men known as Christians. I shall try to make clear when I am dealing with most, many, or even average ordinary Christians, when I am dealing with exceptional Christians, and when I am trying to set up a Christian type, or ideal, or pattern.

Second, Christianity began as an apolitical movement, indeed, as a quite

[11] Robertson, *Short History of Morals,* Part IV, Chap. I. Gibbon himself was not above the effort to have his cake and eat it: "The religion of Constantine, achieved, in less than a century, the final conquest of the Roman Empire; but the victors themselves were insensibly subdued by the arts of their vanquished rivals. *"The Decline and Fall of the Roman Empire,* ed. by J. B. Bury, New York, Macmillan, 1914, Vol. III, p. 227.

literally unworldly, even antiworldly, movement of protest, and became within a few generations an established church, with its own government, its own property, its own hierarchy, increasingly and in the end inextricably woven into the whole texture of organized, governed, working Western society. Perhaps just because its original ethical tone, still clearly put in many a New Testament passage for all to read, is so completely unworldly—or millennial, or Utopian, or spiritual—later Christian adaptation to this world has seemed a particularly glaring instance of the gap between word and deed. Christian attitudes toward wealth make a familiar instance, especially dear to Enlightened anti-Christians of the eighteenth century and after; these critics were more than willing to admit that the church had indeed achieved one miracle—many a camel had gone through the needle's eye since Christ had advised the rich young man to give up his wealth.[12]

Yet Christians—a St. Francis, and many another—have said quite as harsh things about a church that enjoyed wealth, power, display, pride, that gave by its whole existence the lie to the good news of the gospels, a church that seemed to accept this world in all its ethical imperfections. You will not understand the Christian tradition, nor the twist the Enlightenment gave that tradition, if you do not realize that the violent—yes, *violent*—repudiation of the wickedness of ordinary human nature and of the society in which ordinary human nature has full and free play has never quite been suppressed in Christianity. The threat, or the promise, of a newborn, millennial society is always there. Christianity has never, for long, ceased to be a revolutionary faith for the few; nor has it, for long, ceased to be a consoling, conservative, routine faith for the many. But even that routine has not for long lapsed into moral depths like that of Renaissance Rome without provoking rebellion.

Finally, the good Christian has always had, at least until quite recently, still another spur to activity, to something more than routine acceptance of whatever exists. Christianity is a monopolistic faith in that, like the later Judaism and Islam, it claims to be the one true faith, a faith destined to prevail for all on earth. The Christian wants to spread Christianity and he has often spread it with the sword; moreover, he wants the right kind of Christianity, his own, and he will insure the prevailing of the right kind with an Inquisition. Another glaring repudiation of all that Jesus came to say and do? Another use of religion to cloak what *really* makes the missionary spirit, the desire for wealth and power? Again, the anti-Christian—and the uneasy, the rebellious, the saintly Christian, surely often his brother under the skin—

[12] Matthew 19:16-24.

150

distort and oversimplify our human dilemma, our human tragedy. Christianity is an uneasy, a tragic, an impossible faith, in high tension between the real and the ideal, the "is" and the "ought"—that is one of the sources of its strength; above all, that is how it came to spawn its long string of heretics, from Tertullian to Marx and Lenin.

It is perhaps easier, though more dangerous, to begin with the general than with the particular. Christian concepts of ethics are related to how the believer thought and felt about the universe; and such thought and feeling are related to the temper of the Greco-Roman world in the first century A.D., to the conditions of living, not just to the "mode of production," in that modern, troubled time. We are dealing in big, vague, imprecise terms; but it looks as though there was in the first century A.D. a *need* for Christianity, in as rigorous a meaning for that somewhat disputed word "need" as the social psychologist can give it.

The commonplaces, once more, are unavoidable. Christianity brought consolation to the unhappy, satisfaction—some of it, through communistic sharing, material satisfaction—to the poor and deprived, meaning and excitement to the bored, adjustment, if I may speak the language of our time, to the maladjusted. Christianity was in its origins a proletarian movement, a religion for the humble, for the weak, but, notably, as Nietzsche himself, I suspect, really knew, for the fiercely rebellious humble, the violent weak. It became very rapidly, as we have just noted, also a religion for the strong, even for the proud, with no more of paradox or of inconsistency than is the way of this world. Individuals, many of whom sincerely felt themselves to be Christians, have enjoyed wealth and power and conducted their lives in ways the man watcher has to note as *logically* irreconcilable with the ethics of the Sermon on the Mount. Yet many Christians at all times have clearly been aware of the origins and the spirit of their religion. Christianity, to revert to the abstract, has never ceased to do what it set out to do, to give to the meek their inheritance of the earth, the poor in spirit their kingdom of heaven. Christianity is indeed, as Marx should have known, since he was so representative a Judaeo-Christian revolutionary, the food of the people. It has filled, nourished, quieted them; but it has also at times stimulated them just because it fed them, prodded them on in the eternal, impossible Christian endeavor. We are back at the Sermon on the Mount.

The need for religion in the early years of the Roman One World is certainly not to be established statistically, nor by any retrospective poll of opinion. We do know that there were at the time a great number of competing

151

cults, a welter of cults, a variety worthy of our own day. This fact alone would establish the need. But we can perhaps go a bit further in defining the need. Some of it, surely, was the need of the deprived, the physical suffering of the poor, the starving, the beaten slave, the slum dweller of the great cities, cities of hundreds of thousands almost without what we call public utilities and with hardly more of what we call social services. For them the Christian communities, as we shall see, gave concrete material aid. We cannot be sure that there were relatively more of the physically deprived in this Greco-Roman world than, say, in the world of Hesiod, or of earlier agricultural communities. Since nothing like our own industrial revolution and use of power-driven machinery added to the total economic productivity of this Greco-Roman society, it may be that the poor really did become poorer as the Greco-Roman One World developed after the second century B.C. But we can be quite sure that many of the social supports, the traditional steady ways, the routine, unthinking acceptance of the human as well as the natural environment, which go with small rural communities, and which are the *real* and natural "opium of the people," were lost to the slum dweller of Alexandria, Antioch, Corinth, and Rome.

Nor did the physically adequately nourished in this society always have the equivalent of those traditional comforting supports. We Americans, unfortunately, are likely to be naïve believers in a crude economic interpretation of history; in spite of the evidence about us, we believe that collective human action of a revolutionary sort—and early Christianity was such revolutionary action—must spring from a sense of purely physical, purely economic, deprivation. But what millions of at least adequately fed and housed human beings in the Greco-Roman world seem to have suffered from was spiritual deprivation. They could not wring religious meaning out of the Olympic pantheon; the gods were not really any better off than *they* were; they could not feel for the Empire, nor for the no-longer-free polis, nor for any political entity, satellite or the like, the emotions men need to feel. Stoicism was enough for some; but, unorganized, with no ritual, no communion, not indeed, a religion at all, less so than the least sacramental and communal of our own contemporary secular or surrogate religions, no more than a philosophy, Stoicism was not a faith for the many. This was a big, busy, still-growing society, unstable certainly at the imperial level, a society in which men moved about a good deal, a society in which, had there been sociologists and social psychologists, there would have been a good deal written about social mobility, rootlessness, lack of inner direction, frustration, lack of community, and even, I feel sure, about the obvious alienation of the intellectuals.

I shall insist on what I have just written; millions of rich, moderately well-to-do, and just ordinary men and women suffered in those days from spiritual deprivation. But if a reader cannot find meaning in that word "spiritual," I am willing to use the language of the hard-boiled. Millions of such men and women suffered from anxiety, from a feeling of insecurity, from sheer boredom. Theirs was a society in which the established groupings of human beings, which were also rankings, assignments of accepted status, were in part, and in very significant part, especially in the cities of the Mediterranean coasts, breaking down and leaving the individual, a human being, almost identical, as Cicero said, with other human beings. Theirs was, in our language, a society with a strong egalitarian and individualistic drive, a society in which individuals *felt* they were not born to a place, but had to make a place for themselves.

I exaggerate deliberately. There were many, many spots, not all, by any means, backwaters, in the Greco-Roman world where the old reassuring steady ways continued. Many men and women, even in the great cities, must have gone on quietly doing, believing, being, what their ancestors had done, believed, and been. They crop up to the end, even among the literary, an Ausonius, a Sidonius, an Ammianus Marcellinus. But read—and it is fine reading—those few specimens of the social historian's treasured source, approximations to the novel, which we have from those days, the *Satyricon* of Petronius and the *Golden Ass* of Apuleius, and add for good measure some skits of Lucian's. You will, I think, conclude that this was a world in which ordinary men and women did feel uprooted. Poor Trimalchio, for all his self-won wealth, if not, indeed, because of it, was at least as insecure as anyone Arthur Koestler ever drew.

To the poor, the bored, the unhappy, and, let us never forget, to the men of good will, to the ambitious, to those extraordinary men the professional revolutionary leaders, those organizers of disorganization, as well as to their successors, the reorganizers of organization, and, in a sense most important of all, to the millions who did what others did, the joiners, the conformists, the accepters of fashion (without whom there would be no fashion)—to all of these Christianity brought meaning, and opportunity. H. L. Mencken puts it neatly: "Try to imagine two evangelists on a street-corner in Corinth or Ephesus, one expounding the Nicomachaean Ethics [of Aristotle] or a homily by Valentinus the Gnostic and the other reciting the Sermon on the Mount or the Twenty-third Psalm; certainly it is not hard to guess which would fetch the greater audience of troubled and seeking men."[13] Christianity—I must repeat that I am writing from a historical-naturalistic point of view—in its first days satisfied the needs and gave scope for the gifts of many different kinds of men—Christ himself, John the Evangelist, Peter, Paul, the many now unknown who must have contributed to the canon of the New Testament.

An ethic is always closely related to an attempt to understand the universe, to a theology, a cosmology, or, at the very least, to water such great concerns down as much as they ever can be, a *Weltanschauung,* or world view. Christian ethics could hardly be what they are and have been had Christianity not given the kind of answers it did to the problems that troubled the men and women of the first century A.D. Of first importance for understanding the extreme *anti*worldliness of early Christianity is the doctrine of the Second Coming. The first Christian Jews, as we have noted above, were prepared for a Messiah, for a leader who would carry out the word of the Hebrew prophets. As Christianity spread to the gentiles, the doctrine of the Messiah who was to restore Zion was transmuted into the doctrine of the risen Christ who was to return shortly indeed at the end of this world, at the final judgment day, when the saved should enter on an inheritance of eternal bliss, the damned on one of eternal misery. Christ himself is authority: "Verily I say unto you, there be some of them that stand here, which shall in no wise taste of death, till they see the Son of man coming in his kingdom."[14]

Now to many of us, perhaps born tough-minded, but certainly molded by a culture in which such dominant strains as philosophic rationalism, instrumentalism, and the practice of natural science are most unfavorable to Messianic beliefs of just this sort—that is, to beliefs based on a supernatural Saviour and an interruption of the ordinary natural regularities—the doctrine of the Second Coming is incomprehensible nonsense.[15] Yet if you really

---

[13] *Treatise on Right and Wrong,* p. 181. I have no space for the interesting subject of what the competing cults brought, and why Christianity won out over them. Broadly, Christianity brought everything they did, and more, notably a more immediate, concrete promise of salvation and a much better-served, better-organized, better-loved Church Militant. I refer the reader to the books I suggest on p. 567 of *Ideas and Men* and on this topic especially to two of the older ones, Franz Cumont, *The Oriental Religions in Roman Paganism,* and T. R. Glover, *The Conflict of Religions in the Early Roman Empire.*

[14] Matthew 16:28. The Synoptic Gospels are in agreement on this point.

[15] The above was written not with irony, merely with caution. Messianic, or at least Utopian, beliefs of another sort, based on eighteenth-century belief in the natural goodness and reasonableness of man, still survive the twentieth-century intellectual climate, though I think they are wilting a bit.

thought and felt, were really sure, that to secure, even to desire, what your appetites seek vigorously in this world—food, drink, sexual satisfaction, right on through the long list of satisfactions of the flesh, and of the spirit guided by the flesh—were to mean eternal pain, very soon and very surely, you would not be much attracted by the doctrine of the Golden Mean. You could not tell yourself comfortably that you were avoiding in matters of sex, for instance, the neurotic extremes of Don Juan on one hand and of St. Anthony on the other. You would almost certainly do your best to imitate St. Anthony.

We know that even in our own world, in which it is still easy and fashionable to be worldly, there are men and women who reject the world. Our psychiatrists tell us that—to continue the specific, concrete example of matters sexual—some individuals they, and we, consider abnormal find that the act of sexual intercourse is repugnant, impossible, hateful. All that is needed to get back to the early Christians is to add "immoral." The problem of understanding the origins of Christian ethical extremes of repudiation of "normal" and "natural" satisfactions of appetite is not one of finding individual ascetics. The Stoics, even the Epicureans, furnished plenty of such individuals. It is to explain why such extremes got incorporated in a great universalist faith, became *fashionable,* to use an accurate word with no derogatory intent. One can give a vague sociological answer of the sort I have tried to give above: in a sophisticated egalitarian world the very fact of luxury and self-indulgence in a small privileged class cast discredit on the flesh, bred a contrary asceticism. St. Anthony is a delayed response to Messalina; the decencies of ordinary Christian self-control are healthy human reactions against the self-indulgence of the masses with their "bread and circuses."[16]

Yet the historian must not quite dismiss the accident of greatness. In these earliest formative years Christian asceticism or antiworldliness may have taken on its extreme form in part because of the personalities of the men who made it so much more than another Jewish splinter group. It may even be that Christianity has had such heavy but on the whole remarkably successful going with some of the facts of life because that extraordinary revolutionary tamer of revolution, St. Paul, held that it is better to marry than to burn —and held, also, that even those who desired to speak with tongues should do so decently and in order.[17]

16 Anthony is, of course, much later. Reference books date him hopefully 250?-350? By this time the belief in an immediate Second Coming had probably lessened greatly; earlier ascetics would not have felt the need to go to the desert, in their view as impermanent as Alexandria itself.
17 I Corinthians 7:9 and 14:39, 40.

The first Christians were not—at least, many of them were not—respectable people, above all, not tame, moderate, controlled bourgeois. The perpetual indignation with which, during the last few hundred years, idealistic Christians and idealistic anti-Christians have proclaimed and deplored the obvious fact that most Christians are respectable and even, in the West, bourgeois has surely a justification and explanation; Christianity is in origin a religion of protest against the ordinary life of men on earth, against *l'homme moyen sensuel* and all his works. Some of what St. Paul reproaches the congregation at Corinth with is the disorderly enthusiasm, the emotional running amok, the Holy Rollerism and camp-meeting frenzies we Americans know so well. We know it so well that we still have the folk belief that many a child, not always a legitimate child, has been conceived in the pious excitement of camp meeting. Men—and saints—like Paul, who prize order, know well that other men need curbing. They know that sex is a strong and potentially dangerous appetite that can lead to jealousy, fighting, disturbances of all sorts. They know that man really is not what the hopeful made of Aristotle's famous phrase, a "political animal" in the sense the philosophic anarchist gives the words, an animal whose appetites, desires, impulses, lead him automatically to the ethically and communally good. Christian ethics *do* repress, surely in part because the early Christians, perhaps a bit more than the run of mankind, needed repressing.

In our day, when Christianity, even among the seekers, is most respectable, the violent rebelliousness of early Christianity needs underlining. Many of these Christian men and women, in spite of the ethics of gentleness clearly present in their canons of belief, were firmly, ferociously, unparadoxically tough. They were not, even at their gentlest, "liberals," rationalists, humanitarians, not, let me underline and repeat, not *respectable*. They could hate as well as love, and both fiercely. The first ascetics did not go to the desert as a social service; they went there because of a great disgust. It took a long time to transmute that disgust to love, love for one's fellows as they are. There are those who hold that the transmuting has never been complete in Christianity.

Nietzsche, of course, felt this profound early Christian revulsion against things as they are, above all, against men as they are, and sympathized with it more than he liked to admit. Established Christianity was to spread its net as widely as Western life at its fullest and most varied. Nietzsche was no historian, and he was quite wrong in identifying all Christianity with what he called "slave-morality," the revolt of the weak against the strong. But the element of revolt is there, unmistakable, irrational, as mad a transvaluation of values as any the West has experienced. One little detail: the "poor" of the famous phrase we know as the "poor in spirit" is, in New Testament Greek, the word πτωχός, *ptochos*, or cringer, hence beggar, a damning word indeed, not the more usual πένης, *penes*, the working poor man, a word no more scornful than most such by which we in the West commonly reflect our daily disagreement with the spirit of the Sermon on the Mount. But the good news remains literally: blessed are the cringing, the cowering, the beggars, in spirit.

The Goodspeed "American translation" makes this "blessed are those who feel their spiritual need." Talk about bowdlerizing! Liddell and Scott comment on πτωχός, "the word . . . always had a bad sense until it was ennobled in the Gospels." They are right, and Nietzsche wrong: the πτωχοὶ τῷ πνεύματι, become the poor in spirit or even those who feel their spiritual need, have indeed been ennobled. But they seem hardly cringers any more; they are Bernard of Clairvaux, Innocent III, Loyola, Calvin, Jonathan Edwards. They are not even any longer near those mystical quietist goals, *theoria, ataraxia,* nirvana.[18]

III

I have in the preceding pages done violence to the modern principle that "facts" should first of all be established before they are discussed. Actually, the facts of early Christian asceticism, otherworldliness, revulsion against pagan license are well-established. And they are extremes, heroic extremes— so heroic that calmer leadership soon got to work to tame them. St. Simeon Stylites will do as one example, up there on his pillar sixty feet high in the Syrian sun (the top does appear to have been railed in) eating, drinking, sleeping, defecating—all very little—and preaching a great deal year upon year. The excesses of the monastics suggest, indeed, that the old Greek spirit of the agon had been transferred to a sport that would hardly have appealed to the Greeks of Pericles's Athens.

The ideal of antiworldliness in conventional Christianity is hard enough for the innocent rationalist to accept; monasticism even in its tempered later Western form with the Benedictines must seem to him regrettable nonsense. We should have no difficulty understanding why the amazing feats of the

---

[18] The verse is Matthew 5:3. The Goodspeed *New Testament: An American Translation,* Chicago, University of Chicago Press, 1923; Liddell and Scott, Greek-English Lexicon, 8th ed., revised, New York, Harpers, 1897, s.v., πτωχός, p. 1342.

earlier monks and hermits disgusted historians like Lecky, formed without benefit of Freud.

There is, perhaps, no phase in the moral history of mankind of a deeper or more painful interest than this ascetic epidemic. A hideous, sordid, and emaciated maniac, without knowledge, without patriotism, without natural affection, passing his life in a long routine of useless and atrocious self-torture, and quailing before the ghastly phantoms of his delirious brain, had become the ideal of the nations which had known the writings of Plato and Cicero and the lives of Socrates and Cato. For about two centuries, the hideous maceration of the body was regarded as the highest proof of excellence. St. Jerome declares, with a thrill of admiration, how he had seen a monk, who for thirty years had lived exclusively on a small portion of barley bread and of muddy water; another, who lived in a hole and never ate more than five figs for his daily repast; a third, who cut his hair only on Easter Sunday, who never washed his clothes, who never changed his tunic till it fell to pieces, who starved himself till his eyes grew dim, and his skin "like pumice and stone," and whose merits, shown by these austerities, Homer himself would be unable to recount.[19]

Lecky himself goes on recounting instance after instance. They have the accuracy, and the misleading quality, of any modern series of *faits divers* and horror stories. It is unfair, and unsound psychologically, to equate St. Simeon Stylites and Kelly the flagpole sitter, the record-breaking monk with the record-breaking sophomore. Yet there is a simple residue of truth in such comparisons. Early Christian asceticism does display this element of paradox, the obvious willingness of the man who flees the world to accept the wondering attention of the world. These mortifiers of the flesh look in the long perspective of Christian experience to be dangerously close to the great Christian sin of pride. They are, however, in some sense victims of the thirst of the masses for wonders and wonder-workers.

Yet the outsider may be safer if he notes simply that historical Christianity has always produced men, women, and movements that reach out and over the bounds of any disciplined good, even the good of humility, into the wilds, the depths. At any rate, there is no use in our adding to the rationalist horror of the *philosophes* at the spectacle of the filth-covered anchorite the smug satisfaction of popularized psychiatry at so evident a display of its rightness. It does not seem enough to appeal to any of the catchwords, not even to "psychosis." At most, we may concede to modern intellectual fashion that the anchorites who fled the world were maladjusted in that world, perhaps that their flight was a sublimation of drives frustrated in that world.

[19] W.E.H. Lecky, *History of European Morals*, Vol. II, pp. 107-108.

Later, more disciplined monasticism may even look to some of us a morally better sublimation for frustrated virtue and consequent great moral disgust than, shall we say, writing a newspaper column.

The rush to the desert—it really was almost a rush—must seem in part a fashion, a minor mass movement in which many took part because men are imitative animals. But the leaders would have been sure that God had sent them to the desert that they might bring home to their fellows how sinful the world had grown, how much in need of no mere reform, no mere preaching, no mere conferences, but of root-and-branch destruction of the cancerous growth of worldliness. Perhaps we can leave it at that.

Of course, not even at the height of the movement to the desert were the masses of Christians involved. For us it is perhaps more important to try to estimate what degree of personal asceticism, of repudiation of the world of the flesh, penetrated into the rank and file. Clearly no good answer is possible, but it seems likely that in the first few centuries the drive of Christian asceticism did go wider and deeper than it has gone since, save perhaps in such renewals of this element of Christianity as Calvinist Puritanism—and Calvinism, as we shall see, was not ascetic after the manner of the early Christians. This early asceticism trusted no appetite, not even the simple appetite for food. When Tertullian writes that "through love of eating love of impurity finds passage," we may well believe that many of the faithful did find all bodily enjoyments dangerous, all potential passages for evil.[20]

Christian asceticism, then, is real and extensive. Certainly most Christians did not pursue the ideal into saintly depths. But the tone, the coloration, of ordinary lives was altered from the tone that had been imparted by the very effort of the pagans to attain the beautiful-and-good. A dignified, rhetorical, but, one feels, sincere avowal of Christian asceticism comes out in the poetry —classical in form—of the convert Paulinus:

Time was when, not with equal force, but with equal ardor, I could join with thee in summoning the deaf Phoebus [Apollo] from his cave in Delphi. . . . Now another force, a mightier God, subdues my soul. He forbids me give up my time to the vanities of leisure or business, and the literature of the fable, that I may obey his laws and see his light, which is darkened by the cunning skill of the sophist, and the figments of the poet who fills the soul with vanity and falsehood, and only trains the tongue.[21]

20 Tertullian, *De Jejunis*, Chap. I.
21 *Carmina*, x: 22.30. Quoted and translated in Dill, *Roman Society in the Last Century of the Western Empire*, p. 398.

Paulinus found "business" a vanity. We come to the old accusation that Christianity unmanned men, and women, and made them unfit for the world's work. It is true that the monks fled this world in all its aspects. It is probably true that for some centuries Christianity did turn many less radical rebels against the daily round of duty done—civic, soldierly duty. Tertullian can always be trusted to blurt it out plain: *nec ulla magis res aliena, quam publica.*[22] The first Christians were pacifists of a sort, pacifists who would not fight worldly fights. There are classic texts in the Sermon on the Mount:

Blessed are the peacemakers: for they shall be called children of God.

but I say unto you, Resist not him that is evil: but whosoever smiteth thee on thy right cheek, turn to him the other also.

but I say unto you, Love your enemies, bless them that persecute you:[23]

Paul himself occasionally sounds like a moderate pacifist:

Render to no man evil for evil. Take thought of things honourable in the sight of all men. If it be possible, as much as in you lieth, be at peace with all men. Avenge not yourselves, beloved, but give place unto wrath: for it is written, Vengeance belongeth unto me; I will repay, saith the Lord. But if thine enemy hunger, feed him; if he thirst, give him to drink: for in so doing thou shalt heap coals of fire upon his head. Be not overcome of evil, but overcome evil with good.[24]

Yet Christianity was not and is not faith in passive resistance, to say nothing of Laodicaean or skeptical lying down before the facts of life. The charge to the apostles is the familiar text to bring up against the Sermon on the Mount:

Think not that I am come to send peace on the earth: I came not to send peace, but a sword. For I came to set a man at variance against his father, and the daughter against her mother, and the daughter in law against her mother in law: and a man's foes shall be they of his own household. He that loveth father or mother more than me is not worthy of me; and he that loveth son or daughter more than me is not worthy of me.[25]

We have to get beyond the balancing of texts one against another, Christians for the most part have never really believed that the truths of their faith

[22] "No thing more alien [to the Christian] than the public thing." Tertullian, *Apologeticus*, Chap. 38.3.
[23] Matthew 5:9, 39, 44.
[24] Romans 12:17-21.
[25] Matthew 10:34-37.

would impose themselves magically on the wicked of the world. The many figures of struggle, even of fighting with the sword, so obvious in the New Testament and among the Fathers, we know historically turned out to be no mere figures of speech. At least as early as the Arian controversy at the end of the third century Christians were resorting to bodily violence to further the work of God. Such conduct ought not to surprise and shock us as it appeared to surprise and shock the Victorians.[26]

It is a clear induction from Western history that the old spirit of the Homeric agon is not subdued but heightened when the individual fights, not primarily or solely for his honor or his prestige, but for the Right, for the word of God, for Fatherland, for the word of Dialectical Materialism. From martyrdom to crusading is but a step, an easy and a natural step, for martyrdom itself is a form of crusading. I do not mean here to make the cheap assertion that the Christian who turns, and keeps turning, the other cheek is merely using "tactics" he will change when he thinks he or his cause will profit. I mean, rather, that the Christian drive toward realizing the good right here on earth is so strong as to amount to a ruling passion; the Christian cannot avoid resisting evil.[27]

Otherworldliness running to the extremes of asceticism and even, among ordinary men, to an indifference to the call of citizenship is surely present in early Christianity. So, too, to complete the catalogue of attitudes alien to most of us today, is what must be called the anti-intellectualism of early Christianity. The later Greco-Roman formal culture, as we have noted above, was strongly tinged with rationalism. Christianity was in the beginning a faith of the poor and humble who disliked and distrusted the higher education and the higher educated of their time; it was a transcendental faith that could not for a moment stomach such fashionable beliefs as Euhemerism nor, perhaps even more repugnant because so high-minded, Stoic or Epicurean deism. The texts are there, St. Paul himself providing some of the best:

If any man thinketh that he is wise among you in this world, let him become a

---

26 See Westermarck, *Origin and Development of the Moral Ideas*, Vol. I, p. 348 ff., and especially his back reference to Lecky, p. 349 n. Lecky had argued that it was only the influence of the struggle with Islam that turned the Christian church from merely "condoning" war to "consecrating" it.

27 Note the trouble Matthew 5:39 has always given. The Greek πονηρός, *poneros*, is literally "evil." But the text "resist not evil" has been interpreted commonly as meaning do not resist with actual physical violence the man who is doing an evil thing. The Christian *must* resist evil, regarded as what we moderns would think of as a "force," just as he must hate sin; he must love, as ultimately images of God, all men, sinners or saints. Christianity is an exacting faith.

fool, that he may become wise. For the wisdom of this world is foolishness with God. For it is written, He taketh the wise in their craftiness: and again, The Lord knoweth the thoughts of the wise, that they are vain.[28]

The Fathers are more explicit. Here is the third-century *Didascalia Apostolorum:*

This says bluntly, "Have nothing to do with pagan books," and gives some rather surprising grounds for this injunction. What connection can any Christian have with all the errors they contain? He has the Word of God—what else does he want? The Bible not only provides for the supernatural life but for all cultural need too! Is it history he wants? There are the Books of Kings. Eloquence, poetry? The Prophets! Lyrics? The Psalms! Cosmology? Genesis! Laws, morality? The glorious Law of God! But all these outlandish books that come from the Devil—they must be hurled away.[29]

Yet, fixed though the eyes of the early Christian were on the next world, it is clear that he sought to lessen actual suffering in this one. We moderns should have no trouble recognizing the very real aid and comfort the evangel —in Greek, "good news"—brought simply in terms of psychological satisfaction. Christianity at its minimal was surely a triumph of faith healing not remotely rivaled by the best we moderns have been able to do outside or on the margin of organized Christianity. Whatever their hopes of a Second Coming, the early Christian also took some care of the animal man. The apostles themselves began the communistic sharing of things of this world as of the next which was to be the great strength of the new faith:

And all that believed were together, and had all things common; and they sold their possessions and goods, and parted them to all, according as any man had need. And day by day, continuing stedfastly with one accord in the temple, and breaking bread from house to house, they did take their food with gladness and singleness of heart, praising God, and having favour with all the people. And the Lord added to them day by day those that were being saved.[30]

Charity in something like our modern sense was almost from the first a part of Christian ethics. That it was later taken up into high theology as part of the doctrine of good works does not by any means lessen its reality or its importance. The Calvinists did hold that the Biblical "the poor ye have al-

[28] I Corinthians 3:18-21.
[29] H. I. Marrou, *A History of Education in Antiquity,* p. 320. Marrou on pp. 318-321 handles this subject briefly and thoroughly. For more detail, see C. L. Ellspermann, *The Attitude of the Early Christian Fathers towards Pagan Literature and Learning,* Washington, D.C., Catholic University of America, Patristic Studies, Vol. LXXXII, 1949.
[30] Acts 2:44-47.

ways with you" had an ethical as well as a cosmological implication, poverty being a proper punishment as well as a God-made necessity; in their way, the nineteenth-century utilitarians, who were most dubiously Christian, went even further, holding that charity was both ineffective, for it never really "solved" the problem of poverty, and also most damaging to its recipients, who were kept enough alive to procreate more poor, quite contrary to the intentions of Organic Evolution. But in spite of all this, over the centuries Christian ethics has enjoined the feeding of the hungry, the clothing of the naked, the alleviation of pain, the kindly treatment of the stranger. There *is* a humanitarian strain in Christianity, though there it clearly is feebler, or, at any rate, more resigned, than in the religion of the Enlightenment.

We are back to Nietzsche. Christianity did set up as virtues much that looks in common sense quite the opposite of the warrior virtues of Homer —and of Moses.

Most gladly therefore will I rather glory in my weaknesses, that the strength of Christ may rest upon me. Wherefore I take pleasure in weaknesses, in injuries, in necessities, in persecutions, in distresses, for Christ's sake: for when I am weak, then am I strong.[31]

Christianity did urge that love should replace rivalry; it did seek to lessen the competitiveness of the classical agonistic view of life. In modern terms, there was in early Christianity a strong vein of insistence on what we should call co-operation, altruism, even, perhaps, social security. I must come shortly again to the problem of the paradoxical nature of Christianity; but, for the moment, let me simply say that Christianity does sound firmly a note not so clearly heard before in the West: the note of the agape, the lovefeast, the common weal that is common woe to none, not even the outsider.

The note is sounded most clearly in the Beatitudes, which must be read along with the Ten Commandments:

Blessed are the poor in spirit: for theirs is the kingdom of heaven.
Blessed are they that mourn: for they shall be comforted.
Blessed are the meek: for they shall inherit the earth.
Blessed are they that hunger and thirst after righteousness: for they shall be filled.
Blessed are the merciful: for they shall obtain mercy.
Blessed are the pure in heart: for they shall see God.
Blessed are the peacemakers: for they shall be called children of God.
Blessed are they that have been persecuted for righteousness' sake: for theirs

31 II Corinthians 12:9-10.

is the kingdom of heaven. Blessed are ye when men shall reproach you, and persecute you, and say all manner of evil against you falsely, for my sake.[32]

The two codes—if one may call the Beatitudes a code—are *both* parts of the Christian ethical inheritance, and though the sentimentalist is likely to find the one affirmative and kindly, the other negative and harsh, they do belong together.

IV

Historical Christianity is no monolithic faith. It is not sufficient to say that it is a complex set of beliefs and practices always subject to heresies and splintering. One must note that Christianity is a religion full of quite deliberate paradoxes of the emotions:

He that findeth his life shall lose it; and he that loseth his life for my sake shall find it.

But many shall be last that are first; and first that are last.[33]

The Fathers, too, were fond of this striking weapon of paradox, so suited to the defiant challenge Christianity makes to common sense. Tertullian will do: *Certum est, quia impossibile est.*[34]

The verbal and literary paradox, which is not quite the paradox of the logician, is likely to be thought today to be somewhat cerebral, typical of the way a mind like Oscar Wilde's or Aldous Huxley's works. In high philosophy it smacks of the Hegelian thesis-antithesis-synthesis. But in the logic of the emotions this sort of paradox simply expresses the human condition, the eternal "I hate and I love . . . and suffer." In Christianity the paradox can be stated simply and tritely: the Christian can neither accept nor deny this harsh world of the flesh, cannot—save for a few mystics who are perhaps not really Christian—*feel* this world as illusion, as evil, as something to be wholly transcended. Neither, of course, can he accept this world as pleasant, or interesting, or amusing, or, indeed, as quite necessary and permanent, as it stands, a mere product of historical necessity.

Against the extremes of otherworldly ethics that I have brought forward

[32] Matthew 5:3-11.
[33] Matthew 10:39; 19:30.
[34] Tertullian, *De Carne Christi.* "*It is certain* because it is impossible." This form is much more powerful than, indeed, quite different in meaning from, the corruption often quoted, *Credo quia impossibile* (or, in some versions, *absurdum*), "*I believe* because it is impossible" (or absurd). I do not wish to be understood as citing Tertullian as a *typical* Christian, but he certainly is a *good* Christian.

above, the historian can bring out many characteristic Christian compromises, even from quite early days. One may argue that Christ himself had no theology. It is quite clear that there was in early Christianity a strong current of distrust of things of the mind, a preference for the wisdom of babes and sucklings. Yet within a few generations Christianity had developed a subtle and complex theology which enlisted the best minds of Greco-Roman culture. The Fathers were worried over the temptations set forth in the pagan classics, but even so Rousseauistic or Carlylean a character as Tertullian held that the pagan authors simply had to be mastered if the new church were to maintain proper educational standards. As for St. Jerome, though he regretted that he had read Cicero, he continued to write a fine polished Latin; one suspects that he didn't really regret Cicero.[35]

Extreme pacifism was early qualified, and by the time of St. Augustine this foremost of Western founding fathers could write that when Christ said "all they that take the sword shall perish with the sword" he referred to such persons only as arm themselves to shed the blood of others without either command or permission of any lawful authority—in short, to common-law murderers and unsuccessful wagers of civil war, not to legitimate soldiers or policemen.[36] The formula had been found much earlier, early enough to get into the canon, though it is surely unlikely that Christ himself found it: "Render therefore unto Caesar the things that are Caesar's; and unto God the things that are God's."[37] Christians could and did fight in the armies of the Empire. But the swing was not unlimited; they could never fight in the gladiatorial games, never, as good Christians, fully identify themselves with the pleasures of the Roman people.

Even—perhaps, above all—on sex the Christians made their compromises. After all, St. Paul's most famous pronouncement on the matter did not enjoin total continence; marriage became early, and remained, one of the Christian sacraments. Among the highly placed of the Christian world the line between Caesar and Christ was drawn rather freely: the Christian emperors and empresses were for the most part not appreciably more chaste than had been the pagans. But, again, the swing was not complete. Even for ordinary folk Christian *moral standards* in sex relations were of a Hebraic strictness. Critics find a continued harshness toward the sinner who strayed outside

[35] On Christianity and classical education, see Marrou, *History of Education in Antiquity*, Chap. IX.
[36] Augustine, *Contra Faustum* in Migne, *Patrologiae cursus completus* (Latin series), XXII, 70.
[37] Matthew 22:21.

the permitted connubial intercourse. Westermarck, for instance, points out that if Christian feeling for the sacredness of the individual soul made of infanticide a crime punishable by death, and even perhaps lessened the number of actual infanticides, Christian feeling for the enormities of fornication led to great harshness toward the mother of illegitimate offspring.[38]

Christians have over the centuries conducted themselves variously in matters sexual; and even Christian ethical principles as to sex are by no means monolithic. We may as well face at this point the anti-Christian's charge that Christianity has by its ideas on the subject perverted a fine, natural, simple instinct: without Christianity, we should all come of age, and stay of age, serenely and enjoyably, as in Samoa. If this and similar charges are made from a naïve "naturalistic" base of belief that if men, and women, would but let their natural instincts guide them in sexual relations all would be well, they start from nonsense and must end in nonsense. Just as a sport, sexual intercourse requires for success acquired skills; poor Homo sapiens cannot even swim without lessons. But sex is much more than a sport, and the regulation, in some senses even the suppression, of sexual relations has been the concern of all societies and all ethical systems. All this should be truism.

But has not Christianity suppressed too much, made learning sexual skills more difficult, turned women, whose physiological evolution seems to have inclined them on an average away from easy sexual satisfaction, into actual frigidity? I do not think we know nearly enough about the physiology, psychology, and sociology of sex in humans to answer that question. Purely from the record, it must be said that there are Greek and Jewish precedents in our own tradition for the rigorous control of sex conduct, and for feelings, sentiments, that the business of sex is in some sense shameful, and certainly is so if it is public or promiscuous. And to anticipate, it must be noted that many, many Enlightened anti-Christians of various freethinking sects since 1700 have been at least as prudish, as repressive, about sex as any Christian. John Stuart Mill is, perhaps, an extreme example, but there he is.[39] As it has worked

[38] Westermarck, *Christianity and Morals,* New York, Macmillan, 1939, p. 241. The theologians had difficulty over the problem as to just when the immortal soul entered the embryo. They finally decided that forty days after conception the *embryo informatus* was endowed with a soul and became the *embryo formatus,* the killing of which was a crime punishable by death. See Westermarck, *Christianity and Morals,* pp. 243-244.
[39] Mill's Mrs. Taylor is surely the most high-minded of frigid females we know from the record—and somehow high-minded frigidity seems much worse than the merely neurotic kind. See for the curious story of Mill's nonsex life F. A. Hayek, *John Stuart Mill and Harriet Taylor,* London, Routledge and Kegan Paul, 1951.

out, ordinary parish Christianity has allowed for a fine range of sexual "naturalness," notably in the great Christian centuries of medieval times. I incline to the belief that recurring phases of what the vulgar call "Puritanism" in sex matters are in Western history usually symptoms of deep-seated social problems—as are recurring phases of widespread sexual license.

Finally, it is true enough that historic Christianity has been what the Enlightened would have to call antifeminist. Christianity has blamed a lot on Eve, and taken it out on her daughters. But here again, only a very unhistorically-minded polemicist can maintain that Christianity has elevated man and lowered woman more than did the earlier cultures from which it derived, and into which it breathed new life, notably the Jewish and the Hellenic. Feminism as a faith is a product of the eighteenth-century Enlightenment. Roman women in the upper classes of the Empire did gain an extraordinary degree of personal freedom; but Christianity did not end a nonexistent Roman feminism, for the old classical culture was definitely a masculine one. Here, as throughout, the never-quite-effaced Christian doctrine of the equality of all souls, even female souls, preserved a base from which the Enlightenment was later to work. And it should be obvious that anti-Christian writers have, by their emphasis on some monkish writings, greatly exaggerated the extent to which Christianity condemned women as women, and blamed them as the source of evil. Ordinary parish Christianity, the Christianity of the cure of souls, if it wanted women kept in their place, also wanted that place to be a dignified and honorable one, far nearer the old Roman than to the old Athenian place of woman.

Here, too, Western Christianity made one of its most fateful compromises: complete celibacy, impossible and, therefore, undesirable, for the many, was made necessary for the clergy. There was for centuries a struggle within the Roman Church over this requirement, and the matter was not finally settled for the lower secular clergy in the West until the great Cluniac reforms of the eleventh century. But almost from the first, as the clergy began in practice and in law to be distinguished from the laity, there were voices to urge that celibacy is essential to the priesthood. Yet here again the church as established avoided the extreme. It accepted, or, rather, made, a distinction between clergy and laity; that distinction was real, tangible, and important, but at the bottom it was a functional distinction, as a distinction of status, though a very holy one, not a distinction of kind or essence; nor was it, since the ranks of the clergy were never wholly closed to the poorest lad with a vocation, even in the less democratic phases of the church, a distinction of caste. The Cath-

167

olic priest was held to more rigorous standards of conduct than the layman, and he had privileges that went with his responsibilities; but he was not a different sort of being, not fundamentally holier, than the layman. The saint *is* holier than the ordinary Christian; but the church has carefully avoided canonizing anyone as saint until after death. The Catholic Church avoided here the Manichaean, and, later, Albigensian, heresy, in which a caste of perfect ones, Cathari, was so sharply separated theologically from the common run of the faithful as to seem different beings, a caste in the Eastern sense that the West has always repudiated in ideal, and, therefore, in the long, long run, in practice.

The church has avoided the trap of *formal* dualism in theology and metaphysics. The simple—relatively simple—moral distinction between good and evil sets an unavoidable problem to the monotheist: a God all-powerful, all-knowing, and all-good presents to human logic a challenge. There have been many solutions to this problem of theodicy in Christianity; Job's seems to me still the basic one:

Then Job answered the Lord, and said, I know that thou canst do all things, And that no purpose of thine can be restrained. Who is this that hideth counsel without knowledge? Therefore have I uttered that which I understood not, Things too wonderful for me, which I knew not. Hear, I beseech thee, and I will speak; I will demand of thee, and declare thou unto me. I had heard of thee by the hearing of the ear; But now mine eye seeth thee, Wherefore I abhor myself, and repent in dust and ashes.[40]

One humanly tempting solution has remained heretical from the Manichaeans to John Stuart Mill, who fell from freethinking into this heresy in his old age: this is the dualistic solution of making God all-good but not all-powerful. God in this view wants the good to prevail, but he cannot eliminate evil, Satan, the Dark One, his opponent. We human beings ought to fight for God, not for Satan, but we cannot be sure of being on the winning side. To put things crudely, the religious difficulty of this solution is that a God whose intentions are no doubt good but whose proven capacities are not much greater than man's is not a very useful ally in the moral struggle, and soon becomes quite as superfluous as the deist's watchmaker god—indeed, the lower case letter "g" heralds his superfluity. To the dualist's argument that the fighter for the right who goes into the struggle quite uncertain as to who will win is morally superior to the monotheist who knows he, through God, cannot possibly lose, the Christian monotheist has an effective

[40] Job 42:1-6.

168

reply: On this earth the outcome of any given struggle is highly uncertain, for God does not rig the struggle here; He has ordered the universe as a whole in accordance with His wisdom, not ours, and the dualist argument above is in fact an argument for theological humanism, not for Christianity.

But these are high and ultimate matters. The historian adhering to the merely empirical can assert that over the centuries the dualistic solution of the problem of evil has been rejected as shallow, commonsensical, morally inadequate. A church that accepted dualism as an ultimate would soon cease to satisfy human needs for an ultimate. Not only Roman Catholic, but the great majority of Protestant Christianity, has refused to set up the patent, unavoidable Christian *tension* between this world and another, between Nature and God, as a dualistic *antithesis,* a polarity of equals. Christian morality accepts competition, conflict, the agon, even a touch of pride, but only in tension with loving kindness, altruism, co-operation. In simplest terms, Christianity since Augustine certainly, *accepts* war on this earth as necessary if it is just—if it furthers Christian purpose; but its heaven, its ideal, its ultimate moral tone, is peace.[41]

V

Christianity so sets the way Westerners, even Westerners who would hate to think of themselves as Christians, think and feel about morals that it is worth our while here, at the risk of some repetitiousness, to put the broad lines of that way and its difficulties as succinctly as possible.

The individual, endowed with an immortal soul of priceless value, is a free moral agent. Once he is mature, he knows, by the grace of God and through the teachings of the church, right from wrong. If he chooses to do wrong, the conscience God has made part of, or a function of, his soul tells him he is guilty. He can perhaps plead physical duress, and, to a limited extent, ignorance, but he cannot plead total irresponsibility, cannot claim that he acted under cosmic necessity. He is, through his conscience, aware of the "civil war within the breast," aware within himself of something that drives him to sin, and of something within himself that urges him to virtue. Put in another way, he is aware of the contrast between his soul and his body, and

41 Denis de Rougemont in his *Man's Western Quest* brings out well this Christian contrast of this world and another, a contrast that never—while orthodox or even mildly heterodox—approaches the Eastern (Asian) denigration and denial of this world of the senses, and of the agon. Americans, who are put off by epigrammatic cleverness, at least when it is displayed on the side of the angels, should realize that M. de Rougemont, who writes with epigrammatic cleverness, is deeply serious as well as obviously *sérieux.*

aware that the soul ought to be the master of the body. This attitude I should like to put as the "minimal Western puritanism," an attitude never totally absent in the Christian moral outlook.

Now this minimal puritanism is not menaced—indeed, is greatly reinforced—by deterministic theological and metaphysical ideas that might seem at first sight to destroy the free moral agency of the individual. There can hardly be in matters of Western morals a safer induction from experience than the above statement. The Christian who believes that everything he does is foreordained by an omnipotent and omniscient God *never* goes on to say: Since God is responsible for all my thoughts and desires, he has clearly put into my mind my present desire to fornicate; I shall therefore fornicate, since God so clearly wants me to.[42] We shall have to return to this matter with those two great modern variants of the doctrine of determinism, Calvinism and Marxism.

This minimal Christian puritanism, this *basic* but not *radical* dualism, has had to struggle with determined foes in the long course of Christian history. At the most theoretical, there have been many kinds of theological and metaphysical doctrines that deny, gloss over, or exaggerate the dualism of soul and body, Higher and Lower, such as pantheism on one hand and Manichaeanism on the other. Most of these intellectual deviants are present in one form or another in those great earliest centuries of Christian heresies.

At a much less intellectually respectable level, Christianity has been menaced in this basic moral position by the persistence of many forms of early ("primitive") cosmic beliefs centered on the concept of wrongdoing as a kind of plague, a visitation from gods not really interested in human beings, a possession by demons, a consequence of the individual's breaking, through accident or bad luck, absolute rules made by powerful nonhuman forces "out there," controllable, if at all, only by magic and conformity. This is the moral attitude of Piaget's little children, and it clearly has no place for our concepts of individual moral responsibility. It is not as near extinction in the modern West as we once liked to think. It survives in many ways, from simple superstitions like newspaper astrology to the concept of guilt by association —the latter not without roots in common sense, but, as we all know now, spreading into much deeper and less pleasant soils.

[42] My "never" above was no doubt an exaggeration. The enemies at least of the radical sect known as the Antinomians in the sixteenth century accused them of justifying all sorts of excesses by some such reasoning as the above. Still, the generalization holds up: somehow deterministic doctrines do not explain, let alone justify, wickedness in individual action. Sin is a mystery.

In modern times, however, the chief threat to minimal Christian puritanism has been a heresy as profound as any Christianity has faced, the doctrines that gave direction in the eighteenth-century Enlightenment to the belief in the natural goodness and/or reasonableness of man, and its corollary, the belief that evil is a product of environment—partly of natural or geographic environment, but mostly of human or socio-economic environment. As we shall see, in the actual struggles of ideas this doctrine of the environmental origin of evil does not by any means banish the concept of wicked and virtuous, of morally responsible individuals. To the Marxist, the capitalist is a villain, responsible for the evil he does, even though he would seem to be, like the rest of us, the innocent product of the means of production. Indeed, Marxism is a "primitive" determinism which has borrowed much of Christian ethics. To all this we shall have to return.

VI

Christianity will be a constant theme for the rest of our study. To the outsider certainly Christianity on this earth has changed, developed, had a history. Here again the theme we have just discussed is apposite; there is in Christianity a tension, a contrast, which to some has appeared a contradiction. Christianity, it is maintained, is a revealed religion; it is true; truth does not change; Christianity was in the beginning what it is today. Therefore, obviously, Christianity has not changed and the changes historians record are either not real changes or they are not *Christian* changes (that is, they are temporary and in this world successful heresies). The position briefly outlined above is known to Americans as Fundamentalism, and though with elaborate exegesis on the adjectives "real" and "Christian" it could be made acceptable to a wide range of Christians, in its simple form it is by no means representative of Christian attitudes toward this world and the history which is here made—though not in heaven, which is well beyond history.

Here on this earth the church has a history; it has failures and successes. It grows, develops, for it is alive with human life. Cardinal Newman put the matter provocatively in his *Development of Christian Doctrine,* written, it is true, just before Darwin, but fully abreast of nineteenth-century acceptance of ideas of growth and evolution. Just because the church is in part human, it *must* change: "—in a higher world it is otherwise, but here below to live is to change, and to be perfect is to have changed often."[43]

43 J. H. Newman, *Essay on the Development of Christian Doctrine* (1845), p. 40.

These early centuries in which Christianity was fighting—I use the word advisedly—its way to success are not quite the years from which one would try to draw the Christian moral ideal, embodied or not. It is profoundly true that Jesus Christ is the Christian moral ideal, but not in the sense I am using that phrase in this study. Christ is, save to the extreme Unitarian or "humanist," God, and an *imitatio Christi* must have elements not found in simple moral emulation, which is always to a degree prudential. What Christ did during his ministry on earth is of major importance in the moral content of Christianity, above all, to re-emphasize what I have noted above, because in the balance that ministry rejects the Homeric agon and its successor for the beatitudes and for the greatest of these, love. But to draw the outlines of what Christianity brought in place of the Homeric hero, the Periclean beautiful-and-good, the Stoic servant of duty, we shall do better to wait until in the next chapter the saint and the knight of the Middle Ages appear. Both owe much—in a sense, everything—to the first Christian centuries, but they are not, historically, contemporaries of the martyrs and the Fathers.

We must, however, come back briefly in conclusion to two problems of direct historical pertinence here. On the old question of the part played by Christianity in the fall of the Roman Empire we can be quite brief. Unless the naïve anti-intellectualism which says that men's beliefs in the big and dignified matters of religion and ethics have no relation whatever to their actions, then one has to conclude that a set of beliefs which, as we have seen, is neatly pointed up by Tertullian's "nothing more alien to us than concern with the public thing" must have been one of the variables the historian will list and roughly measure as elements in the collapse of the Greco-Roman One World. But there are many, many such variables, among which Christianity is, I think, no more than of middling importance. I do not think that even if the soldierly Mithraism so strong in the armies had also won over the civilian population of the Empire the outcome would have been very different. Gibbon's famous "triumph of barbarism and religion" remains what it has always been: good Gibbon, but poor sociology, poor history.

The historian is always confronted with a post-mortem, and must always wonder whether anything could have saved the patient. I think it clear that what I have a bit loosely called the "civic virtues"—disciplined obedience to law and authority, steady ways of ritual communion with one's fellows of the common weal, self-identification of the individual with the society, expectation of the need for self-immolation in war, and, to use a modern instance not misleading, a degree of willingness to put "guns before butter"—these civic virtues simply did not exist among the masses of the Roman Empire. Their existence, often as strong sentiments, among the few who held the armies and the civil services together was clearly not enough. Now Christianity was later to give abundant proof that it is wholly congruous with a high degree of the civic and military virtues; it is sufficient to mention the Teutonic Knights, the Cromwellian New Model Army, the help Christianity has given—to the regret of many Christians—to the modern nation-state in war.

But—and it is a big but—there is a whole side of Christianity that cannot accept the civic and military virtues, as they get focused in this world, as virtues at all. Some Christians at all times are fighting pacifists, rebels against the political in-group, condemners of the great, the high, the mighty; some Christians really do not believe in rendering anything at all to Caesar, for they do not think there should be Caesars. We are here at a point far more important than the old chestnut about the role of Christianity in the downfall of the Roman Empire, a point to which we shall have to recur. Deepest of all the problems and contradictions of historical Christianity is this basic, this fundamental, this recurring—if in this extreme form heretical—Christian motif: the world *is* bad, success in it *is* failure, satisfaction with any part of it *is* the mark of the false, the spurious Christian. Church organization has ruined the Christianity of Jesus Christ, theology has falsified the gospel faith, spontaneous religious emotional life has been strait-jacketed by dogma, the Letter again and again has killed—but the Spirit will not quiet down. For ye have the Kierkegaards always with you.[44]

A Kierkegaard in a nineteenth-century Lutheran Church which was about to blossom in the great German Empire had but little effect, was really no more than a reminder that the martyr is indeed a witness. But in the early years of Christianity the martyrs were rather more than forerunners of Existentialism. The lift of the otherworldly ideal was strong, so strong that though we cannot "explain" the fall of the Roman Empire in Gibbon's terms, we can and must note that Christianity contains in it a menace to all worldly empires. Tamed, it is a marvelous discipline, a nurse of the civic virtues. But it is hard to tame, hard to keep tamed. We must return again and again to this theme,

---

[44] Many a great work has been built on one form or another of this Christian contrast or tension, for instance, Harnack's great history of dogma. The reader will find in Philip Rieff's excellent introduction to a modern reprinting of Harnack's own one-volume summary of his life work, a very succinct statement of this conflict between what I may perhaps too lightly call comfortable and uncomfortable Christianity in history. Adolf Harnack, *Outlines of the History of Dogma*, intr. by Philip Rieff, Boston, Beacon, 1957.

for the ethical implications of Christianity tamed are quite different from the ethical implications of Christianity wild.

The other favorite freethinker's denigration, that the noble ethical principles of Christianity had no effect whatever on human conduct in these first four centuries of the Christian era, that men continued to murder, gamble, whore, and generally conduct themselves in ways the freethinkers, the Enlightened, in the modern West disapprove, deserves short shrift. If we must reject the naïve anti-intellectualist assertion that ethics have no effect on conduct, we must reject—perhaps a little more forcefully and with a little greater effort, for we are more conditioned to it—one sort of idealist's assertion that ethics *ought to be* synonymous with conduct, and *would be,* if only . . . well, usually because there are a few, just a few, villainous men, villainous beliefs, villainous traditions, or villainous institutions about. I shall come again to this difficult relation, difficult in reality as it is difficult in analysis, between ethics and conduct. Here it should be sufficient to note that Victorians like the freethinker Robertson gravely oversimplified the relation. In very brief statement: Christian ethics set very high standards, not for a privileged few, such as the Aristotelian ethics very specifically did, but for the many, for everyone. We should not be surprised that the many then and now failed to live up to these standards. We should not be surprised that Christianity failed to suppress immediately the cruelty of the arena, the obscenity of the stage, the fearful agon of imperial politics. Surely we should be surprised only if the whole Roman world had suddenly started to live up in practice to the Christian ethic.

The historian, at any rate the historian with sociological leanings, may perhaps be permitted to ask whether a religion that does set high, in a sense humanly unnatural, ethical standards achieves as good a level of conduct as might a religion less exacting in ethics. This, and the closely related question of the reality of moral "progress" or "evolution," we must ultimately come back to, though here we may note that neither history nor sociology as social or behavioral sciences are yet old enough, well-enough developed, to give us good answers. Certainly they will not give us neat answers of the sort Robertson gave, for he and his fellows actually set their standards quite as high as Christianity ever did—and proposed to realize them with no help from God, nor even from that rather pale but not wholly ineffective substitute for God, the Greek sense of the dangers of *hubris,* with help only from a highly intellectualized "conscience."

Though Christianity sets very high ethical standards—go over once more the Ten Commandments and the Sermon on the Mount—those Christians who have the cure of souls have usually tempered the wind to the shorn lamb. At all times some Christians, and at some times a great many, are spurred—we really do not know why, how, under what conditions—to attempt to realize here on earth these lofty standards. But for the most part, the church of Christ, and, after the separation of East and West, the churches, have acted in accordance with the Christian estimate of human nature, which is not that men are naturally good and/or reasonable, but that they are naturally sinful, though through God's grace they may even here on earth conduct themselves rather better than they would by nature. Oddly enough, this Christian estimate of human nature was by no means inadequately stated by Alexander Pope, who did much to help the rationalist Enlightenment on its way to its heretical belief that men are by nature good.

> Plac'd on this isthmus of a middle state,
> A being darkly wise and rudely great:
> With too much knowledge for the Sceptic side,
> With too much weakness for the Stoic's pride,
> He hangs between; in doubt to act or rest,
> In doubt to deem himself a God, or Beast;
> In doubt his Mind or Body to prefer,
> Born but to die, and reas'ning but to err;
> Alike in ignorance, his reason such,
> Whether he thinks too little or too much:
> Chaos of Thought and Passion, all confus'd,
> Still by himself abus'd, or disabus'd.[45]

Such an estimate ought, in fact, to be acceptable even to the anti-Christians and the varieties of the Enlightened who hold that man is simply an animal who has come out on top after a long course of organic evolution. This animal is clearly not—or at any rate not yet—a social animal in the sense that the bees and the ants are social animals. If we are as close to the higher mammals as the materialist believes we are, then Christianity, seen simply in naturalistic-historical perspective, is a magnificent achievement, and a highly suitable faith for Homo sapiens—far better than an Oriental faith like Buddhism, which will not in the end tolerate or accept the animal at all, far better than the modern Western secular faiths like Marxism and anti-Christian democratic nationalism, or cosmopolitanism, which hold that animal to be already by nature tame, domesticated, a freethinking mammalian bee—a paradox, in short, far more incredible than the Christian one.

[45] Alexander Pope, *An Epistle on Man,* Epistle II, 3-14.

The Middle Ages

THE MIDDLE AGES began, after the collapse of the Roman Empire in the West, with several centuries of violence and primitive political and economic life, centuries that used to be called the Dark Ages. They still look dark on the record, though we note with less surprise than did our Victorian predecessors that to its own contemporaries the record of these Dark Ages seemed to reflect the obvious fact that God, the orthodox God of the Trinity, was in His heaven and all was as right on His earth as He had intended. Gregory of Tours, whose work is as much a *locus classicus* here as that of Tacitus for the early Roman Empire, is certain that God was pleased with the Frankish King Clovis; Gregory has, when he makes this remark, just finished recounting a series of murders and betrayals by which Clovis did the work of the Lord.[1]

Once again, the facts are substantially clear, and we need not spend much time on them. Gregory's ample record of the struggle for power in Merovingian Gaul—actually, already France—in the fifth and sixth centuries is surely no unfair sampling; but almost any of the other chronicles of the time, such as that in which the British monk Gildas recounts the horrid deeds of the pagan Anglo-Saxons, or lives of missionary saints like Boniface which reflect the conditions under which these devoted men labored, are full of deeds —murders, poisonings, patricides, matricides, adulteries, incests, gluttony, drunkenness—at least as bad as any in Western history.[2] It is true that we are

[1] Gregory of Tours, *The History of the Franks,* II, 29 (40).
[2] The reader should go direct to Gregory; the rivalry of those two remarkable women

once more in the presence of the familiar and unavoidable fact that the wicked deeds are interesting, dramatic, and get recorded; and we have also for this period an added factor that makes for bias. All our records are in fact monkish or priestly chronicles, written by firm, excited, uncritical believers in an order of the universe that is not at all our world of science, and social science. Do not ask semantic concern from Gregory and his fellows; do not even expect them to worry over the distinction between the normal and the abnormal in human nature.

Yet there is no need to question the facts established above. The conduct of ruling classes in the West in these centuries is bad enough to need explaining. That explanation can hardly for us lie in the nice rationalism of recent generations. Lecky throws light on the nineteenth, but not on the sixth, century when he writes:

It would be easy to cite other, though perhaps not quite such striking, instances of the degree in which the moral judgements of this unhappy age were distorted by superstition. Questions of orthodoxy, or questions of fasting, appeared to the popular mind immeasurably more important than what we should now call the fundamental principles of right and wrong.[3]

Lecky probably did actually believe that questions of orthodoxy were *not* fundamental questions of right and wrong. The old and dangerous figure of speech does better for us: these centuries are centuries of youth, immaturity, crudeness, barbarism. However tricky this figure may be—the protagonists, in spite of the suddenness and frequence of death by violence, in spite of lamentable lack of hygienic measures, were not in years significantly younger than in other societies—it seems unavoidable. These grown-up men and women do behave with a child's bright violence, a child's lack of adult sense of proportion, or merely sense of probable consequences, a child's cruelty and love of being loved. And, like children, they are romantics, always to be blest or damned. Like children, they know regrets, but not conscience.

The Victorians, who did not worry much about using figures of speech, knew that these Germanic barbarians of the West in the Dark Ages were children, that theirs was a "young" society. But since most Victorian writers were victims of Wordsworth's ideas about childish innocence and virtue, and since children like Clovis and Frédégonde behaved wickedly indeed, they

---

Frédégonde and Brunehaut, as recorded in Books VII and VIII, will leave him in no doubt as to their wicked conduct. The morally outraged Lecky, *History of European Morals*, Vol. II, pp. 235 ff., summarizes in detail.
[3] *History of European Morals*, Vol. II, pp. 242-243.

faced a contradiction. Charles Kingsley, who, incredibly, was elected Regius Professor of History at Cambridge, wrestled with the problem in his inaugural lectures on the barbarian invasions. He felt as he was bound to, that the Germans were blond and good, the Romans dark and bad. Of course, the Romans corrupted the Germans, who were too inexperienced to withstand temptations of the "troll garden" (the Empire!). Kingsley actually calls the Germans children, "often very naughty children," but, of course, at bottom virtuous and good muscular Christians.[4]

There remains for us the puzzle of Gregory's moral attitudes, a puzzle we shall not solve, for if no man can know another among his contemporaries, the best of historical imaginations will not take him back to a man as remote from us as was Gregory. Yet clearly Gregory, of an old and cultured Gallo-Roman aristocratic family, was no barbarian. I do not think he was consciously making what *we* call propaganda. When he wrote that Clovis was doing the Lord's work, he was not urging an Orwellian "doublethink," nor even quite the Nice Lie by which Plato sought to reconcile the inferior men of brass to the rule of the golden philosopher-kings.[5] He meant, if I may be anachronistic, that Clovis, the heathen converted, not to the devilish heresy of Arianism, but to God's own orthodoxy, was doing God's work in his, and His, world—but not in the world of Mr. Gladstone and the Society for the Prevention of Cruelty to Animals. Gregory did not, could not, have expected his Franks to conduct themselves as private persons other than as they did; he did not condone the wickedness of high politics, any more than we condone the weather. He accepted but did not necessarily like or approve evil, as we accept the weather. He was still an early Christian, for whom this dark world is but an entrance to another, much better, or much worse; and the necessary way to the better world, the way people *ought* to go, is through Christian orthodoxy. Gregory did not say that murder, betrayal, adultery are good; insofar as a priest he exercised cure of souls, he most certainly held such conduct up as sin. What he did say was that the victory of the Roman Catholic Church here on earth is the great good.[6]

The medieval man was bound to feel and classify as *normal* in fact a kind

[4] See my *English Political Thought in the Nineteenth Century*, London, Benn, 1933, p. 128.

[5] *The Republic of Plato*, trans. by A. D. Lindsay, London, Dent, 1948, pp. 99-103.

[6] I am aware that this argument is bound to seem casuistical to most twentieth-century Americans of good will; but it seems casuistical basically because, as heirs of the Enlightenment, we expect so much better conduct from everybody—and especially from our rulers.

of melodramatic violence that we, in spite of the tabloids, in spite of our own prophets of doom, in spite of the H-bomb, are at heart convinced is *abnormal,* a preventable, curable, *moral* delinquency. Huizinga has put it well, not only for these early years, but for the whole of the Mi•dle Ages, that most Faustian time:

So violent and motley was life, that it bore the mixed smell of blood and of roses. The men of that time always oscillate between the fear of hell and the most naive joy, between cruelty and tenderness, between harsh asceticism and insane attachment to the delights of this world, between hatred and goodness, always running to extremes.[7]

Even if you find the explanation of figurative youthfulness in a society inadequate, the facts are there. Not the least conspicuous of the extremes of this society is the width of the gap between the ideal and the real, between profession and performance, the gap everyone notes in Gregory's lying murderer Clovis, the favorite of the God of Moses and Isaiah, the God who had sent his only begotten Son to redeem us all.

Men in the Dark Ages, and to a degree in the Middle Ages and the Renaissance, too, faced a life of insecurity everywhere—an economic order still at the mercy of drought, flood, inadequate transportation, inadequate finance, a political order that could not *administer* effectively any large territory—with the economic consequence that markets, too, were small and "inefficient"—a moral order that in the face of violence and insecurity did not, could not, expect men to be sober, steady, cautious, restrained, to have, in short, what I have called for the Romans at their best the "civic virtues." As the Western world grew into modernity, political order and some of the civic virtues followed; but the haunting fear of both this world and the next never quite left medieval men, and it gave their lives a tone of desperation— not for the most part Thoreauvian quiet desperation—which later historians in their own security have been able to find romantic, heroic, fascinating in vicarious experience.

Some mark of this excess of excessiveness, then, remains throughout the Middle Ages; but the naïveté of these early years is lost. It is a grave mistake to regard the Middle Ages as a perpetual childhood. Most of what the later medieval centuries were to fashion into the complex and subtle moral ideals of the saint and the knight have their immediate origins in this crudely violent society of the Dark Ages. At the very least, these centuries are the matrix out of which came the great heroes, the great achievements, of the High

[7] J. Huizinga, *The Waning of the Middle Ages*, p. 18.

Middle Ages. They are to the High Middle Ages what the days of Moses were to the Jews, the days of Achilles to the Greeks. But not even the best known and most important of all these sources, the epic poem of the *Chanson de Roland,* took on its transmitted form this early. For us, certainly, what the poets later made of Charlemagne is more important than what contemporaries like his biographer Einhard made of him. What the twelfth and the thirteenth centuries were to make into the academic culture of the Middle Ages is more important than the rather pathetic "Carolingian Renaissance" in which the clerics staged the first major rally of learning since the breakdown of the fifth century. We may then proceed directly to the developed ideals of the knight and the saint.

II

At the outset we run into a difficulty that can be no more than acknowledged. The Middle Ages regarded both the knight and the saint as complementary facets of a single ideal, the Christian; both were needed servants of God and of His order on earth. Since the spirit is in Christian formal belief loftier than the noblest flesh, the saint, if there must be a ranking, comes before the knight. The first estate of the medieval assemblies was not the nobility, but the clergy. Now such, if we will be moderately honest, is by no means our ranking today. We not only put the warrior, the politician, the judge, the captain of industry, the magician of science well ahead of the man of God, but we suspect that the Middle Ages did not *really* put the spiritual first, did not *really* rank the priest ahead of the noble. Yet this suspicion of ours is unjust, and leads us astray. We shall not get far inside the men of the Middle Ages unless we recognize that they "believed in" their ideal representation of the universe in a way we can hardly believe in ours, unless we are better Christians or more naïve materialists than most of us are. The medieval man knew that spirit primes matter; he did not, of course, expect the spiritual as a rule to be crowned with material success here on earth—that would indeed have been a transvaluation of values in his eyes. But he was no hypocrite; he knew that in the next world God would surely set matters right.

To the knight, then, is, in theory, assigned the task of keeping this earthly social frame we must inhabit in good order. He is soldier, landlord, governor, fitting neatly into a hierarchy that reaches its top in kings and in the emperor, Western successors of the Caesars. And in fact the knight is the man who gets things done at the top, the member of what is until fairly late in the Middle

Ages a comparatively homogeneous ruling class. The priest, who alone at first could read, was needed in lay affairs from the start, for he alone could keep records; and the beginnings of the lawyer, the civil administrator, the entrepreneurial merchant, even of the efficient professional physician, go farther back than we used to think. Still, it is substantially true that the feudal nobility are the representative figures of the lay *vita activa* right up to that seedbed of our times, the fourteenth century.[8]

Now the knight was first of all a fighter. He was trained from childhood in the skills, in those days before gunpowder most exacting athletic skills, necessary to the fighter on horseback. It was, however, a training in one important respect excessively individualistic, even anarchic. The medieval knight was by no means wholly undisciplined; the physical rigors he had to live through and the technical skills he had to acquire involved hard practice and much self-denial. Moreover, the final form of Christian culture to which he was subjected, itself the forerunner of the duty-filled education of the Western resident country nobility of early modern times, was very far from irresponsible anarchism. Yet the knight at arms was never trained to fight in close and disciplined battle order; he was at the opposite pole from the Spartan hoplite, trained to perfectly timed shield-to-shield dressing with his fellows in the line of battle. The knight was never really melted into the soldier; he always stood out.

He stood out so much that in fact he is one of the prime exemplars of that eternal theme in Western moral history, the agonistic competition. The knight seems at least as determined to excel as ever the Homeric hero was. His supreme virtue is honor; and though at its best the concept of honor is much more than this, it has always an element we nowadays cheapen in the term "face." Honor consists in being honored, honored by coming out on top and being recognized in that position. It seems odd now that anyone should have believed that the individual in the Middle Ages did not stand out as an individual, that this was an age of collective effort and submergence of the ego (in the old use, not the Freudian one, of the word) in some noble common thing.

The Middle Ages did not have the vulgar word "publicity," but they had

---

[8] I cannot begin to discuss the socio-economic aspects of medieval culture in a book of this sort. The reader who wishes to refresh himself in these matters can start with some of the books suggested on pp. 30-31 of Brinton, Christopher, and Wolff, *Modern Civilization*, Englewood Cliffs, N.J., Prentice-Hall, 1957. For the complete beginner, Will Durant's *The Age of Faith* is recommended; also W. C. Bark, *Origins of the Medieval World*, Stanford University Press, 1958.

exactly what that word means. Here is Jean Froissart quoting a feudal lord setting the conditions of one of those public-private combats of knights, the "combat des Trentes," that unfortunately did not settle the business of war even then: "And let us right there try ourselves and do so much that people will speak of it in future times in halls, in palaces, in public places and elsewhere throughout the world."[9] But the point hardly needs driving home. The thirst for glory was surely a medieval thirst. It is familiar enough in silly forms, as in the career of a Richard Coeur de Lion. But do not be misled by our modern superstition that the successful are above illusions. Richard's hard-bitten and practical rival Philip Augustus of France was also a knightly type; his *gloire* was at least as far from Christ's as was Richard's.

But the knight was a Christian. Surely was not the bitter competitiveness of the old male warrior society somewhat softened over the old Homeric standards? It was unquestionably so modified. In the first place, the code insisted on gentleness toward women and children, respect for the clergy, and for the masses at least some protection, exemption from the actual pressures of combat. If, in the second place, the code was, especially in respect to treatment of social inferiors, often violated, if the knight in a temper was capable of shocking cruelties even toward the weak, let alone toward a conquered foe, he was also subject to painful and exceedingly real bouts of conscience-stricken horror when he woke to what he had done. As I wish to keep insisting, he did believe in his religion, he did know right from wrong, and he knew, in a way the first Frankish warriors did *not,* that his God punished sin. This knowledge did not keep him from sin, but it did insure, the clergy aiding, frequent and sometimes spectacular repentance. The knight who had had a beaten enemy castrated in a fit of anger might take up the cross in penance, or make some religious endowment, or even do something for the family of the ruined man.[10]

The code, moreover, by no means existed solely in the breach. There were knights of impeccable physical prowess who nonetheless deserve that then-new word "gentleman"; they were gentle, not harsh, not forever challenging. The

[9] "Et là endroit nous esprouvons, et faisons tout que on en parle ou tamps à venir, en sales, en palais, en plaches et en aultres lieus par le monde." *Oeuvres de Froissart,* ed. Kervyn de Lettenhove, Brussels, 1867-1877, Vol. V, p. 292. Note that these knights want admiration not only from their peer groups, but from the "public."
[10] I know of no single work in which this phase of the knightly soul, this more than black-and-white contrast between shocking cruelty and deeply felt repentance is better brought out than in Zoé Oldenbourg's admirable historical novel *The World Is Not Enough,* New York, Pantheon, 1955. The original French has the title *Argile* (clay).

knight of Chaucer's "Knight's Tale" has become a set example, but he is real enough. Best of all, perhaps, is the actual Jean de Joinville, whose memoirs are one of the most valuable of medieval documents. Joinville was devoted to his king, the Louis of France who became St. Louis. He followed the king on his futile and outdated crusade and tells simply and quite uncritically the story of these bungled wars. He does not seem at all aware that they were bungled, at all aware that the French feudal nobility were an ill-disciplined, prideful, and inefficient set of fighting men. But the knightly ideal has—and this is important—very little place for the critical intellect. The normal dose of neurotic complaining, which goes with the knightly real life as with all forms of real life, had to be rather severely repressed, one guesses, with some of these gentlemen, and crops up most obviously in their bouts with their conscience, their concern with their honor, and, as we shall shortly see, in their extraordinary later preoccupation with courtly love. We are today so thoroughly used to associating brightness with complaining that a Joinville, who never complains about the structure of his society, the policies of his king, the state of the universe, seems not quite bright. Clearly he was by no means unintelligent; he managed his own affairs well, he wrote simply and clearly, and he knew his own limitations.

It must not be assumed that the medieval knightly ideal, to say nothing of knightly practice, was a static one. Over six or seven centuries from Carolingian times there is a clear process of growth, and of decline or corruption. That noble document of the early years the *Chanson de Roland,* a recited epic poem of one of Charlemagne's expeditions against the Moslems in Spain, is no contemporaneous document. It represents a long line of professional troubadours or minstrels who worked over traditional materials, and it is surely not without a touch of deliberate "primitivism." The paladins seem so noble, so simple, so innocent, so athletic, so damned knightly that they can hardly have been real. They clearly live by violence, but it is a nice clean violence, with no hint whatever of matters later to be associated with the name of the Marquis de Sade. They do God's work against the infidel, but again with no worries, and certainly with no trace of theological hatred. They hold their honor very dear indeed, far dearer than success, especially military success. They are lions, in fact, with no fox in them.

As in Western Europe from the eleventh century on all the material indexes start on upward, as the self-sufficient feudal-manorial society gradually turns into a modern capitalist society, as the modern state, in fact, takes shape, lawyers, bankers, accountants, all sorts of professionals begin to take over the real work of running things; rather soon, indeed, in view of the modern liberal's notion that the soldier is particularly stupid and unenterprising, the professionals take over even the business of war. The individual knight could, and did, sometimes adapt himself to these changes, especially in Great Britain and in the Low Countries. Still, the class of knights as a whole was left with nothing like enough to do and with a fine impractical set of ideals as to how to do it. I am here obliged to scamp a good deal of importance to the social and economic historian, but the upshot of a process that begins to be noticeable as far back as the thirteenth, "greatest of centuries," is the creation of a privileged class molded and trained for an occupation and status that had in reality ceased to exist—that of feudal seigneur. But the class continued to enjoy its privileges; and it made use of its abundant leisure to push the knightly ideal into two related extravagances, the combat of the tourney and courtly love.

Individual combat between champions goes back to the very beginnings of knighthood in the Dark Ages. A perhaps too optimistic or intellectualist sociological concept suggests that in their origins all institutions arise to fill a need, and at first do fill it well enough. At any rate, it can be argued that where these fights were struggles between champions of given sides in a real conflict, they were socially useful. Intellectually, once you accept the premises they were based on, trial by combat and even trial by ordeal are nice, clean-cut methods of deciding disputes among us poor fallible humans. If God directly and immediately and constantly intervenes in the daily happenings of the world, then obviously he *does* decide which of two fairly matched knights wins in a judicial combat, and he decides it justly.[11]

Even at the beginning, these knightly combats were in part agonistic sport as well as private war or a method of judicial decision and a necessary training for the wider actual battlefield. As true law courts, in our sense, grew up, as with the Hundred Years' War vulgar infantry began the long process of making war serious and deadly once more for the many, these joustings came to be little more than ostentatious mock war, an organized aristocratic sport. As time went on the rules and conventions of the jousting got more and more complex, the armor got more complete, more rhinoceros-like, and the sport got somewhat less dangerous to life and limb, though to the very end it

---

[11] God himself, of course, would not approve a hopelessly *unequal* combat, as, for instance, between a completely inexperienced fighter and a tried and mature champion, or as between a heavyweight and a flyweight.

must have taken great courage to run full tilt into an oncoming opponent. These tourneys, as might be expected, exhibit full cultural lag, and survive well into the Renaissance. By a nice irony, the Cromwell family owed at least as much to the jousting prowess of Sir Richard Cromwell, who got himself knighted for his victories by Henry VIII, as to Richard's Uncle Thomas, the able, realistic, unscrupulous, and "modern" liquidator of monastic wealth.[12]

The knight in these tourneys, it is well known, was fighting for his lady love. We come now to a much more important phase of the late Middle Ages than the sport of jousting. Courtly love has an elaborate and, unless you are prepared for it, fantastically unreal literature, but it is much more than a phase of literary history. Courtly love is an ethics, a religion, an obsession. It is to the historian of Western morals one of those exceptional developments, one of those aberrations, *in this one respect* analogous to Greek pederasty, in which the physical facts of sex, complicated enough in themselves, get blown up into something huge, something that comes to take up the whole of living. Unlike Greek pederasty, however, courtly love is still with us, transmuted, popularized, seized upon by the octopus we call publicity, so altered that the noble lords and ladies who once pursued it would hardly recognize it. But Isolde still dies her love-death—and not only on the operatic stage.

We must have a brief preliminary here. Perhaps nowhere does our contemporary reluctance to come out solidly with a neat formula of separation between normal and abnormal show up so often as in the matter of sex. Yet the journalist-psychologist formula that "We are all abnormal, therefore we are all normal" is surely great nonsense. Ethics and conduct in the field of sex relations are indeed most varied; study of non-Western cultures has driven this home firmly. Even in the West, there is, so to speak, no compact norm, certainly not what the Victorians thought of as a norm. Still, there is over the centuries a kind of wide zone of normality, a zone in which, above all, matters sexual do not fully occupy every moment of waking and sleeping, even for those privileged few who are not obliged to work for a living, a zone in which matters sexual are *not* thoroughly mixed with matters philosophical, religious, cosmological. In short, medieval courtly love *is* an aberration. Whether its modern variants, literary romantic love, Hollywood love, or any other mass-produced love, are aberrations is another, more difficult question.

The literary origins of courtly love lie in the Mediterranean, and specif-

[12] Maurice Ashley, *The Greatness of Oliver Cromwell*, New York, Macmillan, 1958, p. 27.

ically in the troubadours who sang in Provençal from the twelfth century on.[13] There are, no doubt, deeper origins in Greek and Roman culture, for these admirable pagans clearly did not quite take sex in their stride. Aphrodite and Eros are an uncomfortable pair, and their suppression by Christianity was quite incomplete. Yet, the rise of the cult of love and of the woman—the Woman—must have had deep roots in the whole situation of the knightly class: its heritage of excessive masculinity, its counteracting inheritance of Christian ideas of love and gentleness (remember, ideas do have consequences, if not always obviously logical ones), its exasperations, frustrations, and, above all, its increasing divorce from the real work, the real rewards, of this world. These gentlemen needed the aid and comfort the *ewig weibliche,* the Woman, can always bring. Fortunately, men can always invent her in their hour of need.

The church found it useful, and probably, so great was the fashionable rage, necessary to adapt the Woman to its needs. Hence the cult of the Virgin, which, in spite of all the talk about a syncretic Isis and Earth Mother, is much more a medieval phenomenon than one of early Christianity. And as the Virgin of common conventional Christianity, the Woman was indeed tamed, disciplined, caught in the unconstricting net of common sense, so that she became almost the pure consolation that the unhappy Henry Adams writes of so warmly—for an Adams—in *Mont-Saint-Michel and Chartres.* Our Lady, duly rendered orthodox, was a symbol quite as devoid of the meta-erotic complications we all know so well nowadays as of the more rugged sexuality of the driving flesh. She remains, in spite of Protestant and free-thinking reproaches, a triumph of priestly wisdom, well understood of the people.

Not so the Woman of the troubadours. Through whole cycles of transmuted legends, of which the Arthurian cycle, and, within that, the Tristan theme, can be fairly singled out as central, she made her devastating way, sometimes *femme fatale, la belle dame sans merci,* Isolde of the White Hands, Laura or Beatrice, in the end pure longing, pure swooning, pure death.

[13] Denis de Rougemont, *Love in the Western World,* p. 75. This is a book indispensable for the student of the theme. The American reader must not be put off by M. de Rougemont's cleverness; this is a serious scholarly work, though admirably compressed. M. de Rougemont's ingeniously established link between the Cathari of the suppressed Albigensian heresy and the troubadours is not essential to the rest of his book. It is one of those interesting scholar's affiliations of ideas, and by no means implausible; but I suspect there is more in the developed Tristan myth, the love of love, than a Manichaean revenge on Christian monism. So, to be fair, does M. de Rougemont.

The Middle Ages

In dem wogenden Schwall,
in dem tönenden Schall,
in des Welt-Athems
wehendem All—
ertrinken—
versinken—
unbewusst—
höchste Lust.[14]

It was a twisting and devious way, above all—and this is of much importance —a way that hardly ever touched, and then never for long, the bedroom. We are, of course, dealing with very subtle matters. It is crude to say that courtly love is a deliberate playing with fire, but the fine old cliché has its uses. One suspects that the fire was rarely a great consuming conflagration. The chemistry of human sex has pretty unheroic limits, as compared with the capacity of the human soul for wanting something more.

It is not that courtly love was usually, or even often, of the kind sometimes miscalled "platonic." By a firm convention among the literary, it could not possibly be love between man and wife. It could not by an even more obvious convention—without which, no poem—run smoothly. It had to confront and overcome obstacle after obstacle, the more unlikely, the more unnecessary the obstacle, the better; it had, to paraphrase the familiar misquotation from Tertullian, to go on the principle of *amo, quia absurdum*. One may distinguish two lines of development of the tradition, both present in the *Roman de la Rose*, a thirteenth-century poem put together from the work of two quite separate and different poets, Guillaume de Lorris, of the first half of the century, Jean de Meung, of the second half. The Lorris part is all allegory, a

14 These are Isolde's last words. They are quite untranslatable—thank God—into so pedestrian a language as my English. The "Authentic libretto" of Wagner's opera as published by Crown Publishers, New York, 1938, makes the following inglorious attempt (p. 347):

> In the breezes around,
> in the harmony sound
> in the world's driving
> whirlwind be drown'd—
> and sinking,
> be drinking—
> in a kiss,
> highest bliss!

Our American insistence on having these operas in the original tongue is not mere social snobbery, nor even realistic concession to the need of hiring German singers. Isolde's last, last word, "Lust," is certainly not "bliss"; I suggest, in our own undignified American, that "superlonging" comes close.

sort of symbolic and almost, but not quite, platonic investment of a lady whose virtue is both obstacle and reward. The part contributed by Jean de Meung is more clearly in what Americans think of as the Gallic tradition; the language is the language of sensual enjoyment, and the dénouement is not at all uncertain or allegorical.

As M. de Rougemont points out, these two lines run on well into modern times, the first or meta-erotic one through Dante and Petrarch to Rousseau's *Nouvelle Héloïse* and even to the modern French novel of love, which until very recently was most cerebral, if not precisely spiritual, and by no means "broad" or naturalistic in its details; the second or realistic one through "the lower levels of French literature—to *gauloiserie* and the schools of broad Gallic jokes, to controversial rationalism, and to a curiously exacerbated misogyny, naturalism, and man's reduction to sex."[15]

For the moralist, both strains have this in common, that they represent a turning inward to introspection, a spiritualization or a materialization, of the old agonistic competitive drive, and this precisely in a society originally most masculine, soldierly, extraverted. Courtly love, however, by no means softened or extinguished the bitterness of the agon. The Woman in this tradition is far from the Virgin of Christianity, however much the poets of the Middle Ages may confuse them at times. There is no doubt that over the medieval centuries courtly love and its accompaniments did bring to the European nobility refinements of manners, a kind of civility that was by no means without its value as a moral instrument. But in the sense I have sought in the previous chapter to define one essential moral strain of Christianity— the disciplining of human competitiveness into co-operation, spiritually the *extinction* of pride and the exaltation of humility—courtly love brought no help to Christianity, but, rather, set itself up against Christianity. Courtly love at the least sublimated was a sport in which there was a victor and a loser; at its most sublimated it was a series of mutual stimulations to a perpetual longing for more, more of something—more, certainly, of suffering.

> *E perchè 'l mio martìr non giunga a riva*
> *Mille volte il dì moro e mille nasco.*[16]

Tristan and Isolde were, after all, adulterers. The device of the love potion

---

[15] De Rougemont, *Love in the Western World*, p. 176. Like all such dualisms, this is an imperfect one in face of the complexities of human nature. Is there a scientist's concern with sex that fits neither category?

[16] Petrarch, Sonnet CLXIV (164). Literally, "And since my martyrdom does not come to end, I die a thousand times each day, am born a thousand."

and Brangäne's fatal error seems just that—a literary device, and no reflection of a tragic destiny or necessity. Or, if the poets were appealing to a pagan concept of necessity, they were thereby underlining their heresy. In Christian terms, the lovers were sinners who never did repent sincerely, who relapsed, and ended in a most un-Christian, but perhaps quite Freudian, fulfillment of a death wish.

It would be unfair to the medieval knightly ideal to dismiss it with these perversions of the jousting tourney and the tradition of courtly love. At its best and simplest it deserves high rank among the working ideals of this imperfect world. It has suffered from the praises of the literary romantics of the school of when-knighthood-was-in-flower, has, like other phases of medieval culture, been used as a stick to beat the present with. Most of its central concepts as summarized in the word "chivalry" run contrary to the deep egalitarianism of our own day. But it was of remarkable civilizing power. Dip, if only briefly, into Gregory of Tours and then into Joinville, seven centuries later. Something has happened that one is almost tempted to call moral progress.

III

The saint is the Christian hero. His life, too, is an agon, for the church accepts as real and important this world of change and struggle. The saint's struggle is not with his fellow men but with evil; his victory is not an athletic or artistic or intellectual first, but a conquest of evil in himself and in others. His glory is not a personal glory. His victories are God's, for the saint is always what the pristine sense of "martyr" implies, a witness, a living evidence, of the grace of God, of God's governance of the universe, which is not to be proved or witnessed by ordinary naturalistic means as in law, politics, or natural science.[17]

So much for the ideal. The real here is not so much spotted, not so much in obvious contradiction with the ideal, as richer in concrete detail, more varied, more colorful. There are many saints from the earliest centuries about whom in a naturalistic-historical sense we know almost nothing at all reliable; such lives as we do have are no more than documents for social and intel-

---

17 "Saint" is for the sacramental Christian churches, Roman Catholic, Eastern Orthodox, Anglican, and the like a word with an exact meaning. It refers to what one may call a status; in this sense even evangelical Protestants are no longer as afraid of it as they were. "Saint" and "saintly" have also loose vulgar uses as no more than emphatic ways of saying "good" or "holy," but I have the impression that this loose usage is not, in fact, very common. As words go in ordinary discourse, "saint" is a precise one.

lectual history, full of miracles, sufferings, echoes from the primitive past. But of the saints real to us, and to come down no further than the High Middle Ages, a sampling must show a wide range of human personality, of role, even of *Weltanschauung.* From Paul himself through Jerome, Augustine, Gregory the Great, Boniface, Bernard of Clairvaux, Thomas Aquinas, Thomas à Becket, Francis of Assisi, Dominic, Bonaventura, Louis of France, to take only familiar names, the range is wide indeed.

No polar dualism will work, even for these few. The contrast, suggested by the vocabulary of the Middle Ages themselves, between the *vita activa* and the *vita contemplativa,* will not stand up, even if it is interpreted not so much in terms of role as in terms of temperament, disposition, philosophy. St. Paul, as would be clear had we no more than his letters to the Corinthians, was a gifted organizer and administrator. But those words to an American hardly suggest the mystic, the eloquent preacher, the seeker—and Paul was all of these, and, perhaps more than these flat words suggest, a troubled soul. This list is full of great men of action, men who guided the church in this world with such skill that in the High Middle Ages it was able to challenge, for a time, politically, and in this world, all political organizations in the West. Gregory simply as a lay ruler would have won from history his title of "the Great." Bonaventura must figure in any history of Christian mysticism, yet this Franciscan played an important part in the organization of his order and belongs also to ecclesiastical history in its narrow sense. Bernard of Clairvaux disliked intellectual reformers such as Abelard and fought them; he himself was an emotional reformer, one who has left a great mark on the history of monasticism.

There is no doubt a clear limit toward the pole of practical administrative skills and successes. The Christian saint as an ideal, and to an extraordinary extent in reality, is never merely a this-worldly manipulator of men and things. Our vocabulary of clichés—always useful to historians—lets us talk about captains of industry, indeed, about Napoleons of industry, but never about saints of industry. The anti-Christian, or merely the anti-medievalist, will reply that of course the respectability and prestige of the church prevents any such picturesque and fruitful comparison entering into our common language. This is no doubt true, and hardly a discredit to the church, but it does not exhaust the meaning of the facts. The Christian saint, no matter how well he has done his work in this world, has by his life given evidence that to him this world is not enough.

But is the other one? It seems clear that the saint shares often a great deal of the primitive Christian revulsion from, emotional rejection of, hatred for, this world of eating, drinking, lusting, idling, bickering, damaging, and conforming. Yes, you may pursue these dull formulas on until you get to the realities of madness and the Freudian death wish. There is all this in Christianity, because there is all this in us Westerners. The Christian church and after Luther, in the long run, most of the *churches* have, unlike many of the surrogate secular churches of the Enlightenment, recognized that this dark, rebellious, impatient lusting after an end to lusting is there, in us, not to be denied but to be controlled, tamed, disciplined, perhaps even to be transmuted into a kind of conformity.

The church, in short, has had its troubles with the mystic vein in the Christian heritage. With the quieter, pietistic sort of mysticism the church has been successful indeed. There is too much historical uncertainty about the life and personality of Thomas Hammerken, known as Thomas a Kempis, and about the authorship of the *Imitation of Christ* for canonization of the person; but if it were possible to canonize a book, outside of the Bible, the *Imitation of Christ* would have been canonized long ago. Here the prospect of another world is a consolation and a steadying support in this one, no goad to rebellion, no stimulant to the passions. The outsider cannot be so sure about those two Spanish mystics of the Catholic Reformation, St. Theresa and St. John of the Cross. Their passions look dangerously clinical, and most inadequately sublimated, from the point of view of quiet, conforming Christianity. The church has accepted as saints some of the earlier German ladies, such as Elizabeth of Hungary, whose mystic exaltation looks from this distance quite compatible with the sobrieties. It has always had its doubts, however, about Meister Eckhart, who, already in the fourteenth century, seems too German to be true:

> God is all things; all things are God. The Father begets me, his son, without cease. I say more: he begets in me himself, and in himself me. The eye with which I see God is the same eye with which God sees me. . . . My eye and God's eye are one eye.[18]

Pantheism must always get short shrift from orthodox theology, for it destroys the whole central drama of Christ's epiphany, to say nothing of what I have called the minimal moral puritanism of Christianity. Aggressive, mystical pantheism like that of Meister Eckhart is a dangerous invitation to rebellion. The Germans are no doubt quite justified in regarding these German and

---

[18] Quoted from Kuno Francke, *A History of German Literature as Determined by Social Forces,* New York, Holt, 1903, p. 110.

Dutch mystics of the late Middle Ages as precursors of their Reformation, if not of Kant and Hegel.

St. Francis of Assisi sets the problem of the saint and conformity in its sharpest focus. His life, after his conversion in the midst of a youth of worldly pleasure, seems to catch once more that note of primitive Christianity so difficult for most of us, touched as we are by the natural science, the rationalism, the liberalism, the comforts, and the sentimentalities of the modern world, to hear at all. Francis, it is often said, really did seek to imitate Christ, to relive the life of Christ on earth, but, do not forget, the Christ who said, "There be some of them that stand here, which shall in no wise taste of death, till they see the Son of man coming in his kingdom." There is in Francis more than a touch of the chiliast. To him the imitation of Christ was not gentle, sober, polite conformity to the ritual, the decencies, the conventions of a church that had long since accepted this world as not to be greatly changed. It was perhaps not quite imitation of the angry Christ who overthrew the tables of the money-changers in the temple; it was not quite imitation of the Christ who delivered to the multitude in Jerusalem that sermon—fit and proper foil to the Sermon on the Mount—in which there resounds the most Christian curse "Woe unto you, scribes and Pharisees, hypocrites!"[19] Francis is nearer the Christ of the marriage of Cana, of the woman taken in adultery, of the advice to the young man who had great possessions that he sell all and give it to the poor.[20] But the love Francis preached and practiced was not the modern humanitarian's desire that we should all be comfortable and therefore good here on earth. There is in Francis, though the modern sentimentalist must fail to see it, the vein of iron that runs through all Christianity, at least until modern times, a vein that has sources in the Stoa as well as in Sinai. Franciscan poverty was not a form of enjoyment, not even, though the doubter with a smack of psychology will continue to doubt, a perverse and masochistic form of enjoyment. Francis was in fact a very medieval man, one very hard for a modern to understand.

Poverty was to the first Franciscans not merely abstention from the comforts and prestige and all the rest that goes with what we call wealth; it meant also abstention from the kind of possessions Francis abhorred at least as much as wealth, that is, learning, theological skills, all the possessions of the intellect. One suspects that Francis himself had he lived would have been even more indignant at the reputation of his order for learning than at its great

[19] Matthew 21:12; 23:13 ff.
[20] John 2:1; 8:3; Matthew 19:21.

192

material wealth, both achieved in a short generation after the saint's death. The wealth was, after all, a corporate wealth, and, as individuals, members of the mendicant orders did not often fall into worldly self-indulgence, as had some of the earlier monks; but the reputation of a Robert Grosseteste or of his pupil Roger Bacon, both great scholars, both precursors of modern natural science, was an individual reputation.

Perhaps a profounder and more useful polarity in medieval saintliness than that of action and contemplation would be one between the intellectual and the anti-intellectual. The two terms are strained by contemporary abuse; and they are, of course, exceedingly imprecise. But they will do as well as any to indicate the gap between a Thomas Aquinas or a Bonaventura on one hand and a Bernard or a Francis on the other. There is a strain in Christianity, clear in much of what our sources tell us of Christ himself, that distrusts the ratiocinative, analytical, organizing, conforming, and also disturbing, but wrongly, devilishly, disturbing intellect. The Christian of this strain distrusts the intellect as the basic seducer, the serpent in Eden, the goad to a flesh that might otherwise accept peace. This strain is clear in medieval Christianity, clearest of all in the greatest of its saints, Francis of Assisi.

The most striking, and to some no doubt most painful, of the contradictions of saintliness lies in the fact the living saint is almost always a disturber, who disturbs the comfortable, well-behaved, in our ordinary sense of words by no means wicked or perverse, conformist; and the dead saint, duly canonized, is taken up into the very order of imperfection his life had protested against. You may soften the contradiction, if your temperament permits you to do so, by insisting that the saint's own real life is such that even his least worthy worshiper cannot be wholly untouched by this holiness, this leaven. But I do not think you can challenge the fact that the living saint is no merely conventionally good man, no humanitarian reformer, no "liberal" complainer, not even a good practicing Christian, but a man who will not have this world at all at the price most of us pay for our share of it.

IV

The note of distrust of the conclusions arrived at by the established, conforming mind is also clear in the less heroic field of ordinary medieval ethics. In this age of extremes one would expect to find examples of return to primitive simplicities, dislike of the learned, dislike of those in power, dislike of wealth and privilege; and so one does. The rebellions and the heresies from the tenth century on, from the Pataria through the Waldensians and the Albigensians to the revolting peasants of the later Middle Ages, within the church itself in the waves of reform from Cluny to the coming of the friars—all these lively conflicts are reflected in the political and ethical theory of the time. The range of this writing is great, and some of it sounds like a muted version of the great religious repudiation of this pharisaical world we have heard before.

But one may risk a generalization for the High Middle Ages: the normal ethical tone is not set by the rebel, but by the conformist; it is not an ethics that appeals to the heart against the head, but quite the opposite, a very rationalist ethics; it is not heaven-storming, but moderately and modestly worldly; it is, substantially, the ethics expounded for the learned by Thomas Aquinas, and brought to the many from countless pulpits and confessionals and even in the sculptures and stained glass of the churches, and to a degree in the written word, for the High Middle Ages were not by any means wholly illiterate outside the clergy.

We can here touch but very generally on this standard medieval Christian ethics. But first of all we must note that it is an ethics centered on a Christian cosmology and theology as yet untouched by natural science, still strong in its literal theism. God was so real to the medieval man that, if the word could be stripped of its many unfavorable connotations, one would have to say that his was an *anthropomorphic* God. Here, for instance, is Aquinas himself:

If we compare murder and blasphemy as regards the objects of those sins, it is clear that blasphemy, which is a sin committed directly against God, is more grave than murder, which is a sin against one's neighbour. On the other hand, if we compare them in respect of the harm wrought by them, murder is the graver sin, for murder does more harm to one's neighbour, than blasphemy does to God. Since, however, the gravity of a sin depends on the intention of the evil will, rather than on the effect of the deed, as was shown above (I.-II., Q. LXXIII., A.8), it follows that, as the blasphemer intends to do harm to God's honour, absolutely speaking, he sins more grievously than the murderer. Nevertheless murder takes precedence, as to punishment, among sins committed against our neighbour.

This sounds strange, for our own rationalism would put God far above so human a concern as honor.[21]

But do not be put off by such instances. If you turn to Aquinas on private

---

[21] St. Thomas Aquinas, *Summa Theologica*, II.2.13.3. I quote this largely for the sake of the thoroughly medieval phrase "God's honour," but the whole passage is a fine example of Aquinas at his most Whiggish. You *do* on this earth have to crack down harder on murder than on blasphemy.

property, he will surely not sound at all strange. Private property, he finds, is not originally an institution of natural law, but has been added to natural law by human reason working on the materials given by long experience of human society. It is justified by its utility; a person will take care of his own in a way he will not take care of things not his own—this is just a fact. Such ownership is subject of course to Christian duties of charity; private property must be in part shared property.[22] And so throughout, Aquinas is always sweetly reasonable, always willing to compromise where compromise seems to him required by nature and human nature, never, strangely enough in a medieval man, advocating the excessive gesture of rebellion—or of defiant Tory conformity to an idealized past.

There are certain major assumptions of this medieval ethical orthodoxy. There is, as in all orthodoxies, a clear line between right and wrong, an authority that draws that line. In matters of faith the church is that authority. We know, for instance, that the doctrine of the Trinity is true, that we must believe it, because faith is above questioning. But in the immense majority of problems this life presents us with, we must judge in accordance with our reason, which is guided by natural law. Men do, however, most obviously differ in their use of reason to find the right decision in concrete cases. Is there not still a problem of authority? Who rightly interprets natural law?

Modern students of the Middle Ages have answered this—to us, certainly —key question variously. The hostile anticlerical from the Enlightenment on has tended to believe that the whole fabric of medieval philosophical devotion to natural law was no more than a device to fool the many, to consecrate what to them was the *real* ethical principle of the Middle Ages, that what the church says is right. We need not take so partisan a position to admit that in accordance with the ethical conservatism of the time, there was in fact a great reliance on established practice, on what had been done time out of mind, on consensus and common agreement, on what most men would have thought to be "natural." All this is something very different from the arbitrariness and unreason that the Enlightenment, and the Renaissance before it, loved to attribute to the Middle Ages.

What the Middle Ages called a "just price," for instance, was not an arbitrary one in the sense that it was dictated by the will of any individual or even of any small group. The just price was in theory that price which enabled the worker to live at his accustomed standard of living while he was

[22] *Summa Theologica*, II.ii.66.

working on the goods so priced, and make his customary profit. In practice it was no doubt the price that had prevailed in the trade in that particular market, a price always threatened by the endemic inflationary tendencies of the growing medieval economy, a price always defended as the "natural" price. Adam Smith's price, set in theory by the naked play of supply and demand at a given moment, would have seemed to the medieval man to be an arbitrary and unjust price, one that might be too low to guarantee to the laborer the fruits of his labor.

The medieval man never thought of this order of nature as arbitrary—at least not in our sense, which implies an *unjust and preventable* arbitrariness. He knew God could change everything root and branch, but he did not really expect God to do so. On the whole, medieval man was no chiliast, and he did not think God would intervene in any upsetting way with the order of nature. (God did, of course, constantly intervene in specific normal ways, guided nature, so to speak, which is why prayer, reasonable prayer, duly accompanied by works, is effective.) The world as it now stood was far from perfect, but neither was it unworthy of God and man. It had gone on a long time, and we knew a good deal about how to get along in it.

In fact, the medieval was an Age of Faith in a somewhat different sense from the theological one we usually give the familiar formula. This was the last time in the West when most men believed in a quite literal sense in what we call the *status quo;* or, put negatively, and perhaps to us more clearly, these men did not believe it possible by planning, inventing, research, to alter in any important way the sum total of existing "arrangements," culture, institutions, ways of getting things done. Piecemeal, local change, yes; but even then the medieval mind, as in the familiar process of development of statutory law, liked to think of this as a finding, even a rediscovery, not a making, of a law already there, somewhere, where the over-all plan exists, at bottom, of course, in the mind of God. All this is even better illustrated by the almost universally accepted metaphor of society as an organism in which each individual, or, better, each group, had its appointed place and function. The rulers, lay and clerical, are the soul, the mind; the soldiers are the heart; the workers are the belly, and so on. This is one of the oldest of Western political metaphors. That the belly is as necessary as the head is crystal clear, but it is also clear that the belly has not the same adornments as the head, the same position as the head. The lesson is obedience, acceptance of one's earthly lot, acceptance of the order of rank of society.

Yet the record of the Middle Ages is by no means one of general obedience and conformity, and certainly not one of unchanging ways. We now know well that from the eleventh century on the medieval economy was a dynamic one, that all the material indexes start on upward, that not even the Black Death really stopped them; and, of course, we know that in fact civil disorders, risings of the underdog, the discontented, were common. It is true that there is by no means general agreement among our medieval specialists as to the socio-economic history of the late Middle Ages, especially of the fourteenth and fifteenth centuries.[23] But in the balance it is clear that there were important and disturbing changes, some of them making in the long run at least for economic progress, and most unsettling to those of steady ways, to ordinary medieval men, no matter what their social class. This is the familiar paradox once more, the gap, greater in the Middle Ages than is usual even in the West between the ideal and the real, the profession and the practice. But the paradox itself here needs a bit of explanation.

First, and this is particularly true of earlier rebellions, there is the revolutionary ingredient in Christianity. I have tried to make clear that primitive Christianity was not originally a "social gospel" of the full dinner pail and comfort for all. But the New Testament does have eloquent passages against the rich, the powerful, the successful. It is easy enough to turn much of Christianity from mere repudiation of this world to its alteration, alteration in something like the sense that the phrase "social revolution" carries for us today. Moreover, even when, through triumph of church organization, consolidation of dogma, assimilation to the world of war and politics, Christianity had become a prop of the established order, there remained in its cultural tradition an irreducible minimum of ethical idealism, a feeling that cruelty, pride, injustice are not necessarily in the order of nature. There was no reason why Zeus or Jupiter should be sorry for slaves; there was every reason why Jesus Christ should refuse to back up a wicked baron or a corrupt bishop. There is, as Nietzsche saw, almost as much moral dynamite in Christianity as in socialism.

Second, in no mere perfunctory bow to the Marxist interpretation of history, we may note that the very success of the medieval synthesis in enabling men to live and work together in *comparative* peace and good order contributed to the overthrow of medieval ethical conservatism. It is the full, or at least partly full, belly that revolts against the ignoble, if essential, role the head and the heart have combined to give it. Or to put the matter less

---

23 On this see the *Cambridge Economic History,* Vol. II, ed. Postan and Habbakuk, Cambridge, England, 1952.

metaphorically, a reasonably widely accepted feeling that a given society is in fact a just one, a society in which co-operation and integration are normal, expected, and conflict abnormal, or not really there, simply cannot last in a complex dynamic society such as Western Europe had already begun to be by the High Middle Ages. The fact of change cannot be forever concealed, even by legal fictions; and change means conflict in this real world, if not in the world of ethical, or of economic, theory. When the feudal baron and his lady really were the heads of a kind of expanded Great Family on the almost self-sufficent manor, patriarchal theories, metaphors of shepherd and flock, and a lot more pleasant notions would do very well; when the baron and his lady had become absentee landlords, when the steward had become in fact an entrepreneur in the production of wool, and the serfs had become free peasants with money incomes they could hope to increase, when, in short, the Great Family had broken up, it was not possible to go on forever insisting that the father was still a patriarch. The medieval ethical synthesis, attractive though it was, and still is, to the wistful who want the lion to lie down with the lamb, could not last.

V

To discuss the actual conduct of medieval men and women we do well to take their own picture of society with its first, second, and third estates. Inevitably, we know more about the leaders in each group and more about the ordinary members of the clergy and the nobility than about the common folk. We by no means know enough in terms of statistics and the like to be at all confident about our generalizations. But we can hazard something.

The record of the clergy is extraordinarily varied and uneven, exceedingly difficult to summarize in a short chapter like this. I trust the reader will forgive me if I make the dull and Whiggish remark that the record seems to me by no means as bad as most freethinking and Protestant historians have made it out to be, nor quite as good as some Catholic admirers of all things medieval feel that it has to be. Take at random concrete cases. As an individual bad example, Gregory of Tours has an abundance; perhaps the Abbot Pagulf will do. Pagulf, after trying in vain to get rid of, indeed to murder, the husband of a woman he coveted, slipped into the house one night in the husband's absence, and got what he wanted. The injured husband took a brutal revenge, burning up house, abbot, and wife, but the right did not always triumph so clearly in those rough days.[24] As a group example, almost any of the chapter

[24] Gregory of Tours, *History of the Franks*, VIII, 19.

visitations collected and translated by Coulton will do. Here is one for Rouen cathedral in 1248.

We visited the Chapter of Rouen, and found that they talk in choir contrary to rule. The clergy wander about the church and talk in the church with women, during the celebration of divine service. The statute regarding the entrance [of lay folk] into the choir is not kept. The psalms are run through too rapidly, without due pauses. The statute concerning going out at the Office of the Dead is not kept. In begging leave to go forth, they give no reason for so going. Moreover, the clergy leave the choir without reason, before the end of the service already begun; and, to be brief, many other of the statutes written on the board in the vestry are not kept. The chapter revenues are mismanaged [*male tractantur*].

With regard to the clergy themselves, we found that Master Michael de Bercy is ill-famed of incontinence; *item*, Sir Benedict, of incontinence; *item*, Master William de Calemonville of incontinence, theft, and manslaughter; *item*, Master John de St. Lô, of incontinence. *Item*, Master Alan, of tavern-haunting, drunkenness, and dicing. *Item*, Peter de Auleige, of trading. Master John Bordez is ill-famed of trading; and it is said that he giveth out his money to merchants, to share in their gain. [19 March 1248][25]

It is, however, easy enough to balance these instances of vice with instances of virtue. In Gregory's own day many a missionary to the heathen north and east gave the example of devoted Christian zeal. The accounts of the lives of saints are often, in our eyes, naïve and historically unreliable, but the residue of saintliness is there, not to be denied. Even the freethinkers, though they recoil in horror from the earliest Eastern hermit monks, have good things to say about Western monasticism in the first years of the Benedictine rule. These monks did live arduous lives of real labor on the land, in the library, in the missionary field. Nor can even the hostile observer question the reality of the successive waves of renewal that restored the discipline and the ardor of Western monasticism through these centuries. Whenever monastic life seemed to have gone the way of all flesh, when monks had become well-fed, lazy, lustful, worldly, there was certain to be a reform, a renewal, a new order or a reformed old order, right on down to the Reformation.

Even Coulton, an admirably trained professional historian who somehow failed to fall in love with his subject, and who managed to collect a whole series of damaging pieces, nonetheless occasionally brings in a favorable one, even, at times, an instance that has a touch of humor. Here is one from the thirteenth-century Franciscan preacher Berthold of Ratisbon:

25 Coulton, *Life in the Middle Ages*, Vol. I, pp. 95-96.

When I was in Brussels, the great city of Brabant, there came to me a maiden of lowly birth but comely, who besought me with many tears to have mercy upon her. When therefore I had bidden her tell me what ailed her, then she cried out amidst her sobs: "Alas, wretched girl that I am! for a certain priest would fain have ravished me by force, and began to kiss me against my will; wherefore I smote him in the face with the back of my hand, so that his nose bled; and for this as the clergy now tell me, I must needs go to Rome." Then I, scarce withholding my laughter, yet speaking as in all seriousness, affrighted her as though she had committed a grievous sin; and at length, having made her swear that she would fulfill my bidding, I said, "I command thee, in virtue of thy solemn oath, that if this priest or any other shall attempt to do thee violence with kisses or embraces, then thou shalt smite him sore with thy clenched fist, even to the striking out, if possible, of his eye; and in this matter thou shalt spare no order of men, for it is as lawful for thee to strike in defence of thy chastity as to fight for thy life." With which words I moved all that stood by, and the maiden herself, to vehement laughter and gladness.[26]

We may risk a general summary. There is, especially for the higher clergy, the bishops and the abbots, a long and deep trough in the Dark Ages, the years of the fighting prelates, fighting with their battle-axes alongside their lay cousins, years when the higher clergy were assimilated almost wholly to the political ruling classes, years no doubt of maximum sexual license for the higher clergy. They are the years when, for the lower clergy, sheer ignorance and the example of their betters kept them also in a trough. Clerical concubinage was very nearly transformed, for the lower clergy at least, into legitimate marriage. Then in the tenth and eleventh centuries there came one of the most remarkable waves of reform, of moral renewal, in the Western record, a wave comparable in depth and force, though in many ways very different from, the reforms that followed on the eighteenth-century Enlightenment. This medieval reform, centering in the tenth-century reformed Benedictine foundation at Cluny, seems clearly to have been a reform initiated and carried through as a reform, not a revolution, by a self-conscious and mainly clerical minority which by the eleventh century had captured the papacy. But this was also a reform movement that had to win over, if not the millions of serfs and peasants, at least the many thousands of the ruling classes. Our sources are certainly inadequate for a study of what we may nonetheless call "public opinion" in the eleventh century. But we can be sure that the Cluniac movement was one of the first in a long line of modern Western efforts to achieve through propaganda, pressure groups, electioneering—intrigue, if you like— the kind of social change we may unblushingly call "voluntary."

[26] Coulton, *op. cit.*, Vol. I, p. 125, quoting Berthold of Ratisbon, Lib. II, Chap. xxx, p. 290.

It was a successful reform. It did not achieve anything like what its most ardent proponents—for example, the monk Hildebrand, as pope, Gregory VII—may well have wanted. Some of the Cluniacs wanted a European society ruled by the Church of Rome, a true theocracy; and though there have been briefly and locally pretty complete theocracies in the West—Geneva, Boston, Paraguay—the whole temper of Western life has been against such rule. Spurred by the partial success of the reform, the later medieval popes went on to assert claims to supremacy on earth, but by 1300 they had clearly failed. We may guess that some of the reformers hoped to transform men and women right here on earth into what Christian ethics wanted them to be, but we cannot be sure of this, as we can for many later secular reformers.

What the Cluniac reformers did achieve was a good deal. They established clerical celibacy as the law of the church, a law certainly violated again and again, but always, since, not only a sin but a scandal. They helped along the process of disentangling the clergy from the full play of the complex feudal system, though they by no means succeeded in making complete separation of clerical and feudal persons. They helped initiate, in the Peace of God and the Truce of God, some social control of the private warfare among the second estate, and thus, in a very real sense, helped found the modern state. Against the sin of simony they were at least as successful as against the sin of clerical incontinence; simony was never again as open, nor as common, save in the worst days of the Renaissance popes, and then largely in Italy alone and at the top of the hierarchy. In short, the Cluniac movement raised, if only what in our day we might think of as "a few percentage points," the standards not only of clerical, but of lay conduct. It did not make over human nature, but it did make certain extreme forms of misconduct unfashionable.

There was, however, a lapse. By the early sixteenth century the clergy over most of Europe had once more fallen into a trough. The prelate with the battle-ax was gone forever, and so, too, in its pristine form, was the feudal nobility. The temptations that beset the higher clergy in the late Middle Ages were perhaps simpler than those of the ninth century; they were chiefly temptations of the flesh in a society, judged by previous standards, with a considerable margin of wealth for conspicuous consumption among the possessing few, a society of fashionable sophistication, indeed, as Huizinga's masterpiece *Waning of the Middle Ages* has made clear to us all, a society of self-conscious preoccupation with all sorts of things one need not be a Sorokin or a Toynbee to recognize as signs of cultural decadence. Here is a good sample:

In the fifteenth century people used to keep statuettes of the Virgin, of which the body opened and showed the Trinity within. The inventory of the treasure of the dukes of Burgundy makes mention of one made of gold inlaid with gems. Gerson saw one in the Carmelite monastery at Paris; he blames the brethren for it, not, however, because such a coarse picture of the miracle shocked him as irreverent, but because of the heresy of representing the Trinity as the fruit of Mary.[27]

Here, surely, in this almost Hegelian world of ours in which an excess seems to breed its opposite, is one of the reasons for Reformation puritanism.

I have perhaps said enough about the second estate under the heading of the moral ideal of the medieval knight. I have there hardly overstated the extent to which in its earlier days this class was a professional fighting class, the most undisciplined in Western history, and at least as unintellectual, or anti-intellectual, as the Spartiates. Here is Bertram de Born, an average knight, complaining about the clerically sponsored Truce of God, which sought to stop private feudal warfare between Wednesday evening and Monday morning, and on holydays:

Peace does not suit me; war alone pleases me. I am not at all concerned over Mondays or Tuesdays. Weeks, months, years—all that is to me a matter of indifference. At all times, I want to destroy [*perdre*] anyone who does me harm.[28]

These early and deadly private wars were modified into the jousting tourney and the duel, both a bit less murderous; still, over the later centuries there can be no doubt that the class, in part deprived of its roots in the soil and its local governing functions, committed suicide in wars such as the English Wars of the Roses. It and its successors—who were not actually in very large part its descendants—the European aristocracies of early modern times, never wholly lost an anti-intellectualist stamp, in part imprinted by a genuine rivalry for power with the clergy, the intellectual class. As late as the sixteenth century, we find English gentlemen protesting vigorously against the new fashionable education at Oxford, Cambridge, and the public schools, where their sons were actually studying Greek and Latin like any narrow-chested, nearsighted clerk, instead of whacking away at each other on the exercise ground.[29]

The second estate had, it must be admitted, some of the virtues the romanticist cherishes in the knights of old. They were not, as ruling classes go, addicted to the corruptions of the rich, perhaps in part because they were

[27] Huizinga, *Waning of the Middle Ages*, p. 140.
[28] Bertram de Born, cited in Villemain, Cours de Littérature Française. *Tableau de la Littérature du Moyen Age*, Paris, Didier, Libraire-Editeur, 1850, Vol. I, p. 103. My translation.
[29] Fritz Caspari, *Humanism and the Social Order in Tudor England*, Chicago, University of Chicago Press, 1954, pp. 136ff.

never for the most part exceedingly rich. All Europe was poor in the earlier medieval centuries, and as Europe grew rich it was not the knights, but the new merchant and capitalist classes, and their helpers in the new model monarchic state, who got most of the spoils. The knight was, as a businessman, inhibited by the rules and standards of his order, and by an upbringing that stifled any inventiveness he may have been born with. The class was sexually promiscuous enough, for this was a sexually promiscuous time, but it was comparatively free from the not unusual addiction of a military class to homosexuality—a practice, moreover, very vigorously condemned in Christian ethics. Many of its members were later sidetracked into the wastes of courtly love. Even its sense of honor was not quite what the nineteenth-century admirers thought it was. Like all sporting classes, it was taught respect for the rules of the game, but it was also taught by life to want very much to win. One feels it to have been closer to current American sporting ethics than to that, say, of the British Victorian upper classes, who really almost did, sometimes quite did, put virtue above winning.

Toward their inferiors the second estate were by no means the insufferable tyrants later democratic propaganda, mostly stemming from the French revolutionists, made them out to have been. They were certainly not humanitarians or egalitarians; they were full of pride of rank, and contemptuous of commoners, especially of successfully wealthy commoners. But—and this needs to be hammered home to Americans—they were constrained by habit, by unthinking respect for custom, by lack of enterprise, if by nothing else, from what the Marxist means by "exploitation" of the lower classes. By the High Middle Ages, chattel slavery had almost vanished from Western Europe; commoners, including many of the peasants who formed the bulk of the third estate, had the juridical status of freemen, and they were protected by what is one of the firmest marks of the medieval mentality, respect for status, for the established order. All this is less than Lord and Lady Bountiful— though such existed; but it is a great deal more than the wicked seigneur, fattening on the blood of his serfs, enjoying his right of first night with their brides.[30]

I do not wish to exaggerate in my effort to redress the balance upset by

---

[30] Such did not exist, certainly not in law, as modern research has made clear. The *jus primae noctis* is probably the invention of some French eighteenth-century political propagandist of talents worthy of Madison Avenue. In real Western life, the men of a privileged class are rarely as enterprising in rape or seduction of women of classes inferior to them as our modern class-warfare-conscious tradition makes them out to have been, if only because the women of their own class are usually too exacting of their energies. I trust this remark is not a mere *obiter dictum* inspired by the spirit of our own age.

our eighteenth-century democratic belief that an aristocracy of privilege is not only wicked but abnormal. Clearly there were oppressive landlords in the Middle Ages, as there were rebellious peasants, disputatious peasants, peasants addicted to moving boundary stones on the sly. Certainly the rosy picture of medieval society painted by the great literary rebels against nineteenth-century industrialism, a Carlyle, a William Morris, is no piece of realism. I am here maintaining, as often in this book, no more than the difference of a "few percentage points" in the sum total, a difference made by, a consequence of, at a minimum a reflection of, a widespread world view, an expectancy based on a generally held interpretation of the nature of man and the universe. The medieval second estate, though it numbered grasping, cruel, above all, unrestrained individuals, displays over its whole history at the very least the decencies of an unprogressive class.

The third estate in the Middle Ages was almost wholly a peasantry, though by the end of the period there was a small but well-developed urban middle class, especially in Western Europe. Most of the broad generalizations we shall risk about the actual conduct of the masses are, however, roughly true even of the higher classes. Ordinary folk in the Middle Ages were by no means puritans. There were gusts of revivalism, sometimes in unlikely places, in which the laymen were swept up into forswearing the ways of the world. Of these the best known is the brief Florentine madness under Savonarola at the end of the fifteenth century, but in these last centuries there were many less excessive religious excitements throughout the West. And always the masses held what they deemed genuine saintly otherworldliness in enthusiastic admiration. Still, there is no gainsaying the earthiness, the coarseness, sometimes the exuberance, of the common people of the Middle Ages. Folk tales, such as the French *fabliaux,* and their reflection in such a literary man as Chaucer, the details of many of the carvings of medieval churches, the many complaints the preachers make of the evils of dancing and feasting, all mount up to impressive evidence. But you can see this best in anything Breughel painted. It is true the actual painting is later than the medieval period, but these peasants at their quite unspiritual tasks and pleasures are surely unchanged from their medieval predecessors.

Bastardy was certainly not uncommon. We do not have adequate statistics; it may well be that the ratio of illegitimate to legitimate births was in many parts of Europe no greater than it was to be in the nineteenth century. But the attitude toward bastardy was very different from that of the nineteenth century. The Christian sacrament of marriage, the whole structure of family law, made the status of the bastard inferior; but men found something amusing in the fact that nature had overcome the priest. For the layman, at least, sexual continence was hardly an obligation, and the remedy for frigidity or indifference in a wife was clear and easy. Again, there are no good statistics, but it does not seem that this far back there exists much difference between the hot-blooded South and the cold-blooded North. Bastardy was no disgrace in the Italy of Leonardo da Vinci, but neither was it a necessary trauma in the Netherlands of Erasmus. And Erasmus was actually a priest's son.

In fact, in the eternal warfare between Christianity and the natural animal man, Christianity among the masses in the Middle Ages had to settle for what must look to the Christian ethical idealist—who, since the eighteenth century, has frequently been an enlightened freethinker—as a pretty empty victory of mere prestige. Medieval anticlericalism, which is genuine anticlericalism from within the church, not the anti-Christianity that often goes by the name of anticlericalism in modern Catholic countries, is evident from the slightest acquaintance with the age. The priest was for many commoners the agent of a great power indeed, a God whose existence they never doubted, but who somehow was not quite the loving God of Christian sentiment. To avoid the errors of the traditional rationalist freethinker is this matter of medieval faith —those of a Harry Elmer Barnes, for instance—I shall have somewhat reluctantly to use the language of popular psychology, which is no doubt full of its own errors: there is a deep-seated *ambivalence* in the sentiments of the medieval masses toward all the priest stands for.

The facts are there. I cite from Coulton once more:

In certain districts I have seen men when they meet priests [the first thing in the morning] forthwith crossing themselves, saying that it is an evil omen to meet a priest. Moreover, I have heard on sure authority that in a certain town of France wherein many of all conditions died, men said among themselves, "This deadly plague can never cease unless, before we lay a dead man in his grave, we shall first cast our own parson into the same pit!" Whence it came to pass that, when the priest came to the edge of the grave to bury a dead parishioner, then the countryfolk, men and women together, seized him, arrayed as he was in his priestly vestments, and cast him into the pit. These are inventions of the devil and demoniacal illusions.[31]

A simple partial explanation is obvious. The priest inherited from ages and ages of magic and of religious belief heavily weighted with fear of utterly

---

[31] *Life in the Middle Ages,* Vol. I, p. 35, no. 15. These are two other instances, less extreme and more amusing, cited on these same pages.

inhuman forces. The priest was a magician, but also a man, and as a man he might not really be in control of these forces. Better cross yourself. . . .

The age was fully as superstitious as its detractors have pictured it. Once more, there is clearly an irreducible minimum of superstition, taken in its widest sense, throughout Western history. It can be argued—not proved— that one kind of superstition slips into the place of a discarded superstition, that the sum total of superstition is roughly constant in our brief Western history. But the range and variety of superstitions in the Middle Ages was certainly great. The order of nature was no succession of scientifically established uniformities, but a colorful, only partly predictable, melodrama mixed with comedy. Nothing was untouched by the elaborate network of associations that composed the Christian tradition, swollen by hundreds of local pagan survivals. A whole book could be written about the superstitions centering on Friday, that dark day of Christ's suffering which was yet the bright day of our redemption. It would take volumes to record what happened to the relics of saints, and much of the record would be black.

These superstitions, or, if you prefer, these naïve folk beliefs, do often show the freshness, the touching innocence of the child on its good behavior, the engaging immediacy of symbolism lovers of the Middle Ages dwell upon. Here, for the sake of fairness, is one of these:

A certain lay-brother of Hemmenrode was somewhat grievously tempted; wherefore as he stood and prayed he used these words, "In truth, Lord, if Thou deliver me not from this temptation, I will complain of Thee to Thy Mother!" The loving Lord, master of humility and lover of simplicity, prevented the lay-brother's complaint and presently relieved his temptation, as though He feared to be accused before His Mother's face. Another lay-brother standing behind the other's back smiled to hear this prayer, and repeated it for the edification of the rest. *Novice.* Who would not be edified by Christ's so great humility?[32]

Finally, there is that acceptance of violence and sudden death that makes the Middle Ages so different from our own. The alert reader will here detect two contradictions, or, at least, difficulties: one summarized by Belsen, Hiroshima, and other contemporary horrors, the other an apparent contradiction with my previous insistence on the traditional, stable, conservative side of medieval culture, which should make for regular ways, not violence and insecurity. The first I find no difficulty at all, for today we do not "accept" the violence of total war as *natural and unavoidable,* not, even, as such, the domestic violence Europeans find so great in the United States. To this subject

[32] Coulton, *Life in the Middle Ages,* Vol. I, p. 65, no. 35.

I shall have to return. Nor is the second a genuine difficulty. Violence was to the medieval mind a part of God's plan, part of the expected regularities that govern the world. Disease—above all, disease at its most catastrophic in plague—as well as madness, hysteria, violent repression of heresy, the whole range of conventional crime, and, most important, perhaps, of all this, and something quite unknown to Americans for generations, the ever-present threat of famine in an economy wholly incapable of transporting staple food-stuffs very far or fast—all these made for suffering, insecurity, violence.

The Middle Ages, then, could not be humanitarian in our sense of organized humanitarian movements. The Christian heritage did insist on the obligation of charity, and the church did what it could in the vast field of what we should consider necessary social services. There is no lack of the milk of human kindness in the lives of these people. Medieval piety is full of tales of Christian sharing with the unfortunate, from the familiar one of St. Martin of Tours, who slashed his cloak in two to warm a beggar with half of it, right on through to the end of the period. There is no question of hypocrisy here. But certainly to the rationalist humanitarian of the eighteenth century and later there is definitely something that shocks him, something that seems to him wrongheaded. This something is best put as the acceptance, the expectation, of violence and suffering as part of nature and human nature. The medieval mind would have accepted as a truism the favorite reproach of the later rationalist humanitarian that Christian charity is mere alleviation of symptoms, no cure of disease. The man of the Middle Ages was sure that there is no cure—no cure here on earth and in this life, though a certain cure in eternal salvation.

We sometimes like to imagine the admiring amazement with which we suppose, somewhat naïvely, a medieval man brought to our world would confront, say, an airplane in flight. Actually, fear might well be his first but not at all unusual emotion. And since he was quite used to attributing to the Devil at least as much ingenuity as we now attribute to ourselves, he might on reflection be neither puzzled nor surprised. Were he an educated medieval man, what would really astonish him, confront him with something utterly beyond his comprehension, would be an exposition of our belief in progress, natural science, heaven on earth to come. Machines he could take, but not the beliefs that made and were made by the machines. Happiness, salvation, heaven were certain enough to him, but not in this life, not on this earth, not even as remote goals of earthly progress.

Salvation was a moral certainty of God's universe, though no single individual Christian could be sure of his own salvation, not certain in the meaning the word has for common sense. We moderns have, however, so confused the common-sense meaning of "certain," the statistical sense science gives the word, and the surviving moral sense we inherit from the Middle Ages, that we find it very hard to feel the word in its medieval sharpness, except perhaps in our moments of reverence for the wonders of natural science. Deep within some of us, at least, and perhaps surprisingly, in view of the newness of the sentiment, there is this *opposite* of the medieval attitude: the feeling that what we consider evil is *not* a part of the structure of the universe, that evil is *not* something we must struggle against with no hope of eradicating it, but *is* something we can destroy root and branch. No medieval man could really understand this point of view. It is significant that when the kind of writing we call Utopias reappears—the Greeks, of course, had Utopias, notably the *Republic* of Plato—we are already in the Renaissance. The Christian heaven was Utopia enough for the Age of Faith; but it was a sure possible haven, not a "no place"—which is what Utopia means in Greek.

VI

This last brings up a final problem, one not to be avoided, but certainly not to be solved with universal acceptance. The Middle Ages in the West was indeed a time—the last in Western history—when, at least on the surface, all men had the same religion. To be more cautious, we may say that in the Middle Ages all Westerners were members of one church, the Roman Catholic. What effect did this unanimity, this existence of One Church, have on the conduct of men, on their moral attitudes?

But first, was there unanimity? Was even the thirteenth century quite the irenic Age of Faith its apologists make it out to be? The actual incompleteness or imperfection of medieval spiritual unity is not to be denied. Heresy was endemic, and after the quarrel between Philip the Fair and Boniface VIII at the beginning of the fourteenth century schism was so deep and open that one may say that ecclesiastical unity was never really restored in the West. There were among the ruling classes who leave a record behind many hard-boiled political realists like Peter of Dreux whose conduct can hardly be reconciled with membership in the church even by a most extreme accepter of the gap between word and deed.[33] More important, there is evidence that laymen

[33] Yet the gap was indeed huge in the Middle Ages, if only because the whole structure of the word was so real and so perfect and so unattainable *here on earth*. I should guess Philip the Fair thought he was a good Christian—perhaps not as good as his grandfather had been, but, still, a Christian.

sometimes went beyond the normal anticlericalism of the age into expressed doubts about articles of faith. The view that nobody *dared* express his doubts in the Middle Ages is simply not true. Here is a thirteenth-century Belgian cleric:

Certain men of note in this world sat drinking in the tavern; and, as they grew warm with wine, they began to talk together of various things; and their talk fell upon that which shall be after this life. Then said one, "We are utterly deceived by those clerks, who say that our souls outlive the destruction of the body!" Hereupon all fell a-laughing. . . .[34]

True enough, the anecdote ends with the scoffers taught a lesson, but the scoffers could talk freely in their tavern, and they did question the doctrine of immortality. Finally, in formal philosophy, in metaphysics and epistemology, the range of medieval thought is quite as complete as it had been in the ancient world.

Yet the fact of One Church and One Faith remains; and, moreover, for the ordinary thinking and feeling man there was no real alternative to the Christian cosmology, such as the Renaissance and, more particularly, the Age of Reason were later to provide. The medieval Tom Paine or Ethan Allen, or, for that matter, Thomas Jefferson, had to take it out in straight heresy on Christian grounds. We must try to estimate what difference this degree of formal unanimity made in medieval life.

Two negatives seem clear. First, the unanimity was not by any means so complete and far-reaching as to preclude those differences of opinion or attitude that are essential to change, or, if you wish, "progress." In all sorts of ways, from technology and economic organization to the fine arts, the four centuries after 1000 are centuries of conspicuous, though not by our standards rapid, change. Second, in terms of such familiar ethical codes as the Ten Commandments and the Sermon on the Mount, it has to be said that there is no good evidence that medieval conduct was among the many any better than it had been in earlier times. It is very hard to disprove the freethinker's favorite assertion; the Middle Ages are not a period of lofty standards of loving-kindness, gentleness, honesty, chastity, refinement of passions. They are not, to a sympathetic student, the centuries of ignorance, cruelty, and filth they appeared to later freethinkers to be. But they certainly are not in practice "Christian" centuries; there have never yet been such centuries.

The existence of this formally united Christendom does, however, help explain a good deal that went on in the Middle Ages. Without it, the Crusades

[34] Coulton, *Life in the Middle Ages*, Vol. I, p. 131.

would have been impossible; and the Crusades were of great importance in the formation of our modern world. Without it, the West might never have been able to carry into modern times that tenuous sense of belonging to some society bigger than the nation-state, which it has never quite lost. Above all, this feeling that there is One Faith had as a logical, indeed inevitable, consequence certain medieval habits of mind hard for doctrinaire modern liberals to understand—though they ought to try to understand these medieval attitudes, since they are human habits of mind not wholly banished, let us say, from the liberal's own unconscious mind. If you really *know* that x is evil and by its very existence threatens to destroy y, which you know equally well is good—*the* good—you can hardly avoid concluding that x must be got rid of as completely and as certainly as possible. Such certainty here on earth only death affords. I do not quite dare in these days suggest that the problem of toleration is one of pure logic; but there is a logic of the emotions in which the medieval attitude toward heretics, the institution of the Inquisitions themselves, is clear, and untainted with the abnormal.

Indeed, the heretic was to the medieval mind the abnormal, the corrupt. Here is Etienne de Bourbon in the thirteenth century:

Heretics are refuse and debased, and therefore they may not return to their former state but by a miracle of God, as dross may not return to silver, nor dregs to wine.[35]

Another chronicler tells how, after the orthodox crusaders had successfully stormed the Albigensian stronghold of Béziers, their leaders came to the Abbot of Citeaux, spiritual guide to the operation, and told him there were Catholics mingled with the heretics in the city.

"What shall we do, Lord? We cannot discern between the good and evil." The Abbot (fearing, as also did the rest, lest they should feign themselves Catholics from fear of death, and should return again to their faithlessness after his departure,) is said to have answered: "Slay them, for God knoweth His own." So there they were slain in countless multitudes in that city.[35]

I think the reader will understand how ordinary medieval folk felt about heretics and the way they should be treated if he will reflect on how ordinary newspaper readers, and some judges, feel about "sexual psychopaths" today.

There is, finally, the question, I think unanswerable, but surely unavoidable for us in our multanimous times: Did this broad medieval unanimity (save for a small heretical minority) on matters of religion, this common

[35] Coulton, *Life in the Middle Ages,* Vol. I, pp. 87; 68.

acceptance of an *explanation* of man's fate, even of the whole universe, help make men less unhappy, give them a mental and moral security we lack, make them, to come out with the stereotype, less *neurotic?* We cannot give statistical estimates of any value as to the relative incidence of mental "disturbances" of all sorts as between 1850 and 1950, let alone as between 1250 and 1950. Our literary sources make it perfectly clear that madness—insanity—was common enough in the Middle Ages; they also make it clear that the medieval explanation of madness—essentially, in one form or another, possession of the soul of the madman by agents of Satan—together with the medieval habit of violence, and other factors, such as the cost of care, combined to make the lot of these unfortunate madmen unhappy indeed, most shocking, to our notions. But for the great majority of medieval people the question, whether put in the form "Was there less neurosis then than now?" or in the less pretentious and more familiar form "Were these morally and theologically convinced people *happier* than we are?" is quite unanswerable, and, not merely in the narrow logical-analytical sense, meaningless. I should grossly answer, they probably were not happier. But the Matthew Arnold who wrote in those rosy Victorian times felt differently.

> The Sea of Faith
> Was once, too, at the full, and round earth's shore
> Lay like the folds of a bright girdle furl'd.
> But now I only hear
> Its melancholy, long, withdrawing roar,
> Retreating, to the breath
> Of the night-wind, down the vast edges drear
> And naked shingles of the world.[36]

And so, too, do our own contemporary publicists who worry over our obvious many-mindedness in these great matters of world view. They give, or at least imply, another answer, that medieval men had a spiritual serenity and, therefore, a happiness we have disastrously lost. The skeptic can do no more than conclude, not proven. German is a great help when one wants to be vague. Sorrows these medieval men and women had, if not our world sorrows; but how real are *Weltschmerzen?*

[36] *Dover Beach.*

The Reformation

THE PAIRING RENAISSANCE AND REFORMATION, consecrated in American undergraduate terms as "Ren and Ref" in many a college, is now of such long standing that it will probably survive the attacks of the revisionists. The two coincide roughly in time, at least in the climactic sixteenth century, and they are related, as all parts of Western culture are related. But to tag the sixteenth century as "Renaissance and Reformation" is no more sensible than it would be to tag the nineteenth century as "Nationalism and Natural Science." The reformers and humanists, even though there were individuals, like Erasmus, whose lives linked them personally, were different men trying to do different things, as different as the nationalist Mazzini and the scientist Darwin. For the historian of morals in particular, Reformation and Renaissance are different worlds, not easily yoked in any metaphor, not even as obverse and reverse of a medal struck against the Schoolmen.

The Reformation belongs essentially to the history of the Middle Ages. The movements symbolized—yes, let us avoid the trap of materialist determination and say frankly, in part initiated and guided—by men like Luther, Zwingli, Cranmer, and Calvin were but the last of a long series of medieval outbreaks of the profound Christian not-acceptance of things as they are—but outbreaks from a Christian fortress, not freethinking attacks on that fortress. I have used dull and flat words indeed; the matter can be put more eloquently, and perhaps, therefore, more accurately: The Protestant reformers and those of the Catholic Reformation, too, were the heirs and successors of Benedict of Nursia, of Hildebrand, of Bernard of Clairvaux, of Francis of Assisi, of

212

Wycliffe and Hus, and of many others who throughout the ages sought to tear the church from its compromises with this world of success, wealth, power, comfort, cruelty, thick-skinned "realism," men who sought to bring back in all its freshness, all its revolutionary immediacy, the good news of the Gospels; they were *not* precursors of Locke, Voltaire, Rousseau, Franklin, Jefferson, and Bentham.

Every one therefore which heareth these words of mine, and doeth them shall be likened unto a wise man, which built his house upon the rock: and the rain descended, and the floods came, and the winds blew, and beat upon that house; and it fell not: for it was founded upon a rock. And every one that heareth these words of mine and doeth them not, shall be likened unto a foolish man which built his house upon the sand: and the rain descended, and the floods came, and the winds blew, and smote upon that house; and it fell: and great was the fall thereof.[1]

There are, of course, great differences between Luther and Calvin and their medieval predecessors; the Protestant reformers broke the unity of Western Christendom. Their heresies founded successful schismatic churches, which have gone on multiplying to the point where neither heresy nor schism really comes into many a modern Protestant's working vocabulary, any more than such to him obsolete words as "brook" and "village" come into the Coloradan's vocabulary. Note, incidentally, that the cultural environment can be as tyrannical as the geographic. Until Luther, the church had either institutionalized, tamed, softened—I do not mean this in a bad sense—the passionate other-worldliness of a Francis, or buried under the weight of academic disapproval the incipient, and dangerous, rationalism of an Abelard, or simply exterminated or, at least, driven underground by firm suppression threatening mass heresies, as with the Albigensians. That Luther and Calvin had another fate we must in fairness admit is due in part, indeed in large part, to a great complex of causes, some of which the analyst must list as economic, political, institutional, and the like. But the fact remains that Luther and Calvin were not entrepreneurs, nor nationalists, nor—above all not this—"modern" rationalists, democrats, workers for the eventual establishment of the Jeffersonian-Jacksonian-Rooseveltian republic of the United States. They were medieval men: Luther an Augustinian monk who owed a great deal to his founder, Calvin a serious-minded medieval lawyer, a member of that middle class that had long been taking over the work of running things that the knights could not or would not do. Neither Luther nor Calvin, for that matter

[1] Matthew 7:24-27.

not even the mildly "rationalist" Zwingli, thought of himself as tearing the seamless web of Christendom, as setting up a church that would settle down in comfort with hundreds of other schismatic churches. They were all setting up what they thought, if I may use the political language of our time, was the One Church, the *église unique.*

That the Protestant Reformation helped greatly to make the world we live in should be most obvious. In important senses, Protestantism is "modern," as modern as science and technology. But this modernity, I must insist, was not planned by the fathers of Protestantism, was, in fact, unforeseen by them, a fine example of something obvious to all but the very naïve rationalist, that a planned reform, once introduced into the infinite nexus of concrete human relations, can have quite unpredictable results. Once the break with Rome was in the making, even Luther, driven by the break to appeal against authority, against tradition, power, status, was put in the posture of defending freedom, innovation, individualism, "modernity." Luther, and the other reformers, for the most part, wanted men free from Rome, but not free from a God who was no anarchist, no scientific naturalist, who was a churchman and a Christian; but any challenge to authority, any challenge as eloquent as theirs, can stir the anarchist in us all, the anarchist who refuses to listen to the old argument that *true* freedom for the individual is not his doing what he wants, or thinks he wants, to do, but his doing what is *right,* what you want him to do. Protestantism did *help* make the non-Christian world view of the Enlightenment.

That the Protestant reformers so broke up the formal unity of Western Christendom against their original intentions is due to the course of events dependent in part on quite other than direct religious or theological concerns. To such concerns we shall come soon enough. Meanwhile, our starting point must be the same as Luther's, Calvin's, and even Loyola's: how to do God's will on earth, or, if you insist on the moral side of it, how to make men more truly Christians. Now it is true that the reformers, though they were agreed that the Catholic Church of the early sixteenth century was not fulfilling its mission on earth, were in broad disagreement as to just what this mission should be. The range of Protestant opinions as to the true Christian mission is great, almost coextensive with the range of human nature. On the rejection of certain specific Catholic institutions, such as monasticism, celibacy of the clergy, and a few others, there is nearly unanimity among the early Protestants. Theologically, however, it is hard to weave a blanket wide enough to cover all the Protestant reformers. Luther at his most excited—which is very excited—pushed the doctrine of salvation by faith alone to the point of anarchy, a point at which his own new Lutheran Church never arrived, and where Luther the administrator did not stay for long. In a very general sense it may be true that religious rebels appeal to faith as against works just as political and moral rebels appeal to liberty against authority, but the generalization is too broad to be very useful; the facts resist this particular dualism more clearly even than usual. Some of the reformers seem to have wanted no more than to take over the governance of the church from Rome; a "high church" party is present from the start in the Anglican and the Lutheran Churches, a party that hardly feels at all the evangelical need to make the good news revolutionary, earth-rending.

If now you ask what moved these reformers to want the particular kind of evangel they preached, and if what moved them to various expressed religious aims was not simply various changes in their concrete cultural environment—the coming of nationalism, capitalism, science, technology, and the like—we are right back at the old, unsolvable, unavoidable problem of circularity of causation. I can only repeat that the problem seems to me really unsolvable. But I think that one reason why Luther, Zwingli, Calvin, and perhaps even Henry VIII wanted what they wanted was because they could read, and being able to read, they could read such prodding sentences as:

Take heed that ye do not your righteousness before men, to be seen of them: else ye have no reward with your Father which is in heaven.

No man can serve two masters: for either he will hate the one, and love the other; or else he will hold to one, and despise the other. Ye cannot serve God and mammon.[2]

II

We may go direct to what is, certainly for the historian of Western morals, the most important spot on the Protestant spectrum—the way of life associated with that big word "Puritanism," or, almost as big a word, "Calvinism."[3] "Puritanism," especially, is one of those imprecise words that irritate the semanticist, no doubt unduly. It does have a hard core, which I suggest can be reasonably well located as a belief that the individual, the person, has a

[2] Matthew 6:1; 6:24. "Righteousness" in 6:1 may be "almsgiving"; but the central notion is clear.
[3] I cannot here go into church history and history of dogma sufficiently to cover the varieties of Protestantism. For a brief survey I can send the reader to my *Ideas and Men*, pp. 316-333, and to the works suggested for reading with that chapter.

spiritual component (not a phrase the Puritan would like—he would say simply a soul) which can and ought to control rigorously the demands of his fleshly component, his body. Such demands are many and varied, and the Puritan, historically considered, in his sixteenth- and seventeenth-century setting and in his modern one, has varied in his estimate of their badness as well as in his measures to control them. The Puritan ought, however, to be distinguished from the Christian mystic and the Christian ascetic, much though he has in common with these protesters against the *chrétien moyen sensuel*. The Puritan does not flee this world, does not deny the flesh, does not by any means seek to annihilate the flesh; he does seek to control the flesh, which means under certain conditions refusing its demands.

Now "Puritanism" is the semanticist's despair—as are so many of the words the moralist, and the social scientist as well, must use—not so much because of taxonomic sloppiness in the way it is used generally, but because of the human sentiments of love and hate that inform, and deform, its use. Especially for the English-speaking peoples, it is important to note that certain tendencies of earlier Puritanism were incorporated into the way of life we call "Victorian" and were, in the process of incorporation, twisted in ways Calvin or John Knox would not have recognized. When in the early twentieth century the literary led a mass onslaught against everything Victorian, Puritanism was one of the first and most often buried of the victims. We when young knew the Puritan was life-denying, joy-killing, and a hypocrite in the bargain. The balance has swung back again, but the echoes of the great noise set up by Mencken and many another are not wholly stilled. It takes an effort to get back to the Puritanism of the sixteenth and seventeenth centuries.[4]

What the Puritanism of Calvin, Knox, the Mathers, and all the others meant for morals is, of course, closely tied to the systematic thought of these leaders on matters of theology. For us, their central position is a very firm insistence on the absolute omnipotence of God and on the wormlike insignificance of man. But these thinkers differ greatly from the author of the Book of Job, who ends with one of the most eloquent assertions of God's inscrutable might and man's presumptuous weakness. The Calvinists do not—so the

---

[4] The reader should go to the soundly balanced studies of Perry Miller, *The New England Mind: The Seventeenth Century*, New York, Macmillan, 1939, and *The New England Mind: From Colony to Province*, Cambridge, Harvard University Press, 1953. George F. Willison, *Saints and Strangers*, New York, Reynal and Hitchcock, 1945, tries to redress the balance in a way all too common, by asserting that what is usually said about the Puritans—at least about those in and around Massachusetts Bay—is the opposite of the truth. But then, historians have to make discoveries, just as scientists do.

outsider must conclude from their actions—quite find God's will inscrutable. God might indeed have condemned us *all* to hell. Adam's sin was reason enough, but the Calvinist's God does not need reasons, not reasons tailored to poor human understanding, and there are moments in the sermons of Puritan divines when it seems as though God, turned Freudianly anthropomorphic, sadistically enjoys our suffering, and intends to keep piling it on. This is surely true of Jonathan Edwards's "Sinners in the Hands of an Angry God," notably the famous passage:

> The God that holds you over the pit of hell, much as one holds a spider, or some loathsome insect, over the fire, abhors you, and is dreadfully provoked: his wrath towards you burns like fire; he looks upon you as worthy of nothing else, but to be cast into the fire; he is of purer eyes than to bear to have you in his sight; you are ten thousand times more abominable in his eyes, than the most hateful venomous serpent is in ours.[5]

If, however, you read the whole sermon unsympathetically enough, you will have no trouble concluding that Edwards was skilled in what the complainers nowadays worry over as "motivational research," that he was a gifted but by no means "hidden" persuader.[6]

The Calvinists were desirous of saving men's souls, and of getting them to act on earth in such a way as to make salvation at least not impossible. They were surprisingly practical men, not anchorites, not mystics; they were men for whom the cure of souls meant saving souls to further the good on this earth. This in turn meant knowing something about God's wishes. If you assumed these Calvinists to be rationalists, you might accuse them of both inconsistency and pride. But they were not rationalists, and they did not need to account to anyone for their knowledge of God—except to God, and in a very exacting, if not rationalistic, accounting. But as outsiders, we may distinguish two contradictions between their theology and their ethics.

The first we have already dwelt upon, for it runs through Western moral and intellectual history. Theologically, the Calvinists were extreme determinists; ethically, though the orthodox ardently repudiated those *doctrines* of mere "conditional" predestination and even outright freedom of the will later grouped as "Arminianism," they were clear that their duty was to fight evil here on earth, and thus make the necessary prevail. The Calvinists, especially during their great debates of the seventeenth century, are most interesting because they are ferociously determined to *solve* this puzzle of predesti-

---

5 *The Works of Jonathan Edwards, A.M.*, London, Ball, Arnold, 1840, Vol. II, p. 10.
6 I hesitate to make so rationalistic a suggestion as that Edwards knew what he was doing.

nation, to keep their insufferably powerful God from appearing to poor humans quite the tyrant he looked like—indeed, had to be. Their leaders wrestled with the problem; the ordinary Calvinist had to live with it. He lived with it as, fortunately, human beings even in the West have lived with their metaphysical anxieties, by solutions adjusting, somehow, sentiments, emotions, habits, and at least a minimal demand of the intellect. The commonest solution was not far from Job's: man cannot know all God knows, or he would be God, which is unthinkable; therefore, the individual cannot *know,* cannot be certain, that he belongs to the predestined saved (as the antinomian John of Leyden was said to have believed of himself) instead of to the predestined damned; the individual is not, however, wholly without *some* light on the differences visible here on earth between saved and damned; the saved are likely to do the ethically right thing, a thing clear in the whole community of the Puritans, the damned to do the ethically wrong thing; therefore, the individual who feels any inclination to do what he knows is wrong will suppress—he is as yet without benefit of Freud—any such inclinations; he will behave as if saved, in the hope that he is saved, according to rigidly predestined plans made by God in eternity for this testing earthly prelude to eternity. It is no test for God, who knows how it will come out; but it is a fearfully uncertain test for the tested.

The second Calvinist difficulty does indeed, at least in its historical aspect, deserve to be called an inconsistency. The Calvinists at their most extreme made the sharpest of distinctions between the very few saved, the saints, and the very many damned, the sinners. This sort of distinction in worldly matters is clearly one between the *aristoi* and the *polloi.* The Calvinists were aristocrats of the spirit. Yet they appear in some senses to have fathered democracy, both of the flesh and of the spirit. Again in terms of historical development, there is no real difficulty here. In the first place, the Calvinists were for the most part, save in France, where some of the great nobles made use of Calvinism in their unsuccessful fight with the crown, members of the landed gentry, caught in the squeeze of inflation, the professional classes, or the merchant classes. They did not like what was left of the old feudal nobility, and said so firmly. They at least helped discredit an older and quite different kind of aristocracy. Second, Calvinist ethics, as Max Weber pointed out, had its part in the long process by which capitalism and its complex of values, some of which made for egalitarian democracy, prevailed in the West. Third, Calvinism got its start in rebellion against the established church; and in the West rebellion of any consequence has always had to appeal to the individual to make the decision to break with habit, law, established right, and such a break must be made in the name of the individual's *right* to think for himself, to be a "free" man. In short, Calvinism carried with it *seeds* of a way of life very different from that of Geneva, Amsterdam, Edinburgh, and Boston.

In those places, and wherever it flourished pristinely, however, Calvinism was not democratic, not libertarian, not really "modern." An American's mind at these words leaps at once to the Salem witchcraft trials. The historian is not surprised at these trials, but, rather, at the fact that there were not many more of them. For the Calvinist at bottom saw the universe as his medieval ancestors had seen it, as the universe of Christian cosmology, not by any means the universe of the "Newtonian world-machine." That from Calvinist societies there came so much so different from what the first Calvinists could possibly have planned or expected or wanted is in part explicable, as we shall shortly see, in terms of the theoretical explanations made by men like Weber and Tawney. But it is in part also explicable by the fact that in ethics and politics ideas can have consequences not clear to those who first develop these ideas; or, in a familiar figure of speech, idea seeds do not always grow into quite the plant the sower had expected.[7] Calvin, Knox, and the rest did not knowingly sow what we have recently been reaping.

Much of the way of life that developed out of their leadership did prove congruous with the channeling of human energies into the great increase in material wealth, in human command over natural resources, that made the modern West unique. We have come to the "Weber thesis," one of those ideas, or "leads," or simply "interpretations," that are now part of the slowly cumulative study of human conduct.[8] Greatly simplified, Weber's thesis—which he insists is a *sociological,* not a *psychological,* thesis—is this: the Protestant, and more especially the Calvinist, worked hard on this earth in the station to which he had been called—usually in what we should now call "business" of some sort or a profession like law or medicine; he worked hard because he believed God wanted him to follow his vocation faithfully, and

[7] The stock example is the relation between the Locke-De Lolme-Blackstone concept of the separation of powers in eighteenth-century Britain—in itself to some extent objectively erroneous—and its later development in American constitutional history. On this see A. L. Lowell, "An Example from the Evidence of History," in *Factors Determining Human Behavior,* Harvard Tercentenary Publications, Cambridge, Mass., Harvard University Press, 1937, p. 119.

[8] The reader had best go direct to the *locus classicus,* Max Weber, *The Protestant Ethic and the Spirit of Capitalism,* ed. by T. Parsons, New York, Scribner, 1930. Also R. H. Tawney, *Religion and the Rise of Capitalism,* new ed., New York, Harcourt, Brace, 1947.

also, no doubt, because "the devil lies in wait for idle hands"; he believed, also, that success in his worldly enterprises was a sign that God was with him; he had no scruples about the morality of interest-taking, nor in general about the whole economic structure of nascent industrial capitalism; he was ready, once technology had got that far, to put his capital into new power machinery which in turn snowballed into the great productive capacity of the modern world. If, as a consumer and an encourager of consumption, he was certainly no ascetic, the kinds of products his tastes and his ethics impelled him to turn out were the solid goods of large-scale production, mass market, profits plowed back, not the luxury goods of the artist and craftsman working to provide noble and churchman with "superfluous" end products. Even his churches were bare of the kind of ornamentation that costs heavily in support of "unproductive" artists. In short, the Protestant turned great moral energies, such as inspired the best of medieval monasticism, not, so to speak, *away from* this-worldly economic productivity, but directly *into* it.

Weber himself had been influenced by Marxism, and seems to have felt that the Protestant ethic helped the capitalist to justify what was "exploitation" of the workers. The Englishman Tawney, and others who have pursued this line of study, have gone further. They are clear that the Calvinist ethical concept of worldly success as a sign from God that the successful was not unlikely to be numbered by God among the saved was extended by the successful capitalist to include the convenient notion that failure to make money —remaining in the status of a paid worker with no capital save his capacity to work for a bare wage—was a sign from God that the worker was perhaps damned, or had somehow sinned, if only by being lazy and incompetent. Even ordinary Christian charity might seem interference with the will of God; to this may be added the general Calvinist notion of predestination, which could be used to justify any established relation, and also the common Protestant appeal to the individual as against authority, which could be used to justify economic individualism, or *laissez faire,* as it was later called.

The sum total puts too much of a burden on the Protestant ethic. By the eighteenth century, many other ideas and influences were coming to bear on the economic structure of the West. But even to limit the discussion to the sixteenth and seventeenth centuries, one must first of all show that there was in fact "exploitation" of workers. Absolutely, in terms of real income, it would seem difficult to show that workers were worse off in these early modern times than in medieval times. Relatively, in terms of a comparison between what the middle classes and what the workers gained from the slowly increasing economic productivity of the early modern centuries, it may be that the workers, no longer effectively protected by their obsolescent medieval guild and companionship organizations, did fall behind. But one would be safer with a Scots verdict of "not proven." The fury with which the twentieth-century attack on capitalism, industrialism, the Protestant ethic, has been carried out is in part simply a manifestation of sentiments of revolt, not very different from those that inspired Menckenian attacks on Puritanism.

An even greater difficulty with the Weber thesis taken as a blanket explanation of modern capitalism is the fact that so much of the spirit of capitalism is discernible in the late medieval world before the Protestant revolt. There is a good symbol here: the ledgers of the fourteenth-century Florentine merchant Datini—two centuries before Calvin—are headed "In the name of God and of profit." Datini was one of those obsessive persons who can destroy no papers, and by extraordinary luck the life record of this otherwise ordinary person is available to us. It shows much the same combination of business and religious anxieties, of concern for his far-flung business interests and for his future life, that come out in Weber's *Protestant Ethic*.[9]

Well before the Protestant revolt, firm foundations of modern capitalism had been laid in Italy, in the Low Countries. Capitalist careers, those of a Jacques Coeur in France, of the Fugger family in Germany, had been made by men untouched by the Protestant ethic. Venetian trade with the Levant, the English wool trade, the Hanseatic trade are all medieval examples of highly organized marketing methods dependent on banking and on "business" mentality. The Protestant ethic was an important *contributory* factor in the rise of capitalist society in those nations of Europe which, on the whole, were later to be the leaders of the industrial world: Britain, North Germany, Holland, the United States. But the map of nineteenth-century industrial leadership does not exactly coincide with the map of Protestantism: Belgium, Northern France, the German Rhineland, Piedmont-Lombardy remained Catholic countries, and yet full of the "spirit of capitalism." Some of what went into the frame of mind that made capitalism is not specifically Protestant nor specifically Catholic, but, rather, Western, a product of the long moral history we have been tracing, and no doubt of the long moral prehistory we cannot trace. The agon, the Western ritual of formal competition, or combat, if you

[9] Iris Origo, *The Merchant of Prato*, New York, Knopf, 1957. Datini's ledger is quoted on p. viii. See especially the Marchesa Origo's perceptive introduction.

prefer, at some point in the Middle Ages, perhaps as early as that marvelous thirteenth century, began to take economic channels that were to lead to the Napoleons of industry. We cannot fully understand why human energies took this turn, but once it was taken, the Weber thesis, and the Marxist thesis, help us to understand why these energies were so effective. Protestantism helped weaken that contempt for the banausic that dominated the Western warrior aristocracies so long, and that contempt for everything this-worldly—including the banausic—that filled the minds of some of the ablest and most energetic of the priestly aristocracies.

It is, finally, worth noting that as long as Protestantism in any of its forms—including, very notably, Calvinism—remained what I have elsewhere called an "active" religion it by no means encouraged the worldly way of life Weber, Tawney, and others have analyzed. The Christian who takes his religion to be his *whole life*—and this is true of the active phase of any form of the Christian religion—cannot possibly be first and foremost an entrepreneur or a capitalist. He need not—the Protestant did not—flee this world as did the anchorites. But he cannot make worldly success even one of his major goals; his mind must be on other things, even if those other things are minding other and weaker, or, at any rate, less religious men's business. Calvin's own Geneva was by no means a progressive industrial center; nor is the Boston of the Mathers very clearly as yet the germ of the Boston of the Lawrences, the Lowells, the Forbeses.

Once the fire goes out of Calvinism, once it becomes sober, respectable, a matter of routine—*not*, be it understood, therefore a matter of *mere* form, or hypocrisy, or pharisaism, though it always seems such to the next set of rebels—once Calvinism is "inactive," then the Weber thesis does seem to hold. The moral residue of Calvinism, after the intense fusion of theology and ethics in the heart of the believer no longer obtains, is congruous indeed with the "spirit of capitalism." But so, too, under favoring conditions, is the moral residue of Catholicism. Modern, industrial capitalism found less good soil in many Catholic countries, such as Italy, in large part because such countries lacked coal and iron. Moreover, Catholic habits, traditions, its network of established values, certainly made for conservative resistance to change—and change is the essence of capitalism. But once, as in Belgium, Northern France, Piedmont, the new capitalism got a start, it found in the disciples of established Catholicism a by no means unfavorable spiritual climate.[10]

[10] I owe this point to David Landes, who in his studies of the very Catholic textile center Roubaix-Tourcoing has found a living "Protestant ethic" in Weber's sense.

III

This central world-view of Protestantism, which we have to call Puritanism, was by no means limited to the formal Calvinist sects. Puritan ethics and Puritan morals are found in wide sectors of the conservative state churches, the Anglican and the Lutheran, and they inspire many of the wilder sects of the Left of Protestantism. Now many of these groups, both of the Right and of the Left, by no means shared the determinist theology of the Calvinists. Puritanism as a moral ideal and as a way of life is broader than any theology. Calvinism is its core, but there is a wide margin around that core, a margin unmistakably Puritan.

The Puritan as a moral ideal in the sixteenth and seventeenth centuries is more difficult for us today to understand than the Greek beautiful-and-good, the feudal knight, or the medieval saint, perhaps because the Puritan ideal, very considerably altered, and often not recognized as such, is nonetheless so alive with many twentieth-century Americans. We do not, I think, see the ideal embodied in an ecclesiastic, not in Calvin himself, nor in Knox, Beza, nor even in some less-known and presumably more typical Puritan divine. Though we refer freely to the Puritan "theocracies" of Geneva or Boston, we do not think of the Puritan ideal in clerical terms. Cromwell comes closer. He is certainly, in the Carlylean sense of the word, the Puritan hero. His awareness of—"intimacy with" is not quite the fair way to put it—God, his troubles with his conscience, his mastery of discipline for himself and for his men, his Puritan orthodoxy in dress and manners, his practical gifts of command and persuasion—all this fits in with the ideal.

But for what I have called the moral ideal one does not go to the great, the geniuses. The moral ideal is never perfectly embodied in anyone. It is a concrete abstraction built up from many sources. A good many Americans, in spite of the work of the debunkers, still see the Puritan as the conventionally handsome young man the sculptor Daniel French made into a bronze John Harvard, or the grave, mature, sturdy Puritan of St. Gaudens's Deacon Chapin in Springfield, Massachusetts. And it does seem again that physically the Puritan ought not to be frail, ought not to look (to use a favorite word of the nineteenth century) too "spiritual." Nor ought he, though John Milton was indeed a Puritan, be poet or artist. Tawney to the contrary notwithstanding, he ought not to be a London or an Amsterdam merchant or banker.

Our best lead here is David Riesman's phrase "inner-directed." The Puritan was alive to the civil war in the breast, and knew that he had to fight it.

God was on his side, wanted him to win, would even, in the sense of the typical Puritan adage that "God helps those who help themselves," be his ally. Still, the war was no war of coalition—not on the Puritan's side at least. He had to fight himself with himself, alone. The outside world of nature and of other men did not necessarily seem hostile to him in his struggle, though in comparison with later humanitarian and universalist faiths Puritanism is pessimistic, has in its full strength the vein of iron that runs through Christianity, both active and inactive. The Puritan was not antisocial, asocial; he knew he had to get on with his fellows. He knew that charity was enjoined on him as a duty, and that he had to do his duty.

His commanding general in this war with himself, which did often involve war with others, was his conscience. He would not, I think, even were he a strictly orthodox Calvinist, have easily thought of his conscience as "determined" by something quite outside him, even if that something were God. His conscience was himself. (Here, incidentally, is the heart of the intellectual difficulty with unconditional predestination I have discussed above.) As outsiders, we may hold that his conscience responded to the voice of a particular cultural tradition, to the pressures of his fellow Puritans, to the demands of the body he was disciplining, to an unconscious he had never heard about. He was always sure it was his voice, and always hoped that it was echoing God's.

Concretely, his conscience told him to obey the Ten Commandments. The Puritan's dependence on the Bible is a commonplace, and so, too, is his tendency to go first to the Old rather than the New Testament. This last point must not be exaggerated, however, or we shall fall into the errors of the debunkers of the 1920's, who made out the Puritans to be ferocious devotees of a revived Jehovah utterly forgetful of the Sermon on the Mount. Here, as so often in matters of morals and taste, one needs a hairspring balance. The Puritan, like most morally earnest men in the Western tradition, had at least a touch of the Stoic. His inner-direction would not let him wear his heart on his sleeve, but it is not fair to say that he had no heart. He liked order, discipline, neatness, and these things he did not find in the undeserving poor who are the usual objects of charity. But he was even harder on himself than on others, if he lived up to the ideal; and the world he wanted this one to be was surely not a cruel world.

Nor was it a gloomy one, a prison for the flesh. We must continue to step carefully. The Puritan was certainly no hedonist. Much that in normal Western practice, and even in normal Western ideal, is at worst harmless pleasure, he felt was following the Devil's lead. In those few times and places when the strongly Puritanical were in full power, they translated their ideal into blue laws, sumptuary legislation of all sorts, the laws of a "republic of virtue." A rigid Sabbatarianism has long been the symbol of this phase of the rule of the saints, one that sticks firmly in the craws of their many opponents and that gave rise to the well-known squib:

> To Banbery came I, O prophane one!
> Where I saw a Puritane-one,
> Hanging of his Cat on Monday,
> For killing of a Mouse on Sonday.[11]

The Puritans passed laws to compel non-Puritans to behave in certain ways because, like good heirs of a long Western history, they thought this was the way to regulate morals. They had not had Political Science 104 in a good American college, and did not know that sumptuary and suchlike legislation was ineffective. Moreover, in ideal, and to a great extent in practice, the Puritan required no more from others than he required from himself. If he believed the community should have rigorous codes of conduct, he had already been rigorous with himself. There were Puritan hypocrites, of course, but Robert Burns's Holy Willie is no fair sample; besides, Willie's trouble was not hypocrisy, but pride. There is nothing perverse or unusual about the legal phases of the blue laws, nor nearly as much as we once thought is perverse in the moral phases.

The Puritans were strict Sabbatarians because they felt strongly that the Catholics from whom they were revolting had profaned the Sabbath by letting all sorts of worldly activities go on then, by making it into what in English is now called a holiday, instead of making it what God meant it to be, a holyday. Much of the rest of their prohibitions are a defiance of the old nobility against whom also they were in revolt. Their simple clothes, their dull, somber colors, their short-cropped hair, their avoidance of the dance, music (save for hymns, in which the modern psychologist might say they found an outlet for much that was otherwise repressed), the drama, all are protests against the conspicuous consumption of an upper class. These prohibitions, and the deep Puritan distrust of the arts in particular, no doubt have deeper roots than this

---

11 Richard Brathwait, *Barnabae Itinerarium: Barnabee's Journall,* ed. by D. B. Thomas, London, Penguin Press, 1932, p. 17. Brathwait's Latin (p. 16) is better:
Veni Banbery, O prophanum!
Ubi vidi Puritanum,
Felem facientem furem,
Quia Sabbatho stravit Murem.

protest against an old nobility and an old, and by the sixteenth century very much painted and adorned, church; but the protest, the inevitable human version of Hegel's dialectic, is there.

The other roots are no doubt many as well as deep, not altogether exposed in their entirety even by psychoanalysis. Macaulay's well-known epigram that the Puritans stopped bearbaiting in England when they were in power, not because it gave pain to the bear, but because it gave pleasure to the spectators is true—a bit over half true, anyway—but not just. The Puritans shared the common Western acceptance of the facts of pain and violence, an acceptance not challenged by large groups in the West much before the eighteenth century. You cannot expect them to feel for the bear. As for the spectators, the Puritans felt that they were demeaning themselves at bearbaiting; they felt that this was a low pleasure, and they did not hesitate to ban what they thought to be low pleasures. There were, in their opinion, many such, though the long list of them comes almost wholly under a broad head of long-recognized vices, or temptations to vice—gambling, drunkenness, lewdness, boasting, conspicuous consumption. These pleasures all seemed to them a threat to what they valued most in externals, in conduct—self-control.

There were, however, it must be insisted, allowable pleasures for the Puritan. He did not approve of gluttony, which appears in the sermons along with other vices. But he was not greatly worried over it, and in matters of food and drink he favored solid, sound fare and enough of it. He was not notably abstemious if his digestion was good, and contrary to the opinion of the young of the 1920's his digestion often was good. He took the commandment against adultery at least as seriously as he took the others, but within the due bounds of monogamous marriage there is no evidence that he felt about sexual intercourse any of St. Paul's obvious doubts. The empirical evidence that he enjoyed the pleasures of the bed is overwhelming, especially for the American Puritans, for whom large families were an economic asset. The simpler pleasures of life, those of work, good health, exercise, the weather, all were open to him; if you are going to make much of Milton the Puritan, you had better accept the poet of *L'Allegro* and *Il Penseroso* as well as the poet of *Paradise Lost*. There were the pleasures of the mind, for though the Puritans were by no means all intellectuals, their average was high; they seem often to have found pleasure in such matters.

But they did not like Art. They closed the playhouses, stopped dancing on the green, where folk habit encouraged warmly boisterous embraces, or anywhere else, discouraged the arts of architecture and decoration in their barnlike churches, banished for a time all music but the pounding hymns. This bill of particulars is not quite fair, but it is true enough that the Puritan at his most ardent moments distrusted the higher pleasures of art as well as the lower pleasures of the flesh. I am tempted to take a cue from Macaulay, and note that what the Puritan objected to was not art, but the artist. Not all artists had by the seventeenth century become deliberately, and certainly had not yet become commercially, Bohemian. Even today, there is an occasional artist or poet who behaves like an insurance executive, and even is one. We shall come to this revolt of the artist against the Philistine again with the Romantics of the nineteenth century. The process of making the artist disreputable had, however, begun, and had gone far with the stage and was visible in the studio, and in most un-Puritan lands like Italy. The Puritan, who did not like disorder and what he thought was irresponsibility, had no patience with this incipient Bohemia. The artist has paid him back, and did not have to wait until the early twentieth century for his revenge. On the whole, from *Hudibras* on, the artists of the word have been harsh on the Puritan. Butler on the Puritans already sounds like the emancipated readers of Mencken:

> Compound for sins they are inclin'd to
> By damning those they have no mind to:
> Still so perverse and opposite,
> As if they worshipp'd God for spite.[12]

The hangers-on of the world of art, the social environment in which it thrived, also struck deep into the hates and fears of the Puritan. The English stage had produced the immortal Shakespeare, but even if the Puritan had been able to understand and accept the un-Christian realism of Shakespeare, what he could not stomach was the easygoing manners and morals of the playhouse, audience as well as actors. As for the fine arts, they were in the Puritan's mind indelibly associated with the old church and the old nobility, both of which he had rejected. Still, no doubt one must try to get at the something else in the Puritan that made him distrust, perhaps fear, the arts. We are back again at the inner-directed man, fearful, above all, of loss of self-control, aware that this world is full of temptation, indeed, taught, and believing, that such temptation is no working out of natural sequences, but the direct, ever-present intervention of the Devil himself, whose eye, like God's, is ever on the sparrow though with very different aims. I have said above (p. 155) that much would look very different to us if we really thought, with the first Chris-

---

[12] Samuel Butler, *Hudibras,* Part I, Canto I, lines 213-216.

tians, that the world would end tomorrow or the next day. It would surely also look very different to us if we felt every time we had even a slight fantasy of doing something not approved by our conscience—our superegos, if you like —that the fantasy in itself was a sign that we were likely to spend eternity in fearful suffering. I am not maintaining that this belief of the Puritan was a reasonable belief, nor even that it was a useful belief, but merely that, given the Puritan's cultural inheritance, it is an understandable belief, indeed, I fear I must say, a "natural" belief.

The lover of the high arts may still not be satisfied. Is not the Puritan's fear of art really pretty perverse at bottom, for do we not all know that high art, great art, is *catharsis,* an emptying of the soul of pettiness and evil, an elevating thing? Low art may stir the genitals, but high art, though perhaps only a John Mill would hold that it achieves a happy spiritual castration of the rapt appreciator, still has to the genitals a relation that can only be described in terms like transcendence, sublimation, ennoblement. Perhaps Dante, for one, knew better; or were Paolo and Francesca reading a work of low art that day? As always in this obstinate world—obstinate to the work of the simplifying systematist—both sides can appeal to the "facts." It is very hard to imagine anyone led astray from even Puritan morality by *Oedipus Rex.* But *Tristan und Isolde?* Give the Puritan his premises, and he has a case.

Still another major interpretation of the Puritan ideal demands our attention. Erich Fromm, who knows both the Marxist-Weber literature and the Freudian, holds that the way of life that came out of the Protestant Reformation puts too great a strain on ordinary human nature.[13] The Reformation, he maintains, broke down the complex medieval network of social, economic, and religious institutions, ritual, and beliefs which combined to give the individual some material security and much spiritual security. The ordinary man in the Middle Ages knew where he stood, had, so to speak, to make to a minimum extent the kind of decision that puts a strain on him. In Riesman's terms, he was "tradition-directed." Then Luther and the rest of the reformers came along, working, it is true, in consonance with changes in the mode of production, and emancipated the individual from all or at least a great many of these restraints. They freed him. But to the psychologist looking back on the situation, it seems clear that for *most* men these medieval ways had been not so much restraints as supports. Such men did not really, in their unconscious, *want* to be free. To the sturdy, and exceptional, Protestant individ-

[13] Erich Fromm, *Escape from Freedom,* New York, Farrar and Rinehart, 1941.

ualist, Lutheran doctrines such as justification by faith and the "priesthood of the believer" were challenges to do his best in this world without the priest's "interference," to work hard, to face the need to make decisions on his own, to be in matters of the spirit as well as in matters of business his own master.

But the majority proved incapable of this exacting way of life. In purely economic terms, they had to put up with what amounted to exploitation by the stronger. It took a long time, and presocialist and socialist effort, before the workers once more could be organized. Psychologically, as well as institutionally, no really adequate substitute for the assurances that the medieval synthesis gave ordinary men was worked out in the West, with the result that in our own times the masses "escaped from freedom" into the arms of the totalitarian dictators of Right and Left. We shall have to face this problem of the moral difficulties of modern libertarian democracy in a later chapter. Most of us today, however, touched as we all are by some popular versions of psychology, are more likely to think of Protestantism in its active Puritan form in the seventeenth century as suppressing, not liberating, as putting on *restraints,* self-imposed by the good Puritan on himself, and, through blue laws, imposed on others.[14] Yet the psychological interpretation is not here inconsistent; for the good Frommian, the artificial and harsh external restraints of later capitalist Puritanism were made necessary in part by the earlier loss to Luther and his allies of the natural and accepted supports which the old institutions and beliefs once gave the now-unsupported individual. Whether the new harsh codes were imposed by the Puritan on himself by his conscience or on the others by laws and institutions, the net result was that natural psychic drives or energies, driven back into the unconscious, took all sorts of revenges in psychoses, neuroses, maladjustments that had piled up to plague us now. We must then ask the question: Is it sensible to apply modern notions of "repression" and its evil consequences to our classical Puritan?

The question cannot be satisfactorily answered. The relativist that dwells in every historian, comfortably or not, must insist that all modern psychological theories or doctrines may turn out to be quite impermanent, that it is absurd to apply to the seventeenth century the fashionable ideas of the twentieth, and so on. And it is true that one can hardly imagine a seventeenth-

14 I use "blue laws" as a handy American term for all the complex Puritan attempts to "legislate private virtue." The reader should be warned that to the purist in matters historical the phrase means only a specific set of laws in seventeenth-century Connecticut. See W. F. Prince, "Peter's Blue Laws," American Historical Association, *Report,* 1898.

century Puritan on a modern psychoanalyst's couch. We shall never know what horrors of infantile experience lay behind Oliver Heywood's self-reproach:

Oh my Lord, I am here at Thy footstool, a worthless worm, an unprofitable branch, a sinful wretch, fit for nothing but to be cast out as unsavory salt.[15]

At the very start, it may be urged that the problem is unreal. The Puritan, it may be argued, was not suppressing, but merely "controlling." Now that the first wave of popularized Freudianism has receded, we do not regard any and all interference with the child's, let alone the adult's, wishes to be suppression, and bad. We guide, control, even punish. There is a familiar semantic situation here, the complete clearing up of which would be difficult indeed: "suppression" will for a long time not lose for us its pejorative sense. Even so, I must insist that at least for such periods of Puritan dominance as the 1640's in Britain, the rule of the saints in Geneva and in New England, and within the congregations themselves for much of these early centuries of the Reformation, "suppression" is the accurate, the necessary word. American traditions about early New England, molded still more by *The Scarlet Letter* and its like than by the debunkers of the 1920's, are not altogether misleading; the Puritans said No. Calvin's own Geneva was so fully regulated that one wonders how even the political theorists could have dug libertarian influences out of pristine Calvinism. Here is a recent popular historian's summary:

To regulate lay conduct a system of comiciliary visits was established: one or another of the elders visited, yearly, each house in the quarter assigned to him, and questioned the occupants on all phases of their lives. Consistory and Council joined in the prohibition of gambling, card-playing, profanity, drunkenness, the frequenting of taverns, dancing (which was then enhanced by kisses and embraces), indecent or irreligious songs, excess in entertainment, extravagance in living, immodesty in dress. The allowable color and quantity of clothing, and the number of dishes permissible at a meal, were specified by law. Jewelry and lace were frowned upon. A woman was jailed for arranging her hair to an immoral height. Theatrical performances were limited to religious plays, and then these too were forbidden. Children were to be named not after saints in the Catholic calendar but preferably after Old Testament characters; an obstinate father served four days in prison for insisting on naming his son Claude instead of Abraham. Censorship of the press was taken over from Catholic and secular precedents, and

[15] Oliver Heywood, quoted in W. Notestein, *Four Worthies*, New Haven, Yale University Press, 1957, p. 214. The whole essay on Heywood is worth reading as a good sampling of the minor Puritan divine. Heywood's language is the then-fashionable language.

enlarged (1560): books of erroneous religious doctrine, or of immoral tendency, were banned; Montaigne's *Essays* and Rousseau's *Emile* were later to fall under this proscription. To speak disrespectfully of Calvin or the clergy was a crime. A first violation of these ordinances was punished with a reprimand, further violation with fines, persistent violation with imprisonment or banishment. Fornication was to be punished with exile or drowning; adultery, blasphemy, or idolatry, with death. In one extraordinary instance a child was beheaded for striking its parents.[16]

This would seem to be almost the opposite of "freedom" in any sense, except for the few who made and enforced the laws. It is not that in ordinary Protestant societies the individual was left, in the sense the philosophical anarchist gives the word, "free"; it is, rather, that for the old medieval set of conformities there was substituted in Protestant countries a new one, one which in the Calvinist range of Protestantism was a great deal stricter, more repressive of ordinary human drives, than the old had been. The question then becomes: Was the new nexus of controls unsuited to the task of cementing a going society?

In its extremist forms at Geneva, in Holland, in New England, in the English Puritan Revolution, I think the answer must be yes. At any rate, by pragmatic test, these societies in their strict form did not endure. The rule of the saints at its fullest anywhere was an attempt to push and pull poor human beings to heights—and they are heights, not depths—they appear to the realistic observer not to have been designed for. The rule of the saints I have elsewhere classified with the rule of the Jacobins and of the "old" Bolsheviks, as the effort under the pricks of an active religious drive to make this earth some kind of a heaven.[17] As the Puritan drive slowly subsided, as the greatly moderated Calvinist groups became part of conventional Western society, the moral implications of their way of life change. To these we must come later, for they set their stamp—no longer by any means quite the stamp of Calvin himself—on a great deal of the nineteenth-century West, and in particular on the English-speaking parts of the West.

But even at the height of their drive to their ideal, there is no clear evidence that Calvinism "produced" more of what we call *mental disturbances* than earlier phases of Western society. I do not think that Oliver Heywood was insane, or even neurotic. Statistics, as I have had to remark often, are just not good enough to test so woolly a thesis as that Puritan suppressions

16 Will Durant, *The Reformation,* New York, Simon & Schuster, 1957, p. 474.
17 See my *The Anatomy of Revolution,* New York, Norton, 1938; in Vintage Books, New York, Knopf, 1957, especially Chap. VII.

produced mental disturbances on a large scale. For one thing, since they were small societies, for the most part, and men are mobile, the most recalcitrant could and did escape, in New England to life among the Indians of the frontier, in Europe to neighboring lands. For another, we must remember the vulgar German proverb "The soup is never eaten as hot as it is cooked." The Americans of the 1920's were not the first "scofflaws" under this kind of prohibition; even at Geneva, one could commit adultery, and procreate bastards; in England, a large country for those days, traces of Merry England survived here and there all through the Puritan revolution. It is impossible, save in inverted Utopias like *Brave New World* and *1984,* to repress all of the people all of the time.

In summary, the Puritan ideal, even when pushed into fanaticism, is at the very least one of the fascinating efforts human beings have made to tame themselves. The romanticist is no doubt right: we are indeed wild animals, barely domesticated enough to keep our species going. But the dream of an ordered society keeps recurring, spurs men on to transcend themselves and history. Puritanism is by no means the harshest of these dreams, and, in its effort to make itself real, by no means the least effective. Liberal cant in this country, which has shut so many off from so wide an area of human experience ("the liberal is a man who will not read anything he is going to disagree with"), has been especially unfair toward the Puritans. They deserve better from us; we can perhaps learn from them almost as much from the Zuñi, the Hopi, or the Samoans.

IV

Puritanism, Calvinism, though I believe they are central to the moral experience of Protestantism, by no means exhaust the varieties of such experience to be found in the Reformation. Once more using a convenient if imperfect dualism, we may distinguish between "hard" and "soft" Protestantism, or, indeed, Christianity. This distinction is not by any means that suggested by Paul's contrast of Letter and Spirit, nor that between staying in this world and fleeing from it, nor is it quite that between the organizer (Gregory the Great, Bernard of Clairvaux) and the withdrawn mystic (St. John of the Cross). The soft Protestant is no wastrel, nor is he by any means a rationalist. But he shies off from the harsher and more aristocratic doctrines of Calvinism— unconditional predestination, not to speak of such refinements as infant damnation, restriction of God's grace to a very few elect, and the Stoic bearing that goes with Puritan dignity. Though they flourished more particularly in the eighteenth century, the origins of these softer Protestants go back to the very beginnings of Protestantism. Already in the sixteenth century, Menno Simons, founder of the Mennonites, anticipates much with his doctrine of a "new birth," itself a signal of salvation. German Pietists, British Methodists, French Quietists—the latter formally Catholics, but hardly orthodox—are almost always on the soft side of the line. The Quakers, those peculiar people, have their soft affiliations, conspicuously in their pacifism and their escha- that their emotions were not those of the romanticist in revolt. They were optimistic and truly democratic Calvinists, as in a sense they are. But the taxonomy of Protestant sects is a bewildering task. The Methodists had their Calvinist wing, and they, the Baptists, and other sects were, in matters of private morality, drink, dancing, card-playing, often quite as "puritanical" as the saints had been. The Bible was their common source book. They did not precisely welcome the Age of Reason. They, and not Yankee Congrega- tionalists, and certainly not Boston Unitarians, are in twentieth-century America the last of the Puritans.

Positively, these softer Protestants do have in common an acceptance of some form of the doctrine of free will, and at least a tendency toward, if not precisely universalism—each sect believed firmly it was the true form of Christianity—at least a belief that God had basically good intentions toward the human race and would welcome a significant increase in the number of the saved. What they have most conspicuously in common is an emotional piety which in their meetings might rise to the excitements their enemies of the Age of Reason regarded as indecent, and described with the horrid word "enthusiasm." They were not for the most part wild men, however, and it is clear that their emotions were not those of the romanticist in revolt. They were simple people, mostly from the humbler ranks of society both in Britain and in Germany, and in the North American colonies. Lecky thought that the Methodist movement in Britain probably saved that country from grave difficulties with its lower classes, who had to bear the brunt of the Industrial Revolution; the miners, the workers in the new industrial towns, the deprived village laborers, found in the sharing of religious emotions, in the whole conservative fabric of Methodism, a satisfaction that saved them from the allurements of French-inspired revolutionaries. This thesis was expanded and extended by the French historian Elie Halévy.[18]

[18] W. E. H. Lecky, *A History of England in the Eighteenth Century*, New York, Appleton, 1888, Vol. II, pp. 691-692; Elie Halévy, *A History of the English People in the Nineteenth Century*, London, Benn, 1949, Vol. I, *England in 1815*, pp. 424-428. Lecky could hardly have picked up the Marxist tag about "opium of the people," and Halévy no longer needed it.

Though the pietistic sects attracted a by no means negligible number of the evangelically inclined among the educated classes—Wesley was an Oxford man, and Zinzendorf a count—they must be numbered among those who have pushed Christianity away from the intellect and toward the emotions. Their theology was relatively simple, their clergy often uneducated, and their distrust of the highly educated great indeed. But this very anti-intellectualism helped them resist much more successfully than did the hard Protestants the pressures of the Enlightenment. The Puritans' contempt for the damned of this world, their self-insulation from common sense, their intense desire to remake human conduct, would seem on the surface to be more proof against the natural science, the rationalism fondly supposing itself common sense, the often sincere belief in toleration of the Enlightenment, than would the gentle piety of the Methodists and Pietists. And no doubt in its first fire, its active stage, Puritanism was quite safe from pure rationalism. But the Puritan was essentially an intellectual; he had to think, to understand, and his warfare with himself was in part the war of the head with the heart. When the active phase of Puritanism was over, its prosperous third and fourth generations, no longer driven to bring heaven to earth, began the process of reconciliation with this earth as it stood, a reconciliation that brought some of them to Unitarianism or freethinking. The intellectual history of Boston is an excellent illustration of this movement.

Not so with the pietist sects. They not only resisted the rationalist current of the Age of Reason; they for the most part also resisted the closely interflowing current of sentimental humanitarianism. They damped the hell-fires a bit, but they did not extinguish them. They worked with the poor, the unhappy, the wicked, and welcomed their conversion or even their reformation, but they did not altogether equate sin with a bad socio-economic environment. In fact, they believed in original sin, not in the natural goodness and/or reasonableness of man. The intellectuals have not much liked them. They are not very exciting, but they were numerous, and perhaps a useful brake on our madly progressing modern world. They are still with us, almost wholly apart from the intellectuals, almost wholly, as real living persons, unknown to the intellectuals.

V

Protestant tradition, naturally enough, has held that the Reformation reformed, that human conduct improved under Protestant successes, that even the Catholics, tardily learning a needed lesson, put their house in somewhat better order in what the Protestants call the "Counter Reformation." The freethinkers of the Enlightenment had a bit more trouble in estimating the moral value of the Reformation. They felt that the Protestants had at least been an entering wedge for the Enlightenment, and they discerned in Protestant attacks on Romish superstition and corruption much of their own sentiments; still, they could and did read, and they realized that early Protestantism was Christian, in fact, superstition. And, of course, debunking has been long an irresistible temptation to all sorts of historians, including the Enlightened. We may then start with some of these doubts about the reforms of the Reformation.

The complex most consonant with the temper of our age goes back at least to William Cobbett, a testy radical journalist of early nineteenth-century England, who wrote a history of the Reformation in England.[19] Cobbett has been expanded and extended by the positivists, by the Marxists, by Weber, Tawney, and Fromm, and, naturally enough but perhaps not altogether wisely in such company, by Catholics. At its broadest, this line of attack maintains that Protestantism substituted for the communally responsible medieval society with its guilds, its organized charities, its notions of a "just price," its obligation to make life as secure as possible even for the poor, the modern unrestrained scramble for wealth. Released from these good medieval Catholic Christian restraints, the followers of the reformers, above all, the new modern territorial rulers and their hangers-on, grabbed all they could, no matter who suffered. Henry VIII in England suppressed the monasteries and confiscated their wealth, which he used to reward his courtiers and build up to support his own upstart dynasty the *nouveau riche* Tudor nobility and gentry who we mistakenly think were real nobles of Norman lineage. The German princelets, the Dutch burghers, all got their share of the spoils, and the French Huguenot nobles would have got theirs if they could—obviously it was hope of spoils that attracted them to the Calvinist allegiance.

The new rich, the attack continues, in spite of their canting Protestantism, which did not last very long anyway, conducted themselves in matters of private morality at least as badly as the rich usually do. Public morality in politics, already undermined by the unscrupulous power politics of the Italian Renaissance, was surely not improved in the North by the Reformation.

19 *A History of the Protestant Reformation in England and Ireland: Showing How That Event Has Impoverished and Degraded the Main Body of the People in Those Countries. In a Series of Letters, Addressed to All Sensible and Just Englishmen,* London, 1824-1825.

Public morality in economic life, as we have noted, was, according to this thesis, greatly worsened. Now the limits were off in competition, and the Devil took the hindmost. The new wealth came from commerce and investment, not primarily from land; its possessors lacked the steadying customary morality and the sense of duty to their dependents that the old class had had. "As truth spread," wrote J. A. Froude, "charity and justice languished in England."[20]

There are two obvious criticisms to be made of this general thesis. First, and simpler, is the criticism we have already made of the Weber thesis, that whatever the facts of change from the medieval way of life to the modern— and these facts are no doubt partly those of an expanding economy, and the transfer of the agon, the competitive spirit, from the life of the knight and the cleric to the life of the courtier allied with new capitalistic wealth— these changes greatly antedated the posting of Luther's Ninety-five Theses in 1517. Protestantism in some of its phases was part of these changes, and was affected and made possible by these earlier changes. What I have said in comment on the Weber thesis holds for this extension of his thesis: unscrupulous "Renaissance" politics in the struggles of the twelfth and thirteenth centuries between pope and emperor, not to mention the Hundred Years' War, grave neglect of the poor by their superiors, clear evidence of popular unrest all through the fourteenth century, beginnings of the ejection of farming peasants by "capitalist" landlords anxious to make more money by sheep grazing in fifteenth-century England, very modern "class struggle" conditions, the *popolo grasso* against the *popolo minuto,* the revolt of the *ciompi* in the Florentine *trecento*—the list of these unidyllic conflicts of the "serene" Middle Ages could be long indeed.[21]

Second, and more complicated, there is the criticism based on doubts as to whether there was in fact a *general* increase in conventional immorality among the ruling classes, a *general* increase in suffering, deprivation, neglect, among the ruled. We shall have in a final chapter to attempt to put into understandable order those changes in actual group moral standards and conduct that we can roughly establish. There are such changes, but they will probably not turn out to make the kind of sense the proponents of the thesis we are here commenting on try to make. There are sudden and usually impermanent collective accesses of puritanical conduct—the brief rule of Savonarola, for

[20] *Henry VIII*, Vol. I, p. 74. Even though Froude was a Victorian and a bitter anti-Catholic, I suspect there is irony in that "truth."
[21] For the Florentine class struggles, see Iris Origo, *Merchant of Prato,* pp. 66-67.

example. There are, at least in modern times, accesses of particularly striking unpuritanical conduct among those who can afford luxury, often reaction to the opposing kind of excess, such as the period of the Stuart Restoration in Britain after the Puritan Commonwealth. There are, to anticipate a bit, all sorts of long and short "cycles," varying with different classes or other groups of a given society. Ethics, conduct, morals do change between 1250 and 1700, but not as simply as the critics of Protestant morality make out.

As to the general moral level of those who could afford to live loosely—and many who tried to live as their betters lived—Huizinga's *Waning of the Middle Ages* shows clearly that the luxury, the overrefinement, the fascination with death and corruption, the morbid excesses of the sixteenth century are all present in the fourteenth and fifteenth. The same holds true of the sufferings of the poor, and of the relation between the rich and the poor. This last relation was never, at the height of the feudal-manorial system, one of mutual Christian loving-kindness. The class struggle, which the Marxists are perfectly right in insisting is a constant of Western history, was intensified and made more open, but not by the Protestant Reformation, for the process goes back much further in time. Clearly, individuals and sometimes large groups did suffer in these changes. There were evicted peasants, victims of technological change, victims of the bitter foreign and civil wars, which also antedate Protestantism, though here they are clearly stepped up by the new hatreds Protestantism brought with it. But, as I have already noted, real income, even real income for the many, the "people," subject to the ups and downs of a reasonably free market economy and to the grave local shortages inevitable in those days of primitive transportation and primitive economic administration and no doubt to many other variables, has been going up, on the whole, ever since about 1000 A.D. I do not think that the most morally outraged economic historians have shown, again on the average and over the long run, that "workers," "proletarians," even "peasants," any "lower class," has been *wholly* excluded at any time from at least a share of this increased real income.

But has not one of the marks of the modern world been the unhappiness, the discontentedness, of large numbers of those at the base of the social pyramid? Is not Fromm perhaps right, after all, that the upshot of the Protestant Reformation has been to leave the masses forlorn, spiritually uprooted, victims of a freedom to change they could not adapt themselves to, mass men deprived of all that makes for human dignity? The broader implications of this very broad generalization we must face in a later chapter. In its specific

237

application to the Protestant Reformation I think the thesis cannot be well established, and certainly needs many qualifications.

First, in terms of charity, seen as what we now call social service, the situation was not nearly as bad as some historians, like Cobbett or even Froude, have made it out to be. Even in England, the Elizabethan Poor Law of 1601 is merely the culmination at the center of national government of a long process whereby the secular authority took over the major share of responsibility for those we nowadays piously and democratically call the "*under*privileged." Once more, Puritanism is in principle harsh and disapproving toward the poor. Like that last Puritan, George Bernard Shaw, most Puritans felt the poor must be undeserving or God would not have made them poor (for Shaw, it was lack of the Life Force that made them poor). But here I think we might reverse the usual order of the puzzling relation between principle and practice; the Puritan did better by the poor than his preaching would show. I grant that he did not love them (does anybody?), but he did not let them starve.

Again, over the whole wide range of Puritanism, above all, in its less intense forms, it can be argued that men got at least the satisfaction of bringing the ideal and the real into closer approximation than has been usual in Christianity. Grant the lapses in conduct the novelists build on, grant the aesthetic poverty of the ideal, grant much of all the anti-Puritans say, it is still true that Puritans lived in communities where much that the general voice of the West has long regarded as virtue was practiced, where much that that voice has regarded as vice was kept at a minimum. The Puritan way of life for many approximated the Puritan ideal. Plain, not ascetic, living was the common lot; high thinking, exhortatory and introspective, was by no means an uncommon lot. The Puritan was far too self-conscious, at bottom too touched with a kind of rationalist drive, to take the label "primitive"; he was not even, as some of the softer eighteenth-century humanitarians became, a conscious seeker after a primitive past. (The Protestant appeal to the Bible and to "gospel Christianity" seems to me by no means genuine primitivism even in groups like the Mennonites and the Quakers.) But the Puritan way of life does have analogies with that of simple, well-disciplined, tradition-directed societies, where from top to bottom there is no luxurious living, no conspicuous consumption, no open vices, no intellectual vices like irony and cleverness.

It could not—or, at any rate, it did not—last. Puritanism had its part in the Victorian ideal and reality, and it is not without its part in our own lives.

But the Puritanism of the seventeenth century has ceased to live. The Marxist is no doubt, as usually, at least partly right; the very productivity of a Puritan society was bound to increase wealth, and to set before the successful temptations to luxurious living they could not withstand. But the Puritan respect for education, indeed, for the life of the intellect, was also a danger to the Puritan way of life. If men's "lower" appetites and feelings tend to lead them to the vulgar vices, their "higher" intellectual drives tend to lead them to even more dangerous and more varied vices—to originality, to the high disgust we call in America "liberalism," to cleverness and irony, to that attitude, most objectionable to the Puritan, for which we must, since it is usually such a *thing,* use the sophomoric *word* "sophistication." In a sense most important of all, in the specific historical situation of the West in the seventeenth century, to encourage the free use of the intellect—and to encourage the intellect at all is to tempt it to free thinking—meant to encourage the development of modern natural science. And, again, whatever it might or ought to have done, natural science has proved in fact the greatest dissolvent of the cosmology central not only to Puritanism but to all Christianity. Perhaps the central element of the "Protestant ethic" that helped make our world of mid-twentieth century was not the glorification of hard work and of worldly success, but the glorification of the intellect. Plain living the Puritan could often stand without yielding to temptation; but high thinking proved too much for him.

We may use a more concrete and perhaps more suggestive metaphor. The Puritan society was, though less simply so, one like the Spartan, the early Roman, the feudal lords of the early Middle Ages in some of their aspects, a society of lions. But the Puritans, though they disapproved of the *morals* of the foxes, were not without some admiration for the *brains* of the foxes; or, as some might prefer to put it, the Puritans themselves as men of business, the men Weber depicts, and finally as men of politics, were themselves foxes. In the human, if not in the animal world, the fox ultimately destroys the lion.[22]

VI

To return to our starting point, whatever its ramifications in politics and economics, the Reformation of the sixteenth century, both Protestant and

[22] The metaphor is Machiavelli's. It is developed at length by Pareto, whose lions are conservative, tradition-directed aristocrats guided by sentiments he calls "residues of persistent aggregates," whose foxes are innovating, clever, unscrupulous leaders guided by sentiments he calls "residues of instincts for combinations." It is hard to plunge into Pareto; but see his *The Mind and Society,* New York, Harcourt, Brace, 1935, para. 2178, 1480.

Catholic, was in the minds of many of its leaders, and their followers, too, an effort to renew the moral crusading spirit Christianity is born with. Some of them—who can be sure?—were perhaps inspired by a stepping up of that spirit into a heresy most dangerous and yet endemic in Christianity, a heresy deeper even than Manichaean dualism, a heresy anticipating that of the eighteenth-century Enlightenment. Some of them may have hoped to destroy evil on earth, to "cure" evil, a task the moral realist finds as meaningless as the physician would find the "curing" of death. At any rate, if you want to measure the success of the Reformation by the degree to which it turned all men into morally perfect beings, you can say quite simply that the Reformation was a failure.

If you take a modest standard and ask what specific reforms were relatively successful, you get a different answer. Much that outraged the reformers in the church of the late fifteenth century was ended, and has never come back in so scandalous a form. The Catholic Reformation was a striking success. The Roman papal court that so shocked Luther, and not only Luther, has never returned. It is no doubt impossible, and perhaps undesirable, to eliminate entirely the politician from the ecclesiastical administrator; but the vices symbolized for us all by the Borgias cannot possibly persist for long in any Christian clergy, and they have not persisted at Rome. The Catholic Reformation was a renewal all along the line, renewal of missionary zeal as the geographical discoveries opened up new worlds, renewal of organized social work as new orders filled with charitable zeal were founded, renewal of confidence that inspired the counterattack so successful in Central and Eastern Europe. There were relapses, even among the clergy, as the Enlightenment brought temptations of a different sort, and as the old ones were, at least for the upper clergy, renewed in an atmosphere like that of the French *ancien régime*. Yet even for France, the state of the church in 1789 does not look to modern research anywhere nearly as bad as it looked to the French revolutionaries and their faithful historians—a degree of indifference, yes, much ignorance and incompetence among the poorly paid lower clergy, but nothing like the fleshly corruption of the fifteenth century.[23]

This Catholic Reformation, be it noted, was a moral reform in a church that at the Council of Trent firmly refused to change its theology or its government. Even the rather extreme extension of the doctrine of good works which

[23] Pierre de la Gorce, *Histoire Religieuse de la Révolution Française,* Paris, Librairie Plon, 1925; André Latreille, *L'Eglise Catholique et la Révolution Française,* Paris, Librairie Hachette, 1946.

had started Luther off, the sale of indulgences, was corrected in practice rather than in theory, for at Trent the fathers decided that there was indeed a treasury of good works on which mortals under proper conditions might draw. The Catholic Church has not in matters of ultimate philosophical concern been quite the monolithic survival of the Middle Ages some both inside and outside it like to maintain it has been, but in comparison with Protestantism it has certainly resisted the later complexes of heresies I shall here call simply "optimistic-rationalist-humanitarian" and to which I shall shortly return in considering the Enlightenment of the eighteenth century.

As for the Protestants, they, too, failed to cure evil. They may, as a man like Tawney thinks, have added to the miseries, and the relative number, of the poor, have set up a new and worse Pharisaical middle class. They may have added to the number of what the modern psychologist would consider the unnecessarily self-tortured. They may have condemned many a fine artist to mute ingloriousness or vain rebellion. They may have been most responsible for the perhaps dangerous multiplicity of modern Westerners on all matters of ultimate philosophical concern. These are all most debatable propositions, and I feel wholly justified in putting them in the conditional mood. As the reader will know, I incline to think that in all these matters the requisition against Protestantism has been drawn up too strongly in recent years. But no one in his senses will accuse the Protestants of *encouraging* the Borgias in their midst. The Puritans, in fact, were for the most part reasonably—sometimes most unreasonably—pure. Even the conservative established churches, the Anglican and the Lutheran, though not unfairly accused of Erastianism at times, though they have always had numerous conventionally un-Christian Christians, have also never been conventionally corrupt. To a Kierkegaard, the nineteenth-century Lutheran Church was truly corrupt; but Kierkegaard was sicker, or madder, or more Godlike, than almost anyone in the long record of Christianity. He needed the third-century desert, but had only nineteenth-century Denmark. To all but the Kierkegaards and their lesser likes, the Protestant, like the Catholic, Reformation was a true reform; in both, it seems likely that the level of laymen's conduct was raised somewhat; in both, the open scandal of a clergy living in clear and simple sins of the flesh was ended, at least in the West.

The Renaissance

If ever an élite, fully conscious of its own merits, sought to segregate itself from the vulgar herd and live life as a game of artistic perfection, that was the circle of choice Renaissance spirits.[1]

ALL CONCEPTS OF MORAL EXCELLENCE are aristocratic, for their holders know well that the many do not live up to them. Even the most innocent of American democrats knows that, at the very best, most of the people have hitherto been fooled most of the time. There is, however, a great difference between two kinds of Western aristocracies, well brought out in the contrast between the Renaissance and the Reformation. Huizinga is quite right: the choice spirits of the Renaissance, the men of *virtù*, the humanists, the courtiers, asked only that the many not trouble them. In a few circles like that of Pico della Mirandola there was a vague, Platonic-Utopian feeling that the whole world might be much nicer if everyone knew Plato, but there really was no true reforming zeal in these people. These aristocrats of the soul and body not only did not dream of making the many into men of *virtù*, of learning, of civility; most of them did not worry at all about the conduct of the many, as long as they were not themselves interfered with.

The Protestant reformers, more particularly at the Calvinist center of Protestantism, were, as their enemies have always loved to point out, aristocrats, elitists, spiritual snobs. The elect were few, and knew it; the damned

[1] Huizinga, *Homo Ludens*, p. 180.

were many, and were kept constantly aware of their unhappy state by the few saved. Here, put with no real malice on my part, is the clue to the difference between these two aristocratic attitudes. At the very lowest point, the Puritan saint could not be indifferent to the conduct of the damned—the predestined —multitude, if only because, as a Puritan divine said, their conduct stank in the nostrils of the faithful. The Puritan may have felt he could not save the many, but he certainly could not let them sin in peace. Actually, as I have insisted, his practice was much more hopefully melioristic and Christian than his theory. He wanted his fellows to behave themselves, and he did his best to make them do so. As for the less heroic forms of Protestantism, they never quite lost, any more than did the Catholic Church, the basic Christian drive to achieve a society in which all men should live up to the aristocratic Christian ethical ideal—but to achieve it without violence, and without the heroism that destroys.

The Renaissance return to the Greeks and Romans, then, was not simply a return to round arches, Ciceronian Latin, Plato, and the rest; nor was it a return to anything so vague as a healthy paganism, the spirit of individual freedom, the revolt against authority. It was an attempt made by another aristocratic minority to live again the life of the beautiful-and-good, the Aristotelian Golden Mean, the enjoying—but not uncomfortably original, not worried, not frustrated—mind in the graceful body, the life recommended by the Just Cause of Aristophanes, "redolent of ease," the serene divorce from sweaty reality so nicely reflected in my quotation from Seneca (see p. 116). "Courtesy," wrote Paolo da Certaldo in the fifteenth century, "is nothing but the [Golden] Mean, and the Mean endures."[2] But the mean in this sense is about as far from "average" as one can get.

Now the men of the Renaissance did, like their Greek models of the Great Age, make a real effort to combine in one the excellences of the two major Western aristocratic roles, so often separated in fact and in ideal. They sought to be best with their bodies and best with their minds, to combine the warrior-statesman and the priest-artist-intellectual. They were not by any means as successful as their modern admirers have made them out to be. The Renaissance scholar-humanist, unaided by our modern lexicons, reference books, indexes, and well-catalogued libraries, had so colossal a

---

2 Paolo da Certaldo, *Libro di buoni costumi*, ed. by Aldredo Schiaffini, Florence, Felice Le Monnier, 1945, no. 82, p. 79: *Cortesia non è altro se non misura, e misura dura.* There are touches of Polonius in this little fourteenth-century book of moral advice, much folk wisdom and common Christian sense, and faint echoes of the beautiful-and-good.

task that he can hardly be expected to have had time to develop his body. Some of them did their best, but on the whole the European scholar was as tied to his desk as the Schoolmen had been. Indeed, only in England was the attempt to bring together in higher education the young of both aristocracies, the doers-to-be and the thinkers-to-be, destined to survive in partial success in Oxford, Cambridge, and the public schools. On the other side, the men of *virtù* had nothing for the exercise of their bodies quite as good as the Greeks had had in their games and their wars. The knightly tournament persisted, more than slightly ridiculous, in the sixteenth century of the High Renaissance in Northern and Western Europe; the hunt and youthful games were available. But gunpowder had begun to spoil the sport of war, or, at least, to spoil its aristocratic side, and there was never a continental equivalent of the playing fields of Eton. As for the artists, their favorite sporting exercise was usually taken in bed.

We shall, then, defying the tradition that makes the Man of the Renaissance a glorious union of the artist, scholar, and man of action, do well to consider separately the ideals of the humanist and of the man of *virtù*. Of course, the two ideals worked often in the consciousness of the same man; more particularly, the artist was likely to try to have the best of both worlds—sometimes, as with a Benvenuto Cellini, with a degree of success. At the court of Lorenzo de' Medici, the artists and the men of letters strove for courtesy and *virtù,* and the courtiers strove to be humanists. Symonds, Burckhardt, and the other lovers of the Renaissance—they were usually also haters of the nineteenth century—were not wholly wrong: these Renaissance athletes of the spirit tried hard to be Apollos. They tried, perhaps, a little too hard.

II

The *humanist* ideal gets neatly, but, as always, imperfectly, embodied in a culture hero, Erasmus. The humanist, who was a scholar and often also a man of letters and a moralist, was not what we know as a natural scientist. If, like Erasmus, he were distinguished enough, he did, however, acquire among all interested in formal culture something like the prestige of the physicist today. Had there been newspapers and news weeklies, Erasmus and a few others would have figured prominently on their pages, as an Einstein or a Bohr has in our day. How far down into the masses this reputation went in the sixteenth century is hard to measure. There was hardly yet in the

West, even in Florence, Paris, or London, the equivalent of the big sophisticated cities of antiquity, Athens at its height, Alexandria, Rome, no doubt, certainly Constantinople at the height of the fight over Christian heresies, where your man in the street is a kind of debased intellectual, lively and interested in debate on matters of taste, philosophy, or religion, almost, but not quite, as much as in sport and scandal.

The figure of Erasmus suggests some negatives about the humanist ideal, negatives with which we may frankly begin our attempt to understand the ideal as it really was, for they must be cleared out of the way. The humanist was no democrat; he had no illusions that Plato would do for the many. It is a commonplace that the first few generations of humanists after the invention of printing felt toward that mechanizing of a beautiful art the kind of scorn the artist has ever since felt for the machine-made. Printed books they disliked perhaps also because such readily distributed learning threatened to make learning easy and not a rare distinction. They need hardly have worried. The humanist was proud of the skills he had laboriously acquired, proud to the point the democrat would call snobbishness. These skills were the traditional skills of grammarian, literary historian, critic, philosopher, amassing bits from the already immense body of work in Latin and Greek; apart from a touch of archaeology, then at its very beginnings, they were not the skills of experimentation, concrete observation, case histories, in short, they were not the skills of the scientist who dirties his hands. The humanist was not a man who had nobly and in anticipation of the modern world emancipated himself from the authority of custom, the printed word, the accepted; only, unlike the Schoolmen, he did cut away as far as he could patristic and medieval tradition, and went back directly to his beloved Greeks and Romans. He merely substituted one authority for another. Toward the Schoolmen a rebel, toward the giants of classical antiquity he was the humble disciple.

But he was humble only toward the long dead and their works. He was contemptuous of his medieval predecessors, whom he regarded as benighted barbarians ignorant of good Latin and of any Greek, subservient to the reputation of an Aristotle they had never read in the original. Toward his contemporaries he displayed that curious form of the Western struggle for prize which prevails among the learned, and which has rarely been as naked, as vehement, as Homeric, since the great era of the humanists. Erasmus himself was a vain and prickly scholar, justifiably aware of his gifts and his prestige, but certainly guilty of the great Christian sin of pride. Here, as a sample of the controversial manners of the age—an extreme one, no doubt—is Poggio Bracciolini addressing his fellow humanist Tomasio Filelfo:

Thou stinking he-goat! thou horned monster! thou malevolent detractor . . . May the divine vengeance destroy thee as an enemy of the virtuous, a parricide who endeavorest to ruin the wise and good by lies and slanders, and the most false and foul imputations. If thou must be contumelious, write thy satires against the suitors of thy wife—discharge the putridity of thy stomach upon those who adorn thy forehead with horns.[3]

It is true that these quarrels of humanists have a touch of the unbuttoned that one does not find in later and purely academic versions—not even in the nineteenth-century German version—of the *entremangerie professorale.* There is Renaissance gusto in all but the driest of them, a sense of emancipation rare in the scholarly tradition. This same Poggio Bracciolini, when in middle age he found it prudent to marry, "was obliged to dismiss a mistress who had born him twelve sons and two daughters."[4]

Yet for the historian of morals the important thing about the Renaissance humanist is that in him it is possible to see, faintly indeed—it is not more than the old reliable small cloud on the horizon—the beginnings of the alienation of the intellectual that is so important a phase of our own moral climate. The attitude described in that nowadays-familiar phrase is not altogether absent from the ancient Greco-Roman culture. But not even in Plato, or the Roman satirists, or in Lucian does one see the formation of a corporate spirit, of what we call a "class," aware of itself and of its differences from any other social and economic grouping, convinced that it does not really have its rightful place at the head of all other groups. Among the Renaissance humanists there is by no means the sentiment that vulgar businessmen are doing what the humanists ought to do; there are no leagues of artists against the Philistines, the bourgeois. We must not deal in anachronistic fancies. But there is a strong consciousness of kind, a sense of belonging to a privileged group, a group so privileged not by birth but by talents, and disciplined by hard work, in short, an aristocracy of the mind, an elite. That aristocracy was at the height of the Renaissance treated very well indeed by the other aristocracy, that of the body, of political and economic power. There is not yet alienation. But it will come, and the successors of the humanists and artists of the Renaissance will be ready for it.

[3] All this, of course, in good Latin. Translated in M. W. Shepherd, *Life of Poggio Bracciolini,* 2nd ed., Liverpool, 1837, p. 282.
[4] Shepherd, *Bracciolini,* p. 282.

Among the artists, there is clearly in the Renaissance that sense of not being held to the conventions and decencies of ordinary life that was later caricatured in nineteenth-century "Bohemianism." Again, the word itself is an anachronism. Not even late medieval circles like the one that produced Villon, though they were raffish and disreputable enough, are much like the self-conscious, virtuously loose-living modern Left Bankers, Greenwich Villagers, or beat North Beachers. For one thing, there was no Victorian respectability to revolt from—that is, no organized and powerful middle class. Cellini himself, for all his crimes and disorders, so proudly reported in his autobiography, is no Bohemian. Yet the signs of what was to come are there, as they are among the scholars. The artist is the man set apart to do great things, the man made to break rules, the man who cannot be expected to put up with the dullness of life. He is still the greatly honored Michelangelo, still the Protean Leonardo da Vinci, still, even as a minor artist, the Cellini who hobnobs with a king of France. His successors will not take as kindly to their middle-class patrons.

Once more, and at the risk of being unduly tedious, I must point out how thoroughly the Renaissance ideal of humanist and artist bears the stamp of the struggle to prevail in an intense competition. I would not for a moment contest the fact that the scholar and the artist were inspired by lofty ideals of Truth and Beauty. I am willing to grant that it is nobler, more useful to mankind, altogether morally better, to produce the best piece of statuary, the best critical edition of Aeschylus, the best plan for St. Peter's, than it is to run the fastest race, knock out the most opponents in prize fights, joust best in a tourney. But we should not forget, as we tend to forget when we feel the prizes of a contest are noble, that the contest still was a fight, that there were more losers than winners, that the winner almost certainly enjoyed winning, that, in short, the Sermon on the Mount was no part of it all. The Renaissance so many have admired from a distance, the Renaissance the textbooks strew with nice words like "individualism," "free spirits," "gusto," was in fact one of the most violent free-for-alls of Western history, one with a great deal of infighting, and no referee.

III

The most important and all-inclusive of Renaissance ideals is that of *virtù*. It is an ideal that descends clearly in many ways from the medieval knightly ideal, and in one of its phases, that represented by the familiar *Courtier* of

Castiglione, employs the same term the troubadours used to designate the ideal of *courtly* love. It is an ideal for the first aristocracy, the men of affairs, though certainly many a member of the second aristocracy was inspired to follow it. Cellini, for instance, was sure that he had achieved *virtù*—as, indeed, he had.

Etymology can help here, and clear up the difficulty that springs from the fact that *virtù* is not virtue. Both words come from the same Latin root, which means simply "male strength," and has survived in the English "virile." In modern English and French, however, Christianity has scored at least a verbal triumph and has succeeded in divesting the word "virtue" of its masculinity, pugnaciousness, and general aura of magic potency, and investing it with its current and relatively peaceful ethical content. The Italian *virtù*, the great word of the Renaissance, kept its more primitive associations; but even so, when taken over bodily into English in the eighteenth century, it came to mean there a passionate connoisseurship of art objects, became merely a part of that great Mignon complex, or fallacy, that has so distorted our Northern understanding of the Italians.

Virtù for the man of the Italian Renaissance meant doing supremely well, gracefully, and, if possible, with no sign of effort, what his society esteemed most worth doing. Now as I have already noted, it is true enough that in the Renaissance many of the things scholars and artists do were esteemed as permitting the exhibition of *virtù*. (No lonely *virtù*, of course; it has to be exhibited to others.) Castiglione would have his courtier

more than passably accomplished in letters, at least in those studies that are called the humanities, and conversant not only with the Latin language but with the Greek, for the sake of the many different things that have been admirably written therein. Let him be well versed in the poets, and not less in the orators and historians, and also proficient in writing verse and prose, especially in this vulgar tongue of ours; for besides the enjoyment he will find in it, he will by this means never lack agreeable entertainment with ladies, who are usually fond of such things. . . .[5]

But Castiglione's man of *virtù* has much more firmly the markings of the aristocrat of the great Western tradition of bodily gifts, of the warrior spirit and training, tamed vastly, softened perhaps, and certainly civilized, in comparison with the simple sword wielders of old, but still a full hormonal male. Again, an excerpt or two will do:

[5] Castiglione, Count Baldassare, *The Book of the Courtier* (1528), trans. by Leonard Eckstein Opdycke, New York, Scribner, 1903, p. 59.

. . . I am of opinion that the principal and true profession of the Courtier ought to be that of arms; which I would have him follow actively above all else, and be known among others as bold and strong, and loyal to whomever he serves. And he will win a reputation for these good qualities by exercising them at all times and in all places, since one may never fail in this without severest censure. And just as among women, their fair fame once sullied never recovers its first lustre, so the reputation of a gentleman who bears arms, if once it be in the least tarnished with cowardice or other disgrace, remains forever infamous before the world and full of ignominy. Therefore the more our Courtier excels in this art, the more he will be worthy of praise. . . .

I wish, then that this Courtier of ours should be nobly born and of gentle race; because it is far less unseemly for one of ignoble birth to fail in worthy deeds, than for one of noble birth, who, if he strays from the path of his predecessors, stains his family name, and not only fails to achieve but loses what has been achieved already; for noble birth is like a bright lamp that manifests and makes visible good and evil deeds, and kindles and stimulates to virtue both by fear of shame and by hope of praise. And since this splendour of nobility does not illumine the deeds of the humbly born, they lack that stimulus and fear of shame, nor do they feel any obligation to advance beyond what their predecessors have done; while to the nobly born it seems a reproach not to reach at least the goal set them by their ancestors. And thus it nearly always happens that both in the profession of arms and in other worthy pursuits the most famous men have been of noble birth, because nature has implanted in everything that hidden seed which gives a certain force and quality of its own essence to all things that are derived from it, and makes them like itself: as we see not only in the breeds of horses' and of other animals, but also in trees, the shoots of which nearly always resemble the trunk; and if they sometimes degenerate, it arises from poor cultivation. And so it is with men who if rightly trained are nearly always like those from whom they spring, and often better; but if there be no one to give them proper care, they become like savages and never reach perfection.[6]

The *Courtier* is, like so much else in the Renaissance, deliberately Greek. Sir Harold Nicolson has put this well:

Castiglione had at the back of his mind the twelve great virtues which Aristotle defined as essential to the perfect man. He assumes above all that the good courtier will possess the two virtues of Magnanimity and μεγαλοπρέπεια, which is generally translated 'magnificence,' but which also signifies 'grandeur controlled by taste.' It is greatness of mind and nobility of soul that differentiate good manners from such things as deportment and etiquette, which can be taught 'by any dancing master.' Moreover, the function of courtier might be humiliating, were it not for the end, or *telos*, that it serves. A courtier should train himself to become a man of such character, ability and standing as to be able to direct his

[6] Castiglione, *The Book of the Courtier*, pp. 25, 22.

prince along the paths of liberality and justice and to keep him always within 'la austera strada della virtù.' Were it not for such high ideals and purposes the position of a courtier might appear parasitic.[7]

Castiglione, who seems to have been a nice man and who, after all, was writing a book of etiquette, even though it has high philosophical touches, does not really underline the extent to which *virtù* is a masculine thing. But note a significant detail from the history of costume. The fifteenth and early sixteenth centuries are, as far as I know, the only period in the history of the West when the male wore very tight lower garments ("hose"), with a conspicuous codpiece, which was often ornamented. This fact "proves" nothing but symbolizes a great deal. The man of the Renaissance admired masculinity, one may hazard, but was a bit uncertain as to whether he had it; hence, he must display what he undoubtedly had. Remember, the old feudal fact of maleness, untouched by art and letters, was still fresh in men's minds. Indeed, one may hazard a broader and even riskier generalization: in the Western tradition, the pursuits of the artist, writer, scholar, priest have never been accepted generally as *fully* masculine pursuits. The codpiece accompanied naturally enough the highest masculine flight of the artist and thinker.

A special kind of *virtù* came from the successful application of this heightened ethics of competition to politics. We think, once we have got over our first normal Western identification of Renaissance with Art—an identification not necessarily made by the men of the Renaissance themselves —of the Borgias, of Machiavelli, of the *condottiere*, of the Renaissance popes, as typical figures of their age. And so they are. High politics, it need hardly be said, is not a pursuit in which the participants have generally lived up to the best ethical concepts of the Western tradition. But the politics of Renaissance Italy survives in our memory, along with that of the Roman Empire at its worst, as peculiarly immoral, as combining the refinements of a high culture with the ferociously unprincipled struggle for power of Merovingian France. The world of Machiavelli does, however, seem to most of us somehow worse than that of Gregory of Tours—though the fact remains that in the end both justify acts that are certainly contrary to the rules of Christian morality. Perhaps we are all victims of our feeling for history: Cesare Borgia should have known better; Clovis the barbarian could not have known better.

Nor was the politics of *virtù* by any means limited to Italy. Burckhardt, who did not like being the safe Swiss bourgeois he was, admired the *virtù*-filled actors of European politics, as he admired most of what went on in the

[7] *Good Behaviour*, Garden City, N.Y., Doubleday, 1956, p. 152.

sixteenth century. They made the state a work of art, he felt. And as artists they could hardly expect to be what the bourgeois call moral. Certainly the personalities stand out. The struggle for power between Charles V and Francis I, with Henry VIII strutting the sidelines, with all Italy boiling with men of *virtù*, with Protestantism in the North in its first heat of passion—all this, heightened by the beauties of art and letters, makes a picture most attractive from a safe distance. But the potlatch touch is there, in fact, rather more murderous in its ultimate extension than it seems to have been among the aborigines of the Pacific Northwest, and absolutely, if not relatively, even more expensive. No Kwakiutl ever bested those two Renaissance tribesmen Francis I and Henry VIII at their meeting on the Cloth of Gold near Calais. Indeed, for those who like to line up the perfect transitional moment from medieval to modern—Dante, first modern and last medieval writer, Bouvines, last medieval and first modern battle, and so on—the Field of the Cloth of Gold (1520) makes an excellent, if rather late, moment. The Field was a medieval tourney, the armored knights tilting away as of old; but it was also an international conference "at the summit," and it was conducted with some awareness of what we call "public opinion."

One final carping word about the Renaissance ideal. These aristocrats were reasonably secure in their superiority, clear that they were above the common herd. They did not, it is true, seem to worry much about their inferiors. And yet, they seem, from our remove in time, to be not quite as assured as the Greek gentlemen were; they seem to be *consciously* different from the vulgar, on the edge, at least, of worrying about their superiority. Castiglione can be read as being somewhat on the defensive. The reader may remember the line from Homer cited in Chapter III, which I have crudely translated "always to be best in masculine excellences and come out on top of others" (see p. 65). Here is the Renaissance George Chapman's version: "that I should always beare me well, and my deserts enlarge beyond the vulgar. . . ."[8] One should not hang too much on a single instance. But Homer says not a word that can be remotely associated with the concept of "vulgar." The man of *virtù* knew the vulgar were there, not altogether unmenacing.

I have no doubt painted too black a picture of the two great Renaissance ideals of the humanist and the man of *virtù*, or, at any rate, of men trying to live up to these ideals. The humanist was not always vain and quarrelsome

[8] *Homer's Iliad*, trans. by George Chapman, London, Routledge, 1886, Book VI, line 218 in the translation.

with the peculiar defensive vanity and purely verbal violence of the scholar; and in the ideal he should not have been vain and quarrelsome. The Florentine Platonists were apparently gentle souls, no more than agreeably proud of their great learning. Ficino, in an age when the scholar might in an economic sense exploit his patrons and often did, remained as poor and devoted to his tasks as any medieval monk. The many Christian humanists who before and after the hotly combative Luther and the coldly assured Calvin sought to bring the new learning to purify but not disrupt the old church were often as good Christians as it is permitted men to be, modest, temperate, kindly, firm, unposturing. Guillaume Farel, John Colet, St. Thomas More, or, among those who left the church, Zwingli and Melanchthon, must be put as a balance against the more violent and prideful. *Virtù* itself need not, and did not, always take the course it took with Cellini, or Cesare Borgia, or the other Renaissance earth stormers. Lorenzo de' Medici was worthy of his circle. Castiglione's *cortegiano* was no mere exemplar of the will to shine, but a cultivated, disciplined, considerate gentleman, trained to reconcile in conduct and in ideal the beautiful and the good.

"Reconcile" is not the word the Renaissance man would use here. The ideal has the attractiveness most of us find in the old Greek identification of the beautiful with the good—to which one might as well add the true, even the natural. These great and good words, no matter how they may annoy the naïve semanticist, mean much, and very specifically. The beautiful means inevitably to us Westerners much that the puritanical strain in our Christianity cannot quite accept as good: guiltless sensuous pleasures of all sorts, from pleasure in human nakedness to pleasures in sounds that lull instead of inspire. The true must seem to many of us not quite the unavoidable and not very pleasant thing the realist—or Nature herself—sometimes thrusts under our noses. Somewhere, outside the cave Plato himself did not quite escape from, beauty must be truth, truth beauty, and both good and natural. Why not in Medicean Florence?

IV

Why not indeed? For one thing, because a Florentine monk, Girolamo Savonarola, who does not figure in the Mignon complex, did not feel that the beautiful is the good. Savonarola's brief bonfire of books and paintings seems out of place in the Renaissance, and so it is, for the Renaissance is not a "period," but, rather, the lives and achievements of a small group of artists, scholars, men of *virtù*. Unlike Puritanism, the Renaissance never did touch the many, even in Italy. No doubt the Florentine masses were aware of the reputation of their city, and proud of it; so were the Parisians of the nineteenth century aware that theirs was *la ville lumière*. But this is the vicarious satisfaction of "pooled self-esteem." Neither morally nor aesthetically were the masses of either city lifted to the level of those they admired.

Savonarola's brief career as a Puritanical fanatic at least as extreme as the Calvinists is a reminder of several things that need saying here. First, although no Puritanism imprinted itself as a way of life among the many in the so-called "Latin" nations as did Calvinism in the North, the notion that Puritanism plays no part in the moral history of these lands is not true. The Puritan temper is in its characteristic forms passionate indeed, dedicated to ends utterly opposed to the ideal of the beautiful-and-good, excitable, perfectly congruous with our stereotypes about the Latin temperament. Historically, Puritanism was born in the Mediterranean, with Moses and with Plato, and it has never ceased to crop up there. Most of the great renewals of Latin monasticism were inspired by the Puritan desire to subdue the old and too-comfortable Adam in us all. From Arnold of Brescia through Francis of Assisi to Savonarola and Socinus, Italy has produced in all their varieties these passionate men of single purpose, who do not remind one at all of the brilliant polymaths and sunny artists of the Renaissance—the Leonardos, the Ficinos, the Raphaels . . . and the Sodomas. Spain, of course, does even better with the austere, tortured, proudly militant or raptly mystical Christian whom we English-speaking people cannot think of as Puritans, largely, no doubt, because our own Puritan ancestors thought of Spaniards as their antitheses as well as their enemies. The list is long, culminating in Loyola, St. John of the Cross, and that Greek who *must* have been a Spaniard, though he goes by the name of El Greco.

Savonarola may remind us not only of the fact that even in the South there are, especially for the historian of morals, many great figures in the chronological "period" Renaissance that do not fit with the "real" Renaissance, but also of the fact that Savonarola and many of these other dark rebels against even the beautiful-and-good in its resurrected form could move the people, the many, in a way the Politians, the Ficinos, the Erasmuses, the painters and sculptors could not—and indeed did not *want* to move them. They remind us who are Protestants that the passions, the great mass movements, the killings and the torturings, the series of revolutions we call the Reformation are no Northern thing, but cover all the West. Spain again is a good symbol. The *siglo de oro* was not for most Spaniards a time of great artists and writers; it was a time of searing religious conflicts between the conservatives and the reformers, conflicts quite as bitter as if Lutherans and Calvinists had actually won a foothold in Spain, conflicts that bred among the masses that extraordinary tension that is the mark of social revolution, successful or abortive. This is what happened to the body of St. John of the Cross:

Hardly had his breath ceased than, though it was an hour past midnight, cold and raining hard, crowds assembled in the street and poured into the convent. Pressing into the room where he lay, they knelt to kiss his feet and hands. They cut off pieces from his clothes and bandages and even pulled out the swabs that had been placed on his sores. Others took snippings from his hair and tore off his nails, and would have cut pieces from his flesh had it not been forbidden. At his funeral these scenes were repeated. Forcing their way past the friars who guarded his body, the mob tore off his habit and even took parts of his ulcered flesh.[9]

Something like this can happen anywhere, anytime, as long as the Christian eschatology has meaning for the many; if sin, damnation, and salvation are real to them, men are going to grasp excitedly for available salvation, as they would for available gold.[10] But there was too much of this kind of religious frenzy, too many signs of deep popular disturbance and unrest, in the centuries that culminate with the sixteenth for the historian of morals to dismiss all this as simply another constant of human conduct. We come to the most important and difficult part of our subject, the estimate of the level of moral life of an age. It looks as if for such a purpose the chronological period really appropriate is the last few centuries of the Middle Ages— Huizinga's "autumn" of the Middle Ages, roughly the fourteenth and fifteenth centuries—and the sixteenth century itself, the golden age of the Renaissance. These look like disturbed, unhappy, difficult centuries, especially for the many, a period of moral lapse, a kind of trough in the diagrammatic account of human conduct in the West.

It is difficult, and perhaps impossible, to show an actual decline in the kind of conduct easiest described as the domain of conventional private morality. Was there over all the West a relatively greater number of men and women who commonly lied, raped, murdered, fornicated, committed adultery, stole,

[9] Gerald Brenan, "A Short Life of St. John of the Cross," in *The Golden Horizon*, ed. by Cyril Connolly, London, Weidenfeld and Nicolson, 1953, pp. 475-476.
[10] It began to happen not many years ago over the grave of a priest in greater Boston; church and state combined to stifle so un-American a manifestation of the primitive in Christianity.

got drunk, idled unprofitably, behaved, as our self-conscious generation puts it, "neurotically," in 1490 than in 1290? The reader knows already that I do not think this question can be answered at all in accordance with the highest standards of the historian's profession. National, local, class variation in these matters forces itself on our attention ever more vigorously as our sources improve in quantity. Nevertheless, I think it worth while to try to guess at some answers, which add up to a "yes, there is more private immorality on an average and among the many in these centuries."

The preachers, the moralists, are vigorous enough. Here is a final lead from Savonarola, who writes to his father in 1475:

In primis: the reason that moved me to enter religion is: first, the great misery of the world, the iniquities of men, the rapes, adulteries, larcenies, pride, idolatries, and cruel blasphemies which have brought the world so low that there is no longer anyone who does good; hence more than once a day I have sung this verse, weeping: *Heu fuge crudelas terras, fuge littus avarum!* And this is why I could not suffer the great malice of the blind peoples of Italy, and the more so as I saw all virtues cast down and all vices raised up. This was the greatest suffering I could have in this world.[11]

And here is a less exalted moralist, the English Elizabethan translator— Grub Street is already near—Aegremont Ratcliffe:

For who ever saw so many discontented persons: so many yrked with their owne degrees: so fewe contented with their owne calling: and such number desirous, greedie of change, novelties? Who ever heard tel of so many reformers, or rather deformers of estates and Common weales; so many controllers of Princes, and their proceedinges: and so fewe imbracing obedience? whiche beginneth nowe (the more pitie) to be lagged at the carte's taile. And to be short: such straunge and souden alteration in all estates? . . . The Merchant, doth he not tickle at the title of a Gentleman? The Gentleman, doth he not shoot at the marke of Nobility? And the Noble man, hath he not his eye fixed uppon the glorie and greatnesse of a Prince? What Prince could not be contended to be Monarche of the whole world?[12]

Finally, even earlier there are ample signs of the kind of social unrest that makes, if not for private immorality, at least for the kind of personal difficulties over status, security, discipline which our contemporary alarmists seem to find so unprecedented. As early as 1381, John Ball wrote:

By what right are they whom men call lords greater folk than we? . . . how can

[11] Quoted in Ralph Roeder, *The Man of the Renaissance,* New York, Viking, 1933, p. 4.
[12] "Dedication to *Politique discourses,*" quoted in Ruth Kelso, *The Doctrine of the English Gentleman in the Sixteenth Century,* University of Illinois, *Studies in Language and Literature,* XIV, No. 1-2, Feb.-May, 1929, p. 32.

they say or prove they are better than we, if it be not that they make us gain for them by our toil what they spend in their pride.[13]

Now it is true enough, as I have pointed out in my introductory chapter, that there is in Western tradition almost a constant of complaint of this sort, generation after generation of intellectuals who tell us the men and women of their time are wicked, more wicked than usual, and who say so with an eloquence that makes my report of what they said seem inadequate. Yet we must not conclude that such complaints are of no use to the historian seeking to find out how men really did conduct themselves; these moralists must be used with care, with due reference to all other sources, and to the full record of other kinds of history, but when so used may help us in our attempt at retrospective man watching.

There is, then, in the writings of these men of late medieval and early modern times a surprising degree of unanimity about the moral failings of their age. Their tone is quite different from that of what was, after all, a great Age of Complaint and even Conflict, the Victorian. The Mills, the Carlyles, the Renans, yes, even the Kierkegaards and the Nietzsches, make their chief attack on mere stuffiness, "middle-class morality," and insensitiveness to the good and the beautiful. The moralists of the eighteenth-century Enlightenment center their attack on the privileged classes; they clearly for the most part believe in the natural goodness of the common man. But the late medieval and early modern reformers, from Wycliffe and Hus to Luther and Calvin, spare no one. They are, of course, preachers by calling. What they say is backed up, however, from many sources. It is no doubt unwise to swing completely around to the "realist," and insist that Chaucer, Boccaccio, Marguerite of Navarre, and the others are simply reporters, social scientists desirous of arriving at the typical in human behavior. It would be dangerous to call in and take at their word the deliberate shockers, an Aretino, the proto-Bohemians, a Villon, the cheerful skeptics, a Rabelais, the concerned skeptics, a Montaigne, the inverted idealists, a Machiavelli. But when taken with several grains of salt their evidence is impressive: a troubled, lively, fascinating, and immoral age.

When, therefore, all this is put together, when much social history is added in confirmation, one gets the firm impression that the Reformation, Protestant and Catholic, was needed, and was indeed a moral reformation. Again, no single item is necessarily more than a bit of the *fait divers* which were there before there were newspapers to record them. When we read that

13 Quoted in Kelso, *English Gentleman*, p. 31.

Charles the Bold in 1468 witnessed a Judgment of Paris in which the three goddesses were appropriately naked, we may regard this as just one more example of the way the great misconduct themselves. When we read that women danced naked in some of the taverns, we may feel we are simply dealing with the eternal Folies-Bergère, one of the great constants of history.[14] But when to many details of the sort one adds the fact that in the history of female costume these centuries, starting from the full, modest robes of the thirteenth century, witness the gradual development of exposure and emphasis until décolletage, front and back, becomes as complete as possible—and is accompanied by that helpful egalitarian device we call "falsies"—we begin to see the light of a process, a describable social change.[15]

Indeed, the historian of morals, who should realize that deeds are often closer to other deeds than words to deeds, must pay careful attention to the history of human dress. Clothes are one of the chief forms of conspicuous consumption, one of the chief signs of great success in any agon. There is certainly no universal co-ordination between clothes and sex morality, but within one cultural tradition, such as that of the West, female costume is at least some indication of how far in a given class strict, male-dominated monogamous marriage is an expected and even realized thing. We must return eventually in considering our own society to this puzzling problem of the relation between the outward recognition—even the flaunting—of sex differences, the display of the female breasts, the male genitalia (as in the above-mentioned codpiece, symbol of *virtù*), and the morals and the *morale* of a whole class or society. We may modestly rest content here with the obvious fact that in the late Middle Ages and in the Renaissance the facts of sex were flaunted.

There are other indications of a high-living age. The arts of luxury, not merely dress but furniture, cookery, private and public building, all flourish. The ideals of the humanist and, on the surface, the man of *virtù*, pay respect to the "classical" or "Apollonian" feeling for moderation, self-discipline, restraint, respect for the opinions of one's peer group, the old Greek wisdom of "nothing in excess." Yet the fifteenth and sixteenth centuries were among the wildest, most excessive, most exuberant of times. Painting, sculpture,

14 Friedländer, *Roman Life and Manners*, Vol. II, p. 93, quoting Falke, *Deutsche Trachten-und Modenwelt*, Vol. I, p. 278. Friedländer thus emerges from his own "period" for the good purpose of showing that the looseness of imperial Rome was not unique.
15 On all this see Durant, *The Reformation*, pp. 766-768, with many useful references to secondary literature.

architecture were so directly in the classic tradition that we tend to be fooled by these works of art, which do look restrained, restrained notably in comparison with the later baroque. But the life behind the paintings and the sculptures was unrestrained, rowdy, given to extremes, consciously lived as something for the record. These immoralists, had they not been orthodox Latinists, might have gone us one better with that horrid prefix "super." The men of the Renaissance lived romantically, anticipating and often in real life outdoing the romanticism of the Romantics of the nineteenth century. These latter had to take out their wild desires, for the most part, in printer's ink.

And always, right through the Renaissance, there is the familiar violence that had so long been man's lot. There was the uncertainty of daily life in the face of the never wholly absent threat of famine, plague, the diseases of filth and contagion, and, in most of Europe, the cold of winter. There was the still, by modern standards, most imperfect public order. Police, beyond a few night watchmen in the cities, did not exist. Bands of beggars could be violent and dangerous; highwaymen were an accepted risk of travel. The atrocious punishments for what are now minor crimes—the famous example is the English penalty of death for sheep stealing—added public executions to the violent flavor of all life and clearly did little to diminish crime. It must be repeated: however real in the West today, and especially in the United States, are the problems set by violence, from juvenile delinquency and adult gangsterism to highway accidents and the fearful threat modern war presents, however persistent in "human nature" whatever drives men to these violences may seem, the fact remains that the problems of violence in our world are set in so different a framework of social and political institutions, of actual human expectation and habit, that they are quite different problems. We think of much if not all violence as preventable; the men of the Middle Ages and the Renaissance did not. The haunting fear our intellectuals have of the atom bomb is a different thing from the fear everyone then had of famine, plague, and their fellows.

After such serious matters, it may seem trivial to come to the topic of cleanliness, even if there is an English proverb that cleanliness is next to godliness, and should, therefore, be a concern of the moralist. But one of the many eddies of the modern current of thought that sees the Middle Ages as good and later ages as bad has a little eddy on cleanliness. The Middle Ages, it is maintained—at least as far as towns and cities went—were relatively clean, and physically a good human environment, if a trifle cramped; people took baths. With the growth of the modern way of life, and especially after capitalism, the cash nexus, the businessman, the mad scramble of the market place had taken over and ended medieval togetherness and mutual responsibilities, towns and cities got crowded, dirty, ugly, and people stopped taking baths—the capitalists would not let them.[16]

I am afraid this thesis cannot be proved. It can hardly apply at all at any time to the great majority of Europeans, peasants whose housing, sanitation, and the like were probably not very different in 1550 from what they had been in 1250—cramped, filthy, unhygienic, and not even lovely. Peasants did not bathe. As for the towns, still walled, they had often grown considerably by the sixteenth century, and were more crowded, and hence perhaps less agreeable to live in. But I do not think that medieval towns were as clean and pleasant as the lover of the Middle Ages—who is almost always a hater of the present—makes them out to have been. I do not think that the moral, or immoral, equivalent of the cash nexus was quite absent from Western society even in the thirteenth century.

There is not much doubt that the West in the sixteenth, and right through the eighteenth century, was what we should consider very dirty and unsanitary indeed. Individuals who prospered could often live as comfortably and as cleanly as they wished in their own interiors; housing in the countryside in Western Europe did clearly improve considerably in early modern times. But urban filth was an Augean stable. The most ardent lover of eighteenth-century London—and there are many of them nowadays—knows well it was a stinking place.[17] In the Louvre, and at Versailles, those great palace cities, there was a most inadequate provision for what Americans now call "rest rooms." The male courtiers, at least, commonly simply retired to a corner behind a door; as a result, the odor of urine was a permanent thing in these abodes of luxury. It seems farfetched to blame this on the spirit of capitalist enterprise.

The historian of morals must be careful to record the moral reputation an age has left behind it; that reputation may seem to him not entirely deserved, and, in particular, the reputation may rest on the conduct of a class or group by no means typical of other parts of the society. But there will always be

---

[16] Mr. Lewis Mumford will do as an example of this attitude. I do not much caricature his position in my brief account. See Lewis Mumford, *The Culture of Cities*, New York, Harcourt, Brace, 1938, pp. 42-51.

[17] My older readers may remember the late Leslie Howard in *Berkeley Square*, a play in which the sentimental twentieth-century lover of the eighteenth gets transported back to his beloved eighteenth-century London—and is horrified by its stench, its dirt, its harsh class-lines, its violence.

some fire behind the smoke, some truth in the cliché. The Renaissance has left us the evil moral reputation of Italian life at its height, and the beginnings of the firm belief among Northerners, at least, that in Western Europe the distinction between North and South is no mere geographical cleavage, but a moral cleavage.

The best-known exhibit of Renaissance immorality is the papal court under popes like Alexander VI and Julius II. No sensible person nowadays would think of trying to deny the personal immorality of the conduct of Alexander Borgia, which is quite down to that of Clovis, nor the worldliness and corruption, the shocking struggle for prize, of the papal court in much of the fifteenth and sixteenth centuries. One need not consult Protestant or freethinking historians: the great Catholic historian Ludwig Pastor is quite frank about it all, indignant as a good man should be, and aware as a historian should be that no evil is quite unprecedented. Homo sapiens has been on earth enough to give a full indication of his capacities for both good and evil.[18]

A sounding almost anywhere in contemporary writing should convince the reader that this Italian Renaissance, for all its glories, was a violent and immoral age. Almost any page of Cellini will do for the artist. Here is a passage from Boccaccio's *Decameron* which shows a breakdown of *morals and morale* far worse than what Thucydides tells us about the comparable plague at Athens:

Some thought that moderate living and the avoidance of all superfluity would preserve them from the epidemic. They formed small communities, living entirely separate from everybody else. They shut themselves up in houses where there were no sick, eating the finest food and drinking the best wine very temperately, avoiding all excess, allowing no news or discussion of death and sickness, and passing the time in music and suchlike pleasures. Others thought just the opposite. They thought the sure cure for the plague was to drink and be merry, to go about singing and amusing themselves, satisfying every appetite they could, laughing and jesting at what happened. They put their words into practice, spent day and night going from tavern to tavern, drinking immoderately, or went into other people's houses, doing only those things which pleased them. This they could easily do because everyone felt doomed and had abandoned his property, so that most houses became common property and any stranger who went in made use of them as if he had owned them. And with all this bestial behaviour, they avoided the sick as much as possible.

In this suffering and misery of our city, the authority of human and divine

---

[18] The reader should dip, at least, into one of the fifteenth- or sixteenth-century volumes of Ludwig Pastor, *History of the Popes*, English translation, 40 volumes, St. Louis, Herder, 1910-1955. This is sober, conscientious historical writing, in no sense alarmist.

laws almost disappeared, for, like other men, the ministers and the executors of the laws were all dead or sick or shut up with their families, so that no duties were carried out. Every man was therefore able to do as he pleased.

Many others adopted a course of life midway between the two just described They did not restrict their victuals so much as the former, nor allow themselves to be drunken and dissolute like the latter, but satisfied their appetites moderately. They did not shut themselves up, but went about, carrying flowers or scented herbs or perfumes in their hands, in the belief that it was an excellent thing to comfort the brain with such odours; for the whole air was infected with the smell of dead bodies, of sick persons and medicines.

Others again held a still more cruel opinion, which they thought would keep them safe. They said that the only medicine against the plague-stricken was to go right away from them. Men and women, convinced of this and caring about nothing but themselves, abandoned their own city, their own houses, their dwellings, their relatives, their property, and went abroad or at least to the country round Florence, as if God's wrath in punishing men's wickedness with this plague would not follow them but strike only those who remained within the walls of the city, or as if they thought nobody in the city would remain alive and that its last hour had come.[19]

Finally, here are a few entries from the diary of the Florentine Luca Landucci. They are, like our newspaper stories of today, accounts of what the reader most wants to read, the horror story; they are not sociological studies. Still, this is surely a world far more violent, more insecure, more "natural" and undisciplined, more immoral, than ours:

21st June. We heard that the French had gone with our troops to encamp before Pisa, and the Pisans had fired upon the French and killed several of them. The French leader came here, and it was said that the French went in and out of Pisa as they chose. Treachery was suspected, and this suspicion was justified.

At this time the plague appeared in several houses, and many people were suffering from French boils.

On this day certain women came out of Pisa clothed only in their chemises; but our troops took them, suspecting that they carried messages, and decided to search them. The soldiers were so shameless as to search them to their skins, and they found letters to the Pope's son. Think what wars bring about, the innumerable cases that happen, and the sin of those who cause it all.

At this time we heard that there had been a tumult at Perugia, and that the Baglioni had been expelled, 100 men having been killed. Also that the Sienese were in arms, and that the father-in-law of Petruccio had been killed.

[19] Trans. by R. Aldington, New York, Covici, Friede, 1930, pp. 3-4. The reader should go to the whole of this introduction to the First Day.

11th August. Pistoia rose in arms, on account of internal disputes.

During these days all the people here were discontented, chiefly because of the *barzello,* which had been very hard upon them, and also because they could see that no conquests were made, and there would be large costs to pay. The Pisans had sacked Altopascio and taken Librafatta.

17th August. We heard that the Pistolese were still fighting amongst themselves, and that 150 men had been killed, and houses burnt down; and the church of San Domenico was burnt down. The people from all the country round, and from the mountains, rushed to the town; and it was said besides that Messer Giovanni Bentivogli had sent men on foot and horseback.

19th August. We heard that the Pisans had taken the bastion, and killed everyone in it, and that they were encamped at Rosignano; and our leaders did not send to relieve any place, it almost seeming as if they were stunned. We were without soldiers, in fact, or to speak more correctly, with but few; their number not sufficing to go to the succour of a place when needed, so that we were between the devil and the deep sea. It was a very distressing and perilous time, so much so that on the 20th August, the day of San Bernardo, the bells of the *Palagio* were not allowed to be rung, on account of the dangers within and without; but God has always helped this city.

30th August. Soldiers were hired and sent to Pistoia and to Livorno and to garrison the castles.

1st September. Many people passed through here on their way to the Jubilee.

5th September. We heard that the Turks had taken Corfu and Modone, and had killed everyone, and razed Modone to the ground. And it was said besides that the Turks had defeated the Venetian fleet and captured it; and that 30 thousand persons had been killed, on board the vessels and in the cities together.[20]

Something of this laxity, corruption, and violence is visible in other parts of Europe than Italy. The fifteenth century, notably, is everywhere one of social unrest, endemic violence, of widespread fears and pleasures of the senses, an age that seems to deserve Sorokin's label for our own: sensate. And in the sixteenth century, the Northern Renaissance itself, if it does not equal the achievements of the picturesquely sinful Italians, is not an age, even in those homes of virtue, England, the Low Countries, and Germany, of chastity and simple moral virtue among the great. Elizabethan England would have—I almost wrote should have—shocked Victorian England.

[20] *A Florentine Diary,* trans. by Alice De Rosen Jervis, London, Dent, 1927, pp. 170, 171, 172-173. The "French boils" are almost certainly syphilis, a new disease which people of a given state usually named from their favorite enemy. The year is 1500.

But, though as Protestants many of us register firmly Italian immorality for these centuries, general opinion in the West has been willing to forgive the Renaissance its sins, as it has not been willing to forgive imperial Rome, or Byzantium, or—much much less sinful, in fact—the aristocracies of the *ancien régime* in France and her imitators. Partly, no doubt, we are, in spite of ourselves, heirs of the Victorians, who held that, particularly for the Renaissance, great Art redeems everything. We feel, and perhaps not without justification, that the unprincipled struggles, the exaggeration of pride into *virtù*, the romantic, Faustian effort to bring back to life classic, Apollonian Greece and Rome, the tremendousness, the sheer hyperbolic drive of these men of the Renaissance, was somehow nonetheless not without a most paradoxical aesthetic measure and restraint. (Paul Bunyan, pure and revolting hyperbole, is no Renaissance character.) Their saving graces make their immoral conduct somehow fruitful, at bottom, moral. Perhaps more soundly, we judge, from the vantage point of time past, these disorderly centuries of the late Middle Ages and the Renaissance to have been signs of an age of growth, of progress, those of imperial Rome and Byzantium to have been signs of decay and death.

As to the second major aspect of the reputation of the Renaissance, the establishment of a division between a moral North and an immoral South, we must note that Northern opinion greatly exaggerates for the fifteenth and sixteenth centuries the reality and degree of that difference. Nevertheless, the division is by no means wholly unreal. Calvinism, whether you think it economically or spiritually determined, took root in the North as it never did in the South. The South, as I have insisted above, has had its Puritan rebels, its crowds inspired by brief and quite unsunny passions; it has never had a large middle class endowed or afflicted with "middle-class morality." There is that much truth in the Mignon complex, even in the forms it takes with a Norman Douglas or a Robert Graves.

Moreover, to balance the laxities and the corrupting rivalries of court life and high politics, there was throughout the North an aristocracy and gentry, formed in just these centuries from the fourteenth through the sixteenth, varying certainly in its ideals and conduct in different lands, but, on the whole, as I shall point out in the next chapter, a disciplined, serious-minded, conscientious, privileged class, much maligned in our tradition. The English landed gentry, the Dutch nobility, the French provincial noblesse, the Prussian *Junkers*—these were not much like the Italian upper classes of the Renaissance. They were, substantially, lions, not foxes, and they as much as

the Protestant reform and the rising middle classes gave to the next few centuries of European life its stamp of high seriousness.

V

What we are dealing with in this chapter, however, exceeds the bounds of
private morality, of a history of morals taken in a narrow sense. What seems
to be happening in these centuries is a widespread disturbance, a loosening
of the old steady ways, a social syndrome of the kind that the philosopher of
history calls by some phrase suggesting death or decay, with or without overtones of coming rebirth. Intellectuals of our own day, feeling that we ourselves
are on some horrifying descent, have been fascinated with syndromes of this
sort in the past of civilization. We do not understand them; we are not even
sure that we can identify them. After all, the West survived this crisis of the
fifteenth and sixteenth centuries—if there was a crisis. Perhaps what happened was simple enough: wealth increased markedly over these centuries
and, however bad the condition of the masses may have been, a very great
number of people were by 1500 able to do something besides work, eat, sleep,
and procreate. They could afford luxuries, afford to play, afford to sin; and
this they proceeded to do, and to worry vocally about it.

At the very least, this innocent economic interpretation must be accompanied by recognition that for many whose wealth permitted the pleasures of
the flesh, as well as the pleasures of high competition, of *virtù,* there was a
haunting memory of the fact of sin. The tensions, the excitements, the tortured awareness of the macabre, the *excessiveness* of the age must have their
theater of action in the human soul. But we can go much further. Surely new
and increasing wealth and its consequences have their place in the syndrome,
but so, too, must a major fact of the history of ideas, and therefore of the
history of morals: from the fourteenth century on there was slowly formed
a new cosmology, a new attitude toward man's place in the universe—"new,"
as always in human affairs, implying much survival of "old"—a new view of
reality which could not always or readily or forever sit comfortably along with
the old medieval synthesis in the mind of any one normal man. We shall be
much concerned with this new view of reality—better, new views of reality
—for the rest of this book. Summary of so complex a thing is impossible; we
may for the moment content ourselves with a good symbol, the title of a
book by the late V. Gordon Childe, a distinguished Australian anthropologist

and non-Christian: *Man Makes Himself*.[21] I feel sure there are no medieval books with titles remotely like this.

With the Reformation and the Renaissance we have at last come to the end of the Middle Ages. An older way of looking at historical periods did see in both Reformation and Renaissance the modern age born fully formed, ready for life, liberty, and the pursuit of happiness. There is no use quarreling over so adjustable a matter as a historical period. It is a long way from the thirteenth century to the eighteenth century, and in all these years the Middle Ages as a way of life was slowly giving way to what we call the modern, or, in Toynbee's despairing words for our own contemporary generation, the "post-Modern." The historian who focuses on international politics, national history, art, letters, technology, will naturally emphasize quite different dramatically notable points of break between medieval and modern, or insist there is no such break, but only a long slow transition. For the historian of morals, however, the break, though far from sudden, comes rather in the seventeenth and eighteenth centuries than earlier, and it comes out fully only when those two great factors in the modern Western moral outlook, the nation-state and the complex of science, technology, and business enterprise have come into being, and man has before him the alluring promises of the religion of the Enlightenment with its doctrine of progress.

There remains, in a brief retrospect of the Middle Ages from the point of view of the historian of morals, a whole interrelated set of attitudes, theses, theories, and just plain notions, which add up to the view that, despite their violence, social and economic inequalities, superstitions, poverty, and all the rest, the way of life of the Middle Ages was somehow more suited to *la condition humaine* than our own, that they were, or at least had, a Golden Age. Some form or other of this view, though it is still almost unknown to many Americans, has had a great revival in our own day, a revival quite different from what seems to us the naïve and romantic "Gothic revival" of the early nineteenth century. Even in this brief survey we have come across the names of several associated with one form or another of this view—even if their emphasis is often less on exalting the medieval than on damning the modern. Weber, Fromm, Tawney, Riesman, Sorokin, Lewis Mumford, James Joseph Walsh—but the list could be very long.

Few of these writers would dare, or perhaps care, to assert frankly that

21 London, Watts, 1941 (1st ed. 1936). This book is a very good brief specimen of an attitude, a world view, we shall be much concerned with, under the broad name of Enlightenment. It is available in a paperback, New American Library, Mentor Books.

265

men were "happier" in 1250 than in 1950. Some, though not the best balanced of them, have asserted that the morals of 1250 were better than those of 1950. The best of them, I think, assert something like this: the "organically structured" society of the Middle Ages, with its peasant communities, *accepted* social hierarchies and economic inequalities, or a relatively stable set of peck orders, if you insist, tradition-guided nexus of mutual obligations, guilds, "just prices," common membership in the great community of Catholic Christendom, common acceptance of Christian theism—this society enabled men to live more serenely, securely, *normally* than can we in the mad free-for-all of modern society, where many, many men are insecure in status, insecure in means of livelihood, insecure in standards of taste, insecure in manners, insecure in faith.

First of all, I must insist that the medieval synthesis so admired lasted briefly indeed, hardly more than the thirteenth century. From the Black Death of the fourteenth century right on through the Renaissance, the modern age, with its cash nexus, its economic growth, its new dynastic states, its overseas expansion, is in the making. In these centuries the medieval Christian world view is slowly undermined for many intellectuals, though only in the late seventeenth century does another world view, which I have called the religion of the Enlightenment, fully emerge. Those two world views, the Christian and the Enlightened, are different enough, as I hope to show. What is really puzzling is how much difference the holding of these different views has made in human *conduct*. I feel very sure that it has made a difference; but I am quite as sure that that difference is exaggerated in our tradition. We are—if I may be permitted a methodological aside—quite unable to measure human differences as we measure chemical differences. Any culture is at least a compound, indeed a mixture; but we cannot measure its components, and can only try quite crudely to describe them.

The world view of any culture is but a component of the total culture; yet from the inside, even to a degree from the outside, we think and feel, we experience, that culture through its world view in a way you may find suggested in such terms as "holistic," "Gestalt," "style," "form." So experienced, even vicariously, as the historian must always experience, the West of 1250 is certainly very different from the world of 1750. Yet I do not feel confident that the questions suggested by this contrast of medieval and modern can be answered at all out of our analytical and empirical knowledge. Here I wish to do no more than point out that not the least of the difficulties in our way is a grave and obvious contrast between the real and the ideal in medieval life itself, a contrast that can be at least partially established empirically. *If medieval life were what it seems in analysis of its "values," "social structure," and "world view" and so on, one might grant that men were then secure, serene, balanced, "human," in a way they are not now.* But we know the violence, the uncertainties, the breakdowns of nice theories of mutual obligation, the peasant wars, the cruelties, the fanaticism, the ignorance and superstition—I refer the reader once more to Zoé Oldenbourg's admirable *The World Is Not Enough*—and the rest of the long tale of suffering of life then as it was really lived. I am not sure that a degree of unanimity—it was only a degree, for heresies were endemic—on matters of religion was quite a balance for all these uncertainties.

We are at the dead end that seems always to come when one tries to test broad theories of moral development in the West, a dead end blocked more firmly by the fact that such theories, divorced from transcendental a priori standards to measure development, progress, or retrogression, tend in our time to drift into the impossible attempt to measure whether men were "happier," "more comfortable," "better off" in the past than now. The attempt is impossible if it is made with purely naturalistic standards, if the process of moral development is judged as though the process itself automatically gives us standards with which to judge its results. If you judge the course of history by standards ultimately *beyond history,* as the full Christian must, you may then at least say, not that medieval men were happier than we are, but that they were better than we are, for they knew, they believed, what millions of us cannot bring ourselves to know and believe, that there is something beyond history. *Within history,* men seem always essentially the same in their differences, and Talleyrand quite irrefutable: *Plus ça change, plus c'est la même chose.*[22]

[22] "The more it changes, the more it's the same thing." The attribution to Talleyrand is uncertain, but appropriate.

The Seventeenth Century

IF THE LATER MIDDLE AGES may be regarded as the seedbed of modern Western culture, the sixteenth century as the bare beginnings of sprouting, then in the seventeenth century, one may say, the plant begins to show above ground. The metaphor is imperfect, for in the long slow process of change in human culture so little disappears entirely; the Middle Ages are still alive in our midst—and not merely in some rural pocket in Europe. The Hearst property at San Simeon was certainly not the mere "ranch" it was called, nor even a modern rich man's "estate"—it was a barony. Baron Hearst—himself a human palimpsest—was a medieval lord, a man of *virtù,* a freebooter, a late nineteenth- and early twentieth-century American entrepreneurial survival of the Gilded Age. The personality is indeed a persistent Western, if not human, one; the total cultural pattern, I repeat, seems to me to involve a social process hard to put in words, even in figures of speech. The central point is this recapitulation, this reviving, this persistence of a pattern from the past. Of course, the persistence is often deliberate, a conscious harking back, in its weakest and perhaps final form no more than the intellectual's peevish regrets in the style of Edwin Arlington Robinson's Minniver Cheevy. But I find terms like "archaism" (Toynbee), "fossil" (Guérard, Toynbee), and the heavily metaphysical "pseudo-morphism" of Spengler unsatisfactory, for they all imply a conscious fakery, or a mere seeming, an unreality by no means always present in this little-understood process of *keeping* (not just reviving) the past in the present.

Three aspects of modern culture do show themselves clearly in the West in this seventeenth century: the new state, without which our sentiments toward the territorial in-group could hardly have taken the form we call "nationalism"; the new natural science, without which our modern metaphysical rationalism might have been as shallowly rooted and as limited to a small intellectual class as was the Greco-Roman, and without which our modern economic and technological development would have been impossible; the new Puritanism, without which—and to hold this one need not accept everything Weber and his followers have written—science, technology, and entrepreneurship could not have combined as they did in our modern world. The reader who has persisted this far need hardly be reminded that none of these aspects of culture are "new" in any absolute sense, in, for example, the sense very prettily illustrated by the astronomer's nova, the new star that appears where nothing at all had been visible in the blackness.

Puritanism is so immediately a part of the whole Protestant Reformation that I have dealt with it under Chapter VIII above; but even for Puritanism, as I noted there, the alliance with capitalist commerce and industry, the new power of the state, all that was to give our modern Western world its quite unprecedented mastery of material resources, is not at all obviously begun in the sixteenth century, nor indeed very conspicuously even in the seventeenth. We shall encounter this Puritanism again, in the English eighteenth and nineteenth centuries when as "dissent" or "nonconformity" or "Victorian morality" it has really outgrown its medieval beginnings. Here we must consider at some length the new state and the new science. But we shall conclude with a moral ideal most characteristic of the century, one which flourished then at its height, that of the noblesse of the old regime in the West.

II

We cannot in a book of this sort concern ourselves with the details of the long and varied process by which, from out of the "feudal disintegration" of early medieval times, states already by 1500 so firmly "sovereign" and so modern as England, France, and Spain had grown, or been made. The process, surely by no means well understood, is by no means without interest to the historian of morals. If, as some think, the central moral problem of the mid-twentieth century is how to prevent war among "sovereign" states, it might be possible to learn something from the way in which these sovereign states came to preserve peace within their own boundaries. Within what by 1500 had become France, it had been, only a few generations earlier, legal and moral—*not* contrary to the commandment "Thou shalt not kill"—for a Burgundian to kill a "Frenchman" in organized warfare. Within the new France, it had become murder for a Burgundian to kill a Frenchman, for the old duchy had been incorporated in the French state. And only a few generations earlier yet, what the historian calls "private warfare," wars between mere feudal barons, had been fitting and proper.

Now much that is central to any understanding of Western political morality is wrapped up in the processes that made France out of a feudal congeries. Did the Burgundian, or the Breton, or the Gascon feel that he had been *forced* into becoming a French subject? Was the process one of pure violence on the part of the French crown? If so, why was it so successful? Or, perhaps the most fundamental problem of all, was the process of uniting France—or England, or Spain, or even those late-comers to national unity Germany and Italy—a "natural" one, one fairly put as "growth," one that therefore had to "come about" in due and often very slow course? Or was it an "artificial" one, one best put as "making," one that, therefore, we can say was "planned" and put through by human conscious effort, and that can perhaps be copied by us and our children on an international, even on a world, scale?[1]

We shall here take the sovereign state of early modern times as already formed. The degree of unity under the crown—or, in a few instances, mostly surviving medieval city-states like those of the Hansa, under the republic—varied greatly. But everywhere, even in Germany, the new state is to be found; and wherever it is to be found, it demands the final *earthly* allegiance of all its inhabitants. There survived everywhere a great deal of the old medieval particularism, and in terms of culture, and often of pure tourist bait, there still survives today much of the variety of old. But this new state was the matrix of the modern nation-state, the legal entity within which what we call nationalism was to develop, adding to the state as ultimate legal authority the claim of the state as ultimate moral authority, indeed, ultimate teleological authority.

Long before with the great French Revolution of 1789, however, this focusing of the moral and emotional loyalties of citizen (or subject) on the

[1] The reader no doubt knows my own answer—it was *both* natural and artificial. But the sorting out of the two, and the gradings in between, is a very difficult matter. I have tried in a little book, *From Many One* (Harvard University Press, 1948), to sketch out the importance of the problem, and suggest possible lines of approach. There lies in the offing, of course, that particular form of the old problem of determinism which has reached an acute form in our own day as "historicism": Were both France of today and Germany of today "determined" by Charlemagne, or, for that matter, by Adam and Eve?

nation-state had become evident, the new state—call it as yet no more than the dynastic state—had set in a new and still-troublesome form an old moral problem. This is the problem that confronted Antigone (see above, p. 103), the problem of conflict between moral and political law. The statesmen of these early modern centuries set up for the new state the claim to be above the accepted ethical principles that were supposed to guide the conduct of the individual in his private life. There is certainly a link between this modern doctrine of "reason of state" and the old Greek doctrine, or better, perhaps, traditional assumption that life of and in the polis is the realization of the beautiful-and-good, that, in our terms, the state is the supreme moral end of life. It is clear, however, from the *Antigone,* and from Aristotle's *Politics,* that even in antiquity this doctrine by no means banished the difficulty in a concrete case: What course of action is in fact the one consonant with the supreme good which is the state?

To this last phase of the problem some distinguished leaders of the new dynastic state—I am simplifying here, but not, I hope, distorting—gave what was essentially the reply Plato makes Thrasymachus give in the *Republic* to the question What is justice? Reason of state dictates as the right course, the *moral* course, what human reason, working on the stuff of experience, judges to be the most likely to succeed. And what is success? Well, for Cardinal Richelieu, perhaps the most representative exponent of reason of state, in theory in his famous testament, in fact in his whole unpriestly and un-Christian life, success would be something like this: first and foremost, the retention and improvement by France of its newly acquired position as leader in the struggle for prize of Western international politics, its hegemony (what the United States now has in the same scramble of world politics); this position to be maintained if possible by diplomacy, if necessary by war; the means, whether diplomacy or war, to be the most efficient, the most likely to succeed, regardless of how many ethical principles are violated, and how often; similar "rational" (or pragmatic or instrumental) tests to be applied to internal or domestic French policies, always with the aim of making the entity France strongest among other states in the struggle for prize, which is so much, much more than the struggle for life or survival; this victory to be achieved, these tests to be applied, always with a prudent, if possible well-disguised, disregard for the principles of morality. Richelieu, in fact, is a better representative of reason of state than the better-known Machiavelli, whose name springs naturally to one's attention as a representative immoralist of high politics. Machiavelli, for all his defiance of Christian morality, did have as a test of success, even for his Prince, a state in which the good life showed traces of the old pagan ideals of the beautiful-and-good. Richelieu seems to have wanted no more than that France, that haunting, not-quite abstraction, the France he ran, the France that was *his* team, should place first and stay first in the Big League.

What all this meant in terms of human careers is the creation of a relatively small but well-trained class of civil servants, diplomatists, and domestic administrators, really dedicated to the success of the state, the *rational,* the efficient success of the state. They were to prove skillful indeed, professionals, not amateurs like their medieval predecessors. Without them, the economic advances of the modern world, even of our whole developed culture, would have been entirely impossible, for they built the frame of public order, of security for private property, within the state—and to a degree even in international relations, which were by no means anarchical, but, rather, an organized struggle for prize—without which nothing else could have been done. They were, even when socially mobile, for the most part gentlemen, and they had the manners and morals of gentlemen. Even as agents of reason of state in international relations, the diplomatists were not quite the villains of our current popular conceptions, not Hollywood-conceived diplomatists. Like Talleyrand, who is a superior specimen of the breed, they did not believe in the *unnecessary* violation of the principles of morality, and they were fully aware that open and avowed immorality even in international relations is not wise. They knew that vice always owes its tribute to virtue, and that the tribute should be a graceful one. But there can be no doubt that both in domestic and in international relations this new class was strongly influenced by the doctrine of reason of state, and by the feeling for rational efficiency, for rational organization, that was so much a part of that doctrine. At the very least, if they were not wicked oppressors, they were insensitive managers, firm believers that what was good for them was good for France, or Prussia, or even England.[2]

Reason of state was, both as ethics and as conduct, profoundly anti-Christian, and in the perspective of time seems far the most dangerous menace to the Christian view of life that came out of the Renaissance. The Middle Ages could hardly have entertained the doctrine. Grant, as in this book I have perhaps too freely granted, that the spotted medieval reality was bad,

---

[2] The doctrine of reason of state as formal political philosophy was never very popular in England, but the practice surely was—or so we non-English have long believed.

that private and public conduct was often most un-Christian, it remains true that medieval man could not have thought that all things are Caesar's. A medieval Antigone, supported by her confessor, would have confronted a feudal baron ordering her to violate canon law without much sense of being heroic, and she would have been well supported by the organized church. In fact, the international church was better organized than the international state (the imperfect empire of the High Middle Ages); in theory, the doctrine of the two swords, lay rulers and spiritual rulers, each with his own province, left to Christian ethics a very great sphere. A medieval cardinal might have had quite as strong a will to power as Richelieu—many of them clearly did—but he could not have possibly exercised that will to power as Richelieu did, and have kept the good opinion of the world. It is a measure of the difference of the climate of opinion in the two cultures that, though he had his critics, Richelieu was accepted in his own day as, if not a good man, at least as one not to be greatly blamed.

One may risk a broad generalization: with the rise of this class of professional servants of the new state, who were not only necessarily in close relations with men of "business," but had in a sense to be themselves men of business, the characteristic agon of the West begins its spread into activities that the ancients considered banausic, and that the ruling classes of the Middle Ages considered low. The reader must recall that I use the word "agon" not as a synonym for human competitiveness, let alone for the full range of the Darwinian "struggle for life" among human beings, but for the ritualized, almost sportive, competition for the great honors of a given society, for the satisfaction of the will to shine perhaps even more than the will to power, and often with extreme disregard for the will to survive. With the possible exception of the late Greco-Roman world, the agon had hitherto been limited to the kind of group and the kind of activity suggested by words like "aristocrat," "gentleman," "amateur," and the like. Even in the society of the Roman Empire, the newly rich Trimalchio is a figure of fun, the devoted soldiers and administrators for the most part Stoic gentlemen full of scruples, basically amateurs, and quite incapable of an expressed concept like reason of state.

It is certainly true enough that the old prestige of the warrior-aristocrat and the priest-aristocrat continued. Indeed, even in these United States today, the opinion polls always show the heirs of Achilles, Odysseus, and Socrates, the soldiers, judges, politicians, scientists—yes, even the college professors—ahead of the businessman or banker in the agon. But the businessman and the banker are there, in the midst of the agon, along with a great many others who were not there in earlier times.

Here the question—unanswerable, as usual, in this form—inevitably arises: Did the new economy precede, "cause," the new state and its morality of efficiency, or did the new state and the new morality "cause" the new rational and dynamic economy? We Americans, children of the Enlightenment, like the Marxist grandchildren of that great change in our views of the universe, tend to put the economic horse solidly before the linked carts of morals and politics. Actually, we are dealing here with a process of historical action and reaction, of multiple causation, in which no horse-and-cart metaphor helps, nor any metaphors of roots, or watersheds and tributary streams, or trigger pulls. Richelieu, Colbert, Cromwell, Heinsius—not to mention John Law—are all part of a long process in which millions of now-forgotten men made millions of decisions that made the modern world. You cannot, except in a frame of purely metaphysical thought, say if there had been no great administrators like the above, then no Watt, no Stephenson, no Rockefeller, no Ford. But you can say that in the historical process as we know it, the new economy and the material gains it brought in its train were impossible without the new state, the new bureaucracy, the new standardization and efficiency in administration. If you are still dissatisfied with this formulation, consult your sentiments, which should, as always, give some kind of answer to the unanswerable. My own lean toward: In the beginning was the Word.

III

But surely did not Francis Bacon, Galileo, and Newton have a part in the great transformation of values that has put a Henry Ford not, indeed, in the place of an Achilles, but at least in a place of honor not totally unlike his? Natural science is certainly one of the major components of our contemporary view of the universe, and therefore of our morals. But the relations between the development of modern natural science and the whole social and cultural matrix out of which science grew are most complex and ill-understood.

As systematic knowledge of "events" in the external world and their probable interrelations—including the possibility of predicting them—natural science goes back to the ancient Near East. So, too, does the helpmeet or auxiliary of science, mathematics. The distinguished historian of science the late George Sarton devoted several long volumes and hundreds of articles to

274

his chosen subject without ever getting very far into modern times. Nor was ancient and medieval science—there was indeed science in the Middle Ages —simply "deductive." The present elaborate social and material equipment for testing, experimenting, verifying did not exist, but the fundamental concept of Western science summed up as the imperative to submit "theory" to the test of "facts" was as well known to Hippocrates and Archimedes as to us.[3]

Yet we do quite rightly assume that "modern" science is different from earlier forms of science. First and most obviously, it clearly occupies a more important place in our culture, in terms appropriately if only roughly measurable in man-hours devoted to it. It is, as a corpus of learning, immensely greater and more varied. No matter how you decided to measure it, your lines of graph would skyrocket from the seventeenth century onward. Second, and quite obvious to us today, the work of the "pure" scientist was to prove useful to the "practical" engineer, technologist, craftsman, entrepreneur, and through them to make possible the extraordinary material success of the modern West, a success neatly summarized by the fact that at the present apex of this process, the ordinary American has in his garage the power-equivalent of a princely stable of former times, or of a whole plantation full of slaves. Third, less obvious but more important for the historian of morals, modern natural science has buttressed, extended, in a sense made possible, a whole set of heresies of Christianity, or, if you prefer, an anti-Christian world view, for which I have used the no-doubt-inadequate blanket term "Enlightenment." I now offer the reader a wide assortment of terms: materialism, rationalism, "humanism," scientism, naturalism, secularism, evolutionism, positivism, ethical culture. Again, with the great name as symbol; no Galileo, Newton, Darwin, then no Locke, no Herbert Spencer, no Marx—or, at the very least, no such great secular religions associated with such names as these last, no modern democracy, no widespread belief in "progress," no Communism.

Although for us, concerned with the history of Western morals, the third factor is of major importance, it is worth noting briefly that both the other factors have a moral aspect. Science in itself, as an intellectual discipline, could hardly have flourished as it did after 1600 had it not been for the long tradition of disciplined thinking, and disciplined scholarly patience, that had inspired even so unscientific an intellectual achievement as medieval scholas-

[3] On "facts" I refer the reader back, through my note on p. 4 to L. J. Henderson.

ticism. The banausic virtue, or necessity, of sheer hard dull *work* had well before Calvin been an acquisition of the second or intellectual aristocracy of learning as, in spite of the need for a degree of "practice" in athletic training, it had *not* been for the first, or warrior-statesman, aristocracy. Catholic Christianity, especially in its monastic form, had made work honorable and habitual among the learned. This same extension of the banausic virtues had to come about before science and technology could begin their modern collaboration. That collaboration is not as old—not, at least, in the form we know it—as is commonly thought. Francis Bacon does foresee it, with the scientist leading the way. But for a long time in these early modern centuries it is the craftsman, the empirical inventor of instruments, the metallurgist who make it possible for the pure scientist to do more and more refined and effective work. But for the two to come together at all, the scientist had to be conditioned, not merely to the intellectual attitude implied in his Antaeus-like return to earth after flights of thinking and imagination, but to the moral attitude that the search for facts cannot be identical with the pursuit of the beautiful-and-good, cannot be done with the old Greek grace, cannot, indeed, be done with Renaissance *virtù*.

We do not, I repeat, understand how this came about; but somehow the virtues of the workshop became also the virtues of the laboratory and the office or *bureau*. The modern German gift they vulgarly call *Sitzfleisch*—you will hardly find it in the Germans of Tacitus, or of the Song of the Nibelungs —came into honor in the West. We can, however, once more be sure that the process was not one of idea-horse pulling matter-cart, or vice versa, but the long, slow mutual interaction of millions of human beings variously motivated, variously environed, a process circular, or spiral, but not neatly unilinear. This is quite as true of the process by which the modern heresies above so generously named came into being. Science had a most important part in the process, but in no sense was its only begetter—but this last, too, is an unsatisfactory figure of speech, for in such processes the begetter is also begotten by what he begets.

Once it had begun to seep down into the awareness of the educated and later of the partly educated classes, which it had done in Western and Central Europe and the United States by the last of the eighteenth century, science-*cum*-technology had its major effect in reducing immeasurably the areas within which a man might assume a will at least remotely like his own to be operating. Medieval Christianity, as we have noted, still left an immense field for a God—yes, let us use, though not in scorn, the word "anthropomorphic"

—who even when He did not "interfere" with Nature, still guided and controlled Nature and, above all, gave purpose to natural processes. Science and many scientists themselves were not long in coming to the point Laplace at the end of the eighteenth century had arrived at when he could say of God, "I have no need for that hypothesis."

We need not here consider how legitimate, wise, or valuable was this leap from the specific study of scientific problems to a religion, or at least a cosmology, which we commonly call "materialist" or "mechanical." The fact is that men made the leap, and that they were encouraged to make the leap by the extent to which science already had succeeded in accounting for much in nature that had hitherto defied "rational" accounting. Thunder and lightning, that old favorite, will do as an example. Admittedly, even the illiterate Christian probably did not see his God in the storm in the role of Jove or Thor actually wielding bolts of thunder, but neither could he account for the phenomenon, save by common sense, which never really accounts for anything, never satisfies our need for a metaphysics; he could not, as a matter of fact, account in this way for wood floating in water, and iron sinking. Historians of science are quite justified in pointing out that scientists themselves, qua scientists, by no means "produced" the world view of the new Enlightenment, and certainly not the doctrine of the natural goodness of man. But the upshot of the popularization of science among the upper and middle classes was an invitation to a world view that would dispense with, or at least greatly curb and confine, the activities here on earth of an immanent godhead.

A concrete instance may help the modern reader. Henry VIII of England had his marriage with Catherine of Aragon annulled (it was not a divorce) no doubt in part for reasons of state. The *arriviste* house of Tudor needed a male heir, and though poor Catherine had had numerous miscarriages and had borne short-lived infants, only Princess Mary survived. It is easy for us to say that Henry acted out of selfish and hard-boiled motives. But he *said* he believed his marriage with Catherine had been contrary to canon law (she was his brother Arthur's widow) and that God was punishing him for this sin by denying him a male heir. Why should he not believe this sincerely, since he found it convenient to so believe? Henry knew much less about the physiology of human reproduction than does the ordinary schoolboy today; in fact, from the point of view of modern science, he knew nothing. Even today, the fundamentalist Christian can believe that God directly guides the spermatozoa on their heroic way to the ovum and can and does sidetrack them if He likes. But most of us, Christian and non-Christian, would turn our minds first, in a specific case such as this, to anatomy, physiology, and the mathematics of probability.[4]

Earthquakes, terrifying indeed, and occurring at no regular intervals and with no obvious "natural" causes, are an even better example of the gradual encroachment of natural causation upon divine intervention. They were until the eighteenth century almost universally regarded as acts of God in a literal sense hard for most of us, even if we are honest Christians, to recapture—by no means acts of God in the sense covered by that phrase in our insurance policies. The disastrous Lisbon earthquake of 1755 is nearly at the dividing line for the educated classes. The general public still interpreted the catastrophe as a warning and an intervention of divine power; the *philosophes,* though they believed the disaster had natural causes, nonetheless launched themselves from it in vigorous moralizing, as did Voltaire in his *Candide;* the scientists, or natural philosophers, as they were still known, though very much in the dark, went to work gropingly on what became the science of seismology.[5] The scientists, let it be repeated, have won, for the great majority of Westerners, even though they are Christians, cannot see directly, concretely, as the metaphor requires, the hand of God in specific chains of "natural causation."[6]

But was not common sense enough, and had not common sense already in the Middle Ages pretty well banished primitive animistic notions, and even expectancy of the kind of miracle Christian tradition enshrined? To a degree, this is no doubt so. But just what did go on in the medieval mind when it faced the traditional water test for a person accused of witchcraft, whereby

[4] For the facts of Henry's belief see C. W. Ferguson, *Naked to Mine Enemies: The Life of Cardinal Wolsey,* Boston, Little Brown, 1958, pp. 331-332. The familiar story of how Charles II roared with laughter when he heard that the scientists of his Royal Society were trying to weigh air is another case in point.

[5] "In 1750 a writer on the subject [of earthquakes] in the *Philosophic Transactions* of the Royal Society of London apologized to 'those who are apt to be offended at any attempts to give a rational account of earthquakes'." K. E. Bullen, "The Interior of the Earth," in *The Planet Earth,* a Scientific American Book, New York, Simon & Schuster, 1957, p. 19. For the fascinating intellectual and moral history of the aftermath of the Lisbon earthquake see T. D. Kendrick, *The Lisbon Earthquake,* London, Methuen, 1956.

[6] I had written the above when I saw an arresting newspaper headline: GOD'S ROLE IN THE RECESSION. Further reading, however, as is not infrequently true of headlines, actually confirmed what I had written and showed that my first impression, that here was a good old-fashioned fundamentalist, was wrong. Someone had written the evangelist Billy Graham asking why God allowed the unemployment crisis of 1957-58 to be thrust on the people, and Mr. Graham began his reply: "Certain things that come upon nations are not necessarily ordained of God, but are the result of the law of cause and effect. God doesn't as a rule go against the laws of the universe." It is quite possible in our world that the headline writer or the questioner or both were Enlightened, attempting to needle Mr. Graham. San Francisco *Chronicle,* April 19, 1958, p. 12.

the accused was thrown into deep water, considered innocent if the water swallowed him and guilty if he succeeded in keeping above water, presumably on the grounds that the innocent water rejected an evil thing? Clearly there is a normal expectancy here, not wholly irrational by any means; but equally clearly there is a view of the properties of water hard for the most convinced Christian today to entertain. I think it clear that common sense—even Western common sense, which is perhaps to a degree inclined toward what becomes natural science—is, unbuttressed by that science, unable to question seriously the full Christian cosmology. Common sense alone would never have the courage, or the foolhardiness, to question the possibility of the miraculous. Even at the height of the Middle Ages, common sense could and did question the *probability* of the miraculous in the daily round of life, but not the *possibility* of the miraculous. To conclude that miracles in the Christian sense of the word are impossible took a bolder, newer, less experienced, more ruthless mental discipline than common sense, or even "pure" philosophical rationalism, could provide. This natural science did provide.

Natural science also helped fill out, extend, and implement in many ways that form of rationalism that is best called "efficiency" and that I have already called attention to as one of the goals of the new state. Indeed, natural science is the most efficient tool man thinking has yet developed to help him realize certain definite aims or goals; sufficient here to mention our modern conquests of wealth and power. *In itself,* and in spite of the deep belief of the heirs of the *philosophes* that it does provide such, science does not provide what the moralist as well as the theologian has to call ends, goals, purpose. The growth of natural science in the modern West is, as we have noted already, and shall have to pay much more attention to in the next chapter, intimately connected historically with the rise of full cosmological *rationalism*. But in itself science merely helps us do what we want to do, blow up Hiroshima or reconstruct it. The help is the help of a giant, and no doubt the knowledge that the giant is there has deeply and subtly affected our feeling for what is desirable, if only by so enlarging our feeling for what is possible. Science probably does add to our Western *hubris;* but the *hubris* was there, very strong, long, long ago. More important—I shall return to this point—science normally supplies no such restraint on, discipline of, that *hubris* as that which orthodox Christianity supplies.

Finally, natural science played a great part in the growth of the modern doctrine of Progress (the capital letter is necessary). At the very end of the seventeenth century, in the great debates over whether the moderns could ever equal the ancients, the concrete evidence of scientific progress was useful to the proponents of modernity. Dean Swift's attack on the scientists in the Academy of Laputa, though by no means the last attack on scientists, was perhaps the last brilliant attack in which they were accused of living in a Cloud-Cuckoo-Land of utterly impractical projects, made to seem in their way quite as unworldly or foolish as the Renaissance humanists had made the Schoolmen seem, debating how many angels could sit on the point of a needle.[7] By the end of the eighteenth century, French scientists were being formally organized to help the revolutionary government in that most practical of human activities, warfare. Men in hot-air balloons, after small animals had previously been sent up, had begun the conquest of the air. The fact of technological progress, and its relation to the work of the pure scientists, had begun to be evident to the general public. The men who planned and made the great French encyclopedia in the mid-eighteenth century were well aware of this conquest of the scientists and technologists; soon, with St. Simon, Fourier, Robert Owen, men were to assert the modern conception that there could be a social science modeled on natural science, and that, just as natural science bore fruit in technological "progress," so social science would inevitably bear fruit in moral progress or, what their thinkers regarded as identical in meaning, social, economic, and political progress.

Yet the seventeenth century was by no means simply the first of the modern centuries, the century of the triumphant new secular state, of the beginnings of organized science, of increasing capitalistic production, of the final swing of power—and of cultural leadership, too—from the Mediterranean to the Atlantic. It was also the century that saw the culmination in practice and in ideal of a way of life that was destined to die out in our time as completely as any such way of life can in our history-ridden Western world. Though what is suggested by words like "aristocracy," "noblesse," "gentleman," *"Ritterlich,"* "hidalgo" still carry some weight of associations, favorable or unfavorable—in fact, as always for most of us normal human beings, mixed and ambivalent associations—the style of twentieth-century culture has no place for the reality behind the words. Even where, as with the "new conservatives" in the United States, there is an attempt to uphold the linking of privilege

IV

[7] Howard Mumford Jones, in his recent defense of research in the humanities, points out with satisfying irony that Swift was accusing the scientists of exactly the kind of silly pedantry it is now fashionable to hold against the humanist scholar.

and duty, the full overtones of *noblesse oblige,* the dignity, good taste, restraint, *pietas* (capacity for feeling reverence), and distrust of innovation and bright innovators that characterizes the ideal of the gentleman of the *ancien régime,* there is rejection of what was, after all, a fundamental of this actual European aristocracy—inherited title, privileges, wealth, protected as far as seems possible in the West by caste restrictions on marriage with outsiders, or *mésalliances.* Our new conservatives want an open aristocracy of merit—an aim the historian of the West is bound to insist seems as Utopian as when Plato first announced it in the *Republic.* As for the remaining nobles in the flesh, two centuries have been very hard on them, even in Britain. A duke, like a queen, does not even *look* quite right in modern dress.

The aristocracy of the European *ancien régime* was in fact the last *natural* aristocracy in the West. The "nature's nobleman" of the sentimental eighteenth century, the "aristocracy of talent" of hopeful intellectuals, above all, no doubt, the horrid "superiors" emerging from the cauldron of modern racist, elitist, and even crankier thinking and feeling all seem unreal, synthetic, unnatural. Our notions of excellence—I use the word deliberately instead of another with more suggestions of social hierarchy—have been splintered, atomized, specialized, though by no means destroyed or even, in a sense, lessened, in our world of egalitarian ideals and prize-seeking realities. In our world a cat cannot only look at a king—if he can find one—but, if he is a prize-winning, pedigreed, best-of-show champion, is himself a kind of king. The European aristocracy of old was founded on a conception of general excellence, of hierarchical superiority, not merely the old Greek effortless and amateur superiority of the beautiful-and-good (though that was an important part of the aristocratic ideal), but on a conception of an order actually *cosmological,* not merely psychological or sociological, on a belief that the aristocrat was a part of God's and nature's plan for the universe. It is almost impossible for a modern American to understand the sentiment that made of this aristocracy a reality. I can hardly do better than revert to a concrete instance that brought the reality to me sharply in the midst of my early researches in the history of the French Revolution. A servant was brought before the revolutionary authorities for smuggling in roast chicken to a nobleman imprisoned during the Terror as a suspected "counter-revolutionary." The unrepentant servant explained his act simply: "But M. le Marquis was born to eat chicken."[8]

8 Crane Brinton, *The Jacobins,* New York, Macmillan, 1930, p. 269n. I think there is a symbolic truth, and not mere irony, in the fact that in our United States chicken is no longer in any sense a luxury food.

It must not be assumed that either in theory or in practice this aristocracy was an *absolutely* closed caste. What I have said above does not so much need qualification as completion. Outsiders could enter the aristocracy, but according to the theorists, only for some outstanding merit, such as great service to the country; and even those formally ennobled, or, in England especially, granted the legal right to use a coat of arms, and thus enrolled among the gentry, could at best hope that their sons or grandsons would be fully and completely assimilated to the quality of gentlemen. We can today, of course, look back and say that precisely the reason for the vogue of manuals of "courtesy," of self-help in learning how to behave like a gentleman, which from Castiglione on are very numerous in the West, was that the successful bourgeois were pressing very hard and Marxistically on the class above them. And there is some light thrown on human conduct by the obvious though not Marxist truth that the early modern bourgeoisie sought to imitate the manners, the "values" of the noblesse, and that the nineteenth- and twentieth-century proletariat sought to imitate the manners and values of the middle class. This latter imitation would appear to have been especially close and successful, if, by our current aristocratic Western artistic standards, unfortunate, in the Soviet Union.

Still, the tone of these sixteenth- and seventeenth-century manuals of behavior is very different from that to which the American disciples of Emily Post and her fellow writers on etiquette are accustomed. Sir John Ferne was simply more outspoken than his colleagues when he concluded the long title page of his *The Blazon of Gentry* (1586), "wherein is treated of the beginning, parts, and degrees of gentlenesse," with the specific injunction: "Compiled by John Ferne gentleman, for the instruction of all·gentlemen bearers of armes, whome and none other this worke concerneth."[9] That tone is already, by the close of the sixteenth century, the tone of a group on the defensive, aware that it is defending if not a lost, at least a menaced, cause. Ferne must have known that the "Mercers, and shopkeepers, retaylors, Cooks, victaylours, and Taverne-holders, Millioners, and such lyke" who, he complained, were "suffered to cloath themselves, with the coates of Gentlenes" would make up a large part of the public for his book.

These gentlemen, if, as all such classes must be, they were sure of their

[9] Quoted in Ruth Kelso, *The Doctrine of the English Gentleman in the Sixteenth Century,* University of Illinois, *Studies in Language and Literature,* XIV, No. 1-2, 1929, p. 208. The reader will find in Dr. Kelso's bibliography an admirable guide to the literature of "courtesy" not only for Britain, but for the rest of the West European countries.

standards of value, were not at all sure that they would be allowed to realize them in this real world. One may hazard the guess that in the West, at least, no privileged aristocracy has been entirely unaware of some danger from below, though it is hard to read such awareness into either Homer or the *Chanson de Roland*. But there is a difference between fear of the masses and fear of those barely below—perhaps, in actual economic position, above— who are pressing hard for a share of honor, glory, prestige, all goods much less readily divisible than mere money. The Duc de St. Simon spends pages recording with full moral indignation his efforts to maintain his right to have the *président à mortier* of the *parlement* (a noble indeed, but of the newer nobility of the civil service, not, like St. Simon, one who could claim to be of the old feudal warrior nobility) doff his hat in the ducal presence. St. Simon seems to us abnormally sensitive, his insistence on such points of etiquette petty. He was indeed a great writer, but there are no grounds for holding that he was otherwise very different from the rest of his order. He is at the end of a long tradition, an exhausted tradition, in which manners and morals have been frozen into a ritual exactness and exclusiveness which paradoxically sharpens and intensifies the struggle for prize the ritual is intended to tame, or at least control. The French royal levee, as described in a famous passage of Taine, is a good example: the queen was sometimes left shivering in the damp chill of the ill-heated palace of Versailles as successive delayed arrivals of ladies of precise but varying rank and privilege prevented the rapid execution of her ritual clothing.[10]

I had written these last sentences about the fantastic order of rank in the *ancien régime,* and the intensification—the rendering ridiculous—of the struggle for prize that it produced when my mind reverted to my own brief experience as a civil servant, and to certain difficulties over a rug in one office, a bare floor in another. Sociologists of business have reminded us that in the great corporations rank and privilege go along naturally enough with stomach ulcers; and we academics, aware that the *entremangerie professorale* is not unconcerned with external signs of rank, should be careful not to cast the first stone. Yet the conclusion from these parallels should not be that the struggle for prize, seen as a whole, never changes. Western man is the eternal contestant, and there are never prizes enough; but the nature of the contest, its goals and its prizes, the relative numbers of those who may participate in it, even its rules, vary greatly—or we should have no history of morals, or

[10] H. A. Taine, *The Ancient Régime*, trans. by J. Durand, New York, Holt, 1896, p. 107, footnote 1.

history of any kind. What the Duc de St. Simon was fighting for was truly a lost cause, and because it was lost we are likely to be unfair to those who fought for it. Especially in France, where the fight reached a climax in bloodshed and terror, the vanquished have either been damned by the triumphant democracy or made by their descendants and admirers into very much gilded lilies of the field. We in the United States, with no more than an incipient squirearchy in the North, an insecure group of country gentlemen in the South, nonetheless managed to follow the French lead in this matter. We damn an aristocracy we never had.

This last European aristocracy was indeed, as we have noted above, keenly aware of its honors, felt and announced superiorities over the commoners, defended them as well as it could; but it was not a harsh, ruthless, Spartan ruling class—not even in East Prussia—and it was not, *as aristocracies go in the West,* lax in its private morals, luxurious and dissolute in its tastes. It was, in its core and majority, which I am here taking as typical of it, the country gentlemen of varied title—sometimes, in Britain, no more than "Esquire"—by conventional moral standards one of the best aristocracies in our Western history. I do not quite dare fly in the face of common knowledge and maintain that even in France its virtues were responsible for its downfall; but in the midst of a culture that is clearly the product of the aggressive, innovating, restless energies of the foxes I confess to a certain wistful fondness for the virtues of these rather tired lions, the unprogressive gentlemen of the *ancien régime.*

The gentleman was culturally—though, so great is social mobility even in the Middle Ages and early modern times, not by 1700 in most cases genetically—a descendant of the feudal knight. The apparatus of titles, coats of arms, possession of a landed estate, are a direct inheritance from medieval society. So, too, is the dedication to arms, though arms and the dedication had greatly changed. Great nobles might still raise and command regiments, but they were regiments of the royal army, under professional command, and ultimately subject to the direction of what was already a national ministry of war. The officers of these armies were indeed mostly gentlemen, and among them such feudal survivals as the duel still obtained. The knightly code of honor, the knightly awareness of caste and privilege still survived, heightened, as we have just noted, by the rise of rival groups, into a systematic defensive code. The medieval knight hardly needed to feel contempt for underlings— though nineteenth-century fiction sometimes pictures him as so feeling—and he certainly was not, until late in the Middle Ages, and then only in advanced commercial societies, in danger of being tempted to go into trade.[11] The landed aristocracies of the old regime, however, very self-consciously erected barriers between themselves and the "fund lords." To *vivre noblement* one had to be above the need to work, not merely at the banausic occupations, but in theory at least, at any form of what we should call "business." The pure landed noble looked down a bit even at those who practiced law, or administered the growing state. Highest political posts, posts as officers in army and navy, and general supervision of his estate just about ended what a noble was supposed to do without derogation of his rank in established society. The church, Catholic, Anglican, Lutheran, in certain societies, Calvinist, would do, especially its highest posts, but usually these were refuges for younger sons. Court would do, and indeed the pensions, sinecures, the whole network of privilege surrounding the royal or princely court was essential to the economic survival of the class. The class as a whole, and on the average, did not do well in terms of economics, though it is not fair to blame its failures entirely on its inability to adapt itself to the new world of capitalist industry. Moreover, its more enterprising individual members often did well by themselves, for, whatever theories of *dérogeance* might have been, participation in finance, speculation, the dignified and really profitable end of the new business world was open to nobles everywhere, even in that supposed home of the aloof noble, France. The improving agricultural noble landlord, who profited economically as well as culturally by his improvements, is a familiar figure in England, and by no means unknown on the continent.

Yet the core of the class, the smaller landed nobles and gentry, at its economic worst hardly above the peasantry in parts of Europe, was old-fashioned, unenterprising, economically "unfit"—and relatively law-abiding and morally sound. They were good conventional Christians, according to the accepted faith of their land; the Prussian *Junkers,* notably, were God-fearing Lutherans. The Jansenists, who were rather more than conventional Christians, were strong among the administrative and judicial noblesse of France;

---

11 Much of the above does not hold for the Italian aristocracy, which, as has often been pointed out, never got as divorced from urban life as the feudal aristocracies of the North, never became as "medieval," as "Gothic," and was not until 1860 to become part of a major state organization. I am in this chapter following culture on its western way, and am writing chiefly of the trio that will rule the Western world of power, wealth, and culture for some centuries, Britain, France, and the Germanies, and of the smaller but culturally important states around them, Netherlands, Switzerland, Scandinavian countries. Spain, as always, was strange, intense, apart; her hidalgo class deserved to have its Cervantes. I shall at the end of this chapter note briefly the fact that the "European" aristocracy had by the seventeenth century already developed conspicuous national differences.

and the members of the corresponding class of small nobles in the Hapsburg dominions were sober, steady, practicing Catholics.

The rural landholding nobility were through most of Europe at the very least no more oppressive toward the peasantry than their medieval predecessors had been. The fashion among recent British historians has been to exaggerate the novelty of the actual suffering that the two great waves of enclosure, that of the sixteenth and that of the late eighteenth and early nineteenth centuries, brought on the peasantry. At any rate, the Carlylean picture of a French, if not, indeed, a European, noblesse doing nothing useful and living riotously off the labors of their oppressed inferiors, can no longer be accepted. Many a country gentleman did his best, as tradition directed him to do, for those dependent on him. For England this is admitted, if reluctantly, of the Squire Allworthys and many others, even of the nobility, carrying out their duties as justices of the peace, as customary landlords, as dispensers of charity. But even in France, where propagandists of the new order since 1789 have made us see the noblesse as irresponsibly hounding their stewards to get every penny out of their peasants—and, on their rare trips to the country, enjoying the right of first night with peasant brides and forcing the men to beat the frog ponds to stop croakings that spoiled sleep—even in France the responsible country gentleman doing his duty by his dependents is by no means a rare figure.[12]

Their private morals seem to me to have been, even if judged by conventional Victorian standards still prevailing amongst us today when we judge others, on the whole rather better than those of most privileged classes. I am not, of course, referring to the very small group of courtiers, the top of the social pyramid, about whom I shall shortly say a word. But the small nobility and the gentry, save for the inevitable black sheep, were not dissolute. As gentlemen in the great tradition, they hunted, rode to hounds, drank as a gentleman should, conducted themselves as a gentleman—who is after all and above all, in the great tradition, a male—should. As to sex, they believed in and practiced what is known as the "double standard," an attitude so far as I know not seriously challenged among laymen in the West before the last

---

[12] My favorite instance is the Marquis de Ferrières, deputy from the noblesse of Poitou to the Estates General of 1789, whose memoirs and letters back home to his wife have, because of this political post of his, been published. His letters show just the kind of concern with everybody on the estate one expects from the best eighteenth-century English squire. I realize Ferrières is no statistical fact, but neither is the wicked, oppressive absentee. On the general state of our studies of the European noblesse of early modern times—studies that I think confirm what I say above—see A. Goodwin, ed., *The European Nobility in the Eighteenth Century,* London, Adam and Charles Black, 1953, also Marquis de Ferrières, Charles Elie, *Correspondance inédite,* Paris, A. Colin, 1932.

years of the eighteenth century. But they were not heroically promiscuous, certainly not in the way later republican propaganda on the Continent was to paint them. Their arranged marriages certainly lasted; divorce, in spite of the virtuously interested efforts of a John Milton in its favor, was nowhere generally accepted. Even at the top there were loyal, chaste, and continent husbands, from Cromwell, of whom it would be expected, to Louis XVI and George III, of whom it would not be expected. Among the rank and file of gentlemen, the slightest dip into the source materials of social history, now beginning to be abundant, shows many a happy marriage, adultery-free.

The resemblance of this class to other privileged hereditary classes with steady moral ways, with the "lions" of Machiavelli and Pareto—with, for example, the early Roman aristocrats—increases when one realizes that they were not very intellectual. They had, of course, both refinement and culture if they are compared to their early medieval predecessors. They were literate, and those who had literary or artistic tastes could readily satisfy them. They were exposed to higher education, in England already to the sequence of public school and Oxford-Cambridge, on the Continent more often to private tutors, though there the Jesuit schools were most influential in Catholic lands, and the military schools were beginning to rise. Still, though it was by no means illiterate as were the nobles of Charlemagne, the tone of the class was against the innovating mind, against the disturbing doubts the new rationalism was introducing, against the kind of sensibility coming into fashion with the advanced. Faintly, the outlines of the coming separation between Horseback Hall and Heartbreak House were already visible.

Though there are survivors of this class of small and middling landed nobles in our contemporary West, they survive as relics, sometimes nicely refurbished relics, like Williamsburg, Virginia. This is now true even for the Prussian *Junkers,* who survived longest in the modern world, and who are in many respects an extraordinary group, closest Christian parallel to the old Roman aristocracy of the Republic. The *Junkers* held themselves together long enough to play a major, though by no means a determining, role in the making of modern Germany. The un-Jeffersonian democratic imperial Germany—or, if even so qualified, "democratic" here offends you, I will settle for "mass- or *Volk*-based" imperial Germany—that finally in 1870 emerged from the rivalries and complexities of the early modern Germanies was not a society in which the *Junker* could ever feel at home; indeed, the feeling many *Junkers* had about their own Bismarck, that he had with their help made an empire out of the wrong material—industrialists, bankers, Jews, intellectuals, liberals, all sorts of peoples who sought to ape the ways of the dissolute, unmanly, and materialistic West Europeans and Americans—is fully understandable in the light of their past.

The *Junkers* were the descendants, spiritually and often genetically, of the Teutonic Knights, those organized pioneers and crusaders of the late Middle Ages who led the Germanic conquest of the less well-organized Slavs. They were a landed aristocracy, not quite in the desperate position of the Spartiates toward their Helots, but, still, a reasonably purebred Germanic minority ruling over a much more mixed group of serfs in an agrarian military economy, almost a frontier economy, one conquered from an enemy people. They were early and almost automatically converted to strict Lutheranism. By early modern times they had consolidated into a landed upper class loyal to their Hohenzollern rulers, who wisely did not interfere with basic *Junker* interests at home, a fine reservoir of officers for the Prussian army, masters of their own estates, which they administered with no nonsense about progress and humanitarian enlightenment, but which, in contrast with some of the West European nobilities, they did administer. The *Junkers* have suffered in Western opinion from their association with two great German nationalist efforts to gain supremacy in the Western state system. And it would be absurd to deny that many of the class had a part, not only in the conventional aggressions of Wilhelm's Germany, but also in the insanely romantic aggressions of Hitler. They were, after all, loyal soldiers, professionals loyal to a whole set of values which did not include critical political thought. Still, the class did not at heart like Hitler, nor the modern world. The *Junker* was one of the last of the old lions—a disciplined, God-fearing, traditionalist, a believer in the order of rank in which his birth had placed him on top, a soldier by faith and profession, an uninquiring mind hostile to the foxes of this world, an anti-intellectual, but of the simple old sort, not at all like the neurotic intellectual anti-intellectuals we today all know too well. The *Junkers,* though they were aristocrats, remind one of the Boers of Oom Paul Kruger, children of a simple agrarian culture, patriarchal, rigid conformists to a code straight out of the Old Testament; they would have no truck with "liberty, equality, fraternity," nor in general with the religion of the Enlightenment, and the Western liberal has rightly felt that they do not belong in his world. But they should not be confused with the wild men of racist creeds, the naïve imperialists, the economic expansionists, the mass of nationalists, the unprincipled idealists, who have made the recent German attempts to dominate, or secede from, the West.[13]

[13] See W. Goerlitz, *Die Junker,* C. A. Starke, Glücksburg, 1956.

To this general account the very top of the upper classes, the active court nobility, is almost everywhere in the West a partial exception. Even of the court nobility of the later Stuarts, or of the last three Louis of France, or of the big and little German princely courts, it must be said that they look pretty Victorian in comparison with the Roman privileged classes we read about in Tacitus, Suetonius, Martial, and Juvenal, or with the upper classes of Renaissance Italy, and look very Christian in comparison with the untamed Merovingians we read about in Gregory of Tours. These people suffered even more than the rank and file of their class in the virtuous republican propaganda inspired by the "principles of 1776 and 1789," since their doings stood out so firmly; they were newsworthy, historyworthy. Still, there can be no doubt that theirs was not the life of sober, steady, principled adherence to high moral standards in the Christian tradition. Many of them were caught in the intense competition of high politics, and at just the time when the new doctrine of reason of state was ready to still any conscience that needed stilling. The political morality reflected in the *Memoirs* of Cardinal de Retz, for instance, is low indeed, and the record of British politics from 1640 to 1660 and 1660 to 1689 does not remind one very much of the career of Clement Atlee.

Nor is the private morality of these courts a loftly one. Kings had to have mistresses, as part of the display of royalty, even if they were not sexually very enterprising. The notorious laxities—sexual promiscuity, drinking, gambling, extravagance of all sorts—the cynicism reflected in the theater of the age, and the general abandonment of the English Restoration of 1660 are not quite typical, though they are hardly exaggerated in our history books. This moral relaxation was general, by no means limited to the court of Charles II, and seems to be one of those interesting and essentially modern phenomena, a cyclical swing in revulsion from a great collective effort to achieve moral reform, a phenomenon akin to the French Thermidorian reaction of 1794, and also to the less-complete and violent twentieth-century revulsion from Victorian standards.[14]

---

[14] There is a familiar, apt, and perhaps even authentic anecdote here which helps us understand English folk feelings on a more important matter than the private immorality of the court. There were two chief mistresses of Charles II, Louise de Kéroualle, a Frenchwoman and a Catholic, and the English Nell Gwynn, a former comic actress. The Frenchwoman, made Duchess of Portsmouth, was hated by the English people, as the full-blown Nell was not. Nell, royally ensconced in a coach, was once mistaken for her rival—or collaborator—and hearing the angry shouts of the mob, leaned out of the window and said firmly: "Good people, I am the Protestant whore." The temper of the crowd changed at once, and she was loudly cheered. But what if she had said: "I am the English whore"?

The conduct of the nobles of the court of Louis XIV, especially in his early years, was, however, hardly any better than that of the nobles of the court of Charles II, and is not to be explained as a revulsion, except perhaps from the tensions—not exactly puritanically inspired—of the Fronde. The German courts, which imitated the French in everything, of course imitated the French in morals. We confront once more the usual list: sexual promiscuity, in these very upper groups often, but not always, extended to permissible promiscuity for married women as well, a kind of single standard of laxity, as well as unscrupulous rivalry in the struggle for place and power, the potlatch spirit in conspicuous consumption, a fashionable fondness for the wit that shocks and sounds like cynicism—*is* sometimes cynicism—and the inevitable minor vices of gambling, drinking, idling.

Yet even the conspicuous consumption, even the minor vices, were at the height of this culture in the best year of Louis XIV redeemed—or, at the worst, very agreeably gilded—by high standards and high achievements in taste and manners. Indeed, one can go further and assert that the ideal of French classicism *at its best* was one of the great moral ideals of the West, an ideal to be ranked with that of the beautiful-and-good, the medieval knight, the man of *virtù*. Like them, it was an aristocratic ideal for an aristocracy, though it was not untouched by an even more serious Christian sense of duty toward lower classes than that which had suffused the medieval ideal. It shared to the full the respect for the mind of the Greek ideal. It held high as virtues dignity of deportment, good manners, which inevitably means consideration —*thoughtful* consideration—for others, *mesure,* that very French version of the Greek "nothing in excess," the Christian moral code—taken, duly, with *mesure.* It is not a heaven-storming ideal, but it is not a conventional one. From the classic Greek and Roman ideal that these gentlemen held so high it differed, as any Christian ideal must, by something rather more than what I have called the minimal puritan touch—witness the court preachers, and, further on toward the central Christian tensions, Racine, Pascal, and—yes— La Rochefoucauld himself. It is, for many reasons, chiefly perhaps because of its great respect for dignity, hierarchy, "those rules of old discover'd, not deviz'd," its deep underlying pessimism, never romantically on exhibition, and its high aesthetic content, the most difficult of all Western moral ideals for us Americans to understand. It is the Christian ideal nearest the old Greek ideal, nearer by quite a bit than the morally disordered Renaissance ideal of *virtù.*

Like most such ideals, it is not easily embodied. The French are no doubt quite right; Louis XIV, all of him, his whole career, even with the mistresses, even with the devastation of the Palatinate, is as good a French classicist of the great age as one could find in the world of action. But no American can take Louis seriously. I should not dare suggest any of the great literary figures mentioned above, though, just as is true for the work of the great Athenian dramatists as examples of their culture, the total work of Corneille, Racine, and Molière is no bad sampling. Perhaps, in spite of her femininity, one could take Madame de Sévigné as representative. She has, for an American, the great advantage of not wearing the periwig, that symbol of what we call the stuffed shirt—which is just what these aristocrats were not, not even Louis XIV.

Finally, we must note here that what has been written above about the rank and file of the European aristocracy of the old regime has made the not wholly justifiable assumption that there was such a *European* aristocracy. Was there not in reality nothing more than an English nobility—which the honest historian would never equate entirely with the gentry, as I have tended to do— French noblesse, German *Adel*, Spanish hidalgos, even that squabbling, undisciplined, ill-fated lot the Polish *szlachta?* Most certainly by the seventeenth century the process of national differentiation in Europe was well along toward its modern form of nationalism, and had come to include in part the aristocracies. A Prussian *Junker* was already a very different man from a French provincial noble—though, indeed, the medieval Teutonic Knight was in some ways very different from a Joinville or a Froissart. But we are going to have to cope with the many and difficult problems of the moral implications of modern Western nationalism soon enough. This nationalism, though it engulfed the aristocracies almost completely by the nineteenth century, was not primarily a product of these aristocracies. For the treatment I have in this chapter given the noblesse of Europe as a whole, I can bring out two justifications. First, there was among aristocrats everywhere, even as far east as Poland, a survival of the medieval feeling that nobles belong together, that there is a *European* nobility above mere newly fashionable nationality. This feeling is admirably brought out in Shaw's *Saint Joan* in the conversation between the nobleman and the chaplain, one of Shaw's stock Englishmen.

THE CHAPLAIN. . . . I feel it, my lord: I feel it very deeply. I cannot bear to see my countrymen defeated by a parcel of foreigners.
THE NOBLEMAN. Oh! you are an Englishman, are you?

THE CHAPLAIN. Certainly not, my lord: I am a gentleman. Still, like your lordship, I was born in England; and it makes a difference.

THE NOBLEMAN. You are attached to the soil, eh?

THE CHAPLAIN. It pleases your lordship to be satirical at my expense: your greatness privileges you to be so with impunity. But your lordship knows very well that I am not attached to the soil in a vulgar manner, like a serf. Still, I have a feeling about it; and I am not ashamed of it; and [rising wildly] by God, if this goes on any longer, I will fling my cassock to the devil, and take arms myself, and strangle the accursed witch with my own hands.

THE NOBLEMAN. So you shall, chaplain: so you shall, if we can do nothing better. But not yet, not quite yet. . . .

THE NOBLEMAN [airily] I should not care very much about the witch—you see, I have made my pilgrimage to the Holy Land; and the Heavenly Powers, for their own credit, can hardly allow me to be worsted by a village sorceress—but the Bastard of Orleans is a harder nut to crack; and as he has been to the Holy Land too, honors are easy between us as far as that goes.

THE CHAPLAIN. He is only a Frenchman, my lord.

THE NOBLEMAN. A Frenchman! Where did you pick up that expression? Are these Burgundians and Bretons and Picards and Gascons beginning to call themselves Frenchmen, just as our fellows are beginning to call themselves Englishmen? They actually talk of France and England as their countries. Theirs, if you please! What is to become of me and you if that way of thinking comes into fashion?

THE CHAPLAIN. Why, my lord? Can it hurt us?

THE NOBLEMAN. Men cannot serve two masters. If this cant of serving their country once takes hold of them, goodbye to the authority of their feudal lords, and goodbye to the authority of the Church. That is, goodbye to you and me.[15]

Second, and quite as important, the French aristocracy held in this seventeenth century, and continued to hold in the eighteenth, a degree of cultural and social primacy so great that it can be not unfairly taken as setting standards for all. Certainly it is at least as fair to take the France of Louis XIV as "typical" of Europe as it is to take the Athens of Pericles as typical of Greece. But the caution is very real: the future does not belong to the aristocrats, certainly not to French aristocrats. Within a few generations, even the British, even the Prussian aristocracies will be swallowed up in the new world, to which we must now turn.

[15] *Seven Plays,* New York, Dodd, Mead, 1951, "Saint Joan," pp. 838, 839, used by permission of the Public Trustee and The Society of Authors.

The Age of Reason

IN THE COURSE of the eighteenth century a "New Moral World," to borrow the phrase of Robert Owen, one of the most hopeful prophets of this world, came into full competition with the complex of older moral worlds we Westerners had been living in. By this sweeping statement I do not at all wish to deny that the origins of the "new morality" go back well into the medieval centuries; nor do I wish to imply that the new wholly replaced the old then or now. I trust I have sufficiently insisted throughout this book that we are all, whether or not we are devoted to the study of history, deeply marked by all history, all prehistory. But there are in history periods of great and identifiable innovation—"revolutionary" periods, if you like—and the eighteenth century was one of these. The French call their history from Louis XI to 1789 "modern," from 1789 to the present "contemporary"; and though the particular bitterness of the French political struggle no doubt accounts for this, to us Americans, fantastic nomenclature, the conception has applicability to all the West. We are still struggling with the fundamental problems the eighteenth century posed; some of us, especially in the United States, are still proudly, but a bit worriedly, living in the eighteenth century.

In accordance with our tried, and not very empirical, method, we may begin by attempting to state in as broad terms as possible the fundamental positions of this new morality, this new world view. To start with the broadest: the eighteenth-century Enlightenment sought to substitute—take that word literally, as "put in place of"—for the *transcendental* God-determined Christian otherworldly heaven a this-world *transformed* by human reason guiding human action into . . . well, the phrase is inadequate, but "a heaven on earth" will have to do.

Now Americans today are so used to this basic article of faith of the eighteenth-century Enlightenment—though not by any means in its fresh, revolutionary, immediacy of 1789, when it took on intensities worth comparing with early Christian expectance of a Second Coming, when, indeed, this eighteenth-century eschatology was a messianic belief—that it is hard for us to realize that, as at least belief that for *all* human beings the "pursuit of happiness" and the attainment of comfort here on earth are normal and expected aims, this world view is new indeed. Yet the bright and ruthless young French revolutionary Saint-Just quite naturally, and, one suspects, almost without thinking, tossed off in an oration in 1793 the remark *Le bonheur est une idée neuve en Europe*. For once, translation has no traps; this is simply, "Happiness is a new idea in Europe."[1]

There is, of course, a trap here: just what is meant "operationally" by happiness—or *bonheur, Glückseligkeit*? Nothing, surely, that we can agree on as, one hopes, we can agree on the chemical definition of "water." Is happiness positive, a state of rapture, joy, or at least enjoyment? Is it negative, the absence of suffering, frustration? Is it a process—did not Jefferson write "the *pursuit* of happiness"? Is it a goal, something attainable once and for all? The word surely means all of these, in all their myriad combinations in the human being.[2] As a kind of minimal expectation among most modern Westerners, the happiness to which he has come to feel he has a "right," the happiness he "expects," includes the physical comforts, the material satisfactions, the absence of preventable physical suffering—and most such suffering he has been taught to believe is preventable by the miracles of science—and, quite as important, such degree of success in whatever kinds of agonistic competition he takes part in as can satisfy his self-esteem, his desire for a standing among his fellows. Parenthetically, the obvious needs stating here: In our pluralistic world there are so many such competitions, so many real "societies"—even,

---

[1] Saint-Just is so cited in an interesting essay by Raoul de Roussy de Sales which throws a good deal of light on this whole topic of the novelty of the world view behind that deceptive phrase the "pursuit of happiness." The historian will note with no surprise that M. Roussy de Sales implies that Saint-Just said this of all the world, though he actually said it of Europe. As a good conventional child of the Enlightenment, Saint-Just no doubt thought of Americans as, if not quite children of nature, at least already well acquainted with the idea of happiness. Surely was he not right in 1793? R. de Roussy de Sales, "The Idea of Happiness," *The Saturday Review Treasury*, New York, Simon & Schuster, 1957, p. 206.

[2] On many phases of this topic, see H. M. Jones, *The Pursuit of Happiness*, Cambridge, Mass., Harvard University Press, 1953.

let us not forget, the family, which obstinately refuses to disappear in the face of the prophets of doom or bliss—that most of us *do* have a degree of success, esteem, of loving and being loved, or the Fromms and even the Orwells would be more than right.

This new moral concept of heaven on earth was not without its static or negative side; its happiness is certainly cessation of care, pain, grievous struggle. But was—is—the conventional Christian heaven much more than that? There is not, for the ordinary Christian, in heaven much of the kind of expectation embodied in heroic Valhallas or Elysian fields, nor even in what the Westerner understands to be the Moslem heaven. Granted that the saved Christian will be resurrected in the flesh, granted that the popular imagination has rather vaguely filled heaven with material satisfactions, it is still true that Christian distrust of the flesh in this world has spilled over into Christian ideas of the next world. "Bliss" is the favorite word of the theologians for the heavenly state of man, and it is a very sedate and unsensual word.

In contrast, the new eschatology insists on the continuing struggle. Indeed, in what is so far its most extreme form among major organized religions, the Marxist faith of the Soviet Union, the coming heaven on earth will be embodied in a "classless society" in which struggle—even that of the agon—having ceased to be the evil-producing class struggle, will be the good-producing, the happy emulation among contented men, which we will call "Progress." The concept of Progress is, however, central to all forms of the new eschatology, including most emphatically our own democratic form. As a systematic interpretation of the universe as it seems to man, the idea of Progress is a creation of the eighteenth century. In accordance with the usual process in human affairs that I have called reinforcement (*not* the well-worn vicious circle), this idea emerged from a late medieval and early modern world in which the new state was creating better public order and wider markets in which, in turn, merchants were increasing wealth, and inventors, given some margin by that wealth, were increasing mechanical power, and philosophers, benefiting from a similar margin, were mulling over ideas which were to lead to the idea of Progress. Once clearly stated and developed, which was not until the end of the seventeenth century, the idea of Progress reinforced the new state, the new economy, the new technology, and set us on the merry way of exponential increase we are still on.[3]

---

[3] I cannot here go into the general history, and especially the intellectual history, necessary for the full consideration of the place of the idea of Progress in Western history. The best brief introduction seems to me still the "old" book of J. B. Bury, *The Idea of*

The historical process which the eighteenth century elevated into an eschatology under the name of Progress was, to use another great term of the century, considered a *natural* process. And by this word "natural" the men of the time came increasingly to mean, at a minimum stage of opposition to Christian orthodoxy, a process misunderstood, not really described or accounted for, in the Christian canon and tradition, and therefore demanding modification of Christian orthodoxy; and at a maximum stage of opposition to such orthodoxy, they meant a process that had gone on in spite of willful Christian attempts to deny and resist it, attempts that could not stop the process, but had indeed—paradoxically, of course, but is not all evil a paradox of the emotions?—slowed down this inevitable process. The conclusion for these latter *radically Enlightened* was therefore clear: Christian orthodoxy had not to be modified, but destroyed root and branch, or it might be a more serious obstacle to inevitable Progress.

The Christian—and we are still pursuing these ideas among the extremists, the atheists or materialists—had to believe in a God who could and did interfere with the order of nature, had to believe in some "supernatural" which to these advanced thinkers was—and they were free with the word—quite simply "superstition." The true nature of the universe, and of man's place in it, was gradually being disclosed to the natural philosophers, headed by the incomparable Newton, who together had already made it certain that the time scale of Genesis was quite wrong, that the sun did not revolve about the earth, and that most of the miracles recounted in the Bible were contrary to what these natural philosophers—our "scientists"—called the "laws of nature." Common sense, the Enlightened of the eighteenth century believed, had always had its troubles over miracles like that of Joshua's stopping the sun and had come independently to a good deal of healthy skepticism; but the scientists had set the seal of highest truth on what common sense had only suspected. Man is a part of nature; a God who is not part of nature is an illusion; a god who is a part of nature is a superfluity.

Such rigorous conclusions were by no means common in the eighteenth century. Before we go on to some of the implications of the new eschatology

---

Progress: An Inquiry into Its Origin and Growth (1920) now available in a paperback (New York, Dover, 1955). Bury was a late Victorian freethinker who "believed in" Progress. But see also Carl Becker's admirable summary in the *Encyclopedia of the Social Sciences* under the word Progress and his *Heavenly City of the Eighteenth Century Philosophers,* New Haven, Yale University Press, 1932. For a brief bibliography of the Enlightenment, I refer the reader to my *Portable Age of Reason Reader,* New York, Viking, 1956, pp. 26-34.

for Western moral life, we must try to be clear about a difficult and complicated matter. The new view of the universe did not destroy the old; Christianity did not die out. Now, two centuries later, there are more Christians on earth than ever before. We shall return to this topic in a later chapter. Here it must be enough to point out that the kind of challenge to ultimate Christian beliefs presented by the system of beliefs just outlined was met by Christians with a great variety of adjustments, from a deism or "natural religion" that could hardly be called Christian at all, through moderate compromises on the time scale and literalness of the Bible, to forms of "fundamentalism," Catholic as well as Protestant, that seem to repudiate entirely the new world view of the Enlightenment. In the eyes of naturalistic-historical observer, however, no one not wholly insane can entirely repudiate what the last few centuries have brought with them. The American fundamentalist driving his Ford through Mencken's "Bible Belt" cannot be what his sixteenth-century predecessor was, if only because he is driving a Ford—and may live to see his son drive a Lincoln. More important, and more simple, he is bound in this world to feel beleaguered, to be aware that his are no longer the beliefs of the majority of his fellow Americans. As we shall shortly see, it is not even quite true that Christian ethics have survived unchanged in an era that has witnessed so successful an attack on Christian cosmology and theology.

Moreover, we must be clear about another important modification in what has just been written about the new world view of the Enlightenment. Its leading eighteenth-century exponents were intelligent, cultivated men, by no means contemptuous of history, by no means pure theorists unaware of the facts of life. The best known of them—Voltaire, Rousseau, Diderot, even Bentham, indeed even Kant—nourished all sorts of reservations about Progress, human goodness and reasonableness, the immediate perfectability of men, the attribution of all evil to socio-economic environment.[4] The formation of a kind of canon of belief for the religion of the Enlightenment is a process still going on; already it is clear, however, that many of these subtle and difficult thinkers who in the eighteenth century helped make the new faith would be quite unable to accept it now, either in its American or its Russian form. Some such process, I must insist again, has, from

---

[4] I cannot here go at length into the many problems of intellectual history suggested by this last, but I strongly recommend to the reader Henry Vyverberg's recent *Historical Pessimism in the French Enlightenment,* Cambridge, Mass., Harvard University Press, 1958, which has a very useful bibliography.

the historical-naturalistic point of view, marked the growth of all our Western higher religions. The fact that the religion of the Enlightenment often claims to base itself wholly on a historical-naturalistic world view (or "method") would not appear to have exempted it from this historical adaptation to the needs and nature of the many, who never yet have been subtle and difficult thinkers.

With these necessary warnings, we may continue to pursue into the field of ethics some of the implications of the radically anti-Christian "materialist" position we have been outlining. The new Enlightenment had made much of what Christians had traditionally accepted as true seem literally false. In the first rationalist flush—recall Euhemerus and Greco-Roman rationalism—a great deal that to a less-confident and tamer rationalist nowadays seems quite possible or even probable as an event, however much he still refuses to accept the full Christian explanation as implied in the word "miracles," came in the eighteenth century to seem as untrue and impossible as the actual stopping of the sun by Jehovah through Joshua. I mean, for example, the whole effect on us of what is fashionably called the "psychosomatic," and of much modern psychology, animal as well as human, which can easily enough accept as "facts" the story of the Gadarene swine, and even that of Lazarus. The more naïve rationalism of the eighteenth century —though even in this matter there are many hints in the work of the subtler thinkers of anti-intellectualism and existentialism to come—felt it had to question even the facts of the Christian tradition, had to find the source of these lies in priestly villainy, in deliberate charlatanry, in the conspiracy to fool the innocent many.[5] Now, as I have perhaps unfashionably insisted in this book, the Western ethical tradition is overwhelmingly intellectualist in the sense that it refuses to accept the false, the lie, as necessary, or, save in the most innocent of forms of the "white" lie, as useful.[6] To many a sincere convert to the new views of the Enlightenment, historical Christianity seemed hopelessly stained with falsehoods, whether or not they had been propagated in good faith. A new start seemed needed.

But as the movement of ideas developed, emphasis was turned from the

---

[5] On this whole subject of eighteenth-century rationalist attitudes toward the "irrational" in religion and mythology, see the forthcoming book by F. E. Manuel, *The Eighteenth Century Confronts the Gods.*

[6] There is a strong-minded minority, perhaps dying out, that holds the absolutist position that no falsehood at all is ever justifiable. A distinguished Boston physician not long deceased maintained that the physician must always tell the patient the full unadulterated truth as he, the physician, sees it. Confronted with such intransigeance, I feel inclined to twist the well-known dictum of Lord Acton into "virtue tends to corrupt, and absolute virtue corrupts absolutely."

falsehood of Christian cosmology to what seemed to the Enlightened to be the harmful moral effects of a conventional Christian upbringing. Some of these attacks on Christianity merely echoed the familiar pagan and Renaissance humanist complaint that the Christian was taught to suppress natural instincts and appetites he ought not to suppress, that he could not enjoy life or let others enjoy it, that he was inevitably either a frustrated, truncated human being or a hypocrite. The important, and relatively new, line of attack in ethics, however, questioned the philosophical and psychological basis of the Christian "civil war in the breast." Robert Owen, who was born in 1771, put the matter at its clearest and simplest: Human conduct is wholly the result of the action of the environment—the cultural as well as the physical environment—upon the individual. No man is, therefore, "responsible" for his conduct. We are, unfortunately, as Christians taught that we have a "free will," that we can follow a nonexistent, yet somehow invented, "conscience," that we can *choose* between good and evil conduct. On this false foundation the whole fabric of religion is erected, the sufferings of the poor, the tyranny of the rich, the crimes and misdemeanors of us all explained and even justified by the preposterous notion of original sin, and thousands and thousands of deluded individuals driven by the sense of guilt Christianity inculcates into unhappiness and despair, into a state of mind which, men being the product of such conditioning, drives them into the vicious circle of evil.

Evil, then, is no consequence of an imaginary fall; Christian theology and all that is built on it is harmful nonsense. Evil is a consequence of the bad environment we grow up in from infancy, our constricting family, that nest of selfishness, our schooling in error, our church, our politics, our absurd social structure. And all this bad environment has been built up on the sole basis of human ignorance. Man is by nature good—that is, he comes into this world equipped to respond to stimuli from his environment in such a way that he will be happy, well adjusted, and, therefore, in the only meaning of the word that makes sense, *virtuous*. But the infant from its very first gurgle is subject to stimuli from a vicious and corrupt environment. Naturally, inevitably, he responds in such a way that he is unhappy, maladjusted, and, therefore, in the only meaning of the word that makes sense, *wicked*.[7]

[7] I have used a few words, like "maladjusted," that Owen would not have used, but I do not think I have misrepresented his position. The reader should go direct to Robert Owen's *A New View of Society and Other Writings*, ed. by G.D.H. Cole, London, Dent, 1927, in Everyman's Library. If he has any doubts as to the persistence of Owen's view into our own times, I suggest he read B. F. Skinner, *Walden Two*.

We need not here worry over the problem of how man, that naturally well-adjusted creature, got so badly maladjusted. Owen seems not to have worried over it, nor did many of the Enlightened, save an occasional subtle soul like Diderot, who came to question the dogma of environmentalism. But we must note that, having reached this point, the Enlightened tended to divide, roughly, into two schools of thought as to what must follow. Both agreed that existing environment produced evil. They did vary somewhat in their emphasis on which particular environment, mostly actual institutions, was most responsible for this evil. Someone at some time in the eighteenth century no doubt blamed every institution that ever has been blamed, but in contrast with later tendencies to blame economic and political institutions, the thinkers of the eighteenth century reserved their heaviest fire for religious institutions, and in particular for the Church of Rome. Still, they spared very little of what existed. Theirs was to be a new moral world. Where they divided was on the problem of how to bring about the transformation of the bad environment into the good.

One group, of which the most clear-cut, logical, and extreme representative turns out to be no logic-loving Frenchman, but a man of that nation of distrusters of logic, the English, William Godwin, author of *Political Justice* (1793), we may call the *philosophical anarchists*. Godwin held that if each man did what he wanted to do, free from all compulsions put on him by *any* "organization," if he were free from the laws, rules, and, above all, the rulers of any institution from the family to church and state, he would so act that he and all men would be happy and virtuous. What we have here is the purest, and the most naïve, consequence drawn from the great environmentalist dogma of the natural goodness and reasonableness of man. The anarchist believes that man is born with a kind of self-regulating instinct—if the somewhat unfair and gross metaphor may be pardoned, with a kind of very complicated and effective spiritual automatic regulator, or thermostat—which always works perfectly if its possessor does not try to improve on it, tamper with it, and, worst of all, try to replace it in other human beings by exercising power over them.

The great tampering that has made this thermostat so useless in our society is, for the anarchist, *law,* the attempt to regulate, which means to treat as identical, repetitious, and, therefore, predictable what in reality is varied, spontaneous, ever-changing. Marriage will do as a sample of the vain, or, rather, harmful, attempt to regulate human conduct by law. If the thermostats of both partners are working the way nature intended them to work, the legal formality of marriage and the absurd promise to love, honor, and obey are unnecessary; if, in this particular relation, the miraculous little thermostats indicate that all is not well, then there is no loving and honoring, and should be no obeying—there is no marriage. Basically, the anarchist blames the bad environment that makes for evil on what he considers a perverse attempt to construct an *artificial* environment. All that needs to be done, then, is to remove this environment, remove all institutions that prescribe, regulate, compel human action; all that needs to be done is to leave the individual *really* free ("really" is, of course, the greatest of Western adverbs). This anarchistic position is in ethics really and at last the "immanentist" position Mr. Stace attributes, somewhat too confidently, in my opinion, to the Greeks (see above, p. 56). Unlike the Greeks, the anarchist is untroubled by worries over necessity, fate, *hubris,* or any of the other cosmic troubles that haunted those sunny Greeks. The position of the philosophical anarchist is the gentlest, most hopeful, of positions men have taken toward the universe; it is the position modern sentimental Christian liberalism—influenced by whatever also influenced the anarchists, including, such is the nature of what I have called "reinforcement," the work of the anarchists themselves—often assigns quite anachronistically to Jesus.

The other group is, in respect to the problem of how to deal with the bad existing environment, at a polar opposite from the anarchists. These are the *planners,* the manipulators of environment, the "enlightened despots," to use a consecrated historical term. Many, perhaps most, of them were good enough children of the Age of Enlightenment to hold that all men are naturally good and reasonable, and that once the crippling effects of the present bad environment on the mass of human beings have been remedied, once they have become whole men, enlightened men, then the program, or absence of program, of the philosophical anarchists can be followed. But right now they hold that the many *are* crippled, their natural instincts warped or suppressed, their natural intelligence undeveloped in a world that leaves them ignorant, or, worse yet, full of mistaken ideas. They are sheep led by bad shepherds. But fortunately there are good shepherds available, the small but potentially adequate minority of men who really understand the situation, and who have the good will to remedy it—the Enlightened. The necessary steps are then clear. First of all, the bad shepherds, the present rulers in church and state and society, must be supplanted by good shepherds. The good shepherds will then gradually bring the sheep along the path to transformation into the human beings they were meant to be. They will educate, they will make laws, they will enforce laws, they will even have recourse to dictatorship—a virtuous dictatorship, such as the later Marxist "dictatorship of the proletariat." They will not, and certainly not at the beginnings of the process, consult the sheep, let alone allow the sheep themselves to choose their shepherds. We have perhaps worked a rather worn figure of speech to absurdity. The point is clear: the position of the thinkers of this group is not a democratic one. They are authoritarians for and of the moment, however much, like their contemporary Marxist-Leninist successors, they may claim to be libertarians for and of the future.

Neither of these groups of moral revolutionaries of the eighteenth century included violence in their prescriptions for society. We are today, whether we like revolutions or not, thoroughly used to the process of violent change in high politics. But until the French Revolution astonished the world, the men of the eighteenth century, true to their upbringing, expected the Enlightenment to do its work in the minds and hearts of few or many in such a way that the transition to the new moral world would be peaceful and gradual. The French Reign of Terror added a new intensity of hope or fear to political morality in the West.

In real life, neither of the groups I have just sorted out by analysis into the polar opposition of anarchist (libertarian democrat) and enlightened despot (authoritarian elitist) comes out so neatly separate. The plans and the practices of thinkers and doers alike were generally a mixture of the two. This is especially true of some of the most influential of the great thinkers, of none more so than Rousseau. There is still a debate, into which we need not go here, as to whether the *Social Contract* comes out on the side of liberty for the individual or on the side of authority for the enlightened ruler, or "society." Rousseau, who was, after all, a philosopher if not a *philosophe,* was sure he had solved the problem implied in the antithesis of liberty-authority; the individual who obeyed the general will was wholly free, since he was thereby obeying himself—his better self, his true self, his *moral* self.[8] Rousseau was driven in the course of this abstract analysis to the famous conclusion that the individual who failed to recognize his true self in the general will could be "forced to be free," presumably by those who did recognize his true self for him.[9]

[8] Jean Jacques Rousseau, *The Social Contract and Discourses,* trans. by G. D. H. Cole, new Amer. ed., New York, Dutton, 1950, Chap. VII, p. 13.
[9] A brief note here may keep us from getting deeply involved in one of those nagging philosophical questions I have tried in my introduction to sidetrack. (See above, p. 8.) The nominalist, the tough-minded, the realist of common sense will reject Rous-

Even among the theorists, then, the two logical extremes were barren poles indeed. The authoritarians did not urge that we all be slaves to the wisest man on earth; the anarchists did not urge that all regularities, habits as well as laws, be banished from human life. In the balance, however, it is safe to say that the Enlightenment was generally on the side of authority— virtuous, enlightened authority, it goes without saying. The *philosophes* were bright, clever, gifted men, who have to be called intellectuals, for they were already marked out as a group that dealt more with words than with things, and more with words as signs of "reality" and "values" than with words as a *direct* means of commanding, or manipulating, human beings. Such bright clever men can hardly be democrats at heart—not even when they call themselves New Dealers. The democrat—may I say, without much irony, the *true* democrat?—has got to be patient with human imperfections, even with human stupidity, has got, I suspect, to feel in his heart that stupidity (stupidity in matters dear to our Western philosophical, ethical, and aesthetic tradition, stupidity in matters verbal) is not the *real* form of original sin. Voltaire was no more a democrat than was Calvin; both would have agreed with another nondemocrat, John Mill, that "ordinary human nature is so poor a thing."[10]

Yet the overwhelming, the abiding effect of eighteenth-century thought on man and his destiny was to reinforce mightily all that was making for modern democratic egalitarianism. The century of the uncommon man paved the way for our century of the common man. Voltaire and Mill are heroes of the democratic tradition; so, too, is Squire Jefferson, founder of a republic he thought of, at bottom, as Roman, based on free, virtuous farmers, and who would surely have been horrified could he have foreseen the America of another squire, Franklin D. Roosevelt.

There is no great difficulty here. The thinkers of the Enlightenment merely helped on—their help was essential—a process begun long before, a

---

seau's "solution." If I, in the only conscious mind I have got, do not want to do something, and if anyone or anything human, from policeman through priest to a majority vote of a group I "belong to," forces me to do that thing, then I am not at that moment "free." But the toughest-minded realist must admit that some such piece of thought-feeling conditioning as that of Rousseau's "general will" does seem in the long run to reconcile many of us to giving in to, to obeying, *persons,* other wills; as children of the West, and especially of the West of modern science, we no longer regard, as our ancestors of not so long ago did regard, our relations with a to us impersonal "nature" as involving any other will than our own.
[10] J. S. Mill, "The Claims of Labour," *Dissertations and Discussions* (*1874-1875*), Vol. II, p. 288.

process we have traced in the history of morals through Renaissance, Reformation, the new state, and the new science, a process of the utmost complexity, from which I wish now merely to single out a single element of great
importance in understanding the process: the many—not all, but the millions,
nonetheless—came to want, to expect, a great deal, both in material satisfactions and in spiritual (substitute "psychological" or any other word that will
do the same work for you if, as one end product of just the process I am
trying to understand, you cannot face the word "spiritual") satisfactions that
had hitherto been limited to the few. The many came to *expect* to be happy,
comfortable, and, what is more important and much more difficult to analyze,
they came to expect as *individuals* some, at least, of the satisfactions that go
with participation in the Western, ritualized competitions I have called
agones, or the struggle for prize. This, nothing less, is what lies behind modern
Western egalitarianism: prizes for all.

Traditional Christianity, which did emerge from a society with egalitarian
elements, had through its promise of salvation given to the humblest in this
world equality with the proudest, if it had not, as the Nietzscheans have always insisted, given the weak, the botched, the failures, an absurd promise
of superiority.

But he that is greatest among you shall be your servant. And whosoever shall
exalt himself shall be humbled; and whosoever shall humble himself shall be
exalted.[11]

But the effect of the moral revolution of early modern times—for once the
word is not just rhetoric—was to cast grave and spreading doubt among the
many as to the reality of the Christian afterlife, and to suggest to them that
they had better try to get the promised satisfactions of salvation right here on
earth. Do you wish to feel the difference? Read again in its context the passage from the Gospel quoted just above, or, better, that passage from Mary's
hymn to the Lord:

He hath scattered the proud in the imagination of their hearts.
He hath put down princes from their thrones, and hath exalted them of low degree.
The hungry he hath filled with good things; and the rich he hath sent empty
away.[12]

This last is, for the Gospels, pretty earthy and concrete and fully in the

11 Matthew 23:11-12.
12 Luke 1:51-53.

Judaic tradition; but put it beside the preamble to the Declaration of Independence, or, better yet, that good, unexalted, commonsensical poetic assertion of the modern egalitarian:

> The rank is but the guinea's stamp,
> The man's the gowd for a' that.[13]

Let us then recapitulate, simplifying and certainly exaggerating in the process. The traditional Christian world view was that God had created the world just five or six thousand years ago as described in Genesis, that he had made it for man, that man through Adam had sinned, was banished from Eden and condemned to suffer, that through the miraculous intervention of the Son of God, sinful man, though cursed by Adam's fall with original sin, might, as a Christian sacramentally made part of the church, gain salvation in an afterlife, that conduct in accordance with membership in that church and with the rules of morality canonically prescribed—*both faith and works* —was the best sign that a man would be saved, and conduct markedly not so in accordance, above all, such conduct not repented of and sacramentally absolved, was a sure sign that a man would be eternally damned. Add to this world view the general tone of orthodox Christianity in favor of established social and economic inequalities, a conservatism not really breached by periodic revolts to restore "primitive" Christian *unworldliness* or *antiworldliness* (both of which were quite different, as I have insisted, from eighteenth-century egalitarian democracy) and the Christian unwillingness to make sensuous pleasures quite free from dangers, and you have something very different from what most of us Westerners now accept as a world view. The Christian could and did enjoy himself even in fornication—but, unless he was very stupid or very wicked indeed, he had a sense of guilt about it; the Christian could and did accept this ordinary world of cause and effect, of predictable regularities—but, unless he was a very advanced skeptic, he believed that God could turn everything topsy-turvy if He wished, and, what is more important, that God actively and yet inscrutably made the regular perversely irregular, as we all know it to be, from the fall of the dice to the fall of kings. But I am unnecessarily wordy: to the traditional Christian the other world of heaven, hell, and purgatory was there, real, visible, certain; Dante, if I may use a word I suspect has never been used of him, was in these places a *reporter.*

---

[13] "For A' That and A' That," *The Poetical Works of Robert Burns,* New York, Oxford University Press, 1948, p. 328.

The new view started from a different cosmogony. Newton had finished what Copernicus had long ago begun; the earth was just a minor planet spinning on its axis in orbit around the sun, clearly not the center of the universe. By the end of the eighteenth century geology and paleontology had, at least for the Enlightened, disposed of the chronology of Genesis, and, for the really advanced, suggested that the "hypothesis" of God was hardly necessary. The universe in this view was the vast mechanism we call "nature," and man was wholly a part of it; the French physician La Mettrie wrote a book entitled *Man the Machine* (1748). At death, obviously, the machine stops and begins to disintegrate; there can be no afterlife, no immortal soul, indeed, in the Christian sense, no soul at all. What we call a soul is really no more than consciousness, a function of the central nervous system which behaviorist psychologists like Condillac, with leads from Locke, had already begun to study. This vast mechanism of the universe is, however, one in which there is the rather mysterious phenomenon of organic life, sentience, a not-quite-mechanical, at least not-quite-predictable, apparently related series of responses to stimuli from the environment. At this point, or somewhere near it, the Enlightened found room for—the Christian, I think, has to say smuggled in—a teleology, in fact an eschatology, an ethics, a religion, one which, like all Western religions, was to proliferate in sects, heresies, and schisms, a religion which, in constant mutual interaction with Christianity, is the new religion of the modern West.

We shall be for the rest of this book much engaged in the task of tracing some few of the myriad forms of this interaction between the world view of the Enlightenment and that of Christianity. Note carefully that I write of interaction, not of polar, mutually exclusive opposition. It seems clear that no Christian, not even the fundamentalist, can be in the 1950's what he would have been in the 1650's; but it is also clear that there could have been no Enlightenment had there been no Christianity. I do not think that in any sensible foreseeable future either world view will vanquish the other; one cannot say, *ceci tuera cela,* this will kill that. But there does exist in our West this great, Enlightenment-born religion which in many of its forms specifically declares itself to be anti-Christian, or non-Christian. I am going to use from time to time, as the generic term for this religion, the term "free thought," but the fact is that, as I have already mentioned (see above, p. 148n.), unfortunately, there *is* no accepted generic term. Orthodox Marxism-Leninism (it is now proper, I take it, to omit "Stalinism"), which is in some ways the free-thinking analogue to Calvinism, is, thanks to its success in the Soviet Union, the most clear-cut and powerful of these sects, very explicit in its intolerant repudiation of Christianity. At the other extreme are some exceedingly "liberal" forms of what their holders claim to be Christian faiths, but which to an outsider trying to be objective seem to have scrapped too much of historical Christianity to have the claim granted. Such, for example, is American Unitarianism, in its Left Wings, at any rate; there is still debate among the Unitarians as to whether or not they wish to be called "Christians." Almost all these variants can be traced back to the eighteenth century; even Marxism-Leninism, though it does owe its actual form to these two prophets, has very clear origins in eighteenth-century thought. [14]

It is impossible to make good quantitative estimates of the number of believers of these shades of opinion, either for the eighteenth century or, for that matter, for the present. Even in the Soviet Union, to say nothing of the satellites, it does not seem as if Communism has wholly destroyed Christianity. In the free world, statistics of actual membership in organized religious bodies are in themselves inadequate measures of actual individual attitudes. There is the great obstacle of the religiously "indifferent," typified in a country like France by the anticlerical Radical Socialist who calls in the priest at his deathbed, in America by the Sunday golfer who goes to his Protestant church on Christmas and Easter, and even more by the churchgoer, even church member, who conforms for social and economic reasons but who really sees the universe as the freethinker sees it. This last type, by the way, is very different f: the medieval conformist Christian, or the indifferent, comfortable, shallow Christian of any past age, for these simply had no alternative world view; in those moments when they had—as we all do—to face metaphysical anxiety, they had to fall back on the Christian cosmology. All in all, we had better give up attempts at statistics, and conclude simply that there are in our modern West millions of freethinkers of all shades, none of them theologically, eschatologically, ethically, emotionally quite Christian.

[14] I must relegate to a footnote the actual spectrum or ladder of *eighteenth-century* religious attitudes, which would go up or down, depending on the position of the observer, from Roman Catholicism of the extreme Right—say, that of the eighteenth-century University of Salamanca—through the sacramental "revealed" religions, the Leftist sects, to Unitarianism, deism, "natural religion" in all its forms, most of them religions of the heart, of a nice nature, "pre-romantic," to its end in materialism and atheism. There is not much room for skepticism or Pyrrhonism on the ladder, and no one had yet coined the word "agnostic." It is almost certain that a respectable deism was the ordinary position of the Enlightened. Leslie Stephen, *History of English Thought in the Eighteenth Century*, 3rd ed., 2 vols. (London, Smith, Elder, 1902), gives in great detail the niceties of these theologies for England, a representative country. I have dealt with the subject briefly in the Introduction to my *Portable Age of Reason Reader*.

II

This last statement may seem to contradict the often-made assertion, to which something I have written earlier may seem to give support, that the Enlightened, though they rejected the theology and ritual and the rest of organized Christianity, retained Christian ethics. It would be more accurate to say that many of the Enlightened did preserve what they thought was Christian ethics, or the *best* of Christian ethics, and that they could find in the immense range of Christian historical experience some justification for almost all they considered ethically right; but also that at the many points where their own theology or metaphysics—words they would never have used of their own world view—implied some modification of Christian ethics, they made very important modifications, modifications that have often worked back into accepted Christianity. I must insist that the range of freethinking is very great, that, like Christianity, this new religion is not monolithic, and that therefore generalizations I make about the new ethics are subject to the usual caution: exceptions abound. It may even be possible that somewhere on earth a vigorous, vocally anti-Christian freethinker had a set of ethical values identical with those of some Christian of old. I must confess I am at loss for a specific example of such a freethinker; no gentle and respectable Victorian, not even that ascetic hedonist John Stuart Mill, so incapable of anything you or I could accept as *hedone,* or pleasure, will quite do. With this caution, then, I shall consider the new directions the Enlightenment gave to ethics, the new content—though also in part old—it gave to morals, under two broad headings, humanitarianism and utilitarianism.

Eighteenth-century humanitarianism is newer than you think it is.[15] I do not mean that no human being in the West ever felt sympathy for the sufferings of his fellow men before the eighteenth century, nor ever sought to alleviate the miseries he saw all about him. There is a vein or strand of this direct, emotional recoil of pity in Christianity. There is abhorrence of human gamecock victors in that vulgar physical agon that the Christian firmly condemned, and there is, perhaps in all but the saints a bit weaker than this damning of the victors, a sympathy for the losers, the victims, the underdogs. Pity is an emotion shared by many of the old pagan world of the Greeks and the Romans.

[15] I refer the reader to my article "Humanitarianism" in the *Encyclopedia of the Social Sciences,* Vol. V, pp. 244-248, and especially to the book of Hermann Kantorowicz, *The Spirit of British Policy and the Myth of the Encirclement of Germany,* trans. by W. H. Johnston, London, Allen & Unwin, 1931.

But the humanitarianism of the modern world differs from the pity or charity of earlier times in many ways. It was based, as we have just seen, on the very different world view that sees suffering, not as part of the order of nature and human nature, above all, not as ordained by God, but as unnatural, as the product of accumulated human errors happily remediable now that we know what the errors were. Hence the new humanitarianism was organized in a manner familiar to us all today, not after the pattern of Christian charities, which to the Enlightened seemed stopgaps, part of the old errors, but in pressure groups aiming at legislative measures to cure or prevent given suffering, or as official or semiofficial governmental bodies with similar aims, or as outright political parties organized to bring heaven to earth. By the nineteenth century all these organizations were full-blown, perhaps clearest in Britain: voluntary societies like the Society for the Prevention of Cruelty to Animals (1824) or the Society for the Prevention of Cruelty to Children (1884); the new Poor Law administrative system (1834) designed under Benthamite auspices as the "scientific" way to deal with the problem of poverty, and a good example of the difficulties of diagnosis and treatment of such evils, for a whole wing of the radical humanitarians thought the New Poor Law shockingly harsh; and, finally, such political radicals as the Chartists, the British form of the revolutionary plan to bring heaven to earth, or, better yet, the many American communist experiments from Brook Farm to New Harmony. All these movements have clear origins in the eighteenth century.

I have used Britain for most of my examples partly because many humanitarian reforms, such as the abolition of the relatively new Negro slavery, were in fact first achieved there, partly because the variety of organizations, from private to public, was greatest there, and partly because the British, more than any other people, extended their sympathies to the whole animal world, and especially to horses and dogs. But France, which most English-speaking people think of as a land inhabited by logic-ridden individuals relatively insensitive to the sufferings of other individuals, incapable of the *sentiment* of sympathy, would do quite well as an example. As Professor Shelby T. McCloy has shown in a recent study, the French in the eighteenth century were keenly aware of the demands of *humanité* and instituted concrete reforms in a wide range of fields.[16]

16 *The Humanitarian Movement in Eighteenth-Century France,* Lexington, Ky., University of Kentucky Press, 1957. Professor McCloy studies the deed as well as the word, institutional as well as intellectual history, and in his brief introductory chapter

The simple rationalism that made suffering out to be no more than the result of bad environment, bad "arrangements," is, however, only part of modern humanitarianism. The emotional elements are vastly more complicated. The favorite reproach of moderate and conservative men, that radical revolutionaries and even plain reformers do not so much pity the failures, the weak, as envy and hate the strong, the successful, is like most such stereotypes, unfair but by no means wholly untrue. There is such a component in the great protesters, a Rousseau on the edge of paranoia, a Voltaire too bright for love but not for vanity; it is even stronger, one suspects, in the professional rebels, the Tom Paines, the Marats. Even in such men as these, however, the particular form of not-quite-hypocrisy here involved is not only even better concealed from the not-quite-hypocrite himself than in cases where more private vices are involved, but it is also more thoroughly mingled with what one has to call genuine pity, genuine moral indignation. Violent radicalism is at least the tribute selfishness pays to altruism.

There are other, and deeper, emotional currents in humanitarianism, currents that have so far escaped the rational analysts, that, indeed, some historians like to maintain do not exist. I refer to those great shifts of taste, fashion, emotion, surely not subject to regular periodicity, but still cyclical, during which men revolt in the name of what they feel is simpler, fresher, more "natural," against the *complications* of their civilization; and since the intellectual content of our education, our literature, our arts, our legal and moral codes does tend to get complicated, these revolts tend to have a strong component of what is nowadays fashionably called "anti-intellectualism." The eighteenth century, century of rationalism, of formalism, of artificiality, was also the century of romantic emotionalism, of appeals to natural simplicity, of revolt against not only the *bad* environment, but the *whole* environment. Our new moral world came not only out of the relatively simple and rationalistic world view I have outlined just above; it came out of a deep-seated, widespread movement among the determining groups of Western society; a movement articulate enough, often put in terms that sound misleadingly intellectualist, but at bottom, like early Christianity, a really ferocious, irrational, and

---

gives a useful survey of expressions of the humanitarian ideal—including a reference (p. 3, note 5) "where Voltaire speaks of being dominated by 'love of the human race.'" I think it clear that no early or medieval Christian could have used that exact phrase, so definitely omitting God, Voltaire himself, surely, was not so dominated, even though he said he was.

highly successful revolt against what the rebels liked to call tyranny, but which was actually more often nothing but convention, tradition, the routine and the dullness of the settled, the established, the unpricked. But, of course, these common constraints are sometimes felt as tyranny by the Faustian temperament—and perhaps, up to a point, even by the Apollonian.

For the most part, the articulate eighteenth-century rebels of the heart had high hopes for the future. Against society and its tyrannical conventions they set the free natural man and his life-seeking, life-giving spontaneity. They found, most of them only through the printed page of travel and exploration, existing examples of the natural man, virtuous but not dull, dignified but not vain, above all, spontaneous, tearful, joyful, sentimental, and unashamed. Such were the Hurons, the South Sea Islanders, indeed most savages; such, a little more deliberately wise, a little more formal, but still not corrupt and vicious, like Europeans, were Chinese, Hindus, Persians; such, perhaps a bit too calculating, a bit too laden with Christianity and other hindrances from their original homeland, were even the North American white colonists, led by those children of nature Franklin and Washington. We are tempted today to believe that much of the cult of the primitive in the eighteenth century was insincere, affected; some of it, I suspect, was the work of publicists—we really are already in modern times, and you may give the word its full modern content—glad to furnish the public with the guidance they thought it wanted.[17]

The writers of the eighteenth century had no trouble finding models of virtue nearer home—nor, for that matter, did the artists, devoted also to the good cause. Novels, plays—especially the *comédie larmoyante*, practiced by no less a person than Diderot—essays, didactic paintings, all celebrated the same truth: among the poor, the simple, the peasants, the workers, the inspired and exceptionally gifted and sensitive even among the upper classes, there is still to be found in our corrupt eighteenth century the virtues of gentleness, loving-kindness, mutual help, true charity (not the corrupting "works" of Christianity), and, where a wicked civilized person or a wicked

[17] Such, I think, was Lahontan, one of the earliest, whose work is not available in English. Baron de Lahontan, *Dialogues curieux entre l'auteur et un sauvage de bon sens qui a voyage, et Memoires de l'Amerique septentrionale*, Baltimore, Johns Hopkins Press, 1931. Voltaire's Huron came, no doubt, out of Lahontan's. Surely Voltaire, Montesquieu, and even Oliver Goldsmith wrote tongue in cheek when they had their savages, their Persians, their Chinese, show up the injustices, the pretenses, the many defects of European society. Still, this is a curious variant of a genre, satire, which is never easy to classify as sincere or insincere.

civilized institution does not interfere, true happiness. Here, in short, are the humanitarian's prized virtues.[18]

We are with the eighteenth century in modern times in many ways, in none more clearly than in its variety, its multanimity. Since with the eighteenth century the reading public was already numerous, numbering certainly in the millions, though still far from universal literacy, since printing and engraving were relatively cheap, it is quite true that some of this variety can be attributed to the fact that we have more specimens surviving. But not all. Some of it, like the multanimity of the late Greco-Roman world, is a sign of the times, a fact. Along with the literature and the painting of the simple life, of the children of nature, there is the formal poetry of the heroic couplet and the Alexandrine, the witty comedies of a Marivaux, a Sheridan, the not very natural pornography of a Restif de la Bretonne, the work of so many, many men of all sorts in no sense children of nature, and quite incapable of pretending to belief in natural virtue as a foil to civilized vice—a Samuel Johnson, a Burke, a Diderot in most of his moods, a Voltaire in all of his, a Kant (whose abounding virtue is very far from the primitive), a Goethe who recovered very quickly from *Werther* (was that perhaps the really big dishonest Hollywood job of the century?), a Choderlos de Laclos, a Sade, both still well ahead of most of us on sex—the list could be long indeed. And remember that Boucher was quite as popular as Greuze—and probably with much the same people.

Nevertheless, what I have called humanitarianism, or, better, perhaps, humanitarianism plus romanticism, is the eighteenth-century translation into emotional terms of the new world view that man is born to happiness, that now at last we human beings know enough, feel enough, to conduct ourselves as the morally perfect—nearly perfect, at worst—beings we were meant by Mother Nature to be. Still, among the intellectually enlightened it is possible to discern already the beginnings of one of the great and painful stresses we still suffer from—the conflict so evident among contemporary American liberals between the love for common men that their principles, or at least their sense of history and tradition, tell them they ought to have and the compound

[18] A sampling: Rousseau's *Nouvelle Héloïse* or, among the forgotten, any novel by Robert Bage or Thomas Holcroft; for a play, Diderot's *Fils naturel,* or that play of Kotzebue's, *Kabal und Liebe,* which in English adaptation they played in *Mansfield Park;* for more formal philosophical treatment, Shaftesbury's *Characteristics;* for didactic painting, almost anything of Greuze, which should be compared with some of Hogarth's moral sequences to bring out what happened as the century wore on.

of fear, distrust, and contempt for the common man that brews somewhere inside them.

This conflict is in its most rudimentary stages in the century of the Enlightenment, hardly visible on the surface even in such scorners of system and consistency as Rousseau. It was still too easy to find a few appropriate villains who were responsible for the evils. I do not suppose any conspicuous eighteenth-century thinker on the side of the angels could ever let himself go as did that culture hero of American liberalism Walt Whitman in praise of animals and dispraise of men, common men, democratic men, men Whitman *ought* to love.

They do not sweat and whine about their condition,
They do not lie awake in the dark and weep for their sins,
They do not make me sick discussing their duty to God,
Not one is dissatisfied, not one is demented with the mania of owning things,
Not one kneels to another, nor to his kind that lived thousands of years ago,
Not one is respectable or unhappy over the whole earth.[19]

Nor could an eighteenth-century European, even in a Europe where only man was vile, feel like the present-day American fanatics whose skill at pressure-group politics has set aside thousands of acres of our "wilderness areas" to be free even from the corruption of the wheel (perhaps that first one was, after all, the wickedest of inventions). For these American primitivists of our own day the only prospect that can please is one with no trace of humankind at all. The great hope in mankind for them has ended—and not only for them, if we may judge from the intellectual temper of our age—in the great disgust, a disgust so universalist as to have little consoling power.

It was, however, in the eighteenth century a great hope indeed. The old wicked world was to end in a First Coming of Reason, Nature, Humanity. These men of the Enlightenment, whom the Victorians saw as cold, sapless, unimaginative, unemotional rationalists, were in word and deed religious enthusiasts, youthful, daring, full of gusto, founders of a faith men still seek to live by. It is a hard faith for us today to live by, as we cannot help learning. Its kingdom is so definitely of this earth that we find it hard to await a Second Coming with due patience and hope. But for the men who had seen the American Revolution followed by the French Revolution, the great day was

---

[19] Walt Whitman, "Song of Myself," No. 32, in *The Complete Poetry and Prose of Walt Whitman*, ed. by Malcolm Cowley, New York, Pellegrini, 1948, I, 89. There is an amazing amount of "liberalism" packed into these lines, a great disgust that spills over onto something more than mere environment-as-evil.

at hand. Condorcet, outlawed and in hiding from the Jacobins who had misunderstood the new gospel, sat down to write his philosophy of history, published after his death in prison as *Esquisse d'un tableau historique des prog-
rès de l'esprit humain.*[20] From primitive man onward, Condorcet traced in
nine epochs the gradual rise of man, his progress toward the immanent goal
of history. With his own time had begun the tenth epoch, the end of history
and the beginning of . . . shall we call it the attainment of universal happiness? With Condorcet we find the religion of the Enlightenment in perhaps
its purest form.[21]

III

The utilitarian strand is interwoven with the humanitarian in eighteenth-
century ethics. The century was certainly conscious of the conflict between
the head and the heart. Indeed, the man of feeling in Diderot rebelled violently against the stodgy rationalist Helvétius, and he composed a long com-
mentary on the latter's extreme version of the thesis that human beings can be
rationally manufactured according to the best standards.[22] Perhaps even a
Condorcet was dimly aware of the difficulty underlying the world view of the
Enlightenment—and of the twentieth century: the naturalistic humanitarian
sentiment must basically push toward letting men do what they want to do,
think and feel at any given moment what they want to; for men, like most
other mammals, do not like cages; the utilitarian rationalist must keep trying
to induce, or even to force, men to do what he knows they *ought* to do, what
would be "best"—*most useful*—for them. But the ordinary enlightened man
in this century of the beginnings of our modern hopes was not yet aware of the
full import of the distinction I have made above between the way of the
philosophical anarchist, the way of the heart, and the way of the enlightened
despots, the way of the head.

Though the term "utilitarianism" owes its success to John Mill in the next

[20] Trans. by June Barraclough as *Sketch for a Historical Picture of the Progress of the Human Mind,* London, Weidenfeld & Nicolson, 1955.
[21] So pure that the mild paradox is irresistible: this world has with Condorcet become quite the other world. I owe to the work, as yet unpublished, of a graduate student at Harvard, Gerald J. Gruman, M.D., now engaged on a historical study of ideas on what he calls "prolongevity" a really extraordinary parallel with Christianity: according to Dr. Gruman, the full implication of Condorcet's work is nothing less than corporeal individual immortality here on this earth, eternal life in this flesh, for everybody, an eschatological concept indeed.
[22] Diderot, *Réfutation d'Helvétius* in *Oeuvres complètes,* ed. by J. Assézat, Paris, Garner, 1875, Vol. II.

century, the whole moral outlook it summarizes is the work of the eighteenth, and in one form or another permeates the writings of most eighteenth-century moralists. Helvétius and Bentham give a good cross section, though it should be noted that the famous phrase "greatest good of the greatest number" originates in the *On Crimes and Punishments* (1764) of the Italian *philosophe* Beccaria. The systematist classifying ethical ideas has, of course, to list a broad group as *hedonist,* and, as always when his groups are broad enough, finds the ancient Greeks start the line. But eighteenth-century hedonism in its utilitarian form is by no means identical with Epicureanism. The eighteenth-century attitude was widely held among the many of the newly enlightened, but the Epicureans were few and aristocratic; the eighteenth-century attitude could base itself on a naturalistic rationalism that, again in contrast to that of the Greco-Roman world, was widely held, and, in addition, supported by the new faith in natural science; finally, the eighteenth-century attitude was optimistic, even messianic, that of the original Epicureans resigned, cosmically pessimistic.

Briefly, the utilitarianism of the eighteenth century starts out with the basic assumption that human beings are endowed by "nature" with the suitable physiological equipment to guide their conduct in such a way that they can do what is right and avoid what is wrong. But "right" and "wrong" are, especially to Bentham, words stained by Christian and other erroneous notions about human nature. We had better remove the stain by saying that men "naturally" seek pleasure and avoid pain, and that if they do so unimpeded by such fantastic notions as that there is a God who has prescribed otherwise, that suffering is here on earth a passport to eternal bliss in another world, that many kinds of pleasure are in fact wicked, instead of merely not useful, and so on, each man will, by maximizing his own pleasures and minimizing his own pains, so conduct himself that society as a whole will achieve the "greatest good of the greatest number."

We may note briefly here that from the eighteenth century on—for, as we have seen, that century was indeed multanimous in these matters—critics have found the attitude thus baldly outlined wicked, oversimple, above all, an invitation to human beings to wallow in self-indulgence disastrous to themselves and others. As held by a Helvétius, a Bentham, utilitarianism of the eighteenth-century sort must offend the Christian, not so much because the actual conduct that the *philosophes* found pleasurable and therefore useful and therefore good is very different from what the Christian approves, but because these eighteenth-century thinkers reject the Christian theology and cosmology, and do so vigorously. We must eventually come to grips rather more closely with the problem of what if any differences in human conduct appear to result from—or merely accompany—the differing ethical bases of Christianity and Enlightenment. Here I prefer to call attention to the closeness of the actual content of Christian *ideas* of the good and the *ideas* of the good held by such very articulate anti-Christians as were many of the eighteenth-century utilitarians.

Those sovereign masters of men pleasure and pain combine to repeat a good deal of the Ten Commandments and the Sermon on the Mount. Is there pleasure in fornication? Yes, but in the felicific calculus of Bentham and his followers the pains will in the long run outweigh the pleasures—pain from awareness of having yielded to low instincts, of having broken a community rule, monogamy, that long experience has shown to be socially *useful,* and therefore *moral,* possible pain of having to provide for a bastard, the likely pain, if indulgence is promiscuous, of actual venereal disease. No, the *real* pleasures are the lofty ones, not the swinish ones. The English utilitarians in particular were righteously indignant when their Christian opponents made against them the old reproach "a hog from the sty of Epicurus." They were wholly justified, for anyone who took the trouble to read Bentham's *Principles of Morals and Legislation* (1789), in which he makes a most elaborate classification of pleasures and pains, the famous felicific or hedonistic calculus, would note at once that my example above is not unfair: what—exception made of the theological provisions, such as the first four of the Ten Commandments—the calculus shows to be useful is substantially what the Christian tradition shows to be good. There is here no anticipation of a Nietzschean transvaluation of values, no praise of the bright flashing sword of the warrior, nor even much hint of social Darwinism to come. The utilitarian would not, of course, encourage the lazy poor; but he would insist that by making the pains resultant from laziness greater than the pleasures, you could solve the problem of poverty.[23]

The moral values of the eighteenth-century utilitarian, then, were conventional late Christian, those of the unheroic Christian, not those of the saint, not those of the rebel, above all, not those of the mystic. This is the "middle-class morality" that we, when young, following our master Bernard Shaw,

[23] The key documents are Bentham's *Principles of Morals and Legislation* and J. S. Mill's compact essay on *Utilitarianism.* The great critical study is still Elie Halévy, *The Growth of Philosophic Radicalism.* The French are no doubt a bit more fleshy than the English, but I think a reader who can struggle through either Helvétius's *De l'homme* or *De l'esprit* will not feel that Helvétius is advocating a life of sensual self-indulgence, or even of Renaissance *virtù.*

found so dull, so full of hypocrisy. But in the eighteenth century they were the moral values of the fighting radicals; they were a goal to be fought for, and attained, an earthly paradise of universal peace, comfort, and rational pleasure. The utilitarians were never quite sure, however, of just how to go about reaching the goal. As Halévy pointed out, Bentham himself never clearly faced the problem of distinguishing between what Halévy called the "natural identification of interests" and the "artificial identification of interests." The basic assumption of the utilitarians, as, indeed, of all but a few of the thinkers of the Enlightenment, was that something inside each individual *if it is allowed to work as it was designed to work* would guide his conduct to moral goodness. In utilitarian terms, the individual's rational interest, following the felicific calculus, would show him the right path.

But is the rational interest of each individual always congruous with the interest of society as a whole? The English utilitarians, who were determined nominalists, would not quite like the term "interest of society," since they thought of society as merely a term, dangerous like all such terms, for the total number of actual individuals in any organized group. But they gave to the old and troublesome problem behind this phrasing, the problem of the relation of the individual to the group, about as firm an answer (and surely as disputable?) as has ever been given: "The greatest good of the greatest number" means precisely what it says—when it is attained each individual is as happy, *has as much realized moral good,* as possible, and—the utilitarian would here insert "therefore"—all individuals, or that feigned entity "society," would have as much realized moral good as possible.

But how was this greatest good of the greatest number to be attained? The natural identification of interests might in theory be attained by the way of the philosophical anarchist, by leaving each individual absolutely free— a way not much in favor with the utilitarians; or it might be attained by the democratic way of a majority vote, on the assumption that the greatest number knows its own greatest good, and that the minority "ought" to consent to obey the majority. Toward this solution the utilitarians, and, for the most part, all the Enlightened from then on, have been of two minds. It would be unjust to them to say that they give this democratic principle mere lip service; for one thing, their basic faith and their quite honest sentiments hold that common men are potentially good and reasonable. But there arises this nagging difficulty: How can the many, unaided, make the bootstrap-lift out of the morass in which they now are?

Most clearly to the Enlightened, those children of Newton, one does not defy gravity by trying to lift oneself by one's bootstraps. The many, the common men, have to be helped—helped, not forced, not frightened. Here enters the artificial identification of interests. The man who does not, cannnot, in this corrupt world, understand his own *true* interests must, at least for a period of transition, be provided through planned institutions with clear rewards (pleasures) and clear punishments (pains) so evident to him that, though he would not unaided have thought out for himself the proper "other-regarding" action, he can by following his sovereign masters, pain and pleasure, do the right thing. The Benthamites were in their way enlightened despots; they certainly were ingenious planners, social engineers, and on a big and thoroughly modern scale. They seem in retrospect to have given more attention to the punishments than to the rewards. W. S. Gilbert's libretto for the *Mikado* has immortalized in circles normally not much interested in criminology Bentham's effort to devise a punishment to fit the crime, a punishment just sufficiently painful to the criminal to outweigh the pleasure he had felt, or anticipated, from the crime, and therefore just sufficient to act in his mind as a deterrent to future crimes.

The reader will see at once that even though they distrusted the many too much to rely on the natural identification of interests, the utilitarians—indeed, the whole of the Enlightenment—relied even in their plans for the artificial identification of interests on universal human rationality. The bait, the inducements, these shepherds devised for the sheep assumed that the sheep were sensible, even rational, animals; the utilitarians were in no sense anti-intellectual. The Enlightened could not have accepted either in its Christian or in its Freudian form a concept of original sin; something of what the Christian calls "sin" was to them careless "error," as it is to scientist and magician, the rest "shocking superstition." The death wish would have seemed to them sheer nonsense, as it still seems to their twentieth-century followers. Working under their formula, the utilitarian-humanitarian-enlightened radicals, as we shall shortly note, achieved many concrete reforms, reforms all but the most skeptic or the most saintly will call "good"—notably, for example, in the treatment of just those mentally disturbed persons then called simply the "insane" whose behavior most clearly contradicted utilitarian rationalism. Their Enlightened voice is still strong in the land, still echoes down—"Let me assert my firm belief that the only thing we have to fear is fear itself."

IV

We have now with the eighteenth century reached a point of modernity where it is difficult to discern a single generally accepted moral ideal, such as the Homeric hero or the Renaissance man of *virtù*. So little, contrary to the hopes of just the radical Enlightened we have been studying, dies utterly in our history-conscious West. The Age of Enlightenment is indeed short on canonized Christian saints, but the Christian ideals remained alive, and in Methodism the century produced one of the great Protestant sects. The old aristocratic ideal, directly descended from that of the medieval knight, flourished, especially east of the Elbe. The man of taste, the *honnête homme* of classical moderation, survived far into the century, amused rather than outraged at the new man of feeling, and sharing with such moderate *philosophes* as Montesquieu a sympathy for Greek rather than Christian ideals. The *philosophe* saw himself rather as a fighter for the new ideal than as its embodiment, though the intellectual classes, more numerous relatively and absolutely then than in the sixteenth century, made of writers like Voltaire, Rousseau, Montesquieu, of enlightened rulers like Frederick the Great, or even more enlightened public figures, since they were closer to nature, like Franklin, culture heroes more firmly enshrined than any of the Renaissance had been in their own day. No English intellectual save Newton, who was hardly a moralist, figures in such a list. Of Bolingbroke, the nearest English analogue to a *philosophe*, Burke was not long after his death to write the damning sentence: Who now reads Bolingbroke? Already that great moral myth and reality, the idea of the national character, which we must treat at length in the next chapter, was taking shape in the West.

Yet there *is* a moral ideal figure that emerges from the Enlightenment. I think it not unfair to say that for the first time in Western history that ideal is the common man—idealized, of course. The eighteenth century preferred to speak simply of *man, l'homme, Mensch*. Later critics—Taine's embittered analysis in the *Ancien Régime* is an excellent sample—have complained that this "man" is an especially unreal, "abstract," and therefore dangerous conception; the *philosophes* planned their new world for a *man* who never existed, forgetting that real *men,* creatures of habit and prejudice, infinitely varied in character and temperament, and only rarely capable of rational thought, could not possibly follow their plans. Such plans for abstract and unreal man when they are applied to real men end in a Reign of Terror. Now behind this criticism there is one of the great and abiding political and ethical positions Western men take, one better stated by Burke than by Taine. This is the position, which we may label that of philosophical conservatism, that the factors, the variables that count, in any given problem of human relations are in real life so infinitely many, so wholly inseparable and unpredictable that if the human mind tries to sort them out and take specific measures to *change* any of them, and especially, *one* of them, then, first, these measures will turn out to have consequences the thinker-planner had never contemplated; second, the wider and more extensive the changes planned, the greater will be the discrepancy between plans and real consequences; third—and this is crucial to this philosophic position—these unexpected consequences will tend to be undesirable ones, to be *bad*.[24]

Yet to reproach the *man* of the *philosophes* with being peculiarly abstract and unreal is to miss the point. All the ideals of human conduct we have hitherto examined are abstract but real. The men of the eighteenth century knew just what they wanted other men—and, no doubt, themselves— to be like. Their ideal figure inherits much from those of the past, but he is by no means identical with any of these, nor even a recognizable compound of them. For one thing, as we have already noted, this man is potentially, and in the real and close future, *all* men. It is true enough that there is in historical Christianity a never wholly suppressed drive to transform all human beings into Christians—Christians in the heroic, aristocratic sense of the saintly ideal; but the drive always petered out, and in the eighteenth century is hardly discernible, even in its one major renewal of Christianity, that of Methodism, Pietism, and the evangelical movement.

The ideal man of the Enlightenment owes much to the primitivists; he is in part the uncorrupted, sweet simple Child of Nature, innocent of worldly vanities, ready with sympathetic tear and rallying smile—but read, or at least dip into, Bernardin de St. Pierre's *Paul and Virginia* or Thomas Day's *Sandford and Merton*.[25] But the man of feeling, the man of nature, was only an element in the ideal man of the Enlightenment. Deep down in this man there was the rebel against all culture, all civilization—shall we say, against life?— whom we shall meet again in the twentieth century. But in the eighteenth century this revulsion from the "artificial" of civilized life is no more than a dash, a seasoning; there is no touch of fine existentialist despair in this optimistic man.

Indeed, this man is essentially the thinking man, the rational man. His feelings, not without help from his adrenal glands, tell him that a duke is an

[24] I simplify unfairly a position Americans for the most part have difficulty understanding at all. Still, the philosophic conservative does apply to human relations the Hippocratic "do no harm"—use if you must political placebos, but leave the real job of curing to nature. This nature is not by any means the nature of the primitivists, the romantics, but, rather, the total cultural and institutional heritage of the group. Only very wise conservatives, however, allow for the fact that a big part of that heritage in the West is the work of the radical, innovating, planning intellect; those medical radicals the surgeon and the experimental internist are rarely tempted to let ill enough alone.
[25] Both these books were very popular in the nineteenth century—a significant fact— and were often reprinted. They are still readily available.

artificial creation; but his reason tells him the same thing. Head and heart are in happy union. They agree on the good life for all, a life that must be good for all, since if any are deprived, all are deprived. Virtue and *la vertu* now take on firmly their modern meaning. The Enlightened man, the man of virtue, will be honest, kindly, respectful of the rights of others, firm in defense of his own, will satisfy normally and sensibly his natural appetites, including, though only in the normal and sensible institution of marriage, his sexual appetite. He will be a loving but firm parent, a responsible citizen—even a "patriot," which in eighteenth-century English and French did not mean a nationalist, but precisely this perfect Enlightened man of virtue and citizen of the world.[26] He will be neither rich nor poor, for virtue is impossible at either economic extreme; he will not—and this is important—*want* to be rich, nor, of course, in the perverse Christian sense, want to be poor. And, it goes without saying, he will avoid the vices—the personal vices of indulgence, gambling, eating or drinking to excess, whoring, laziness, the greater vices of vainglorious search for power and wealth, cruelty, the magnifying of self at the expense of others. Above all, he will put his mind to the mastery of the arts and sciences of this great age, and use that mastery in the service of his fellows, that we may all be better, and therefore happier—or happier, and therefore better, for, like truth and beauty, happiness and goodness are nice interchangeable identities.

Is this a stuffy ideal, a vague and dim ideal clad in fearful clichés, the greengrocer's paradise of Robespierre in which no one would have, or want to have, much more or much less than three thousand francs a year, parent of the even stuffier—because more nearly realized—Victorian ideal? Is it a long dull sermon, its generalities unseasoned by the spice of a real and present hell, since hell has been abolished, a sermon all promises and no threats, hardly a sermon at all? So it must seem to many of us in a twentieth century that is not without constant threats of a real and present hell; so, indeed, it began to seem to the Byronic of the next generation.[27]

Yet the ideal did not look like this to the young, the advanced, the bright vanguard of the 1780's; to them it had the freshness, the moral compulsive-

[26] It is unfortunate we so often quote Samuel Johnson—"patriotism is the last refuge of a scoundrel"—without knowing what he really meant. He meant, of course, by "patriot" the enlightened citizen of the world, not the nationalist patriot. Actually—though many of his admirers will be offended by this statement—I think Johnson himself was an English "patriot" in our modern sense of the word.

[27] I must confess that some of the more smoothly worn phrases of the Enlightenment—*humanité, bonté naturelle,* Nature and Reason, virtue, *Aufklärung,* the system of natural liberty, and many more—grate on me as I read in the eighteenth century the way, in the debunking decade of the 1920's, George Babbitt's word "service" used to grate on all the young intellectuals.

ness, of any active religious faith. For a while, the religion of humanity, too, had its crusaders, its martyrs—apostles it had never lacked in this century of Enlightenment. If now the ideal seems stale, this is partly because any religion in the West seems bound to lapse into an inactive state of acceptance of irremediable imperfections, into ritual and conformity among the many, doubt and conformity among the few, until a new moral rebellion flares up. In the West, as I hope to show, what may be called the first, or early orthodox *church,* form of the religion of Enlightenment is democratic nationalism. The national state became, in fact, the church visible for the new faith—though many a believer in the fundamentals of Enlightenment stayed outside the church as far as he could, or even joined a heretical sect, Chartist, "positivist," pacificist, and the like. Democratic nationalism on the whole has made its compromises, and is now an inactive religion, but very much alive. The major heretical rebellion against democratic nationalism, Marxist socialism, has now, duly organized as a state religion in the Soviet Union, reached in the West at least a stage of comparative inactivity as regards its moral ideal, though, unfortunately, not in respect to its desire to expand as a church.

If the ideal of the Enlightenment has lost its first Promethean will to make men into more than men, it is still, I repeat, very much alive, is still for most of us a guide and an aim. There are still those who would renew the drive of the men of 1776 and 1789; there are more who, struck with the enormous gap between what Condorcet, for instance, thought the twentieth century would be and what it has so far been, would radically alter, or throw overboard entirely, the "principles of 1776 and 1789." But for the most part, we are good democrats, good nationalists, good believers in progress and in the pursuit of happiness, complaining a lot, but not, at bottom, expecting a lot, not at any rate, heaven on earth. Ours, in short, is an inactive religion.

V

It is inactive, however, in part because so much of what it promised has in fact been realized. We must be careful here. To the god-ridden, statistics are meaningless, save perhaps in such instances as the parable of the lost sheep.[28]

---

[28] "How think ye? if a man have an hundred sheep, and one of them be gone astray, doth he not leave the ninety and nine, and goeth into the mountains, and seeketh that which is gone astray?" Matthew 18:12. This parable is a good illustration of the difference between what I call an active and what I call an inactive religion—which is basically a moral difference. I should suppose that during most of Christian history no one having cure of souls could have taken the parable as a literal guide to action. In inactive periods, a religion *has* to put the ninety and nine first.

Statistics show that over the last two hundred years all sorts of standards of living have gone up. The life span of a twentieth-century American is now at least twenty years longer than that of his eighteenth-century ancestor. But to the ardent moralist the question remains: Are those seventy years better spent than were the fifty years of old? Have we made moral progress?

By the standards of the eighteenth-century *philosophes* we at least have made some of the sort of betterment of the environment that in their philosophy must lead to a better life here on earth. The "middle-class morality" that has its origins in this century may well be an inferior sort of morality, but it has in some respects come closer to filling the gap between the ideal and the real, between ethics and conduct, than ever before. For the first time in Western history, what we may call the condition of the masses began to improve in respect to public order, public health, public manners, the whole material side of life. The base line at the beginning of the eighteenth century was certainly low, as a look into social historians like Lecky and Trevelyan, into the memoirs of the period, into the *Beggar's Opera* of Gay or the *Gin Alley* of Hogarth will show for England, one of the more advanced nations. But we may perhaps best start with a passage from Aldous Huxley, a writer not inclined to glorify the present at the expense of the past.

Such, then, was the kind of world in which the new parson had been brought up— a world in which the traditional sexual taboos lay very lightly on the ignorant and poverty-stricken majority and not too heavily upon their betters; a world where duchesses joked like Juliet's nurse and the conversation of great ladies was a nastier and stupider echo of the Wife of Bath's; where a man of means and good social standing could (if he were not squeamish in the matter of dirt and lice) satisfy his appetites almost *ad libitum;* and where, even among the cultivated and the thoughtful, the teachings of religion were taken for the most part in a rather Pickwickian sense, so that the gulf between theory and overt behavior, though a little narrower than in the mediaeval Ages of Faith, was yet sufficiently enormous.[29]

By the end of the eighteenth century there was surely some justification for

---

[29] *The Devils of Loudun*, London, Chatto & Windus, 1952, p. 14. It must, however, be pointed out that even in the late seventeenth century the beginnings of the modern, middle-class version of Puritan morality are clear in writers like Defoe and Bunyan, in German Pietism, in French Jansenism. In our modern world, not even "trends" are to be taken as neat entities. The witty, irresponsible Restoration playwright already fears the respectable:

> "To gain your Favour, we your Rules Obey,
> And Treat you with a Moral Piece to Day;
> So Moral, we're afraid 'twill Damn the Play."

Sir John Vanbrugh, *Complete Works*, London, The Nonesuch Press, 1927, Vol. II, p. 156. From the "The False Friend," first performed in 1702.

the concept of "progress." In the great field of technological control of our material surroundings, the Industrial Revolution had well begun, the statistical curves were turning upward, gross national product, real incomes, and the rest all increasing, and, on the whole, the working class as well as the middle class was benefiting from a rising standard of living. Even in the early eighteenth century, signs of this material progress were clear: the Industrial Revolution does not come out of the blue.[30] By the early nineteenth century the humanitarian movement had begun to achieve concrete results. Slavery was abolished in the British dominions in 1807, after a long and very modern campaign by abolitionist groups inspired chiefly by that Christian adaptation of humanitarianism known as the evangelical movement. The French Jacobins set up briefly and on paper something that looks like the modern welfare state; by no means all these reforms were abandoned in the subsequent reaction. Even the much-attacked Speenhamland system of poor relief in England, whereby doles from local authorities were paid for home use to make up for inadequate wages, was in accord with the spirit of the age. Later historians were shocked at the system because it corrupted the poor, discouraged initiative, and kept wages down; we may see the system as permissive, kindly at bottom, and inspired by a number of motives, some of which were consonant with the Enlightenment.

There is before the eighteenth century not much feeling of sympathy for the convicted criminal. There *is* admiration for the conspicuous and dramatic criminal, yet I think it clear that what we here call "humanitarian" thought and feeling are hardly discernible in these centuries. And the severity of penalties, the horrors of prison life, are well known. The eighteenth century saw a fully developed humanitarian-utilitarian theory of criminology, best summarized in Beccaria's *Crimes and Punishments,* one of the clearest examples that books do work in this world; it saw in many lands a beginning of improvement in actual physical conditions of prisons, and, even more conspicuously, it saw the gradual abandonment of enforcement of the old dire penalties for petty crimes still on the statute books.

[30] It is clear that the view of the Industrial Revolution as one long and unrelieved tale of man's inhumanity to man—as exemplified in the work of economic historians like the Hammonds—is no longer tenable. It would seem quite impossible for the population of Western Europe to have increased as it did had the purely physical conditions of life for the masses been worse than in earlier times. The moral effect of the factory system is another problem, to which I shall return in the next chapter. The English Labour Party intellectuals—one of the most powerful of Enlightened sects—have long held that the Industrial Revolution was a work of iniquity. See the representative work of J. L. and Barbara Hammond, *The Town Labourer,* new impression, New York, Longmans, Green, 1920; and for a corrective, T. S. Ashton, *The Industrial Revolution,* New York, Oxford University Press, 1948.

One phase of this development is an admirable illustration of how the world view of the Enlightenment worked through humanitarian and utilitarian values to alter Christian ethical attitudes. Christian theology condemned suicide as a sin, morally a form of murder, since God alone could rightfully end the sojourn of a soul on this earth; Christian society had made suicide a crime, punishable by burial of the body outside consecrated cemeteries, transfixed by stakes, at a crossroads. Christian pervasive moral sentiments had made suicide a serious disgrace for the family of the guilty person, a painful one to bear. Now the Enlightened—if enlightened enough—simply denied there was a soul or a God, denied what I have called the minimal Christian puritanism of the body-soul relation. Suicide was to the fully enlightened neither a sin nor a crime, but entirely a matter for the individual to decide. It should certainly carry no disgrace to the suicide's family, who were entirely innocent. It was not even, in view of its rarity and the certainty that it would never be common, harmful to the common good. Indeed, Beccaria makes a comparison, characteristic of the utilitarian moral attitude, between the emigrant and the suicide. Both leave their country, but neither of them in numbers large enough to do any harm. The emigrant may by his labor benefit the rival country; the suicide does not and therefore is even *less* a criminal than the emigrant.[31] It should be noted, however, that in mid-twentieth century, suicide is still a grave disgrace for the family in all but very advanced circles.

So, too, long after the orthodox Christian view that insanity is actually possession by demons really has almost disappeared, is mental illness. The illness of the soul or psyche or central nervous system many of us still find disgraceful, a matter for guilt, as we do not find illness of the body. Yet the eighteenth-century thinkers were clear in this matter. Here the humanitarian and the rationalist strands were interwoven to produce a new attitude toward the mentally ill. The rationalist could not believe the insane were possessed of demons; the humanitarian could not believe the insane were perversely guilty and therefore to be held responsible for their actions. The old harsh ways of exorcising the demons by whipping, the easy way of chaining the insane up, the horrid way of putting them on exhibition in "Bedlams"—all this came to seem absurd and wrong to the Enlightened. Gradually, under the leadership of physicians and—a new thing—research psychologists; most of them French, there arose the concept of mental illness, and of therapeutic treatment. By 1800, the best opinion had long since given up harsh and punitive treatment, had given up the feeling that somehow mental illness is

31 *An Essay on Crimes and Punishments,* trans. from the Italian, London, 1770, pp. 132-134.

the patient's fault in a way that ordinary somatic illness is not.[32] The general public was still far behind the experts in this respect, but widespread deliberate cruelty toward the insane had ceased to be normal in the West.

The guillotine itself, that instrument of the Terror, was an invention inspired by humanitarian motives. Dr. Guillotin sought a way to bring death quickly and surely to criminals condemned to capital punishment. You may build a good deal of symbolism around the guillotine and its successors right down to the kindly lethal gas chamber. We kill, we avenge, we protect society, we recognize in the deed something not quite consonant with the Enlightenment, something that goes better with Dante than with Bentham—but we kill as gently as we can. I do not think there is in the past of Western civilization any exact precedent for the *institution* of the guillotine. The humanitarian temperament crops up as far back as we can go; the humanitarian institution is new.[33]

It is permissible perhaps even for us in mid-twentieth century to believe that rising standards of comfort and literacy and security, the ubiquitous moral preaching the Enlightenment loved so much, the contagion of fashion for decency, respectability, *humanité* had *some* effect on the conduct of men in the eighteenth century. The effect is not statistically measurable; but surely is it not at least possible that the familiar adage about smoke and fire may apply to virtues as well as to vices? We shall, however, return to this topic with the Victorian middle-class morality of the next century, the classic case. That morality was as yet no more than building up in the eighteenth century.

Moreover, even among the upper classes conduct in the eighteenth century in the West is hardly as bad as the moralists preparing for the French Revolu-

[32] The Victorian Samuel Butler in his Utopia, *Erewhon* (1872), has illness of any sort punished by imprisonment, and crimes treated by hospitalization. This bright idea is no doubt chiefly inspired by an intellectual attitude common among intellectuals, an attitude with important moral consequences, the attitude that the polar opposite of what is commonly believed must be right; but it is also in part a logical conclusion from the eighteenth-century dogma of the natural goodness of man, coupled with a belief in individual free will.

[33] I have no more than sampled in abolition of slavery, lessening of harsh penalties in criminal law, gentler treatment of the insane, what is really a vast range of eighteenth-century humanitarian reforms. I refer the reader once more to McCloy, *The Humanitarian Movement in Eighteenth-Century France,* for a full treatment for at least one country. Note that actual material, technological progress of all sorts, progress of the kind many twentieth-century Americans think of as limited to their own point in space and time, had by 1800 brought widespread improvements in material production and distribution; the common man was, in fact, beginning to have it better, if not to be better. But does, perhaps, the second follow from the first? So, at least, the Enlightenment believed.

tion have made out. The French aristocracy itself was a society open to the rich, the clever, the interesting—sometimes to the charlatan—a society certainly not puritanical, though there were puritanical Jansenist circles in it, a society that cultivated the usual vices, that liked witty irreverence, that no doubt had too much leisure, too few responsibilities. Yet only very devout French republican historians, and their followers abroad, have been able to make out this aristocracy as cruel, heartless, or even, as Western aristocracies go, morally very lax. Throughout the privileged upper classes in the West, already nationally differentiated, there were many converts to the Enlightenment, landlords seeking to improve the lot of their tenants, men of feeling, earnest students of the new ideas. The *salon,* typical social institution of the age, was surely the most serious-minded gathering of the sort yet to appear. Lafayette, a portent, if not a type, reminds one much more of the Gracchi than of the Augusti.

In respect to conventional morality, the lowest point of the century was the "Thermidorean reaction" immediately after the fall of Robespierre in France.[34] Here for a few years, until Napoleon promoted respectability in private life and regularity in public life, there was one of those almost mass revulsions from the high standards of private and public virtue the radical revolutionists seek to impose, a revulsion not unlike that of the English Restoration of 1660. The French danced, gambled, consumed conspicuously and in bad taste, and, of course, had fun in bed. The historian of morals cannot claim to understand the dynamics of such periods of looseness, but he can recognize the phenomenon as a particular phase of his history. So, too, with the phase from which the Thermidorean reactions themselves are a reaction, the phase particularly clear in our great modern revolutions since Luther's, clearest of all in the French Jacobin Republic of Virtue and its accompanying Reign of Terror: the historian still can but record these accesses of collective virtue.

Indeed, to many the Terror is the most immoral thing in the eighteenth century. Quantitatively—it had perhaps 20,000 victims in a population of

[34] I am considering only relatively large groups in making such a generalization. You can find individuals—a Sade, for instance—of surpassing wickedness of conduct; and you can find all sorts of smaller groups, all sorts of specific places, where sin was open and serious. For the first, the immediate circle of the Regent, the Duc d'Orléans, in France immediately after the death of Louis XIV (1715) will do as a sample; Orléans was bright, witty, corrupt, self-indulgent, yet, in a general political way, well-meaning. For the second, the city of Venice will do, already in the eighteenth century what we call a tourist center, a *ville de plaisir,* indeed, where the facts of life really were close to what good English evangelicals thought they were on the Continent.

about twenty-two million—the Terror cannot compete with any good modern war, or with the Nazi attack on the Jews. But it was a series of religious persecutions, its victims sacrificed to a religion of humanity that makes a poor screen for such deeds. The Terrorists had mixed motives, and their Terror was no simple thing. But one element, without which the Terror would not have been what it was in fact, was the effort to force millions of men and women to conduct themselves as the ethics of the Enlightenment prescribed. Reason unreasonably proved to be quite as jealous a god as old Jehovah had ever been.

The Terror was brief, but coming as it did in a land in the forefront of the Enlightenment, after the shining and universal hopes of 1789, accompanied and followed as it was by a great World War, it was a shock, and made an epoch. "Mankind has always made this earth a Hell when it has sought to make it a Heaven," wrote the German poet Friedrich Hölderlin—poet, not historian, for the French Revolution was surely the first attempt to make this earth a heaven for all. The attempt still goes on, as it went on all through the nineteenth century; for the rest of this study we must grapple with the problems set by the attempt. But the spiritual atmosphere of the attempt has never been the same since 1792-1794; the new religion has never quite caught again the first incredible rapture of hope of 1776 and 1789. Its major heresy, Marxism, was born in hate and great disgust. Nor has the intellectual atmosphere ever again been quite the same as it was when Wordsworth cried out his still-familiar

> Bliss was it in that dawn to be alive
> But to be young was very Heaven.

The natural science that played so large a part in building up the world view of the Enlightenment has in its still-incomplete and imperfect application to the study of *human* nature in the behavioral sciences almost wholly undermined the fundamental dogma of the Enlightenment, the natural goodness and/or reasonableness of man. That dogma is now at best a Sorelian myth for all but the truest of true believers; for many today it is a dangerous falsehood. But to this topic, too, we must return.

The Nineteenth Century

WITH THE NINETEENTH CENTURY we are full in the floodstream of contemporary Western life. It is quite possible that the range of human conduct, the varieties of human conceptions of the universe, the sheer multanimity of men were as wide during the great years of the Roman Empire as in our own day. It is even possible that the limits of human variation within Western culture were set long ago in the ancient Near East. But for the historian the important fact is that so much of the record of human activities for the last two or three centuries has survived physically. With widespread literacy, relatively inexpensive printing and illustrating, with the newspaper and the periodical press, all flourishing by 1800, the historian of ideas, the social historian, the historian of morals, all are confronted with far more source material than they can ever hope to exhaust.[1]

Yet all this complexity is no more than the working out of what had come to a head in the Enlightenment. Metaphors are never quite perfect tools of analysis. Here that of seed-sprout-growth misleads, for the "plants" we are dealing with in this kind of history crossbreed in quite impossible ways. You might think of a vast musical composition, the plan and certainly the authorship of which no one really understands. The themes are, however, stated by 1789, and what follows has been development, wild orchestration, frequent

[1] Our twentieth-century trivia will not survive so long, thanks to the invention of cheap wood pulp. Indeed, the "yellow journals" of the late nineteenth century have already faded beyond yellow into disintegration, and the cheesecake and the gow that shock on our newsstands will not survive to shock our descendants. But the good rag paper of the eighteenth and early nineteenth centuries preserves everything.

recapitulation, occasional harmonies, some whopping dissonances. More conventionally, we are still in a "period," still best put as modern or contemporary, which can be said to begin roughly with the eighteenth century; much has been new since then, in science and technology, in art and in all our culture, but nothing as new "across the board," nothing as fundamentally revolutionary, as the challenge the world view of the Enlightenment—let us symbolize it as the Newtonian world-machine—set to the world view of Christianity—let us symbolize that by the concept of Father, Son, and Holy Ghost.[2]

II

For the historian of morals, the most important development of the nineteenth century is nationalism. The nation-state came to be the societal frame, the "church," or organized group of true believers, within which the new world view of the Enlightenment took on rituals, emotional satisfactions, gave to the faithful a sense of belonging to an *identifiable* group, brought the difficult abstractions with which this science-born, indeed physics-born, cosmology had clothed itself right down to earth. Humanity, mankind, all men, the universalist and cosmopolitan ideals dear to the theorists of the Enlightenment turned out for most men to be unable to bear the earthly weight all ideals have to bear when they get to work among ordinary people. Only a minority of intellectuals has been able to maintain, unchurched, so to speak, the pure religion of humanity; and they keep trying to find themselves a church that will be *truly* universal.

We need not here attempt to go into the development of Western nationalism in most of its aspects, nor, above all, to worry over the exact definition of what—common language, common "race," common institutions, common history, and much else—we shall hold to be essential to constitute this particular in-group, the modern "sovereign" territorial nation-state.[3] So far,

[2] I do not find Arnold Toynbee's "post-modern" for the years since 1914—or 1875—a useful concept. I think he makes use of the term to persuade us that the world view of the eighteenth-century Enlightenment is dead, bankrupt, which better and more clear-sighted Christians than he know is not so. We will need more than another general war to start a new "period" in Western history. See Arnold J. Toynbee, *A Study of History,* abridgement of Vols. I-VI, D. C. Somervell, London, Oxford University Press, 1946, p. 39. For a most interesting periodization, see C. S. Lewis, *De Descriptione Temporum,* Cambridge, England, Cambridge University Press, 1955.
[3] Boyd C. Shafer, *Nationalism: Myth and Reality,* New York, Harcourt, Brace, 1955. With Shafer as a start, the reader can go on into this very important subject from the leads he offers.

at least, there is a clear condition for achieved nationalism: the nation must be "independent" or "sovereign," not subject to formal political control, nor to too obvious informal political and economic control, by any organized group outside its borders. The Russians do claim that they have succeeded within the Soviet Union in providing full cultural independence for national groups while merging them all in a common political and economic federal union. In most of the West, however, those who feel that "consciousness of kind" that makes a familiar loose definition of nationality are content with nothing less than "independence" and at least the minimum symbolic evidence —flag, diplomatic recognition, armed forces, rituals, and the rest—that goes with independence.

Morally, membership in a nation means that the individual shares what the English essayist Arthur Clutton-Brock, who did not like nationalism, called "pooled self-esteem"; and such membership satisfies, in part, and for many who could not otherwise satisfy it, the agonistic drive for triumph so characteristic of the West—satisfies it in a sense vicariously, but quite concretely. The nation, even the very large nation, makes a fine outlet for the team spirit, the better just because such participation is vicarious. I recall a public lecture at the Sorbonne in 1920, after victory had brought back to France the iron ore of Lorraine. The lecturer, using big units or ratios the exact nature and size of which I forget, came out at one point with some such figures as these: French iron production in 1914, 9 units, German production, 20 units; French iron production in 1920, 14 units, German production, 9 units. The audience, which was composed of the kind of people who go to such academic "extension" lectures, burst into loud applause at this point. It seems highly unlikely that anyone in the audience stood to gain directly in the way the economist measures gain from this increase in French national production of pig iron. In fact, the comparison with football scores is suggested by much more than the mere figures. Here were people, in psychological slang, *identifying* with France, the France of the "Marseillaise," the tricolor, *France, mère des arts, des armes, et des lois*—and pig-iron production.

It is surely impossible even for those who find terms like "religion of nationalism" misleading, inexact, or simply offensive, to deny that the individual does have this emotional relation to the common thing, that much of the hymns, symbols, and public ceremonies of the nation-state at least suggest religious ritual, and that there are national holy writings, declarations, bills of rights, consecrated orations by a Webster, a Danton, a Farewell Address, other pronunciamentos, that are comparable to canonical writings in recognized religions. There are clearly national saints—Washington, Lincoln, Lenin—and those near-saints, the culture heroes—Shakespeare, Dante, Goethe.[4] But, those who reject the analogy with recognized religions ask, where is your armature of theology, eschatology, ethics, all essential to a true religion? The answer is partly, of course, that nationalism is clearly not a theistic religion, and if you so define religion as to make a *theos* and a supranatural view of the cosmos the essential mark of a religion, you must abandon the analogy between religion and nationalism. You will, however, have thereby abandoned a useful tool for understanding human conduct.

I prefer to retain the analogy with accepted religions, and suggest that, first, many organized Christian churches have contrived very well to adapt themselves to nationalistic beliefs, so that to many individuals the need for a supranatural faith has proved quite congruous with ardent participation in the nationalist common thing. The range of actual adjustment between Christianity and nationalism has been great indeed. The great gateway of "render therefore unto Caesar the things that are Caesar's and unto God the things that are God's" has proved a wide one, no mere loophole. Very little, it has sometimes seemed, of pure earthly concern is left as God's. The freethinkers in 1914, when the Great War really did surprise the world, gloated over the fact that the Germans and the British in particular were each vocally assured that the one true Christian (Protestant) God was firmly on their side. But the freethinkers themselves, heirs of eighteenth-century cosmopolitan belief in the equality of all men before nature, were of divided allegiance. German

---

[4] On the worship of Lincoln, see Ralph Gabriel, *The Course of American Democratic Thought*, New York, Ronald Press, 1940; on the worship of Washington, see Marcus Cunliffe, *George Washington: Man and Monument*, Boston, Little Brown, 1958, especially Chap. I, "The Monument"; on the French Jacobin ritual and worship see my *Jacobins*, Chap. IV. Note that both Mt. Vernon and the restored Kentucky cabin where Lincoln was born are almost *always* known as "shrines," to which "pilgrimages" are made. I have often had the irreverent thought that no one has yet filled out our Trinity —unless the American Constitution will do. Neither Jefferson nor either of the two Roosevelts has made the pantheon, in spite of efforts of their ardent admirers to get them in. But Washington—remote godhead—and Lincoln—warm, human, both god and man—are safely enshrined. I think it true that the British have not made use of these same forms of nation worship to the extent the Americans and the French have done; theirs are older, and more assimilated into Christian forms. I do not think, however, that from the point of view of a rigorous Christian idealist the British are less idolatrous than are we or the French.

socialists and French socialists, sure that God does not exist, were quite as sure that the nation does.[5]

Even more important, however, nationalism in itself—or, rather, each specific nationalism—did to a degree incorporate much of eighteenth-century thought, which, as I have insisted in the previous chapter, is a full cosmology, or world view. The ordinary nineteenth-century Frenchman, the Englishman, the American, even the German "believed in" self-government and a degree, at least, of democracy, believed in Progress, took part in the pursuit of happiness, hoped for some, at least, of that heaven on earth the eighteenth century had promised them—and felt, thought of, political activity, in which as citizen he played a part, as one way, perhaps *the* way, of attaining that heaven. It should hardly be necessary to point out that no medieval commoner expected anything of the sort out of "politics." The good citizen ought, of course, to be a good man. Except in regard to relations among sovereign states—even here, formally, professedly—modern nationalism took over conventional Western moral codes, Christian and Enlightened, in various mixtures. The French *bon républicain,* who was a great preacher and moralizer, never tired of trying to teach through nice little manuals of what we should call civics a sound lay utilitarian morality of love and help-thy-neighbor.[6]

The critics and enemies of nationalism—and they are many among Western intellectuals in the twentieth century—hold that as the "real if unavowed" religion of most of the West (Toynbee) it encourages the individual to indulge in infinite hopes and fears, and does little to discipline him into accepting earthly limitations, that it feeds his more ignoble side, starves his nobler possibilities. Now since, as I have argued, nationalism is the most important of successful forms of organized belief or church which the new cosmology of the eighteenth century takes in our world, it is not wholly unfair to attack under the name of nationalism that cosmology itself. But what most of these attackers, including Mr. Toynbee, are really getting at behind nationalism in their attack is the whole world view of the Enlightenment.[7]

[5] I suppose that generally in the West the freethinkers in 1914 tended to side with the Western allies, for the Central Powers stood as symbols of "autocracy," France and England (with the dubious inclusion of Russia) for "democracy." Free thought, as heir of the Enlightenment, has tended to side with democracy and to oppose absolutism and has also thought of England-France as the Palestine of the new faith. For the extremists, now, Moscow is the Rome.

[6] F. V. A. Aulard, *Eléments d'instruction civique suivis de résumés et questionnaires. Cours Moyen,* Paris, E. Cornély, 1902.

[7] In many ways the frankest and clearest of these attacks is still the work of the late Irving Babbitt, and especially the *Democracy and Leadership* (Boston, Houghton

A History of Western Morals

Few today put the central *moral* issue between Christianity and Enlightenment as baldly as the eighteenth century, even the seventeenth, often put it: Is the ultimate sanction of a supranatural God and perhaps even a supranatural hell necessary to insure that men conduct themselves in society with a minimal degree of decency? The eighteenth century debated this question earnestly, and came often to the conclusion that the outright atheist at least is a dangerous influence, that the common man cannot stand the undermining moral example the atheist affords. The nineteenth and twentieth centuries, however, were to quiet that particular debate. In spite of the undoubted spread, not so much of sheer atheism as of effective reduction of the areas of human experience in which the supranatural or the transcendental could seem real and pressing, the level of conventional morality in the West has clearly not been lowered. The Victorian outlook, to which we shall come shortly, is in itself evidence that the old supranaturalism and the new naturalism can be combined into a way of life that certainly is no new Sodom and Gomorrah.

I think it can be maintained, however, that the paling for many, and the disappearance for some, of the orthodox Christian world view, the substitution for Christendom as church of the national commonweal as church, has for the believer meant a real loss. Christianity would seem to be, even in comparison with other higher religions, the most consoling of faiths, the faith that, not so much by the aspect the freethinkers love to deride, its heavenly reward in an afterlife for suffering here on earth, as by the ritual, the ministry of the cure of souls, the long experience of the human soul (or psyche if you are an anti-Christian), can steady the individual in his misfortune. Marianne of the French Republic is a lively and charming lady, whom we all know from the cartoonists' sketches; but she is no substitute for Our Lady of Sorrows. Nationalism has its surrogates for the saints; but not even Abraham Lincoln seems to fit into prayer. The patriotic rituals, the hymns, the oaths, the exercises, even when all these are very deliberately heightened as in Nazi Germany, even when the faithful take them seriously, are at best substitutes for

---

Mifflin, 1924), and the *Rousseau and Romanticism* (Boston, Houghton Mifflin, 1919). The American "new conservatives" have echoed this attack, which takes as its central point that what came out of the eighteenth century—call it nationalism, romanticism, democracy, humanitarianism, even, in the United States, "liberalism"—prods human desires but does not satisfy them, puts no limit, no end to them, denies the basic fact of human life, that men want and need restraints, limits, boundaries, want to know them and feel them as such; they do not *really* want to be infinitely free, expansive, aggressive; their nature, their *composition,* to use a materialistic term, is not able to stand Enlightenment.

the revivalist side of Christianity; they do not sound through the pains and boredoms of daily life. My parallel above between French-German iron production and football scores was not wholly superficial. Nationalism is fine when our team is winning, but there is no joy left when it loses, and precious little consolation.

The moral indignation many men of good will feel in the twentieth century toward nationalism is centered not so much on its lack of consoling power as on the fact that in theory and in practice the nation as guided by its rulers is subject to no higher law. In international relations, say the critics, though lip service is duly paid to concepts of right and wrong, naturalistic or supranaturalistic, we really are in a situation where might makes right crudely and simply, where all that counts is success in beating the other fellow, where, as time goes on, even the old conventional rules of the horrid game of war, such as formal declaration of war, Geneva convention on prisoners of war, and the like, are cynically flouted.[8] To many men of good will, the great moral evil of our time is war; and war in our time, they hold, is made the shocking thing it is by the complex of human relations we call "nationalism." Many of them, led by Mr. Toynbee, are in effect saying of the nation-state what Voltaire said of the Roman Catholic Church—*écrasez l'infame,* "crush the infamous thing."

Combined as it is with the threat of the fusion bomb, biological warfare, and many other fearful threats, the fact of modern nationalism is most certainly one of the major problems the moralist faces today, and we shall return to it. Here we may content ourselves with trying to put nationalism into its proper historical perspective by asking the obvious question: Is the component added to international politics by the cosmology of the Enlightenment as what we call "nationalism" of such innovating importance that it makes a radically new situation?

The answer is, I think, no. There has long been debate over why men organized in groups kill, maim, imprison men organized in other groups in what we call warfare, and over the right and wrongs of warfare, ultimately

---

[8] Lip service is, of course, a kind of tribute; but our conscience even as nationalists does bite deeper than the prophets of doom allow. The famous toast of Stephen Decatur at Norfolk, Virginia, in 1816, "Our country! In her intercourse with foreign nations may she always be in the right; but our country, right or wrong," admits a *difference* between right and wrong, shows, as a matter of fact, a conscience at least faintly disturbed. I do not think you will find in the early days formulas like "Athena, may she always be in the right, but . . ." or "Jehovah, right or wrong!" The ardent nationalist today realizes he is on the defensive. The familiar quotation from Decatur will be found in almost any dictionary of quotations.

as to whether it is an evil or a good.[9] As a matter of fact, we shall in the very next section of this chapter take up one of the sharpest and most novel phases of the intellectual history of the warfare over warfare, that brought to a head by the publication of Darwin's *Origin of Species* in 1859. The anthropologists leave us in no doubt as to the fact that, in spite of the noble savages who practice hospitality toward the stranger, many, if not most, territorial in-groups will fight with others. And here another piece of folk wisdom obtrudes itself: "All's fair in love [that is, male Western pursuit of female] and war." We must be clear on this matter: the morality, or immorality, of organized warfare is no new thing.

The historian of the West can leave no doubt as to the empirical facts. From the days of Homer and Moses on, even from much earlier, warfare has been endemic in the West. There have been variations in the material and human damage war does, in the extent to which war has been in effect regulated by law, convention, the "rules of the game," by notions of what is right and wrong in warfare. But, as with most of these variations in history, the sorting out of the variables, the plotting of the curves, is a difficult and often impossible task. A glance at the account Thucydides gives of the violence at Corcyra that got the Peloponnesian War off to its worst phases should convince anyone that, weapons apart, there is precedent for all the moral horrors of our contemporary warfare.

Certainly from a survey of war in the West one cannot conclude that the human, the moral, elements that enter into warfare vary in any one sure direction, forward or backward. Two tendencies which, if they could be firmly established as such, are worth noting as possibly valid analyses may be suggested. First, wars that enlist the active emotions of the many, that employ the many as actual fighters, tend to be more ferocious, above all, harder to settle with a tolerable peace, than wars fought by the few, the professionals. Modern democratic nationalist wars are "worse" wars than the "limited" wars among eighteenth-century dynasts, but they are not the first or the only wars that have so enlisted the emotions of the many. Second, and closely related, wars we used to label "ideological," wars fought to make the true God, or dialectical materialism, or the Nordic myth prevail over unbelievers are worse wars than wars—say, like our Mexican War—which are wars of

[9] Here is a fine bit of Hegel: "Just as the movement of the ocean prevents the corruption which would be the result of perpetual calm, so by war people escape the corruption which would be occasioned by a continuous or eternal peace." *Philosophie des Rechts,* §324. Such a sentiment is clearly that—a *sentiment,* not to be disproved, but simply disapproved.

mere aggression with a minimum gloss of moral justification. Both these ideas are suggestive as leads for further study, a study not assured in the beginning that they would prove true. They are, however, by no means the assured truths they seem to be to many of our contemporary proponents of a brand-new international order. And even if they are diagnostically true, we have surely no ready remedy at hand.

On one count, at least, the Enlightenment can be cleared of responsibility for one of the moral weaknesses of nationalism. The doctrine that the agents of the state in their dealings with agents of other states are not held to the rules of ordinary morality, indeed not held to any moral code, but are concerned solely with the success of their states in war and diplomacy is no invention of the eighteenth century; it is, indeed, specifically opposed by most of the *philosophes*. As we have noted, in its specific modern form of the doctrine of "reason of state," it is well formulated in the sixteenth and seventeenth centuries and well practiced. At least in the sense of accepted formal obligations to a growing body of international law, the eighteenth and nineteenth centuries in the West saw a *comparatively* good period in the morality of international politics. There has been, no doubt, an obvious lapse in the last twenty years, but one scarcely attributable directly to the Enlightenment.

It seems hardly possible for even the most extreme nominalist to deny that the "nation" that gives us so much trouble is real, that differences in language, art, the whole reach of culture among nations are real. There are moral differences among the nations of the West, nothing like as great as the convinced nationalists think they are, and like other aspects of the national character, difficult of definition, almost impossible of statistical definition. Most Anglo-Saxons believe that the French in particular are loose, promiscuous, in the matter of sex; and it must be admitted that many articulate Frenchmen do their verbal best, and sometimes more, to give support to that belief. Yet any one who knows the French knows well that the actual range of conduct in such matters is probably much the same as elsewhere in the West, and he knows that many Frenchmen are chaste and continent. The Russians since the Bolshevik revolution have done their puritanical best to banish the familar traditional outward and public allurements and display of sex, much as in other outbreaks of puritanism, or rather *Vulgärpuritanismus,* in Savonarola's Florence, in Cromwell's England, in Robespierre's France—and they have held the line longer than most of their predecessors. On the other hand, in twentieth-century America the mass media concentrate with increasing frankness on all that used to be known here as "sex appeal." Our rare Soviet visitors are apparently as shocked at one of our newsstands as our grandfathers used to be at Parisian ones.

We are back at one of the unsolved puzzles that confront the historian of morals: Just what is the relation between profession and performance, between word and deed? Even in the comparatively simple matter of sex relations, no firm answer can be given. I feel very sure that the Russians have not risen above sex, and equally sure that we have not sunk—as Mr. Sorokin holds we have—into obsessive indulgence, both direct and vicarious, in matters of sex. The Russian moral style has for a surprisingly long time been out of line with Western, if not with human, traditions in such matters; someday cheesecake and gow will come to Russia. Our own in the United States has in the last generation or two, perhaps, as liberals think, under the pressure of selfish commercial interests, but more likely from a whole syndrome of causes, including what may well be called *Vulgärfreudismus,* been out of line with our own traditions, and may be expected to return at least part way back to the old restraints.

But we cannot here allow ourselves to get involved in the concrete facts and the fascinating theories of the national character. They are worth all the careful study they can be given, for they are real even when they are part of a myth, above all, when they are part of a myth. We may content ourselves here with a few general cautions. First, each nation has an image of itself, slowly built up and hard to change, and images of other nations with which it has relations close enough to permit the building up of such images. Where specifically moral elements enter into these images, they are bound to be greatly simplified and exaggerated, and, it goes without saying, tend to reflect moral credit on one's own nation, moral discredit on others. Yet the enemies of nationalism go too far if they pursue the line set by the definition of nationalism as "pooled self-esteem" to the point where they maintain that the nation as an entity—or, if you prefer, national public opinion—is wholly incapable of self-criticism. To drop into metaphor, there *is* such a thing as the national conscience. It is not as sensitive, or as varied, as the conscience of sensitive individuals, it is not a unanimous feeling among all nationals, and, perhaps even more than an individual conscience, it finds that success is usually good. Still, the best observers grant that a large number of Germans really felt guilty about Nazi excesses; and there are stirrings of national guilt over Hiroshima even in the United States.

Second, national differences in conduct are apparently greater in public morality than in private. In such matters as sexual conduct, the big and little vices, personal honesty, all of what I have called conventional morality, I should think it pretty certain that actual differences among Western nations are not nearly as great as our national images or myths or clichés make out. In a matter actually marginal to public morality, that of ordinary commercial honesty and trustworthiness, most Americans think most French businessmen are untrustworthy, and most Frenchmen think American businessmen are excessively sharp and unprincipled. The British in these matters are likely to feel, and, in spite of their reputation for reticence, to express, a greater holiness-than-thou. Actually, formal bankruptcy, for instance, which Americans take in stride, is morally a disgrace in France. In such matters as law-abidingness, honesty in the face of the tax gatherer, public neatness, and general civic goodhousekeeping, on to actual crimes of all sorts, there are no doubt among Western nations real and sometimes measurable differences, sometimes almost as great as they appear in the images, myths, and clichés to be. But even in such matters, an all-inclusive national moral peck order based on the facts of human conduct cannot really be established. There is a very rough moral peck order based on general Western opinion, or, rather, many versions of such a peck order varying with each national opinion. Perhaps there might be tentative agreement among good non-Western observers not committed to either of our great conflicting secular faiths of Communism or Democracy to put Britain and the virtuous little democracies of Western and Northern Europe on top, the unhappy French rather lower than they deserve to be, and neither ourselves nor the Russians as high as we think we ought to be.

To sum up, necessarily inadequately, this vexing and important question of the morals of nationalism: in the pure and exacting moral tradition both of Christianity and of the Enlightenment, the worship of the nation-state that has grown up in the contemporary world is a poor thing, a shabby thing, at best, at worst, a wicked pooling of the selfish, the prideful in human nature. Even in its more subdued manifestations, even in the most virtuous of democracies, nationalism is a denial of the Christian equality of all souls before God, of the Enlightened equality of all men before a righteous Nature; in the best of us it is a form of Pharisaism, what the Christian tradition calls a snobbish claim to a high place in a peck order, a blindness, a failure to see ouselves as others see us, a hypocritical assumption of a burden—"the white man's burden"—which is, in fact, a prize of victory in the agon. In its madder forms, in the posturings of a Mussolini or the frothings of a Hitler, it is one of the great degraded moments of our history. Surely there can be no doubt:

whatever it is that has in our Western past made saints or *philosophes* must drive the best of us to fight against, crusade against, this evil thing.

And yet, and yet . . . crusades, too, break heads and hearts. The strain of moderation, of acceptance of the world as not radically and immediately alterable, is a real, if, among contemporary intellectuals, commonly under-valued, part of Western moral traditions; the moderates, too, even the mod-erates who have no other principles than moderation, are not outside our ethical tradition. In that tradition, one must note that nationalism has long and deep roots in the Western past, however recent its actual present flower-ing; one must note that nationalism is somehow "natural" to the West, and, to judge from twentieth-century developments, a part of the Western culture most attractive to the rest of the world. Perhaps men have got to pool their self-esteem somehow, and perhaps the noblest crusader can do little to change the nature of that pooling. We have not yet found in the concept of mankind any such pool. For the present, we may do well to try to palliate the evils and excesses of nationalism, reading the famous aphorism of Francis Bacon—no saint, and no *philosophe*—as "Nationalism is not to be conquered save by obeying it."[10]

There is still more to say. Into the service of the nation-state there have gone loyalty, courage, devotion, hard work, and a good deal more that we should all accept as morally good in our tradition. One need not agree with the naïve apologists for war and struggle to admit that our moral history would be poor without the record of these imperfections. Here is one more of those moral paradoxes that are strewn so liberally in our way in the modern world: If the kingdom of God or of Nature is at all to be realized here on earth, must it not be so in a *place,* somewhere before it is everywhere? This moral difficulty is at its gravest and most concrete in our world for the Jew. To many Jews, the Zionist movement, even—indeed, above all—in its present partial success in Israel, has been an immoral betrayal of the mission for which God long ago chose the Jews. For them, Zion is no hill on this earth, and certainly no nation-state with flag and army and a seat in the United Nations. To others, Israel is truly the earthly Zion, without which no heavenly

---

[10] Bacon wrote *Natura non vincitur nisi parendo.* Of course, thinkers have long sought a way to pour into the concept of mankind as a whole the kind of emotions and senti-ments that men have always poured into some concept of more parochially grouped human beings. See the work of an interesting contemporary, Gerhard Hirschfeld, Di-rector of the Committee for the Study of Mankind, 53 West Jackson Blvd., Chicago, Illinois.

one, without which, indeed, no chosen people. I do not think the mere historian can chose here, for them or for us.

III

I have said that the nineteenth century produced no such completely revolutionary new idea as the idea that the eighteenth-century Enlightenment fashioned into a new world view of a universe without God, a universe where everything was natural, nothing supranatural. This is true enough, but the nineteenth century did produce a major corollary to the great theme of the eighteenth, or, better, a great explanation and justification of that notion of Progress which had played so great a part in the world view of the Enlightenment. Darwin was the culture hero of the nineteenth century as Newton had been of the eighteenth. Especially as philosophers, moralists, and publicists developed what seemed to them the correct social, moral, indeed metaphysical consequences of Darwin's work as a biologist into social Darwinism, the somewhat static and un-Faustian picture of the universe provided by the Newtonian world-machine gave way to a picture of a vast organic universe, growing, evolving, and, above all, improving, with improving man, Homo sapiens, at once its master and its creation.[11]

Darwin himself, though he was quite aware of what men were making of his work, kept pretty much to his biological last. The Huxleys, Spencers, William Graham Sumners, and many others showed no such restraint; they went straight to what has come to be called "social Darwinism." Given the multanimity of the nineteenth century, social Darwinism could not be a simple, agreed-on set of dogmas, but the major articles of its faith are clear. Briefly, the social Darwinist held that men, like other organisms, compete among

---

[11] I must emphasize that in moral, intellectual, cultural history—I suspect in any kind of history, except the history of an individual—change is slow and incomplete, not to be given even the kind of dramatic force of, for example, 1859: Darwin's *Origin of Species*. The "Darwinian" controversy in its broadest sense—the old "Conflict of Religion and Science"—goes back to the eighteenth century, and still goes on, though not quite in the same verbal forms as in the nineteenth century. Compare the following from 1785, not 1885:

Some drill and bore
The solid earth, and from the strata there
Extract a register, by which we learn
That He who made it, and revealed its date
To Moses, was mistaken in its age.
—Cowper, *The Task*, Book III, lines 150-154.

The *form*, I grant, could only be eighteenth century, even though Cowper did not write heroic couplets.

themselves for food, shelter, and the chance to reproduce their kind. Variations, very slight ones in a given generation, allow some individuals to succeed better than others in the competition, and to reproduce themselves more successfully. Their progeny will tend to inherit these advantages, and in the long slow course of evolution will add to them. On the other hand, those not adapted genetically, constitutionally, to their environment will tend to fail to reproduce themselves. In the long run, this "struggle for life" which we human beings must take part in along with other organisms—though we are so far the most successful of them, and are able to make planned use of many of the other organisms to further our own evolution—makes for the continued improvement of the species through the "survival of the fittest." All you need now do is translate into simple ethical terms: if in the inevitable competition among human beings we let nature take its course, the good will prevail, the bad die out, and once more we shall all—yes, in a sense, even the failures, the defeated—live in the best of possible worlds.[12]

Now one important radical wing of the social Darwinians went on to draw some simple conclusions from this analysis of the struggle for life. The struggle must be, among men, as "free" as it is among, say, wildcats. A wildcat born with good muscles and just that extra sense of timing in his spring gets the extra rabbit; a wildcat born with weak muscles in his hind quarters gets no rabbit, and dies young. No misguided Christian wildcats, no sentimental eighteenth-century Enlightened wildcat lovers of their kind, no "liberal" wildcats, can take care of and feed the weak-muscled cat. Wildcats remain, then, perhaps, from our human point of view, not altogether admirable creatures, or at least not useful ones for us, but splendid examples of the working of evolution. We moderns ourselves, these social Darwinians insist, have somehow managed to interfere with the natural and normal course of evolution of our own species (that absurd problem of the origin of evil will keep cropping up, but here is a place we had better not notice it). We protect the weak, allow them to mature, and even to pass on their weaknesses to prog-

---

[12] I want to underline once more that I am writing as a historian of morals, not of natural science. As *biologists* the Darwinians were fully aware of the complexities, of unfavorable turns in the process of evolution in a given species, of degeneration, of much else that many, certainly, as *moralists* tried to shrug off, or explain away, or, better yet, just not notice. Not noticing is fatal to the scientist—in fact, it is to him immoral. Those naïve persons who still think natural science itself is a complete and adequate morality are likely to put undue stress on the scientist's "intellectual honesty." Compare Huxley, "The foundation of morality is to have done, once and for all, with lying." T. H. Huxley, *Science and Morals,* quoted in Mencken, *Treatise of Right and Wrong,* p. 197.

eny whom we also protect. Poor relief, hospitals, a medical profession with a simple ethical imperative, "keep them all alive as long as you possibly can," and nowadays full social security—well, the list of what we do to stop evolution, stop progress, would be a socio-economic history of our modern West. But Western intellectuals being what they are, this last fact only served to sharpen the zest of the radical social Darwinians; they were going to get evolution back on the track through revolution.

I simplify, but do not really caricature, let alone satirize, the theoretical position of these devotees of untrammeled struggle among individual men. They realized, of course, that Homo sapiens has a most complex central nervous system, that variations in it added to the complications of successful adaptation, that sometimes an unusually sound mind in an unsound body might triumph even in the struggle for life, as Evolution (the capital letter is needed here) intended it. But since they thought that the sound mind in a sound body was no doubt the *real* intention of Evolution, they believed all would come out right in the end. Meanwhile, they saw the struggle for life as essentially an economic one, and took their practical stand on an extreme economic *laissez-faire;* the entrepreneur who fails, the worker who loses his job, are both "unfit" to survive, and ought—the "ought" is here clearly the old moral ought—to die.

Actually, most of the radical social Darwinians were also aware of the fact that, whatever his origins, Homo sapiens has in fact evolved into a kind of social animal, and that "culture" and "society" as well as individual mind and body must be taken into account. Their usual minimum allowance for these factors was to grant to governmental institutions the functions of defense of the national group (until the world state is achieved), policing against criminals (again, until we breed out criminals, for they must not be allowed to reproduce), and enforcing contracts; on the role of religious and educational institutions they were less certain, but these should, of course, promote the cause of the faith in Evolution. Finally, though these thinkers might feel that ideally the unfit as tested by free economic competition ought to die a useful natural death, usually from starvation, they were quite aware—after all, most of them were Englishmen—that the ideal is not yet the practical. They tended, after the model set up by the English utilitarians, to advocate that the demonstrably unfit, the poor, the criminal, the defectives, be, as far as possible, isolated, kept from reproducing their kind, and maintained at a minimum cost. Such, substantially, was the view of many by no means cruel Westerners in the Victorian heyday. It is well reflected in much of Herbert Spencer's work, especially his angriest, *The Man versus the State* (1884).[13]

Yet for most men of good will in the nineteenth century, even in Manchester, even for the less-angry Herbert Spencer who wrote the *Principles of Ethics* (1879-92), what they drew from Darwin's work conflicted with ideas and feelings they had been brought up with, which they knew were part of a long and valued cultural heritage. They were genuinely, honestly, and deeply disturbed by the contrast between the concept of a fine free-for-all in which the defeated simply went down and the gentle altruistic concepts of the Sermon on the Mount, or of the Enlightenment. Confronted with this difficulty they went to work with the laudable and very human intent of smoothing it over, of reconciling its oppositions, of having their cake and eating it. They did not do nearly as bad a job as the first anti-Victorian critics of the 1890's and the early twentieth century thought they had done.

Their great discovery may easily be made to seem naïve; perhaps it is naïve, now. They discovered that Christian and humanitarian ethics, properly understood, were a part of nature's plan all along, fully consonant with Darwin's discoveries, indeed, a necessary adjunct to the workings of Evolution among men. Our ethical inheritance is basically a set of rules for conducting the struggle for life as nature certainly, and perhaps even the Unknowable (Spencer's very Victorian effort to hedge a bit on Pascal's wager), intended all along. The traditional virtues, honesty, loyalty, law-abidingness, obedience

---

[13] Those interested in the affiliation of ideas, in a sense more a part of intellectual history than of the history of morals (the two cannot and should not be rigorously separated), will note that nineteenth-century radical *laissez faire* of this sort is a stage in the development and paring down of "pure" anarchism. The pure doctrine (see above, p. 300) accepts complete environmentalism, and insists on no interference whatever with the "free" natural response of the human organism to stimuli from the environment and on no "rigging" of the environment. The *laissez-faire* variant of the nineteenth century accepts the "fact" of hereditary variations, and comes somewhat reluctantly to the conclusion that government, society, in the hands of the strong, must rig the environment a bit to dispose of those with "bad" heredity, but leave those with "good" heredity in an anarchistic freedom. In the twentieth century the basic idea of anarchism has been further altered, though it still maintains its close affiliation with those agreeable symbols Nature and Liberty. I think in our own time the anarchist theme is heard chiefly in the form that takes backing from biological concepts of ecological balance, of a natural homeostasis or equilibrium, of "do no harm," of preserving the elaborate existing nexus of social relations. The modern of this sort, taking his cue from nature's by no means simple plan, would argue that we must not destroy the wildcats and other predators, or we shall have too many deer and rabbits, and perhaps a horrid epizootic, which might spread as an epidemic to us human beings. Besides, Nature wants variety, wants even wildcats. What was once a radical has become a conservative doctrine.

where obedience is due, even honor, tainted though that virtue is by medieval knightly abuse, all these reinforce the strong man in his struggle, help prevent the victory of the *merely* clever, the sly, the rule breaker, the man who might even set Evolution back a stride by winning—temporarily, of course, but still regrettably—by means of dirty tactics. But there are other traditional virtues, especially emphasized both by conventional Christianity and by the new humanitarian ethics. How about gentleness, pity, loving-kindness? Spencer and his fellows had room for some of these, though they could not, of course, go quite as far as our Lord went in the matter of the meek inheriting the earth, and could not quite accept a great deal else in the Sermon on the Mount. Man, they pointed out, is a social animal, and in particular his institutions, less grandiose in scale and less dangerous to Evolution than the state—notably the family, but also the school, the vocational group, the neighborhood group, and the like—are actually held together by the hard cement of what looks at first to be softness, by love, by mutual aid, by self-sacrificing altruism. Our natural sympathies are useful. There need be no transvaluation of values to carry out the work of Evolution.

But on the other hand there must be no exaggeration. We must be firm about the unfit, firm, above all, not to let the marginal person slip up the wrong slope. We must listen to the voice of our conscience, and feed the poor —but we must not feed them so well that the naturally lazy will not mind being poor. Nature has implanted feelings in us, which, distorted and corrupted by Christianity in the past, we must cleanse of their impurities. "Pervading all Nature," wrote Spencer in a famous sentence, "we may see at work a stern discipline which is a little cruel that it may be very kind."[14] We must not be misled into a perverse sympathy for the unfit. Loving-kindness must not flow out, as so often it does, in an uncontrolled stream over the just and the unjust, or, as we now in the nineteenth century say more clearly and scientifically, the fit and the unfit.

Finally, another group of social Darwinians found a formula that gave rather less logical difficulty than did the middle-of-the-road formula we have just discussed. These thinkers decided that for Homo sapiens the struggle for life among individuals of the same species, which the Darwinian biology had emphasized, is actually a struggle for life among groups or societies of individuals. In the late nineteenth century, the in-group that inevitably was chosen

---

[14] *Social Statics* (1851), p. 149. Another Spencerian aphorism: "The ultimate result of shielding men from folly is to fill the world with fools." *Autobiography* (1904), Vol. II, p. 5.

as the key competitor was, of course, the nation-state; but as the twentieth century progressed, the most vocal of the school turned to an even vaguer in-group, a "race," the Nordic, Germanic, even the "white" or "Caucasian."[15] Whatever the in-group chosen, the formula was simple indeed: *Within the group,* the struggle for life among individuals was called off—by Nature, of course; but the same sovereign mistress had ordained that *among groups* the struggle should go on with unsparing ferocity. War was the final and most satisfactory form of the struggle, and in war the fit group won and the unfit group lost. Within the group, then, there must be co-operation among individuals. If only because these writers put so much emphasis on war, an activity not effectively carried on, as a rule, at least not in the modern mass armies, by warriors indulging in democratic egalitarian discussion, they preached a kind of discipline we now call authoritarian, a hierarchical society of strict discipline and conditioned obedience, not by any means the "natural mutual aid" of anarchists like Kropotkin. Success in war, they held, went obviously to the group best disciplined, best able to meet the test of the battlefield. And yet in the nineteenth century it was clear to the most benighted surviving feudal warrior that the factory stood behind the armed forces; and in economic and industrial life the fashionable pattern was unbridled competition among individuals. It was all very confusing.

Racists and their like were chief among the social Darwinians to emphasize an obvious conclusion from the scientist's own direct work in biology. The good and the bad (fit and unfit) variations are constitutional, and therefore genetically determined. Obviously a fit human pair is likely to produce fit progeny, if not fitter progeny than themselves; the unfit, too, tend to breed true. The racists and other conservatives were all for proper human breeding. Blonds, being better, should marry blonds. There was a good deal of what we now know was erroneous genetic theory in all this, and even more in the work of a small and never more than mildly lunatic fringe group who saw heaven on earth as attainable only through planned breeding of humans, through what came to be called eugenics. Moreover, the general influence of Darwinism in matters of social ethics was definitely *not* in the direction of

[15] There is a huge bibliography for this nationalist and racist variant of social Darwinism. A start may be made from Richard Hofstadter, *Social Darwinism in American Thought,* rev. ed., Boston, Beacon, 1955. It must not be assumed that the Germans were the sole or even the most important of the school. In the present revulsion of "Afro-Asians" against "Caucasians" the writings of English-speaking peoples, including Americans like Madison Grant and Lothrop Stoddard, figure most conspicuously. An American who feels surprised and grieved at the attitude of these Afro-Asians toward us will do well to dip into this literature.

redressing the balance between heredity and environment, nature and nurture, upset by the environmentalism of the eighteenth-century Enlightenment. Logically, perhaps, the social implications of Darwinism should have brought home to men the immense difficulty of making rapid changes in the human material with which the reformer works. In the long run, it is not impossible that the influence of the natural sciences on the social sciences will go toward curbing the Utopianism still marked in the social sciences; indeed, there are signs that this is happening.[16] But for the nineteenth century the natural sciences implied, above all, human control of the environment: the science of Darwin meant then clearly that, knowing that progress is adaptation to environment, we can rig the environment! Products of Evolution, we can alter what produced us.

None of the schools of social Darwinians, not even the most intransigent of laissez-faire economists nor of the all-out-for-war school, could quite avoid the nagging difficulty: human beings did compete among themselves, to the point of killing, to the point of confirming the view of nature as "red in tooth and claw"; but they also did co-operate among themselves, did display the emotion called love, seemed at times to confirm the view of nature as a wise and kindly "impulse from a vernal wood." Men seemed not quite to behave like wildcats, nor even, in spite of Thomas Hobbes, wolves; on the other hand, they clearly could not be trusted to behave like soldier ants. The wiser thinkers realized that men were *both* competing individuals and collaborating, or at least obeying, members of groups. Walter Bagehot's prescient *Physics and Politics* (1875)— we should call it *Biology and Politics*—is a work still worth reading, not just by the historian of ideas, but by anyone interested in the attempt to study human behavior, human relations, in something of the same way the natural scientist studies the behavior of the birds and beasts. Especially on the problem of why some organized human groups—tribe, state, and the like—do subdue, control, and sometimes absorb others in what certainly looks like a kind of Darwinian struggle, Bagehot is wise and temperate.

Three general comments on the place of Darwinism in our intellectual

16 One ironic sign: Sir Charles Galton Darwin, grandson of the naturalist and himself a distinguished physicist, has written a little book, *The Next Million Years* (London, Rupert Hart-Davis, 1952), of which the burden is that man as a "wild" creature cannot improve himself through planned breeding, and has already had a long-enough history to show all he can achieve. Since it takes roughly a million years to evolve a new species, we shall have to face another million years much like the last few tens of thousands.

and moral life may conclude this brief account. First, although perhaps our received tradition of historical writing, right on down to the textbooks, does perhaps exaggerate the extent and importance of the specific theological and cosmological debate started by the publication of the *Origin of Species*—there were millions of printed words, and heaven knows how many spoken—still, the shock of Darwinism on Christianity was a great one. No doubt the eighteenth century had marked the spread to the educated many of what Galileo had begun; no doubt the continued development of geology and paleontology, of the whole world view of the Enlightenment, should have meant that Darwin's ideas brought no surprise. But the fact is that Darwin's work widened and sharpened the difficulties many Christians had with their orthodox cosmology; they even made serious what in the eighteenth century with Lord Monboddo had seemed a rather bad joke, the possibility that men are "related to" monkeys and apes. For the Protestant countries, and the English-speaking ones in particular, which had never quite known the anti-Christianity (miscalled anticlericalism) of the French Revolution as it was known in Catholic countries, Darwin, kindly, unironic, uncomplaining though he was, did the work of a Voltaire; he challenged dramatically the old established religion.

Second, Darwin's whole work and influence served to bring to the eternal Western preoccupation with the agon, with the organized struggle for prize among men, the immense prestige of that natural science and its ally technology which had first made the doctrine of Progress seem a fact of life. The theme of struggle—profitable, desirable, struggle, not, if you had the right perspective, tragic, even for the losers—dominated Western thought for years, and, in shapes not quite those given it by the nineteenth century, still dominates it. Much as the Marxists dislike to admit it, the Marxist concept of the class struggle is deeply indebted to the climate of Darwinian thought. Much as Nietzsche in the flesh refused to admit it—he thought of Darwin as an ignoble English shopkeeper—there is much more of Darwin in *Also Sprach Zarathustra* than of Zoroaster. The basic concepts of social Darwinism are hard to get out of our minds: we want a society ever-changing, dynamic, progressive, and we see in competition among variously endowed individuals, or even groups, a necessary condition of such a society. We feel and think of Progress in a frame essentially Darwinian.

Third, with Darwin the doctrine of Progress took almost complete possession of the Western mind. Darwin's ideas, as we have noted above, gave an explanation for the dynamic or changing element of human historical experience, an element not well explained in terms of Newtonian mechanics. But they also gave directions, purpose, a teleology, something barely short of an eschatology, for these observed changes. In the mind of the educated man in the street—there were millions of him—in the West, Darwinian terms, originally used with scientific caution, and without teleological implications, terms like "fit," "unfit," "adapted," even "higher" and "lower," came quite simply to be translated into simple ethical terms, into "good" and "bad." Organic life started low, primitive, and, though blamelessly, of course, at that stage, bad; it has evolved ever since, perhaps with a few backslidings, but on the whole in a regular way ("unilinear evolution") toward the higher, more civilized, and therefore good; its high point so far is the species Homo sapiens.

This neat unilinear ranking guided the first anthropologists, and gained widespread acceptance among the many in the West. In this view, there were three stages of human social progress, that of the savage, that of the barbarian, that of the civilized man. Auguste Comte translated this into more abstract terms. The intellectual evolution, which, of course, paralleled, probably even "caused," the moral evolution, was one from theology to metaphysics to natural science (positivism). Of course, there were many in the nineteenth century who felt that the fact of moral progress among men was much less clear than was the general course of organic evolution, and less clear than "material" progress since the cave men. But still, for the confident Victorians, even when with Spencer they put the matter in weighty social-scientese, as progress from the homogeneous to the heterogeneous, from militant societies to peaceful industrial societies, or as progress from adherence to the "cake of custom" to innovating individual liberty, to "freedom slowly broadening down from precedent to precedent," the process was one that made sense, moral sense, as progress from the lower to the higher, world without end.

IV

There is no grave inaccuracy, and much convenience, in using "Victorian" as an epithet for Western culture in the nineteenth century. Great Britain set the tone for the West in many matters of morals, manners, and even of taste, something in the way the France of Louis XIV set the tone in the seventeenth century. The alternative to "Victorian" is "middle class" or "bourgeois," both overworked, and both too closely tied with the economic interpretation of history. I shall use Victorian, without further apology, as a label for the predominating, or characteristic, or typical set of attitudes of the nineteenth-century West. Whether there was any such characteristic set of attitudes involves the old and still-unsolved problem we have dodged so successfully thus far, the problem of generalization from complex data and, perhaps, even the philosophical problem of the "reality" or "truth" of universals.

The Victorian era is coming back into good repute, if only because it was in bad repute forty years ago, and there seems to be in the modern West a tendency for a given cultural generation to scorn its immediate predecessor and admire the cultural generation one or two removes from its immediate predecessor.[17] Beginning in the 1890's and culminating in the 1920's there was a great condemnation of the Victorians, one that put special emphasis on Victorian prudery and Victorian unnatural restraints on everything natural and especially on good unashamed genital sex life. More profound critics went on to condemn as unlovely, or unheroic, or unjust, almost everything the Victorians most prized. The condemnations were many, varied, and, taken as a whole, full of contradictions. Still, the central themes were clear: the Victorians were middle-class, middle-of-the-roaders, middle always in the sense of mediocre—and intolerably satisfied with their mediocrity.[18]

We must admit at the outset that the Victorians were indeed Victorian. The social historian who cares to dig up instances of what must seem to almost all of us incredible prudery can fill volumes. Perhaps the original of the common verb *to bowdlerize* will do for us, who have more important concerns in this book. Thomas Bowdler published in 1818 a book entitled and subtitled: *The Family Shakespeare in Ten Volumes, in which nothing has been added to*

[17] The above is a grave oversimplification. But the problem of the cultural generation —which includes the problem of whether there really is such a thing, since the annual supply of young humans is relatively constant—is rather one for the historian of ideas than the historian of morals. It does seem likely that our contemporary willingness to recognize that the child—the real individual child as well as the figurative child, the cultural generation—"naturally" rebels against the parent, even hates the parent, has some moral implications for our culture. On this problem of the "cultural generation" see Karl Mannheim, *Essays on the Sociology of Knowledge,* New York, Oxford University Press, 1952, pp. 276-322 and J. Ortega y Gasset, *Man and Crises,* trans. by Mildred Adams, New York, Norton, 1958.

[18] There is a whole library of books in which the early twentieth century damned the Victorians but not to my knowledge any single critical study of this theme. For the cheap criticism of the Victorians as prudes, sex-starved and repressed but scandal-loving, see Leo Markun, *Mrs. Grundy,* New York, Appleton, 1930. For serious criticism, G. B. Shaw seems to me the best single example, and of Shaw a good sampling is the following prefaces and plays: *Man and Superman, Pygmalion, Candida, Major Barbara.* Shaw himself was a good Victorian in many ways; see H. M. Jones, "Shaw as a Victorian," *Victorian Studies,* I, no. 2 (December 1957). For the *feeling* of a cultural generation in revolt, see Malcolm Cowley, *Exile's Return,* new ed., New York, Viking, 1951. Note how firmly established is our American feeling that even decades—the '20's, the '30's—vary in spirit.

the original text, but those words and phrases are omitted which cannot with propriety be read in a family. He later did a Gibbon, cutting out the author's cold and erudite obscenity and his more inescapably anti-Christian ironies. Or, we may take Byron's indignant poem "The Waltz" (1813), in which he condemns this indecent dance as though it amounted to fornication, or rape. The worrier can make a sequence of shocking degeneration from minuet through waltz to fox trot and rock-'n'-roll. But I do not think that sequence is one of moral degeneration, and certainly not one of increasing sexual promiscuity. I think such matters are matters of taste, concerns of social history, and only partly and indirectly of the history of morals.

One final instance and we shall have done with this all-too-obvious subject. We were prudish in the United States. Here is the virtuous Frances E. Willard, writing with something less than innocence:

When I was first a boarding school pupil at Evanston, in 1858, a young woman who was not chaste came to the college there through some misrepresentation, but was speedily dismissed; not knowing her degraded status I was speaking to her when a school-mate whispered a few words of explanation that crimsoned my face suddenly: and grasping my dress lest its hem should touch the garments of one so morally polluted, I fled from the room.[19]

There were also protests against prudery. "Indelicacy is often manifested by affectations of purity. The woman who talks about 'limbs' of the table and the 'bosom' of the chicken is unrefined, and exposes herself to merited ridicule and contempt."[20]

It is surely much more important, and more fair to Victorian culture, to see as the central theme of their moral struggles an effort to reconcile the Enlightenment and Christianity; or, if you prefer, an effort to arrive at a working compromise between the heroic, the Utopian, the chiliastic in the new religion of humanity and progress and the apparent need of ordinary folk to lead ordinary lives, a compromise that involved the salvaging of much of conventional Christianity. The compromise was often, especially among the

---

[19] *Glimpses of Fifty Years,* quoted in Leo Markun, *Mrs. Grundy,* p. 506. Each age, each group, has its necessary Pharisaism. The reader of the mid-twentieth century who goes back to Markun's book ought to be quite as impressed with Markun's own kind, exhibited on his next page, where he notes that the employers of the Lowell mills in the early nineteenth century housed and supervised carefully the girls they employed —not, of course, because they *really* wanted to protect their virtue, but because they wanted to keep them away from trade unions and efforts to raise their wages! *Mrs. Grundy,* p. 507.
[20] Alexander M. Gow, *Good Morals and Gentle Manners for Schools and Families,* New York, American Book Co., 1873, quoted in Leo Markun, *Mrs. Grundy,* p. 560.

intellectuals, one that left tensions, doubts, all sorts of spiritual discomforts, as with Arthur Hugh Clough, who lost his faith but felt he had to keep on hunting for it; yet more often it was, at least for the time, a consoling compromise, and one that guided many useful lives.

The nature of the compromise is clear in Victorian ethical thought, neatly symbolized by T. H. Green, from Tory Oxford, home of lost causes, idealist in metaphysics, much influenced by the Germans, a moderate liberal reformer, and Henry Sidgwick, from progressive Cambridge, usually listed as the last of the English utilitarians, much influenced by everything gentle and worthy, including psychic research, a moderate radical reformer. Ethically, the two seem at this distance to be in almost identical positions. Of course, the range or gamut of nineteenth-century ethical ideas seems, if only, as I have noted above, because of the abundance of our surviving source materials, very great indeed. To the usual schools of Western tradition there were now added more conspicuously than ever before—though still well short of full cultural interpenetration—all sorts of Eastern influences. Westerners were converted to Islam, or to Buddhism, or to a great number of theosophies of varied intellectual and geographic lineage. Two of the more striking Christian sects originating in the nineteenth century, which was not a fecund one in the creation of major sects, both have exotic elements; with the Mormons this exotic touch is contrived and superficial, vanishes under examination, but with the Christian Scientists it is truly theosophic, out-Hegeling Hegel.

We shall return to some of these variants, but for the present we may continue with the core, the center, of the Victorian ethical attitude. Sidgwick puts, perhaps more wistfully than usual, the initial difficulty that faced the seeker: how to find a moral order in a universe in which the work of Newton, Darwin, and their like has found only a physico-chemical order and nothing else, found only nature—lower-case nature, at that—and lost God.

I don't know whether I *believe* or merely *hope* that there is a moral order in this universe that we know, a supreme principle of Wisdom and Benevolence, guiding all things to good ends, and to the happiness of the good. I certainly *hope* that this is so, but I do not think it capable of being *proved*. All I can say is that no opposed explanation of the origins of the cosmos—for instance, the atomistic explanation—seems to me even plausible, and that I cannot accept life in any other terms, or construct a rational system of my own conduct, except on the basis of this faith.[21]

[21] A. and E. M. Sidgwick, *Henry Sidgwick, a Memoir*, London, Macmillan, 1906, p. 347. From an autobiographical fragment. Note that Sidgwick wrote "happiness of the good," not "of the greatest number."

Sidgwick, whose father was an Anglican clergyman, had resigned a college fellowship on the ground that he could not claim to be a Christian; yet he never ceased to consider himself a theist, and he seemed all his life to be a happy man. This search for God, enjoying the search even though not finding Him, and confirming one's ideas of the good on the way is very Victorian. Sidgwick was a member of the Metaphysical Society, a group of English leaders with backgrounds and commitments running from Roman Catholicism to Unitarianism and agnosticism which met in the 1870's in a London restaurant, dined well, and discussed the Ultimate in comfort and equanimity—itself a very Victorian procedure, and one that may tempt a critic in the 1950's to the unfair conclusion that these men were not really what they professed to be, Catholics, Anglicans, agnostics, that they were just successful Victorian intellectuals, safe in London. They were, rather, honest Victorian intellectuals who still hoped, having found that compromise worked so well so often in politics, in economic and social life, in morals, to find the Ultimate Compromise. We today have either given up the hunt for the Ultimate or feel convinced that the Ultimate, once more, is no matter for compromise.

Yet there is a real problem here, one we may well symbolize by this Metaphysical Society: Why do men with mutually incompatible sets of ideas of ultimate concern to them (you may say to yourself, with differing "ideologies," but do try to keep an open mind) at times try to exterminate one another, at times accept one another in apparent respect and even liking, at times dwell uneasily together in all sorts of degrees of toleration and mutual adjustment? The likes of Cardinal Manning, T. H. Huxley, J. A. Froude, and Henry Sidgwick could hardly have dined together in London in 1645; their likes in Italy could not have dined together in Rome in those very 1870's. Any very close equivalent of the Metaphysical Society seems unlikely in the United States of the 1950's, not because we do not accept multanimity, but because we feel a bit ill at ease about admitting that we do not, as Americans, agree on fundamentals. We accept, but we do not cherish, our multanimity.

Now I find unsatisfactory any answer to the central problem of conflict over ideas which insists that the conflicts are not at all over ideas, that ideas are pretexts, fakes, window dressing, in vulgar Marxist language "ideology," perhaps most damning of all, "abstract." Ideas are at least necessary battle cries, army uniforms, ways of distinguishing the fighters; no civilized groups ever fought without some differences of ideas. But the naïve "materialist" position in this matter does serve to remind us that the ideas are neither independent of human beings nor absolute masters of human beings. The central problem can perhaps be put: What feelings, attitudes, compulsions work on human beings in ways likely to sharpen the prick of ideas, or what ones so work as to diminish the prick of ideas? This is surely one of the critical problems of our own age, which loves formulas like "the world cannot exist half x and half y—to say nothing of the poor n's."

We do not know nearly enough to give even a partial answer to the problem. If we wish to approach it as a problem to be studied in the way the scientist works, we shall have to go at it by the method of case studies. The Victorians make a fine study of this sort, for theirs was a society full of stresses and strains, class conflicts, a rapidly growing society, certainly a dynamic one in economic terms, by no means an old and tired society, in fact, a society pursuing to the full the Western hunt for prizes. Yet it was not a murderous society, not even, in the perspective of Western history, a very warlike one; the nineteenth century was not in terms of international politics quite as peaceful as it thought itself, but even here it was a society that put limits, "rules of the game," on much conflict that nowadays has very few such rules. We are back to Manning and Huxley, Catholic and freethinker, not just appearing together on a platform in public for a worthy and harmless cause—their corresponding personalities have done that even in the United States—but in private, unnecessarily, not at all, perhaps, for show.

But is not the clue in that phrase "rules of the game"? These prosperous, educated English gentlemen were, after all, at play. They did not suffer deprivations, a sense of inferiority either as individuals within their own nation-state or as members of such a state in relation to members of another; their self-esteem, separate or pooled, was satisfied; above all, they did not have the fears so common and so justified in our own world. No doubt much of all this must figure in the equation—if it can ever take a form even remotely like that of an equation. The Victorians themselves would have insisted that they had a positive, vigorous belief in toleration of all sorts of differences, from differences over theology to differences over taste and fashion, not a weary acceptance of human differences as incurable, but a real delight in them as the spice of life. Most Victorians would have added, with J. S. Mill, that they welcomed differences of opinion right on up through matters of ultimate theological and metaphysical and ethical concern because they were convinced that in the open forum of public discussion the truth will in the long run— and not in such a fearfully long one at that—prevail. Though the Victorians made many a compromise with the immediacy of the rational optimism of the Enlightenment, they remained true to its belief in process as Progress, in its own rationalist version of "ye shall know the truth and the truth shall make you free."[22]

The members of the Metaphysical Society would, however, have been in quite substantial agreement not to differ in their conduct in most important respects. Indeed, their ethical difference would have been largely a matter of metaphysical foundations of belief, not a matter of code. Perhaps in their freshness and bitterness of youth, metaphysical beliefs incite to violence, as theological beliefs most surely have done. The idealist may seek to rid the world of materialists—and, of course, the materialist may seek to get rid of the idealists. Or, as we are told of the East, the thinker who thinks the world is an illusion may *behave,* briefly but critically, as if he thought it an illusion. But nothing of the sort for the Victorians. For one thing, the Western tendency to take the sense world as real, or at least as worth fighting over, has meant that, save for the very few addicts of what Aldous Huxley hopefully calls the "perennial philosophy," most Western idealism, transcendentalism, "tender-mindedness," has so far compromised with the sense world as to welcome a fight. Our Western believers in nonresistance, in absolute pacifism—the early Christians, the Quakers, Thoreau—turn a ferocious other check. For another thing, the Victorians found that the idealistic formulas of conduct— say, the Kantian universal imperative—and the nonidealistic formulas—say, the Benthamite greatest good of the greatest number—cried out for reconciliation in their code of morality.

Once more, the code is basically the standard Western Christian code, modified a bit by humanitarian concern, a bit less exacting of the flesh in some ways, more so in others, than at more difficult times, in my opinion rather better observed on the average in conduct than at most times, but still the standard code. Not even in matters of sex relations is the code greatly out of line. What the rebel generations from the 1890's all emphasized as Victorian prudery is more a matter of taste and fashion than of morals. The Western code had always frowned on fornication, adultery, perversion, had at least since Christ always insisted on monogamous marriage; in its unofficially emended form it had long accepted the so-called double standard, whereby conformity was more rigidly insisted on for the female than for

[22] John, 8:32. In the previous verse, Jesus had said to his disciples "if ye abide in my word." This was just what worried the Victorians.

the male; but in Victorian times a John Stuart Mill, who thought all sex intercourse low and disgusting, is more of an exception in middle-class circles than he would have been in this respect among the early Christians.[23]

In this, as in so many other ways, the Victorians were authentic modern descendants of the Puritans, who did not so much seek to subdue the flesh as to control it. Perhaps among the many in the nineteenth century the motive behind the control, and the inspiration for ways of control, is best described as respectability rather than as conscience. Yet one may suspect that even in the seventeenth century, Puritan conduct among the many was conformity; and as for the sensitive few, a nineteenth-century Arthur Hugh Clough is as much hounded by conscience as anyone in the seventeenth century. For the many, the virtues are the virtues Weber has made us so aware of—and doubtful about—those of thrift, hard work, cleanliness, self-restraint, self-help, high-mindedness. There is more than a trace of holier-than-thou, of course; one would not try to revise out of existence the anti-Victorian view of the Victorians. It is hard to think of the many in the West save in terms of x-than-thou; and "holier" may come to seem rather better in the formula than "more interesting," or even "more natural."

Nor was the Victorian code nearly so heartless in its insistence on laissez-faire economics as we have been led to believe. After all, even Darwinism was no more than a theory; but by Victorian times, especially in England, humanitarianism had become a fashion and a habit. The very indignation that filled the "condition of England" debate is a sign of the times. We are misled by the no-doubt-useful unscrupulousness with which the proponents of the New Order, from socialists of all stripes to just plain lovers of the underdog, attacked the existing order; and, of course, neither we today nor their opponents then really bothered to read those cruel and inhuman advo-

---

[23] Mill's belief that among women pleasure in sexual intercourse is limited to the professional few is actually a fairly wide-spread Victorian belief. Modern studies of frigidity in women do give some basis for a statistical difference between men and women in this respect, but the grounds of the Victorian belief remain a bit of a puzzle. There is in terms of intellectual affiliation perhaps a line, difficult to trace, from the medieval exaltation of The Woman. But this is in the Middle Ages an upper-class attitude, very ambivalent, as we have seen. Medieval commoners were nearer the Chaucerian Wife of Bath. For that matter, Victoria herself enjoyed the pleasures of the bed very much; by a nice irony, the Empress Eugenie was almost as frigid as Mill's Mrs. Taylor. F. A. Hayek, *John Stuart Mill and Harriet Taylor;* Simone André Maurois, *Miss Howard and the Emperor,* trans. by Humphrey Hore, New York, Knopf, 1958. On the Victorian "double standard" see a long chapter of Westermarck, *Origin and Development of the Moral Ideas,* Chap. XLII.

cates the Classical Economists. From Adam Smith through Mill, in fact, the economists were by no means fanatically insistent that government must have no role even in economic life.[24] As for the ordinary Victorian, he was too sure that human suffering was an evil, one that now for the first time might be overcome, to follow Darwinism to its logical conclusion and let the incompetent suffer as they should. He would, of course, be against pampering the poor and the unfortunate, and he would not, unless he were a radical, sympathize with efforts to achieve social security by state action; but he might be all the more willing to back up his numerous charities.

The Victorian moral code is in its main line clear enough; the Victorian moral ideal, the admired figure, is not. At any rate, the grammatical singular here would be an even more dubious construction than usual. For the men of the nineteenth century, history was already an enormous warehouse full of attractive ideals. In the freedom and intellectual promiscuity of the times, one could always find a cause and a hero. In effect, all the ideals we have hitherto encountered in this book found admirers, even followers, somewhere in the multanimous West in these years. From this distance, the result looks not like any effective synthesis or syncretism, but, as in nineteenth-century domestic architecture, a mere juxtaposition. The medieval knight seems as ill assimilated in the nineteenth century as the Gothic style of architecture; the beautiful-and-good of Athens, the Roman Stoic, as unnatural as classical place names in the land of the Iroquois Confederation. The Greeks and Romans that the liberally educated of the West—some of them —came to love and admire were surely not the Greeks and Romans who had made their own moral ideals; the world of the Waverly Novels was not the world of the Middle Ages.[25]

A full-scale history of morals, quite as much as a full-scale cultural or intellectual history, would have to try to sort out these many "uses of the past," try to put into the complex whole—if it was a whole—such varied parts as political Philhellenism, which enlisted strong moral sympathies, the attempt to revive as moral guides the heroic ages of the Germanic, Celtic,

[24] Lionel Robbins, *The Theory of Economic Policy,* London, Macmillan, 1952; especially Lecture II, "The Economic Functions of the State," pp. 34-61.
[25] We are here at the very real problem Spengler saw only to try to dismiss it under the phrase "pseudo-morphism." This problem we cannot get entangled with here; suffice to say that the beautiful-and-good as it appeared to Pericles was not the beautiful-and-good as it appeared to Matthew Arnold. The two beautiful-and-goods are sometimes related, to use a misleading and certainly dangerous metaphor, *genetically;* sometimes the relation appears to be no more than verbal association. But there *is* a relation—even though as with the sirens of Homer and the sirens of our modern fire engines, the relation seems tenuous, even absurd.

and Slavic peoples, European fantasies about America, and about Asia, the persistence, though not generally in a form quite so innocently ignorant of the facts of anthropology, of the eighteenth-century "noble savage." We cannot here do more than note their existence, and make one comment. "Escapism" does not explain them, any more than "pseudo-morphism" does; or if you must use concepts like "escapism," then grant that all the arts always have a touch of escapism. Once more, the Victorians were not unique.

The problem of the existence of the varied gallery of the nineteenth-century moral ideal persons is not so much that of their historicity, nor of what needs they satisfied, but of their variety, of their being a gallery, not a pantheon. Anyone who could solve this problem would know more about human relations than is now known. That obsessive parallel with the late Greco-Roman culture is hard to put down: the nineteenth-century hash of beliefs and ideals, these archaisms and futurisms, this cultural free-for-all can look like the beginning of the end. But it is worth noting that it did not look at all like this even to most Victorian intellectuals, who nonetheless were great complainers. And the man in the street took it in his stride. Somehow, the free-for-all among ideals had marvelously got translated into the decencies, the orderliness, the respect for the rules of the game you may symbolize, if you like, by the English Victorian bobby, the only policeman so far in Western history beloved by all.

There is, then, no single nineteenth-century ideal moral figure; national, class, professional, indeed, in a sense, individual, differences are too great, make for a bewildering variety of such figures. But the century did have its own originality, molding some of these figures from the past into shapes never seen before. We may sample some of these briefly.

Two we may take from the sphere of the mind—or, in sociological terms, from the intellectual classes. This is the great century of the romantic hero, who turns out on examination to be almost as complex as that Protean "ism" romanticism itself. He may be the lonely Stoic aristocrat—de Vigny; the ineffably sensitive loving soul, a St. Francis seen through the secular distortions of the Enlightenment—Shelley; the far-from-lonely and not very aristocratic aristocrat, laughing ironically through ironic tears and always very visibly—Byron; the man of letters, man of the world, man of affairs who has lived all life, all lives—Goethe, Hugo (the English appear to have refused to have produced such). Even in its more vulgar forms the ideal has range and variety. Perhaps its central form is the Bohemian artist, upholding nature against the unnatural Philistines, merrily, tearfully starving in his chilly garret, but still warming his Mimi's cold little hand. But there is also the excessive individual, the super-something, who was a people's hero long before Nietzsche fooled the high-brows into thinking his Superman was one of them; there is the explorer, the record breaker, the lay saint of social service, nursing, and many more.

For the historian of morals, the most obvious fact about the romantic ideal in all its phases is that it sets up the rebel, the man who will not take the world at all as he finds it, and who usually will not even trouble to notice what this world is like. The romantic is the seeker, the man who, in the fine simple words of the most romantic of romanticists, Nietzsche, wants *etwas mehr*—something more.[26] He is often not very critical in his choice of "more." And he is a good child of the Western struggle for distinction; he wants the prize, wants to be noticed. We have met him often before in these pages, in cultures by no means usually called romantic. What distinguishes him in the nineteenth century is the amazing variety of his activities, which, as we shall shortly see, include many the ancients would have thought hopelessly banausic, and some the Christians think immoral. As an ideal, however, even the excessively active romantic ideal of the perpetual rebel and seeker had for the many its pleasantly quieting side of vicarious enjoyment. The moralist of the school known in the United States as the new conservatives—Edmund Burke gives them their start—holds that men need curbs, not spurs, calming, not exciting, and that our cultural inheritance from the romantic movement is a dangerous excess of spurring for a beast already galloping off wildly. There is here one of the innumerable unsolved problems we have encountered in this study. Is the immense body of Western art, good and bad, that we may call, with no intent save a classifier's, "erotic," a stimulant, or a sedative, or merely a surrogate? The search for a few concrete instances—*Madame Bovary, Tristan und Isolde,* a more-than-nude of Boucher's right on down to the latest American novelist attempting to be a clinician—is enough to indicate that the answer must be all three at least, and more, the mixture varying greatly with time, place, and person. I incline to believe that for the Victorians, at least, the net effect of the romantic ideal was to a great extent consoling, quieting, even a kind of discipline, something to keep them from actual adultery, lawlessness, and other interesting sins.

Yet the conservatives may in the long run be right. The mutually rein-

---

26 Nietzsche said this, naturally not without irony, of the German people—*wir Deutschen wollen etwas von uns, was man von uns noch nicht wolte—wir wollen etwas mehr, The Will to Power,* p. 108.

forcing ideals of romantic individualism and romantic love, old as the troubadours, the great Western tradition of the prize contest, the agon, reach down
at last in the nineteenth-century West to the millions. If even a few of the
millions really attempt to translate these ideals into action, our gloomiest
prophets may well be right. All for love or the world well lost may do for
Anthony and Cleopatra (though only on the stage); for Jack and Jill, romantic love—unless it gets worn out soon in the daily rubbing of the world
—will end, not in high tragedy, but in the divorce court, or in some other un-
pleasantness, from which no one gets catharsis. We of the twentieth century
have certainly inherited from the eighteenth and nineteenth centuries an
unsolved problem: how to put up with millions of would-be heroes and
heroines.

A second moral ideal taken from the work of the intellectual classes
was no doubt often assimilated to the ideal of the romantic artist, but not
always; and it has a somewhat different afterlife in our time. This is the
ideal of the hero as scientist, which can, not unfairly, be put impersonally as
the ideal of Natural Science. This ideal is a direct descendant of the ideals
of the Enlightenment, and must be considered as part of the effort to create
a new cosmology as independent as possible of traditional Christianity. But
with the nineteenth century it focuses more closely than in the eighteenth
on the natural scientist, as contrasted with the *philosophe,* a process indicated
by the substitution of the word "science" for the older "natural philosophy."
As a folk figure, the scientist grows in stature all through the century, and
has not diminished in our century. We must return to him and his Science.

Outside the intellectual classes, the nineteenth century found a hero
where he had not been found before, though the way had been prepared for
him by previous centuries. This is the hero as the practical man in fields of
activity not those of statesman or soldier. I phrase this last awkwardly and
deliberately, and do not say the hero as businessman. In spite of what many
contemporary American liberals believe, the many have never looked upon
business as a heroic activity, nor have they made the businessman a hero.
What has happened is that in modern times the agon has been extended to
many activities once thought beneath it, and those successful in certain
specific phases of economic activity have attained honor and esteem, or envy
and admiration, have helped by their lives to set up new moral patterns of
the ideal. The nineteenth century is so obviously in this respect a seedbed for
our own century that I shall here but note some of the seeds that sprouted
then.

The most striking is the ideal of the "self-made man," nicely embodied in the work of the Victorian Samuel Smiles, nicely exaggerated in good American fashion by Horatio Alger. A great deal of Calvinism, at least of Calvinism à la Max Weber, gets woven into the ideal, which survives vigorously in our contemporary America long after the intellectuals have pronounced it dead. A great deal of Victorian belief in progress through free competition, in democracy as essentially the career open to talents, as well as a great deal of the essential belief of the Enlightenment, the romantic doctrine that Nature doesn't really approve of any system and certainly not of established social hierarchies, will be found in this self-made man. Another seed sprouts in the United States more clearly than elsewhere, though it can be found in Balzac and in real life as well; and it is full-grown in the familiar Gilded Age of the late nineteenth century. This is the unscrupulous great entrepreneur, the manipulator of finance, rich and rich-living, James Fisk, Jay Gould, and their slightly more decorous European counterparts. These men are not moral ideals, any more than Robin Hood or Captain MacHeath, but they are envied and even admired, and they help make up the strange gallery of Western heroes. They remind us once more that our great Christian tradition has always made the Devil interesting.

Finally, and as merely one sample of a particular national form of the moral ideal, we may consider briefly that familiar American figure the Pioneer—or, since he often appears in more special shapes, the hunter, trapper, mountain man, scout, prospector, miner, cowboy, herder, and very first—but only the very first—farmer. There is a whole folklore, a whole tangle of something only a cultural anthropologist could begin to disentangle, that has grown up around the American frontier; there is—the already old-fashioned and somewhat disapproved word has to be used—a fascinating *myth* of the American frontier, the West. Bernard De Voto has taken the myth of the frontier apart, lovingly, skeptically, and with a fine indignation for those who have in our time sought to make it an exhibition, a piece of advertising, synthetically folkish—and foolish.[27] I do not dare engage us in this subject here. We all know the virtues the frontier taught—or imposed: self-reliance, ingenuity, distrust of established authority, dislike of all but the democratic snobberies, refusal to accept the conventionalities

27 See especially his "The Anxious West," *Harper's Magazine*, December 1946 (CXCII), pp. 481-491. Note that De Voto, who was no man to use concepts just because they are fashionable among intellectuals, could not avoid that word "myth." I'm afraid none of us can.

of law, order, and hereditary rank, the masculine tradition of egalitarianism which, nevertheless, knew well that all men are not equals with the six-shooter or at poker. We all know that the virtues of the frontier are not by any means the virtues of an old, established, complicated society, such as that of present-day San Francisco, Denver, Reno—or even of Monida, Montana. But they survive, and not only as myths, nor perhaps only as examples of cultural lag. Franklin D. Roosevelt's favorite song was "Home on the Range."

V

We come with the nineteenth century full into statistical riches. And yet for the historian of morals who would like to be able to make sociological generalizations about the actual conduct of masses of men and women, the statistics are still by no means enough. Especially for the ordinary private vices—sex once more will stand well enough for the lot—they remain inadequate. There are, for instance, statistics of illegitimacy. But how many cases get well covered up? And, of course, illegitimate births are no measure at all of deviations from strict Christian monogamous marriage. There are statistics of all sorts of "sexual offenses," where these are formal crimes. But whether or not they are crimes depends on the country concerned; there are variations as between, say, Scotland and Sicily, Massachusetts and Sonora. There are variations in accuracy of reporting, in the statistics themselves. But we may come to the now-classic example, the Kinsey reports. Who can be sure how true the replies of the persons interviewed, of just how much allowance should be made for what the historian—especially the historian of art and letters—knows is the firm Western tradition of honoring sexual prowess?

We are back at the rough generalizations which are all that is possible. The Victorian moral ideal was premarital chastity for both partners, with some lessening of the rigors for the male, and complete fidelity for both partners after marriage; and, in the strictness of the ideal, no divorce. There were the usual and expected variations by country within the West, and the usual attenuations and permitted but not encouraged lapses, notably for the males. But even in France, Anglo-Saxons should be reminded, the code was basic Christian monogamy; the exceptions were most interesting, and without them there would be few novels or plays; but this, as I have just pointed out, is the traditional role of Satan. As for sexual deviations, they were all, from simple masturbation to the worst a Sade could devise, morally wrong.

And actual conduct? Surely nothing that had been done before in this field lacked imitators in the nineteenth century. I think it extremely likely that on the whole there was, in the nineteenth-century West at least, less sexual promiscuity of all sorts, less deviation from the moral code in this respect than in the immediate previous centuries, the usual difference of a few percentage points. For one thing, the lives of most Westerners of the middle and upper classes were more closely surveyed in this century of publicity, police, family discipline. Middle-class standards of propriety, which in England reached as high as the throne, had a far greater influence on the upper classes than most of us, victims of clichés, will admit. There was no great and conspicuous group in the West that could quite equal some of the famous loose-living groups of the past, imperial Roman, Renaissance, Restoration. There was indeed much loose living in the nineteenth century, many centers of vice, attractive and unattractive, from one end of the Western world to another. But much that in earlier centuries could be public had in the nineteenth century to be hidden; and if only because hiding is always a burden, even if sometimes an added excitement, one can conclude that what the undeniable refinement and strictness of manners did set up as external standards were not wholly flouted in private. In fact, the generation of the early twentieth century used to reproach the Victorians with having repressed *l'homme moyen sensuel et sexuel* too successfully. I think it more likely that this reproach is partly true than that the Victorians were all complete hypocrites, symbolically destroying at night, like Penelope, all they had built up in the day—though the anti-Victorians of the early twentieth century were fond of maintaining that the Victorians had both suppressed their drives in public and in words and had shamelessly and hypocritically let them loose in private and in deeds.

The debunkers of the era of Mencken loved to discover the seamy side of Victorian life, a discovery that certainly required no great ingenuity or patience in research. Of course there were prostitutes in Victorian London; there are always prostitutes in Megalopolis, whether it is called Alexandria or Rome or New York or even Moscow. But here is a good debunker at work:

Taine thought there were about 50,000 harlots in London in 1870. . . . Colquhoun, a magistrate of the City, estimated there were 50,000 prostitutes as early as 1796. The estimates for 1840 ran as high as 80,000. Sometimes the figures were much lower. For example, the London Metropolitan police thought there were 2,071 well-dressed prostitutes in brothels in 1841, only 921 in 1857; 19,994 well-dressed prostitutes walking the streets in 1841, 2,616 in the latter year; while the number of harlots "infesting low neighborhoods" went down from 5,344 to 5,063 in this same period.[28]

At any rate, what in the last chapter we discerned as definite and even, in terms of public health and the like, statistically measurable improvements in conditions of human life surely of concern to the moralist continued in the nineteenth century at a greater rate than in the eighteenth. Some good psychological measure of how far Westerners had come, in the more favored parts of Europe and the New World, to expect good public order, freedom of travel, safety, relative cleanliness, the many decencies of a free and tolerant world—or, negatively and importantly, absence of the perpetual and overriding violence of life in earlier Western centuries—is afforded by the well-known fact that most of us in 1914 really did feel that what has become in our current vocabulary World War I was not possible; we were honestly surprised by the outbreak.[29]

In spite of the dissenters, to whom we shall come in a moment, the nineteenth century was the great century of reform, enacted in legislative bodies after long and ardent campaigns, thoroughly in the spirit of the Enlightenment. Ye shall make the law, and the law shall make you free—and good. It was the victory of those who took the side of planning, regulation, good shepherding as against those who believed that freedom meant philosophical anarchy. The range of this regulation had already begun to horrify an old-school liberal like Spencer well before his death in 1903. We are all familiar enough with it, from police measures against vice to complex social-security legislation of the kind the English love to joke about as protection "from womb to tomb." In some senses, its culmination in the United States, at least as far as direct and large-scale attempts at moral reform of private lives go, was, of course, the famous Eighteenth Amendment. But the failure of this attempt to eliminate entirely one of man's oldest temptations, the obvious persistence of much else, gambling, prostitution, crimes of all sorts, the steady chorus, particularly in the United States, of publicists' complaints about juvenile delinquency, sensual self-indulgence, general moral letdown, should not blind us to the fact that the nineteenth century did achieve in human conduct some of the reforms its leaders sought—and that in many ways these reforms have endured.

[28] Leo Markun, *Mrs. Grundy,* p. 268. My own conclusion from these figures is that figures are not much use in a history of morals—and also that the term "prostitute" presents certain semantic difficulties.
[29] I do not mean to deny the tensions, the "sword of Damocles," especially of the decade 1904-1914. Still, Norman Angell's *The Great Illusion* (New York, Putnam, 1910), remains symptomatic.

Through most of the West, outright physical cruelty to men and animals was vastly lessened in the two centuries from 1700 to 1900; the notion that most pain, especially the pain of disease, is natural and inevitable, and even, in some Christian thinking, good, had almost wholly vanished by 1900. Refinement of manners had spread far down in the social scale, to the point where the conventional vices were at least concealed, or even, as seems to be probable, statistically somewhat diminished. Public order in most of the West had been greatly improved. Public morality had at least reached a point where such affairs as the Crédit Mobilier in the United States, the Panama Canal affair in France, the Marconi affair in England, were outright scandals, occasions for legal prosecutions, not, as they would have been in the era of Walpole, accepted practice, condemned only in satire. The effort to bring heaven to earth had apparently succeeded at least in diminishing some of the more hellish aspects of life on earth.

VI

The moral and intellectual history of the nineteenth century is by no means summarized as a compromise between the immediate Utopia of a Condorcet and the spotted reality of human nature. The major line of development, the orthodoxy of the new faith in progress, happiness here on earth, bigger and better all around, is the one I have called the Victorian compromise, and which I have outlined briefly on previous pages. But the orthodoxy was challenged on many fronts. First, there were those who wanted to widen the break with a Christian past and develop ever more radically the religion of the Enlightenment with its belief in the natural goodness of man; second, there were those who sought to preserve the essential pessimism of traditional Christianity as to human nature and human perfectability here on earth; third, there were those who repudiated both Christian and Enlightened world views and sought to develop a non-Christian, even anti-Christian, pessimistic outlook on human nature, on democracy, on progress. Like all such classifications of human attitudes, this one is subject to all sorts of variations, exceptions, contradictions; there is possible a paradoxical membership in all three classes at once. I note this fact dutifully, and pass on.

First, those who push beyond Enlightened orthodoxy, the heretics, are indeed many and varied. The historian of political ideas or of economics can find a crude blanket word here: "socialism." Most "socialist" and related systems find that the nationalist-democratic orthodoxy of the Victorian compromise fails to translate "liberty, equality, and fraternity" into reality because it does not really believe in fraternity, gives to equality the inadequate—and, in fact, incompletely realized—meaning of political equality in the vote, legal equality before the law, and means by liberty the Darwinian free-for-all. The historian of morals will content himself with a simpler formula: Socialism and its allies are all efforts to preserve, even to increase, the extreme, the violent, the Utopian effort of the Enlightenment to bring heaven to earth, to end moral evil and achieve moral good, here, now, completely. The socialists and the other radicals are the protestants of the new faith in the principles of 1776 and 1789, principles tarnished, compromised, in the eyes of these protestants by the new Rome of nationalist popular governments or semidemocracies, of societies without the fundamental equality of the new religion—equality of income, "material" equality.

Like the Protestants of the sixteenth and seventeenth centuries, the socialists show a marked tendency toward sectarianism. Out of Marx's life and work there develops as the nineteenth century comes to an end what begins to look like a church, not merely a sect. But the development of social democracy and communism must await our next chapter. Here we may be concerned all too briefly with what for the "behavioral scientist" is one of the fascinating pages of recent history, the many attempts, some of them of Christian rather than of Enlightenment inspiration, to achieve in the "consociate family," the small experimental community, that complete reform of human conduct the eighteenth century had clearly not achieved in the great society. What the Marxists often contemptuously dismiss as "Utopian socialism" is surely one of the most important beginnings in Western moral history. These communities were the first experiments in what we may call "social or cultural engineering."

They were not, the historian is bound to note, entirely new. Even in ancient times, groups of men—sometimes, even, of men and women—had left their parent societies, not just as colonists expanding, but with intent to flee what was in their minds a bad or at least defective society and found a better one. From the Jewish Essenes, the Greek Pythagoreans, and on through the many Christian monastic movements, men had sought to live in small groups a better life than they thought possible for the many in the great society. Plato's *Republic* is a planned society, at least on paper. Yet the communistic experiments of the nineteenth century were new in many ways, more particularly in the way suggested by the very term "cultural engineering." The Jesuits in Paraguay had accomplished remarkable feats of such engineering with the Guaraní Indians. Some of these consociate families were efforts to flee rather than reform the world; but even such groups as the Mormons, who had an "ideology" not at first sight obviously related to that of the Enlightenment, were quite clearly making social experiments.

Of them all, those of older and more direct Christian inspiration lasted longest and fared best; but Shakers, Amana, Amish, Hutterites, and suchlike groups are fossil remnants of the great sectarian drive of the late Reformation, less compromised with the world than groups like the Quakers, who stayed in the great society. These small and relatively isolated religious groups were disciplined into simplicity, living evidence, if that were needed, that closely knit, tradition-directed, small groups, their members' conduct open to their own community supervision, their morals defined and sanctioned by supernatural authority, their minds closed to what we may loosely call "major innovating ideas," at least in morals and politics, can survive very well in a great society that tolerates them. They did not, in nineteenth-century America, much affect that great society.

All the groups directly inspired by the Enlightenment, such as the Fourierist, Owenite, and Icarian, or by the Enlightenment with Christian gloss, like the Oneida community, were, as consociate families, as efforts to surpass the conventional democratic society around them, dismal but often fascinating failures. There can be no one reason for that failure, no one overmastering defect of the kind the simplifiers seek; their members were not all eggheads, not even at Brook Farm; they were not all victims of persecution by their conventional neighbors; they were not all lazy, maladjusted, incompetent; they did not all aim at standards of conduct impossibly lofty, even for Christians; they were not all seduced away from consociate living by their success in producing marketable goods; they did not all break down under the strain, so hard for good Americans to bear, of being different. Certainly all these factors bore a part in the failure of some of these communities. But perhaps the success of the great society in providing many of the comforts, the satisfactions, the measurable "progress" these secular groups sought has the largest part of all to play in their disruption.[30]

As for the second current, few major organized Christian churches were able in the nineteenth century to maintain intact the traditional Christian attitude toward nature and human nature. All had to go part way in compromise with what the Enlightenment had brought to a head. Even the so-

---

30 On these "consociate families," see Mark Holloway, *Heavens on Earth: Utopian Communities in America, 1680-1880,* London, Turnstile Press, 1951, with a good guide to further reading, pp. 232-234.

called Catholic reaction to the French Revolution, though it produced in Joseph de Maistre a writer who did seek to undo the work of the eighteenth century, gave way as the nineteenth century went on to mild modernism, to Christian socialism, to all sorts of compromises with the facts of the new democratic society. I do not wish to be misunderstood here. I am not asserting that nineteenth-century Christian leaders abandoned all their positions, sold out to the new world of the improved flesh. On the contrary, the great majority of the Christian churches maintained the reality of the supranatural, the fallen nature of man, the minimal Christian moral puritanism of the "civil war in the breast." Most Westerners were Christians of one kind or another, Christians enough not to expect heaven on earth at once, for all, or even for themselves. Still, leaders and led alike among Christians in the nineteenth century seem either to have gone at least halfway toward the new world view of nationalist democracy or else to have been fighting a defensive battle, to have been "reactionary," in the nineteenth century a deadly term indeed.

The third current that swung against the optimistic assumptions of the Enlightenment was one that reaches full development in practice and in ideas only in the twentieth century; it is a current of many eddies and branches, many by no means new. It bears no clear name generally accepted. I think it can best be understood as centering on a fundamental repudiation of the eighteenth-century belief in the natural inborn ability of all men to reason clearly and well, as the mathematician or the natural scientist reasons; or, put metaphysically instead of psychologically, it repudiates the eighteenth-century belief that the universe is so organized that all "rational" men can agree in a description and evaluation in whole and in part of that organization. It is often, in an obvious sense, pessimistic about man or nature or both, but this pessimism has overtones very different from that of Christianity. This current is usually at least as hostile to Christianity as was the Enlightenment. I shall call this current, with much regret that I must use a negative and in many ways unsatisfactory term, "antirationalism."[31]

[31] Semantic accuracy is difficult here. The essential thing to note is that this current of thought and feeling tends to repudiate both Christian and Enlightened concepts of an order in the universe which is 1) at bottom friendly to men, and 2) understandable by, or at least somehow communicable to, men. But it is not really skeptical about the existence of such an order; it *knows* there is no such order, *knows* the universe is hostile to man. I may add that I personally find the concept of "Christian existentialism" —as far as I can understand it—a difficult paradox of the emotions, or, in common-sense terms, an impossibility.

The Nineteenth Century

In its first fashionable form, antirationalism appears as nineteenth-century romanticism. Now romanticism is many things, but in this context it is an assertation of the primacy of feeling over thought, of the unfinished, unending, infinite over the finished, the completed, of the unknown over the known. The romantic will take over from the eighteenth century the concept of process, even that of Progress, but he will insist that it is not a process that can be planned, thought out, or even, in the sense the word has for the mechanist, invented. It is a process that can be guided, perhaps, by human will, but only by that will itself guided by intuition, instinct, the hunch that will not be put into words, and certainly not into logic. The immediate moral effect of romanticism as a fashion was no more than a reinforcement of that phase of the Victorian compromise that sought vicarious satisfaction in art and literature, that tried to balance nature and society, dreams and reality. Quite early—in German culture, in the eighteenth century—the romantic insistence on the variation, the uniqueness, the organic quality of givenness that made each nation a thing in itself came as a strong reinforcement to nationalism. But romanticism itself was hardly an explosive. It could reconcile the romantic with his lot, give him the satisfaction of knowing that he was more sensitive, more unhappy, more misunderstood, than the vulgar satisfied philistine. It made him sure that the eighteenth-century *philosophes* were a shallow lot, but it did not drive him to conduct markedly out of the Western tradition. This is true even when as a romantic artist or art lover he became a Bohemian rebel, an alienated intellectual. Even then, he had no desire to blow things up; that desire was to come in the next century, when antirationalism had become anti-intellectualism.

In retrospect, however, it is clear that at least for the intellectual classes who had been most markedly affected by the Enlightenment itself all these confused nineteenth-century currents of thought that questioned or pushed further the world view of the Enlightenment had by the end of the century begun to have a cumulative effect. The famous decade of the nineties was among the intellectuals a decade of doubt, wit, sophistication, even, in what must seem to us a mild way, despair, a fit prologue for the twentieth century. The Victorian synthesis, the genteel tradition, was beginning to break up. The intellectuals were bracing themselves to face the facts of life once more. But all this is no more than a prelude to our own times. What is more important for the understanding of the direct tradition of the Enlightenment —the tradition we like to think as the true democratic one, the tradition that edges over clearly on the side of freedom for the individual to go his own

369

common-sense way—is the growth of serious doubts among the Enlightened as to whether the common man, free, and free in particular from the fear of punishment in an afterlife, free from the "irrational" but real sanctions the traditional religion had given to the necessary public and private virtues, would actually conduct himself suitably.

These doubts no longer took, in the nineteenth century, quite the simple form of the eighteenth-century debate as to whether an atheistic common people could be a satisfactorily moral people, though essentially the problem is closely related to that old one. In the work of a now nearly forgotten moralist, Benjamin Kidd, who in his own day saw his *Social Evolution* (1894) a best seller, the problem is, rather: Now that most men clearly *believe in* Progress and Evolution, now that their minds are at least in part swept clear of the old static world view, will they in fact make the sacrifices, the abstentions from complete self-indulgence, the *savings,* necessary to just this process of social evolution we call "Progress"? Or will they not in effect say to themselves: We can enjoy the fruits of our labor only here and now, since there is no afterlife, since we are in no useful sense immortal as individuals; so let us do so; in a good short cliché, after us the deluge. Kidd was greatly worried over this possibility, and as a simple-minded accepter of the rationalist belief that men are motivated by clear economic self-interest, he could see no reason why John Jones should work hard, save money, pay taxes, and in general act as a responsible citizen, unless he could somehow be induced to believe that such conduct would pay off. He therefore worked out the outlines of a fine purposeful religion of humanity, in which the individual would be motivated to the proper moral conduct by a worship of the future, a pale god he called "projected efficiency."[32]

We know now—or should know—that John Jones in his millions, and in particular the John Jones of the better neighborhoods, is in no danger of living up to the maxim "after us the deluge." The more extreme of Keynesian economists in our times have expressed regrets that poor John is in fact such

[32] There were, of course, many attempts in the nineteenth century to make the religion of the Enlightenment into a somewhat better organized church, above all, one better equipped with a cosmology and a dependent moral code than the loosely organized democratic society and the nation-state, buttressed by surviving Christianity, afforded. Comte's positivist religion is the most famous, and indeed survives today as a very small and ineffective sect. For a sympathetic but not quite worshipful treatment of Comte see F. S. Marvin, *Comte,* London, Chapman and Hall, 1936. For true worship, see Jane M. Style, *August Comte, Thinker and Lover,* London, Kegan Paul, Trench, Trubner, 1928.

a cautious, saving, hard-working fellow.[33] It is fairly clear that the fear of hell-fire does not in our time really get into the emotions of a very large number of individuals who nonetheless conduct themselves reasonably well. The focus, the conditions, of our moral problems and our thinking about them have changed greatly with the twentieth century. The generation that has grown up in the great vogue of psychology, which is to our century what physics was to the eighteenth century and biology to the nineteenth, has got used to the notion that men, for good or for evil, are not calculating rationalists. But there is enough of the old eighteenth century alive in us so that a great many intellectuals still wish they were, and still hope they soon will be.

[33] The best economists continue, of course, in spite of the claim of some of them to be nothing but scientists, to be good moralists. As such, they by no means advocate a complete transvaluation of our traditional values. If they rarely take the ant ("go to the ant, thou sluggard") as their moral symbol, they do not want us to be butterflies, or grasshoppers, or insects of any sort. Note the sound moral basis—even in conventional senses—of the deservedly successful recent book by J. K. Galbraith, *The Affluent Society,* Boston, Houghton Mifflin, 1958.

XIII

The Twentieth Century

WE CANNOT SEE OURSELVES as others will see us. It is one of the marks of our own time that there are probably more people than usual in Western culture since the hope-fear of the Second Coming of Christ really faded for most men, who hold that we shall not be seen at all, our history having ended, after our prolonged whimpers, with a grand bang. We do indeed label our own times quite freely and with self-conscious scorn the Age of Anxiety, the Aspirin Age, the Age of Confusion, the Age of Tranquilizers, and much more of the like; and we underline such labels by thinking—if we think at all about such matters—of the quite recent past as a time of faith, optimism, security, the Age of Reason, the Century of Hope, the Victorian Age. I do not seek to make light of our present difficulties; but here I shall risk a somewhat different emphasis, and shall even go so far as to suggest that future historians—I am confident there will be such—will see us as essentially part of a "period" continuous with the last two centuries, as grandchildren of the Enlightenment, as wrestlers with problems set us by the last two centuries.

We have added little save our fears to the mixture; and it is indeed a mixture. There are those—I am writing solely of the West—who still think the world is flat, and those who think the world is an illusion. There are those who hold that homosexual intercouse is a sin, which will be punished—unless duly and ritually repented—by an eternity of hell, those who think it an unfortunate abnormality, and those who think it nobody's business but the participants'. In this matter of homosexuality there are those who make all sorts of variant diagnoses, recommend all sorts of variant action, or none at all, who really hold a greatly varied set of moral sentiments in the matter. Denis de Rougemont has written:

For all, the whole lot of us, lead our lives of civilized people quite without suspecting that those lives are being led amid a strictly insensate confusion of religions never completely dead, and seldom altogether understood and practised; of moral teachings which once upon a time were mutually exclusive but now are superimposed upon one another; or else combined in the background of our elementary behaviour; of unsuspected complexes which, because unsuspected, are the more active; and of instincts inherited less from some animal nature than from customs entirely forgotten, customs which have turned into mental furrows or scars, that are unconscious, and, on that account, easily confused with instinct.[1]

This quotation can do more for us than point up what a moment's reflection should drive home to everyone, the fact that ours is a world of great multanimity, a world of which it can perhaps be said that almost no general statement or "proposition" can be made and get complete, unanimous acceptance—not even, as conventional educated Americans need to be warned, a statement labeled as "scientific truth." M. de Rougemont's words, few as they are, bear the mark of two phases of the intellectual life of the twentieth century rooted in the past but characteristic of the turn our century has taken, at least among the intellectual classes. These are pessimism about man's fate, and awareness of the relatively small part rationality plays in men's lives. We cannot here attempt an analysis either of contemporary pessimism—it sometimes goes so far as a pervasive sense of doom—or of what, for want of a better name, must be called contemporary anti-intellectualism.[2]

Both attitudes are, of course, responses to what two centuries of experience have done to the dream, the ideal, of the eighteenth-century Enlightenment, to the hope of a heaven on earth. Let me repeat: a great number of men had by 1789 come to believe, with Condorcet, that—I put this mildly and cautiously—at the very least a large proportion of what most men most of the time think and feel as *evil,* wars, physical suffering, poverty, frustrations, above all, frustrations clearly assignable to human willing and human power, would cease to be. But the matter deserves to be put more sharply, in no mere loose comparison, but in terms of lasting human sentiments: the true believers in the religion of progress and humanity at the end of the eighteenth century, like the Christians of the first few generations, were millenarians who believed there would be an immediate and total alteration of

1 Denis de Rougemont, *Love in the Western World,* p. 115.
2 I refer once more to my *Ideas and Men,* Chapter XIV, and the books therein suggested for supplementary reading.

man's state. For them, the French Revolution of 1789 was a true millennial event—a First Coming of Reason. We and our nineteenth-century predecessors have been struggling with the task of adapting the new faith to an old world that would not *totally* alter, would not, in fact, alter anything like enough to satisfy any dreamer.

But we must not expect our history to *follow* in detail in any useful sense the history of the first three Christian centuries. To make an analogy on an analogy: no clinician would expect a complicated illness to take an identically or even necessarily very closely detailed course in two quite different individuals. He would try to use a finished case to help him understand a current case, but he would be at least as alert to note differences as to note similarities.[3] The differences between the first three Christian centuries and the first three—or two and a half—Enlightened centuries seem already marked. Our present-day Christianity seems more persistent under Enlightened attack, above all, more adaptable, than was paganism under Christian attack. The new faith of the Enlightenment is related, subtly and in complex ways not understood of the many, or indeed of the few, to a way of using the human mind relatively little developed in the Greco-Roman culture, that of natural science. The new faith is related to a political organization, the modern nation-state, that did not exist in the One [Western] World of the Roman Empire, and that, in spite of the Toynbees and other prophets of doom, is still a very sturdy political organization. To have been even approximately parallel in this respect, Christianity would have had to appear during the great balance-of-power struggle among the superpowers after the death of Alexander the Great, that is, three centuries or so earlier than in fact it did appear. The new faith has an ethical code that makes material satisfactions in themselves a good; or, to put it negatively, the new faith has no distrust of the flesh as such, no anchorites who flee the world, no condemnation, at least in its orthodox forms, for the world as such. The new faith has a melioristic, even an idealistic, ethics, and makes a somewhat illogical recognition of what in Christianity is minimal moral Puritanism; and in its orthodox form of nationalist democracy it has made the kind of compromise with its ideals that the rigorous, the pure Christian holds Christianity had made by the time of Constantine, if not before. Yet the heresies of the new faith lack the variety of early Christian heresies, even seem in the twentieth century to have

---

[3] My conscious mind tells me firmly that I do *not* mean that a religion, or a cosmology, is a kind of disease; as a good child of my age, I cannot wholly disavow my unconscious mind, which may mean just that, or worse.

been incorporated into a single one, Marxism, which in its turn has made extraordinary compromises with the nation-state. In short, the differences between the total situation of early Christianity and the total situation of the new faith in progress, democracy, material satisfactions, the natural goodness and reasonableness of man, science culminating in cultural engineering—in short, the faith of the Enlightenment—are very great indeed, so great that no sensible person would attempt to predict the future of the new faith from the past of the old.

One cannot, as I have insisted, even name the new faith, which has no single name of its own, and no single church, and to many does not even seem to be a religion. Democracy, which both the free world and the Communist world claim as theirs, is perhaps the most current term for the new faith and the new church. But in the free world Christianity and democracy have made mutual adjustments, and the word "religion" is for most people reserved for Christianity and other theisms, and for what the anthropologist calls religion. In the Communist world and among the anti-Christians in the free world rebellion against Christian theism is so strong that the word "religion" is for them an indecent word. It would be nice if we had another word that would do the work of "religion," and tie together instances of human behavior that the classifying intellect finds it useful to put together, not at the species level, but at the genus level. But I know of no such useful word, and refuse to coin one.

It may, however, be wise to avoid altogether the Toynbean pitfalls of comparison between the Greco-Roman world and our own and simply put the matter in terms of our modern history. In the eighteenth century an important number of human beings in the West came to take toward man's fate here on earth an attitude only a few human beings had taken previously, an attitude nowhere better summed up than in the words of one of the leaders of those who took this new view: all men on earth have rights to "life, liberty, and the pursuit of happiness." These rights were the more important because Jefferson and many of his fellows were fairly sure that no one had any other life anywhere save his own present one on this earth. They held that these rights could be realized here on earth by reforms in political, educational, economic, and social institutions, reforms men could agree on if they were allowed the free use of a faculty hitherto cramped and perverted in most men, the faculty of *Reason,* which has to be given an initial capital letter. The more extreme of them held that the reforms must include a reform ending forever the kind of institution known as "churches," which had in their eyes been chiefly responsible for the cramping and perverting of Reason in men; even the more moderate among them looked forward to a gradual withering away of the Christian churches, or to their transformation into institutions of the kind Americans will recognize under the term "Unitarian."

Now I shall call this set of attitudes toward man's fate the "faith" of the Enlightenment, thus dodging temporarily at least the word "religion," though clinging through the word "faith" to what seems to me inescapable in man's fate: for us all, both "seeing is believing" and "believing is seeing" are true and necessary statements, but the latter usually prevails in a conflict. The rationalism of the eighteenth century of course denied the second proposition, partly under the mistaken notion that the natural scientist denied it in his practical life. I propose in this chapter to examine in very broad lines what has happened to this faith in the West in the twentieth century, as I have already done for some of the things that happened to it in the nineteenth century.

II

First of all, the continuities of the faith of the Enlightenment need emphasis, if only because so many twentieth-century intellectuals, especially, but by no means solely, in Europe, have bemoaned or cheered its extinction. It is very much alive, and growing as faiths grow, in the midst of setbacks, quarrels, and adaptations to changing conditions. The twentieth century, as we all know, confronted the new faith with two general wars separated by a great world-wide depression, and with an ever-present threat of a third general war to be fought with weapons that many experts believed were powerful enough to destroy the human race, or, at the very least, to make what we call "civilization" impossible after the apocalyptic horrors of this general war. Nearly two centuries after Condorcet, his "tenth epoch" to come could, now that it has come, be made to look even worse than the "ninth epoch" he believed was ending in his time. No one in his senses would call the world in the 1950's heaven on earth, Utopia, the realized promise of the Enlightenment; few intellectuals at least, even in the United States, would be willing to call it morally a clearly *better* world than that of 1750.

And yet in some ways, if he could analyze parts instead of facing the whole, or the defective parts, that would probably first strike his *philosophe's* mind, a Condorcet brought back to earth would not be altogether disappointed. With respect to what had been achieved by "Reason," as he would call it, working through science and technology to increase human ability to get some of the things men want through command over natural resources, Condorcet would surely find his greatest hopes fantastically exceeded. This hardly needed saying, but let us say it. I incline to the belief that he would be impressed with what "Reason" has achieved even in the fields of social or behavioral science. He would, of course, be shocked at the evidences that superstition, the fanaticism called "Christianity" had not been wholly eliminated; but he would meet many kindred souls well above such superstition, would perhaps recognize that for the faith of the Enlightenment, also, the blood of the martyrs—of which he was one—has been the seed of the church. He would find millions who believe that they can and should be happy here on earth, that happiness consists, in important part, at least, in the satisfaction of what common sense has long regarded as normal or natural human wants for good food, good shelter, good sex life, good family life, good work, good amusements, good self-esteem, that they and their children and their children's children will get increasing increments, so to speak, of such happiness, that this process is Progress, world without end, and a good thing, an end, a purpose, an eschatology.[4]

Concretely, some of what I have noted above, with no ironic intent, has been achieved. In many parts of the West in the 1950's—not by any means solely in the United States—more people have more material satisfactions than ever before. For many, many people the simple, clear, indubitable forms of actual physical suffering which, as I have insisted throughout this book, have been endemic in all Western history—the violence and uncertainty of life men long took as simply given—have been greatly reduced. And as part of this reduction there has come the whole set of changes in our moral attitude I have summed up as "humanitarian." Actual cruelty and, more important, indifference to suffering felt unavoidable have indeed greatly diminished in the last few centuries. Belsen and Hiroshima, the threat of the H-bomb, are real enough, and as symbols must stand for grave and continuing moral dangers. But they do not make a paradox; we have not grown crueler as we have grown more secure from violence and sudden death in the daily round of ordinary life. We have not been able to eliminate the moral evils of war and race conflict, but the new faith, like Christianity, does consider these as evil, an evil to be resisted, destroyed.

---

[4] On the strength of these beliefs in the United States, see C. A. Chambers, "The Belief in Progress in Twentieth Century America," *Journal of the History of Ideas,* Vol. XIX, April 1958, pp. 197-224.

That whole aspect of the new faith summed up by the word "democ-racy"—it is, of course, an aspect that is separable only in analysis from the ethical and cosmological attitudes I have just discussed—is one of the continuities that link the twentieth with the eighteenth century. Here, too, one can argue that twentieth-century opposition to what we Americans understand by democracy is, save for a few intellectuals, rather heresy than denial of the faith. Certainly the Communists continue to insist that theirs is the only *real* democracy; and even the various fascist sects, though they insisted that our parliamentary democracy is corrupt and decadent, though they were chary about claiming themselves to be true democrats, nonetheless paid firm trib-ute to one of the fundamentals of the new faith: the individual here on earth should be happy, secure, well-off. Highest happiness is, indeed, in some of these totalitarian theories the service of the state, self-sacrifice for the state. But this concept, too, is not strange to the Western democracies, and is clear already in Rousseau. And the relentless pressure from the many to translate their right to happiness into material goods, consumer goods, is clear where-ever the Western culture has penetrated—that is, throughout the world.

It is hardly necessary to dwell on the fact that nationalism is still very much alive, that the nation-state is all over the West the nearest thing to a church for the new faith. The normal Western way remains in this respect, as in so many, a middle way. The extreme fascist position that the nation-state, always in essence at war with other nation-states, should be for the individual the whole of life, a Sparta of the soul, hardly was real even for the most consecrated devotees. In this modern Western world, the paradox of a comfortable Sparta, or of a self-denying devotion to the delights that modern science and technology have made available, was too great for the many. On the other hand, complete transcendence of the nation-state in some form of world government or world federation, the actual concrete limitation of national "independence" or "sovereignty" was still in mid-twentieth cen-tury the aim of a relatively small high-minded minority everywhere. Pacifism, conscientious objection, passive resistance of the sort associated with the name of Gandhi, all such efforts to live down the long Western tradition that makes the struggle for prize in the end a *fight* are still in the West the views of the crank, views of a not very effective minority. Meanwhile, as Western culture spreads around the world, nationalism in its characteristic Western form spreads around the world. To most Americans, this spread seems a good thing. American sympathy goes out to Arabs and Asians as it once went out to Irish and Greeks and Poles struggling against their foreign masters; and not the least clear of the survivals of the optimism of the Enlightenment among us is the belief that a self-conscious oppressed national group, once it has become a free nation-state, will get along with other nation-states in the concord Nature intended.

Most important of all, there survives, and at its strongest, no doubt, in North America, the belief in the natural goodness and reasonableness of man. This belief has certainly been 'qualified, chastened, stripped of its revolutionary implications of *immediate* revolutionary perfectability of man. It has, as we shall soon see, been very seriously challenged by many modern thinkers. It was never held as an absolute by the man in the street, certainly not held as a description of the way he and his neighbors conduct themselves. But it does survive as a negative in a strong distrust of what I may crudely symbolize as any form of the shepherd-sheep relation among human beings, including that of the planner to those for whom the planning is done, and it survives as a positive in the conviction that somehow or other out of long, free, complete discussion there will result, even on the scale of the populous nation-state, a "sense of the meeting," decisions, on the whole, wise, certainly the best available.

Democracy—a fine, loose, accurate word here—has in the nation-state its church, with, of course, its rituals, in happiness for all here on earth, its eschatology, by now no longer chiliastic, and a most complicated and elaborate network of approved ways of reaching its ethical ideal, the "sense of the meeting." Much of this elaborate network it owes to the long past, and particularly to Christianity. To Christianity it owes the feeling for the individual as an end, for the "dignity of man."[5] To Christianity it owes the form its moral awareness takes, the form I have called "minimal puritanism." Nothing is more striking than the persistence through the last two centuries of this feeling of conscience, moral responsibility, the civil war in the breast. The Owen we took in Chapter XI as a sample of the logical extremist of the Enlightenment (see p. 299), the Owen who carried the simple environmentalism of the age to the point of fixing on the inculcation of a sense of individual moral responsibility as the source of all evil has never been taken seriously by many in the West. The complainers have seen this individual sense of moral responsibility disappearing under the influence of belief in the natural goodness of man, or belief in utilitarian ethics, or belief in progressive education, or belief in Freudian psychology—or even belief in economic

[5] I see no need to apologize for this language as vague and woolly; it is very precise.

determinism. The man watcher can only note that under any and all modern systems of belief in the impossibility of the individual's choosing between good and evil, better or worse, and of belief in the irrationality of guilt feelings, the individual goes on choosing between what he thinks is good and evil, and goes on feeling guilty if he chooses what he thinks is evil.[6]

The individual in our society does not by any means agree with other individuals completely as to what he thinks good and what he thinks evil. Our modern Western democracy is, in fact, reconciled to, perhaps can be said to rejoice in, sometimes and in some ways, a good deal of ethical relativism. In practice, it has a strong instinct, or, what may be better, a habit, historically developed or "cultivated," for accepting variety. It has also, as a system of regulating human relations, a good many ways of promoting uniformity. In big broad lines, democracy, developing the healthy ambivalences of real life, values both variety and uniformity, both liberty and equality. One has to live in a given democratic society to know where it draws the line between these two apparently antithetical aims. The bulk of recent critical literature finds the achieved balance less than happy, and insists that modern democracy, notably in its dominant American form, leans unduly toward the side of conformity, equality, leveling toward a dead, if materially fairly high, level.[7]

I do not greatly quarrel with this verdict, but I should like to point out here that in practice so far democracy has meant no end to the various traditional Western ways of giving external emphasis to the "fact" that men are

[6] Of course I cannot "prove" this assertion, but I do not think it is a mere *obiter dictum.* Any alert observer of current events, any reader of the miscellany we call literature over the last few centuries would come to a similar conclusion. Note that I am not discussing the relative prevalence of the Thrasymachan doctrine: the good, the just, is for the individual what he can get away with. I shall try in the next chapter to come to grips with the question of how far this moral "cynicism" (the popular name for it, adequate enough, though not fair to the original Greek Cynic school) does prevail at different times and places. If I may briefly anticipate here, it clearly cannot prevail in a simple, well-knit small society (early Rome, early Boston, or, *with respect to the ethics of the group,* such a group as officers in the armed forces or physicians). On the other hand, this "cynicism" is always present and often preached in any great, developed, complex civilized society, but is rarely if ever dominant. Really frantic "moralists"—Mr. Sorokin will do as a sample—who hold that our entire "sensate" culture has gone to the dogs morally seem to me simply not to register, not to see what's there, not to be man watchers at all.

[7] Two examples, from very different points of view: David Riesman, *The Lonely Crowd,* New York, Doubleday, 1955, and Eric von Kuehnelt-Leddihn, *Liberty versus Equality,* London, Hollis and Carter, 1952. Good reporters like F. L. Allen, *The Big Change* (New York, Harper, 1952), and Max Lerner, *America as Civilization* (New York, Simon & Schuster, 1958), are aware that ours is indeed a pluralistic society, full of human variation; but both tend to emphasize the leveling of the last fifty years which has made us all, from millionaire to sharecropper, "middle class."

by no means identical, no end to the struggle for prize—indeed, its extension, rather—no end to the economic pyramid, the peck order, heroes and hero worship. The century of the common man so far has turned out to be the century of the record breaker, the century of Lindbergh, Babe Ruth, stormers of Everest, spreaders of charisma in all directions. We in America are still against dukes, but not against "brand-name" aristocrats.

In sum, in the rather less than bird's-eye view we have in a book of this sort been able to give to the record of Western man as a moral person, he still looks recognizable, looks almost natural, in this mid-twentieth century. He still looks more like that man of Alexander Pope, still on the isthmus of his middle state, than the lower-case god that the Enlightenment hoped for, or any of the numerous creatures—ape, lion, ass, dog, worm—he has been compared to.[8]

III

No one, not even a hearty, cheerful complainer like Mencken, sure that this is the worst of possible worlds, and a damned good thing, ought in these days to make light of the temper of Western thinkers. In my first chapter I insisted that there is indeed a gap, of the sort Mencken himself loved to emphasize, between the common man, worried perhaps over his little concerns, but clearly not harassed by world trouble, and the intellectual classes, some of whom are always Platos, always Juvenals, always Abelards, always Luthers. But the gap is not a wall; there is always some communication, better or worse, across it. There are also great variations in the temper—let us simplify, and say in the quantity and quality of complaining—among the critical intellectuals of a given age.[9]

[8] Once more, I do wish to drive home the Utopian implications of the pure faith of the Enlightenment. We might get an effective symbol if we telescoped the titles of two well-known books by twentieth-century Enlightened believers: *Man Makes Himself* by V. Gordon Childe and *Men like Gods* (New York, Macmillan, 1923) by H. G. Wells, into *Man Makes Himself like Gods*. Let me repeat, this faith does survive in our culture.
[9] There is great need for a good modern history of the intellectual classes in the West. Such a history would at least attempt a morphology of such classes in historic societies, and, an even more difficult task, an account of relations in time among them, that is, a genetics or dynamics of their evolution. Or if this is too ambitious—as I guess it is—it would be helpful to have a comparative study of samples of intellectual classes in different societies from the point of view of the nature and extent of their "alienation"—what they complain of, and how vigorously, what they want in place of what they dislike, and how much success they have in furthering their hopes.

Ours would seem to be an age of grave fears. The intellectual temper of our age is a gloomy one—an indignant gloom, for we are still children of the fighting West. The well-trained scientific mind distrusts the single instance, above all, when it is made to carry symbolic weight as a generalization. But the nonscientist may still be quite impressed by putting Condorcet, after all, a philosopher of history of a sort, square up against our own Toynbee. The difference is one of those immeasurable differences that confound the measuring mind. I contrast them, not so much for their views of what the future will be like, but for their feelings about their present. Condorcet in the midst of the Terror, outlawed and in hiding, death at hand, seems ready to burst into a prosaic freethinker's version of Pippa's song:

Reason's a-working—
All's right with the world

Toynbee in the midst of the highest standard of general prosperity the West has ever known shudders at the horrors around him.[10] Toynbee has lived his life in our paradoxical day of great material improvement for the common as for the uncommon man, two shocking wars, a world depression, and the threat of another war of apocalyptic horror. As a sensitive man, he could hardly help contrasting this reality with the hopes, not only of the Enlightenment, but with those of his own Victorian teachers. Something had gone wrong.

It is by no means clear as yet whether the numerous critics of the world view of the Enlightenment and its Victorian emendations have in our time gone very far toward a shared world view of their own. They are not in agreement. The "return to religion"—that is, to some form of Christianity—has hitherto been far from universal, though it is certainly in mid-twentieth century real enough. There remain throughout the West solid groups of free-thinkers, all reluctant to give up the eighteenth-century dream. There are less

[10] Simply as historians of civilization, there is an interesting difference. Condorcet clearly has no explanation at all for how one of his epochs grows into another, no notion of a dynamics of civilization. Toynbee is acutely aware that he has to explain just how one of his climbers on the cliff hoists himself up; he has to account for change by something less vague and more consistent with evidence than Condorcet's "reason" or "enlightenment." Toynbee's debt to Darwin, however, clashes with his hopes from Jesus and Buddha, and he takes refuge in a vague eschatology. But he cannot quite escape the intellectual heritage of much scientific work of the last two centuries, a sense that cultural evolution among men is a long, slow, irregular process, timed and worked out on a different scale from our human hopes and fears, our dramatic, and our moral, senses. He wants a miracle, but unlike Condorcet, he cannot quite believe in miracles—or, rather, he has to try to persuade himself to a belief in miracles.

solid but more numerous groups of the indifferent, worried often enough, but hearing no good news. A great number of churchgoers, especially in North America, are still firm adherents of a belief that ought—if "ought" were a part of ordinary logic—to separate them from the class of Christians; this is the belief that "man makes himself." There are indeed nuclei of traditional Christians in the Roman Catholic and in other communions; and in neo-orthodoxy there has been a revival of traditional Christian insistence on original sin.

The major philosophical movement of our time most directly set against rationalist optimism is secularist existentialism, a revival of Stoicism peppered with heavy dashes of modern aesthetics and psychology. The two obvious general currents of mind in our time, historicism and anti-intellectualism, are both currents set against the rationalism and optimism of the eighteenth century, but they have not yet flowed into any great common reservoir. Our awareness of history has so far not gone very far toward putting limits on our inherited belief in comparatively sudden, even planned, permanent change; indeed, the simplifier might be tempted to say that for the eighteenth-century hope of immediate universal bliss we—or, rather, our intellectuals—have substituted fear of immediate universal catastrophe. Similarly, some currents of modern anti-intellectualism, though they are free enough from belief in the natural reasonableness of ordinary men, have ended up with programs of cultural engineering, the skilled engineers working with Madison Avenue methods but fine humanitarian ideals on the raw irrationalities of human beings to produce just what Condorcet foresaw. No doubt our awareness of history and our awareness of the role that drives, prejudices, sentiments, habits, all the long role of unreason, play in all we do have combined to make a great many modern Westerners aware also that the hope of heaven on earth was itself unreasonable and unhistorical. But all this has not by any means been molded into what I must continue to apologize for calling by the unlovely term of "world view." Our Western faith has not in mid-twentieth century been given the organization, the codification, the clarity of central beliefs, that we should have if we are to find in our faith, our world view, the moral guide, above all, the moral support we need. But to this topic we shall return in conclusion.

Meanwhile, the specific moral evils our prophets call to our attention must be briefly noted. One whole class of such evils one may hesitatingly call the "private vices of self-indulgence." It should be clear to the reader that I find the realistic study of the extent of these vices in any society difficult indeed.

They are not even very private, for indulgence in them affects all those close to the indulger; moreover, especially since the current of eighteenth-century humanitarianism mingled with that of puritanism, society through government has in many parts of the West sought to regulate and sometimes prohibit such familiar human conduct as gambling, fornication—especially in the form of organized prostitution—consumption of alcoholic drinks, cruel sports, the duel, and many others. I doubt if the most extravagant philosophic anarchist would maintain that the sum total of these efforts has actually *increased* the sum total of human self-indulgence they were directed against. On the contrary, it seems clear that in most of the West sports like bearbaiting have been eliminated, the duel reduced to sheer eccentricity, and gambling somewhat reduced. The extraordinary attempt to prohibit entirely the use of alcoholic drinks in the United States by constitutional amendment is now accepted by all save fanatical prohibitionists as a failure; but in most of the West more moderate regulation of the use of alcohol has, if one takes the early eighteenth-century West as a point for comparison, greatly reduced public drunkenness. We are beginning to recognize chronic alcoholism as a form of mental disease.

Those who believe that conduct in the twentieth-century West has fallen to a low point as measured by our traditional—or at any rate by our modern best—standards of morality usually place great emphasis on our modern attitudes toward matters of sex.[11] There is no doubt that we talk, write, and print more freely on all aspects of sex relations than did our nineteenth-century predecessors. There is a great deal of pornography in print and illustration which seems to me fairly constant over the centuries, and which has been under the moral ban of Christianity from the beginning, and was certainly not held consonant with the beautiful-and-good of the Greeks. Most of this material has come under the ban of the kind of humanitarian-puritan legislation I have mentioned above, and has been driven in our day even further underground than in the past; but of course it is still there. What our moralists are really concerned with is the extent to which seriously meant art and literature—not necessarily *good* art and literature—and the conventions of good manners are infiltrated by words and sentiments that to them bear the stamp of pornographic concern. As far as externals go, it is clear that the twentieth century permits much the nineteenth century forbade. Whether we have got

[11] I shall in this bird's-eye view of this whole phase of morality—sex, family, divorce, juvenile delinquency, crimes of violence—concentrate chiefly on twentieth-century United States. If we may believe our European critics, we set the pace in these matters, and should therefore provide a fair sample.

back to eighteenth-century standards is a nice point for critical discussion. That latter century for the most part enjoyed the salt of sex in its art and letters, but it liked a gloss of refinement, and avoided what we call "realism" —no four-letter words, at least, not in print, no uncomely nudity, no pseudo-clinical relish. We have not, in my opinion, got back to the grossness of the late Middle Ages, nor to the extraordinary frankness of a Latin writer like Martial.[12]

But the ultimate concern of those who feel we are far sunk in sexual excess goes deeper than the externals of old-fashioned pornography. They hold, though they might not put it at all this way, that the tradition of courtly love and romantic love has in the twentieth century got vulgarized, has spread through popular literature, the movies, and even through the popularization and simplification of the work of Freud and other psychologists, and now holds the many in its obsessive coil. American youth, in particular, assaulted by all the mass media, encouraged even in formal education, has come, it is maintained, to regard the pleasures of sex as a kind of supreme good. Sexual prowess, always in the West a form of distinction, part of the struggle for prize, has for the many been lifted to the highest prize of all, within the reach of all. The result is sexual promiscuity, frustration, failures, rivalries without end, a grave moral contagion in a world already sinking.[13]

With this alarming diagnosis the historian will hardly agree. Much of the actual conduct reported in the two Kinsey reports cannot have surprised him, and must have surprised even less a practicing physician, a counsellor, any-one exercising cure of souls, or anyone who knew anything of Western world literature since Homer and Moses. Today, as in the long past, much human concern with matters of sex remains vicarious, a consolation, a surrogate, and not a stimulus. The high-minded in a democracy have difficulty forgiving the low-minded, who in our modern times are very numerous and very noticeable. Moreover—and this is most important—a moderately high-minded observer of the American scene in particular ought to recognize that many of the young today are high-minded indeed about sex relations, children, the family. They want what they consider normal genital satisfactions, they want children

---

12 The reader of German—and anyone who can look at pictures—can follow this line between art and pornography for the centuries from the Renaissance through the nine-teenth in Eduard Fuchs, *Illustrierte Sittengeschichte,* Munich, Albert Langen, 1909-1912. The text is a very full social history of sex *mores* in Western Europe, but it is not a history of morals.
13 I refer once more to P. A. Sorokin, *The American Sex Revolution,* a most un-clinical and unrealistic study.

—the sudden leap in the birth rate among the American upper classes in our time is surely a challenge to the naïve alarmist as it is to the demographic behavioral scientist—and they want a successful married partnership. The books on sex and marriage that they read, part of the great American do-it-yourself literature, are essentially manuals of piety, and indeed many of the young succeed in being most unco' guid about sex. In all seriousness, I think an objective reporter on the American scene would have to conclude that, with the exception of what is sometimes called "café society," or "Holly-wood," that characteristic modern American equivalent of a fine corrupt old-fashioned aristocracy, the sexual morality of modern America is rather stricter than at many periods of Western history. And even café society itself, in these days when more of the middle-class proprieties survive than the alarmist will admit, cannot indulge itself as freely and publicly as many such privileged groups in the past. Messalina could not survive long even in Los Angeles.[14]

But the divorce rate? The rate is high indeed, particularly in the United States, and reflects in part, surely, the inevitable disappointments of a sexual relation exalted into something ineffable. It also reflects the gradual loosening of religious sanctions for strict monogamy, the gradual development of hedonistic ethical attitudes, the wide acceptance of the view that marriage is simply one of many forms of human relations—a job, a club membership—which can and should be broken off if either or both parties find it an unsatisfactory one. All this is true. It is true also that divorce is often bad for the children. But in itself our high divorce rate is not a sign of sexual looseness or promiscuity; indeed, as continental Europeans accustomed to such age-old institutions as the mistress like to point out, our American addiction to divorce is in itself a tribute to our high standards for marriage. The really grave aspect of the whole American sex problem is not so much one of sex morality in its narrow sense, but of its part in the larger context of our discontents and fears, to which I shall come at the end of this section.

Juvenile delinquency? Statistics would seem to show an increase here. The increase comes for the most part, however, not from precocious crimes of serious nature, robbery, murder, gangster violence, but, rather, from a great

[14] My guess is that we have passed in this country the peak of serious-minded pseudo-"Freudian" sex. Frigidity in women—or, at least, inability to get a fine explosive or-gasm—is beginning to seem not quite so immoral as it did a few years ago. Even light-minded folk sex may well be receding, not to Victorian suppression, but, still, to somewhat less conspicuousness in American life.

increase in just old-fashioned bad behavior, from truancy and showing-off to indiscipline and what Hollywood has christened the "blackboard jungle." Here, too, there are obvious explanations. The movement for permissive or progressive education, like most social experiments—perhaps I should write, like most experiments—has borne fruits not expected by its pioneers. Parental discipline has surely been greatly relaxed. Some of the blame put on the mass media belongs there, belongs on the makers of movies and on television. But, above all, we have here in the United States attempted to occupy several hundreds of thousands of adolescents in what, with all the abatements made by educators in the rigorous classical training of Western tradition, with all the basket weaving, ceramics, physical education, and preparation for twentieth-century living, is still a formal schooling. Never before in the West has there been anything like such universal formal education. It is pretty clear now that for a very significant number of these young people such education is too great a strain, affords a constant temptation, granted the whole atmosphere of our culture, to active rebellion. If we can afford to "educate" them, we must surely educate them even less classically than we try to.[15]

Crimes of violence? Those who complain that such crimes are the mark of our age, those who are shocked and surprised by continuing gangsterism, by the criminal elements in American labor unions, and all the rest show even more than the usual American unwillingness to recall the unpleasant past. Two strands of violence go far back in our relatively brief history; there is the violence of the frontier, caricatured as well as glorified in the "Western," and there is the violence of our great cities packed with a steady stream of immigrants ignorant of our ways. One of these strands, that of lynching, has almost disappeared from American life, and has not yet re-emerged even in the current crisis over integration in Southern schools. The dramatic drop from a high point of 130 lynchings in 1901 (mostly Negroes) to zero in 1952 is difficult to explain, and impossible to explain if you take the position of the prophet of unrelieved doom. Actually, with continued improvement in police methods there has been over the last few generations a gradual relative lessening of crimes of violence in the United States. We are still the most dis-

---

15 I am not making light of the conditions revealed in such studies as that in the New York *Times* in March 1958, which showed how the well-meant slum clearances in New York had helped breed new adolescent gangsters. But first, these problems are not at all new; they have always been part of great urban complexes. Second, we are very aware of them, and work hard to do something about them. The Western drive to reform, to clean up, seems to me in no sense diminished in mid-twentieth century. We are still very moral people, in no field more desirous of doing the right thing than in education.

orderly country in the West, but we have by no means got back to our own frontier days.

Finally, there is a whole broad field of public morality, ranging from sharp commercial practices through the vast reaches of what Americans call "graft," through mink coats and paid-up hotel bills, and on to treason. Here once more common sense, and perhaps the social sciences, must reach a whiggish conclusion: the total situation is not as bad as the professional complainers make it out to be, nor as good as the professional happiness boys make it out to be. In a culture as competitive and as multanimous as ours there is bound to be a good deal of cheating, a good deal of pretense. But the growth of public regulation and even, in part, the very competition that spurs on the evil help correct it. Public-health measures, and especially regulation of food and drugs, have in a major field reduced the evils summed up in the old phrase *caveat emptor*—a traditional phrase which, by the way, should give pause to the lovers of the economic past. All but the very "liberal" would agree that American business morality is, notably in regard to trusts, better now than in 1900. The era of the Robber Barons is well over. Political and economic competition, if it heightens the nervous tension of our lives, also makes it difficult to continue for long any major fraud save what to a few Westerners must seem the fraud of all life on this earth. The voice of a modern Cicero against a modern Verres gets magnified and broadcast by all the means technology gives us. The whole apparatus of publicity, the sales apparatus, that terrifies or disgusts an Ortega, an Orwell, a Koestler, can be, and sometimes is, used on the side of the angels; indeed, some of our most articulate angels of the Enlightenment have learned to use the apparatus of the mass media with almost as much skill as the demons.

There is, however, a different category of moral ills of our time as the exacting critics see them, a category even less easy to observe and measure than the conduct we have been surveying. This category may perhaps be grasped best as failure of *morale,* as not so much indulgence in evil as apathy, Laodiceanism, lack of moral fervor. One whole aspect of this approach to the ills of the modern West has come up often already in this study: the view, to state it at its broadest, that we are getting to be too conformist, too much alike, too much social animals, and that, conversely, we are losing our individuality, originality, our interesting wildness. This view is often, perhaps usually, coupled with the view that although *within* the state or society—the given beehive—we are taming the agon, there has grown up *among* the new beehives, and particularly between the two biggest, busiest, and best organized, the wildest and most murderous competition ever yet known. To this last point I shall shortly return. In the meantime, the broad assertion that modern Western society is getting too conformist, too "security-conscious," too "other-directed," is in fact so broad, so vague, that assent to or dissent from it must be a matter of one's sentiments, indeed of one's moods. Even the sketchiest attempt at empirical testing of the thesis is difficult and confusing.

One special phase of the master generalization, the assertion that in the United States the younger generation want security, not adventure, want a job, better, a position, not to be their own boss, that they want to be "organization men," not "captains of industry," might be tested along such lines as the following: first, a historical approach, comparing the United States with the older countries of Europe, from which it might appear that some of what the complainers dislike is due to economic and social maturity, which is not necessarily senescence; second, an analysis of the way inventions, innovations, improvements of all sorts, do get made today, for they undoubtedly do, and a further analysis of the almost innumerable forms of real competition in our society and our economy; third, a good study of the extent to which the young actually *do* succeed in one way or another in being their own bosses, in being nonorganization men—for nothing is commoner in the study of human relations, even among those hardheaded men the economists, than the premature announcement that "x is no more."

I incline personally to the judgment, certainly a subjective one, that Homo sapiens, even in his American variety, is still closer to his mammalian cousins —and not to the most sheeplike of these—than to the social insects. The publicists, sometimes the same ones who find the young lacking in adventurousness, in *true* competitiveness, complain that they accept no moral restraints on their will to win, on their part in the struggle for prize. Here the favorite instance is the one of the West Point football players who cheated on examinations even though this was against their officer's sense of honor. The historian might here be tempted to point out that the Roman or medieval military honor from which that of our officer's caste is derived would not have been as exacting in an analogous case—the field of an examination of this sort is banausic, vulgar, and the temptation of winning is, after all, the strongest of temptations—as in one that equated honor and physical courage. There is no doubt however, that these young men violated a real moral law of our culture. True enough, they were themselves a group, and, within that group, no doubt very imitative and inner-directed. And the essential element in their behavior was the old and human desire to come out on top; one even hears remotely the echo of the Homeric *aien aristeuein*—always to be best in masculine excellences. This, one supposes, never comes out in the beehive or anthill, not even among the warrior insects.

We have yet to face what is to the prophets of doom, and to many publicists who do not merit that emotion-charged label, the full horror of our age, the ultimate source, the final justification, of our doubts, our worries, our despair. Specifically, this is a threat of what the journalists call "World War III," a war that, to judge from the precedent of the last two and the known achievements of technology, might destroy so many people and so many things that what we call civilization would be impossible anywhere on earth, war that certainly would bring about fearful suffering of the sort repugnant to our whole moral tradition. The human imagination has had its full range on the possibilities, which at the most extreme include the extinction of all forms of life, plant and animal, on earth. The point I wish to make here is simply that once more the horrors of the Book of Revelation begin for many to seem real and present.

Yet only an alarmist would detect in our Western society sure signs of the apocalyptic moral abandon, the collapse of *morale* our best clichés from history illustrate well enough: "after us the deluge," "fiddling while Rome burns," *je-m'en-foutisme,* "the handwriting on the wall," the death's head at the feast. I have perhaps already insisted sufficiently that diagnosis of the state of mind and heart of a whole contemporary culture is exceedingly difficult, and in any scientific sense, impossible. But I do not feel around me today the atmosphere of mass despair Huizinga and his fellows have described for the late Middle Ages, nor the seething of mass unrest that comes out of almost anything written in and of the decades just before and just after the birth of Christ. It is, indeed, possible, if one may apply to large groups, even to a whole culture, the terminology of a science based on the study of individual behavior, that there may be states of collective psychopathology, and that we may now be in one even more widespread and serious than that of the fifteenth century.[16]

The fear of a third World War may, then, be driving us all—all of us Westerners at any rate—into mass madness. But if so, that madness is not yet reflected in the sum totals that record man's daily round of work, of social routine, of conventional behavior. That sum total, as I have tried in this

[16] In a perceptive essay, "The Next Assignment," *American Historical Review,* Vol. LXIII, January 1958, Mr. W. L. Langer suggests that the collective trauma of the Black Death may well have been an important determinant of the behavior Huizinga and others have recorded.

chapter to urge against the newspaper headlines, comes out at least no worse in terms of conventional moral standards than at other times in Western history. Let me attempt a final symbol: in the United States some hundred million individuals, many of them adolescents, their skills, their bodily and mental health and capacities subject to no more than most casual testing, have each at his command on open roads vehicles capable of greater speeds than their grandfathers' steam locomotives, which were tied to rails and driven by trained professionals subject to rigorous and frequent tests of health and ability; yet these millions of automobile drivers in 1956 killed only one person for about every ten million vehicle miles they drove in the state with the worst record, one person for about every forty-three million vehicle miles in the state with the best record. There are, of course, many variables involved —the work of automotive engineers and of highway engineers, the education and conditioning of Americans from youth up, and many others. But I think it hard for anyone to deny to our old mythical friend the "average" American some sense of moral responsibility in his dealings with the almost incredible power he commands at a touch. What the alarmist finds a very bad sign of human failings seems to me, in fact, a sign of human capacities and sense of responsibility. If men were as bad as some moralists hold, we should kill many more than 40,000 a year on our roads.

Our moral tradition insists that we refuse to accept any death in an automobile accident as necessary; it insists, indeed, that we must not even put the statistics as above, but that we recoil with horror and indignation from that simple net figure of some 40,000 traffic deaths per year, that we feel the need of all sorts of concerted measures and campaigns to reduce that figure. No one should complain of this very human and probably very useful moral attitude. If it is true that the statistics show that juvenile delinquents, sexual psychopaths, kidnapers, wife beaters are still in the United States relative to the total population very few indeed, it is also true that our horror and alarm at the conduct of such persons is in full accord with our moral tradition, and in particular with our Christian tradition as modified by the humanitarianism and hedonism of the Enlightenment. Modern Western democracy is, its critics notwithstanding, at least as much committed to the "better" as to the "bigger."

IV

It would seem likely—though I should guess almost impossible to prove empirically—that the moral anguish of our age is rather the mark of the intellectual classes in our West than of the many. We must at least attempt here a cursory sketch of a problem worth careful and objective study: the problem of the attitude of the intellectual classes in our own age and in its immediate predecessors toward the universe and man's fate in it. Unfortunately, neither historians nor sociologists have yet given us a really good base from which to start such a sketch: we cannot be confident about the normal, the customary, position of such classes in the West, nor even of their constitution, their make-up.

As a rough definition, we may call the intellectual classes those who write, teach, preach, practice the fine arts, music, drama. These people are not by any means the only ones in the West who use their minds, their "intellect," nor are such people the only *intelligent* ones in our society. Americans, for whom, as for most Westerners, all derivatives of the Latin *intelligo* carry favorable connotations, make, in fact, a pejorative distinction to mark off intellectuals they do not like—or toward whom, to be fairer, they have ambivalent feelings: the slang terms "high-brow," "longhair," "egghead" do this work, and we may without bitterness let them do the work for us. I am, in the next few pages, substantially writing about eggheads, an imprecise and sociologically accurate term.

It is difficult to define for the whole course of Western history any normal attitude of these intellectuals toward the society they live in. A great many of them in any society at any time tend to take toward some part at least of the doings of their fellows an attitude popularly known in the American language as "critical." But the degree of their censoriousness, the nature and the immediacy of the changes they demand, the targets they aim at, their basic acceptance or denial of the goodness of their own society and government, vary greatly in time and space. Again very roughly, the now-fashionable phrase "alienation of the intellectuals" can be applied to this basic attitude of the class at certain times in the Western past. The early Christians, some of whom were eggheads, were alienated from the pagan culture against which they revolted; the Schoolmen, on the whole, were quite as clearly not alienated from their thirteenth-century world. One might even defend the generalization that the intellectuals during the great flowering times of our Western culture in most of the past, during the "Golden Ages," were *not* basically alienated: the records of Periclean Athens (but not the slightly later Athens of Socrates-Plato), Augustan Rome, Elizabethan England, the France of Louis XIV, back up this statement. Perhaps better, the intellectuals of these flowering times were proud, confident, hopeful of the future of their society, moralists, capable of irony and satire, but not addicted to despair, and even—or so it looks from this distance—roughly in agreement as to good and bad, beautiful and ugly, true and false.[17]

Now the intellectual classes of the eighteenth-century West were substantially hostile to the existing order; and the *philosophes* of France, which shared with England the intellectual leadership of the time, stand as a classic instance of a group of intellectuals almost—not quite—unchallenged in their supremacy, and sure that the religious, political, social, and economic institutions of the West added up to a very bad environment indeed, one that had to be radically changed at once. Yet the *philosophes* were sure of themselves and the future, alienated from what they held to be the bad past of their society, but confident they could guide their society to the good life for all. They were not alienated as our modern eggheads—even those ostensibly and ostentatiously recently converted to the American Way—are in part alienated from ordinary Western men and women. We have been over this ground in Chapter XI. Whether they were anarchists or planners, the intellectuals of the eighteenth-century Enlightenment felt no real hostility toward the many, their fellows; indeed, they felt at times that warm glow of love for all men, that *humanité,* their too rarely realized *agape*.[18] They were the true, the recognized leaders of the many, in due rapport with them, in that happy—and, I am afraid, not very common—position Toynbee calls that of a "creative minority" admired by the many linked to it by "mimesis."[19]

The intellectuals themselves came in large part, after they became aware of the melodramatic failure of the French Revolution to follow the course

---

[17] I apologize for introducing so briefly and inadequately this enormous and difficult subject. I do not wish to be understood as saying that the intellectuals of the flowering periods were optimists, those of our own pessimists. There is a sense in which it may be said that all intellectuals always in the West are discontented people; there is a sense in which the extreme romanticism of Thomas Hardy's "thought is a disease of the flesh" comes to plague us all; perhaps it is true.

[18] I think it hard for the most devoted lover of mankind to maintain that the new religion of the Enlightenment did really achieve the loving-kindness that shows itself now and then in Christianity. The French Jacobin effort to achieve surrogate love feasts in their ritual was contrived indeed. See my *The Jacobins,* Chapter IV.

[19] Toynbee, who is, above all, a moralist, holds that the unmistakable sign of failure in a civilization (or society) is the breaking of this link of *mimesis,* or admiring imitation, between the many and the few, after which the creative minority becomes merely a "dominant minority," and the many become a "proletariat," hostile to their superiors; the good integrated society becomes then a class-struggle society, on its way to death and dissolution. Whatever the objective value of this scheme, it is surely a significant one for the understanding of the temper of many intellectuals of our age. They think our conflicts are death throes, not signs of life and growth.

they had plotted for it, to lose their feeling of identification with the lot of the many. It can be argued that the many, even in the America which has coined those scornful epithets of high-brow, longhair, and egghead, have never ceased to entertain toward the intellectuals sound ambivalent feelings, part of which were admiring, if not quite respectful. I suspect there is even today as much mimesis among the many toward the varied few as the interlocking peck orders of a democracy can bear. But there is little doubt that the intellectuals have, though with frequent attacks of conscience, and with a great deal of rationalizing, turned against the many, *the many who obstinately refuse to live up to the standards the Enlightenment had set for them.* In the nineteenth century, the intellectuals generally held that they were turning not against the people, who were sound at heart, but against the middle class, the new and unforeseen obstacle to heaven on earth. For the first romantics, the middle class was, above all, an enemy to beauty and sensitivity, the Philistines against whom to the sounds of the new music the Davidsbündler marched forth to an assured formal victory. It is with these romantics that the artist, the writer, the intellectual, though he existed in his harsh world of economic necessities only because of the patronage of the middle classes—exercised, it is true, not in the old direct noble way, but through the horrid mechanism of the market —became more clearly than ever before in the West a misunderstood person, misunderstood most of all by the many.

For a great many intellectuals, especially, perhaps, in this country, the continuing mess they find this world to be in could be explained still, as the *philosophes* had explained it, by the continuing existence of a bad environment, not yet overcome, and by additional new villainous institutions, classes, entrenched evils. The good fight could and must still be fought. The Marxists are the clearest example of these surviving heirs of the Enlightenment, and so, too, are many of those known in the United States as "liberals." But even in the nineteenth century there were signs of the great disgust, a feeling of anger and despair at the stupidities, the inadequacies, the dullness which the intellectual finds in his less-gifted fellows. Flaubert's *Bouvard et Pécuchet,* in which the efforts of two stupid—and, what is worse, well-intentioned—men to educate themselves result in dismal failures, reminds one that Flaubert, too, felt something like the great disgust that sent the anchorites to the desert— and a great deal of the pride and love of exhibition that sent them there too.

It will not do to exaggerate the alienation of the intellectuals, nor their sense of doom. Many of them, indeed most of them, lead lives not usually, not continuously, ridden with despair. The weight of the universe lies less heavily on them in the United States than in France; in Russia—clearly a case apart —they are presumed to be cheerful and unalienated, and not even to hold the cardinal tenet of their fellows in the free world that nothing fails like success.[20] There is clearly still a public in most of the West for the literature of rosy optimism, for the kind of thing the 1920's associated with the name of Edgar Guest—though one suspects that many of the purveyors of this comforting literature suffer acutely, as do those who provide fodder for Madison Avenue and Hollywood, from a guilty conscience that puts them firmly on the side of the alienated. The creative intellectuals are still complainers; but there are signs they are beginning to complain about, or at least analyze, their own class. We have heard a lot recently about conforming nonconformity, about stereotyped thinking among intellectuals, about minds open *in ideal, closed to reality.*[21]

For the serious writers, thinkers, artists, for those who set the mood and spirit of the high culture of the age, there can be little doubt; the stamp, the style, the flavor is dark indeed, angry, protesting, despairing, sometimes dignified, noble, sometimes—inevitable, symptomatic word—just neurotic. Call the roll, from Faulkner and Hemingway to Sartre and Jaspers and on to Colin Wilson and the latest of the incompletely self-made angry young men of Britain; they are always oppressed, never amused, though often bitterly bright. The best of them, Camus, in his moving acceptance speech of the Nobel prize for literature in 1957 cannot for a moment drop his burden:

. . . As the heir of a corrupt history that blends blighted revolutions, misguided techniques, dead gods, and worn out ideologies, in which second-rate powers can destroy everything today, but are unable to win anyone over, in which intelligence has stooped to becoming the servant of hatred and oppression, that generation [Camus's own], starting from nothing but its own negations, has had

20 Boris Pasternak's novel *Dr. Zhivago* (New York, Pantheon, 1958), smuggled out of Russia through an Italian translation, shows amply that there are alienated intellectuals even in the Soviet Union, and that one of the prime Western moral sentiments the intellectual incarnates and cherishes has survived there. I mean the deep feeling that the ordinary, dull, unpoetic, regulated, satisfied, routine life is somehow evil, as well as "joyless," that the artist must always press the attack on the Philistines, whose joylessness and lack of depth stink in the nostrils of the deeply joyous. Note the rash of recent American books on the horrors (moral evils?) of life in suburbs and exurbs by such writers as A. C. Spectorsky, John Cheever, and many others. The dogma that the ordinary, the conventional, is in itself evil is one of the really extraordinary products of Enlightenment.
21 For example, Morris Freedman, "The Dangers of Nonconformism," *American Scholar,* Vol. XXVIII, Winter 1958-59, pp. 25-32; Paul Pickrel, "The New Books," *Harper's,* Vol. CCXVII, December 1958, pp. 88-92, reviewing Paul Lazarsfeld and Wagner Thielens, Jr., *The Academic Mind.*

to re-establish both within and without itself a little of what constitutes the dignity of life and death. Faced with a world threatened with disintegration, in which our grand inquisitors may set up once and for all the kingdoms of death, that generation knows that, in a sort of mad race against time, it ought to re-establish among nations a peace not based on slavery, to reconcile labor and culture again, and to reconstruct with all men an Ark of the Covenant. Perhaps it can never accomplish that vast undertaking, but most certainly throughout the world it has already accepted the double challenge of truth and liberty, and, on occasion, has shown that it can lay down its life without hatred. That generation deserves to be acclaimed wherever it happens to be, and especially wherever it is sacrificing itself.[22]

Even at their gloomiest and profoundest, then, these Western intellectuals remain fighters; resignation is not for them. They are a long way from Nirvana. Not even Arnold Toynbee, who wants very much to learn from Buddha, seems in his behavior very close to that transcendence of the agon he and his Eastern masters preach. And in mid-twentieth century the intellectuals seem as far from agreement as ever they were in the nineteenth. Our West has surely never been more multanimous than at present.

V

It is at least as difficult to discern for the twentieth-century West a pattern of moral ideals as it is for the nineteenth century. Some of the enthusiasms the Victorians had for the moral as well as for the aesthetic ideals of particular past ages have weakened. The Middle Ages no longer are in fashion; but they are by no means buried, and there are still many who would like to have us go back to the spiritual certainties of the thirteenth century. We have, as the nineteenth century scarcely had, an architectural style of our own, and in a sense we have our own moral style. But just as we are still eclectic enough architecturally so that we can reach into the grab bag of history and build colonial reproductions, or Cape Cod cottages, or other "traditional" styles, so in our varied moral ideals we continue to let very little of the past die. Even in the United States, and after a whole generation educated with almost no Latin and no Greek, there are still those who would like to have us achieve the Periclean beautiful-and-good—but for all, not for the few.

I shall try to outline some of the traits of our twentieth-century moral ideals, concentrating, as seems fit, on the United States at its moment of hegemony in the West. This is a huge subject, to which I cannot hope in this

[22] *Speech of Acceptance . . . of the Nobel Prize for Literature,* New York, Knopf, 1958, pp. xi-xii.

brief space to do justice.[23] I shall try to take a line through the middle, but the reader must never forget that American multanimity is very real, that we have somewhere in our midst representatives of almost every "value," every religion, organized and disorganized, every taste, every moral stance men have taken. Nor must he forget that, no matter what worried intellectuals tell him about the leveling mediocrity and potential tyranny of the masses in this country, our present multanimity is bottomed on strong habits and strong beliefs that make diversity—liberty, freedom, democracy, if you like—a solid part of our pattern of ideals.

First, and at the risk of some repetition, must come a few needed negatives. Pollsters, reinforced by a good many less formal observers, have made it quite clear that Americans in general do not set up as an ideal anti-intellectualism in the vulgar sense of the word—that is, the depreciation of the value of the instrument of thought and dislike of those trained to make good use of that instrument; and they do not set up the businessman as our national ideal. In tests of opinion as to what calling in life is most prized among Americans, judges, scientists, high elective officers, physicians, even college professors and men of God come out generally better than do bankers and businessmen. There are clear signs, not to be denied even in the midst of our national reaction to the Russian launching of the first artificial earth satellite, that the millions now undergoing for the first time in human history advanced formal education are quite aware that they are not potential Platos, Einsteins, or Pasteurs. They know they are not intellectuals, and they do not want to become intellectuals. But this by no means amounts to their being *anti-intellectuals*. They have toward us eggheads the irreverence that crops up in medieval attitudes toward priests and monks, a saving irreverence that probably relieves them of feelings otherwise subject to dangerous repressions. Actually, "egghead" as a term of warfare is chiefly used in the civil war among the intellectuals themselves, no doubt in an ideal world a war that would have to cease, but in our own imperfect world perhaps also of some use as an outlet for emotions best not bottled up. Finally, the American is no immoralist; he

---

23 Even before we attained our present position in the world, books on the American national character, American civilization, the American "style," the American historical mission had been innumerable. Few of my readers can have been spared this subject in formal and informal education, and some of them I expect have had rather too much of it. But it remains a must. There is omnibus treatment in Max Lerner, *America as Civilization,* by a liberal intellectual so conscientious in this book that he sometimes seems neither a liberal nor an intellectual in our usual American sense of those words; and specifically on our subject, a thoughtful book, Roger Burlingame, *The American Conscience,* New York, Knopf, 1957.

wants to be happy, he feels, indeed, he has been taught to feel by the Enlight-ened, that he has a right to be happy, but this happiness is no sodden immer-sion in the mud of sensual self-indulgence, nor a fine Nietzschean transvalua-tion of values. His moral code is still essentially the traditional Western moral code.

Central to an attempt to understand what contemporary Americans ad-mire, what they think is *really* good, is an understanding of how they view that central theme of the moral history of the West, the agon, the struggle for prize. Once more, let me repeat that admiration for the gangster or the Thrasymachan man-who-gets-away-with-it, the mucker pose or the mucker reality, are eternals of Western history which we have no good reason to believe are in fact commoner now than in the days of Celadus, Crescens, and Scorpus (see Chapter V, p. 133) or in the days of Robin Hood. The low-minded are not more numerous, perhaps even not more powerful, than they used to be; it is just that, especially since the eighteenth-century Enlighten-ment, the high-minded have been rather more worried about them, and less tolerant of them. The Christian finds many kinds of actual practical toleration rather easier than does the Enlightened.

Now the agon in twentieth-century America, and, indeed, throughout the free West, is a bewilderingly complex thing. Above all, it displays to the full that state of inner contradiction, of impossible coexistence of opposites, so characteristic of the West, a plaguing, pricking, prodding state of mind that the more worried of us find intolerable. We want everybody to win the prizes, and we do multiply their number and their scope and kind; but there are still only a few prizes, and even fewer firsts. We firmly believe that in a quite real sense one man is as good as another; and we believe quite as firmly that the man who can bat .300 is a great deal better than the man who can bat only .250—and that only in the pitcher can defensive skill quite make up for that deficiency. We very clearly believe that men are equal and that they are not equal. In the daily round of living we have no trouble with the qualifying and saving "in respect to—"; we are all equal in the eyes of the law, equal in the waiting line for tickets, equal at the supermarket, where there are no charge accounts, but not equal in the halfback position, or—let us be fair—not equal as candidates for Phi Beta Kappa. There remains, however, in our final moral summing up a troubled feeling that there is something *wrong,* something un-American, even about so consecrated a formulation as "many are called but few are chosen."

At least such seems to me to be the feeling of a great number of American intellectuals, a feeling that comes out in the unwillingness of many educators to face in all its implications the problem of educating the exceptionally gifted child. It is a kind of backwash from this emotional attitude that helps explain the number and intensity of those who worry over the leveling tendency in the modern West, over the tyranny of the majority, over what they feel is our swift approach to deadening uniformity and mediocrity. If you are addicted to conventional ratiocination, as intellectuals by definition are, and if you believe that others are so addicted, as many intellectuals since the Enlightenment unfortunately are, then from such an obvious premise as, say, the preamble to our Declaration of Independence affords you can go on to conclude that since men think they ought to be *equal,* they are going to try universally to make themselves *identical*—and identical after the pattern of the many, the majority, the average.

I do not think that the man in the street has any such difficulty with the doctrine of equality. He accepts the contradictions and complexities in which this doctrine is in fact embodied in our society and in our working concepts of what that society ought to be. We have in this country set up our own elaborate rules for the agon. First of all, and to my mind of great importance, we have diversified it greatly, multiplied the fields in which it can be played —or fought—out, have come in a sense somewhere near finding some kind of prize for, if not all, at least for a great many. Our almost infinite number of organized groups, from hobby culture to world-saving, seem silly only to those of us who have not recovered from the 1920's. Even for the very top, where the competition is most ferocious and, in societies like that of later Rome, morally and sociologically dangerous, we have somehow taken much of the sting out. In politics, even in business, the defeated rarely revolt or conspire.

This whole topic of the American agon, however, is worth some man-watching work. Anyone who has glanced, for instance, at our varied literature on how to succeed at anything—say, at salesmanship—must be aware of the curious parallels with the literature of the high, the noble agon, from Homer on. The difficulty is to appraise realistically the loss of dignity, of tragedy, of humility, of resignation, that has undoubtedly taken place in the process of democratization. I feel sure that the moral and aesthetic atmosphere of an egghead product like the *Death of a Salesman* is *not* realistic, and, indeed, no nearer high seriousness than the vulgar values it seems to pity and scorn. But there is a problem here, and I repeat that we in the mid-twentieth century have by no means solved it: Can we have a democracy of this world and yet retain the age-old Western tradition of the struggle for prize? Can we find a substitute, a surrogate, for the Christian "many are called but few are chosen," where men, not God, patently, overtly, make the choice?

We have done as well as we have in making men equal, even in combat, in part through the comforting compromises we have made between the realities of daily life and the tenets of the eighteenth-century Fathers—equality before the law, equality of opportunity, and the like, all, from the point of view of the ferocious idealist, hopelessly softened into mere words, mere consolations. We have done it partly by inculcating a genuine respect for the rules of the game, rules that, it is true, the American likes to get around, and that, unlike the Englishman, he will not usually treat as absolutes, but that he firmly "believes in" in principle and that give him a basis for his eternal argument with the umpire. And although in a crowd the American will sometimes shout "Kill the umpire," he feels as an individual with rather better reason than did Voltaire of his shadow deity that if the umpire did not exist he would have to be invented. Again, we have carried the familiar safety valve of free complaint—I mean, of course, free speech—to the point where to some commentators our complaining seems a symptom of a widespread neurosis. But apart from the fact that this term and many others from psychiatry and psychology have in our day become such smooth coins that sensitive teachers of English composition are banning them all, I do not think that Messrs. Drew Pearson, Westbrook Pegler, and Red Smith—and their devoted readers—are in fact abnormal. Complaining is one of the great human habits, which universal literacy and the famous mass media have perhaps simply made more noticeable, not more common. Finally, in our American society there are, contrived or spontaneous, complex gradings or frames ("structuring") of the agon which bring us closer to a kind of realized egalitarianism. One may symbolize this nicely in the world of boxing, with its careful gradations from flyweight (not over 112 lbs.) to heavyweight (anything over 175 lbs.). Indeed, the American would no doubt amend the phrase from Homer we have already found so useful, *aien aristeuein,* into "always to come out on top *in one's class.*"[24]

Socially, class or status in the contemporary United States must seem sometimes to carry to a dangerous excess this multiplying and diversifying—this democratization—of the agon I am here all too briefly analyzing. As the innumerable novels of status, the almost as innumerable "anthropologi-

[24] I have long thought that we needed a good study of sport, professional and amateur. There is the suggestive *Homo Ludens* of Huizinga, but this and most other studies of the sort are too philosophical, too concerned with sport as play. What we need is a sociological study of sport as work, as a seriously meant universe of its own.

cal" studies of Muncie-Middletown, Newburyport-Yankee City, and the rest must bring home to those of us who at least read, if we do not notice, or man watch, our American peck orders are real and exceedingly complicated, as well as subject to change, and most puzzling to foreigners, who sometimes fail to take the word of our more innocent intellectuals that such peck orders do not exist, or, at any rate, are of no *real* importance.[25] Social workers who have witnessed the sufferings of the middle-lower-class family finally convinced that the boy they hoped would have the kind of career that would lift them all into the lower-middle class cannot hope to get that essential B.A. from even the lowest "college" in the local academic hierarchy, cannot hope to raise himself, then, know that this form of the agon is very real indeed—and know that even in our democracy all are not chosen. The career open to talents in this country may be a source of more frustration, indignation, and, ultimately, of sentiments disastrous to our social stability than of the kind of satisfactions that help make us accept the universe and our place in it. On that master question, as the reader will realize, I hesitate to pronounce an opinion. We intellectuals can, I think, indeed have already "existentially" begun to, adjust ourselves to the big cosmological difficulties of the failure of the heaven-on-earth of the Enlightenment; their translation among the many into the concrete hopes and fears of our individual microcosms sets up a much more difficult problem for the would-be man watcher. Tentatively, I should guess that so far we are managing, after a fashion. The next few generations will be a real test of this moral difficulty: Can there be an Enlightened resignation?

For the rest, it must be taken for granted that almost all Americans set for themselves ideals and standards that, in spite of the bad connotations the term has in the history of ethical thought, one must call "hedonistic." I do not think the common preacherly reproach of "materialism" really applies to Americans—nor, for that matter, to Russians, among whom the word is said to be no reproach but a blessing. Still, the ordinary American is far from any purely spiritual or ascetic or mystical ideal, far even from the by no means wholly ascetic ideals of historic Puritanism. He does not—I am, of course, dealing with this real ordinary conceptualized American, and not with an equally but differently real extraordinary individual American—

---

25 Howard Mumford Jones tells me that one of the favorite questions from German prisoners of war we were trying to "re-educate" in democracy—after the obvious one about our treatment of Negroes—was: "How about your Greek-letter college fraternities and 'democracy'?"

distrust radically any of his "natural" appetites. He believes that it is *right* for him, that he *has a right,* to have good food, a good home, a good car, a good family life, a good sex life, in short, happiness. His religion, even if he is a professing Christian, does not tell him these enjoyments are bad, or full of dangerous temptations, or—and this is a crux—difficult to obtain. He does not, of course, by any means feel himself to be a hog from Epicurus's sty. He believes there is a wrong satisfaction of desires, that there are desires he ought not to have. He is still heir of a great deal of the Helleno-Judaeo-Christian tradition of right and wrong. He holds, indeed, a democratic and banausic form—a *vulgarized* form, if the word pleases you—of the old Greek ideal of the beautiful-and-good. Heaven and hell are no longer quite as real to him as they were to his forefathers, but he by no means believes that "man makes himself." He is fond of a gesture, symptomatic and symbolic, which he calls "knocking on wood." It is very old wood, already thousands of years old when Condorcet grew up.

VI

The moral stance of the twentieth-century Russian calls for separate treatment, for it is clearly not quite that of the other societies of the Western world. I do not hesitate, however, to call Russia "Western." Both its old religion, Christianity, and its new one, Marxism, are Western indeed. Of course, as a nation-state it has its own style, and that style has been affected by its "Asian" elements as well as by its "European" ones. Our own American style is itself a compound of Europe and our "frontier." From the point of view of this study, as I have earlier noted, Russian Communism is the latest of the great sects that have in the Enlightenment a common origin; it is, if you wish to put it that way, the most successful heresy of orthodox Western democracy, a heresy that, like most sturdy heresies, thinks of itself as orthodoxy. Needless to say, these terms taken from the Western religious vocabulary are repudiated with great vigor by all Marxists, who share with the followers of a very different prophet, Mary Baker Eddy, the conviction that they are scientists, that they understand the universe and man's fate as scientists in the past understood somewhat more limited, or, at least, more specific, more concrete, matters. Yet the religious parallel seems obvious. The part of God as designer and ever-present cause is, for the Marxist, played by a "theory" of the structure and dynamics of society known as Dialectical Materialism. The good Marxist considers dialectical materialism as a "scientific" theory, analogous, say, to gravity; but certainly among the many believers it is pretty completely hypostatized into something that is at least a surrogate for God, a First and Final Cause. Man's fate as a race here on earth is "determined" by the inevitable workings of dialectical materialism through the "mode of production" which determines class structure and, therefore, the ensuing "class struggle." This class struggle works itself out (the reflexive verb is important) along the lines of the Hegelian dialectic, rescued by Marx and Engels from Hegel's silly idealism about "spirit" and put squarely on the solid ground of "matter." There has been a long history of class struggles, but the one that counts for us is this last: thesis capitalist versus antithesis proletarian, which, after the victory of proletarians, a victory determined, inevitable, and a transitional revolutionary "dictatorship of the proletariat," will produce the final synthesis, the "classless society."

I do not see how an outsider, or even a candid insider, can avoid the conclusion: all this is metaphysics, theology, and, at the end, a fine firm eschatology. The classless society is heaven, a universalist heaven, unbalanced in the end by any hell, a heaven-to-be in a certain if not quite unpostponable future here on earth. The Marxists are increasingly unwilling to be very explicit about either the nature of the classless society or the place and date of its attainment. The orthodox, the official Russian, view does give a plausible and logical explanation of why the classless society has not yet been attained, even in Russia; the victory of antithesis proletarian over thesis capitalist is not by any means complete, and the dialectical process cannot come to its predestined end until proletarians are victorious all over the world—and most notably in the United States. The classless society will be marked—this is one of the most famous and by their enemies most derided of Marxist phrases —by the "withering away of the state." There will in the classless society be no police, no armed forces, no law courts, no compulsion of the sort we have all been brought up to accept as normal. Meanwhile, in Russia and in the lands of her allies, there is—there can be—nothing more than the dictatorship of the proletariat. There is evil, the good Marxist must believe, even in Russia, since there is evil in the United States and in the rest of the so-called "free world." As to the nature of the classless society once it is attained, the Marxists, and in particular their more subtle theorists, are reticent. They feel, I think, that the concept embodies a lofty ethical ideal, that it is in some sense a surrogate for the Christian heaven; but their whole moral and intellectual background turns them away from the admission that they harbor any such concepts. M. Jourdain had talked prose all his life without knowing it; the Marxists have talked idealism, knowing it all too well in their heart of hearts.

Moreover, Marxism-Leninism is the child or grandchild, not only of the Utopian faith in human perfectability of the Enlightenment, but also of the nineteenth-century feeling for process, for change, for an unending dynamics of Progress. Now all the fashionable nineteenth-century explanations of this process, from Hegel to the Social Darwinists, insist on a central dynamic "cause": *conflict, struggle, competition*. Marx himself is most emphatic about the ruthlessness of his own version of this dynamic, the master dynamic of the "class struggle." But in conflict on this earth there are wounds, cruelties, suffering, defeat, not only for the losers, but for the victors, too. So it had seemed in the pure Christian tradition; so it seemed to the Enlightenment. The whole Marxist eschatology is an attempt to imagine a set of human relations *on this earth* in which there will be change, indeed Progress, rivalry (or emulation, about the nicest word available), in short, some kind of conflict but no wounds, no cruelties, no suffering, no defeat, not even any maladjustments, merely victory for all, and no tie games, either. The old Nordic myths had done better; the warriors—it is true not in this world, but in the next—fought lustily all day, and then, their wounds healed, feasted the night in Valhalla.[26]

The Marxist-Leninist world view rejects all notions of a supranatural being or beings, of an immaterial soul, and of an afterlife; good Marxists are infuriated even by the Freudian concept of a psyche, and an unconscious, as violations of the "principles" of materialism. They reject, again on philosophic grounds masquerading as "scientific," the concept of individual free will. But Marxist moral practice maintains a powerful strain of minimal Christian puritanism, of vigorous reforming zeal, of individual obligation among the faithful to help along the inevitable work of dialectical materialism. The Marxist believes in, and puts into effect, systems of rewards and punishments, and, where he has been put into power, goes in for a good deal of cultural engineering. His dialectic tells him that the capitalist by necessity is helping the Marxist cause, but his emotions hardly permit him to love, certainly not to forgive, this enemy. In short, the Marxist, like the Calvinist, is a determinist determined

---

[26] I shall have to return in a concluding chapter to this problem. Our American democracy has, I think, a much less explicit heaven-on-earth than the Communists have, but we, too, have difficulty with our attitudes toward conflict, as I have noted above. Only a very few die-hards can now accept Spencer's opinion that nature is often a little cruel that she may be very kind, which is the essence of the Victorian "solution" of the problem of evil.

to follow what his conscience (a word the Marxist would not use) tells him is right, and to avoid in fear and trembling what that God- or Dialectical Materialism-implanted voice tells him is wrong. This is an old and cherished solution of the insoluble problem of free will, perhaps a necessary one.

The concrete system of right and wrong that has emerged in orthodox Russian Communism is essentially the ethics of the eighteenth-century Enlightenment, rather strongly tinged with the same kind of puritanism that comes out in the French Jacobins, and in the earlier English Puritanism. The Russians were committed by their world view to hold that men's appetites are natural and therefore good; they would have no nonsense about redemption through ascetic self-denial, no self-deprivation here on earth as a passport to heaven. The Old Bolsheviks came to power laden with principles opposed to bourgeois prudery, greed, love of display, ownership of women, all the hypocrisy of middle-class morality; they came, more positively, with all the baggage of free-thinking virtues they had accumulated in the nineteenth century. They at once established at law equality of the sexes, complete freedom of divorce and abortion, access to contraceptives, and they abolished private property, and with it such bourgeois evils as gambling, speculation, everything Veblen ticketed so effectively as "conspicuous consumption." The Old Bolsheviks, Lenin in the lead, were by no means Rabelaisian naturalists; they were, in fact, ascetics. They were, in terms of the old antithesis of liberty-authority, in principle and ultimately on the side of freedom; but they did not believe that the free man, the man of the final classless society, would fornicate, gamble, drink, overeat, show off, dominate others, fight, lie, steal, murder. These and other forms of misconduct, they held, were the result of the mode of production of capitalism. But there these evil doings were, and in the ensuing dictatorship of the proletariat, which under Lenin's own expansion of Marx's thought meant the dictatorship of the fit few, the Bolshevik elite, these evils, and the evil men who committed them, had to be proceeded against by the use of authority. The few modest libertarian or anarchistic measures of the beginning were soon withdrawn, and the Bolshevik version of a Republic of Terror and Virtue began.

After nearly half a century, there is much in Russia that bears the stamp of this Republic of Virtue. There have been, of course, returns to some of the old wickedness. The attempt to abolish the use of alcohol has become under Khrushchev no more than an attempt to lessen it by regulation, as with the British; most travelers do, however, find actual drunkenness, except perhaps at those famous diplomatic parties, less common or at least less obvious than in Western Europe and America. The Russian press has at times got alarmed over juvenile delinquency, "hooliganism," all sorts of corruption seeping over from the Western democracies, such as jazz, "modernistic" art, sex perversions, and the like, not to speak of more serious forms of Leftist and Rightist "deviations"—the current Russian word for "heresies." Clearly, after Stalin's death there was left further room for the old Adam and the old Eve, more chance for what have long been in Christian actuality venial sins of self-indulgence. Yet it is still true that the rare Russian who comes west, and especially to America, is shocked by our mores, by the public lechery—so it seems to him—of our advertising, by the exploitation of sex, conspicuous consumption, downright Roman imperial luxury in our movies, magazines, television. Ethically and aesthetically, Russian formal standards, as has often been noted, have at least since the early triumph of Stalin carried overtones of Victorian times. Even their luxury and display, for the most part limited, as befits a socialist society, to such common wealth as the famous Moscow subways and great new public buildings, seem to us heavy, old-fashioned, bourgeois, in fact. Russian plain living and high thinking seem a still-further-cheapened version of seventeenth-century "business" Calvinism, not an ascetic Christian revulsion from this world, not at all a mystic yearning for higher things, but a driving, no-nonsense desire to produce and share the simpler material satisfactions, the less tempting, less inebriating, less spiritual ones. Such standards are, of course, in the hands of nationalist leaders, a means of putting guns well before butter.

Our own alarmists who insist that Russia and her allies are united in a monolithic block while the free West is divided, hesitating, unbelieving, are at least guilty of turning a difference in degree into a difference in kind. There are clearly in the Communist world today many of those "inner contradictions" the Marxists readily enough find in the free world. It seems most unlikely that the Russians have solved the most obvious difficulty the new faith of the Enlightenment ran into from the start—the fact that this universalist faith never found effective major institutional expression save in the nation-state, by its nature parochial, not universalist. It is not even certain that within the U.S.S.R. the constituent national groups really are satisfied with nice cultural autonomy in a political state dominated by Great Russians. The government of the Soviet Union itself has hitherto behaved toward those states within its system of coalition and those outside it in a thoroughly traditional, which is to say by Christian and Enlightenment standards a thoroughly immoral, fashion.

But contradictions—unresolved tensions—abound in the Communist whole. The classless society is so clearly and so definitely promised that its indefinite postponement will require something of the kind of adaptation in ideas and ritual the Christians worked out with the indefinite postponement of the Second Coming of Christ. It is difficult to imagine how such an adjustment can be made—or come about—in Communist eschatology save by some radical paring down of the Utopian promise of the classless society. The radical egalitarianism of Marxist ideals, quite apart from the concept of the classless society, or, to put it more simply, the specific economic egalitarianism of "to each according to his needs," will surely also need compromise, adaptation, the rationalizing, the glossing over that horrifies the idealist. Orwell's bitter satire "all are equal, only some are more equal than others" will have to have the rankle taken out of it. This can be done, as we in the West know well. It can be made obvious, indeed scientifically true, that a Russian ballerina needs more than a seamstress; or the formula can be reversed, "from each according to his needs, to each according to his abilities."

Not the most unlikely prospect is that the Marxist heresy will slowly be absorbed into its Western parent faith, that the present schism between Communism and Western democracy will turn out to be a rivalry between nation-states organized in traditional coalitions, not, as has sometimes been suggested, a struggle deeply rooted in religion, like the long and still unresolved, though now and for some time apparently stalemated, struggle between Christianity and Islam. I am not suggesting that such a nationalist power struggle would be without its horrors, but if it is true that the hatred theological is the profoundest of human hatreds, it should prove a struggle less likely to be fought to the bitterest of ends than would a religious war. At the very least, it looks as though the Marxist religion must in the long run follow the Western pattern from which it sprang: that pattern is one of a ferocious initial moral determination—a shared determination among the many—to abolish evil, followed by a gradual adaptation of the group to the necessity of living with, coping with, *in a sense* accepting, evil. I state this pattern with excessive and misleading simplicity, but it will stand stating thus.

VII

The historian of Western morals must attempt some account of how the two great twentieth-century contestants for the leadership of the Western world—of the whole world—fit into Western moral traditions. I spare the reader further introspection by either of us as to the nature of scientific objectivity or of intellectual honesty, though some meditation as to whether scientific objectivity and intellectual honesty are in fact identical might be not unprofitable. I shall sum up one conclusion in advance: Some such attempt can be made publicly in the United States, and cannot yet be so made in Russia.

First of all, to judge from the *conduct* and the expressed attitudes of those in charge of public policy and those who comment publicly on it: by the highest ethical standards of our Western culture, both sides in this great agon of the two nation-states are almost equally immoral. We all are wise enough to know that others do not live up to their ideals. Mr. Thomas P. Whitney has no trouble showing, in an article entitled "If Marx Visited Russia Today—" that Marx would not find there "the classless, unexploited society he envisaged."[27]

But one part of our Western moral tradition—it is most familiar even in this age, which the bemoaners say does not know the Bible, in the form of Christ's teaching on the mote in the brother's eye and the beam in yours (Matthew 7:3-5)—requires that we face the facts: a hostile observer, or simply an idealist, could also write most devastatingly on "If Jefferson Visited Washington Today—" or, though one hopes the tone would be different, "If Jesus Visited Washington Today—."

Let me then use frankly the word "idealistic." To the idealist of the Christian tradition that sent the anchorites to the desert, that made St. Francis embrace poverty, that inspired and still to an amazing degree inspires the Society of Friends, the bragging, the posturing, the threats and recriminations, the double talk, the militancy, the holier-than-thou hypocrisy (or, more kindly put, the inability to see the other side), the really intolerable gap between practice and profession *on both sides* must seem simply un-Christian. But more: to the idealist in the strict tradition of the eighteenth-century Enlightenment as well as to the idealist in the deviant tradition of Marxism, the conduct of both sides must seem as immoral as it must to the Christian idealist. This statement, which seems to me incontrovertible, can, of course, always be taken as a condemnation not of the present moral position of the United States or that of the Soviet Union, but as a condemnation of intransigent moral idealism.

Moreover, Americans in particular can stand being reminded—it is almost certainly impossible that anyone could as yet so remind the Russians—that to many Westerners not citizens of either of the great rival superpowers the actual moral situation of the rivals does not look like clear moral whiteness on one side and clear moral blackness on the other. These Westerners, English, French, German, and many others, are unlikely to be intransigent moral idealists—the type is rare—and they may well feel that in the balance

[27] New York *Times*, April 27, 1958, Section VI, Part 1, p. 12.

one side is in fact "better" than the other. But they are in part outsiders, and they can look at us and the Russians without that complete moral narcissism that critics like Toynbee find particularly offensive in "parochial" nationalism, though no doubt they suffer from the same blindness as regards their own nation-parish. At the very least, Americans must expect that quite honorable and honest non-Americans brought up in the Western moral tradition will feel justified in pointing out that by the standards of that tradition our acquisition of the Panama Canal was immoral; that we are in Okinawa and other Pacific islands practicing the "colonialism" against which we preach; that even at home we are progressing but slowly in closing the gap between practice and profession in the treatment of Negroes; that our actual foreign policy since our rapid rise to leadership of one of the rival coalitions has, in fact, been rather clearly in the old historic and not very moral tradition set in early modern Europe, has been—or has aimed to be—"realistic" balance-of-power politics, not a revolutionary new and virtuous extension of the morals and *morale* of our own national in-group to the whole universe of man.

Now the above can be written and published in the United States by an American; nothing like it about Russia can be written and published in Russia by a Russian. This is a great moral difference. It is not, let me insist, a difference that wipes out in this real, imperfect, complicated, bewildering world everything else, not a difference that wipes out all similarity, not a difference that wipes out even similarity in metaphor; or, rather, it is not such from the point of view of a naturalistic-historical approach to morals, nor of a temperate transcendental-religious approach. I grant that for the whole-hog absolutist the United States and the Soviet Union can quite obviously be absolutely different morally—or absolutely identical.

For the rest of us—for the most of us—I think I can make some of the implications of what I am trying to establish quite clear by going back to a clear concrete instance to which I have already made brief reference (see p. 103). In Periclean Athens, a city-state in which the tie between the individual and the state was close, the *Antigone* of Sophocles was staged with the approval of the public authorities. At our distance in time we cannot be sure for just what cause Antigone seemed to these Greeks to have gone to her martyrdom. She was certainly no eighteenth-century enlightened maiden, and she did not sacrifice herself for any clause in a Bill of Rights. She and John Stuart Mill would have had a hard time understanding one another. I grant that it is unlikely that the original Athenian audience felt that the play was in any sense a hostile criticism of the Athenian state or of existing

Athenian institutions. I am even prepared to make the guess, which will shock the true classicist, that some of the original Athenian audience may have reflected: Well, this is the sort of thing that can go on in Thebes, but fortunately not here. Still, Antigone did defy the "government" in the person of the regent Creon in the name of a morality, a "right" that she felt—not without a touch of *hubris*-pride, for this Promethean contradiction is old indeed in our West—was in her and not in Creon, king though he was.

For what was inside Antigone—in her heart and soul, for her moral sentiments, the contents of her conscience, her superego—we have as our long inheritance many names and phrases, not quite synonyms, each stamped with the particular historical circumstances in which it arose, but all central to our moral being. Let me call up some: render therefore unto Caesar the things that are Caesar's, and unto God the things that are God's, *Ich kann nicht anders, e pur si muove* (even though this was but whispered), freedom of conscience, freedom of speech, *non sub homine, sed sub deo et lege,* due process, habeas corpus, juridical defense, the dignity of man, the rights of man, individualism, or just plain liberty. We have also many names for, as we have had much experience with, what Creon *has come* to stand for.[28] Tyranny has come to mean the immoral and unrestrained use of power; but we have caesaropapism, despotism, might makes right, *raison d'état, Realpolitik,* the end justifies the means, my country, right or wrong, the *Fuehrerprinzip,* totalitarianism, and that pathetic phrase of Rousseau's, as full of Western contradiction as any ever uttered, but, to me, definitely on this wrong side of a great moral fence, *it may be necessary to compel a man to be free.*

Now all these words and phrases on both sides are expressions of deep-seated and, within the brief course of Western history, comparatively unchanging human sentiments. As signs or symbols they are imprecise, and when the kind of analysis suggested by a term like "semantics" is applied to them they can be made to seem "meaningless" just because they are so full of meanings. In their totality, each set stands for human conduct directed by very different estimates of what human beings are like and what they ought to be like. In their modern embodiment in the United States and in Soviet Russia, the historian must note that each side sets *as its goal* a society to which the first or libertarian set of sentiments rather than the second or

---

[28] Creon in the play is by no means an embodiment of the attitude that governmental power is above morality, is "amoral"; indeed, he is in a sense converted by Antigone's stand to the belief—or the fear—that he has in *his* stand violated religion; the conversion comes too late to prevent the catastrophe, or there would have been no tragedy. Perhaps I should use the Thrasymachus of the *Republic* as my straw man here.

authoritarian set should best apply: the Marxist ideal, the Marxist eschatology, is still that of the "classless society" in which the state and all its agents, all violence and all constraints have simply disappeared, "withered away." But in fact and in the balance of reality, the free West is freer than the Communist world, so free that in most of the West, Communists may announce their agreement with the Russian Communists' own master contradiction, may make their own firm effort to *compel* men to be free, to achieve gentleness through cruelty, variety through prescription, spontaneity through planning . . . but we need not go on—George Orwell in *Animal Farm* has said it better, if more bitterly. There is, however, a limit to Western contradiction and paradox, for though we can indeed believe because it is impossible, we cannot believe because it is absurd. The Russian claim to be on the side of freedom looks absurd; ours, no worse than imperfectly realized.

We have been dealing, certainly not with abstractions but with the big, overarching general tendency of the free West toward what Antigone stands for, of the Communist West toward what Creon stands for. There are those in the West who stand with Creon, and they are sometimes at least as successful as he was; we may hope that there are those in the Communist world who stand with Antigone, but so far the outside world knows little about them, unless they have fled from Russia. And an Antigone who flees is not quite Antigone.

There are, however, less heroic, more mundane aspects of morality. Honesty should make us admit that from what the travelers say the Russians are closer than we to a morality that has played a great part in our tradition. They are, partly but surely not wholly from lack of material means for self-indulgence in their daily lives, harder working, more austere, simpler, more "puritanical." Dialectical materialism, the facts of national patriotism and the elitist authoritarian inheritance of Leninism helping, has led them far from the Epicurean sty. Make no mistake, the old Adam and the old Eve must be as strong in Russia as anywhere else, and in the eyes of the moral idealist *l'homme moyen sensuel russe* is still, in John Mill's words, a poor thing. I do not think altruism, loving-kindness, the virtues of the Beatitudes, are any commoner in Russia than elsewhere. But, if only because of the scarcity of consumer's goods, and because they are probably still in the active state of their new religion, the Russians do seem to be nearer the moral state, the *morale,* of such societies as Sparta or early Rome than are we of the free West. The danger that Russia may yet prove to have crusading zeal, a social and moral discipline that will defeat us, has worried many of our publicists, and not without reason.

Nevertheless, there are necessary qualifications. First, on our side, the black picture of Western decadence which the more excited prophets of doom paint is not a true picture. The facts of two World Wars show that though many, even most, of us have been brought up to expect heaven on earth, we can live with courage and dignity through hell on earth. In the last war, even civilian populations, not only in the virtuous north of Europe, but also in the lax south, stood up to the test of bombardment from the air far better than the prophets had supposed. Second, on the Russian side, the mere passage of time must gradually lessen the intensity of their religious faith, their revolutionary desire to conquer and convert. Russians moved by nationalism alone, by mere pooled self-esteem, may be less formidable than Russians moved by a spiritual *élan* we do not really understand, but which we have seen in the revolutionary France of 1794, in Christian crusades and in Moslem jihads.[29]

Moreover, unless you can believe that a world view, ideas about the nature of man and the universe, have no effect whatever on the conduct of the many who hold them, you will have to conclude that the Russian world view is ill-designed to preserve for long years the self-denying virtues and the Spartan *morale*. In the symbolic conflict between guns and butter, the Communist philosophical ultimates are all on the side of butter; and though clearly men will put up with what to the pure rationalist seems an intolerable gap between ideal and real, between profession and practice, there is a tendency, confirmed by the historical record, for some men to try to close the gap by trying to realize the ideal and live up to the profession. Such men may not be many, but they make a difference in the long run. When that ideal is material comfort, as it is with the Marxist, these exceptional men get a lot of help from plain men and from ordinary human nature, that poor thing. Russians, like Americans, "believe in" progress, and progress for the faithful is something more, or something less, than the mere successful expansion of the nation-state to which they belong. We have come to one of the central problems that face the modern West, the doctrine of Progress.

---

[29] I am not suggesting that this special spiritual *élan* wins wars by itself alone, nor even that this religiously derived *élan* is the only kind of *élan* that has in the past brought success to aggressive, expanding groups; but it is possible that in our modern world of mass organization some such spirit has to be added to matériel and good leadership to make a successful "imperialist" expansion. No one who knows the record of American armed forces in the last general war and in the Korean war can honestly find much of that kind of *élan* or spirit even among the professional officer caste, and certainly not in the ranks. Many of us in the United States would like to convert the world—but not, and in this we are, I think, honest, by force.

XIV

The Problem of Moral Progress

WHO HAS NOT SEEN in recent years some form of one of the cartoonists' favorite subjects: a monstrous, snarling, apelike, definitely subhuman being holding, or about to manipulate or steer, a complicated machine, an H-bomb, a guided missile, or the like? Perhaps there will be a symbolically good human being in contrast, a white-coated scientist, a kindly humanitarian, even a minister of God, and a caption: Which will win? Verbally the problem, which surely comes home to a great many people in the West today, is commonly put as a contrast between the accepted fact of our great *material* progress and the nowadays equally accepted fact of our much slighter— perhaps nonexistent—*moral* progress. At its sharpest, the matter is pointed to a clear dilemma: We have now the material possibility of destroying our civilization, and, to judge by the recent record, our morals are such in practice that it seems by no means unlikely that we shall avail ourselves of this possibility.

The reader need not be reminded that this problem is both old and new. Western man has long lived under the shadow of impending disaster— famine, plague, war, flood, earthquake. Under circumstances we by no means fully understand, as in the early apocalyptic days of Christianity, or in the troubled fifteenth and sixteenth centuries of our era, great populations have been moved to mass madness by an almost universal sense of impending doom; and, if only because of the intellectual and emotional heritage of primitive Christian belief in a Second Coming, small sectarian groups have been hailing the immediate end of the world at intervals for two thousand

413

years. Indeed, American history affords many examples of groups setting definite dates for the end of the world. One of the latest, when the end did not come, decided that their devotions had swayed God to a postponement. Man as an individual knows he is going to die, and one supposes that his philosophic and imaginative gifts—or, as the real die-hard primitivist romantic would say, curses—have long made some sense of the possibility of a collective death of humanity, or of a given in-group, natural and inevitable.

But the Enlightenment brought something new to the problem of man's fate. In simplest terms it banished, for the fully Enlightened, God and the whole complex of the supernatural from man's hopes and fears of the future, and substituted what we call the "doctrine of progress."[1] The doctrine of progress, coupled with such tenets as that of the natural goodness and reasonableness of man, democratic egalitarianism, humanitarian benevolence, and a continued, even stepped-up, Western or Faustian awareness of history, of process, of growth, had by the nineteenth century put past, present, and future of man's fate in a strikingly new light. There seemed to the Enlightened no longer any grounds for fears of a great, complete disaster. No personal God, his ways inscrutable to man, was left to bring to a sudden end a world he never created. Nature, it was now believed, never produced more than local and occasional disasters; and, moreover, men, the favorite children of Nature, were fast learning how to get around their parent. The willful might still disobey Nature, and be punished for their disobedience; but disobedience, punishment, and, above all, guilt, meant something very different when the power above was a Christian God and when it was the hypostatized Nature of the Enlightenment. Men have always known in their hearts that Nature is an invention of their own; they have not usually felt that way about God.

In sum, though even in the eighteenth century and most certainly in the nineteenth there were isolated intellectuals who held a doctrine of decadence, not progress, most Westerners were confident that human beings everywhere were getting morally better as well as materially better off. We must be careful here: after the first bloom of the Enlightenment wore off with the French Revolution, few expected heaven on earth at once. Most Victorian intellectuals—a Mill, a Carlyle, a Tocqueville, a Matthew Arnold—had fearful doubts as to whether the many could be morally improved, or "civilized,"

[1] Once more, I ask the reader to note my qualifying phrase, "for the fully Enlightened." The main theme of Western intellectual and moral history since about 1700 has been the *coexistence and mutual interpenetration* of two very different broad world views, the Christian and that of the Enlightenment.

fast enough to forestall some disasters worse than that of the French Revolution. They were quite aware of the dilemma: machine master of man or man master of machine. Some of the Utopias of the late nineteenth century, already beginning to sound like inverted Utopias, solve the dilemma by doing away with the machine.[2] Still, these are but premonitions. The central belief of the West was still a chastened belief in progress, well represented by Herbert Spencer of the 1860's among the intellectuals: moral progress lags behind material, especially economic progress, there are still little wars, still backward nations, and even the English still have dukes, foxhounds, Oxford University, and cosmetics, but the majestic evolution of society from the military to the industrial will go gradually on, as the geological record tells us all change in Nature comes about, inevitably, happily, purposefully, as we all should like to have it.

I have pointed out in my last chapter, what hardly needed pointing out, that in mid-twentieth century few intellectuals, and one assumes few of the other educated groups in the West, can hold such a world view without grave doubts. On the other hand, I think it quite as clear that at least in the United States and even among the many nonexistentialists in Western Europe most people have difficulty jettisoning all the cargo of hope and apparent understanding we may subsume in the symbol Progress. I have already pointed out, what some of us do tend not to notice, that the Communist world is deeply committed to a very special form of belief in the doctrine of progress.[3]

Now no one questions the fact—though some may think it desirable not to use in registering that fact a value-charged word like "progress"—that men have in the course of known Western history gained increasing ability to get from their material environment satisfactions of obvious human wants. This "progress" can be measured. A simple instance is speed of travel, which will range from human walking speed to the latest achievement in jet planes. Plotted graphically to cover the last three thousand years, the line representing speed of travel will be nearly flat for most of the period, and then only yesterday, with the railroad, start upward clear off the graph. As an index, speed of travel may well exaggerate the extent to which this whole material progress—man's control over his material environment, including most certainly over his own bodily health, mental and physical—has been very recent

[2] Samuel Butler, *Erewhon* (1872) and William Morris, *News from Nowhere* (1891) will do as samples. But both of these writers sound like optimists if they are confronted with an Aldous Huxley or a George Orwell.
[3] See above, p. 404.

and very great. We are still, physically, less than supermen but no one can question the reality of this change, this "progress," nor its measurability.

If there be an improvement in men's conduct in relation to their ethical standards, or even an improvement in those standards themselves, over the last three thousand years, such improvement can hardly be measured quantitatively, can hardly be given numerical indexes of any sort. The most ambitious effort to apply quantitative measurement to the data of historical sociology, or sociological history, that I know is P. A. Sorokin's *Social and Cultural Dynamics*;[4] and Sorokin, as a good child—an egghead child—of our age, is trying to measure decay rather than progress. He does not succeed, save in affording evidence of "cyclical" movements in Western history, and his indexes must look phony to anyone used to measuring the measurable. I propose in the next few pages the more modest goal of trying to make some rough estimates of the nature and the degree of changes our brief review of the moral history of the West makes possible. They will be but approximations, based on inadequate data, and on inadequate tools for analysis of the data; for the moral sciences are not yet by any means well-developed sciences. Moreover, the concepts of change, of difference, are full of philosophical difficulties. There is good sound intellectual as well as emotional ground for accepting as true such statements as "the morals that find expression in a Nazi concentration camp are *different* from the morals that find expression in the Society for the Prevention of Cruelty to Children," or "the morals of the British aristocracy in 1670 were *different* from the morals of the British aristocracy in 1870." But there are also good grounds, I believe, for the statement that there are relatively *constant* elements in the history of morals in the West, some of which I shall shortly point out. A cook knows that a very small quantitative change—a mere dash of another spice—may make a great difference in the dish he is preparing, though the quantity and quality of the staple he is using, flour, for instance, may remain the same. The analogy is, of course, a more than usually imperfect one, as well as undignified; but I suggest that a society which uses the familiar four-letter words freely in "polite" intercourse is exceedingly different from one in which they are strictly forbidden; and yet its members on *the average* may, even "morally," conduct themselves in quite similar ways in regard, say, to actual sex relations. The spice of language is important, but it is no staple.

---

[4] Four vols., New York, American Book Co., 1937, especially Vol. III, *Fluctuations of Social Relationships, War, and Revolution, with Statistical Tables.*

II

Both as to formal philosophic ethical writing and as to folk notions of ethics incorporated in tradition, codes, aphorisms of folk wisdom, the three or four thousand years of our Western recorded history show an unmistakable constant element. Honesty, loyalty, kindness, self-control, industry, co-operativeness are virtues; lying, treachery, cruelty, self-indulgence, laziness, conspicuous and uncontrolled aggressiveness, and selfishness are vices. There are indeed in-group limitations; lying to an outsider, cruelty to an enemy, are vices only in lofty ethical systems which take in all humanity, not just Western man, let alone just the tribe, as the in-group. Yet there is a strong note of universalism even in popular ethical ideals in the West, a note that had to be sounded both in Christianity and in the Enlightenment, and one that not even the growth of modern nationalism has drowned out. There are variations, often great, in the degree of esteem placed on these common ethical ideals, and on their interpretation. The Stoic notion of self-control and the Irish folk notion of self-control as exhibited at a wake are far apart; but the basic virtue I am trying to describe is there in both. Both try to overcome, to achieve control of grief and despair.

The most striking constant in the history of Western ethical ideals is the general reprobation that intellectuals, men of affairs, and the many alike give to all extreme forms of ethical relativism, which in the West usually takes the form of the doctrine that for the individual and for the group success is right, failure wrong—and success, substantially in this pattern, is doing what you want to do, getting power, wealth, prestige. Add to this the notion that men and groups vary infinitely in what they want. Now from Thrasymachus through Machiavelli to the latest sophomore to discover and misunderstand Nietzsche, this theme does crop up constantly in the history of Western thought, though it is necessarily muted in much of the Middle Ages. Yet such doctrines of ethical relativism are surely never "popular"; indeed, the best-known exponent of one form of the doctrine in modern times, Machiavelli, has become a common noun, a synonym of wicked "realism."[5] The doctrine, in forms such as "might makes right" or *Real-*

---

[5] I grant that Machiavelli was not a Machiavellian; he was not even quite an "inverted idealist," but a complicated and somewhat academic figure very aware of the gap between human practice and profession, and a somewhat premature Italian nationalist. Professor Garrett Mattingly argues, indeed, that *The Prince* is pure satire, that Machiavelli means as moralist the *opposite* of what he here seems to preach. *American Scholar*, XXVII, 1958, pp. 482-490. When you get down to cases, it is hard to find a full, uncompromising ethical relativist, just as it is hard to find full, uncompromising philosophical anarchists, or solipsists.

politik, or just just plain Nazism, and applied to a given in-group, may have seemed sometimes in recent years to have attained respectability and general acceptance among the many; but these ideas have certainly never gained full acceptance throughout the West; and even among the Germans, who have been the whipping boys for a long time for such ideas, they were far from universally held. Indeed, as I have maintained in my first consideration of modern nationalism (Chapter XII, p. 339), all but the most extreme of nationalists are aware that Christian universalism cannot accept nationalist parochialism as an absolute, and that even the one-hundred-percent patriot ought to leave a few percentage points for Christianity or Enlightenment. Western opinion generally holds that those who guide the group are not to be held to all parts of the observance of ethical code; nor are they to be held as rigorously to those that do apply as should the individual in his actions as a private person; but it holds that the group, right on up to the state, *ought* to conform to an ethical code by no means basically different from the code for individuals. Not even *raison d'état* has been widely accepted as dispensing a statesman from the morality of his society, except perhaps among such professionals as the men who really run the state. And even among these latter, and in a democracy, we should ourselves not be very realistic if we dismissed their professions of virtuous intent as altogether hypocritical. Even prime ministers, even secretaries of state, are often true believers.

Still confining ourselves to ethical ideals, we may note as a balance to the real constants above noted that there has always been, more particularly among writers on ethics, a great deal of variety in the expressed set of world views on which they base their actual ethical precepts. I am by temperament and certainly by training inclined to take the position that the precepts which are relatively constant are more important—more directly influence human conduct—than the world views, which vary with time, place, and individual thinker. Yet I suspect it makes some difference whether a man does the same thing under the impression that he is obeying the will of God or whether he does the same thing under the impression that he is maximizing his pleasure—his *true* pleasure. Indeed, I shall risk being somewhat unfashionable and express doubts as to whether under these conditions the somethings done are in fact the same thing. But to recur to a figure of speech used previously, the differing world views here seem to me to be at least no more than seasoning; only if the spice is poured on wholesale are the dishes radically different. Excessive doses of either the

Kantian categorical imperative or of the Benthamite felicific calculus can lead certain individuals far astray in different and not always quite predictable directions. Ordinary doses can sometimes drug, as notably with Kantian idealism, become the conventional nineteenth-century German belief that their philosophic national depth was all that Germans needed in the way of conventional virtue. But for the most part, both the categorical imperative and the felicific calculus led good middle-class nineteenth-century folk to the same unheroic decencies.

Yet one may risk a few generalizations of the range of these approaches to ethics, these "styles" in ethical world views. There have been in the West two well-known periods of maximum range of individual and group variation in this respect, the Greco-Roman world and our own in modern times. In both societies, the variety of these approaches is striking. They range from religion-sanctioned absolutes through many kinds of ethical idealism, even otherworldliness, to high-minded utilitarianism, rationalism, and on to comparatively rare assertions of low-minded utilitarianism, complete ethical relativism, and a cult of the Ego. In contrast, throughout the Middle Ages the approach to ethics was through a generally accepted belief that the rules of right conduct for men had been set by a supernatural power, a God who administered rewards and punishments in judgelike fashion; this God did administer a "natural law," but a law He had set and communicated to man through His son, and the church, not a law or uniformity men made or even discovered by themselves, unaided. In short, the commonplace is correct: formal ethics in the Middle Ages were based on an idealism transcending sense experience, empirical knowledge. Finally, and in spite of the vogue of German philosophical idealism in the nineteenth century, there can be little doubt that the weight of Western thought and feeling on ethics has in modern times fallen away from what William James called "tender-mindedness" and toward what he called "tough-mindedness." Hedonism, utilitarianism, pragmatism, even more ambiguous terms such as "naturalism" or "rationalism," though they invite the philosopher to long discussion, can be thrown loosely as a blanket over the ethical world views of, I suspect, the *majority* of educated Westerners in recent times. Even twentieth-century movements away from what we may vaguely call "naturalistic" or "this-worldly" or "tough-minded empirical" approaches to ethics seem to me not yet to have got many to thinking and feeling very transcendentally. But, of course, the whole Christian tradition *in practice* has always for the many made this world—the world of sense experience filtered through and organized by millions of minds over many centuries—rather more real, or at least rather more certain in all its variety, than any other.

It is perhaps harder to establish a kind of constant in human conduct over the course of Western history. At any given time and for any given group it can no doubt be maintained that there is a rough average conduct, neither very good in terms of accepted ethical norms nor very bad in such terms. Man's biological limitations, the economic limitations that have hitherto pretty well bound the many, the hold convention and conformity have on men, all combine to make real enough, no matter how the subtler, or perhaps merely the protesting, mind may reject its reality, the conception of an *homme moyen sensuel,* a middle of the roader in all he thinks, feels, and does, the man who keeps this world from being a heaven—perhaps, also, from being a hell. From this point it is not difficult to extend such a concept to the brief course of Western history, and come, with Mencken, to the conclusion that in spite of the fantastic, amusing, infuriating, noble, ignominious conduct of some men over these centuries, the bulk of men have as pagans, Jews, Moslems, Christians, freethinkers conducted themselves in a way thoroughly unsatisfactory to most moralists; they have been bad, but not very bad, good, but not very good. They have not for the most part kept to the kind of middle ground suggested by the Greek adage "nothing too much"; they have, rather, oscillated between unheroic bad and unheroic good, never achieving the extremes of the saint or the sinner, but never coming near the poise implied in the Greek ideal. Mencken would agree with J. S. Mill that "ordinary human nature is so poor a thing," but with the, for him, saving comment, "thank God!" Homo sapiens, the good-natured boob, can be led astray by reformers who play on his normally unexacting sense of decency and sometimes get him to behave "unnaturally" for a while; but he has sufficient moral inertia, which actually is a saving kind of stamina, so that he soon goes back to his time-tried and effective normality.

Mencken's bluff assurance that "human nature doesn't change" is stated in language that dates, but the historian of morals must record that some such conception of a constant in human conduct has itself been a constant of Western thought. He must, however, also note that the historical record itself is surely no straight line of any sort, up and down. Or, in an obvious metaphor, the moral landscape history offers us is no even plain, no plateau, but a varied one with great heights and horrid depths as well. It may well be that the great expanse of the middling hills and rolling plains is more monotonous, life there more alike always and everywhere, than on the peaks and in the abysses. But men range everywhere. Alone, often, but sometimes in numbers, sometimes in their thousands, they leave Mencken's comfortable plains, and take to the heights or the depths, or, like those almost medievally symbolic lemmings, swim on in the seas until they drown.

III

But we must return from metaphor to the record. Seen from the mid-twentieth century, the record of human conduct in the West does not seem to be one of clear general moral improvement or progress, not a record of unilinear evolution upward. Of course, not even such evolutionary theorists as Comte or Herbert Spencer, insensitive though they were to the facts of history, quite saw the course of history as an absolutely even straight line or curve, always keeping the upward course. Some lapses, some failures, some retrogression had to be admitted. Nevertheless, the term "unilinear evolution" is not an unfair one to describe the form that the notion of progress applied to human conduct took with many of these eighteenth- and nineteenth-century thinkers. An ordinary Englishman in 1901 *had,* in this system, to be a morally superior being to an ordinary Athenian in 416 B.C. The history-conscious observer will perhaps have noted that these dates are those of Kitchener's organization of concentration camps in South Africa to cope with Boer guerrilla warfare, and of the Athenian attack on the little island of Melos; in the first, some 20,000 Boer women and children died of disease, starvation, neglect, and despair; in the second, all Melian males were killed, and the women and children enslaved. This was progress, perhaps, for in 1901 formal institutional slavery had in fact ceased to exist in the West; but not quite the progress Condorcet dreamed of.

With the recent vogue of Spengler, Toynbee, and other philosophers of history the concept of cyclical variation in human conduct has come back into a kind of fashion. The term "cycle," like the term "revolution," is taken over from mechanics, and has at its root a concept of exact repetition, as with the revolution or turning of a wheel, which is by no means applicable to what we know of human history. Nevertheless, the two terms have both been, in ordinary use, translated into the kind of appropriate impreciseness that will do well enough at the present stage of our understanding of human affairs. I shall use the words "cycle" and "cyclical" loosely to mean the kind of variation that moves roughly from one definable extreme to another, though by no means usually in any repeated and exact time interval nor in equal distances, spiritual or material. We may perhaps get some light on our problem if we consider some of these "cyclical" variations in human morals.

The most all-inclusive of these variations or cycles inevitably must smack of the philosophy of history, with all its often suggestive but, by standards of professional historiography, quite unverifiable hypotheses, hunches, big ideas. I shall, however, hazard the suggestion that there are several forms of swings or cycles in the Western record, movements from one polarity toward another.

The first is a polarity of conservatism, conformity to established ways, on one hand and change, invention, entrepreneurship on the other. I should guess that no one, from St. Augustine and Ibn Khaldun to Hegel and Toynbee, has written on the philosophy of history without claiming as established facts of Western social organization and behavior what he seeks to describe in these or similar polar dualistic terms. The most sweeping and intolerant form that this polarity has been given, the Hegelian dialectic, covering nothing less than all human civilization—the thesis of Oriental despotism, changeless, timeless, then the antithesis of Greek and Western freedom, innovating but irresponsible, anarchic, and, finally the synthesis of Germanic *true* freedom, progressive but orderly—this formulation is so far from the facts as to be almost, but not quite, meaningless. (Not quite, for, unlike the raw facts, just because it is a theory it is something more than mere non-sense.) In more modest forms, applied to smaller societies, not held to any rhythmic or inevitable beat, never taken as meaning that all members of a given society are ever at one pole or another, the basic concept has its own partial validity.

For the historian of morals, the polarity may most conveniently be put in terms borrowed from Machiavelli and taken up by Pareto, terms I have already referred to (see p. 239). In some societies and at some times the feeling, the style, has been set by the lions; in others, by the foxes. The Spartans were lions, the Athenians foxes, though these were contemporaneous societies. The medieval aristocracy of the West were lions; the American plutocracy of the Gilded Age were foxes. Both these latter groups were addicted to violence, and neither conducted life along the best standards of our Western thought. But their moral styles were different. The lions at their best are reliable and unprogressive; the foxes at their best are unreliable and progressive, are at least agents of all sorts of changes, some of which may be morally desirable. Most human societies in the West have been mixtures of the two, with neither so predominating as to produce all change or no change; moreover, lions and foxes alike have been minorities, leaders—the majority, perhaps fortunately, remaining mere men. The lions tend to be corrupted by the material prosperity, which good lion-led armies, helped by a few foxes in government and even in military affairs, bring to a society; the foxes, in the long run of their descendants, turn into lions, but rather stale ones, lacking the fine fresh confidence of the original lions—turn, in fact, into die-hard conservatives, full of radically archaic ideas. No doubt there *is* something in Hegel, after all.

A second and most obvious polarity in our moral history is that between periods, or groups—perhaps whole societies—of great moral laxity and those of great moral strictness. Here even the relatively slight overtones of mechanical regularity we have left in terms like "cyclical" are misleading. The patterns discernible in our brief record are of bewildering complexity. Time intervals between loose and strict periods are irregular; in a big Western society, even in a single nation-state, loose-living and strict-living social classes (to say nothing of individuals) may for a time at least exist side by side; even before the modern nation-state, there have been within the West great regional differences in respect to this polarity of strict and loose morals. Finally, a group or class may in practice live reasonably well according to a code that seems to us strict in many ways, loose in others. Broadly speaking, Western aristocracies at their traditional peaks have had family solidarity, female chastity within the class, children carefully disciplined, have practiced within their ranks the virtues of conventional Christian morality (not *true* Christian morality); but their males in particular have been sexually loose—there were always plenty of women available in other classes—addicted to drinking, gambling, and other customary male vices, and caught up in an often unscrupulous form of the eternal agon.

Nevertheless, there are polar moments discernible, sometimes for these very aristocracies, sometimes for wider groups. The pole of laxity is clear in late-republican–early-imperial Rome and in the disorderly society that culminates in the Italian Renaissance. It is not by any means as clear for the West European aristocracies of the eighteenth century; nor do I think it at all clear for the privileged wealthy classes of the twentieth-century West. Indeed, even for the Romans and the men of the Renaissance, the extent of their immorality is exaggerated by the moral indignation of later historians, by the human fondness for scandal, and by the need to have moral scape-goats. For the last of the old European aristocracies, those of the eighteenth century in West Europe, those of the nineteenth century further east, the propaganda of their victorious revolutionary opponents (who in England did not need a revolution to succeed) has given them a reputation they do not entirely deserve. There were surely among them more Lafayettes and Steins than de Sades, or even Mirabeaus and Charles James Foxes. Our modern world has been spared from the extremes of moral laxity in part, certainly, by the conversion of so many superior people in the moral re-newal of the Enlightenment.

The polar moments of moral strictness are also clear: the early Christian communities, the triumphant puritan communities of early modern times, the brief moments of triumphant freethinking revolutionaries like the Jaco-bins and the Bolsheviks. There are somewhat more spotted, less purely Puritanical times of moral strictness, as in early republican Rome, in the maturing feudal aristocracies, among the Prussian *Junkers,* and among the Victorian middle classes. There is clearly much resistance among ordinary human beings to any widespread attempt to achieve in practice a rigorous moral order of the kind we must call, imprecisely but clearly, Puritanical. It would seem from the record that a degree of moral looseness is far more common than a corresponding degree of strictness. I shall come shortly to the implications of this polarity of looseness-strictness for morale, for the survival of societies.

Two striking examples of a kind of beat, of recurrence in time, again not with mechanical regularity, are afforded by this particular polarity. First, there is the marked phenomenon I have already mentioned, the sequence of rigorous suppression of open indulgence in conventional vices by the English Puritans of the 1640's and the French Jacobins of the 1790's, and the ex-traordinarily corrupt—again in conventional terms—"restorations" or "reac-tions" that followed them. There is a similar though not identical rhythm in the rigors of the first Russian Bolshevik rule and the ensuing relapse into Nep, the "New Economic Policy." These are sudden and dramatic changes, which follow on a given political signal. Second, there is the long record of reform within the Christian community. The record of Western monasticism is familiar: an order is established to practice rigorous and austere morality; it acquires wealth and standing, and begins to be less rigorous and austere, even, in hostile eyes, loose and corrupt; within the order itself in a cell or a branch, or perhaps outside it altogether, a group of reformers initiate a moral renewal, and once more the devoted lead austere lives of Christian goodness—and once more the decline sets in, once more to be followed by renewal. Protestantism itself, and its proliferation into sects, is in part a manifestation of this same process of moral renewal.

There are clear and real regional variations in the Western moral record (note that I am still trying to get that record straight, not yet to judge or even to generalize to any great extent). A familiar form of this variation to us today—it is one that the purest liberal finds it somewhat indecent to mention, or even to admit—is that between North European high morals and South European low morals. The generation of 1900 wrote a good deal of nonsense around his topic, extending the notion to a kind of world-wide moral peck order correlated with a scale from blond to brunette, or from fog to sunshine, or some equally simple measure. Cleanliness, which our Northern folk wisdom ranks next to godliness anyway, served as a nice index for these moralists; they liked to contrast in this respect Amsterdam with Naples, or even San Diego with Tijuana. Now this contrast was real enough, even if it could not entirely bear all the weight the racists put on it. No one, not even an American liberal, who lived first in a North European community and then in a Mediterranean community could fail to see, not only that the Northern community was cleaner, better house-kept, but that its inhabitants were at least *on an average,* as far as an outsider could judge, rather more chaste, more honest, more reliable, more self-controlled, more civically responsible than the Southern. He might come to like his Italians far more than his Swedes or Dutch or Scots; the Mignon complex itself is common among Northerners, who sometimes need relief from their virtue as well as from their fog. But that is another matter.

Tacitus does anticipate some of this theory of Northern virtue, but I do not think that what we know of medieval social history allows one to differentiate greatly between the regions of Europe in respect to these average levels of private and public morality. Chaucer's world seems as far from the world of Victorian England as was that of the French *fabliaux* from which Chaucer drew so much. The conduct of the Crusaders seems not to vary a great deal, no matter where they come from. The Christendom of the Middle Ages, if it was not quite the united world it seems to some to have been, does seem to have been loosely one in morals as in faith.

There remains a polarity that can hardly help taking us into the dangerous regions ranged by philosophers of history, and to the fearsome problems of the decline and fall of whole societies and civilizations.[6] This is the polarity of primitive-advanced, youthful-mature, simple-complex, innocent-sophisticated. Now these polarities are not identical, and they are further confused if one adds the moral one, virtuous-corrupt. Anthropology itself, one of the youngest of the social sciences, has destroyed whatever credit was left to eighteenth-century beliefs in a pristine and universal Golden Age, or to the nineteenth-century belief that primitive cultures are simple, especially simple in that they do not demand much from the human central nervous system. Yet there does remain a kernel of truth in the notion, especially well illustrated in the history of Rome, that there is often a "stage" in the development of a society when *mores* and morals alike are characterized, not by simplicity in the sense of absence of rules, ritual, formality, but by simplicity in the moral sense, rigorous observance of the rules, very little casuistry, little mockery, no irony, firm belief that black is black and white white and gray just nonexistent. But the tone of life in such societies is commonly violent, coarse, masculine, in a harsh sense quite contrasted with the tone of the Enlightenment. Much of its coarseness and violence and few of its virtues appear in the history of the American frontier; but otherwise our Western modern history has not in fact seen any society that at all resembles this idealized simple society.

A closely allied polarity was until quite recently part of our Western moral baggage. This is the contrast between the virtuous countryside and the wicked city, long a part of American folklore, but not unknown in Europe, indeed, originating there in its modern form in the eighteenth century. Whatever basis in fact the contrast had was rather in manners than in morals, and the debunkers were at work undermining the contrast even before modern technology had almost erased it. The novelists found incest and other horrors in New England villages well back in the nineteenth century; and, in a fine display of the competitive spirit, Southern novelists in our own time

---

[6] I would not have the reader conclude from such occasional references that I condemn all attempts at generalizing broadly about the course of history. On the whole, as should be clear from my own rashness in these matters, I am all for such attempts. But they are dangerous. If you find such writers as Toynbee, Spengler, Sorokin intolerable, I recommend A. L. Kroeber, *Configurations of Culture Growth*, Berkeley, University of California Press, 1944, and also his general book *Anthropology*, new ed., New York, Harcourt, Brace, 1948. Professor Kroeber, a trained anthropologist, understands both the strength and the actual present limitations of the methodology of Western natural science—and he knows that science pushes inexorably toward the highest degree of generalization the data will bear.

have discovered even worse things among the magnolias. Like all clichés, the contrast between the honest countryman and the city slicker was not without some element of truth. Great cities especially tend to breed among the many a superficial skepticism about the goodness and honesty of the race, an attitude that in this country the word "sophistication" has been vulgarized to describe. But the last war showed that in Europe and even in Asia the populations of modern great cities are clearly not lacking in the kind of moral fiber that enables them to stand up against bombardment from the air.

IV

We come thus to the difficult problem of the relation of morals in the conventional sense to the prosperity, the survival, of a society; or one may put it, the relation between private and public morals; or, still more simply, the relation between *morals* and *morale*.

At the outset, we can hardly avoid a truism: Western societies have always sooner or later found themselves at war, and therefore in need of good fighting men. To fight well, men need, of course, sustenance, weapons, increasingly complex and expensive, leadership, and luck; but they also need training, discipline, and what we may call simply the "military virtues." Now these virtues can be developed in a professional class, either relatively few mercenary troops, as in early modern Europe, or a relatively large professional army, as in later Rome, or a small professional fighting aristocracy, as in the early Middle Ages. Such professionals can often do pretty well for a society most of whose members clearly do not have the necessary military virtues. At any rate, it is clear that in the One World of the Roman Empire, throughout most of Europe in the Middle Ages, and to a degree right on to the great French Revolution, the many were not directly involved in fighting, did not even, save as producers, have much to do with the ultimate decision of war.

Yet the record of Western history shows many societies and many eras when armies were citizen armies—those of the Greek city-states, of Republican Rome, some few medieval city-states, and that extraordinary phenomenon the modern Western mass army that dates from the French Revolution and has gone on, in spite of knightly aviation, to our own day. In such societies the way the masses of men think and feel about their station and duties, their relation to their fellow men, their relation to the fatherland, is of very great importance. Weapons, supply, geography, leadership, and luck are surely also of great importance, and one of these variables alone may determine victory or defeat. Still, most, even of these variables, seem somehow related to the total strength of the society, a strength that is ultimately the good will of the many as well as the few. No one should question the importance of grave technical military failings in the defeat of France in 1940—nor, indeed, the importance of the simple fact that France is not an island. Yet, the general impression, which the French for the most part themselves do not deny, is that the fall of France stemmed also from a "failure of nerve," from lack of heart and stomach for that particular fight, from a moral failure.[7] And it would seem that even in societies, like the Roman Empire, or the France of the Hundred Years' War, where the many are not directly engaged in the fighting, the feelings of the many, their sense of sharing or not sharing in the common thing, has something to do with the survival of the society.

What are these virtues, what is this state of feeling among the many that makes for a society that can survive the test of war—hitherto, always, the ultimate test in the West? They are clearly not those of conventional private morality, and certainly not those of gentle, pacifist, idealist Christianity. Nor are there in the record—admittedly brief and incomplete—decisive grounds for correlating moral looseness, luxury, urban living with failure, old age, decadence, and collapse of a society. Especially for our modern Western world, the prophets of doom may not have it both ways: we cannot be today completely sunk in sensual self-indulgence and also fine disciplined fighters. And the overwhelming evidence of the last fifty years is that the West is, with all its grave difficulties, by no means lacking in those qualities we associate with youth, growth, even—blessed word—progress. In spite of Toynbee, Sorokin, and all the rest, this society does not *feel* old and tired.

There are, however, on the relation between civic morality and the survival of society a few positive generalizations that seem to come from the record. There is for one thing the striking fact of the expansive success, a success not infrequently achieved in actual battle, of religious groups in what I have called the active phase of a faith. Christianity itself took up the sword as well as missionary work very successfully once it had got established; and there are the Arabs in the almost incredible expansion of Islam, the Western

[7] In our multanimous West, it has, of course, been denied that morals or morale had anything at all to do with the fall of France. Certainly the matter is not as simple as the soldierly tradition makes it out to be. Reluctant soldiers can be quite good soldiers, as we Americans showed in the last general war. But *je-m'en-foutisme* probably does not help win wars, or peace.

Christianity of the Crusades, the secular crusades that followed hard on the establishment of the two most active forms of the faith of the Enlightenment, that of the French Jacobins and that of the Russian Bolsheviks. Even plain nationalism, not raised to very religious intensity, has inspired men to fight and resist with more than ordinary persistence, fury, and intolerance. There is no escaping the commonplace; men do fight best when they fight for a cause, fight best of all to help God, or Reason, or Dialectical Materialism bring about the inevitable.[8]

Yet these crusades have hitherto always been brief, have always burned themselves out quite rapidly. It is much more difficult to account for the place of moral factors in the long pull, in the general good health of a society. Here surely the crux is not the question of how much ordinary wickedness there is among the many, and especially how much gambling, whoring, drinking, gluttony, and the like. These matters, and, even more, such matters as honesty, loyalty, discipline, willingness to accept hardship and disappointment, willingness to collaborate with others, and much more of the sort, *are* important for the good society, even for the going, reasonably good society. But these matters themselves seem to depend in part on men's attitudes toward their fellows and toward the universe, on just the kind of problem of morals and world views we have been dealing with in this study. Their attitude toward their fellows involves a whole series of problems, central to which is the problem of conflict—class struggles, personal agon, the relations between what men want and what they get, and hence the degree to which they are satisfied, "happy." Their attitude toward the universe has an immediate and close relation to all the above complexities of conflict and co-operation.

Now the reader may well be tired of my frequent insistence that in human societies nothing is ever pure X or its polar opposite pure Y, but always a somewhat varying mixture of the two—not to speak of much else which we may call N. But here, if ever, this insistence seems to me fully justified—to the point, indeed, where I should believe that anyone who wholly disagreed with me was not quite sane, or responsible. For in all Western societies on the record, there has been conflict—yes, class conflict, bitter hatreds—*at all times;* and *at all times* there has been co-operation—yes, co-operation, even

---

8 Conceivably they could fight best by not fighting. Yet few generalizations are clearer than that in the West passive resistance, the "general strike," the noble gesture of Lysistrata, just do not work. I suspect they do not work even in India as well as the non-watchers say they do. Gandhi himself came to an unfortunately violent end.

A History of Western Morals

love, between poor and rich, plebians and patricians, low-brows and high-brows. There is no harm in using figures of speech drawn from arithmetic and thinking of, say, some simple range like that of the thermometer, with, then, a freezing point below which lack of conflict of any sort might mean disastrous lack of adaptability to changes in the natural environment, let alone the human environment as represented in a rival society; and with a boiling point above which conflict might be so excessive as to destroy the society altogether. But do not let any such innocent metaphor delude you: even the thermometer can mislead if, accustomed to boil your egg at sea level, you have to boil it on top of Pikes Peak. The variables involved in the stability, the good health, of a given society are never simple enough to be shown on any single unilinear scale.

Nevertheless, we may fairly ask what our bird's-eye view does show us in this matter of conflict, and in particular that of the "class struggle." Our own time has seen two major contrasting interpretations of Western history in terms of class relations. First, for the Marxist, there has been a series of struggles between a smaller privileged rich class, *beneficiaries* of a given "mode of production," and a larger oppressed poor class, *victims* of the mode of production. Between these classes there is—at any rate, in Marxist tradition there ought to be—hatred, the good hatred of the lower for the upper, the bad hatred and fear of the upper for the lower. Second, for Toynbee, the successful responses by which a society achieves and improves its "civilization" are always made by a creative minority (who are in fact an upper class or an aristocracy); the rest of the society, however, the many, do while the society is advancing absorb these civilized advances by a somewhat mysterious process Toynbee calls "mimesis," which, psychologically speaking, is respectful, admiring imitation of their betters. Toynbee does not spell this relation between the minority and the many out closely, but where he seems to think it existed, as in fifth-century Athens *before* Cleon and the plague, it looks a lot like nice English Tory democracy, the many guided by the virtuous few, aristocrats in all of the good, and none of the bad, senses this value-charged word has for us today. Then when the creative minority fails to meet a challenge, as when at Athens this minority provoked or permitted the horrid Peloponnesian War, this subtle nexus of mimesis gets broken, the creative minority becomes a mere dominant minority, and the many sink into a proletariat, hating their betters. You have, indeed, as Toynbee would admit, in such periods of failure of mimesis the kind of class feeling Marx thought *always* prevailed, and would prevail until the achievement of the classless society.

430

Now once more, I think there is some validity in both these analyses. Or, perhaps better, I think our bird's-eye view will show certain societies at certain times almost—but not quite—as ineffably co-operative in class relations as Toynbee's term "mimesis" implies, others at other times almost—but not quite—as desperately at odds as the Marxist class struggle implies. Specifically, the relation among the feudal nobility, the "clerisy," and the peasantry in the West was by no means the idyl it has often been made out to be.[9] Still, it is clear that something of the attitude reflected in the familiar medieval figure of society as an organism, with wise clerical head, brave feudal heart, sound peasant digestive system, did get generally accepted until, roughly, the mid-fourteenth century. If early Athens was not as free from class conflict as the lovers of Greece make out, there is surely a time after Solon when there is something like an era of good feeling; and in Roman history the struggle between patricians and plebeians is by no means a neat Marxist struggle, if only because it is clear that the many were, above all, patriotic Romans. In our own times, Victorian England saw something like partial mimesis among the gentry, the middle classes, and, in part at least, the working class. The American feeling that the Marxist analysis has never really been valid for us is basically sound, not so much because the many here love and admire the few, but partly because so many of the many hope to join the few, and even more because our democratic religion of the Enlightenment, which has always worked best in the United States, does almost as good a job as medieval Christianity did in allaying the feelings that erupt in class conflict.

On the other side, it is clear that the record shows many societies in which class or group or factional conflict has in fact reached a point where the society is on the way to dissolution, decay, death as an "independent" society. What Thucydides describes as "stasis" is surely as desperate and vicious a civil conflict, not quite the Marxist class struggle, as ever ruined a society. The One World of the Roman Empire was certainly not a world of happy mutual co-operation. Here Toynbee's analysis is at its best: the "internal proletariat" of the Roman Empire was profoundly dissatisfied, alienated from its rulers, *relatively* ill-supported either by the props of the small society (family, the old household gods, the familiar steady traditions) or by the vaguer consolations of a higher religi ﹏ that Marxists call "opium of the

[9] I have used "clerisy" in the sense given the word by Coleridge in his Constitution in *Essay on Church and State* (1830) a brief book, and, for Coleridge, a clearly written one, well worth the attention of anyone interested in political ideas. I give a short cut in my *English Political Thought in the Nineteenth Century*, Chap. II.

people." Christianity reflects its origins in a complex but decaying society. The troubles that run from the Black Death to the Peasants' War and Luther are the troubles of a society prey to excessive group conflicts, though until quite recently historians saw these centuries as seedbeds of progress, not decay.[10]

It is by no means easy to fit group tensions in our contemporary West into these older patterns. Here once more we are forced to the conclusion, so unsatisfactory to many minds, that there are signs of both class conflict and of acceptance, by the underprivileged or little privileged at least, of the existence of more privileged groups. Of course, even in the United States there is a social and economic pyramid, or, at any rate, a *figure,* and not the straight line on a graph that would represent a completely classless society. The gap between a Negro sharecropper—or an unskilled Negro worker in the North— and a man in the upper income-tax brackets is very great. There is still a right and wrong side of our railroad tracks, even though they can be crossed. The contemporary American novel of status—John Marquand's *Point of No Return* or Hamilton Basso's *View from Pompey's Head,* for example—seems sometimes obsessively aware of social gradations, and of the frustrations they produce. A great many American intellectuals clearly share with A. M. Schlesinger, Jr., a firm conviction that most American businessmen are fools or scoundrels, or both; and such alienation of the intellectuals has in the past been a sign of instability in a society. As for the European West, we have such clear signs of social discontent as the angry young Englishmen who still find it hard not to be born gentlemen, the notorious perpetual ripeness for revolution all American commentators find in strife-riddled France, the grave difficulties encountered throughout a Europe in which the haves and the have-nots are still morally separated.

Nevertheless, it would be premature to see the West as now hopelessly, or hopefully, prepare for a long bout of overt, desperate, destructive class warfare. There are still widespread sentiments—moral sentiments—of the kind that work to hold societies together, to reconcile the many to their not being the few. Everywhere in the West there are strong Christian elements; and, as we have insisted, historical Christianity has on the whole worked to strengthen those human feelings that make for acceptance of one's earthly lot. Christianity in the realm of ideas denies the Marxist conception of the

---

[10] They still do, overwhelmingly, though sometimes in the form of a transition era in which the medieval society or culture was dying, and the modern rising out of this death. Even Mr. Toynbee puts the beginning of our own end no earlier than the mid-sixteenth century.

class struggle, but so, too, in its most characteristic Western form, does the complex of ideas and sentiments I have called the religion of the Enlightenment. The good, nationalist democrat, even if he thinks he has jettisoned the prejudices of Christianity, has been shaped by Christian culture, including those Middle Ages he despises as priest-ridden, to believe that force alone never settles anything, not even the class struggle; he may suspect, after 1919 and 1945, that force never settles the international struggle; and he holds that men can compromise even their conflicting interests if they will persistently distinguish between right and might, and that there is a natural social order in which violence is wrong. These views may seem to the ardent radical deluded, illogical, opium of the people indeed, but they are strong not only in the English-speaking countries, but throughout the West, strong enough to have withstood the great strain the two general wars of our time have put on victors and vanquished alike. They have not, of course, been strong enough to put a stop to all kinds of conflict within the states that make up Western civilization; for nothing can be clearer in the record than that struggle, the agon, victory and defeat, make the burden of history.

The record is clear also in this respect: warfare among the constituent states of the West is endemic. Indeed, it is almost continuous. I have previously expressed my doubts as to the value of the imposing statistical reckoning of the damage done by foreign and civil war assembled by Sorokin in his *Social and Cultural Dynamics* (see p. 416), but there can be no doubt that the mere listing of these wars and other outbreaks of violence made by Sorokin and his research assistants is impressive. Peace has been rare, war common. There *are* variations in the character of warfare. Sometimes, as in the Middle Ages or in 1914-1918 on the Western front, the defensive primes the offensive; sometimes, as with the Roman legions at their best, or the mass modern armies of Napoleon, the offensive primes the defensive. Sometimes warfare is limited to a professional fighting class, and the people, the many, suffer no more than the inevitable damages to life and property the noncombatant incurs in a combat area, hunger, disease, the general horrors of war. Sometimes warfare and its attendant diplomacy are conducted according to rules, open flouting of which is generally morally disapproved, as in the limited warfare of the Middle Ages and in the formal European warfare of the eighteenth and nineteenth centuries; sometimes warfare and diplomacy maintain but the shadow of lawfulness and morality, as notably in the Greece of Thucydides and in our own twentieth-century Western world.

The historian of morals seeking a clear pattern from the past will find neither a definite cyclical movement from peace to war, or from relatively humane to relatively vicious fighting; nor will he be able, with Spencer and the Victorians of only yesterday, to discern a unilinear movement from the warlike past to the less-warlike present and on to a peaceful future. Professional, limited warfare is certainly less disastrous and less destructive for the whole society, but it is surely never humane, never in Christian or in Enlightened ethics in itself a good. Modern mass warfare with its citizen armies has had outrageous results more perhaps because of the destructiveness brought on by our command of technology than because of the emotional commitment of the fighting men to the cause of the fatherland. There is a tendency, as I have noted just above, for warfare among states with citizen—that is, amateur—armies to be rather more cruel and unprincipled than warfare among statesmen, professional armies of mercenaries, or gentlemen, or of both. Yet such a statement may be no more than a reflection of the last horrors of the great amateur war we have lived through, a war that has simply not begun to seem romantic. Our American Civil War, a highly amateur one, is now hopelessly romantic. Detailed study of any war, even those of the mid-eighteenth century, is likely to impress the student with a sense of the great gap between Western ethics and Western conduct.

I have been considering public morality, or the *morale* of a society, in relation to the survival and prosperity of that society in a competitive military world. Had I proposed instead to survey the relation between such morality and the artistic, literary, and philosophical achievements of the society, I should have had an even harder task. There are certain obvious generalizations. A society that prohibits for religious—that is, surely, also for moral—reasons most of the fine arts will not go down as one that produced a flowering of such arts. Yet in the West radical puritanism, a puritanism that condemns all art and letters across the board, has simply never existed unchecked for long. On the other side of the ledger, there is always the Italian Renaissance, a period of clear and pretty general moral disorder, yet a period of great artistic flowering indeed. Once more, the conclusion is inescapable: we do not understand the causes of any cultural flowering in a society well enough to correlate such flowering with the state of private and public morality in that society. We do know—and it is something worth knowing—that there is no perfect correlation, that the one does not wholly "depend" on the other. Bacon and Milton, Sappho and Sophocles, and many another contrasting pair are there to remind us of that fact.[11]

[11] I cannot here go into this vexing problem of the flowering time, the *Blütezeit* and its relation to morals and *morale*. Sorokin in Vol. I of his *Social and Cultural Dynamics* refers to the important literature of the subject up to the 1930's. And see also A. L. Kroeber, *Style and Civilization*, Ithaca, Cornell University Press, 1957.

In sum, our rapid review of Western moral history has shown no clear evidence that men are in their conduct getting closer to their ethical ideals. There is variation as well as constancy in both conduct and ethics. But the discernible patterns do not indicate any one-way relation between high moral standards in a society and its survival, its material prosperity, or its literary, artistic, and cultural achievement. Nor do such patterns wholly prove or wholly disprove—insofar as empirical evidence is germane to such religious beliefs—the nineteenth-century faith in Progress. They do, I think, make it clear that the kind of change the Victorians labeled as "Progress" is more uneven and jerky, more subject to lapses or "decadence," slower, and much more unpredictable, than the Victorians thought. We may, then, attempt to survey the ground from a somewhat different point of view, and attempt to assess some of our own institutions, some of our own moral attitudes, in the perspective of our brief Western past, knowing well that even our now-apparent gains may not be permanent ones.

V

The prize exhibit of those who can still believe in moral Progress is the Western achievement in abolishing chattel slavery. The achievement is undeniable, not to be seriously weakened by rhetoric about still-existing "wage slavery" and the like. Freethinking historians have made a great deal out of the failure of Christianity in the Roman Empire to eliminate in fact the slavery that Christian spirit and principles condemned, and even more of the failure of Christianity during the great expansion of Europe after 1450 to prevent the renewal of the institution in enslavement of colonial peoples, and, in particular, of Africans. The Marxists, and not only the Marxists, never tire of insisting that slavery has always prevailed where it was economically profitable and has only been abolished after it has been demonstrated to at least most of the slaveowners, condemned to immorality by the mode of production, that slavery is unprofitable. The mere historian will content himself with noting that abolition in our own culture was in fact sealed by a law, and achieved only after long conflict of words—in the United States, of actual fighting, as well—words somewhat beyond the conventional range of the economists. Christians of all shades of opinion, from Catholics to Unitarians, and freethinkers of an almost equal range, worked toward the end of abolishing what they regarded as an evil. Indeed, the honest materialist would have to admit that the completeness of the abolition can be explained only by the fact that the overwhelming majority of Westerners came in a few generations to feel that slavery is *wrong*. Otherwise, there would be in the West pockets of chattel slavery as there are pockets of everything that mere technological progress has condemned, survivals like archery or fencing, or even the horse. There is, we have abundantly noted, always an absolutist *drive* in morals.

The mention of fencing should remind us that the last two centuries have seen the channeling of some of the bloodier forms of the Western agon into a "moral equivalent." We have not as yet found in sport what William James hoped for, a moral equivalent of organized war. But we have abolished the duel, and have driven underground into mere criminality most other forms of *private* warfare. Even in the United States, that classic land of violence, our clan feuds, gang wars, lynchings, are not what they used to be in the last century. Prize fights, and even bullfights are but pallid and still-waning survivals of the cruel exhibitions of the past; indeed, Christianity has never witnessed anything as bad in this respect as the spectacles of the Roman arena. We know and even give a name from pathology, "sadism," to the human desire to witness or to inflict suffering upon other sentient beings. We may even suspect that whatever it is that makes men sadistic is as common a biological inheritance of men as it was two thousand years ago; and we know from the experience of the West since 1939 that whole groups of men can be as cruel in the twentieth century as in the first century. Yet there are grounds for regarding these exhibitions of cruelty as relapses. They have been subject to strong moral condemnation, even by the nationals responsible for them. And over the whole sweep of possible human cruelty and violence, there can be no doubt that we have devised institutional and legal restraints with good roots in the Western conscience. The only form of organized violence that has hitherto escaped some such controls is actual warfare, which we are probably justified in holding to be the great, the critical, moral evil of our time.[12]

There is a whole series of more positive efforts to cope with the evils of actual human suffering on the record. Once more, we may note that not

---

[12] I confess that I had not until I began this chapter read any of the work of our American de Sade for the millions, Mickey Spillane. I do not wish to make light of the moral portent of these shocking—and puzzling—examples of vicious, vicarious, mere paper cruelty, but I do not dare try to explain the fact that in inexpensive soft-cover editions they have sold in millions. It is surely clear that their readers do not for the most part take these books as counsels to go thou and do likewise. It is, however, shocking that there should be a felt need for even vicarious satisfaction of such sentiments. But do not make the mistake of seeing only Mickey Spillane here; his greatest rival in soft-cover sales is not Erskine Caldwell (a more conventional and to-be-expected pornographer), but the celebrated Dr. Spock on how to bring up babies.

merely the notion of "progress," but the whole notion of any specific moral "better" depends on what it is now fashionable to call value judgments. If you think suffering, mental and physical, is a moral good, a needed test of virtue, then you may regard the change from beating demons out of the insane to modern psychiatric treatment of mental illness as no moral progress, even as moral decay. (Do not sneer at the verbal change from "insane" to "mental illness"—that, too, is a kind of moral progress within our tradition.) But the moral concepts of good and evil in their broader senses are a relative constant in the West, and these concepts make suffering an evil against which it is right to struggle.

The list of such modern triumphs or part-triumphs over human suffering is long, and hardly needs recording here. It runs from the treatment of mental illness to the care and feeding of the healthy, and to the comfort and culture of all. Even the two centuries or so of such "progress" shows shifts, variations, tendencies toward taking on vaguely cyclical patterns. This process, which may, nevertheless, also be Progress, is clear in the whole history of education in its broadest sense, and in child development. There are swings from discipline and control to permissiveness, and back again—well, part way back, at any rate. There are swings from what we may loosely call "intellectualism" to "anti-intellectualism," and perhaps, as of 1959, some of the way back again. The brief history of modern education, the first attempt to "educate" in the formal institutional sense of the word almost *everybody*, is full of conflicting ideals and personalities, of evident failures and wrong turnings; it must seem even to the moderately hard-boiled realist rather too much dominated by the goal of ultimate human perfectibility. But the history of education, as of the rest of modern humanitarian effort, does not by any means suggest to the historian of morals who is bent a bit toward the philosophy of history decadence, tiredness, rigidities, a Spenglerian old age of a civilization; it suggests a lively, sometimes almost innocent, youth.

As to the familiar field of personal morality of the sort the Victorian vulgar tended to identify with the sum total of morality, there is neither in the last two nor in the last twenty centuries any very clear sign of the kind of progress one may discern in the lessening of much human suffering in the last few hundred years. Sex morality has, indeed, varied in time and place, as I have abundantly noted. But it is difficult to show that we conduct our sex lives on a higher plane than the Greeks or the men and women of the Middle Ages. The Victorian Englishman thought he and his countrymen had achieved in this respect the kind of progress he saw all about him. We today can hardly do so. It is true that the old-fashioned brothel has tended to disappear under the pressures of legislation and policing in most of the West; but the automobile, though it can scarcely be as comfortable, seems to be an adequate substitute for many. It would be hard to show that fornication, for love or money or both, has decreased significantly in our day. Among the educated—the rather highly educated—there is a tendency to regard the various sexual perversions as a form of mental disease, to be treated as such and not as crime or immorality. Among the many, to judge by recent events in Britain, where there has been an attempt to remove from the list of crimes homosexual activity among adults "constitutionally" inclined thereto, the old strong sentiments of moral condemnation still prevail. The masses, the people, in most of the West are far from being as emancipated from old-fashioned firm morals as intellectuals, either the now few who are hopeful or the many worried about it all, are inclined to assume. The concept of chronic alcoholism as basically a mental illness, on the other hand, seems to be somewhat more widespread. I shall come shortly to the problem of how far the development and spread of such notions—essentially part of the growth of the social or behavioral sciences—may be considered "progress."

As to the other vices of self-indulgence, there again seems to be little sign of consistent improvement, though briefly in puritanical societies and eras many of them are temporarily greatly lessened and driven underground. Gambling, in particular, seems to resist the attacks of Enlightened, as well as those of Puritan Christian, virtue. In old-fashioned language, gambling may even be said to be natural, to be a need. At the height of American Victorian public morality, which came in the early twentieth century, prohibitory legislation in many states had made such usual forms of gambling as that of the race track inconvenient indeed; it was much easier, and almost as much fun, to gamble on the stock market; and there were, of course, in the widespread network of respectable lawbreaking that grew up after the Eighteenth Amendment was passed many opportunities for gambling as well as for buying liquor. There has been since 1929 much relaxation of such prohibitions, and the pari-mutuel has been a great success in some most respectable states of the union.[13] Gluttony, in orthodox tradition one of the seven deadly or capital sins, is nowadays surely one of the least common, in spite

[13] It is an arresting example of the inevitably subjective character of all we are now discussing to realize that for those who really believe in the methods well-enough summed up by the Eighteenth Amendment—and there are many who do so believe—the last three decades have shown moral decline, retrogression.

of (or because of) the relative abundance and security of the food supply of the West. The lover of good cooking will suggest that throughout that large part of the West dominated by the English-speaking peoples there is in fact little to tempt to gluttony; but it seems more likely that fashion, especially for women, has made the consequences of gluttony seem intolerable. And fashion works through the first and deadliest—and most ambivalent—of these sins, pride.

The mere listing of these seven sins—pride, covetousness, lust, anger, gluttony, envy, and sloth—should remind us that whatever it is in men that inclines them to such conduct has certainly not been overcome. We may say in summary with folk wisdom that "human nature hasn't changed." We may say more cautiously and more heavily that in terms of what we think we know about human "personality" the likelihood of some such conduct seems pretty well built into the ordinary adult; and in terms of what we think we know about history and the social sciences we may say that though culture, or "environment," clearly has worked to vary the incidence and intensity of such conduct, to channel and control it in part, no large group has for long eliminated any of this conduct. At this late point in our study, I need hardly point out that, though the freethinker dislikes and usually refuses to employ the term "sin," he does, in fact, usually condemn all Christian sins as morally bad conduct.

The mention of the social sciences does, however, suggest one final possibility of discerning clear "progress" in morals. Is it not possible that, in some way comparable to that in which the natural sciences have opened the way to the unquestionable progress the race has made in its ability to make use of the powers of nature to secure some of the things men want, the social sciences may open the way to progress in our ability to get what we want out of ourselves? Now on this vast subject there is already a whole library of books and articles. We cannot do it justice here. But we can at least try to pose the problem in the frame of the historical record.

But first of all we may dispose of the pejorative statement: There is no such thing as social or behavioral sciences, at least no such body of cumulative knowledge as that which we all recognize as such in the natural sciences. There is, on the contrary, a great and rapidly growing body of cumulative knowledge about human conduct, individual and group, and it deserves the nowadays eulogistic label "scientific." It is not, as a body of cumulative knowledge, as well developed as the natural sciences, for many reasons. It is as an organized effort to use the methods of science much more recent. It has perhaps tried too hard to do exactly what the natural sciences have done, notably in its attempt at quantification. It is severely limited, in its study of human beings, by strong, indeed, for the present, ineradicable, human sentiments which strictly limit the possibilities of deliberate experimentation. It has had to contend with many hostile currents of public opinion, not only among the many, but among the educated few. It has not, probably, in our society been able to compete with the natural sciences in recruiting for its ranks the very best minds. But the list of the handicaps under which the social sciences have labored could be long indeed; and it would have to include the fact that the working out of viable uniformities or generalizations from its data is intrinsically much more difficult than in the natural sciences, both from the complexities and from the inadequacies of its data.

Yet with all these handicaps, the social sciences have progressed; we know more, in the simple sense of the word "know," and we know more systematically, about human personality and human relations than was known in 1700. Our grave difficulty lies in the equivalent, for the social sciences, of the relation between pure science and the technology or applied science or engineering so familiar to us all in the natural sciences—though for the historian and philosopher of science the dynamics of that relation is itself by no means a simple and clear one. Note, by the way, that this problem of the relation between "pure" natural science and technology is itself a problem of the social sciences, not of the natural sciences. On this subject, too, there is already a great library. From my point of view, which I shall try to make clear in the next chapter, the central difficulty lies in a philosophic problem: Does the study of what we call "science," natural or social, give us ends, purposes, even immediate ones, let alone final ones, teleologies, eschatologies? Perhaps such horrendous philosophical problems can be got around comfortably, as I have suggested in Chapter I. There remains for us today at least a difficulty in applied social science harder to get around: such applied science must in real life be "applied" by the few, the expert, the "engineer," who, to judge, as we must, by historical precedent, must stand in relation to those to whom the social-scientific know-how is applied in a position profoundly incompatible with the strong and widespread current that dominates Western, and, most emphatically, American, sentiments. A society bettered—bettered as rapidly, at least, as the alarmists think ours must be— by social engineering *could not possibly be a democratic society*. The relation of the human planner to the human planned-for has, inevitably, elements of the relation between shepherd and sheep; and this relation is in our tradition almost as offensive, as "immoral," as that of master and slave. At bottom, the American distrust of high-minded planners (and most social scientists are indeed high-minded) really is what the worried call "anti-intellectualism," but there it is, fierce and strong. The American today simply will not let himself be improved by his betters—his machines, yes, even his health, but not *himself*.

Yet there is a difficult line to be drawn here. The relation of physician to patient, though it can sometimes be tyrannical and sometimes involves the naïve Machiavellianism of the placebo, can be, and in our culture often is, quite consistent with the sentiments we call "democratic." The comment is obvious: Both physician and patient have the same end in view, the good health of the patient. And although there is plenty of room here for conflict of will, and even for debate over the nature and definition of good health, these difficulties are as nothing compared with the problem of what the economic, social, political, and moral good health of a society is, and what the ends that the skills of social scientists are intended to further should be. Now the social sciences are not at all as advanced as the biochemical sciences on which the expertness of the practicing physician so largely depend; nor is there yet as good a working arrangement between the pure scientist and the applied scientist in any of the social sciences as that shown by the relation between the research biologist or pathologist and the physician, or between the chemist and the chemical engineer. For all the ill-natured fun the caricaturist and the politician love to poke at the economist, there is a clear beginning of such a relation in the field of economics. There is a clear beginning of such a relation in the field of psychology, though here the moral problem of ends is most evident to the worried liberal: 1984 is now less than a generation away.

For all its limitations and, indeed, errors, for all the imperfections of those who built it up, the body of our systematic knowledge of human behavior is greater and more reliable now than it was two hundred or two thousand years ago. In that strong current of Western thought, Christian and Enlightened alike, which accepts human reason as an essential good, the growth of the social sciences must appear cumulative, progressive. The problem of developing *and using* these sciences—a problem to which that of the proper moral place of the expert in a democratic society is central—may well be considered the major problem that faces us today.

VI

In summary, we must say that the cliché is unavoidable: the record shows no moral progress comparable to our material progress. From the beginnings of Western society in the ancient Near East there have been states, societies, which have seemed in no mere Spenglerian metaphor to have been born, matured, and died, to have had a spring, summer, autumn, and winter. Yet this process of rise and fall is still ill understood, and has no immediate and clear relation to the private or public morality of the individuals who make up the state. It would no doubt be comforting to many of us to hold with Thomas Carlyle that "a false man cannot build a brick house," but the record is against the preacher. "False" in this context is no doubt an ambiguous word; but Carlyle meant that a bad man cannot do good work of any kind, and this is simply not so.[14] There are degrees of corruption that clearly lame a society, especially if it is in competition with a disciplined and morally strict society, but not even in warfare is it clear from the record that the simple, old-fashioned virtues always pay off. And as for the record of private morality, it is difficult to show that there is in the record a steady, consistent, unilinear increase in the practice of the traditional virtues, and such a steady decrease in the practice of the traditional vices. There seems to be only a mixture, varying in place and time, and so far never quite lethal for the species.

The idea of Progress in its fully theological form, that of an eschatology, of mankind as a whole moving to some far-off divine perfection, is, of course, not to be tested empirically. I have been seeking in this chapter to answer from the historical record a more modest question: Measured against the known standards for conduct set by the ethical principles of the Western tradition, are we in fact conducting ourselves better, narrowing the gap between conduct and ethics? And I have edged over into another and characteristically nineteenth-century question, one, again, for which some answer from the evidence should be possible: Is human conduct in the West at least sufficiently good by standards that measure group achievement so that we may say that the West is not, in a cultural evolutionary sense, clearly in a *retrogression,* clearly not headed for the kind of extinction a Spengler predicted for it? Yet the answer has to be for both questions something in the nature of the old Scots verdict "not proven," and the whole problem is,

[14] Carlyle, *Heroes and Hero-Worship,* London, Chapman and Hall, 1873, p. 41. I am here working wholly within an empirical, indeed a common-sense, frame of reference. In terms of a theodicy, evil never does produce good—but this is a very different set of ideas and sentiments. There are no brick houses either in heaven or in hell.

unfortunately, hardly to be lifted above the level of the bull session. It can be debated, but there will not even be a sense of the meeting.

Yet most certainly, in this twentieth century our conduct has not been nearly what a Condorcet—perhaps even a Jefferson, young Jefferson—hoped and believed it would be. Raise up the horrid picture of men and beasts dying in the Roman arena, that of Clovis hacking and deceiving his way to a most Christian throne, that of the Borgias intriguing, poisoning their way upward, that of the mass murders of the great French Revolution, that of our own successful genocide of the Eastern American Indians. You can raise up quite equal, if not identical, horrors out of the twentieth-century West, bull-fights, prize fights, dictatorships, purges, concentration camps, attempted and nearly successful genocides, race riots, gangsterism, bloody wars between mass armies. We can all, even the insensitive, even the hard-boiled, even—if such there still be—the optimists, extrapolate in fear and trembling from the facts of Hiroshima. We may indeed be no worse morally than our ancestors, and we may even be on the average a bit less cruel, less brutal, but grouped in nation-states we can do a lot more evil more quickly and more efficiently than they could. Our conspicuously, heroically, wicked are surely no less wicked than the great evildoers of old; the many, again possibly a little gentler at heart than the masses of old, and certainly as always no heroes, seem no more able than of old to halt or contain the heroic few.

But again the record is spotty. It does show over the last two centuries in the West at least a decrease in the violence and uncertainties of daily living in time of peace; it does show over the centuries a widening of the social areas within which a good life—a life not just of struggle to keep alive—is possible; it does show, in spite of the horrors we all know, a slowly and imperfectly extended concept of the dignity of man; it does show the abolition of slavery and many another humanitarian reform in consonance with the ethical tradition of the West; it does show—and this is most important—at least no wide abandonment of the moral struggle and, for the West as a whole, no indubitable signs of moral and civic degeneration. We seem in sum not much better and not much worse, morally, than the Jewish and Greek founders of our moral tradition. A dull, stupid, pussyfooting conclusion? Perhaps, but suppose it happens to be a true one?

There does remain the undoubted fact that, notably in the United States of America, most of us do somehow manage to "believe in" Progress. Here is Adlai Stevenson, and in a campaign speech at that, where he should be telling his audience what they want to hear: "Progress is what happens when inevitability yields to necessity. And it is an article of the democratic faith that progress is a basic law of life."[15] The naïve semanticist—and actually most semanticists are naïve about other human beings—could, of course, make great fun of that distinction between "inevitability" and "necessity." But Mr. Stevenson surely knew what he was talking about. His "inevitability" was a term of common sense, or even, if you like, "scientific," discourse; his "necessity" a term of moral discourse. Here, once again, I shall be unashamedly in the middle—in a livable zone between two bleak poles. To hold that what we believe in moral discourse *must* come wholly true in common-sense discourse, in "fact," just *because* we believe it, is called "fideism," and, though not unknown among human beings, is rightly considered lunacy; to hold that what we believe in moral discourse has *no relation* whatever to what goes on, to what *comes about* in fact, in the world of common-sense discourse is in the twentieth-century West far more common than fideism, and does not therefore always seem the lunacy that it is.

It is true that our American belief in moral, or total, Progress cannot be confirmed from the record by any process like that which the scientist uses to confirm—or reject—his beliefs qua scientist. But the moment faith, or belief in moral values, gets to work in our minds and hearts, it transforms "confirmation" into something not quite what it is to the scientist testing by orthodox scientific methods a hypothesis. Cynic, skeptic, and naïve materialist are quite wrong; faith need not, does not commonly in our Western tradition, deny, neglect, suppress the facts, the data, the realities of this world. It does *use* them to try to get what it wants, what its world view makes moral; it does try to *change* them. We must in a concluding chapter attempt the more difficult task of estimating the moral value and probable or possible moral consequences of some of our contemporary world views, and, in particular, of the doctrine of Progress and the whole configuration that has grown out of the Enlightenment. The question at heart is, not whether the doctrine of Progress is true, but whether it is wise, good.[16]

---

[15] From a radio address, Oct. 24, 1952, quoted by Clarke A. Chambers, "Belief in Progress in 20th-Century America," *Journal of the History of Ideas,* Vol. XIX, April 1958, p. 221. This article brings forward abundant evidence for the widespread and firm American belief in "Progress."

[16] I am aware that what I say above has echoes of late nineteenth-century and early twentieth-century notions such as the Sorelian "myth," the "as if" of Vaihinger, and many other contemporaneous philosophies that sought to rescue teleology from that brute, fact. But nowadays all these terms look a bit too apologetic, concede too much. Even the *élan vital,* even the life force, hardly need disguise themselves nowadays, but may come out openly as the faiths they are. I say quite simply that a faith, too, is a fact.

XV

Conclusion: In Which Nothing Is Concluded

THE CENTRAL PROBLEM that confronts us in trying to draw some conclusions from a history of morals in the West is this: What are the implications for us all as citizens and as private persons of the very great revisions, amendments, in some cases total alterations made in the world view, the religion, of most Westerners since the beginning of modern times? Or, more briefly, what are the moral aspects of the new religion of the Enlightenment? I shall not attempt to rival my colleagues in the philosophy of history, shall not attempt to be a prophet either of doom or of bliss. I shall by the very nature of what I am attempting to do here be obliged to omit consideration of all sorts of factors, economic, political, geographic, biological, and a lot more that would have to go into a—moreover, as yet wholly impossible—chart of "Whither Mankind?" But I shall poke about modestly into a perhaps not wholly unforeseeable near future.

Now whether in alliance with or in opposition to many organized forms of the Christian religion, the Enlightenment, as I have tried to show, has at its base certain beliefs, practices, attitudes that are, as such matters go in this old world, *new,* and which I find it convenient to treat as new elements in world beliefs, even in religions. I am careful to use the plural here, for, like all great religions, that of the Enlightenment is by no means monolithic; it has spawned numerous sects, and has infinite shades of compromise with Christianity and the rest of the real world. Except in Russia, its system of beliefs has never got incorporated in a single intolerant established church. It has inherited, moreover, from its struggles against established and privileged order, a strong initial positive belief in the values of tolerance and diversity, and this belief keeps countervailing the tendency toward intolerance and unification which the faith of the Enlightenment shares with all dogmatic faiths. Indeed, as we have noted for early Christianity, under certain conditions proliferation of heresies and sects is probably a sign of strength in a faith. At any rate, the fact of such proliferation is clear for the faith of the Enlightenment today.

The element of novelty in the religion of the Enlightenment is not the apocalyptic element in itself, not just the promise of a heaven. The novel element is not even the promise of a heaven *on earth*. Christianity was born of apocalyptic hopes; the first Christians felt the perfect promised life was to be, as we should put it, a "natural" extension of this one. There is a touch of this feeling that life right here on earth can and will be perfect for the true believer in almost all of the long series of protesting, if not quite Protestant, reforms that mark all Christian history. Yet the new element in the Enlightenment is real indeed. It is, for one thing, in part a matter of scale, of actual penetration of apocalyptic hopes to the many, all over the West. The Enlightenment spread widely and deeply, as did early Christianity; it is not a relatively limited clerical reformist movement, not even limited in the sense that the Cluniac movement was limited. Again, at least among the many, its apocalyptic hopes are more concrete, more "materialistic," more "naturalistic," with no trace of the monastic, and, again among the many, with little trace of the great disgust, the great revulsion against the world of common sense that marks Christian apocalyptic feeling. There is a sense in which the Enlightenment was from the start a *vague* faith. Finally, the Enlightenment could and did lean on science and technology in a way early Christianity never could; its most characteristic Utopias are full of quite earthly gadgets.[1] Yet the fact is important, and must be noted, that Chris-

[1] Some of these contrasts come out well in a comparison between such representative figures as the twelfth-century Joachim de Flore, whose Utopia is a firm, but most monastic, one, and the Enlightened Condorcet, whose Utopia is certainly no Abbaye de Thélème, but nonetheless contemplates the untroubled indulgence by all of their naturally good appetites. On Joachim there is little in English, but Henry Bett, *Joachim of Flora* (London, Methuen, 1931), will serve as an introduction. The literature of and on Utopias is vast indeed. J. O. Hertzler, *The History of Utopian Thought* (New York, Macmillan, 1923), and Lewis Mumford, *The Story of Utopias* (New York, Boni and Liveright, 1922), will start a student off; but the subject has depths and a scope that escape the sociology of the former and the aesthetic-moral Enlightenment of the latter. Mr. Mumford follows his master Patrick Geddes in preferring to pun Eutopia (good place) rather than Outopia (no-place). My guess is that More himself meant Outopia. I wish to call special attention to the recent R. Dubos, *Mirage of Health: Utopias, Progress, and Biological Change,* New York, Harper, 1959.

tianity and Enlightenment were *both,* in their inception, attempts to do away altogether with evil. Both were movements that we may call, without undue semantic worry, "messianic," "millenarian," "chiliastic," "Utopian." Most of us Westerners today have to live with the difficult heritage of two quite different but, at their most emotionally exacting depths, equally messianic religions, both of which, if we followed their most heroic demands, would make us all saints. Perhaps the ordinary Christian still has over the ordinary intellectual Enlightened the advantage that he knows he will not achieve sanctity.

Still, with this warning against the oversimplification of the assumption that the new faith is a monolithic one—or, even more dangerous, the assumption that it is or ought to be a logically consistent whole—we may proceed to discuss cautiously the moral implications of the basic tenets of the faith, which are perhaps as much held in common as are those of Christianity since Luther. The most striking of the theological-metaphysical tenets of the new faith is that the *real world* (or just plain Reality, capitalized) is revealed to the human mind working on the data of sense experience, aided by such instruments as microscope, telescope, and the like, in a way best exemplified by what we call "natural science." Or, vulgarly, that Science, again with an initial capital, can tell us all we can ever know truthfully about ourselves and the universe. There is among the many, no doubt, much admixture of a hearty and crude common-sense "realism"—Dr. Johnson kicking that stone block on a London street to show that the block is *there,* not just in his mind, nor even just in God's mind, or Bishop Berkeley's. The upshot, for the freethinker fully emancipated, is rejection of the Christian supernatural, of the Christian eschatology of an afterlife, of miracles, and, in fact, most of the traditional Christian world view; *it is often also,* but not necessarily, negatively a rejection of those mental processes we may group together as imprecise thinking, hunch-following, imagination, poetry, romance, the desire of the moth for the star, positively an insistence that all proper, effective thinking is clear, precise, "scientific." This real world is the world a conventionally trained and not very bright freethinking "scientist" recognizes as real, and there can be no other.

Now no religion so far has been able to take the world as it is; and natural science, *while it sticks to its last,* is wholly unable to take the world in any other way than as it is. There is, of course, for the faithful of the Enlightenment a way out of this difficulty: the world revealed by human reason working "scientifically"—let us frankly use for this world the old

447

term "Nature"—this sole real world which is Nature not only is, but has been and will be; human reason working through the materials left by its past learns that this Nature has a plan, *is* a plan, a significant part of which is that what Western men have learned to call good is increasing, and what they have learned to call evil is diminishing. Man makes himself indeed, but according to plans laid down by Nature for the Cambrian trilobites, even for the first earthly atom. Nature, in short, turns out to have moral intentions for us, her favorite children, turns out to be "something not ourselves" (for otherwise how could we resist her by acting unnaturally, evilly?) "that makes for righteousness," turns out, in fact, to be what we all know her to be, a God in spite of herself, and, like *rex noster Maria Theresa,* formally unsexed by her office.

In the meantime, what has become of the nature the scientists have been investigating so fruitfully? This nature has been in the course of the intellectual and emotional process outlined in the previous paragraph quite transcended, transmuted, humanized, and sanctified. I do not think that natural science qua science can find in its researches into nature anything like what we humans commonly call "meaning"—that is, morality, beauty, purpose, in all their overtones for us. Science qua science does not provide us with *ends;* it does not in itself, but only as one example of the working of the human spirit, give us *values.* Or, put in metaphysical and epistemological terms, science does not seek to establish Truth in the absolutist sense, nor Reality; it does not even base itself on "facts" as common sense understands facts, as something existing *independent* of "theories," or "hypotheses" about them, and "conceptual schemes" into which they are fitted by the mind of the scientist. Science has, obviously, its instrumental aspect, but it is strictly the instrument of given human curiosities or conveniences, not, as far as the scientist knows, the instrument of any universal design or purpose.[2]

I am particularly desirous of not being wholly misunderstood in this matter. First of all, my own position here is ultimately a metaphysical one,

[2] On this enormous subject I know no better start than Max Weber's "Science as a Vocation," in *From Max Weber: Essays in Sociology,* trans. and ed. by H. H. Gerth and C. Wright Mills, New York, Oxford University Press, 1946. Most of it is printed, with an admirably succinct introduction, by Philip Rieff in *Daedalus* for Winter, 1958 (issued as Vol. 87, No. 1, of the *Proceedings* of the American Academy of Arts and Sciences). On the philosophical side, see Henri Poincaré, *The Foundations of Science,* Lancaster, Pa., The Science Press, 1946.

on which better metaphysicians than I have taken quite antithetical positions.[3] Second, the bald statement that science gives us only means to ends, never ends, is misleading. The pursuit of science itself is, of course, an end set by human beings, though not an end set by any abstract and hypostatized Science. More important and quite as obvious, the means-ends relation in human life is an intertwining network, in which what is in one respect a means to an end is itself an end for which we try to devise means. It is perfectly convenient to say that in trying to find a foolproof contraceptive—that famous and as yet unfound pill, for instance—science sets up the end as well as the means. But be careful: science itself will not tell you whether or not you *ought* to try to find such a contraceptive, let alone whether you *ought* to promote its widespread use. Social science will give some—not very complete —guidance as to some of the possible consequences of the discovery and spread of such a contraceptive. The social scientist, qua human being, will probably tell you that on the whole these consequences will be good for the race, and, if he is excited enough, will tell you that we *must* find such a contraceptive or face fearful wars and famines. But this is because a Western social scientist today is likely to be a good child of the Enlightenment, and to share its beliefs and values. His Nature God and the Catholic Christian God are neither of them the voice of Science.

The rigorous, exclusive attempt to use the human mind "scientifically" and *only scientifically* is surely impossible; it is perhaps also an attempt contrary to the real nature of man and the universe, and therefore immoral, as the convinced Christian must believe. I will here settle for the impossibility, and try to be concrete. Some—not many—years ago an infant was brought to the Children's Hospital of a great American city suffering from a disease no local doctor had been able to diagnose. The specialists, too, were puzzled, until one bright—and unusual—young pediatrician with some knowledge of the history of medicine got a hunch, quickly confirmed; the baby

---

3 Professor Charles Frankel of Columbia University seems to me the most typical defender in our time of the orthodox position of the Enlightenment, that the pattern of conscious mental activity set by natural science in our tradition does provide us with "objective" moral values, that the good can be derived from naturalistic premises by ratiocination. But it is likely that the foregoing formulation would not be acceptable to Professor Frankel. Perhaps I had better simply list him as a very typical twentieth-century follower and continuer of the Enlightenment. See his *The Faith of Reason: The Idea of Progress in the French Enlightenment,* New York, King's Crown Press, 1948, and *The Case for Modern Man,* New York, Harper, 1956. For a succinct defense of science as a "value," see Barrington Moore, *Political Power and Social Theory,* Cambridge, Mass., Harvard University Press, 1958, pp. 89-110.

was ill with scurvy, a disease American babies, full to the brim with vitamin C, never have nowadays. It turned out that the mother, a European displaced person trying very hard to be American, had learned that boiling kills the wicked germs, and, therefore, secure in this scientific knowledge, boiled everything, including the baby's orange juice!

Now in this matter, which we may put as one of multiple, not single, one-way variables, science does but deepen what common sense knows well enough. In her home country, the mother would perhaps not have had orange juice, but she would, apart from the worst crises of war, have had its equivalent in vitamin C, and she would never have boiled everything she fed the infant. But there are always large realms of thought in which common sense has not had sway, and which science hardly dares try to invade, for it will not get very far. It is a simple fact that something deep in most of us resists the essential position of science, that the variables always vary, that circumstances always alter cases, that even standards of measure are conveniences, not absolutes, that there really is not anything "out there" that stays fixed—except in our minds. Something in us tells us, you sometimes *do* boil even the orange juice. Or, to use in apparent reverse the classic phrase of Galileo the moralist (not the scientist): Something tells us *it doesn't move.*

Finally, in this matter of the relation between science and morals, it must be noted that the pursuit of scientific truth is carried on by human beings who find some part of their own morality in their activity as scientists. But one may argue that, though no doubt we are dealing basically with one of those mostly nonvicious circles, the scientist moralizes the pursuit of science rather than the pursuit of science making the scientist moral. The scientist, for instance, holds himself in his work to a most rigorous standard of honesty, the practical honesty of distinguishing, without too much epistemological worry, between what he registers as observer and what he would like to register as a fully rounded human being. He has, therefore, to discipline himself, to deny himself; he has to humble part of his desiring self, that is, his moral self. Moreover, he must be patient and industrious. He is likely, by training and social class, to favor the gentler virtues. Many atomic scientists, conscience-stricken at some of the results of their labors, are now firmly on the side of the angels.

II

I shall, then, attempt a broad survey and critique of the religion of the Enlightenment as it looks to be in the mid-twentieth century, roughly two hundred years after its establishment. But a survey implies a point of view, a critique implies critical standards. I shall quite frankly attempt to judge this religion in its own terms, as to how far it has promoted the pursuit of happiness, the good life of its inherited Christian ethics modified by humanitarian and hedonistic strains, how far it has succeeded in balancing its principles of liberty and equality, how far it has succeeded in making over human conduct to conform to its concept of human nature. Though I have argued that its aims and standards are not the immediate reflection—a passive and literal mirroring—of an existing "Nature," not even a direct product of the same human effort that produced modern natural science, I have never argued that it has no aims, no standards. Those aims and standards can, of course, be criticized from a point of view wholly—or mostly—outside them, from the point of view, for instance, of a religion that finds this world wholly evil, or wholly illusory, or both, from the point of view of a Protestant fundamentalist, from the point of view of a conservative Roman Catholic, and, in our modern world, from many other points of view. Any such criticism would obviously be quite different from my own. I am, indeed, attempting a task thoroughly consonant with the paradoxical note in the religion of the Enlightenment itself, attempting to stay inside and look on from the outside, attempting to be a mirror that does not distort and yet does more than reflect.[4]

Now the religion of the Enlightenment makes man wholly a part of Nature, at its "materialist" extreme, simply another organization of atoms, as organization perhaps the most complex yet existing, but surely in no sense supranatural. But one of its more obvious inheritances from Christianity and the whole Western tradition is in fact a deep conviction that man is unique, that the gap between him and the highest of animals is enormous. An occasional sociologist, or psychologist, or anthropologist, in some of his moods, will remind us of how much like other animals we are, but the overwhelming trend of the Enlightenment and its tradition is surely to emphasize the fact that "Reason" or some equivalent trait separates us radically even from the anthropoids. There is in the religion of the Enlightenment little touch of what the generally educated Westerner is led to believe is the common Hindu attitude toward animals as essentially linked to themselves, as themselves

---

[4] I write that last sentence carefully as a historian of ideas at work among the many, at least the cultivated many. I think it clear that modern natural science, which is as a world view at least as much the child of Descartes as of anyone else, has in the form of the dualism of subjective-objective actually strengthened the old Christian dualism of soul-body, thus adding an appreciable load for the conscience of most of us. Unlike the old Christian, we have to worry about even our best sentiments, just because they are sentiments.

in another guise. Societies for the Prevention of Cruelty to Animals have indeed been a by-product of the humanitarianism of the Enlightenment; but the Enlightened Westerner loves animals as a reflection of his own self-love, because they amuse him, or flatter him, or seem even to love him. One of the many paradoxes—I use the term as I have generally hitherto, not in its logical sense, but with its full load of emotional connotations—one of the paradoxes of the new religion is that in putting man back into a hypostatized Nature in one sense, it has by the many fillips it has given to his pride, notably by his conquests over nature, made him very conscious of being quite different from the rest of nature's creatures. He is clearly on top of her heap, has indeed—man makes himself—hoisted himself by his bootstraps to this lofty position.

Yet Nature is there, for man clearly cannot bear being alone. And toward Nature man is full of ambivalence. Two French poets set up the poles neatly:

Mais la nature est là, qui t'invite et qui t'aime

O vraiment marâtre Nature![5]

Science has not diminished this ambivalence toward Nature, which like so much else goes back to the Greeks and Romans. For Lucretius, surely, Nature was not even a stepmother, just no relation; yet in the Theocritan idyl Nature is kindly indeed. The relatively modest universe that early modern astronomy opened up profoundly disturbed Pascal, who was more sensitive to disturbance than are most scientists—"le silence de ces vastes espaces m'effraie."[6] Yet I know a modern astronomer, by temperament an enjoying soul, who seems himself to expand with exuberant joy in contemplating the expanding universe, who delights in the thought that among the billions of stars there must be many planets as suitable for life as ours. *Vulgär-Darwinismus* was at once a stimulus to man's self-satisfaction with Nature, for it showed him how he had got his top place with no help from God, and also, with its emphasis on "Nature red in tooth and claw," a reminder that he had got there with no help from, perhaps in spite of, his

[5] "There is nature, which invites thee and loves thee" (Lamartine, *Méditations*, "Le Vallon"); "O really step-mother Nature" (Ronsard, "Mignonne, allous voir si la Rose"). I translate literally. "Marâtre" is a very strong word indeed in French, with secondary senses of "cruel," "harsh"—shall we say, "unnatural"? (I have seen it defined in a modern French dictionary as *mère dénaturée;* we work hard to make Nature a nice humane concept.) Ronsard is no romantic; but De Vigny himself his written as harshly of Nature.

[6] *Pensées,* § iii, 206.

better "moral" self. The "struggle for life" could hardly have even the consoling overtones of its Christian analogue, "many are called but few are chosen," for the struggle was a purely natural, earthly one.

Intellectually, the view of Nature that emerged from the eighteenth-century Enlightenment set a problem quite as important as the emotional difficulty I have just noted. Since Western man always has sought to satisfy his intellect in his world view, since so many of his emotions are intellectual emotions, he has always had difficulty with the problem of the origins of evil. The difficulty that faced the eighteenth century was at least as acute as it has ever been for any theism that postulated a God all-good, all-knowing, all-powerful. In the dogma of the natural goodness and reasonableness of man, the Enlightenment had a postulate that made evil either illusory—and this it emphatically was not to the *philosophes* and their followers—or else unnaturally natural. No such satisfactory solution as Job's was possible, for Western man simply cannot bring himself to regard Nature, no matter how thoroughly hypostatized, as *really* inscrutable, as really possessed of a will and a mind better than his own. I have pointed out in Chapter XI that the Enlightened had to satisfy themselves with blaming evil on the institutional and cultural enviroment—to a minor degree, as in the case, for example, of the Eskimos, on the physical environment—a solution adequate for the very pragmatic reformer, but not for the inquiring mind, since a mind *had* to ask how an originally good environment happened to go wrong.

Two hundred years have indeed modified the bases of this problem for the religion of the Enlightenment. It can be maintained that Freud, crowning a long cultural development, has put both good and evil together, both "natural" to the human psyche-and-soma, almost always intertwined, and yet—for Freud was a good heir of the Judaeo-Christian-Enlightenment tradition—nonetheless distinguishable as good and evil.[7] As a good scientist, Freud was content to leave the ultimate metaphysical and theological problem of how good and evil got there unsolved, perhaps unasked. Certainly there is nowadays abroad in the West, as part of what may be called *Vulgär-Freudismus,* a disposition to accept the naturalness, the thereness, of both good and evil, without undue sentiments as to the uselessness of trying to promote one and to resist the other. Yet two cautions need to be made. First, there is still a strong minority of fundamentalist Enlightened

---

[7] This has been put most effectively by Jerome Bruner in an essay, "The Freudian Conception of Man," *Daedalus,* Winter 1958, pp. 77-84 (Vol. 87, No. 1 of the *Proceedings* of the American Academy of Arts and Sciences).

who refuse to budge from the position that man is a kindly and rational creature by design of Nature, and would be so in practice if only . . . Well, the mad Marat during the French Revolution thought that five hundred heads duly guillotined would do the trick; our modern mad rationalists, to do them justice, seem to feel the guillotine is not quite up to the job. These retarded children of the Enlightenment, who have been very powerful in American public education, cling firmly to the belief that only good is natural, even in the little savages they fail to educate. But it looks as though the power of this entrenched minority of educators is waning, and elsewhere they are not numerous even in the United States. Second, and more serious for the West, we cannot be at all sure that for the many a naturalistic interpretation of evil is desirable or possible. I shall have to return to this point.

Next, as the religion of the Enlightenment has developed historically, it has got tied up with, related to, two complexes of ideas, sentiments, and, no doubt, "objective conditions" that are themselves closely interrelated—nationalism and egalitarian democracy. Christianity, too, has in the last two centuries got itself almost, if not quite, as fully involved with these two complexes. The critic who attempts to estimate how much of the good and how much of the evil to be found in nationalism and in democratic egalitarianism is furthered or lessened by each of these religions, Christianity and Enlightenment, has an impossibly tangled set of human relations to sort out. The ethics, the world view, of both Christianity and the Enlightenment hold that all men are brothers, and that warfare is an evil. Both religions accept, and even cherish, the cultural and emotional ties that bind men in national groups. On the record, neither has had much success in preventing warfare or in transcending in practice the limitations of the modern nation-state. The men of good will who are working throughout the world to achieve an international order that can prevent or at least control warfare are likely to run the gamut from conservative Christianity to all forms of freethinking. I do not think that a critic attempting to be neutral can find much difference here. Certainly neither of the fresher and more youthful forms of the religion of the Enlightenment, socialism and communism, has come anywhere near fulfilling its promise of bringing men together in spite of differences of nationality, race, color, or creed. Their proponents will say, of course, that the mere existence of capitalism, buttressed, they usually add, by Christianity, has prevented the fulfillment of this promise. This kind of argument can hardly be controverted, certainly not among the faithful. But the fact remains that war among nations is an unending threat in our world, and that neither Christianity nor Enlightenment seems able to diminish that threat. Whether one or the other faith seems more suited to enabling men to bear without surrender to despair or to fatalistic numbness the tensions set up by that threat is a matter to which I shall shortly come.

Both Christianity and the Enlightenment hold that in some sense all men are equal; both sets of belief are congruous with much of what we all call, loosely and firmly, "democracy." There is, historically, a very real difference here, however, though not nearly as big a difference as the tradition of the Enlightenment holds. Christianity in its many and long phases of inactivity has indeed buttressed social and economic privileges; but it has by no means always and everywhere put off to an afterlife the achievement of an equality of fact between rich and poor, master and slave. There is always in Christianity the possibility of a new drive inspired by the desire to get nearer equality here on earth; the Christian tradition is strongly melioristic, and even in part humanitarian. This is one of the reasons why so many Christians, both Catholic and Protestant, have since 1700 been able to work together with the Enlightened on concrete reforms basically egalitarian and democratic. And on the other side, it is not true historically that the Enlightenment has always worked in the direction of the egalitarian side of democracy. As I have taken pains to point out, one powerful strain in the Enlightenment is by no means egalitarian; all sorts of planners, from Enlightened despots to cultural engineers have wanted to do away with poverty and suffering—so, too, do many Christians—but not by any means to do away with all order of rank, esteem, privilege, power. Democracy itself in the West has settled for some uneasy compromises between the human desire to be different and the human desire to be alike. A profession on the whole, if only because of its training in the biochemical sciences, fundamentally not very Christian in its world view, that of medicine, displays in the United States especially an acceptance by the majority of its practitioners of some very big gaps between ideal and real —in fact, of differences of class and privilege—as well as a determined effort by a conscientious and reforming minority to close that gap.[8]

Once more, as a naturalistic-historical critic of these two rival but by no means wholly antithetical faiths, I am driven toward one of the key problems of our discussion: How does each of these tend to affect individual human

[8] See, for example, the admirably frank and realistic study of the situation in mental health in A. B. Hollingshead and F. C. Redlich, *Social Class and Mental Illness,* New York, Wiley, 1958.

conduct? What does each achieve in the cure of souls? We may start, not by quite dismissing or considering as solved a very old problem that still bothers many sincere men, but by suggesting that it is not in fact now for us an acute one. This is the old problem, a favorite with many Christians, as to whether a superhuman, supranatural God-judge is finally necessary if men are to conduct themselves at all tolerably well. The early Christians reproached the pagans with having no sanctions against bad conduct, indeed, with encouraging it by their immoral tales of gods and goddesses (see above, p. 62), and, ever since the beginnings of Enlightened naturalism in modern religion, Christian critics have insisted that men who do not fear hell or hope for heaven are likely to misbehave. So good an anti-Christian as Voltaire held the opinion, common to all but the extreme Left Wing of the Enlightenment in the eighteenth century, that sheer atheism among the many would ruin society. This is the origin of one of his best known and least profound aphorisms, "si Dieu n'existait pas il faudrait l'inventer."[9]

To all sorts of alarmists, the history of the last two centuries is a record of steady moral decline, of men who no longer fear punishment in an afterlife rushing into the deadly excesses of our animal sensate culture. I have tried hard in this book to show that the record gives no support to such alarmism, that, on the contrary, the last two centuries of Western history are centuries of a relatively high moral level, certainly not one of general moral decline. It would be difficult to show *empirically* that among Westerners there is any correlation between the degree of acceptance of supernatural sanctions in morals and conduct in conformity with high ethical standards. Indeed, I have a suspicion that because of their recruitment for the most part from serious, otherwise conventional middle-class persons and earnest, ambitious, lower-class persons, the various freethinking sects would perhaps show a slightly higher average of abstention from the lesser vices of self-indulgence than would most Christian groups. As for the more serious moral failings, I repeat that I doubt if there is much difference in level of conduct between Christians and non-Christians. We know enough about the psychology of guilt and punishment to know that no such oddly rational attitude as the classic Christian view of a sure divine judgment based on a clearly known moral code exhausts the range and depth of the human conscience, or even strikes effectively in the middle of that range.

[9] "If God did not exist, it would be necessary to invent him," from a letter in 1770 to the Prince of Prussia, in S. G. Tallentyre, *Voltaire in His Letters,* New York, Putnam, 1919. Voltaire, proud of this aphorism, was fond of repeating it.

Conclusion: In Which Nothing Is Concluded

It will be more profitable to consider the effects of the two faiths on the whole moral tone of the believers, on what, to be fashionable, we may call the mental and moral health of the individual, on his disposition toward one or another kind of conduct. Here, above all, we can but make stabs in the dark, though we can be reasonably sure here, too, that the claims of the extremists of both sides are not justified; neither faith ends surely for the many either in hopeless neurotic or psychotic despair or in a sure serenity and soundness of mental and moral health. The differences between them in this respect may be slight, but nonetheless important.

We may hazard the guess that emotionally and intellectually the new religion in its extreme form does fulfill less successfully than traditional Christianity the useful and indeed necessary role the Marxists call scornfully that of "opium of the people"; or, at any rate, that the new religion is not a satisfactory sedative for the intellectuals, who seem nowadays to need a sedative badly. Since I have used an undignified but clear and, I think, reasonably honest figure of speech, I may as well continue and note that one's fundamental position as to human dispositions in this matter will as usual be decisive. If one holds that men are generally more in need of sedation than of stimulation—I continue to write figuratively, but with an eye on the literal—then one is likely to esteem highly the quieting facets of a religion; if one holds that men are more in need of stimulation than of sedation, then naturally one esteems the troubling, pricking, "inspiring" facets. Now I feel rather strongly—but, of course, quite personally—that men in the West throughout their history, and especially their leaders both in thought and in action, have tended to be overactive rather than underactive, have stood in need rather of being quieted than of being pricked.

Such a judgment, such a diagnosis, is, of course, subjective, and, furthermore, applies only in general and not to special cases. To apply it to the problem immediately at hand with purposes of deciding or curing is, however, no less difficult. I should like to suggest as a mere hypothesis that the two centuries of experience we have had with the religion of the Enlightenment show that this faith is weak in consoling power and, *as a faith,* intellectually disturbing. Now the devout Enlightened, even the conventional Enlightened, may quite rightly insist here that I have put the whole thing in deliberately pejorative terms. The basic Christian position, he will insist, is *resignation,* acceptance of much earthly evil, a position it is the glory of the modern West to have got beyond. The basic position of the Enlightenment—or, as he would prefer to put it, of modern progressive democracy—

457

he must maintain, is that men can, by using fully and intelligently the faculties, the "human nature," they are born with, mold this world to their good desires. The moral force behind this position is, finally, for him, the one thing that today can save us from disaster, indeed from extinction. Consolation, peace of mind, resignation, and suchlike Christian satisfactions are, for him, in this crisis absurd: a human race ruined by fusion-bomb warfare will be beyond consolation. At this point, all we can do is keep on debating. The differences in attitudes, call them what you will, conservative and liberal, pessimistic and optimistic, realist and idealist, are just there, existing, like blond and brunet—with not even a good hair dye available, and few of intermediary coloring.

To continue with my analysis, however, I think it reasonably clear a priori that the new religion can but produce as consoling elements in the cure of souls substitutes that do their work less effectively than did the consoling elements of the old religion. I have already contrasted the Virgin Mary and *la patrie* (we and the Germans are insensitive enough to make it "fatherland," and masculine, or even neuter; the Romance languages at least put it in a grammatical feminine) as consolations in time of need, and found the substitute almost certainly inferior to the original (see p. 334). Protestantism itself, which is *in some ways* a step toward the new religion of the Enlightenment, though it rebelled against the confessional, the priest, the worship of saints, indeed, against almost all Catholic art and ritual, has never quite—not even among the Quakers— achieved a state of "every man his own priest." The various Protestant sects have worked out their own form of the cure of souls, their own rituals and worshiping, in short, their own *churches* in the full meaning of that word. A convinced social Darwinist might insist that they have worked out adaptations suitable to their functions in society and satisfying to their members. But aesthetically and emotionally the Protestant groups tend in one of three directions—toward Holy Rollerism, thumping hymns, and general emotional dishevelment; toward excessive austerity and emphasis on the sermon; toward an increasing imitation of Catholic forms. The Protestant sermon nowadays is perhaps more commonly a sedative than a stimulus, but it is rarely a good consolation.

What has been said of the Protestants in respect of the consoling elements of belief and practice can be said even more strongly of the basically non-Christian forms of the religions of the Enlightenment. Indeed, except in an occasional patriotic ceremony or in moments of revolutionary excitement, as with the Jacobins or the Bolsheviks, the ritual of the Enlightenment is dull and perfunctory; moreover, its devisers, at bottom, are usually not quite sure it is necessary. Good ritual is good art, and the Enlightened—and not only in their Russian Communist sect—are often lacking in aesthetic sense. An Enlightened funeral service is usually a dismal affair indeed, the ritual uncertain, the music bad, the mourners uncomfortable and unconsoled as some of the more sentimental outbursts of Enlightened evangelists—for instance, William Ernest Henley's *Invictus*—are read with more than clerical unction. But then, the Enlightened have all sorts of difficulties with death, as they do with many other facts of life; Freud, a most Enlightened nineteenth-century Jew, was led in the end to his concept of the death wish.[10]

As for the cure of souls, they all try; there is something like the pastoral visit even among the ethical-cultural societies. But the real modern parallel, at least in the United States, is no doubt the extraordinary network of "counselors" of all sorts, from fortunetellers to Christian Science "readers" and professional psychoanalysts. The very profusion and variety of these surrogate priests points up what I am trying to bring out here: if you are rugged enough, you may feel that this proliferation is in itself a sign of life and strength in our society, part of our undignified, fecund, multanimous American democracy; if you are delicate enough, this overwhelming variety of counsel may seem to you madness, the threatening dissolution of all that really holds us together in society. I incline at the moment to the modest, perhaps Whiggish, opinion that with respect to the necessary cure of souls our present American society is probably marginally deficient. We certainly have in this respect achieved liberty and variety rather than equality and uniformity. I am prepared to grant that psychoanalysis when successful is perhaps the most effective form of faith healing yet devised; but think of what a tiny privileged minority can avail themselves of it! The pure Freudian evangel must be the most aristocratic, the most snobbish, of good news. And as for "nondirective" therapy, in which the counselor merely grunts from time to time to prove to the counseled that he is still awake, one feels that not even the philosophic anarchists of the Enlightenment were *that* thoroughly convinced of the natural goodness of man.

The intellectual difficulties implicit in the new faith of the Enlightenment are, however, under critical examination for their logical consequences, quite as obvious, and, to me, quite as serious, as its emotional inadequacies. First,

10 The other end for the Enlightened, I suppose, is the concept of full individual immortality on this earth and in this body. See my mention of Dr. Gruman's thesis, p. 314n. above.

the new faith puts upon the serious but ordinary, conventional, unheroic, ungifted believer an even greater burden than the one that, as Eric Fromm has pointed out in his *Escape from Freedom,* the Protestant obligation of private judgment put upon such believers. Now I think it quite evident that in this respect both Protestantism and the religion of the Enlightenment have their own equivalents or surrogates for the intellectual assurance of being right, of knowing where one stands in this universe, that Catholic traditional Christianity afforded the many. Protestantism and Enlightenment would not at all deserve the name of faiths if they did not give this assurance. The good Baptist, the good Unitarian, the good Marxist, even the good member of the Americans for Democratic Action is by no means obliged to go through a difficult and soul-testing struggle of ratiocination and experimentation to get most of the answers he needs for most of the questions he has to ask; indeed, if he is normal enough and good enough as a believer, he does not need to ask questions at all. As so often, the problem is one of margins. I think it likely that the ordinary devotee of the new faiths of the Enlightenment does face *many more occasions* than does the devotee of older faiths, when he has to go to the pains and stress of thinking about questions for which he does not already feel he knows the answers. It is not very painful, often, in fact, pleasant and relaxing, at most, involving some relieving discharges from the adrenals, to think about questions for which you already know the answers. That relaxing and morally useful satisfaction must come less often to the Enlightened than to the Christian.

One example may suffice: let us take the problem of the sterilization of the unfit. The traditional orthodox Christian has a clear and certain answer to this problem, which, as a matter of fact, he himself would never have raised as a problem: God through the ministers of His church on earth has forbidden any such human tampering with the body which houses an immortal soul. For the traditional orthodox believer in the faith of the Enlightenment, especially if he is really conscientious about his duty to Science (here, essentially, a surrogate for the Christian's *grace*), the problem bristles with unsettled difficulties. How do we in practice define and recognize the "unfit"? What do we know, qua scientists, about the genetic origin for each type of unfitness as defined, for they are unlikely to present the same genetics? What do we know about the effectiveness, in a given population with a given culture, of a maximum achieved sterilization of each type of unfit? What do we know about the effects of a program of sterilization on public opinion? How shall we put such a program across? And, perhaps worst question of all, who shall decide who is unfit, and how? Shall there be appeal from a decision to sterilize, and to whom? The Enlightened may indeed appeal to a favorite stereotype and insist that the orthodox Christian attitude is simply that of the traditional, if not ethologically accurately pictured, ostrich hiding his head in the sand, refusing to face a problem that we had all better face, or else. No good answer here is possible, for any sure scientific answer is bound to be too late.

The answers the scientist gives, even in well-developed fields such as the physical sciences, let alone in the still-groping social sciences, are always tentative, always subject to revision the moment a single fact fails to fit in. For many specific problems, the scientist, perhaps even the social scientist, can be a good deal more sure of himself and his answers than the problem of sterilization of the unfit would indicate. This is so partly because there is a great deal of scientifically established knowledge we can all afford to take as it stands; but it is so also because for some scientists and for many laymen who accept the new faith, the uniformities of science, its "laws," get readily transformed into dogmas, its uncertainties into certainties, and thus, no doubt, its disturbing tensions get resolved into comforting assurance of oneness with the universal plan, of knowing that plan. The Enlightened, fortunately, is not continually held to the highest rationalist tension any more than the Christian is held to the highest spiritual tension. The Enlightened, too, can relax, can even be "natural" at moments.

For the honest intellectual, however, aware of what natural science means in practice, there must remain some awareness of the dishonesty, or at least the laziness, of this leap from uncertainty to certainty, and he is aware of a residue of discomfort. Certainty has been smuggled in; and smuggling, if often an interesting activity, is certainly an immoral one. The good Christian, too, is troubled; he cannot be too much at ease in Zion. But his troubles center in his relation with God, not in God's nature or existence, which he knows but does not—or should not—pretend to understand. The rationalist believer in the faith of the Enlightenment must have moments when he is aware of how great the gap is between what on his own premises he ought to understand and what he does understand.

These intellectual difficulties, which are, of course, also emotional and moral difficulties, have been intensified for the Enlightened intellectual in the course of the last two centuries by evidence, which he is still often unable to face, that the founders of his religion were wrong about human nature, that men are not in fact roughly equal in respect to their capacity to receive the grace of Reason or Science.[11] The *philosophes* expected or hoped all men would become *philosophes,* I think it not unfair to say, in the sense that many of the first Christians must have expected or hoped all men would become Christians. Now Christians have long been aware that all men are not in fact good Christians, but they have never ceased to believe that they have the *capacity* to be good Christians, have never begun to believe that their not being good Christians is a fact of nature not to be overcome even by conversion. You cannot say to a Christian, "That poor fellow over there has an I.Q. of 85, therefore he cannot be saved." But, with no dogmatic assurance as to the scientific value of the technique of the I.Q., indeed, using it merely as a convenience, you can say, "That man over there, who has an I.Q. of about 85, will never become a philosopher, nor even a *philosophe,* cannot ever fully—perhaps not at all—receive your grace of Reason." The overwhelming evidence accumulated since 1700—*though it was available then, and known to many*—that millions of men and women are incapable of using their minds in the way the men and women we may once more call "intellectuals" can and often do use theirs—in the way, reader, you are now using yours—need not mean the end of the world, nor even the end of the religion of the Enlightenment. But it does call for a kind of adjustment in the attitudes of many men of good will, an adjustment in some senses perhaps not altogether unlike that which the gradual awareness that Christ was not going to come back to earth at once made necessary for early Christianity. This adjustment is, I think, going on now among the intellectuals who had enlisted on the side of the Enlightenment, but it is still incomplete, and the process still brings unhappiness to many, still puts an undue strain on the adrenals. The religion of the Enlightenment has a long and unpredictable way to go before it can face the facts of life as effectively as does Christianity, rich with two thousand years of experience of saints and sinners, good and evil, in all their protean—and by no means equal—forms.

The greatest problem that confronts the moralist attempting to criticize the religion of the Enlightenment on its own terms is that of the eternal agon, which throughout this book I have insisted must be a central theme

[11] I am not inventing this parallel. In the famous *Encyclopédie* of Diderot and his colleagues, you will find the following in Volume XII, under the word *philosophe: La raison est à l'égard du philosophe, ce que la grace est à l'égard du Chrétien. La grace détermine le chrétien à agir; la raison détermine le philosophe.* The writer's recourse to the verb *déterminer,* I suppose, was almost automatic. For a translation of most of the article see my *Portable Age of Reason Reader,* pp. 255-257.

for any history of morals in the West.[12] The problem may be put in various ways. We are today likely to recognize it most readily as the problem of the proper balance between individualism and collectivism in a society, or between rival individuals seeking each his own victories and co-operating individuals each seeking the common good. I have suggested, as a figurative way of putting it, as good a balance as possible—admitting we cannot do much about the balance—between the great cat, or possibly the wolf, in man, and the ant or bee, or perhaps the sheep, in man.

In the Christian tradition, this antithesis sets the problem of the constant need to combat in man the most dangerous form of original sin, the sin of pride, which nonetheless is no wholly ignoble sin like that of gluttony, but the "sin of the angels"; for in that tradition, as in common language, there is an ambivalence in the concept of pride, which is not unnatural to man, and can even in some sense be a "good," or "proper" pride (no "good" gluttony, no "proper" avarice). For many of us today the problem is sharpened by a feeling that in the pooled self-esteem of nationalism the spirit of the agon is at its wildest and most dangerous, both in the leaders who face each other in the public arena that is nowadays ironically called "diplomacy" and in the great public that follows them. However one puts the problem, it is hard in mid-twentieth century not to start with a feeling that the presumptions, the evidence, in fact, must lean to the side of controlling, taming, lessening, if possible, the innumerable competitions of modern life, the innumerable temptations we all face to indulge ourselves in the will to shine, or the will to howl, if not in the will to power.

Certainly some such feeling is the burden of the worries which, from Edmund Burke on, philosophic Western conservatives have felt about the effect of the efforts of the Enlightenment to realize men's natural rights to life, liberty, and the attainment of happiness. Burke's sense of outrage over the French Revolution rested on no mere politician's feeling for an "issue." Burke was, indeed, no sensible man, but a Christian, and he felt threatened by the Enlightenment in that fundamental part of any man I have been obliged to label here with the horrid phrase "world view." He saw more clearly than any contemporary that the Enlightenment, too, was not a common-sense matter, but a religion.

[12] I confess to a suspicion that it must be a theme for any study of human beings, even in the East. I do not doubt that "patterns of culture" vary, perhaps even as widely as those of the late Ruth Benedict's Kwakiutls and Zuñis. But I have been careful in this book to confine myself to our Western civilization, where the pattern is certainly far closer to that of the Kwakiutls than to that of the Zuñis.

It has seemed to these Burkean conservatives ever since that the Enlightenment, erroneously holding that men are by nature good, that evil lies
wholly in tradition, convention, institutions, environment, in short, has
worked to dissolve the ties, the disciplines, the restraining supports with
which this Christian-built environment worked to protect men from themselves. Left to themselves, left morally naked, their natural bent toward
satisfying their desires has in fact, so say these conservatives, driven them
to all sorts of irresponsible excesses, toward a series of mad competitions in
all walks of life. What we now need most, these conservatives argue, is
some acceptable restraints on human competitiveness, some means of getting men to accept individual failure, insignificance, an order of rank, the
discipline of reality.

We are back at another phase of the restraining or deterrent effect of
different sets of ideas on human conduct in the large; or, as Pareto would
put it, the specific use of certain ideas, rationalizations (derivations) either
to activate or deactivate certain sentiments (residues). Just as in logic the
fear of the Christian hell should work to keep individuals from sinning, and
the removal of that fear by Enlightened abolition of the idea of hell should
leave the way toward sinning a bit more open, so the Christian dogma of
original sin should act to restrain human self-assertion as well as self-indulgence, and the Enlightened dogma of the natural goodness of man should
work to remove such "unnatural" restraints.

I do not think the record of the last two centuries, however, quite confirms this expectation. There has been in private morality from about 1700
on, in such border areas between manners and morality as dress, an actual
increase of order, form, discipline, and restraint to a kind of Victorian peak,
and an increasing loosening of such restraints since then. But in this key
matter of the agon, and of stimulating or restraining what the Christian calls
"pride," I see very little difference among the believers of the two faiths.
The agon among nation-states seems to me no worse and no better morally
than the agon has been in earlier modern times, and in the days of the
dynastic Western state and in ancient Greece. Death and maiming and
raping in war have always been total; war has always been total. The major
difference between our wars and earlier ones is a difference of scale. There
is some difference in the degree of fanaticism with which wars are fought, as
I have noted, but in this respect over two thousand years there is no clear
pattern, but only a series of oscillations. As for the agon among individuals
in a given society, that, too, has in some of its manifestations, most notably

in economic life, been tamed and partly controlled. The Age of the Robber Barons in the United States is well past, and nowadays some conservatives in America—and even some liberals—are worried lest we have gone too far to eliminate the adventurousness, the competitiveness of the great American tradition.

In fact, if you want to set up a master pattern for contemporary worriers, conservative and liberal alike, it would be something like this: in international relations, the competition among nation-states is absolutely unbridled, unrestrained by law or morality; within each nation-state, however, the tendency is toward an opposite extreme of collectivism, conformity, rough egalitarianism, legal and moral restraints on the individual. Among states, the morality of the big cats; within each state, the morality of the social insects. Toward some such conclusions writers as different as Ortega y Gasset, Koestler, Toynbee, Riesman, Orwell, the younger Schlesinger, and many others, tend to arrive by somewhat varied routes.

Of these two horrors, the first is to the historian-naturalist by far the most threatening. The existentialist disgust that has overcome our Western priestly class, the intellectuals, is indeed in part the age-old and perhaps not very cataclysmic revolt of the sensitive and the bright against the coarsely successful few and the dull, ugly, conventional, joyless many. Over a century ago, when the best explosion men could manage was a mere gunpowder pop, the *Davidsbündler* were prodding away at the Philistine levelers. But the unbelievable threat of a single bomb that has an explosive strength equal to everything fired in the whole course of the last great war does quite realistically justify some of the worries of our intellectuals. The record gives no indication that war can be avoided; the most hopeful Christian, the most positive Enlightened, cannot discern the kind of moral progress in international relations that would make recourse to war unlikely.

An ingenious Christian with a sense of history might bring himself to face the catastrophic destruction—worse yet, the horrid laming—of hundreds of millions of human beings as quite consonant with the apocalyptic strain in his religion. The Book of Revelation has been firmly established in his canon for a long time. But what possible consolation can the Enlightened heir of Condorcet find in the dark prospect ahead? Indeed, much harder for him as rationalist to bear, he must find himself, at bottom, unable to find any *explanation* for what seems to lie ahead. No wonder that under all sorts of disguises, as the unconscious, as the Freudian death wish, as the rather neurotic Stoicism of the philosophic existentialists, as the *Angst* of the Christian existentialists, the dogma of original sin—a belief in some fundamental and on this earth ineradicable flaw in men, not just in environment, not just in institutions—confronts uncomfortably the Enlightened. And perhaps, irrationally, as is fitting, does give him strength to bear up, to face a world he never made. With all its rationalist confusion of word and deed, the religion of the Enlightenment has, perhaps merely as a derivative of Christianity, preserved an illogical and practical moderation, disciplinary power, an ability to cope undespairingly with an evil which should not be there, and, above all, has preserved and, for many of its faithful, strengthened in daily life that "minimal moral puritanism" which quite gainsays its original denial of the "civil war in the breast."[13]

Once more, at the risk of wearying the reader, I must revert to the full religious parallel. Reason does indeed for the Enlightened do the work grace does for the Christian. Though Reason is in the determined world view of the Enlightened the free but uncomfortably mysterious gift of Nature, as grace for the Christian is the free and properly mysterious gift of God, so in this moral world of free will the Enlightened individual must *strive* to deserve (attain?) Reason as the Christian strives to deserve grace. We can all get more Reason into this world of human relations if we will only go to work properly, in the missionary spirit, bearing the good news of Reason, Science, Technology. I am trying hard here to report, not to exhort, not even by that rather ineffective form of exhortation which is irony. The basic *moral* faith of the Enlightenment, that in the natural goodness and reasonableness of man and infinite pliability, is still strong among us Americans. Here is a quotation from a recent source:

Despite all this [our wars and fears of war] we have a kind of strength to which we have given little heed: the fact that human nature is changing at an extraordinary pace; that a new kind of humanity is coming into existence, rooted in current historical trends, especially trends arising from science and the urge toward discovery. Discovery of our own identity, belief in ourselves and in the use of the intellectual weapons of a democratic society—a science-minded and technology-minded society—can strengthen those moral, intellectual, and social devices without which, in such a world as this, there is no strength at all.[14]

In short, one more push and we shall be safe in Condorcet's tenth epoch, only one hundred and fifty years late, which is, in terms of a good philosophy of history, no delay at all.

[13] On that original denial, I refer the reader back to my paraphrase of Robert Owen, p. 299.
[14] Gardner Murphy, *Human Potentialities,* New York, Basic Books, 1958, p. 5.

Yet the doubt persists: If, on the whole, the record has shown that the Western intellectual, for all his bellyaching, can get along with a hope that is never fulfilled, a Promised Land never attained, it is not at all clear that the non- or unintellectual can make such an adjustment. The otherworldly promises the religion of the Enlightenment makes for this world may be too much of a goad for men less used than is the intellectual to taking the word for the deed, less able than is he to transfer to the central nervous system in "sublimation" very concrete appetites. The many are not quite as likely to be taken in by nice words, not even by the activities of those wicked persuaders, propagandists, motivational researchers that the intellectuals love to read about, as are, at their own rather more subtle verbal level, the intellectuals themselves. The many really want what they want. Was not Hitler's thousand years surely the worst of chiliasms?

III

At any rate, we are going to have to put up with this coexistence of Christianity and the religion of the Enlightenment for some time; or, rather, there are no good signs that the present multiplicity of sects, Christian and Enlightened, the present multanimity of Western men in manners, tastes, morals, world views, is going to end—not even with that end of our world the prophets of doom expect. Toynbee, most firmly of all such prophets, has announced a hope that out of these horrors will come a new religion of gentleness and love, Christianity-*cum*-Buddhism, achieved transcendence of the flesh and of the spirit spurred by the flesh, and, one need hardly say, the end of the agon. The Marxists are sure that they, too, will either end, or, better, wholly ennoble, the agon in the classless society. The mere historian should be modest in such matters. He should confess that he does not by any means understand the origin and spread of great religions, certainly not well enough to make predictions. The historian-sociologist of religion, almost inevitably influenced in the West today by the ideas of the Enlightenment, has to say that there does seem to be a relation, a congruity, between the whole culture from which a religion emerges and the religion itself, and that therefore it would be most surprising if a religion of gentleness, love, and "etherialization" of appetites and ambitions—a fully otherworldly religion—were to spring out of the West of nationalist democracy, nationalist Communism, satellites political and astronomical, existentialism, and general interest in a varied, exciting, unavoidable material world. The great disgust, the gut-deep horror of such a world, can indeed spring up anywhere, and in the group may produce a sect, an order, a crusade, and, in individuals, a poet, a revivalist, a saint, or simply a columnist; but I should be surprised if in our time such feelings were to spread to the many and get transmuted into a great religion; for to hate this world enough—or to love it enough—to give it up seems well beyond the powers of the many in our West. It is perhaps already too late for a prophet.

The reader will be aware that I do not regard as a possibility in any foreseeable future a society without any religion at all. Indeed, I consider the concept of a society without a religion as much nonsense as the concept of a human society without human beings. Now and then under the influence of the Enlightenment someone—especially the Marxists—uses as a form of words the statement that a given group or a given individual has "no religion." Now and then in our own time an even more incautious statement is made: Science will take the place of what we call "religion."

Now at the risk of some repetition, I must again go over this ground hastily. Natural science is a method of using the human mind to answer certain kinds of questions. These questions are ultimately always questions about means to ends; which ends are not themselves set, merely, and in isolation within the mind, by that activity of the human mind we call "natural science." The answers natural science provides are always tentative, and, though tested for their truth at the moment in various complex ways, are never so tested by their effects on the tester's personal desires, not even when those desires are of the kind we call "moral." Though for convenience —and out of long habit that goes back at least to the ancient Greeks— natural scientists often talk about the answers they thus get as "true," as descriptions or even reflections of the "real world," the more sophisticated among them will admit that they do not mean by "real world" the world of common sense or the world of morals, theology, metaphysics. The scientist is bred to feel and act toward the task of reaching the kind of truth he works to achieve in ways we have to recognize as "moral." He seeks truth and shuns falsehood. But his truths are not necessarily what we call "morally good," nor his falsehoods "morally bad."[15] Science, in short, has no teleological element, unless you find it pleasing to say that science is its own teleology. Its practice tends among its best practitioners to promote an atti-

---

[15] Just overheard, from an impeccably trained scientist who knows what it is all about: "I didn't say they [your words] were correct; I said they were wise."

tude of tentativeness, of skepticism, of relativism, toward other than scientific questions, but that tendency, no doubt fortunately, is uncommon in the rank and file of scientists, and inevitably incomplete in all of them.

The scientist cannot qua scientist be certain, not morally certain, and as a full human being he is at least inclined to be morally certain at times. Moreover, even in the West, so aware of science, and to a degree so trained in it, the great majority of human beings are probably quite incapable of serious scientific thinking, quite incapable of understanding what science is. I come back again to that imperfect tool the concept of the I.Q., which, nonetheless, is itself a product of the Enlightenment: the many are quite simply not bright enough to be good scientists. Again, even very good scientists often state, and confirm by their conduct, that they need to think and feel about matters of theology or metaphysics, to *know* something about what Spencer, here true to his training as a scientist, wryly called the "Unknowable."

All this should be obvious. But I think the difficulty goes deeper, or at any rate can be put somewhat differently. Thinking and feeling teleologically, morally, metaphysically is quite simply part of the human lot; if you yourself have a firm "materialistic" metaphysics, of the kind historically *associated with* the growth of natural science, you may choose to say that this thinking and feeling are environmentally conditioned activities of the central nervous system—though you will probably be driven to include the endocrines, and thence go on to the total personality. But the point is clear: thinking and feeling teleologically are *there,* quite as much as thinking and feeling scientifically. It would, even on the materialist's premises, take more than a local operation to remove them—you would have to destroy the personality.

It is certainly conceivable—there have even, no doubt, been examples—that there should be a world view, much influenced by the spirit of natural science and the Enlightenment, which should put off fully and honestly into an Unknowable (as poor Spencer with his religion of Progress most certainly did not) *any and all* sets of ideas about the origins and long-run destiny of man on earth, or indeed any big systematic set of ideas about good and bad, or long-run purpose, perhaps accept as good or at least as tolerable that there should be variety, multanimity, more or less of a free-for-all here on earth, and concentrate on doing what seemed possible in limited ways toward getting what one simply wants here on earth. The holder of such a world view might call himself a skeptic, and appeal to the memory of Montaigne. But if

A History of Western Morals

he bothered to read Montaigne he would realize that what the essayist wanted was what any good Christian humanist of his troubled age wanted, that he was—as he is usually labeled in histories of literature—a moralist. Even if our skeptic tried to put his position as an abdication of any private judgment before the great fact that Nature will take its course anyway, he would still have taken thereby a clear—and to some persons most consoling—moral and metaphysical position, one Lucretius tried to take so long ago.

In this world of human nature true "naturalism" is no anarchy, no meaninglessness, not even quite an *acceptance* of things as they are, but a *love* of things as they are. It is, perhaps fortunately, a rare kind of love; among our intellectuals, naturalism is rather more often a hatred for things as they are. And more—even the skeptic's moral stance will not be "determined" in any way any of us can understand and predict more than very roughly; it will be chosen out of many possibilities left us all by the past, and at just this level of world views and similar inescapable generalities, left us by the whole Greco-Romano-Judaeo-Christian-Enlightenment tradition we have been following in this book.

Statistical sorting out of Christian and Enlightened is, just because each has so much influenced the other, a difficult and not very profitable task. In the free West today, at least outside the Iberian Peninsula, neither tries nor, at heart, thinks it possible or desirable to proscribe the other; some degree of practical toleration is the price of our multanimity. The more ardent of each group are given to polemics against the other. The Spanish Civil War of the 1930's showed that both Christian and Enlightened could kill in the name of their religion. But for the most part, even in France and Italy, where the struggle between "clericals" and "anticlericals" has long been endemic, the conflict does not get beyond the bounds within which Western society seems normally to be able to hold itself together. On the continent of Europe outside the Iron Curtain, non-Christians and anti-Christians are relatively numerous, and in France must number something between half and a third of the population. In English-speaking countries, though actual church membership never seems to climb much over sixty per cent of the total population, the number of those who frankly deny they are Christians—they incline to say they have "no religion," which I have insisted above is not likely to be true—is relatively small. But English-speaking anti-Christian Enlightened are nonetheless in total many millions, and are firm, articulate, and often intolerant indeed. Their own faith does teach them that toleration is no negative, but a positive, virtue, and the gentler among them live up to their principles;

470

but many of them are bitter, determined, convinced infighters, no more tolerant than were the *philosophes*.[16] Even the run of the mill of these Enlightened apparently often hold the naïve view that the Christian convinced that he has a revealed, absolute truth incorporated here on earth in a church ought, nonetheless, to behave as if he believed that all religious groups are equal, and that his church is simply another public building, a slightly more dignified cafeteria. But the religion of humanity has long been weak in its understanding of human nature.

We may then for the not too remote future anticipate a continuing interaction between the Christian way and the way of the Enlightenment. Neither world view, to judge from the past, will in such a future wholly annihilate the other—not even in Spain, not even in Russia. Christianity cannot, without ceasing to be Christianity and becoming, as have so many of the modernistic or "liberal" sects nominally still within Christianity, in no way distinguishable from freethinking Enlightenment, wholly give up its other world, its supranatural godhead, in short, its theology.[17] And yet such has been the very great success of natural science and its associated attitudes toward "reality"—that is, such has been and is the Enlightenment—that a great number of Westerners will almost certainly in the future, as they have in the past, be unable to accept this essential supernatural element in the Christian

[16] I am aware that the above statement will give offense to many Enlightened, and that "toleration" is a word that invites semantics—and hence, ultimately, metaphysics. I revert to my controversial statement (see above, p. 11) about moral evil and "weeds." No flower gardener can "tolerate" dandelions. To the Enlightened, *belief* in, for example, the doctrine of the Trinity, has to be a weed, an evil, and surely it is as easy for him as for the Christian to equate *believer* and *belief?* I grant that in principle the Enlightened could not solve in an emergency a problem of toleration in quite the way the Abbot of Cîteaux solved his at Béziers (see above, p. 210); but temperamentally are there not surely Enlightened equivalents of the Abbot? I think Lenin, for instance, might have given a similar response.
[17] This statement, too, will not be acceptable to many Enlightened. But I feel the difficulty is at least more than a conventional one of definition. The Enlightened certainly often try hard to maintain a theology without a *theos*, without miracles, without a supernatural, a naturalistic-historical theology. I can only repeat that this "theology" seems to me no longer Christian *in its basic feeling about men and the universe*—or, for that matter, Jewish. The effort to build a satisfying "liberal" or "modernistic" theology can be profitably studied, for non-Jews perhaps from a relatively objective point of view, in contemporary Jewish thought. See notably two recent books: M. M. Kaplan, *Judaism without Supernaturalism*, New York, The Reconstructionist Press, 1958, and J. J. Cohen, *The Case for Religious Naturalism*, New York, The Reconstructionist Press, 1958. Mr. Cohen writes, "God is that quality of the universe, expressed in its order and its openness to purpose, which man is constantly discovering and upon which he relies to give meaning to his life." Certainly this God is no longer even an heir of Jehovah? Quoted in the New York *Times Book Review*, September 21, 1958, p. 22.

faith. There remains, then, that gap, no more than a gap in ideas, in the "superstructure," but not to be readily filled even by high-minded and subtle symbolisms, by psychological interpretations of miracles, by theologies that make God almost as abstract and unnecessary as Whitehead's—and Descartes's—or that prove that the doctrine of original sin is more consonant with human nature than any other interpretation, a gap not to be wholly filled even by a Barth, a Reinhold Niebuhr, a Tillich. It will, indeed, be so filled for some, and especially for sensitive intellectuals, for there certainly is in our time among the cultivated, as there was in Chateaubriand's time, an appreciable swing back to some form of wished-for Christian participation in what seems to be orthodox communion. But there will remain millions of Westerners, from humanists through the many forms of freethinking to ardent religious atheists, who will refuse to call themselves Christians, and who will not in fact be Christians, though most of them will conduct themselves in the main business of life as do most Christians.

On the other hand, the record shows no more firm signs that the Enlightenment will shortly annihilate Christianity. Through almost all the West, and in all social classes, among intellectuals as among nonintellectuals, there are millions of men who call themselves Christians, and who are, in all but the pathetically diseased Kierkegaardian sense, good Christians. There may even be some good Christians in the Kierkegaardian sense; there are, there must be, by Christian standards and hopes, a few saints, a very few, as saints have always been few. In Russia there has been a concerted attempt to root out Christianity and substitute an extremely intolerant and militant form of the religion of the Enlightenment. We cannot be sure that the attempt will succeed; sound sociological analysis is hardly possible for us in the West as yet. Most travelers—and, frankly, that is all any of us can be in Russia nowadays —seem agreed that Christianity is now practiced almost wholly among the old, that men and women under forty have for the most part been in fact so indoctrinated with the new religion of Dialectical Materialism that they have ceased to have any feeling for, any memory of, Christianity, that, in short, the government has already succeeded in its attempt to destroy Christianity in the U.S.S.R. Yet by no means all travelers agree that the young of the Soviet Union are wholly converted to the official form of the religion of the Enlightenment. We have even less reliable information that the Soviet government is succeeding in stamping out Islam in those parts of the union that had a Moslem faith. Yet it would appear that, during the last general war at least, the government let up designedly on its campaign against Christianity, with the result that the churches in a city like Moscow—true, many fewer churches for more people than in the old days—were filled. I think that, though we cannot yet be sure as to just what has happened in Russia, it is already clear that the Bolsheviks did succeed much more than did the Jacobins in a similar revolutionary attempt to root out Christianity. All the Jacobins achieved in their brief two years of power was to set up in France their own freethinking church, known rather inaccurately as anticlericalism or secularism, in a form so acutely hostile to the Catholic church that France has suffered ever since the tragic rift between *les deux France*. In Russia, it would seem at least that the new religion of the Enlightenment, in one of its more sectarian forms, has really got a state for its church, a Leninist tradition that may work out as an Enlightened variant of the Catholic Petrine tradition.

But let there be no mistake. The church that the Communists are trying to set up as the sole church of Russia is only one sect of the religion of the Enlightenment. I do not think it is destined to be more than a sect, nor, in the long run, to be quite uninfluenced by what goes on in the West, and indeed in the whole world. And in that West men live on and struggle on, it they are intellectuals of a certain sort living best and struggling most fiercely in the deep conviction that life is doomed and the struggle vain. The West—and not only among its intellectuals—is deeply committed to living its para-doxes, its contradictions, its conflicts, postponing to an afterlife or to some other Utopia or to a classless society their resolution, yet deep down not really admitting the legitimacy or necessity for such postponement, always actively at work spinning verbal resolution of its conflicts, always likely to burst forth somewhere on earth in a furious struggle to end struggle, an in-human effort to transcend humanity. Yet this last effort has its own ambiv-alence, for Western man can never quite decide whether to try to transcend his humanity by subduing—by killing—the "natural" man of common sense and desire, or by so indulging that man that neither common sense nor desire remain. On the whole, surely, the self-annihilation of the mystic has not been the Western way, and the climate of the last two centuries has been most unfavorable to the private mystic. The public mystic, of course, is Western indeed, but hardly a mystic, merely another leader, another prize winner.

The variety of these contradictions is great. The intensity with which they are felt obviously varies greatly in individuals and varies in societies with time and place, as does the kind of working solution or acceptable nonsolu-tion of any given contradiction. (Your temperament will tell you which of

473

these semantically identical phrases—working solution or acceptable nonsolution—suits you better emotionally; if neither suits you, you are potentially a saint or a revolutionary, at any rate a troublemaker.) I do not think that a history of men's attitudes toward these contradictions in the last few millennia would show what the Victorians called "Progress" in their resolution. I should like to believe that the humanitarian currents of the last few centuries which have done so much to reduce violence and physical suffering in the West have at least worked to reduce the willingness, the delight with which men *murder* to resolve their contradictions; and in spite of the prophets of doom, in spite of the great wars of our time, it may be that really moral wars—crusades—are getting harder to arrange. The mere *fact* of warfare is at least for us a moral problem, as it hardly was for the ancient Greeks of the Great Age, or for the men of the Middle Ages.

The very doctrine of Progress, however, is one of the acute modern forms of the eternal and unresolved contradictions that are the life of the West. I do not mean merely the obvious contrast between material or technological progress and moral progress. I mean, rather, the horrendous metaphysical problem set by the naturalism and historicism of the classical eighteenth- and nineteenth-century conception of Progress, to which I have already alluded (Chapter XIV) and which is really, at bottom, the old problem of determinism, but this time with no saving God to help out with a solution. Man cannot be at once both inside and outside a process of Evolution which makes him what he is, and makes him want to be what he wants to be, and even ties him up in the metaphysical knot he is struggling with. Nature cannot be unnatural, history cannot be unhistorical, human beings cannot make history or nature or themselves. Yet they most vigorously want to and manage to convince themselves that they can succeed, and have succeeded. Their latest attempt, through belief in a natural evolutionary process of which they are at once the product and the producer, the design and the designer, worked for a while to heighten their efforts as moralists to close the gap between what they say and what they do, between their ethics and their conduct, to make the lower into the higher—an effort not quite identical with what they as Darwinian evolutionists found to be the achieved intention of Nature to make the higher *slowly out of* the lower. It is, I think, still too early to decide whether they will make a happy nonsolution out of the doctrine of Progress. But we are already being urged to go beyond history.

Perhaps the crudest, and one would suppose therefore the most intolerable, of the contradictions that fill the modern West is at its clearest in

Conclusion: In Which Nothing Is Concluded

Russia: the promise, the moral ideal, of the classless society, a society in which men *must* be equals in such a way as to give the lie to the Gilbertian

> When everybody's somebody
> Then no one's anybody.

The reality in Russia of great economic inequalities of income, a social hierarchy of prestige, a political hierarchy of power, a society that gives and takes the wounds of the agon, is clear even through the Iron Curtain. Yet orthodox Western democracy itself has never quite succeeded in filling by means of asserted, and partly realized, equalities of opportunity and of human dignity, the gap between the full egalitarian ideal and the most inegalitarian reality. The conscientious democrat could hardly help feeling that Mr. Elvis Presley's forced giving up for a relatively brief spell as a private soldier his four Cadillacs and one Lincoln and all the rest of his aristocratic privileges was a rather less than satisfactory tribute from vice to virtue—much as the idealistic Christian, the true Christian, in the Middle Ages must have felt about some formal penance imposed on a very rich and very sinful noble. Perhaps the whole West, the whole world, will find, as some of our philosophical conservatives fear, that the contradiction between the ideal of equality and the ideal of individual liberty which really is "built into" the religion of the Enlightenment is in fact a contradiction beyond even the great capacities Westerners have developed for living such contradictions. But for the present, it would seem as though we in the free West had so far managed to get on with this one; it is not yet certain that the Russians, without the help of Christianity, will do as well.

There is not much use repeating the litany of contradictions we have encountered in the course of this book, nor even in trying to pick out a master contradiction of our time. But as a last note of emphasis, I should like to return to the contrast I have set metaphorically as between the great cat in man and the social insect in him. To get the contrast less fancifully put, any good social Darwinian—say, William Graham Sumner—will state the thesis that man is essentially a rugged individualist, competitive with other men, and that in the series of competitions which is life, the good, the fit, win and survive, and the bad, the unfit, lose and die, by the will of Evolution; and Peter Kropotkin, in his *Mutual Aid,* will state the thesis that, on the contrary, man is essentially a gregarious person, who lives by helping others and letting others help him, who is inclined rather to co-operation than to competition—and would be even more co-operative if he could follow his

475

real nature, and not listen to mistaken guides like the social Darwinists. Actually, Sumner does not quite deny that men co-operate as well as compete, and Kropotkin does not deny that some competitiveness among individuals is natural and even good. But each does, especially in the heat of exposition, assert very emphatically that the "nature" of man inclines him unmistakably and markedly in one direction or the other, and each implies that as far as is humanly possible we should all encourage society and Nature to keep men going in the right direction in the future; it is almost as though each feared that the diagnosis of the other was correct. The contrast has been extrapolated into about as distant a future as any of our modern prophets have dared indulge themselves by Sir Charles Galton Darwin in his *The Next Million Years* and by Roderick Seidenberg in his *Post-historic Man*. Darwin holds that man, Homo sapiens, as an animal—which is all he is—has already in something less than 100,000 years shown all he can be and do, has shown that he is basically a "wild animal," not a social one, and that therefore, until another species is evolved in the course of evolution, which we know takes about a million years, men will go on making and destroying states, cultures, churches, in a series so long as to make the historian blanch at the prospect. Mr. Seidenberg, on the contrary, thinks that the future—distant, it is true— will see mankind work out their current heart-rending problems, their conflicts of ideals and ideas, which make for change and therefore for history— and settle down into a state of automatic if high-level, almost spiritual, not at all Pavlovian (no drooling), responses, intellectual and emotional equivalents of, or parallels to, the present responses made by the social insects, an achievement which will mean the end of change, the end of problems, the end of morals, and the end of history, thus closing out nicely another human contradiction, that between "end" as a finish, a death, and "end" as a goal, a life.

We may in mid-twentieth century, with our eyes fixed on no more distant future than the next few generations, be sure that the old contradictions in man's ideas about his own nature and that of his society will by no means be solved. Most intellectuals in the West tend nowadays to believe, either with delight or with resignation, that the burden of evidence shows us moving toward a pole of collectivism, conformity, uniformity, at least within a given state or society. Perhaps, but we shall have to move a long way to get very near the condition of the social insects. Even in the United States, where we have been told from de Tocqueville through Sinclair Lewis right on to this moment that the leveling process is inexorable, a good alarmist about our diversities can point to dozens: the incredible variety of, the complete lack of standardization among, what we call institutions of higher education; the hundreds of organized sects, Christian, Jewish, Enlightened, theosophic, faddist; the continuing concrete variety of our American scene—a physical variety of regions which physiography and climate guarantee against architects, Main Streeters, and essayists who never use their eyes, a spiritual variety which history and geography, and perhaps even the nature of man combine to guarantee for a long time; the sometimes appalling course of fashion, the uniformity of the desire to be different, which in the real world of the man watcher, of time lags, of space not quite annihilated, does indeed make for variation and for differential changes; the continuing American lust for experiment, including socio-economic experiment, which has meant that even in mid-twentieth century, though the great wild decades of Brook Farm, New Harmony, and all the other "consociate families" are past, there still crop up little groups that try to live without machines, or bring up children without a single "No!," or make a university out of one hundred Great Books, or control the flesh by going nude, or go back to the womb of Vermont, or preserve in federally protected "wilderness areas" our innocent Mother Earth and her brood of virtuous animals and plants from her one wicked child, Man. But the list could be long indeed, and I forbear, knowing I can never persuade the many intellectuals not really interested in the world of the man watcher; for them, the United States will still be the land of identical Main Streets tied together by the same interstate highway of mind and body.

There are many real worlds, not the least of which is the real world of morals we have been so cursorily surveying. There is even a sense in which the solipsist and the poet are right: each of us is a world, and surely quite real. Of the worlds we share, Western man in particular has long been quite sure that the most *real* is the world his senses and his instruments—above all, perhaps his eyes and his cameras, for he loves to say "seeing is believing" —present him with; and he has quite recently come to believe that what he calls science is in fact this same world, even more accurately presented— though his good scientists know better, know merely that theirs is the most *inhuman* of the real worlds. One may guess that anthropologists and prehistorians are right, and that men in the condition we think of as primitive culture did not habitually and certainly not systematically separate their sense worlds and their moral worlds, did not think a sensation organized in perception any more real than—perhaps not as real as—a desire (or urge or drive or specifically channeled moment of the life force) organized in sentiment.

But certanly from the Jews and the Greeks on, all those with whom we have dealt in this book have been aware that the world of morals (values) is not identical with the world of sense perception (facts, data), that "ought" is not the same as "is." The great theisms of the West, and in particular Christianity, have taught men that ought eventually becomes is, triumphs over is, "determines" is. Toward that lesson Westerners have long had ambivalent sentiments, but very few have asserted that the ought means nothing at all, that the world of morals does not exist, is not real. Many of the Enlightened thought they had reversed, and corrected, the Christian lesson, and taught that the world of sense perception in its fullness as revealed to science (Reason) is the only real world, and is identical with the world of morals. I have urged that the Enlightened did not by any means make the two worlds identical, that their world of morals was still a set of oughts, and of oughts not *very* different from the Christian oughts.

But the Christian had long since reconciled himself to the continued existence of the gap between ought and is; the Enlightened have, even though they are no longer quite in the hopeful state of mind of 1789, continued to insist that it is in accord with the nature of the universe that the is should slowly but inevitably—this is the doctrine of Progress—catch up with the ought, determine the ought, *be* the ought. Time will then, in the logic of the doctrine of Progress, ultimately cease to be the master contradiction it is for men, and past, present, and future will be one; we shall know what we want and want what we know.

But there are signs that even the more ardently faithful of the Enlightenment are learning the lessons the Greeks themselves finally learned, though at an unhappy cost: "man is the measure of all things" does not mean "man is the master of all things," not even potentially, not even if sufficiently Enlightened. Our morals are the best and truest measure of ourselves, but they are not a measure of the universe; not even our science is quite that, as yet. Mastery of the universe would seem, so far, somewhat beyond us all, scientists, moralists, soldiers, statesmen, priests. Yet I should not care to close this book with anything like a whimper, or even a complaint. Mr. Archibald MacLeish has just rewritten in a modern setting the Book of Job, man helpless but invincible, chastened but never abject. We all are still that man, and still also, perhaps even more, the man of the famous chorus of the *Antigone,* strong, confident, cunning, marvelous to ourselves, but always vulnerable in pride, always less than something not ourselves, πολλὰ τὰ δεινὰ κοὐδὲν ἀνθρώπου δεινότερον.

478

Conclusion: In Which Nothing Is Concluded

What a thing is man! Among all wonders
The wonder of the world is man himself.
He scuds the angry pallor of the seas
Upon the blast and chariot of the storm,
Cutting a pathway through the drownéd waste.
He stirs and wears the unweariable Earth—
The eldest of his gods—with shuttling ploughs
And teams that toil and turn from year to year.

Man the Contriver! Man the master-mind
That with his casting-nets
Of woven cunning snares the light-wit birds;
And savage brutes; and sea-swarms of the deep;
Yea, every wary beast that roams the hills
Hath he subdued through excellence of wit.
Beneath his eye the horse accepts the yoke
And the mad mountain bullock seeks his stall.

Man the Householder, the Resourceful,
Safe from the drench of the arrowy rain
And the chill of the frozen sky;—
The Inventor of speech and soaring thought,
A match for all things, competent, victorious—
Against Death only shall he call for aid,
    And call in vain.

Yea, wondrous is man's Sagacity:
Through this he climbeth on high,
Through this also he falleth.
In the confidence of his power he stumbleth;
In the stubbornness of his will he goeth down.

While he honoreth the laws of the land
And that Justice which he hath sworn to maintain,
    Proudly stands his city.
But when rash counsels have mastered him, he dwells
  with perversity:
    Such a man hath no city.[18]

---

[18] Sophocles, *Antigone*, lines 332-375, trans. by John Jay Chapman, Boston, Houghton Mifflin, 1930, pp. 18-19. Even as late as the time of Sophocles, the word that has to be translated "wonder" had some overtones of its earlier meaning—*fear*.

Suggested Readings

A BOOK of this sort does not need a systematic bibliography. I have tried to give in footnotes such indication of my sources as will enable the interested reader to pursue further specific topics or problems as they strike his interest. I realize, however, in spite of my good anti-intellectualist conviction that most of my readers will have the necessary unshakable convictions as to right and wrong before they open this book, that in our day there are many, many persons sincerely on the side of the angels who would like to know a little more about how both angels and demons got to be what they are—shall I say, how they have progressed? The following is, therefore, a brief set of suggestions for the seeker for a way, insofar as the historical record can perhaps light that way. It should be noted that the categories below are by no means mutually exclusive; many books and authors cited under one head might well also be cited under another.

I · HISTORY

One can hardly hope to get light from a history of morals without some knowledge of history in the conventional and all-inclusive sense of the word. For those—not few in the United States—who have little or no history beyond the amorphous "social studies" of our school curriculums, I suggest the following, chosen to give a Christian as well as an Enlightened view: H. G. Wells, *An Outline of History,* many editions, brief, readable, in all its later editions, thanks to corrections from many readers, accurate enough as to simple facts, and very, very Enlightened; Christopher H. Dawson, *The Making of Europe* (New York, Sheed and Ward, 1934), a study of the essential medieval background by a gifted Catholic writer; Will Durant, *The Story of Civilization* (New York, Simon and Schuster, 1935-1957), which has in the sixth volume reached the Reformation, and will be completed with a volume on the Age of Reason, a longer, detailed history, worldwide in scope, Enlightened indeed, but carefully done from good secondary sources; Edward Eyre, ed., *European Civilization: Its Origin and Development* (New York, Oxford University Press, 1934-1939), a seven-volume collaborative work, most uneven, erratic, but the most detailed work I know written from a conservative Christian point of view. Of orthodox professional academic historical works, which are supposedly without a point of view, or at least without bias, but which in the modern West lean mostly to Enlightenment, the many-volumed Cambridge series—*Cambridge Ancient History, Cambridge Medieval History, New Cambridge Modern History* (in progress), *Cambridge History of the British Empire* (in progress), *Cambridge Economic History of Europe from the Decline of the Roman Empire* (in progress), *Cambridge History of British Foreign Policy, 1783-1919, Cambridge History of India* (in progress), *Cambridge History of Poland*—comprises an enormous and generally reliable encyclopedia of history. Most American college textbooks in European, Western, or world history are at least competent, and accurate as to facts, but they are rarely designed to hold the attention of the general reader; they are nowadays usually well illustrated. For a reader with access to a great library, I recommend the original

Propyläen Weltgeschichte, Walter Goetz, ed., 10 vols. (Berlin: Propyläen-Verlag, 1929-1933), even if he has no German, for the admirably reproduced illustrations are in themselves a fine course in history. D. C. Somervell's two-volume abridgment of Arnold Toynbee's *Study of History* (New York, Oxford University Press, 1947-1957) and J. J. Mulloy's collection of Christopher Dawson's work on general history entitled *The Dynamics of World History* (New York, Sheed and Ward, 1957) will give the reader a start on the modern attempt to construct, or buttress, with the help of history a world view or philosophy. Isaiah Berlin's brief but difficult *Historical Inevitability* (New York, Oxford Press, 1955) will take him into the midst of the great debate over "historicism."

II · ETHICS

This is one of the classical subdivisions of formal philosophy, and there are many introductory manuals, such as W. K. Wright, *General Introduction to Ethics* (New York, Macmillan, 1929); Woodbridge Riley, *Men and Morals* (New York, Doubleday, 1929); R. A. Tsanoff, *The Moral Ideals of Our Civilization* (New York, Dutton, 1942); P. A. Kropotkin, *Ethics, Origin and Development,* trans. by Friedland and Piroshnikoff (New York, Dial Press, 1924); H. L. Mencken, *Treatise on Right and Wrong* (New York, Knopf, 1934), both these latter quite idiosyncratic, Kropotkin at the end of his life a slightly disillusioned Enlightened philosophical anarchist, Mencken a never disillusioned, or always illusioned, sardonic observer of the foolishness of men. Political philosophy is so close to ethical philosophy that it cannot be neglected. Here there is a splendid introduction, George H. Sabine, *A History of Political Theory,* rev. ed. (New York, Holt, 1955).

But the essential is to read the philosophers themselves. There are a number of "selections" designed primarily for use in American college courses in ethics, but usually giving good long excerpts, and useful for the general reader, such as Benjamin Rand, *The Classical Moralists—from Socrates to Martineau* (Boston, Houghton Mifflin, 1909), and G. H. Clark and T. V. Smith, *Readings in Ethics* (New York, Crofts, 1931). Any selection is, of course, in part arbitrary, but the following seems to me a good minimum sampling of the range of ethical philosophy in the West in space and time: Plato, *The Republic, The Apology;* Aristotle, *Nichomachean Ethics;* Lucretius, *De Rerum Natura*—if you have any Latin, try the Loeb Classical Library edition, which has Latin on one page and a good English prose translation by W. H. D. Rouse on the opposite page; if not, there is William Ellery Leonard's labor of love, a "metrical translation" (New York, Dutton, 1916); Marcus Aurelius Antoninus, *Meditations;* St. Augustine, *City of God,* especially Book XII; St. Thomas Aquinas, *Summa Theologiae*—here all but the most assiduous reader will probably have recourse to anthologies and selections, such as those of Rand and Clark and Smith noted above; probably the key sections, especially for those interested in the present revival of Thomism, are the passages on natural law, first part of the second part, Question XC ff.; Machiavelli, *The Prince,* (perhaps a satire—see Garrett Mattingly in the *American Scholar,* XXVII, Autumn 1958, pp. 482-490); *Discourses on Livy* (by no means, a satire); Spinoza, *Ethics Mathematically Demonstrated;* Shaftesbury, *An Enquiry Concerning Virtue or Merit;* Mandeville, *Fable of the Bees;* Hume, *An Enquiry Concerning the Principles of Morals;* Helvétius, *De l'Esprit, or Essays on the*

Mind; Bentham, *Introduction to the Principles of Morals and Legislation;* Immanuel Kant, *Fundamental Principles of the Metaphysics of Morality, What Is Enlightenment?;* Robert Owen, *New View of Morality;* Herbert Spencer, *Principles of Ethics;* Friedrich Nietzsche, *Beyond Good and Evil, Genealogy of Morals, Antichrist;* Henry Sidgwick, *The Methods of Ethics;* T. H. Green, *Prolegomena to Ethics;* G. E. Moore, *Principia Ethica;* John Dewey, *The Quest for Certainty;* and for an up-to-date rationalist, Kurt Baier, *The Moral Point of View* (Ithaca, Cornell University Press, 1958). Many of these books can be read browsingly, as interest dictates. Most of them can be got in inexpensive editions, often in paperbacks.

III · HISTORIES OF MORALS

The classic is, of course, W. E. H. Lecky, *History of European Morals from Augustus to Charlemagne* (1869), now available in a modern reprint (New York, Braziller, 1955). This is a remarkable work, erudite, readable, inspired by deep moral fervor, distrustful of ordinary human nature, convinced of the inadequacy of "theological systems," but not quite serene about Enlightenment. Lecky's *History of the Rise and Influence of the Spirit of Rationalism in Europe* is also a history of morals, and covers a later period not dealt with in the above. It also is available in a new edition (New York, Braziller, 1955). J. M. Robertson, *A Short History of Morals* (London, Watts, 1920), is rather a history of Western ideas about ethics than a history of morals; it is strongly anti-Christian. There are two well-known studies written from the combined point of view of nineteenth-century sociology and anthropology, both much influenced by nineteenth-century evolutionary concepts: L. T. Hobhouse, *Morals in Evolution* (London, Chapman and Hall, 1906; new ed. rev., New York, Holt, 1915), and Edward Westermarck, *The Origin and Development of the Moral Ideas* (New York, Macmillan, 1906-1917). The Westermarck study in particular is a mine of concrete detail. Harold Nicolson, *Good Behavior; being a study of certain types of civility* (New York, Doubleday, 1955), comes close to being a history of morals, admirably brief but covering a good range of Western history.

IV · MORALISTES

I must emphasize that this is a French word, by no means exactly equivalent to our "moralists," who are always exhorters rather than reporters. The line between those I call ethical philosophers above and those I call here *moralistes* is by no means rigid. But I make this category for writers who seem to me to be concerned at least as much with observing human behavior as in trying to correct it. Many of the following writers are deliberately hard-boiled; but I do not wish to be understood as claiming that all under the category "ethics" (II above) are simple-minded, soft-boiled idealists, and all under this category are tough-minded, even cynical, realists. After all, I have listed Machiavelli, Mandeville, and Nietzsche under "ethics" above, and not simply because they might be tagged as "inverted idealists." The wise reader will sample both categories. Here is a small and rather arbitrary sample, but one that will lead the reader on into wider circles: the books of *Proverbs* and *Ecclesiastes* in the Old Testament; Aristophanes, *The Clouds* and *Lysistrata* especially, but any of the plays have touches of the man watcher; Thucydides, the whole *Peloponnesian War,* but especially the Funeral Oration, the Corcyrean Terror, the Melian Dialogue (in the Modern Library, John H. Finley, Jr., ed., pp. 102-109, 184-192, 330-337); Theophrastus, *The Characters,* a most influential little book, first of a genre of great interest to the moralist, the literary vignette not of a specific person, but of a generalized personality—the coward, the surly man, et cetera; Theocritus, if only for Idyll XV, the women at the festival of Adonis, another "first"—the first *New Yorker* sketch; Polybius, *History,* especially Book VI, on the reasons—political and moral—for Roman success; Petronius, *The Satyricon,* a prose satirical novel, a fine source for the historian of morals, as is also Apuleius, *The Golden Ass* (all the above works in Greek or Latin are easily available in English translations); Chaucer, *Canterbury Tales,* all of them, in a modern English version if you like, since you are reading as a *moraliste,* not as a student of the arts; Bacon, *Novum Organum,* especially Book I, and the *Essays;* La Rochefoucauld, the *Maximes,* in French if possible, but there are several adequate translations; La Bruyère, *Caractères, ou les moeurs de ce siècle;* Vauvenargues, *Reflections and Maxims,* trans. by F. G. Stevens (London, H. Milford, 1940)—there are several "oeuvres choisis" in French; Chamfort, *Maximes et Pensées,* preferably in the edition of Pierre Grosclaude, Bibliothèque des editions Richelieu (Paris, 1953); Franklin, *Poor Richard's Almanac* and the *Autobiography;* Burke, *Reflections on the French Revolution,* and J. de Maistre, *Soirées de St. Pétersbourg,* neither quite in line with most of this category, but the best way to get at the conservative Christian response to the Enlightenment; Newman, *Apologia pro vita sua,* a realistic appraisal of a Christian idealism; Nietzsche, the earlier aphoristic writings, such as *The Joyful Wisdom* and *Human, All too Human;* Bagehot, *Physics and Politics,* and almost anything he wrote—he is one of the few observers among English nineteenth-century liberals—if he *was* a liberal; W. Lippmann, *A Preface to Morals* (New York, Macmillan, 1929), which should perhaps be listed above under ethical writings, but is a necessary book to the understanding of his generation in the United States; Eric Hoffer, *The True Believer* (New York, Harper, 1951), a remarkable book, aphoristic in form, but actually a closely knit study of several kinds of fanatics; Aldous Huxley, a complainer and an exhorter, but a magnificent observer of intellectuals. He has written a great deal. There is a selection of his writings, *The World of Aldous Huxley* (New York, Harper, 1947). His essays are more useful for us than his novels; see especially "Variations on a Philosopher," in *Themes and Variations* (New York, Harper, 1950) and "Ozymandias" and appendix in *Tomorrow and Tomorrow and Tomorrow* (New York, Harper, 1956).

V · LITERATURE

Aldous Huxley brings us inevitably to "literature" in the broad and vulgar sense of the word. Literature is surely still our best way of experiencing the past; and it is by no means the worst way of experiencing the present. It gives a range in social and geographic variations of the eternal human that no amount of time and money could permit in the way of direct personal experience, formally social-scientific or informally observing, mixing, hand-shaking, counseling. I should not be heretical enough to suggest that reading is as good as living, or that the library is an adequate substitute for that noble range, field work. But if you know what you are looking for, the library is a fine place to find it.

Suggested Readings

I should not dare make a sampling of world literature for the historian of morals. Almost anything that has survived can be grist to this mill. But the searcher should do his best to sort out in what he reads the work of the observer, the man watcher, the reporter, from the work of the moralist, the poet, the improver, the complainer. The two kinds of thinking and feeling are always present in the work of those who made our literary heritage, and no doubt one can even conceive a measure of their mixture, a scale from near zero to near one hundred. Very near zero for moralizing, poetizing, improving, or complaining, or near one hundred for observing, recording, would be the best of the case histories recorded under the name of Hippocrates, say the fourteen cases in *Epidemics,* in Volume I of the Loeb Classical Library edition, pp. 187-211. At the opposite end of the scale, choice would be freer, more difficult, more disputable. I suggest Kant's *Metaphysics of Morality,* but I am, of course, prejudiced. It is at least an interesting if impious exercise to rate a work of a Shakespeare, a Carlyle, a Balzac, a Tolstoy on one's private scale of such sort.

This is fanciful and a bit pretentious. You can learn a lot about human nature from literature, any literature, great or obscure. But watch your endocrine balance; neither euphoria nor dysphoria really helps us get nearer what we may resignedly call "reality."

Index

Index

Babbitt, Irving, 333*n*.
Babylonia(n), 46, 48, 50, 59, 142, 146
Bacchae (Euripides), 96-97
Bacchic rites, 110
Bacon, Sir Francis, 274, 276, 340, 434; quoted, 2
Bacon, Roger, 193
Bage, Robert, 312*n*.
Bagehot, Walter, 36, 347
Ball, John, quoted, 255-56
Balzac, Honoré de, 361
banausia, 81, 122, 222, 276
Baptists, 233, 460
Barbarians, 17, 68-69, 177-78
Bark, W. C., 181*n*.
Barnes, Harry Elmer, 205
Barraclough, June, 314*n*.
Barth, Karl, 472
Basso, Hamilton, 432
Bastardy, 166, 204-05, 362
"Battle of the Books," 73
Baumann, O., 10*n*.
Beatitudes, 163-64, 411
Beautiful-and-good, Greek ideal, 26, 72, 74-75, 78-80, 83, 86, 93, 96
Beccaria, Marchese de, 315, 324-25
Becker, Carl, 296*n*.
Beggar's Opera (Gay), 323
"Behavior," 4-5; *see also* Conduct
Behaviorism, 4-5, 306
Belgium, 221, 222
Bellona, 62
Belsen, 206, 377
Benedict of Nursia, 212
Benedict, Ruth, 463*n*.
Benedictine, 199, 200
Bentham, Jeremy, 10, 213, 297, 309, 315-18, 326, 355, 419
Berkeley, Bishop, 447
Bernard of Clairvaux, 157, 190, 193, 212, 232
Bernstein, Eduard, 60
Berthold of Ratisbon, quoted, 199-200
Bett, Henry, 446*n*.
Beza, Theodore, 223
Bible, 224, 238, 297, 408
Birth control, 405
Bismarck, Otto von, 287
Blazon of Gentry, The (Ferne), 282
Bliss, 295
Blue laws: defined, 229*n*.; Puritan, 225, 230; Roman, 111
Boccaccio, Giovanni, 25, 256; quoted, 260-61
Boers, 288, 421
Bohemianism, 247, 358, 369
Bolingbroke, Lord, 319
Bolsheviks, 405, 424, 429
Bonaparte, Pauline, 113
Bonaventura, St., 190, 193
Boniface, St., 176, 190
Boniface VIII, 208

Born, Bertram de, quoted, 202
Borgia family, 240, 250, 252, 260
Bosquet, Marshal, 84
Boucher, François, 312, 359
Bourbon, Etienne de, quoted, 210
Bourgeoisie, 282; *see also* Middle class
Bouvard et Pécuchet (Flaubert), 394
Bowdler, Thomas, 350
Bracton, Henry de, 103
Brathwait, Richard, quoted, 225
Brave New World (Huxley), 232
Breasted, J. H., 30, 38; quoted, 40-41, 43-45
Brenan, Gerald, quoted, 254*n*.
Bretonne, Restif de la, 312
Breughel, Pieter, 204
Britain: national character, 337, 339; nationalism, 332-33; *see also* England
Broad, C. D., 7*n*.
Brook Farm, 309, 367, 477
Bruner, Jerome, 453*n*.
Buckle, Henry Thomas, 37*n*.
Buddhism, 118-19, 175, 352, 382*n*., 396, 467
Bullen, K. E., 278*n*.
Bunyan, Paul, 24, 263, 323*n*.
Burckhardt, Jacob C., 244, 250
Burke, Edmund, 312, 319, 359, 463-64
Burlingame, Roger, 397*n*.
Burns, Robert, 225; quoted, 305
Bury, J. B., 295*n*.
Business: attitudes to, 79, 160, 221, 273-74, 285, 360; morality, 339
Butler, Samuel, 73, 326*n*., 415*n*.; quoted, 227
Byron, Lord, 321, 351, 358
Byzantium, 263

Café society, 386
Caldwell, Erskine, 436*n*.
Calvin, John, 157, 212-16, 219, 221, 223, 230-31, 252, 256, 303
Calvinism, 28, 159, 162-63, 170, 215-33, 236, 253-54, 263, 285, 306, 361, 404, 406; *see also* Protestantism, Puritanism
Cambridge University, 178, 202, 244, 287, 352
Camus, Albert, quoted, 395-96
Candide (Voltaire), 278
Canterbury Tales (Chaucer), 20

Capitalism, 218*ff*., 235-36, 454
Carlyle, Thomas, 23, 165, 204, 223, 256, 287, 414, 442
Carter, Elizabeth, 137*n*.
Carthage, 52, 109, 139, 143
Caspari, Fritz, 202*n*.
Castiglione, Count Baldassare, 247-50, 251, 252, 282
Cathari, 168, 186*n*.
Catharine of Aragon, 277
"Catharsis," 100
Catholic(ism). *See* Christianity, Roman Catholic Church
Catholic Reformation, 191, 212, 240-41, 256
Cato, 109, 158; quoted, 110
Cato the Stoic, quoted, 147
Catullus, 114
Celadus, 398
Celibacy, clerical, 167-68, 200-01, 214
Cellini, Benvenuto, 244, 247, 248, 252, 260
Celts, 34, 68, 69, 357
Cervantes, Miguel de, 285*n*.
Chaldeans, 47
Chambers, Clarke A., 377*n*., 444*n*.
Chanson de Roland, 65, 180, 183, 283
Chapman, George, quoted, 251
Charity, 162-63, 309
Charlemagne, 180, 183, 270*n*., 287
Charles the Bold, 257
Charles II, 278*n*., 289-90
Charles V, 251
Chartists, 309, 322
Chase, Stuart, 9
Chateaubriand, Vicomte de, 472
Chaucer, Geoffrey, 20, 25, 183, 204, 256, 356*n*., 425
Cheever, John, 395*n*.
Childe, V. Gordon, 264-65, 381*n*.
Children, morals in, 16-17, 32-33
Chivalry: Greek, 64-65; medieval, 189 (*see also* Knighthood)
Christ. *See* Jesus
Christian Scientists, 352, 459
Christianity: Caesar and Christ, 165, 173, 273, 332, 410; "Christian existentialism," 368*n*., Christian socialism, 368; and Communism, 162, 357*ff*., 375, 457-58 (*see also* Marxism); as consoling faith, 150, 334-35,

488

Index

Index

Index